Also by Frank McLynn

CHARLES EDWARD STUART: A TRAGEDY IN MANY ACTS
STANLEY: THE MAKING OF AN AFRICAN EXPLORER
STANLEY: SORCERER'S APPRENTICE
BURTON: SNOW UPON THE DESERT
ROBERT LOUIS STEVENSON

CARL GUSTAV

JUNG

FRANK McLYNN

ST. MARTIN'S GRIFFIN NEW YORK

A THOMAS DUNNE BOOK.
An imprint of St. Martin's Press.

Library of Congress Cataloging-in-Publication Data

McLynn, F. J.
Carl Gustav Jung : a biography / Frank McLynn.
p. cm.
"A Thomas Dunne book."
ISBN 0-312-19445-5
1. Jung, C. G. (Carl Gustav), 1875–1961. 2. Psychoanalysis. 3. Psychoanalysts—Austria—Biography.
I. Title.
BF109.J8M355 1997
150.19'54'092
[B]—DC21 97-12830
CIP

First published simultaneously in Great Britain, Australia, and New Zealand by Transworld Publishers Ltd.

First St. Martin's Griffin Edition: December 1998

10 9 8 7 6 5 4 3 2 1

For Pauline, Sine Qua Non

CONTENTS

PREFACE

I had better state straightaway that this book does not purport to be a definitive biography of C.G. Jung. Such a work will not be possible until all the relevant documentation is released into the public domain. If we may rely on recent reports of the attitudes evinced by the guardians of the secrets of depth psychology's founders, we may well have to wait until the twenty-second century before we learn the final truth about certain episodes.It is only fair to say that Freudians are just as much to blame for these retentive attitudes as Jungians, and Peter Gay, for one, has frequently had occasion to remark on the irony of excessive secretiveness among depth psychologists, whose stated intention is to bring into the light what was previously in darkness.

Nevertheless, I would be surprised if future discoveries significantly alter our perception of Jung's doctrines and their implications. Future research, when the relevant material is available, will no doubt uncover the names of Jung's many unknown mistresses, the dates of the liaisons and much more along these lines. Whether it will revolutionize our understanding of his doctrines is more doubtful. Interpretation of Jung's theories is notoriously tricky and there are as many rival hermeneutical sects as in biblical exegesis. I am sure my explanations will not command universal assent, and there will be those who claim that the true understanding of, say, the theory of archetypes or the collective unconscious is quite other. But I know of no species of revisionism which holds that Jung did not, after all, believe in any of these things, and I would be amazed if future caches of Jungiana add very much to the doctrinal side of things.

Meticulous care has been exercised to see that no copyrights have been infringed in the writing of this book. And, since Jung is in many ways a battlefield, I deliberately did not seek expert advice or academic readings, so that I would not absorb any of the conscious or unconscious *parti pris* the man and his doctrines provoke. The errors and shortcomings in this volume are mine and mine alone. I gratefully acknowledge the massive commitment of my wife Pauline to the writing of this volume: she has been reader, editor and confidante all in one and sustained me through considerable difficulties in the production of this book. If a 'sea of troubles' is a cliché, perhaps I can best express what I owe to her by mentioning that for much of the voyage towards publication we have been in a severe typhoon. My greatest 'external' debt of gratitude is to the Swiss Pro Helvetia Foundation, who made funds available so that I could visit all the places in Switzerland associated with Jung's life and work. The experience not only helped me considerably in the writing of this book but gave me an abiding admiration for the highly intelligent way Switzerland has approached social problems common to the West. Although I am often critical of Jung in this book, I concur wholly in his feeling of pride in his native land.

CARL GUSTAV JUNG

Chapter One

A SWISS CHILDHOOD

To understand Carl Gustav Jung one must first understand Switzerland, and this is no easy matter. People become puzzled when confronted with a republic that has no president but a communal leadership consisting of an executive council. The technicalities of *confederation* rather than federalism – the technical distinction is that in confederation the central government has powers over the member states but not directly over their citizens – leads to further confusions. Compound this with a geography that produces cis-Alpine, trans-Alpine and inter-Alpine cantons and a political culture not based on a single language and one is already faced with a social complexity that matches the notorious difficulty of Jung's psychological thought. Some observers have even suggested a stricter determinism: that Jung could not have had the theories he had if he had been born elsewhere, since the Swiss constitution is itself 'Jungian'.[1]

Superstitious, xenophobic, conservative, earthbound, introverted, moneyminded – all these epithets have been used to describe Jung, and even more frequently to describe his native country. That Jung was not an untypical 'Switzer' he himself recognized, and he would usually take it in his stride when accused of being 'moralistic', 'mystical', or 'Teutonically confused'. He was quite prepared to admit that he was a bigoted Swiss and even revelled in the idea of being a product of Swiss wooden-headedness.

He conceded that his fellow-countrymen were primitive and said that their love of cattle reminded him of the African: adding that there was still a lot of deeply buried and archaic earth mysticism in Switzerland.[2] As for conservatism, he declared that for the Swiss a new idea was like an unknown dangerous animal which had to be either avoided or else approached with extreme caution – which was why, in his view, the Swiss had such poor intuitive capacity. Their aristocratic posture revealed itself in indifference to the opinions of others.[3] As for introversion, this was a function both of xenophobia and neutrality in the affairs of the world on one hand and the peculiar Swiss political culture on the other, where warlike instincts were channelled inwards into domestic political life.

Jung advanced the paradox that the tolerable social order in Switzerland was a result of having 'introverted' war; Switzerland was ahead of the rest of the world in that it was in a chronic state of mitigated civil war and did not direct its aggression outwards.

The charge of neurosis always upset Jung and he rebutted it as vigorously when laid at the door of his native land as he did when accused of it himself. Although accepting that the Swiss were for geographical and cultural reasons in a precarious position, full of resentments and defence mechanisms (and in this he likened them to the Jews), he thought they had their feet on the ground and their head out of the clouds.[4] It is true that even in the nineteenth century when Jung was born Switzerland had fewer social frictions and less class conflict, but the tendency to melancholy and the high suicide rate were often noted by foreign observers. Above all, the Swiss were thought to be far too interested in money, to have what Jung would later term a 'money-complex'.

'*Point d'argent, point de Suisse*' were the immortal words in Racine's *Les Plaideurs* – said to have been the actual words of Swiss mercenaries in the service of French King Francis I in 1521, when they quit because they had not been paid. Jung accepted that there was some truth in this and liked to tell a story about a relative snubbed at a family gathering on the grounds that he was a 'dreadful person'; when Jung asked what crime the man had committed the answer was short and to the point: 'He's living on his capital.'[5]

The peculiarity of Switzerland as geographical entity and political culture can scarcely be overemphasized in its influence on Jung. Geographically, the Swiss are predominantly a mountain people, and it is a commonplace of political science that such 'highlanders' are deeply religious and politically conservative, with a strong sense of independence and self-reliance.[6] Jung frequently referred to the Alps as *the* central collective image of Switzerland and suggested that a landscape where Nature was mightier than Man produced the characteristic Swiss mixture of obstinacy, doggedness, stolidity and innate pride.

The other salient geographical feature of Switzerland is that it is landlocked – the 'Swiss admiral' has become a stock joke – and to this fact Jung attributed all the qualities of the Swiss, both good and bad: the down-to-earth, limited outlook, the parsimony, stolidity, stubbornness, xenophobia, mistrustfulness, political neutrality and refusal to become involved.[7]

Yet its mountainous and landlocked nature do not exhaust the geographical significance of Switzerland. It is also at the heart of Europe – a fact Jung thought of great significance. This meant that in Switzerland the European was truly at home in his geographical and psychological centre; Switzerland was, so to speak, Europe's centre of gravity.[8] The nodal position of Switzerland has inspired the legend of Saanemoser, a village in Bernese Oberland, where it is said that if you spit into the stream it is an even chance that the fluid will be carried either down various water courses to the Rhone and the Mediterranean or to the Rhine and hence the North Sea.[9]

Yet beyond all these reasons for taking an exceptional pride in his native land, Jung had quasi-mystical reasons of his own for revering Switzerland. As a believer in numerology, astrology and symbols, Jung singled out more obscure aspects of the semiology of Switzerland from which to derive comfort. Obsessed as he was with the dialectical interpenetration of opposites, he pointed to the fact that the red and white in the Swiss flag were themselves 'signs' of the reconciliation he held so dear.[10] Bedazzled by the fact of Switzerland's strength as a nation-state, against all the apparent odds, he liked to point out that the existence of three major languages (Italian, French and German) was no barrier to a sense of nationhood, whereas the received wisdom was that a distinctive language was *the* sign of nationhood and a special political culture. But language in Switzerland was even more important than this in

Jung's view, for there was a fourth tongue, the Romansch dialect, spoken in the remoter Alpine valleys. It was a deeply held belief of Jung's that four was a magic number symbolizing perfection – his work is littered with references to 'the quaternity' – and he saw such quaternities everywhere in Switzerland. The most striking one for him was that Switzerland had four main rivers – the Rhine, Rhône, Ticino and Inn – mirroring the four biblical rivers of Eden (the Euphrates, Gihon, Pison and Hiddekel) – thus establishing his homeland as the true earthly paradise.[11]

Moreover, the Swiss zodiacal sign was an earth sign – Virgo in one tradition, Taurus in another. The stolidity and inaccessibility of the Swiss were, on this view, all marks of the feminine element Virgo.[12] Jung liked to link the Virgo sign to Switzerland's loveliest mountain – the Jungfrau – thus reinforcing his sense of the Alps as a metaphor for perfection.

It is possible to attenuate the deep psychological and cultural impact of one's homeland by exile or emigration, but no-one can shrug off the influence of parents. It is a commonplace that parents are an enduring legacy for good or evil but, beyond this, Jung considered there were two reasons why ancestry was all-important. In the first place he thought that children were condemned to fulfil that portion of a parent's life left undone. Secondly, he believed in a form of atavism: that grandparents could actually have more influence on a child than the parents themselves. This was a particularly important idea in Jung's case, since his grandfathers were more eminent people than his father. Moreover, it is a peculiarity of Swiss history that many of her great figures were sons of pastors who spent their lives wrestling with problems of faith and doubt left unsolved by their fathers. Such were Jakob Burckhardt, Pestalozzi and Durenmatt and so too was Jung. This is what Freud meant when he referred to the 'theological prehistory of so many of the Swiss.'[13]

Jung's ancestry on the paternal side cannot be traced back beyond the early eighteenth century. The Jung family came from Mainz, and it is known that there was a Dr Carl Jung who died there in 1645 and – interestingly in view of Carl Gustav's own later preoccupations – was affiliated to the Rosicrucians, but the early part of the family tree comes to an abrupt end in 1688. In that year, during Louis XIV's siege of Mainz, the municipal archives took a direct hit from cannon fire and were burned to the ground, destroying all previous records of the Jungs.[14] Their history proper begins with Jung's great-grandfather, the physician Franz Ignaz Jung (1759–1831), a Mainz Catholic and an introvert who was known to have had an unhappy marriage with Sophie Ziegler; Jung's 'atavistic theory' links Franz with his own father, Paul Jung (1842–96), since both men had problems with their wife and son. Franz Jung was in charge of a military hospital during the Napoleonic wars, and his brother Sigismund (1745–1824) was Chancellor of Bavaria.[15]

Sophie Ziegler Jung suffered from mental illness whose nature is uncertain. In later life her famous great-grandson analysed her handwriting and found no trace of schizophrenia, detecting instead a 'psychogenic melancholia'; he also speculated that she had an over-intense relationship with her son, which exacerbated the rift with Franz.[16] Partly as a result of Franz's marital discord with Sophie, the rumour sprang up that Sophie had had an illegitimate son by Goethe. The canard was circumstantially plausible, as Sophie and her sister were lively artistic personalities who knew Goethe and did a great deal for the Mannheim theatre (Franz Ignaz transferred the family seat from Mainz to Mannheim), especially at the time of the memorable première of Schiller's *Die Rauberin* in 1782. In his early career Jung was inclined to credit the rumour, and Freud, whether ironically or not, refers to Goethe as 'your ancestor' in correspondence with Jung. The idea of Goethe as Jung's great-grandfather looks like a classic instance of the common fantasy of having celebrated forebears famously analysed by Freud as the 'family Romance'.[17] At the end of his life Jung advanced a more sober explanation for the role of Goethe in the history of his family in terms of a possible 'transference' to Goethe.

What is known for certain is that Jung's great inspiration, his grandfather Carl Gustav, was born in 1794 and converted to Protestantism in his student years. Carl Gustav attended Heidelberg University where he studied medicine though his first love was poetry. His combative personality and taste for radical causes were almost his undoing, for at twenty-three, with his career barely started, he was arrested and spent a year without trial in the Hansvogtei prison. His political activities led him to befriend genuine revolutionaries, one of whom assassinated the Russian privy councillor Kotzebue; in the ensuing hue and cry a hammer and an axe were found in Carl Jung's rooms and he was held as an accessory. Once released, ruined and embittered, he made his way to Paris where he met the famous naturalist and traveller Alexander von Humboldt. Humboldt took him under his wing, found him a job in the Department of Surgery at the Hôtel-Dieu and spotted him as a potential recruit for the Berne academy. When Berne showed no interest, Humboldt presented his protégé's credentials to the new medical school at Basel, and secured a post for him. Jung left for Switzerland in 1820, took out Swiss nationality and made his career in Switzerland thereafter, becoming professor of medicine at Basel University in 1822.[18]

Like his grandson, Carl Gustav was autocratic and pranksterish. Anticipating Gérard de Nerval with his lobster, he had a small pig as a pet which he took on walks as if it were a dog.[19] A strong personality, active, brilliant, witty, voluble and a great organizer, Carl Gustav senior transformed the Basel medical faculty. Before he arrived the faculty had been in a bad way: for many years the anatomist and botanist Johann Jakob Burckhardt had been the only teacher, and between 1806 and 1814 not a single degree had been awarded. Greatly interested in psychiatry – Carl Gustav tried unsuccessfully to endow a chair in the subject at Basel – he founded an institute for psychologically disturbed and retarded children and spent much of his free time with his charges until his death in 1864. Eventually Rector of Basel University, he was an ardent Freemason, became Grand Master of the Swiss Lodge, published numerous scientific papers and wrote plays. He made great friends with the German theologian Wilhelm de Wette (1780–1849), like himself a political refugee, who had been dismissed as professor of theology at Berlin University for his radical sympathies. It was the German Protestant theologian Friedrich Schleiermacher (1766–1834) who brought the two men together and it was through Schleiermacher's influence that he was appointed to the chair at Basel in 1822.[20]

Like all the Jungs, Carl Gustav had a turbulent married life. His first wife died after bearing him three children, whereupon Carl Gustav decided he wanted to marry the daughter of Basel's mayor. When the mayor turned down his suit for his daughter's hand, Carl Gustav decided that to 'spite' the stuffed-shirt dignitary he would marry the first attractive woman he met. He stormed into a tavern and proposed to the waitress there – an exploit that won him notoriety in the university. The hapless waitress died after bearing him two children. Since the mayor's daughter was still unmarried, Carl Gustav decided to try his luck once more, and this time Mayor Frey accepted him. Sophie in turn bore eight children, all of whom remembered their father as a domestic tyrant. The youngest son born to this third marriage was Paul Jung, who was to be the great psychologist's father.

Jung's maternal grandfather was also an astonishing character. Samuel Preiswerk (1799–1871) was a pastor and a Zionist *avant la lettre*, obsessed with Jewish history and culture. Convinced that Hebrew was the language spoken in Heaven, he gave his children Jewish names and achieved such eminence in Hebrew studies that he was appointed to a lectureship in the subject; his greatest source of satisfaction was the knowledge that he would now be able to read celestial newspapers.[21] At first his career was erratic: he taught Hebrew and Old Testament theology in Geneva, was then recalled to Basel as pastor of St Leonhard's church and finally got tenure at the university there. Preiswerk, who first came to Basel in 1833, married twice: his first wife Magdalene produced just one child before dying, but his second, Augusta Faber, a Württemberg clergyman's daughter, bore him no fewer than thirteen. An occultist and spiritualist, he insisted that his wife stand behind him during his sermons to ward off evil spirits. She took less satisfaction from his dealings with the spirits at home, for Preiswerk liked to set out a chair in his study for his first wife's ghost to sit in; during her weekly visit they would have long conversations. The living wife took less kindly to this and, since she was herself clairvoyant and possessed of the second sight, a battle of the psyches was fought out in the Preiswerk household.[22]

Jung's parents Paul and Emilie were both the youngest in families of thirteen children – a fact the superstitious and numerological Carl Gustav junior did not fail to invest with significance. Paul Jung promised great things in his youth and was a brilliant student of oriental languages (principally Arabic) at Göttingen University, but he was a depressive and found himself in his thirties an obscure pastor in the Swiss Reformed Church Evangelical in a backwater in Canton Thurgau. Quiet and unassuming in public, he was quarrelsome and bad-tempered in private, and the marriage with Emilie Preiswerk did not prosper, especially as his dreamy, scholarly nature clashed with her 'uncanny' personality – clearly she had inherited a double dose as a 'psychic' from her Preiswerk parents. Their root problem was sexual. Some have speculated that Paul was somewhat lacking in virility, or that Emilie was terrified of sex; possibly both factors were at play, but it was not a happy marriage.

Carl Gustav, who was born on 26 July 1875, was Paul and Emilie's first surviving child. Emilie had given birth to a boy, Paul, in 1873 but he lived just a few days. Sometimes the shadow of such an earlier sibling can affect the surviving child, as the 'first Vincent' did in the case of Vincent Van Gogh, but the deeply introspective Jung never alludes to his ill-fated predecessor. Carl Gustav was born at Kesswil on the southern edge of Lake Constance, but when he was six months old his father moved to a new vicarage at Laufen castle, above the Rhine Falls. Jung had no memory of Lake Constance but he always adored lakes and wanted to live near one.

Jung's earliest memories were of sensuous experiences: the taste and smell of leaves, the sun dappling the leaves, his aunt pointing out the Alps in the distant sunset, their peaks glowing red. Pressed for his very first impressions, he recalled lying in a pram but there was no mention of his parents. This is significant, as Freud pointed out: 'in every psychoanalytic investigation of a life history, it usually happens that the first recollection to which the patient gives precedence, with which he introduces the story of his life, proves to be the most important, the very one that holds the key to the secret pages of his mind.'[23] It has been argued that Jung's first impressions connote a problem with parental bonding and attachment and suggest a mental universe where the natural world represents security and the interpersonal one insecurity. Even when he does later remember his mother, it is her dress rather than her face or voice he remembers – and this is perhaps a clue to his later obsession with the way women dressed.[24]

Even an infant is aware if there is something amiss with parents, and Jung's childish intuition was not wrong. In 1878 his parents separated temporarily and his mother spent some time in a mental hospital. The trauma for the three year old, who developed eczema and went to live with his aunt, was profound. From then on he always felt mistrustful when the word 'love' was spoken and associated 'woman' with innate unreliability. 'Father', on the other hand, meant reliability and powerlessness.[25] Psoriasis and eczema are well-known psychogenic complaints, and his mother's apparent splitting of personality or 'dissociation' may have been the reason why he always feared schizophrenia in himself.

His feelings about women received a stimulus from two other sources. He remembered his dark-haired maid with the affection most young boys feel for their mother and was later to declare that the maid was an important influence in forming his image of the feminine; and he liked his father's constant companion, the pretty, blonde, blue-eyed Bertha Schenk (later to be his mother-in-law) who often took him out for walks; soon to marry into the rich Rauschenbach industrialist family, she was so friendly with Paul Jung as to raise suspicions that the two might be lovers.[26]

At around the age of four Jung developed a morbid fascination with death and corpses: he was fascinated by the dead body of a four-year-old boy found near the Rhine Falls and, clearly – Jungians would say – at the unconscious level, wished he was that boy. Accident proneness was much in evidence. Firstly he fell downstairs, then he fell against the leg of a stove, scarring himself so badly that the wound was still visible in his senior year at Gymnasium. It is a familiar idea that accident-prone children tend to have problems with their mother and 'self-destruct' because of rage against the nurturer who has failed them. The preoccupation with the corpses also fits the scenario of rage against the mother.

More serious than the falls was an accident on the Rhine bridge at Neuhausen when the child Carl Gustav had one leg under the railing and was about to slip through when the maid caught him. Jung himself attributed these untoward events to an unconscious suicidal urge or a kind of fatal resistance to life in this world. But while still alive and an international figure he explained his 'corpse preoccupation' as simply a means of trying to accommodate to the idea of death. Yet it is of passing interest that it was the maid, not his mother, who saved him.[27]

The death-wish was not the only pathological symptom in the child. He thought he could hear things walking in the house at dead of night and fancied he saw ghosts and other emanations emerging from his mother's room. There was much talk of drowning in the family – the distant roar of the Rhine Falls was always audible – and there were frequent funerals attended by black-coated clergymen. Jung's state of mind at the age of four led the psychoanalyst D.W. Winnicott to conclude that he was suffering from childhood schizophrenia, triggered by a breakdown at three caused by his parents' separation.[28]

Even when his mother returned from mental hospital in Basel, she was no help to him. He remembered his mother as sometimes happy but more often subject to fits of depression. He soon learned to perceive her as two different people, with an uncanny, terrifying second personality. Outwardly she was submissive, but her unconscious occasionally burst through to reveal a deep character of power and resolution. The second personality emerged but rarely, yet each time it did the experience for Jung was unexpected and frightening. There can be little doubt that the dark side of his personality, 'typical of psychosis and psychotic character,' was exacerbated by his mother.[29]

The morbid atmosphere in the nursery was typical of many Victorian childhoods but his neurotic mother added a 'superplus' of anxiety, especially when she taught him prayers like the following:

> Spread out thy wings, Lord Jesus mild,
> and take to thee thy chick, thy child.
> 'If Satan would devour it,
> No harm shall overpower it,'
> So let the angels sing!

Jung later commented drily, with a mordant wit worthy of Bertrand Russell that Jesus appeared to be a winged creature who 'took' little children ('chicks') reluctantly like bitter medicine. That was hard enough to understand, but the difficulty was compounded by the further notion that Jesus ate them anyway, even though he did not like the taste, simply to prevent Satan from getting them.

Not surprisingly, Jung began to associate Jesus with gloomy black men in frock coats, busying themselves with black boxes. A further association of ideas was between Jesus and Jesuits (even though Sir Richard Burton warned, '*si cum Jesuitis, non cum Jesu itis*'). Anti-popery was a strong strain in the Revd Paul Jung's household, and the young Carl Gustav had heard many blood-curdling stories of the nefarious practices of the Society of Jesus. This was probably simply the reflex action of Protestant communities feeling themselves beleaguered by powerful Catholic neighbours. It is difficult at this distance to recapture the peculiar terror that the word 'Jesuit' aroused in the minds of Swiss Protestants in the nineteenth century. In popular belief and mythology the Society of Jesus elicited similar reactions to those evoked by Communism in, say, the USA of the mid-1950s: it was regarded as an international conspiracy by depraved individuals ('the evil empire'), with agents at work everywhere to win power for a foreign ruler (in this case, the Pope). Ruthless, amoral, implacable, fiendishly cunning, served by fanatics and zealots, the Society of Jesus was supposedly responsible for most of the evil in the world.

At the time of Jung's birth about three-fifths of Switzerland was Protestant, but there was an abiding fear among them, based on Catholicism's well-known hostility to birth control, that they could be 'swamped'. The Swiss confederation came under pressure to expel the Jesuits from Switzerland, and the agitation reached its height at about the time of Bismarck's *Kulturkampf* in Germany, which did end there with the expulsion of the Jesuits in 1875. At the same time the Jesuits played into the hands of their Swiss enemies by making a virtue of necessity and switching resources from Germany to Switzerland, where they campaigned against civil marriage and propagandized for papal infallibility. As a further complication, Swiss Catholicism in the 1870s was split between ultramontanes, who accepted the 1870 dogma of papal infallibility, and the 'Old Catholics' who refused to countenance it.

The obvious result of the Jesuit phobia in the Jung household was that young Carl was traumatized by his first sight of a Catholic priest in a cassock walking down the road past his house and fled upstairs in a paralysis of fear. The fact that the priest wore a 'frock' also reinforced Jung's feelings of horror about the breakdown of the 'natural' order, which was why in later life he always reacted so violently to the sight of women in trousers.

In 1879 his father was transferred to a new parish at Klein-Hüningen, now a suburb of Basel but then a small village on the Rhine inhabited by fishermen and peasants. Basel itself, the capital of the half-canton Basel Stadt, was then a small town with a population of 74,247 (according to the 1888 census), of which 50,326 were Protestant.[30] Paul Jung's role as clergyman may sound modest to twentieth-century ears, but the social status of a Swiss pastor was considerably higher one hundred years ago. Two factors are salient. In the first place, in the nineteenth century the presbytery (*Pfarrhaus*) contained an important section of the intellectual élite. It was a social caste of the best and brightest, perhaps comparable with the contemporary Oxbridge élite trained for service in the British Empire. Only the most gifted students were selected for theological training in German, Swiss and Austrian universities, and for the most part the German cultural intelligentsia came from the ranks of its pastors. They served as Protestantism's shock troops in the war against popery, barbarism, paganism and occultism and as a mandarin class were fully integrated into the wider German élite. Organic solidarity was often enhanced by intermarriage among the sons and daughters of ministers, so that it would not have been altogether surprising if the young Carl Jung had thought that most of Basel was composed of clergymen and their families. On the other hand, from an early age, consciousness of belonging to an élite would have been inculcated into the boy, and some commentators trace back Jung's later 'élitism' to this fount.

Secondly, a Protestant pastor occupied an important specific élite position by virtue of his role in the commune. In a country beset by physical obstacles, the federal government was a remote, almost metaphysical entity, and 'the authorities' on all big issues meant the cantons. But on most questions of everyday life and ephemeral administration – the only level on which most people would rub up against 'government' – the local administrative unit or 'commune' was all-important. In the twenty-two Swiss cantons there were about 3,000 communes, some administering an area as large as a town, some a tiny cluster of houses in a hamlet. The more sparsely populated a canton, the greater the number of communes: hence in Canton Geneva there were just forty-four communes, but in mountainous Graubünden there were 205.

Communes, which often owned some land and water in common, were absurdly parochial, to the point where outsiders, even from a neighbouring canton, had to pay a differential tax to switch abode from one commune to another. The commune was Swiss localism at its apogee. Whereas the nineteenth-century Englishman was first an Englishman, then a Londoner and only thirdly, say, an inhabitant of Paddington, in Switzerland the order of priorities was reversed. In the commune of Klein-Hüningen, Paul Jung, as pastor, acted as *ex officio* president of a small council of four men (including a mayor): among the council's tasks would be the provision of primary education and the hiring of schoolteachers.

There were more children of Carl Jung's own age in Klein-Hüningen, but the mere fact of his father being a minister increased his isolation. Whereas a schoolmaster could be integrated into the life of the villagers and often advised them or wrote letters for them, a pastor was regarded as a creature apart and stood outside the mainstream life of the peasants. While his parents continued to quarrel, the lonely Carl Gustav played games on his own, especially with bricks and toy soldiers, or sketched naval battles.

It was just before he went to school that he had one of the most significant dreams of his life; although Jung claimed this occurred when he was aged three or four, clinical evidence points to five or six as the more likely time.

In the dream Jung was in a meadow near Laufen castle and discovered an underground passageway. He descended and in a subterranean chamber found a kind of altar or king's throne on which stood what he thought at first was a tree trunk, some twelve to fifteen feet high and about two feet thick. The object was made of skin and naked flesh, with a rounded head and a single eye on the very top of the head. Later he would recognize the object as a ritual phallus. He was awoken by his mother's voice, as it were from outside, crying out, 'That is the maneater!'[31]

Explication of this dream has divided and taxed the ingenuity of Jungians and others. Much depends on what interpretation we put on the phallus, since for Freudians this is a classic dream of sexual anxiety, while for Jung and his disciples the dream points away from sexuality towards general realms of creativity. There are basically three main hermeneutic perspectives on the phallus: phallus = penis as in the Freudian model; phallus = general creativity as in the Jungian schema; and phallus = name or signifying function (the phallus is a symbol based on absence or lack which manifests itself in the exchange between father and mother of 'signifiers'!) as in the Lacanian universe of discourse,[32] a symbol of absence or lack, denoting what the mother seeks in the father. The phallus is a symbol of power, which is why, according to Lacan, both the mother and the children of both sexes yearn for it; to equate the phallus with the penis and make the desire for it an example of 'penis envy' is on this view absurdly simple-minded.

The penis perspective would suggest Jung's own dread of the organ, his own phallic excitement, fear of encountering the penis inside his mother's body and, more generally, castration fear and sexual anxiety. His parents were now sleeping in different rooms (Jung shared a room with his father) and, as well as being aware of his mother's strangeness, he may also have picked up, unconsciously, his father's sexual frustration; it is not inconceivable that he might have seen his father's erect penis and been frightened by it.[33] Other anxiety dreams experienced by the boy Jung seem to support this, for he later reported a nightmare of telegraph wires festooned with birds (rather in the manner of the Hitchcock movie *The Birds*), where the wires grew thicker and thicker and his fear greater and greater until the terror awoke him.[34] This surely suggests phallic tumescence.

We know that Jung's parents had a disastrous sexual relationship, with his mother full of fears and dread which his father could not assuage, and it is well known from clinical experience that children are insecure if they sense that their parents are not united in a loving sexual way. Even if we did not have Jung's testimony, we would surely wonder what was going on in a milieu where birth control was either unknown or considered sinful and where Paul and Emilie, themselves both from large families, should have taken nine years to produce a sibling for Carl Gustav. At the very least, a sexual-cultural critique of this dream would denote a culture full of sexual repression, possibly one also where dire warnings about masturbation had been issued to the boy. Some biographers have speculated that Jung's eventual break with Freudianism was predetermined by his Calvinist background, which meant he would never be able to reconcile himself to any theory positing the supremacy of the flesh.

But there is much ambiguity and obscurity in the dream, and Jung himself stated that he could not make out whether his mother's cry meant 'That is the maneater' (meaning the phallus, which implied that it, not the Lord Jesus or the Jesuit, was the devourer of children) or '*That* is the *maneater*' – implying that the phallus was simply another in the species of maneaters containing Jesus and the Jesuit or that all three were identical. And since Jung himself always minimized the importance of sexuality in early childhood, it is not surprising to find Jungians opting for 'amplification' rather than, in Freudian fashion, seeking out the latent content beneath the manifest content. Amplification involves exhausting the possible symbolic meanings by drawing in comparisons from mythology, religion, art, ethnology and so on. This reading implies choosing the second interpretation of Jung's mother's ambiguous remark in the dream, and according to this view the phallus dream shows Jung dimly reaching out towards his creative potential on the one hand and disillusioned with his parent's brand of Christianity on the other. If Jesus and the phallus are identical, then both are manifestations that inspire horror and, moreover, Heaven is located in the underworld. Far from representing the law of love, Jesus becomes a dark, almost occult phallic God, whose avatar is 'the Jesuit'.

Whatever the selected interpretation, Jung's mother does not emerge with credit, for either she is guilty of making the boy doubt his faith or she has sown severe sexual anxiety; quite possibly she has done both. In the underworld chamber of horrors where Jung encounters the phallus, his mother far from reassuring him, heightens the terror with her words. This shows the gulf between mother and son, a consequence of the painful separation while she was in the Basel hospital with depressive illness. The result was neurotic anxiety, if not worse, in Carl Gustav – perhaps a manifestation of what John Bowlby called 'anxious attachment'.[35]

One thing the phallus dream did was to exacerbate Jung's 'Jesuit-complex'.[36] Soon after the dream his mother took him for a day trip to Arlesheim and pointed out a Catholic church. Jung slipped away from her, peered in through the door at the richly decorated altar but then, with his customary accident-proneness, slipped and fell and struck his head on a piece of projecting iron. His mother picked up the bleeding boy, who was screaming at the top of his voice; later he was convinced that 'the Jesuits' had made him stumble. Jung relates that for years afterwards he was much too afraid to enter a Catholic Church and that the proximity of a Catholic priest made him uneasy.[37]

Jung's other memories of the early days in Klein-Hüningen were more prosaic. At the age of six he watched a pig being slaughtered; this increased his fascination with death but also hardened him so that later, when there was a flood of the river Wiese and fourteen people were drowned and young Carl found one of the bodies, he was indifferent, whereas his mother was frightened and shaken. In 1881 an aunt took him to a Basel museum to see the stuffed animals. He wandered off into the art gallery section where his aunt found him gazing at the nude sculptures; scandalized, she rebuked him severely: 'Disgusting boy, shut your eyes!' Also that year his mother began reading to him from a richly illustrated children's book, containing accounts of exotic religions and brightly coloured illustrations of Brahma, Vishnu, Shiva and others. Although he had an immediate sensation that these deities had a deep significance for him, his mother, by expressing contempt for 'heathens', forced him to keep his thoughts to himself.

The atmosphere at home continued to be stressful and superheated. His parents were still sleeping apart and young Carl had many anxiety dreams. When he was seven he suffered from croup and choking fits and even in his sleep had nightmares about suffocation. He later suggested that this was a 'psychogenic' factor, and that the atmosphere in the house was beginning to be unbearable. His negative feelings for Jesus were such that he hated going to church except at Christmas, which was the one Christian festival he liked. He began to suspect that his mother had a diabolical side which surfaced at night, and more and more he found it was his father who was the 'motherly' one. One night in 1883 his father got him out of bed and carried him in his arms to the west-facing porch to show him the evening sky, which was lit up with the celestial effects of the eruption of the Krakatoa volcano.[38]

Jung derived little comfort from two new aspects of his life resulting from the move to Klein-Hüningen. At the age of six he went to school and experienced a severe feeling of alienation because of the difference between home mores and those of the local children, mainly sons of peasants and farmers. Trying to ward off the effects of this 'anomie', he became two different people: at home he was studious and devoured books but at school he became a prankster. Bullied at school by a farmer's son, yet rigidly socialized at home against violence, he did not retaliate against his tormentor though stronger than him. The nightmare of bullying went on until the boy suddenly left school to work on his father's farm. Jung remarked that the experience of school alienated him from himself and made him aware of a wider world which seemed in some obscure way hostile. He was now faced by evil on two flanks. His night prayers protected him from the nocturnal peril represented by his mother, but the other evil was there the next day in school and the external world.[39]

Strangely, the aspect of schooldays most Victorians looked back on with horror did not bother Jung: the beatings. He was always an advocate of 'spare the rod, spoil the child' and liked to point out that the Zen masters taught using this method. In the village school at Klein-Hüningen the schoolmaster had a draconian system for teaching the alphabet. The master had a whip consisting of three willow wands woven together into a plait which he held in one hand while he chalked an 'A' on the blackboard. Eight boys sat together on a bench, and as he pronounced 'Now this is an A' the master would bring the whip down on all eight backs simultaneously, thus effectively thrashing knowledge into them.[40]

Universal education had been made compulsory in Switzerland in 1874, and it was the responsibility of every commune containing more than twenty children to provide a primary school. Such schools were attended by rich and poor alike – there was no class division into state and private schools as in England. Every child had to receive six years schooling between the ages of six and twelve. To the thirty hours a week 'class contact' time, forty-four weeks a year, was added an almost equal burden of homework, so that children could reckon to spend ten to thirteen hours a day at their books. It was only half in jest that an English traveller remarked that whereas the Cockney child could look forward to early years of backbreaking manual toil, the child in the slums of Zürich had no choice but to slave over his school chores. This meant that at the age of twelve, when the less fortunate left school to become ploughmen, coachmen, boatmen, woodmen, etc. they were extremely well educated by contemporary European standards.

The other novel feature about the move to Klein-Hüningen was that the Jungs had easy access to both Paul Jung's extended family and the Preiswerk clan: two of Paul's brothers were pastors in Basel and environs, and there were no fewer than six ministers on the Preiswerk side. Jung usually speaks of his relations with contempt and claimed they taught him to notice the inconsistencies in the behaviour of adults. He remembered a relative asking him where he thought he was going on his rocking horse; to which, acting the *enfant terrible*, he asked his mother why the man was talking such nonsense.

One of his Preiswerk aunts was a notorious scold. She was married to an inventor who knew how to make recordings and, one day, tired of her nagging, he made a record of one of her diatribes behind her back. Next day he played it back for her, but his wife was having none of it and exclaimed angrily when she heard her own voice, 'I never said that, it is not true.'[41]

Another aunt, who was a spinster, Jung credited with having first given him the idea for what he later called 'active imagination'. She lived in an old-fashioned house full of antiques, among which was an engraving of a bishop in full regalia coming out of a house: the bishop, his aunt explained, was his grandfather. Every Sunday, in a scene pointing forward to the macabre happenings in M.R. James's *The Mezzotint*, Jung would gaze intently at the picture until the bishop 'came down' the steps. When he explained this to his aunt, she was short with him. Young Carl, however, insisted he had seen the man walking down.[41]

Evidently at some stage Paul and Emilie resumed marital relations, for in 1884, when Jung was nine, his sister Johanna Gertrud was born. This was a shock for Carl, who had become used to being an only child and a genuine solitary besides. He had developed a passion for playing alone with bricks or other materials, and particularly liked to build up towers and then destroy them in an 'earthquake'. Albert Oeri, his schoolmate, remembers him at this time as 'an asocial little monster' who would emerge from his shell only to stir up trouble for his peers.[42] The shock was compounded, for his parents had given him no warning of an addition to the family, had said nothing about his mother's pregnancy, and then insulted his intelligence by giving him the traditional story about the stork. Dismissing this as nonsense, Jung became convinced that his mother had done something he was not supposed to know about.

The dishonesty over the birth of his sister was part of a wide pattern of bad relations between Carl and his mother. She used to humiliate him by calling out detailed sartorial instructions whenever he went to visit his numerous relations; Jung would retaliate by not passing on his parent's greetings. When his mother praised certain well-behaved and neatly dressed boys in the village, Jung was filled with hate for them, and would waylay and beat them up.

By this time Jung had evolved a 'secret' as a means of dealing with his overbearing mother. He had a vision of eternity connected with a conundrum he posed himself by sitting on a stone; he asked himself whether he was the one sitting on the stone or whether he was the stone on which he was sitting. This is the first example of the dissociation Jung would later refer to as the split between No. 1 and No. 2 personalities. It was also the beginning of his lifelong passion for stones and stone carving.

To his 'magical stone' and the mystery of the phallus dream, which he had told nobody, Jung now added a third element. He carved the end of a ruler into a mannikin, about two inches long, adding frock coat, top hat and shiny black boots. He then inked the mannikin over to make it all black and placed it in his pencil case, together with a smooth blackish stone painted with water colours as 'company' for the mannikin. Then he took the pencil case to the attic at the top of the house where he had once hidden from the 'Jesuit' and concealed it under the beam of the roof. Whenever he got into trouble at school or with his parents, Jung would take comfort from his mannikin nestling in a place where no-one could find it. The tormenting sense of being at odds with himself was gone.[43] This 'secret' symbolized the part of himself he was withholding from the world. From time to time Carl would put a 'scroll' in an imaginary language into the pencil case. He later claimed that the mannikin he carved was an archetypal image corresponding to 'Telesparos', the little cloaked god of the ancient world, found on the monuments of Asclepius and, significantly, shown reading from a scroll. The fact that he carved the mannikin without any inspiration from his father's library was one of the facts later leading him to believe in innate ideas.

The words used by Jung to describe his pencil box and mannikin are worth pondering: 'It was an inviolable secret which must never be betrayed, for the safety of my life depended on it. Why that was so I did not ask myself.'[44] Naturally, explanations have proliferated. One view is that the mannikin, like the stone, represents Jung's ability to project his psyche onto material objects and thus enables us to understand his later fascination with alchemy.[45] Another idea is that the mannikin is what child psychologists call a 'transitional object' – cuddly toys are the best example – neither something imaginary nor the objective thing for which they stand. Yet another interpretation is that phallus, Jesuit, stone and mannikin are all symbols of an as yet unapprehended Whole and represent Jung's first attempt at what he would later call 'integration'.[46] Others point to the fact that Jung hid the mannikin in the same place in which he had hidden from the 'Jesuit'; that the Jesuit, like the mannikin, had an unusual hat and frock coat, thus making him also a creature of disguise. The mannikin is phallic shaped, and the 'burial' of the mannikin in the attic relates to an early 'corpse obsession'. So, Jung's childhood secret was 'a secret compounded of a funereally dressed Jesuit and the underground phallus in addition to the contents of his pencil case . . . along with all this phallicism it is important to recognize the central part played by hiddenness, secrecy, mystery or invisibility.'[47] Finally, it has been emphasized that the secret image of the mannikin was a masculine one, and Jung's identification with it gave him a secret 'power' combatting the powerlessness associated with his father. The mannikin marked a boundary which his intrusive and disruptive mother could not cross.[48] Instead of turning vainly to this mother for the love she could not give him, or to his father for the protection he could not give him, Jung turned inwards to his own resources.

If we may take fairly seriously what Jung tells us about his first eleven years, important clues can be gleaned from his other writings about aspects of this period which he does *not* dwell on in his memoirs. Superficially, one might offer the judgement that since Jung moved from Canton Thurgau when he was a few months old, the fact that he was born in the Swiss backwoods is not important and therefore that he cannot be bracketed with those other 'prophets' who were born in remote parts of countries they later dominated. It has often been noted that the national 'giants' are rarely metropolitan figures: Jesus was born in Galilee, Mao in Yenan, Napoleon in Ajaccio, Hitler in provincial Austria, Stalin in Georgia, Franco in Galicia, Mussolini in the Emilia Romagna, and so on. Jung can be assimilated to this tradition in the sense that he never shook off the rural superstitions he absorbed in his early years, and he took over from the peasants he encountered in his youth a sense of things that went beyond space, time and causality.

Outside the big cities, the Switzerland of the 1870s and 1880s was still a remarkably primitive country and the occult was taken for granted in isolated pastoral communities. The peasants believed that glaciers were haunted by the ghosts of the dead and that the pagan god Wotan's host still roamed the lonely Alps in remote cantons.[49] Much of Swiss Christianity seemed to Jung a syncretism of pagan and Christian beliefs. Speaking of an ancient parchment in a Zürich museum on which was written an invocation to Odin and Baldur, Jung was adamant that there was a village in the Canton of Zürich where the peasants were still living by the same book, only instead of Wotan and Baldur it was Jesus Christ and his disciples.[50] During his tours of the Swiss countryside Jung himself came across blood pacts with the devil, pin-sticking and spells for drying up the milk of cattle, and handwritten books of magic. As with the 'conjurors' of Thomas Hardy's Wessex, there were in Switzerland witchdoctors in the guise of the so-called strüdel (wizard). Jung once watched a strüdel take a spell off a stable just behind the St Gotthard railway line. Several international expresses roared past during the ceremony; their passengers can scarcely have suspected that a few yards away a ceremony was taking place that had probably first taken place more than 2,000 years earlier.[51]

The cult of the primitive extended to sexuality too. In some parts of Switzerland in Jung's youth, incest for economic reasons was so common that courts did not even bother with the cases brought to their attention. Jung knew a case of a peasant who wished to marry. His mother put it to him that if he married it would simply mean another mouth to feed and she would have to move in with the couple and be supported. The solution was simple: 'If you want a woman, take me.'[52]

Jung imbibed superstition almost literally with his mother's milk, for Emilie Preiswerk was a psychic and an 'uncanny' to the point where her son was afraid of her at night. Photographs show her as a forbidding woman, and though she bore Jung when she was just twenty-seven, her youthful charms faded fast, to the point where she was considered ugly as well as domineering.[53] At an early age Jung decided it would be dangerous to let her see too much of his inner life. Although after her death he was to claim that he derived from her an earthiness and a 'hearty animal warmth', and that her intuitive gifts gave him the security to explore the depths of the psyche, this was hindsight rationalization. While she was alive he feared her in a very real sense, and her grip on him was such that, just before her death, when Jung was in his late forties, she suddenly appeared in his study, whispered a few 'uncanny' words and then vanished, leaving Jung unnerved by her visit and shaking like an aspen for hours afterwards.[54]

From his mother Jung inherited a not always pleasant ability to see people and things as they really were. Once at a wedding he told an 'imaginary story' to a barrister. An embarrassed hush fell on the company and Jung was later reproached with indiscretion for having told the man's life story; even more worryingly, he could not remember a single detail of what he had said. His intuitive ability was partly because Emilie treated him as a grown-up when he was a child and confided to him secrets she would not divulge to her husband. Jung said that he learned to divide everything she said in her normal mode by two, 'but then came the moments when her second personality burst forth, and what she said on those occasions was so true and to the point that I trembled before it.' It was from observation of his mother's 'split mind' that Jung claimed to have learned 'the natural mind of woman.' It was from her too that he intuited the secrets of 'splitting' and 'dissociation' that he was later to put to such good use in his studies of schizophrenia. His mortal fear of schizophrenic tendencies in himself was based on the knowledge of the genetic inheritance he could expect from his mother. Just as his mother was a loving carer by day and a demon by night, Jung sensed in himself a 'day' and 'night' personality.[55]

But by far the worst aspect of his mother's 'dualistic' legacy was that it made it impossible for Jung in later life to integrate his feelings in a single woman. Because it was from the maid, not his mother, that he had introjected the ideal image of femininity or 'anima', he was ever afterwards interested in the dual-mother motif and in the fact that so many mythological heroes have dual mothers. His later polygamous tendencies can be attributed to a childhood that taught him never to put all his trust in a single woman. He was also left with a deep well of rage, which accounts for the aggressiveness manifested in his adult life, the mood swings and the sudden volcanic eruptions.[56] Yet if his mother had dominated the first eleven years of his life, the dominant factor in his adolescence and young adulthood would be his moody and introverted father.

Chapter Two

TROUBLED ADOLESCENCE

In 1886, when he was eleven, Jung began attending the cantonal Gymnasium in Basel. He was clearly an advanced student, for the parting of the ways in Swiss education normally happened at age twelve, when a trifurcation took place. Those who had completed their education went to work. For a more fortunate minority there was a local secondary school where the division of labour according to sex first became apparent. There was one school for both genders, but boys attended in the morning and girls in the afternoon. Apart from the common core subjects of German, languages and mathematics, the curriculum diverged sharply: boys were taught civics, agriculture, geometry, bookkeeping, drawing and gymnastics; girls learned household accounts, horticulture, needlework and nursing. Boys leaving secondary school at fifteen could expect 'superior' jobs as waiters, farmers or foresters.

Such students could by now read and write fluently, understand politics and government and shoot all types of guns. The high level of literacy in nineteenth-century Switzerland was often contrasted with the analphabetic masses in London, Paris and New York. This was all part of what was referred to as Switzerland's 'education mania'. If Britain was a nation of shopkeepers, Switzerland was a nation of schoolteachers, and the fame of Swiss educationists – Rousseau, Fellenberg, Pestalozzi – was international. In the late nineteenth century, with universities in Basel, Zürich, Neuchâtel, Geneva, Vaud, Lucerne, St Gallen and Ticino, Switzerland was proudly aware that no other country in the world could boast so many seats of learning in proportion to population numbers.

But the literate products of normal Swiss secondary education knew nothing of Latin and Greek and many of the other humanities, and thus had no chance of entering the professions. In some ways Swiss education followed the tripartite pattern laid down in Plato's *Republic*, for an élite class of future professionals followed a third track. This was the course Jung followed, and it made him more conscious than ever of being part of an élite, even if it did point up his parent's relatively precarious financial position.

At the Basel Gymnasium Jung learned history, English and the elements of algebra, trigonometry and calculus. But the overwhelming emphasis was placed on the study of classical languages and civilization. In the high German manner, classical scholarship was seen above all as a matter of close linguistic and textual analysis: to construe a sentence of Latin prose or to write verses in Greek was regarded as a far superior enterprise to literary criticism of, say, Homer or Catullus. It is difficult to overemphasize the dominance of Greco–Roman culture in the schools of German Europe in this era. Ancient Greece, and to a lesser extent ancient Rome, were regarded as exemplars of the golden age. Athenian democracy was dwelt on but not Athenian slavery; the Greek attitude to abstract thought but not to women; the rational and Apollonian side of Greek culture, not the mystical, esoteric or Dionysian.

Greek mythology was a focal point in the literature of German high culture, particularly in the works of its most representative figure Goethe. Goethe's *Faust* – the single book that most influenced Jung – was the sacred text of Germanic culture and was memorized and recited by generation after generation of students in the Gymnasium systems. Through Goethe and the German Romantics, and through the assiduous inculcation of the classics in the Gymnasium, all Swiss and German students could cite copious passages from the classical authors. This widespread knowledge of classical citations and references bemused and bewildered visitors from the Anglo-Saxon world. When Ernest Jones met Jung and Freud in 1907 what amazed him most of all was their ability to quote huge slabs of Latin and Greek from memory and to be thoroughly familiar with each other's classical references.

At the Gymnasium Jung met boys from wealthy families and began to realize that he was simply the son of a poor parson, whereas in the village school, among peasant children, he had been the privileged one. For the first time he became aware of what it meant to have money, and he listened awestruck as his schoolmates told him of four-week holidays on the Mediterranean and, even more miraculous to his ears, of vacations among the snowy Alpine peaks. The Alps were always important to Jung, perhaps because they represented the never-never-land or Eden from which he had been expelled by his calamitous relationship with his mother.[1] But even apart from the feelings of envy and discontent engendered by attendance at the Gymnasium, Jung found the experience a nightmare. He loathed the art classes, as he could not draw still life and other set subjects – he could draw only what stirred his imagination – and he detested gymnastics, remarking that he was going to school to learn something, not to imitate the apes. This was linked with a general terror of the physical world and its potentialities which he later explained as having been caused by his mother's 'abandonment' of him at the age of three.

Worst of all was his first taste of mathematics, which seemed to him gibberish. When confronted with the mysteries of algebra and its hieroglyphic cartouches of 4a–2b+2ab, he asked plaintively, '2b what?' His classmate Albert Oeri described him as 'frankly an idiot at mathematics,' and claimed this was a hereditary failing with the Jungs.[2] Jung, who in later life liked to hold forth about the theory of relativity and quantum physics, was very sensitive on this point and at the age of sixty-five finally said his piece: 'It is an assinine [sic] prejudice that mathematics has anything to do with the training of the mind . . . Mathematics is not a function of intelligence or logic. It is a particular gift like music. You find it therefore very often in families alternating with the inheritance of musical talent . . . You also find a mathematical talent with individuals that are idiotic in every other respect.'[3]

After a number of fainting fits, self-confessedly neurotic in origin, Jung got out of gymnastics by providing a medical certificate, but there was no way out of the academic maelstrom. Sterner measures were called for, and luckily a school bully took a hand. In the early summer of 1887 Jung was standing in Basel Cathedral square waiting for a classmate when a boy shoved him in the back and knocked him off his feet. He fell and struck his head on the kerb, and was unconscious for half an hour. Just before losing consciousness he remembered thinking to himself, that he would not have to go back to school any more. As he later admitted, it was his first experience of the true meaning of neurosis, and was a singular pre-echo of a similar episode in the life of André Gide.[4]

Jung made a meal of his injury. From then on he had fainting fits whenever he was sent to school or whenever his parents asked him to do something he did not want to do. For six months he was off school, loafing, while his condition baffled a succession of doctors. He was sent to convalesce with relatives at Winterthur, where he spent his time reading or gazing fascinatedly at the railway lines. The fainting fits diminished at Winterthur but recurred as soon as he went home and there was talk of a return to school.

Back at home it was suggested that perhaps he was suffering from epilepsy. Jung laughed up his sleeve at this diagnosis, but he was quite content with his life of idling, sketching, reading and unadorned loafing in the countryside. From a modern perspective, while there may be dispute about how much of the illness was consciously faked and how much unconsciously psychogenic, it is easy to assimilate Jung's 'school-phobia' to his problems with his mother, as this is a well-known clinical correlation.[5] But the halcyon period came to an end when Jung heard his father discussing his son's 'epilepsy' with a friend. His father said the doctors had no idea what was wrong with him but thought it might be epilepsy; if this were incurable, he dreaded what would become of his son and how he could earn a living. On hearing this Jung, terrified at the thought of poverty, rushed away to learn Latin. The conflict between his conscious will and his unconscious resistance to school brought on a further three fainting fits in the space of one and a half hours, but after the third attack Jung felt better, and the fits did not recur. A few weeks later he returned to school and never had another attack. He claimed that was when he first knew what a neurosis was, forgetting that he had earlier claimed to know what a neurosis was when the boy pushed him to the ground. At first he was studious and punctilious as a means of assuaging guilt, often rising at 5 a.m. to study for two hours before leaving for school at seven, and occasionally even getting out of bed at 3 a.m. He strove to do something about his passion for solitude which he thought had pitched him into the neurotic crisis, but was continually pestered by doubts and other sensations about his own identity. On one occasion, while walking into Basel from Klein-Hüningen along the river he suddenly felt as if he had come out of a dense cloud and emerged with an intense sense of selfhood. However, this took a knock when he was invited to holiday with some friends on Lake Lucerne and was given a severe dressing down by the friends' father after some horseplay in a boat on the lake. Although one part of him acknowledged the justice of the reprimand, another side was furious that such a 'boor' should rebuke an 'important person' like himself. Wrestling with these confused feelings, he came to the conclusion that he must be two persons; one an unimportant schoolboy, the other an important old man in the eighteenth century. So began Jung's theory of the No. 1 and No. 2 personality, symbolized, respectively, by the schoolboy and the other, 'who lives in the ages'.

Jung's perception of himself as a dual personality was in part an 'introjection' of his mother, whom he had already thought of as two different people, and in part a function of his pre-adolescent neurosis. Jung himself cautions against a pathological interpretation of No. 1 and No. 2: in his view, it had nothing to do with a 'split' or dissociation in the ordinary sense but was something that was played out in every individual.

The fascination with the 'important old man in the eighteenth century' is worth examining. Jung says that he wore buckled shoes and a white wig and drove in a high-slung fly. On one occasion an ancient carriage drove past the house in Klein-Hüningen and Jung had a *déjà-vu* sensation, as if the carriage came from '*my* times'.[6] Often he would find himself writing the date 1786 instead of 1886 and each time it happened he was overcome by an inexplicable nostalgia. The stories he had heard whispered about Goethe – perhaps also the canard that he was descended from him – made an impact, and the description of No. 2 suggests that he might even *be* Goethe. It is certain that Jung always took his inspiration from the past rather than the future. He disliked the twentieth century and felt that his spiritual home was the eighteenth, where German idealism and classicism and even the Romantic Movement provided a world of order and stability – symbolized by such names as Goethe, Schiller, Hölderlin, Novalis, Kant and Leibniz and their nineteenth-century epigones Hegel, Fichte, Schelling and Schopenhauer.

It is significant that the motif of No. 1 and No. 2 personalities, though adumbrated as early as 1886, became of cardinal importance to Jung when he returned to school after his 'epileptic' episode, for the unconscious drives he had temporarily suppressed through willpower simply took another form and breached the surface as theological doubt. Ever since the phallus dream, Jung had had his doubts about Jesus, and on going to the Gymnasium he began to differentiate clearly between Jesus, with the mass of childhood associations – phallus, Jesuit, mannikin, stone – and God, an abstract being with no clear gestalt, to whom he prayed. But his intense feelings about God could not be satisfied with theological abstractions about the 'primordial actual entity'. He wanted a personal relationship with God, and after days of wrestling with a 'sinful thought' about whose nature he was unclear, he decided not to fight his fantasies any more but to go with them; after all, God must want him to think these thoughts. His fantasy took the form of a waking vision, of the kind he would later in his career describe as 'active imagination'. He saw before him the cathedral, etched against a blue sky. God appeared to be sitting on a golden throne high above the world. Suddenly he let fall an enormous turd which fell upon the sparkling roof, shattered it and broke down the walls of the cathedral.[7]

Instead of feeling blasphemous, Jung was suffused with euphoria, joy and relief, and a consciousness of having been let in on secrets denied to others. Yet to an outsider the vision implies rage and fantasies of destruction. Some have interpreted it as a preference for the 'smiting' Yahweh of the Old Testament over the 'gentle Jesus' of the New, or even as wish-fulfilment for the destruction of Christianity; in this connection another youthful Jungian remark has force: to the effect that the church was a repository of death rather than life.[8]

However, it is likely that Jung's parents, especially his father, are the true objects of his rage in this fantasy. Yet if his rage was directed against *both* parents, we can already detect a change of focus as Jung moves his father more and more to centre stage. The first revelation of the fantasy for Jung was that his father had been floundering in theological darkness and had not understood the will of God: he had clung to the God of the Bible and ignored the God of Revelation, who sees to it in his wisdom that no evil comes from tests of courage. The reason Jung felt imbued by grace was that he was convinced he had been obedient to the true will of God and defied the traditional view of religion. When God befouled his own cathedral he showed that he could be a terrible being, that he had a dark side, that he wanted his creatures to sin, and that the so-called sinner was closer to God than the 'unco' guid' – which was why, after all, Christ had founded his Church on the rock of Peter, the one who denies and wavers. By having had a glimpse of God's evil side, Jung felt he had been admitted into the band of the elect, he was a chosen one. Whenever his family spoke about religion after that, he was silently contemptuous, convinced that none of them knew anything about God's true secrets.

Jung's 'struggle with God' was an internalized form of his struggle to jettison the theological and psychic baggage of his father, and his contempt for traditional Christianity an aspect of his contempt for the man who had allowed that dispensation to immobilize him. 'My entire youth can be understood in terms of this secret'[9]: this statement referring to the turd fantasy – has an ironical ring to modern ears, as it ties in with another of Jung's dicta. He claimed that the greatest tragedy of his youth was to see his father cracking up before his eyes over the problem of faith and, as a consequence, dying an early death.[10]

It took some time for Jung to come to a conscious realization that his father clung to blind faith as a means of warding off the void of nihilism or atheism. Carl began by asking his father for an explanation of the Trinity; to his son's astonishment Paul Jung replied that he did not understand it himself. Then his father began to 'prepare' him for his first Holy Communion but Carl was bored by his father's instruction. He was as outraged by his father at prayer as Hamlet by Claudius. It seemed to Carl that his father would neither acknowledge his doubts about Christianity nor engage in any dialogue with him.[11]

At his Communion, Jung felt no spiritual contact with God, but merely a numbing void, and felt the entire ceremony to be a meaningless hoax. Despairing of guidance from his father, he began to read Biedermann's *Christliche Dogmatik* and found there the exhortation to conceive of God after the analogy of the human ego, 'the unique, utterly supermundane ego who embraces the entire cosmos'. However, Jung found this prescription to be both arrogant and blasphemous. Moreover, nothing was said in Bierdermann to make sense of the wrathful, vindictive and intolerant side of God nor to explain why, if He had made the world to his satisfaction, it was so terrible. Jung concluded that Bierdermann and all similar writers of apologetics were purveyors of obscurantist drivel, and he felt sorry for his father, who had fallen for all this mumbo-jumbo. He came to see his father as hopelessly trapped by conventional theology; the true meaning of his early experience was that God had disavowed theology and the Church founded upon it.[12]

Seeing how imprisoned his father was in the traditional teaching of the Church, which he actually used to ward off the possibility of an encounter with the true, living God, Jung decided to talk to his father in the rare intervals when he was not depressed or hyper-irritable – for on these occasions it was best to give him a wide berth. Expressing doubts about Christianity simply tapped into Paul's own suppressed scepticism and led to many angry explosions, so Carl learned to soft-pedal. By gradually drawing his father out in conversation, he eventually realized that he had had not a single numinous experience and, if he had had the courage of his convictions, would have embraced atheism. This suspicion crystallized into a certainty the day he found him perusing Hippolyte Bernheim's book on psychological suggestion, whereas hitherto he had read only novels and travel books; the Bernheim book explained away miracles, such as those at Lourdes, as examples of auto-suggestion. But these new bearings brought Paul Jung no comfort, for the more he fed his own intellectual doubts, the further he lapsed into depression and hypochondria.

The obvious way out for Carl was atheism, but he was convinced that it was precisely because he was a 'chosen one' that he had been cut off from his father's church and the faith he and other Christians so blithely shared. He, Carl Jung, had received God's grace through moral strenuousness, not the sterile formulae preached by parsons. It was his mother, at root a pantheist or animist, with a pagan 'No. 2' personality, who finally rescued him from his intellectual cul-de-sac by introducing him to Goethe and *Faust*. To Jung this was a revelation as he found there confirmation that there were or had been people who saw evil and its universal power, and the mysterious role it played in delivering Man from darkness and suffering. He objected only to the conjuring trick by which Mephistopheles was outwitted. But in general he was bowled over by Goethe and grateful to his mother for the introduction.

Since his mother and father were both in their own way devout, yet approached the problem of faith from such different directions, this tended to be yet another latent factor in their many rows. It is tempting to speculate that the sexual problems in the Jung household might have been a problem of impotence in Paul, mirroring his theological impotence, or, in turn, that his crises of faith might have immobilized him sexually as well as intellectually.[13] Carl felt compassion for his father even as he despised him, and later found more to praise in the paternal than the maternal legacy. He was grateful for the linguistic talents he inherited from this father,[14] acknowledged that he never tyrannized over him, and remembered one occasion as the best gift his father ever gave him. On his return to the Gymnasium Carl had continued to have occasional neurotic outbreaks concerned with his two personalities and in 1889 he was sent to Entlebuch under doctor's orders for a period of rest and recuperation. He recalled that for the one and only time in his youth he solved the dilemma of No. 1 and No. 2 personalities by getting drunk. At the end of his stay his father came to fetch him and announced a surprise. At Lucerne they took a lake steamer to Vitznau, the terminus of the cog-wheel railway that ran up to the snow-capped summit of Mount Rigi, above the clouds. Since tickets were expensive and Paul Jung could not afford for them both to go, Carl, full of joy, ascended on his own.[15]

The Rigi episode was an isolated moment. For much of his youth Jung continued to be plagued by narcissistic vulnerability, frustrated feelings of grandiosity and the need to be idealized; he was assailed by feelings of inferiority and low self-esteem, angry that his father failed him both by being unable to make a convincing case for Christianity and by being too feeble of will to object to his son's incoherent rebellion. Many young men, when failed by their fathers, turn to their peers, but this avenue too was blocked, since Jung was deeply unpopular at school. He began by shining academically and coming top in his class, but hated it when other boys tried to compete with him, and so decided to duck out and settle into a comfortable niche in the middle of the class. He solved his anxiety about the boys from superior social backgrounds by deliberately making friends with those from humble origins. His teachers regarded him as a troublemaker, especially when he arranged a duel between two fellow students in the vicarage garden, as a result of which one of the duellists received a bad cut from a sword.[16]

A decisive turning point in his schooldays came when Jung was twelve. He wrote an essay in the German class which he thought his best yet. The teacher agreed but said it was composed frivolously and effortlessly, and therefore that it was morally worthless. When Jung protested that he had dug deep into his intellectual resources to produce this sparkling piece of work, the teacher lost his temper. Pointing to the boy who had produced the worst essay, he asserted that he had taken trouble over it and would get on in life, whereas Jung would not, for he was all glib cleverness and humbug.[17] After that Jung did not do a stroke of work in the German class for many years, but he liked the Latin teacher, who used to send him to get books from the university library during the regular exercises, since he was so far ahead of the rest of the class; he would then dawdle back from the university, browsing through the volumes as he walked.

Jung's timidity, lack of confidence, self-effacement and apparent desire to avoid fisticuffs – largely because he had had so many unfortunate physical accidents as a child – tempted his peers to try a spot of bullying. This was a mistake, for Jung was big and strong and his repressed aggression and rage were merely awaiting a suitable focus. He was set upon by seven boys, but he seized one of them by the legs, swung him round his head like a scythe and mowed the others down. The stricken would-be bullies fled to report Jung's taste for 'brawling' to the headmaster, who marked him down once more as a 'troublemaker'. Jung was punished, which increased an already burgeoning sense of the world's injustice, but none of his schoolfellows dared to tangle with him again.

At school Jung was morbidly sensitive to criticism and, like K in Kafka's *The Trial*, felt profoundly guilty when he was accused of things of which he was innocent. As he grew older and his intellectual confidence increased, his aloof and solitary manner led him into further clashes with his teachers, and especially his old nemesis from the German class. Thinking that bygones were bygones, at sixteen he composed a precociously brilliant essay based on his reading of *Faust*, but the teacher refused to accept that the essay could have been written by a schoolboy and branded Jung a liar.

From the age of sixteen Jung was an omnivorous reader, which helped to plug the gaps left by his parents' refusal ever to discuss any general ideas at home. Only his maternal uncle, pastor at St Alban's in Basel, gave him any encouragement in his intellectual pursuits, and through him Jung became acquainted with Plato, Aristotle, Kant and Schopenhauer. This intellectual curiosity helped him overcome his shyness and to heal the split between No. 1 and No. 2 personalities, but his omnivorous reading worried his father. At school Jung's new-found confidence led simply to accusations of being conceited, a humbug, a braggart, a charlatan and a cheat. When he mentioned names like Kant and Schopenhauer to fellow students who read only what was on the syllabus, they jeered at him. Even his few friends referred to him as 'Father Abraham', which Jung took to mean that, like Abraham, he was baffled by God's paradoxical demands, but by which his schoolmates meant to indicate their feeling that he was old before his time – another phenomenon 'born old', like 'Father Time' in Thomas Hardy's *Jude the Obscure*. Jung resolved to withdraw into himself once more and to discuss his beloved philosophers only with his uncle.

Yet even in that quarter there were shocks in store. His uncle turned out not to be a truly open man intellectually but to have pet likes and dislikes – Nietzsche and Burckhardt, for example, were beyond the pale. What finished his uncle for Jung was the discovery of his selective attitude towards Kant: the great philosopher was revered when his arguments could be used to demolish the opponents of Christianity, but was dismissed when they were turned on Christianity itself. Carl was forced to prevaricate and conceal his doubts about his uncle's wisdom: the Thursday lunches at St Alban's, which he had at first looked forward to as the high spot of the week, became a dreaded ordeal and Thursday the blackest day on the calendar.

The massive self-assigned reading sessions were designed partly to ward off the assaults from No. 2 personality, and were successful in the sense that from the age of sixteen to nineteen Jung suffered less from depression than in his early years. But, since the 'quarrel with God' sometimes broke through, Jung, on his long walks in the Black Forest, developed a comforting version of pantheism. Struck by the gap between the alienated urban dwellers of Basel and 'God's world' (the world of nature and animals), he developed a Whitmanesque feeling for the dumb beasts. He renewed his mystical kinship with stones, found trees to be the closest things to the real meaning of life and developed a special feeling for Gothic cathedrals. Disillusioned with his uncle, he developed his own thoughts on philosophy. He was attracted to Plato and the pre-Socratics while disliking Aristotle and Aquinas, but was increasingly mesmerized by Schopenhauer, whose sombre picture of the world chimed in with his own observations on evil.[18] However, a close reading of

Kant alerted him to what he thought was Schopenhauer's 'fatal flaw', his central notion of Will, which Jung considered a mere hypostasization of a metaphysical assertion, turning a phenomenon into a thing-in-itself.[19]

Still much absorbed by the problems of No. 1 and No. 2 personalities, the teenage Jung had many dreams and fantasies that he was afterwards to interpret as pointing towards his life's goals. At the age of sixteen, on the three-quarters-of-an-hour walk to the Gymnasium from the vicarage, he had a fantasy of a mysterious castle in whose vault was an apparatus that turned electricity into gold; Jung later thought that this presaged his interest in alchemy and the human psyche as an apparatus.[20] A little later he fantasized that a large four-master was making way in full sail up the Rhine and that Basel was destined to be a port. He oscillated between indulging these fantasies and brooding on them, and casting them aside and turning instead to the construction of fortresses out of small stones. Castles and keeps fascinated him, and he began a detailed study of the fortification plans of the seventeenth-century military engineer Vauban. The zigzag pattern between daydreaming and practicality was part of an ongoing internal debate: which was more important, the fantasies and theological issues engendered by the No. 2 personality or the scientific knowledge of the No. 1? Fearing the No. 2 personality, which he associated with his mother and thus with depression and mental illness, in his late teens Jung overwhelmingly opted for the study of fossils and plants and the reading of scientific periodicals, yet the issues raised by *Faust* would not so easily be denied.

The problem was that he could not reinforce 'No. 1' by contact with either of his parents. In 1891 a visit to his father, who was holidaying alone at Sachseln, gave him the opportunity to visit the hermitage at Flüeli. This hermitage was famous as the residence of the fifteenth-century German mystic Brother Klaus (Nicholas of Cusa), who was later to be so profound an influence on Jung. The visit to the hermitage reactivated all the old concerns from the No. 2 personality. Jung's unbalanced mental state emerges clearly from the story he tells of his first romantic encounter. While strolling up the hill from the hermitage he met a pretty, blue-eyed girl and in a rush of enthusiasm told her all about himself and his secret thoughts. At first he was convinced that their meeting had been pre-arranged by Fate, but then the manic mood subsided, and he realized there was an impenetrable barrier between them and that the encounter was meaningless.[21]

If his first fantasy sexual encounter was associated with his father – for it took place near Sachseln, where his father had a friend who was a priest, and Jung imagined that this priest was the girl's father confessor – his first sexual experience also took place in a sense under his father's aegis, for when Jung was eighteen he was seduced by a male friend of his father's. We know little about this incident other than that the seducer was a man he had once idolized and that the experience left Jung with a personal horror of sexuality.[22] However, it seems reasonable to conclude that the seduction did little to enhance Jung's feelings of trust towards the world, never great at the best of times, and may have swung him back to sympathy for his mother, since his preferred parent (his father) lived, it seemed, in a world that was even more precarious.

Jung's final years at the Gymnasium were clouded with tension and anxiety. At the very time he fell prey to his father's homosexual friend, his relations with his father again plummeted. Throughout 1893–94 there were almost daily clashes between father and son, which sometimes degenerated into overt quarrelling. Paul Jung complained of mysterious abdominal pains for which no organic cause could be found, and spent hours in his study smoking his long pipe, locked in a neurotic attachment to the past, which manifested itself in rambling, sentimental reveries. It seems that Paul now regarded an escape into the 'golden age' of his youth as his only refuge, since his wife, his son, and finally his God had forsaken him. Not surprisingly, Carl worried about the future, for he had a semi-invalid father on his hands, there was little money in the family, and his mother was both unstable and without qualifications. Teenagers who have to deal with domestic insecurity are frequently disruptive influences at school, so it is no particular surprise to find that his Gymnasium report for the second quarter of 1894 records that he was reprimanded for wilful misbehaviour and for disrupting the school outing.[23]

Clearly Jung was worried about his future. Could he even afford to go to university? Even if he could, which direction should he take? His No. 1 personality pointed towards the sciences, but No. 2 indicated the humanities. The choice narrowed to archaeology or the sciences, so Jung conducted an internal debate on the relative claims of No. 1 and No. 2 and tried to look at himself from the viewpoint of both personalities. In the eyes of No. 1 he was a disagreeable, moderately gifted young man with vaulting ambitions but an undisciplined temperament, who alternated between naïve enthusiasm and childish disappointment, and was in his inmost essence a hermit and an obscurantist. As for No. 2 this was, in No. 1's view, a 'dark continent'. From the vantage point of No. 2 things looked very different. The life-tasks set by No. 1 seemed to be part of a thankless moral quest, complicated by a variety of personal faults such as laziness, despondency, depression and inept enthusiasm for valueless ideas; he was liable to imaginary friendships, limited, prejudiced, stupid (as evinced by the mathematical cretinism), lacking in understanding for other people and confused on philosophical and theological issues. No. 2 felt himself to be in secret accord with the wisdom of the Middle Ages, as personified by Goethe's *Faust*.

Seeking to break out of the impasse into which he had been hedged by his two conflicting personalities, Jung had three significant dreams which decided him in favour of a scientific career. In one he was unearthing the remains of prehistoric animals in a burial mound on the Rhine, and in another he discovered a wondrous creature in a deep pool in a wood – a creature he named a giant radiolarian. In the third and most important dream he was making his way through a blanket of fog with the aid of a tiny light he held cupped in his hands and seemed to be pursued by a dark and fearsome creature; on awaking he realized that he had been pursued by his own shadow. Although the first two dreams suggested that zoology was the proper subject for him to study, Jung, mindful of his family's poverty, opted for medicine, which offered better career prospects. He hoped that he had at last solved the conflict between his two personalities: it seemed to him he had to go forward into the world of No. 1 – study, moneymaking, responsibility – and leave No. 2 in abeyance for a while, not forgetting that No. 2 was after all the source of dreams.[24]

Jung passed his final examinations at the Gymnasium in the early spring of 1895 and on 18 April was registered as a medical student at the University of Basel. His school experience shaped his later ideas on child development, even though this was never an area of primary interest to him. He always believed that gifted children should be educated in the same class as their more normal peers. While acknowledging that it was hard to distinguish the wool-gathering of the gifted child from the lack of concentration of a mental defective, he remained convinced that there were no misunderstood geniuses, only 'lazy hounds'. Even the unhappy experiences with the German teacher taught him the hard truth that the gifts of the gods were two-edged: the shadow side of talent and creativity was unpopularity and an exaggerated self-confidence.[25] By now he was a splendid physical specimen, six foot, one inch tall, broad-shouldered, powerfully built, with a deep resonant voice. Since his father could not pay for all the cost of his studies, Jung applied to the University of Basel for a grant, which was awarded, thus destroying a favourite Jung fantasy of his teenage years, that 'top people' were against him.

When his son was ensconced as a medical student, Paul Jung seemed to rally momentarily and emerge from his torpor. Once he attended a meeting of a fraternity Carl had joined and displayed such exuberant spirits in the student milieu that his son realized that in essence time had stood still for him since his undergraduate days; Jung wondered if he too would end up treading the downward path from youthful enthusiasm to cynical and jaundiced middle age. But the irruption of Jung senior into the university ambience was a flash in the pan, and by the winter of 1895 he seemed to be fading from sheer lack of will to live. Soon the strapping barrel-chested Carl was carrying his father around like a helpless child. Finally, on 28 January, Jung returned from an anatomy lesson to find his father dying. Paul rallied momentarily to ask his son how he had got on in the exam. Jung humoured him and said he had done well, whereupon his father lapsed into a coma. Carl stayed with him, heard the death rattle and in a detached vein watched him die, only summoning his mother when all was over. His mother croaked, in her No. 2 voice, 'He died in time for you,' meaning that father and son did not understand each other and that Paul would probably have been a hindrance to Carl in his career.[26]

Jung commented detachedly that his father's suffering and death was a kind of imitation of Christ; unfortunately his father had not seen this and had thought of his suffering as a purely personal affliction.

There were three main consequences for Jung of his father's death, two of them at the theoretical level and the third a pressing material problem. In the first place Jung began to develop his theory that it was the lot of the child to live out or fulfil that portion of the parent's life that was left undone, though he stressed later that the unfulfilled matter was likely to be of a collective rather than an individual nature.[27] His father had warned him to be anything except a theologian. There are some who would say that a theologian, rather than a psychologist, was what Jung ultimately became, and that his true life's work was solving the problems of God and the devil that his father shrank from or could not face.[28] Certainly Jung could not simply shrug off the memory of his father and turn over a completely new leaf. Six weeks after Paul's death he appeared to his son in a dream, and the dream was repeated two days later.

Secondly, the immediate cause of Paul Jung's death was cancer, and this would lead Carl in later years to elaborate a theory that cancer tended to occur when a person came to a halt in his or her personal development of self-realization or could not surmount some obstacle. If an inner process of growth or spontaneous creative activity did not begin then, the result was likely to be fatal. But although Jung believed a carcinoma could develop for psychic reasons, and even disappear for psychic reasons, he stressed that this did *not* mean that cancer was remediable by psychotherapy or could be prevented by any particular psychic development.[29]

Thirdly, the Jung family was at once plunged into financial crisis, since Paul Jung had left just £200. The family moved out of the vicarage and took a cheaper house in the Bottminger Mill area in the Basel suburb of Zinnigen. For a short while Carl came under pressure from his maternal (Preiswerk) relatives to leave university and take a job as a clerk. When he asked one of his uncles for advice, the worthy replied that he would now learn to be a man; initially furious at this glib nonsense, Jung later reflected that the advice was not so bad after all. He moved into his father's room and took his place as the head of the household, doling out a housekeeping allowance to his mother each week. He himself did the household accounts but quickly realized that he was not going to make ends meet, since she was hopeless at domestic management, refused to economize and had a Dora Copperfield approach to money. On one memorable occasion he asked her to buy enough muslin to keep wasps off a bunch of grapes; Mrs Jung came back from Basel with a hundred dusters. However, she was a good cook – food was always very important to Jung – and after some domestic altercation he would usually pick a bunch of wildflowers on the way home to give her as a peace offering.

Jung later claimed to have enjoyed his time of poverty and to have learned from it,[30] but we can take this with a pinch of salt.

In fact poverty deeply distressed him and financial matters looked very bleak until three members of his extended family finally rallied round. An aunt gave him the right to sell her collection of antiques on a commission basis and Jung proved an astute salesman. Meanwhile his mother's youngest brother gave her a small allowance, while a paternal uncle gave him a long-term interest-free loan of 3,000 Swiss francs to keep him at the university. By 1897 the worst money worries were over, and Jung was able to concentrate on a new problem. The Preiswerk family had finally surpassed itself in the realms of the uncanny, or so it seemed, and in Hélène Preiswerk, Jung's cousin, it had produced a genuine medium.

Chapter Three

STUDENT DAYS

Shortly before Paul Jung's death it became clear that his son's seduction at the hands of the unknown 'family friend' had decisively swung Carl back into the maternal orbit, for in June 1895, unknown to her husband, Emilie Preiswerk arranged a series of seances in the Klein-Hüningen presbytery. Carl was the only male present, and the other participants – Luise and Hélène Preiswerk and Emmy Zinstag – were there without the knowledge of their fathers.[1] The star of the show was the thirteen-year-old Hélène Preiswerk, Emilie's niece.

The first session took place at nightfall. Jung's own accounts of them have to be used with care, for he altered the chronology to make it appear that he had first made contact with Hélène in 1899 (i.e. four years later), and he presented the weird happenings in the vicarage as a controlled scientific experiment when they were in fact an example of amateur mediumship of the 'family circle' kind. Most importantly, he concealed the fact that he used hypnotism to induce Hélène's trances, and wrote of them as if they had been spontaneous occurrences.

There were three meetings in 1895, then the series of seances was interrupted by Paul Jung's death and the period of mourning; the sessions resumed in 1897. At the 1895 seances Hélène communicated with Jung's paternal and maternal grandfathers and produced a remarkable impersonation of Samuel Preiswerk's voice and lecturing style. While 'possessed' she spoke in High German instead of her usual Basel dialect and afterwards could remember little of what she had said during the session, except that she was convinced the spirits of the dead had spoken through her mouth.[2]

When the coven of spiritualists regrouped in 1897 – Jung was by now coming to the end of his second year in medical school – Samuel Preiswerk 'came through' again, this time with a proselytizing message, in which he urged Hélène to set up a national home for Jews in Palestine and *then* to convert them to Christianity. This puzzled the listeners, for in his lifetime Samuel Preiswerk had been an ardent Zionist but not a convertor. After about a month, however, Hélène fell into a different sort of trance, which Jung described as 'semi-somnambulic', in which she remained aware of her surroundings while making contact with the spirits.[3] In this state she revealed a secondary personality in herself and said that her name was 'Ivenes'. This new personality was dignified, ladylike, calm, poised and serious, in contrast with Hélène herself, who was inclined to giddiness and instability; Hélène tended to go in for table turning and automatic writing, Ivenes for revelations about the past.[4]

Interested in the possibilities of auto-suggestion, Jung drew Hélène's attention to Justinus Kerner's then well-known book about a visionary, *The Seeress of Prevorst*. The behaviour of 'Ivenes' then changed. She spoke in an unknown language, resembling a mixture of French and Italian, and claimed she had journeyed to the planet Mars whose canals and flying machines she described, and that she had visited the stars and learned to instruct black spirits. Her controlling spirit was still Samuel Preiswerk, with his inspirational sermons. Other spirits manifested themselves, generally falling into two groups, the dour and the exuberant, depending on whether the personality of Hélène or Ivenes was dominant at a given moment. There were visions of occasional struggles between the white and black spirits, which seemed to Jung to correlate with Hélène's 'limbo' position, half in the dream world, half in the external world.[5]

Then came evidence of reincarnation, that Ivenes had lived before. She had been the Seeress of Prevorst herself and before that a young woman seduced by Goethe – which, according to the 'Family Romance', made her Jung's great grandmother. In the thirteenth century she had been a Madame de Valours who had been burned as a witch; in the tenth century she had been the Countess of Thierfelsenburg; in the first century AD she had been a Christian martyr under Nero. Soon she came close to achieving Walt Whitman's mystical sense of identity with the entire world, for she imagined herself to be the ancestor of most people she knew and, by giving birth to numerous children in each of her previous incarnations, was at the centre of an elaborate genealogical mosaic. She displayed considerable ingenuity in weaving into this intricate fabric any new person she met. It was apparent that she displayed a particular interest in Jung, assuring him that a female friend of his had been a famous poisoner in eighteenth-century Paris. Other forays into the 'hidden world' included a description of the structure of the mystic world involving seven circles, with ever-increasing illumination as one approached the nucleus: light and darkness were in the third circle, matter in the second, and the 'primary force' in the central circle.

Although Jung does not make this clear in *Memories* and suggests that the 'occult phenomena' in his household were the *cause* of his making contact with Hélène, it seems that 'undischarged psychic vibrations' were left in the house after the seances, for the family was disturbed in 1898, shortly after the resumption of the seances, by two bizarre events. First there was the freak splitting of the family's seventy-year-old dining table, very solid and made of seasoned walnut wood, when, following a crack like a pistol shot, a fissure appeared along it from the rim to beyond the centre against the line of the joint. Two weeks later, while Jung was at the university, there came another sudden pistol shot from inside a cupboard, and it was discovered that the flawless steel blade of a bread knife had snapped off and splintered into several pieces. When Jung came home he found his mother, his sister and the maid very upset at the mysterious shot, and it was only after a careful search that he identified the cause in the form of the shattered fragments in the cupboard.[6] In *Memories* Jung presents these events as inexplicable, contextless occult happenings, but even at the naturalistic level the two events were entirely reconcilable with the laws of physics.[7]

Soon, however, matters began to take an alarming turn with his cousin, for Hélène began to fall into trances when not at the seance. One night she appeared uninvited in Jung's bedroom, dressed in a white robe.[8] It seems more than a coincidence that almost immediately after this incident Jung invited some of his classmates from the university to one of the seances and they at once caught Hélène cheating. Her latest speciality was to show her audience 'apports', or objects allegedly brought from 'the other side' by spirits, and she was detected producing one like a conjuror from beneath her dress. The situation became clear to Jung: his cousin was in love with him and had fabricated the evidence for the supernatural, having acutely divined his passion for the occult and his 'will to believe'. He quitted the seance in disgust.

But when, later, he reflected on nearly five years of intermittent seances, he realized that, beyond the fraud committed by Hélène, in the end when her considerable powers of acting, impersonation and invention were failing, many important aspects of the human mind had been revealed by his cousin and her *alter ego* Ivenes. Her impersonations of historical figures were associated with the dream images of normal sleep; the split-off part of her personality (Ivenes) used the nearest available material – the Preiswerk family – which was why she spoke in the voice of Jung's grandfather; and there seemed to be a clear connection between her hallucinatory personalities and the delusions of mental patients. It is not surprising that in 1902 Jung said that it was Hélène who had first revealed to him the existence of the unconscious,[9] and it was clearly his experience of seances, not, as he claimed, a 'road to Damascus' revelation when reading the work of Krafft-Ebing, that made him decide to become a psychiatrist.

The existence of an unconscious seemed to Jung to be clearly indicated by Hélène's ability, when in a mediumistic state, to ascend to a level far superior to that of her waking state. And the stories of overt and secret love affairs, the illegitimate births, and the desire for an immense family, were a transmogrification of a secret wish for sexual gratification, thus increasing the probability that Freud, with his theory of dreams as suppressed wishes (published in the very year Jung gave up the seances), was right. Yet there were elements in the experience with Hélène that pointed forward towards the later Jungian theories. The more mature personality of Ivenes suggested a potential as yet unexpressed in Hélène but in the process of elaboration in the unconscious, and her choice of mediumship could be the means adopted by the unconscious to overcome the obstacles to psychic growth posed by a repressive and patriarchal society. Here was the germ of the seminal, later Jungian idea of 'individuation'.

Hélène herself had an uncanny effect on Jung, and he claimed to have learned about women from her first, since her image constituted a key part of his general image of women (or 'anima' as he later termed it). One of Jung's mistresses, Sabina Spielrein, confirmed this a few years later.[10] To put it in technical Jungian language, his anima was 'constellated'. The erotic charge between the two was thus by no means one-way, though it was Hélène who suffered most as a result of the unfulfillable 'affair'. The rapport between Hélène and Jung was unmistakable, for she could read him like a book. She sensed that he was attracted to Jewesses and therefore claimed to be one.[11] Intuiting that he was deeply perplexed about aspects of Italian culture – what Jung would later refer to his as his 'Rome-complex' – she sought messages from 'the other side' from one 'Conventi', supposedly an Italian murderer. Many of Ivenes's personalities came from the Italian Renaissance and in one incarnation she was supposed to have been a princess, married to Ludovico Sforza.[12] Hélène's ability to 'touch' a 'complex' was also revealed by the story of the affair with Goethe, whom she knew to have a special significance for Jung; this was a disguised expression of her own desire to have an affair with Carl and is an important element in the 'kinship libido' between them.

In discharging her erotic fantasies on an impossible object, Hélène was exhibiting in primitive form what would later be recognized as 'the phenomenon of transference'. The Jungian analyst James Hillman has suggested that, with Hélène, Jung enjoyed what he called '*participation mystique*', but that he later integrated his 'endogamous anima' so that he no longer required people like Hélène for projective rapport.[13] Certainly the importance of Hélène Preiswerk for Jung can scarcely be overestimated, and if Herman Melville claimed that the whale boat was his Yale and his Harvard, it may not be hyperbolic to suggest that Jung's true university was the series of seances with Hélène. The irony of it all was that despite his having taken a firm and conscious decision to pursue science and the dictates of the No. 1 personality, Jung's true formation in his Basel University years took place at the hands of the occult and his No. 2 personality, showing once again that the unconscious can never be denied.

The bizarre experiences with Hélène steeled Jung against the mockery he had to endure in the world of No. 1 because of his interest in the occult. He wished to know what was the objective truth about so-called supernatural phenomena but, apart from his mother and the young Preiswerks, nobody seemed interested in what was to him a matter of burning urgency, and some in his circle even indicated fearfully that it was not an area into which any God-fearing person should venture. From having taken the supernatural for granted in his youth, he now found that at the university everybody scoffed at it. He sought refuge in his old idea of the disjuncture between civilization and 'God's world', but this solace was dangerous, for any feeling of superiority, he knew from bitter experience, would make him unpopular. He therefore decided on a new form of integration. Not only would he mediate between the demands of Nos 1 and 2 but he would also divide himself between the studious life and the heavy-drinking life of the 'hearty'.

Jung in his cups was noisy, roistering and abrasive, though seldom seen helplessly drunk. From his physical burliness and his beer-drinking capacity he soon received the nickname 'the Barrel'. His favourite haunt was the 'Breo' tavern in the Steinem district, where he sometimes stayed all night. When he had been on an all-night binge he reverted to his old trick of taking his mother a bouquet of wild flowers as a peace offering. He also appealed to her own No. 2 personality by talking of the dangers of walking home at night to Binningen through the Nightingale woods – an area notorious locally for the number of murders committed there. Although he carried a loaded army pistol with him, he always liked to inveigle one of his fellow students into walking back with him through the wood, through fear not of human assailants but of ghosts, though what the loaded pistol was supposed to do against phantoms of the spirit worlds was not clear.[14]

According to Albert Oeri, Jung was a good dancer who had a decided eye for a pretty girl. At one festival he fell madly in love with a girl from the French-speaking part of Switzerland and decided to get engaged. He went into a jeweller's shop and spotted a ring that would be ideal for his fiancée. When told the price, which was beyond his means, Jung went into a towering rage and asked the jeweller how he was supposed to get engaged with prices like that. He stormed out and ended the romance. The woman once glimpsed who provokes besotment was a recurring feature in the life of the young Jung: first there was the peasant girl at the Brother Klaus hermitage, now the French-speaking girl, and later there would be others who would 'constellate the anima'.

His straitened circumstances, which had led to the débâcle in the jewellers, improved when he got two further jobs, in addition to acting as agent for his aunt's antiques. He obtained part-time work as a junior assistant in the medical laboratory and in the summer worked as a locum in the village of Mannedorf when Dr Heinrich Pestalozzi was on vacation. This was his first experience of the Lake Zürich area, and it involved a great deal of trudging to outlying farms and cottages; the peasants, however, thought Jung had an outstanding bedside manner for one so young. With the extra money he had a telephone installed, but his mother sensed an 'uncanny' rival and loathed what she called 'the sorcerer's box'. Once her cousin rang up and his mother put her ear to the receiver and peered hard into the mouthpiece. 'Yes, yes I hear you but I cannot see you,' she exclaimed, and eventually became so exasperated that she smashed down the receiver and refused ever to go near the telephone again.[15]

Jung's formal studies at the University of Basel were uneventful. He was admitted to the medical school on 18 April 1895 and qualified as a physician five and a half years later. After his introductory course he became a junior assistant in anatomy and in the following semester the demonstrator placed him in charge of the histology course. He hated physiology because of the vivisection involved; Jung was always horrified by cruelty to animals, and this was as much due to his quasi-Whitmanesque empathy with them as to his Schopenhauerian, neo-Buddhist sympathies. The part of the course that interested him most was evolutionary theory and comparative anatomy, which in those days played a much greater part in the training of physicians. Jung shone in zoology, where the professor was Friedrich Zschokke, a newcomer to the chair who had made his name in parasitology but in Basel specialized in hydro-biological ecology.[16] Yet when Jung had to make a choice (in 1898) between surgery and internal medicine and had to forego a career in surgery because he did not have the financial means to sustain himself through the early years, he was increasingly seen as a protégé of Professor Friedrich Müller, the internalist whose favourite research project was correlating the periodicity of menstruation with the tides.[17]

Jung's schedule of lectures, reading and practical work was gruelling, so that it was only on Sundays that he was able to read his favourite authors, Kant, Eduard von Hartmann and Nietzsche, and to continue his theological speculations. It was conventional at Basel to pooh-pooh Nietzsche, but Jung quickly discovered a kindred spirit – all the more valuable for his psychic health as his writings were widely known and he did not have to be yet another 'secret'. The reading of *Also sprach Zarathustra* was as much a revelation to him as *Faust* had been. The personage of Zarathustra was clearly Nietzsche's 'No. 2', and, as Jung saw it, Nietzsche had been driven mad by two things: unlike Jung, he had discovered his 'No. 2' late in life; and he had 'fearlessly and unsuspectingly let his No. 2 loose upon a world that knew and understood nothing about such things'.[18] In theology

Jung elaborated his long-felt dislike of the Christian view of Christ as the link between God and Man. In Jung's view this was what linguistic philosophy would later call a 'category mistake': the true link between Man and God was the third person of the Trinity, the Holy Ghost.

Jung had a pronounced taste for metaphysical disputation and entered with gusto into the proceedings of the Basel section of the Zofingia society, to which he was admitted on 18 May 1895. The Zofingia was a student fraternity particularly associated with the movement for Swiss independence, and at this stage in his career Jung was identified as a liberal. Of 120 members drawn from the four faculties of theology, philosophy, law and medicine, about two thirds could be expected to attend the weekly meetings, and Jung quickly made his mark as a combative and talented debater who could hold an audience spellbound with his exegeses on Mesmer, Swedenborg, Lombroso and Schopenhauer.[19]

In his fourth semester, on 28 November 1896, Jung gave his first talk to the Zofingia on 'The Limits of Exact Science', arguing against materialism and in favour of a scientific study of the occult. This was well received, though Jung in *Memories* liked to portray himself as a voice crying in the wilderness, and therefore played down the degree of acceptance his address commanded. In the summer semester of 1897 he delivered 'Some thoughts on Psychology' – a farrago of ideas culled from Schopenhauer, Kant and David Strauss, in which he deplored the current lack of interest in metaphysics and argued for the reality of spirits and the occult.[20] In 1898 he was elected chairman of the fraternity, and in his inaugural address during the winter semester of 1897–98 he used Basel's stone tower as a central symbol for the contemplative life, arguing that an educated man should eschew political activity – a fashionable attitude among pre-1914 intellectuals. Jung's lifelong taste for strong language was well to the fore; he quoted Blücher, whose late arrival on the field of Waterloo dealt the *coup de grâce* to Napoleon: 'They are damned bastards, those diplomats.'[21] His fourth lecture, 'Thoughts on the Nature and Value of Speculative Inquiry', delivered in the summer of 1898, contained more of his thoughts on Kant and Schopenhauer, but it was in his final address that Jung revealed himself as the theologian *manqué* he always was with a lengthy critique of the theology of Albrecht Ritschl, whom he criticized for ignoring the mystical element in religion.[22]

Jung's final contributions to the rough-and-tumble of the Zofingia came after talks by other students. He pitched into one of his peers who lectured on sleep by pointing out that he had omitted to discuss the most important element: dreams. And in the very last debate he took part in he found himself clashing with Paul Häberlin, the boy who had been born three years after him in Kesswil. Jung, in typical self-confident vein, scouted the idea that God could be experienced, on the ground that he himself had never had such an experience, and argued instead for a correlation between religious feeling and the sexual instinct. This brought Häberlin to his feet, and in a heated exchange Jung was forced to reveal his true colours when he declared that the idea of a good God was self-contradictory.[23] There was never any doubt of Jung's aplomb, eloquence, vitality and impetuosity, but many of his peers resented his stance of 'effortless superiority' and his apparent need for disciples, and noted that, while hypersensitive to criticism from others, he was often tactless and wounding himself.

The Zofingia lectures reveal a fascination with philosophy which other eminent psychologists, Freud especially, never shared. Given Jung's mystical feeling for the number four, it is not surprising to find that in later life he always turned for inspiration and sustenance to an élite quartet: Plato, Kant, Schopenhauer and Nietzsche. Aristotle never appealed to him, nor did Hegel, at that time all the rage in universities throughout the Germanic- and English-speaking world. Jung always felt that Hegel had misplaced his vocation, that his philosophy was a highly rationalized and lavishly decorated version of the unconscious: it was ever his view that Hegel, as a romantic thinker contrasted with the rationalist Kant, was a psychologist *manqué*.[24]

In his first year at the university, Jung had made a vow that he would work more from facts rather than intuition or would try to match the two up.[25] Matching the facts to his intuition meant integrating No. 1 and No. 2 personalities, and 'somehow, somewhere' Jung eventually found the 'open sesame' in psychiatry. He dramatizes the process in *Memories* as the chance reading of Krafft-Ebing's *Lehrbuch der Psychiatrie*, but it seems likely that the process was a more attenuated one and that Krafft-Ebing merely crystallized a process already under way by 1898. In the winter semester that year Jung attended a course in psychiatry given by Professor Wille at Basel, and followed with another in his final semester in 1900; the point was that in order to qualify as a physician it was necessary to attend only one such course. Although psychology was then held in academic contempt as a subject for intellectual lesser breeds, Jung was intoxicated by the discovery of a discipline that united science and the humanities and held out the promise of healing his divided self.[26]

The decision to specialize in psychiatry alarmed and disappointed his mentor, the internist Friedrich Müller, who had been hoping to take his brilliant young protégé with him as chief assistant when he moved to Munich. At first Müller reacted with stupefaction and incredulity, but gradually he accepted the inevitable. Jung's new-found euphoria, though, once again exposed his Achilles' heel of over-confidence. Certain that Fate was on his side – which seemed borne out when he correctly 'question-spotted' in the early papers of the final examination – he made a mess of the paper in his favourite subject, pathological anatomy. This meant that he did not head the list of medical students graduating in 1900, as widely expected, but merely tied for first place with a man he despised as a banal, narrow specialist.

This man could justifiably be seen as Jung's 'shadow' or alter ego, for he soon pitched into the schizophrenia Jung so deeply feared he himself might fall prey to – one of the reasons he was so interested in Hélène Preiswerk was that he was terrified that he might inherit a 'psychotic' gene from the Preiswerks. Widely touted as 'one to note', Jung's rival first drifted around Egypt, then came up with a crackpot scheme for damming up the St Moritz area in Canton Wallis to produce electrical energy for the whole of Europe, and seemed merely disconcerted when it was pointed out that all the inhabitants would either drown or have to be displaced. Next he concocted a scheme for diminishing gravity but by this time he was beginning to be inundated by psychotic delusions. He ended up being confined for life to an asylum.[27] This was not the last time that a fate Jung feared for himself was actually visited on someone else closely connected with him, and it increased his perception of himself as 'psychic'.

There is a suspicion – and lacking the documentary evidence which has never been released it can only be a suspicion – that some of the weaknesses Jung feared might overtake him had settled instead on his sister. It is distinctly odd that Jung never refers to his sister except on one occasion, and then in such a Delphic manner that one immediately senses that something is being hidden. He says that Johanna Gertrud, who died at fifty, was homeloving, conventional, physically delicate, sickly and virtually sexless and in every respect different from him. A spinster, she went into hospital in 1935 for a simple operation but did not survive it. At root she had always been a stranger to Jung.

It was a requirement for the degree of doctor of medicine at Basel that candidates submit a dissertation, and Jung hit on the clever idea of using his experiences with Hélène Preiswerk to illustrate a thesis on the psychological foundations of the occult. When he began work in 1900, new light was shed on his preoccupations by a contemporary bestseller brought out that year by Théodore Flournoy, *From India to the Planet Mars*, which had uncanny parallels with his own experience with Hélène. Flournoy spent five years working with a medium named Catherine Müller, who became better known under her pseudonym in the book, Helen Smith. A convinced spiritualist who worked as a saleswoman in a department store, Smith, an attractive thirty-year-old, had entered semi-somnambulic and full somnambulistic states over the five years, and manifested personality changes in the course of which she offered alleged proof of reincarnation. Smith and her admirers were convinced she was genuinely re-enacting scenes from past lives, but the sceptics considered her fraudulent. Flournoy, however, came to much the same conclusion as Jung on Hélène Preiswerk, that the true explanation was much more complex and interesting. Instead of fraud he postulated cryptamnesia (forgotten memories) and wish-fulfilment, and described the 'revelations' as 'romances of the subliminal imagination'.

As with Hélène and Samuel Preiswerk, Helen Smith had a 'guiding spirit' in the form of 'Leopold' – interpreted by Flournoy as a subpersonality of the medium. By a close examination of the three different 'cycles' of Smith's revelations, he then showed that her alleged previous lives were examples of a reversion of the personality to a different age. In the first cycle Smith had re-enacted her life as a fifteenth-century Indian princess, in the second her life as Marie-Antoinette, and in the third her time as a Martian, in which cycle she claimed to be familiar with the geography, culture and language of the planet Mars and even spoke and wrote the 'Martian' tongue. Flournoy identified all the books Smith had read as a child and then forgotten, and convincingly cited these as the source of the revelations. Then he pointed out that the Marie-Antoinette cycle was a reversion to the age of sixteen, the Hindu cycle to the age of twelve and the Martian fantasy to early childhood.

Further investigations firmed up Flournoy's hypotheses. He had conjectured that the 'Martian' spoken by Helen Smith was a form of French but the linguist Victor Henry established that the vocabulary was mostly composed of distorted Hungarian words, and it was known that Hungarian was the mother tongue of the medium's father. And a close reading of the rapport established between Flournoy and Smith showed that the same erotic 'transference' had taken place as between Jung and Hélène. Flournoy had convincingly demonstrated the activity of the unconscious in the form of creativity, compensation and wish fulfilment and added the important idea of cryptamnesia to the corpus of psychological ideas. Helen Smith's later career also paralleled Hélène Preiswerk's, suggesting the innate perils of mediumship. Flournoy had stressed the 'ludic' nature of the 'romances of the subliminal imagination', arguing that it was an advanced form of play, a kind of mental equivalent of playing with dolls, but warned that the 'play' required a compensating anchor in work, or the fantasies might overwhelm the subject. Unfortunately, Helen Smith became greedy for the material things of life. First she threatened to bring a legal action unless Flournoy shared the royalties from the best-selling book; Flournoy acquiesced. Then she was taken up by a wealthy American woman who paid her a large allowance simply for concentrating on mediumship fulltime. Flournoy's fears were fulfilled, for by giving up her job Helen severed the last link with reality. She died young after a life as a hermit, in which she painted religious subjects while in a somnambulistic state.

Jung was so impressed by Flournoy's book that he wrote to him in Geneva, offering to provide the German translation of the book. Flournoy did not reply for six months, by which time he had a deal with a German publisher, but he sugared the pill a year later, when Jung's thesis was published, with a very favourable review.[29]

In his dissertation Jung posed the question: were psychic powers simply special psychological states or did they relate to the supernatural? His answer was a resounding endorsement of the former proposition, for he generalized from the Hélène Preiswerk experience to the theory that anyone, given enough patience, could make tables move through unconscious motor impulses. Before he had even begun his career as a psychiatrist Jung had made the important discovery, confirmed by Flournoy, that split-off contents of the unconscious could take on the appearance of a human personality, whether projected onto the external world in the form of hallucinations or as a temporary controller of the conscious mind, as in the mediumistic sessions. He advanced the idea that many alleged cases of plagiarism could simply be cryptamnesia, and stressed the inevitable erotic content in an encounter between medium and doctor.

Jung's thesis also shed new light on the question of multiple personality. There had been many famous cases in the nineteenth century, including those of Mary Reynolds in Pennsylvania and

'Estelle' in Switzerland.[30] Psychologists had spent much time on the taxonomy of *successive* multiple personalities – classifying these cases according to whether the different personalities knew each other or not, or whether only one knew the other. It turned out, as William James's researches demonstrated, that the usual pattern was for various personalities to know nothing of each other.[31] The rarity of Helen Smith's case was that she was a *simultaneous* multiple personality.[32] By the beginning of the twentieth century psychologists were adding further refinements to their investigations. One method, particularly associated with the American psychologist Morton Prince, who was later to play a role in the life of Jung and Freud, was 'double hypnosis', in which hypnotic procedures were applied to an already hypnotized patient, thus often eliciting a third personality.[33]

Various explanations were given for the phenomenon of multiple personality. The 'organicist' school speculated that the brain itself had become organically modified; the 'associationists' argued that there was a loss of contact between two main groups of associations; the Flournoy thesis held that the total personality was involved in elaborate games of regression, progression and role playing; and there was a 'sociological' explanation: that the organism became confused by having to live at different times by different value systems. The last hypothesis implied that unitary personality was not a biological given but something the individual had to work hard to achieve, and the idea received impressive backing from literary classics. In Robert Louis Stevenson's *Dr Jekyll and Mr Hyde*, for example, it is suggested that as human knowledge progresses it will be found that the individual is not one, or even two, but many.

Jung's pioneering work on the split-off aspects of the psyche as an explanation for the occult owes much to Flournoy, but Jung himself would take the idea of the split-off aspect or 'complex' much further. It is interesting that at about the time he abandoned his work on complexes, around 1910, critical opinion within the psychiatric profession itself swung against the whole idea of multiple personality, on the grounds that doctors had been duped by 'mythomaniac' patients or had themselves consciously shaped the result. Yet cases of multiple personality, inexplicable on this basis, continued to occur: the most famous in the 1950s was that of the 'Three Faces of Eve'.[34] Just as Jung was to complain in the late 1950s that the study of schizophrenia had made no progress since he stopped working in the field, so might he have said something similar about multiple personality.

Yet if Jung's thesis was a dazzling achievement for a young man, his treatment of Hélène Preiswerk herself was scarcely admirable. To state that he preferred the personality of 'Ivenes' to that of Hélène[35] might have been construed as fair comment had not Jung made it clear that his cousin was in love with him: he was in effect rejecting her love by saying he preferred a split-off phantom from her unconscious to the flesh-and-blood woman. Even more inexcusable was the way he ruined her reputation in starchy, gossipy Basel by revealing her identity. Even if it was not readily discernible in Basel who the medium was, Jung designated her by the codename 'S.W.', which enabled amateur sleuths to notice that there was an 'S.W.' in the commonly used *Textbook of Insanity* who was a seamstress – Hélène's occupation. Nor was the description of 'S.W.' calculated to assuage Hélène's feelings, for she was described as suffering from an 'intensified feeling of self-importance, which found its expression in affected speech and grand airs, now and then attended with evidence of eroticism and coquetry'.[36]

Hélène found herself forced to leave Basel. She continued working as a seamstress, first in Montpellier and later in Paris, returning to Basel, where she died aged thirty. It seems that in his rush to get into print and establish his fame Jung was heedless of the hurt he might do his former friend. Harsher critics of Jung go so far as to say that he ruined Hélène's life by telling her story in his dissertation.

The year 1900 was a good one for Jung. He finished his written examinations, started work on the dissertation, and found himself temporarily in funds after some successful antique deals. The evening after his last examination he indulged himself in the luxury of going to the theatre and soon settled down to read Flournoy, for whose work he always had the greatest respect.[37] Having served in the Swiss army as part of his compulsory national service since 1894, he was delighted to be promoted to officer rank in 1900 following his annual stint in the camps. On his return he was offered a post at the Burghölzli Mental Hospital in Zürich, which he accepted. His mother, having swallowed her initial distaste for psychiatry – so inferior a line of work, she felt, for the son she had hoped would be a great surgeon – seemed to accept the impending separation with equanimity and began to turn away from her son towards her daughter. Jung celebrated his appointment with a final week of holiday in Stuttgart and Munich, where he attended his first opera, *Carmen*.[38]

Jung departed from Basel for Zürich on 10 December 1900. He was glad to shake off the dust of Basel, mainly because it meant putting distance between himself and his mother, but his official reasons in *Memories* speak of boredom, of irritation with being stereotyped as the son of Reverend Paul and the grandson of the eminent Professor Carl; despite the alleged intellectuality of Basel, Jung claimed, the weight of tradition was what really mattered there. Where Basel was stuffy and parochial Zürich was cosmopolitan, as befitted a famous centre of international finance.[39]

Nevertheless, no-one can live in a city for nearly twenty-five years without having some of its peculiarity rub off. What, then, was the unique impact of Basel on Jung, and what was the legacy he carried with him to the more cosmopolitan setting of Zürich? There was, above all, the geographical location, which created a very different, and more sophisticated, world-view from that obtainable, say, in a remote valley of the Bernese Oberland. The Basler shared the insularity of his inter-Alpine brother but balanced this with an acute knowledge of the outside world. The importance of Basel was that it acted as a crossroads for German, French and Italian influences.[40]

Jung left Basel in jaunty spirits, determined to make a name for himself in his chosen field. Ahead of him lay austerity undreamed of. The free-wheeling, self-regarding, medical student, unable to suffer fools gladly and impatient with all authority, was about to enter a way of life where iron discipline was the norm, and the hard-drinking 'Barrel' was about to run into a teetotal regime severe even by Victorian standards.

Chapter Four

BURGHÖLZLI APPRENTICESHIP

Jung reported for work at the Burghölzli hospital in Zürich on a cold Monday morning on 10 December 1900. At the door he was met by the director of the Institution, Eugen Bleuler, who set the tone of austere workaholism that was to be Jung's lot for two years by carrying his new assistant's bags up to his rooms. Jung was informed that he would have to get up every morning at 6.30 a.m. to make his rounds and have breakfast before the daily staff meeting at 8.30 a.m. Moreover, he would have to type up his own case histories, as the Burghölzli employed no secretaries.

Compulsory austerity was never Jung's strong point. Although he could live a spartan life as an ascetic when the mood took him, the essential point was that *he* had to choose to live like that. Additionally, he was a 'heavy grubber', both gourmand and gourmet, and noted at once that the food at the Burghölzli, though plentiful, was plain and monotonous, with no pretence at *haute cuisine*. Jung never cared for Bleuler, but it may be that this was in part because he never entirely recovered from his initial resentment at the monastic regime his chief imposed.

The enigmatic and controversial Bleuler himself elicited very different opinions from the people he came in contact with. Born in 1857 at Zolliken, a peasant village outside Zürich (now a suburb) he made his name as a highly committed psychiatrist, prepared to live among his patients like Schweitzer among the African lepers. He studied with the eminent 'alienists' Charcot and Magnan in Paris, spent periods of training in Munich and London, then worked in the Waldau Mental Hospital near Berne.[1] In 1886 he was appointed Medical Director of the Rheinau hospital, one of Switzerland's most backward institutions, and brought it up to the first rank by sheer commitment and hard work. A bachelor, he lived in the hospital and spent every hour of every day with his patients, thus gaining a unique insight into their troubled mental worlds. At Rheinau he began to develop his idea that patients suffering from schizophrenia (then called dementia praecox) were not recoverable but that their peculiar private universes could be penetrated and deciphered.[2] When a typhoid epidemic broke out, he recruited his schizophrenic patients as nurses, and they performed well – thus adding a new twist to the well-known phenomenon that schizophrenics suffering from severe *bodily* diseases emerged from their twilight mental world for the duration of the physical illness.

Bleuler also became a protégé of Auguste Forel (1848–1931), another remarkable man and the first to put the Burghölzli hospital on the map. Established in 1860 as a cantonal asylum for the insane, with the understanding that it would serve also as the psychiatric clinic of Zürich University, the Burghölzli had a distinctly chequered first twenty years. There were two main problems. The educated doctors and staff spoke High German but the patients – since this was a state hospital – in the main spoke either demotic German or an impenetrable working-class Züricher dialect. Secondly, there was an unresolved conflict arising from the dual role of the Burghölzli director, who had to double as a professor of psychiatry at Zürich University – a research position; it soon became clear that the two duties were largely incompatible. The best psychiatrist of the 1860s, Wilhelm Griesinger, who had a chair at Zürich, resigned and departed for his native Germany rather than accept the dual role. There followed a succession of unsatisfactory caretakers who also quit because of the fissiparous stresses of the two jobs. Finally, in 1879, Forel was appointed director.[3]

Forel anticipated Bleuler in his energy and commitment. The world authority on ants and their behaviour, he also became a strict teetotaller after becoming convinced that a doctor could not cure alcoholism without becoming an abstainer himself. Thereafter a fanatical ideology of teetotallism reigned at the Burghölzli; as Forel and Bleuler became closer and closer as colleagues, Bleuler too signed the pledge and declared war on John Barleycorn.[4] Forel's speciality as a psychiatrist was in hypnosis, of which he became a zealous advocate and expert practitioner. To maximize the productivity of his staff, he used to hypnotize those on night duty to sleep through the night but to wake up if an emergency arose, so that they were rested enough to spend the day studying.[5] Combative and pugnacious, he frequently got into fist fights with intruders on the Burghölzli grounds. Forel took early retirement at fifty in 1898 but intrigued shamelessly to make sure that his fellow teetotaller, Bleuler, then a comparative unknown, succeeded him.

Disliking Bleuler, Jung never cared for his mentor either and resented the way Bleuler allowed the retired director to reappear at intervals and prowl around the Burghölzli. He remembered with irritation the time Forel suddenly burst unannounced into the young doctors' common room and harangued them vehemently for half an hour about the evils of alcohol.[6] Jung liked to tell stories that showed Forel and Bleuler in a bad light. A favourite yarn over Sunday lunch when Jung was a paterfamilias featured the time when a Burghölzli patient jammed a chamber pot over Bleuler's head.[7] As for Forel, Jung liked to puncture his 'do-gooder' image with anecdotes showing him with feet of clay. Forel advocated women's rights but, according to Jung, was a martinet at home who, when he found that the marmalade his wife was making in the kitchen was too sweet, smashed the jar on the floor. Since that kind of behaviour was more typical of Jung himself than of Forel, it may be that what we have here is a very good example of what Jung later called 'projection of the shadow'.[8]

Jung's characterization of Bleuler was consistently ungenerous. He attributed to him the exact fault he did *not* have: being interested only in research and neglecting his patients. Jung said that Bleuler was interested only in describing symptoms and labelling patients, but this is denied by everyone else who worked with him. Moreover, there is the curious fact that in *Memories* Jung never once mentions Bleuler's name. Jung's anger towards his father, it seems, was visited on all successive 'father figures'. Bleuler was the first of these but he would not be the last. Autocratic and quirky though he was, Bleuler was also (apart from his hobby-horses) liberal and broad-minded and happily agreed to be Jung's 'supervisor' for the published dissertation on the occult. A curious mixture of originality and caution, he liked exciting ideas but would frequently have second thoughts and draw back.

The Burghölzli itself was an austere block of unprepossessing buildings on the heights overlooking Lake Zürich, but without a view of the lake, since in those days it was orthodox opinion that the sight of water would trigger thoughts of suicide in the minds of the severely disturbed.

The doctors' regime was punishing. Jung's friend and colleague Alphonse Maeder reported, 'the Burghölzli was in that time a kind of factory where you worked very much and were poorly paid. Everyone from the professor to the young resident was totally absorbed by his work. Abstinence from alcoholic drinks was imposed on everyone. Bleuler was kind to all and never played the role of chief.'[9] After the morning conference, at which three times a week the new patients were discussed and at the other sessions existing cases were consolidated, doctors dispersed to fulfil the individual tasks Bleuler had set them before undertaking evening rounds between 5 and 6.30 p.m. The meticulous notetaking required by Bleuler, who stipulated that his staff had to write down everything said by the patients, whether they understood it or not, meant that Jung often did not complete writing up his reports until 10 p.m. That was the hour at which the main doors of the hospital were locked and bolted. Only senior staff had keys and even they had to get a chit signed by Bleuler, which he provided reluctantly, before they could leave the grounds. Additionally, there were staff seminars, at which attendance was compulsory, when each doctor reported on an aspect of new research assigned to him by Bleuler.

Monasticism, then, was the keynote. In six months Jung read through fifty volumes of *Allgemeine Zeitschrift für Psychiatrie* as well as studying Freud's newly published *The Interpretation of Dreams* – which was the task set him by Bleuler. He saw much in Bleuler's methods to criticize, but liked his 'work therapy' whereby apparently irresponsible patients would suddenly be given tasks of great responsibility. Bleuler worked hard to prevent his charges becoming institutionalized, and liked to discharge seriously ill patients to confront family life again if he felt they were not making sufficient progress; another of his favourite devices was to transfer a patient from one ward to another with quite different patients. Considerable short-term success was achieved by these shock tactics, but Jung felt there was not enough follow-up to determine the ultimate fate of the discharged patients.

Jung used his early days in the Burghölzli to test the validity of certain general hypotheses he had framed on the basis of Hélène Preiswerk's case. He noted that people with periodic amnesia or suffering from spontaneous somnambulism often exhibited marked character changes and went from being meek and mild to being extroverted or even violent. From the many hours of reading in his room, when there was nothing else to do, he drew examples from literature to illustrate this thesis. For his notion of 'psychic excitation' as the trigger for somnambulism he cited the instance in Flaubert's *Salammbô* when the hero, having captured the priestess Salammbô, falls asleep after touching her virginal breast. He worked in the example of Bettina Brentano's suddenly falling asleep on Goethe's knee when she met him and linked this with traditional tales of sorcery: 'Ecstatic sleep in the midst of extreme torture, the so-called "witch's sleep", is a well-known phenomenon in the annals of witchcraft.'[10] The case of Joan of Arc convinced him that there was something called 'teleological hallucination' – a form of somnambulism which enabled people to prevail who would otherwise succumb to apparently insurmountable obstacles. Investigation of his patients, one of whom had frequent visions of the dead and of skeletons, helped him to test the idea he had first encountered in Krafft-Ebing's *Textbook of Insanity* that visual hallucinations were mostly of animals, funerals and fantastic processions swarming with corpses, devils and ghosts, while auditory hallucinations were either of shrieks and crashes or of things with a sexual content.

One of the things that most fascinated Jung was the power of the human mind to 'forget' or blank out memory. He continued to work away on cryptamnesia and even wrote to Nietzsche's sister Elisabeth on the subject.[11] Cryptamnesia seemed to him an unconscious process of remembering an image but not its derivation; hence the supposedly 'original' ideas of scientists, writers and composers whose critics are able to point out their precise source. Jung warned that plagiarism was a charge that should always be made with caution because of cryptamnesia, which was why it was a justified accusation only when a truly remarkable idea was reproduced, when such an argument could scarcely hold.[12] Glossolalia or the gift of tongues was, of course, the cryptamnesic phenomenon *par excellence*.

Most of all Jung was intrigued by cases of 'double consciousness' when a person had a memory blackout and assumed a new identity, totally unaware of the previous one. There were many instances of people going into an amnesiac trance for, say, two months, living a life totally at variance with their 'normal' one, then suddenly waking up and resuming their old identity. There was a famous case of a doctor who lost his memory and failed to return home, took up a new occupation as a storekeeper and, many months later, remembered who he really was when he saw his 'missing' photograph in a newspaper. Jung suggested that in order to distinguish phenomena like narcolepsy, periodic amnesia, somnambulism and double consciousness from neurosis, it might be necessary to correlate the former with the psychology of genius or the supranormal.[13]

Jung's first Burghölzli papers, in which he attempted to summarize his findings on alcoholism and manic depression, concluded that alcoholism was a typical, though by no means invariable, symptom of manic depression; the other common symptoms were criminality, social incapacity or instability and moral insanity. The manic mood disorder was a clinical condition best classified under the heading of psychopathic inferiority, but the hypomanic cluster of symptoms obviously had their roots in youth or childhood.[14]

Jung also used his category of 'psychopathic inferiority' to explain cases of simulated insanity. In an influential paper on the subject he argued that the apparent malingering of prisoners awaiting trial was actually a quasi-hysterical dissociated state. He thus in effect argued that simulated madness was simply another form of mental illness. He pointed out first how hard it was to simulate insanity; you need to keep up the pretence for months and to have both extraordinary willpower and amazing histrionic abilities, whereas most criminals had merely a kind of impulsive energy that faded quickly. However, he conceded that one of his patients at the Burghölzli simulated so well that he was just about to write up his report stating categorically that the man was schizophrenic when he finally became bored with the pretence and confessed.

Jung concluded that there are two categories of simulated insanity: an easily detectable bogus one, as when a prisoner feigned insanity in order to be transferred to an asylum from which he could escape more easily than from prison; and a genuine case, which was a kind of unconscious *cri de coeur* by hysterics seeking to draw attention to their real mental illness. Hysterics, he argued, did not lie even though what they said was not true in an objective sense. However, since the desire to simulate insanity was in itself a pathological symptom, and a convincing simulation therefore possible only in cases of pathological hysteria, it followed that the differential diagnosis as between schizophrenia and hysteria was a difficult one. Jung was inclined to say that simulated insanity was not mental illness in the true sense but a sign of 'psychopathic inferiority'.[15]

He also established credentials as a budding expert on criminality by pointing out that the presence of hysteria in *criminal* acts was entirely adventitious, since moral defects and hysteria were two quite different things; many hardened criminals were not hysterics and many hysterics had very sensitive moral feelings. Hysteria could influence human actions considerably, but only moral deficiency would lead to criminality; nor was moral deficiency the same thing as 'psychopathic inferiority'. Hysteria could enhance a pre-existing moral defect, but it could also enhance a pre-existing admirable moral trait. Jung ended his paper by complaining that there were too many criminals in asylums because courts accepted facile pleas of psychological mitigation: 'Just now in the Burghölzli only one more criminal is needed to make the situation quite impossible'.[16]

Jung's early papers, published in 1903, are noteworthy for the many approving references to Freud, a full three years before he made contact with the great Viennese psychoanalyst.[17] Although Jung always claimed that he discovered the unconscious quite independently of Freud, partly from Pierre Janet and partly from his patients, it is clear that Freud's influence was already being felt. The one area where Freud obviously could not influence Jung, since he had no experience of the field, was schizophrenic psychosis, and here clearly the great influence was Bleuler himself.

When talking of schizophrenia it is important to establish which ideas Jung took over from Bleuler and which he originated himself. His days in the Rheinau had convinced Bleuler that the ravings of patients afflicted by dementia praecox had a meaning. As to what caused schizophrenia, Bleuler thought it had a twofold origin: there was a 'primary', organic schizophrenia, which derived from an unknown cause – possibly a toxic substance in the brain, in which heredity played a large part; and there was a 'secondary' and 'dynamic' schizophrenia which was psychogenic. But although

Bleuler thus seemed to muddy the aetiology of the disease, he also widened the definition of schizophrenia (the word was his own coinage) to include conditions previously thought to belong to diseases distinct from dementia praecox. Bleuler followed Janet in thinking that schizophrenia was characterized by a lowering of the mental level or psychological tension, but he built on Janet by adding his own idea of a loosening of mental associations, similar to those occurring in dreams or reveries, but with the difference that moral notions like right and wrong could no longer be distinguished, and it was these 'dissociations' which led to loss of contact with reality. Finally, Bleuler was an optimist, in that he thought schizophrenia could be arrested at any stage of its evolution.[18]

Jung began at the Burghölzli by careful observation of the form and content of schizophrenia. He noticed that schizophrenics were fond of social affectation, neologisms, 'power words' and magical, exorcistic formulae; the neologisms and word salads often came from dreams. A male patient, if denied anything by the doctors, would threaten them with the words, 'I, the Grand Duke Mephisto, shall have you treated with blood vengeance for orang-utan representation.' A catatonic female used to sing 'verbigeratively' for hours on end a religious song with a 'Hallelujah' refrain. Then she started verbigerating 'Hallelujah' for hours, which gradually degenerated into 'Hallo, Oha,' and finally she verbigerated 'Ha-ha-ha' accompanied by convulsive laughter. Often such patients had a stereotypical fantasy about escaping from the asylum and marrying, which they would repeat and eventually jumble up with neologisms, until in the end the only audible sound was a constant hum, except that sudden stress could make the earlier fantasy sentences reappear. Schizophrenic patients' handwriting contained peculiar flourishes, expressing the contradictory tendencies in the psyche: now sloping and cursive, now upright, now large, now small. Mock-stupid behaviour was a constant, as were lack of consideration, narrow-mindedness and inaccessibility to persuasion. Schizophrenics often confessed they had lost the capacity for feeling or emotion. Most significant of all were the hallucinations or 'voices'. Those who delighted in neologisms were also invariably in thrall to their 'voices', some of which would 'correct' the patient. One of his patients was teased by her voices about her delusion of grandeur, or the voices would command her to tell the examining doctor not to bother.[19]

Two early cases with women patients crystallized Jung's thoughts on the nature of schizophrenia and how it differed from other severe illnesses. The first was the case of 'Babette S', suffering from paranoid schizophrenia with characteristic megalomania. Born in the slums of Zürich in 1844, she had been in the Burghölzli since 1883, an object lesson in dementia praecox and as such exhibited to hundreds of medical students. Babette's father was a drunkard and her sister a prostitute, and at the age of thirty-nine she had finally snapped and plummeted into madness. She was plagued with voices and would come out with apparently meaningless expressions, of which Jung kept an inventory: 'I am the Lorelei,' 'I am Socrates's deputy,' 'I am the double polytechnic irreplaceable,' 'I am plum cake on a corn-meal bottom,' 'I am Germania and Helvetia of exclusively sweet butter,' 'Naples and I must supply the world with noodles.'

Jung learned that her voices were distributed throughout her entire body but that 'God's voice' came from the middle of the thorax. On a hunch he told her that she had to concentrate on that one voice alone and do its bidding. The voice suggested that Jung test her on the Bible; at each visit he assigned her a chapter to read and tested her on it next time. This went on for seven years until Jung realized that her mind was being kept alert by this exercise. The result was that the formerly ubiquitous voices retired to the left half of her body and left the right side free of them. Total cure in such a case was out of the question, but Jung had managed a very satisfactory form of damage limitation by halving the intensity of the hallucinations.[20]

Jung realized that paranoid ideas and hallucinations contained a germ of meaning and that behind the psychosis lay a personality, a life history, or a pattern of hopes. He realized that in such patients there remained in the background a personality that could be called normal and was, so to speak, an onlooker at the psychic drama all around. This personality – in Babette's case 'God's voice' – could sometimes make sensible remarks, and the lifeline it provided was perhaps why, when a physical illness overtook the patient, this personality took charge so that the schizophrenic appeared almost normal.[21]

The other burning question Jung wrestled with was whether schizophrenia was ever reversible and, if it was, did that mean that the original diagnosis of dementia praecox had been a confusion with some other form of mental illness, perhaps a severe form of hysteria? One of his catatonic female patients, aged eighteen, had been in the Burghölzli a year after being seduced by her brother at fifteen. After that experience she became odder and odder and could form no relationship with any living creature except a vicious watchdog. Once admitted to the Burghölzli, she heard voices, would not speak to the staff and refused food. Jung made the breakthrough by communicating with one of her voices. She told him she lived on the moon, but there was a vampire there who preyed on women and children, so all of them lived underground. She tried to kill the vampire with a knife but became enraptured with his beauty and allowed him to carry her off.

Then a period of resistance started. She accused Jung vehemently of preventing her from returning to the moon, relapsed into catatonia, was violently insane for a while and spent an unsatisfactory period in and out of the hospital, still unable to accept that she could not go home to the moon. In the end it was agreed that she would take a job as a nurse at a sanatorium, but she had not told anyone that she went around with a loaded gun on her person. When an assistant doctor made sexual overtures to her, she shot him, though not fatally. During the last interview she had with Jung she handed over the revolver and confessed that she had had it with her all the time she was in the Burghölzli. She added, 'I would have shot you down if you had failed me!' The reports do not make clear how soon after the shooting incident the woman recovered, but the result was that she went out into the world, married, survived two world wars in the Orient and never had a relapse.[22]

Making an inductive generalization from the Burghölzli cases, the Hélène Preiswerk episode and his wide reading, Jung came to the conclusion that the key to severe psychosis was that part of the mind became split up to form an autonomous sub-personality or a number of sub-personalities, which, in a celebrated coinage, he called a 'complex'. The key difference between schizophrenia and hysteria was that in the former case the connection between the ego and the complexes was virtually completely lost, but that with hysteria the split was relative, not absolute. An hysterical patient might suffer from persecution-mania, apparently very similar to genuine paranoia, but the difference was that in the former case one could bring the delusion back under the control of consciousness – an impossibility with genuine paranoia. To put it another way, in a *neurosis* the complexes had *relative* autonomy, but in schizophrenia the complexes had become disconnected so that autonomous fragments did not reintegrate into a totality or, in rare cases of remission, were unexpectedly joined together as if nothing had happened.[23]

In schizophrenia dissociation was normally irreversible: it was as if a mirror had been shattered and the pieces thrown to the four winds, whereas in neurosis the mirror remained intact but had sustained multiple fractures. In the case of a hysterical multiple personality there was a fairly smooth, even tactful, cooperation between the different 'persons', who kept to their respective roles and did not bother each other, almost as if the psyche were a sentimental drama with a central director. However, in schizophrenia the split-off figures assumed banal, grotesque or highly exaggerated characters and names; they did not cooperate with the patient's consciousness, were not tactful, had no respect for sentimental values, but broke in and made disturbances and took a delight in tormenting the ego. The result was a chaos of incoherent visions, voices and characters, all of a strange and incomprehensible nature, all objectionable, shocking, noisy, impertinent, cruel and obscene – rather like Kipling's *Bandar-Log* without a chief monkey in charge.[24]

Two further issues remained to be resolved. Why did 'splitting' and 'complexes' characterize both hysteria and schizophrenia, and where did the vital difference lie? And were the complexes of male and female schizophrenics alike? In hysteria the psyche was brought to a standstill because it could no longer rid itself of a complex: the individual became more unadapted to the environment, and the wish-dreams or wish-deliria of the hysteric were concerned exclusively with the fulfilment of the complex's wishes. Yet many hysterics succeeded after a time in regaining their equilibrium, partly overcoming the complex and avoiding new traumas. In the case of schizophrenia, on the other hand, the complexes became fixed and insuperable, making the causal connection between complex and illness as hard to detect in schizophrenia as it was easy in hysteria. Many dementia praecox cases began as hysteria, but the symptoms 'degenerated' and became fixed. Jung therefore speculated that the Bleuler model of 'primary organic' and 'secondary psychogenic' schizophrenia put the cart before the horse. The true explanation was that all schizophrenia began psychogenically as the problem of an intrusive complex, but that in some cases the complex released a toxin in the brain which made the illness irremediable. In Jung's view the toxins were produced by the split-off complex rather than the body organically considered, as in Bleuler's theory; this would explain the irreversibility of schizophrenia, since the toxins obviously damaged the brain irreparably, particularly impairing the higher functions. For Jung, then, the elusive toxin was the 'epiphenomenon' that was triggered by a complex, whereas for Bleuler the complex appeared *as a result* of the toxin.[25]

The search was then on for the culprit toxin, which, however, proved as elusive as the alchemist's 'philosopher's stone'. A popular theory at the Burghölzli in Jung's day was that snake bites could cause psychosis and the obvious next stage was to speculate that the putative toxin might be identical or similar to snake venom. However, this promising vista later proved a dead end.[26]

The other issue was the differential content of complexes as between men and women. Jung concluded that men had primary complexes to do with money and ambition, with erotic complexes firmly in second place. With women, who were preoccupied with sexuality, pregnancy and children, erotic complexes were primary.[27] In some ways this made the female patients easier to treat. Jung's colleague Franz Riklin had a case of an hysterical patient who vomited whenever she drank milk; under analysis Riklin discovered that a male relative had sexually assaulted her in a stable, where she had gone to fetch milk.[28]

Overwhelmingly, Jung discovered that schizophrenia in his female patients was related to repressed or unrequited love. He noticed that one of them, diagnosed as a hopeless catatonic, made certain odd hammering movements with her hands, as if engaged in some unknown craft or trade. When she died Jung attended the funeral and there discovered from her brother that she had been engaged to a cobbler who had jilted her; on making further enquiries Jung learned that the old-fashioned method of mending shoes involved manual movements exactly like those of his patient.[29]

Another patient, a thirty-two-year-old cook, had succumbed to schizophrenia after having all her teeth out. This had triggered secret anxieties about the clandestine birth of an illegitimate child years earlier – an event she did not want her present fiancé to know about.[30] Another case involved confusion over sex, love, guilt and sin. A young woman had plummeted into schizophrenia after three traumatic events. First, at the age of sixteen, one of her friends provoked a female imbecile into a display of obscene behaviour, as a result of which the pair of them were severely reprimanded by parents and teachers. Then she fell violently in love with a man who did not reciprocate. Finally she went to a religious revival meeting, became suffused with feelings of guilt, and was filled with remorse at ever having been in love. She went to pieces, began hearing voices and seeing 'Christ', and ended by being institutionalized in the Burghölzli.[31]

It is interesting to see Jung in his pre-Freudian period already partly a Freudian at heart, for he made a threefold analysis of the consequences of undischarged sexual energy; in the case of men it usually took the form of feverish obsession with work, dangerous sports or collecting mania; in women it was channelled into philanthropy and the caring activities like nursing; while with creative souls it was sublimated into artistic endeavour, exactly as Freud had said.[32] But following the Freudian furrow involved obvious dangers. In his early days at the Burghölzli Jung had to deal with a case of sexual neurosis so severe he could not cure it. His twenty-four-year-old patient, suffering from hysteria and St Vitus's dance, had developed the neurosis after her mother, suffering from osteomalacia, told her that her illness was the result of having been married. A month after Jung discharged her, the family doctor wrote to the Burghölzli with a complaint from the girl that Jung had done nothing but seek opportunities to talk about sex with her. Here was a cautionary tale, showing that nothing was ever certain in psychiatry. Instead of a pattern of initial resistance followed by a confession, in this case the sexual complex entrenched itself behind aggressive defence mechanisms, seeking to impugn the moral integrity of the doctor.[33]

Already Jung was revealing himself as a highly original psychiatrist, but the very notion of originality is often misunderstood. Nobody creates out of nothing, in a vacuum; it is more a question of rearranging pre-existing strands into a pattern nobody thought of weaving before. Tracing real and alleged 'influences' in the work of major theoreticians has become an overdone pastime, but there can be little doubt that the major influences on the Jung of the Burghölzli years were Flournoy, Bleuler and Pierre Janet. Jung's idea of the 'complex' was an extension of Janet's idea of the *idée fixe subconsciente*. Janet, a pupil of Charcot, took from his teacher the idea that split-off fragments of the personality could follow an independent, unconscious development and could then appear under hypnosis or manifest themselves in illness. Janet then linked these independent mental entities with his 'subconscious fixed ideas' – the source of all mental illness. From Janet's division into hysteria and psychasthenia Jung got the idea of a difference between hysteria and schizophrenia. Most of all, Jung admired Janet's fixing on the *abaissement du niveau mental* as *the* sign *par excellence* of dementia praecox.[34] As Jung had seen over and over again at the Burghölzli, schizophrenia was marked by this distinctive lowering of the mental level, leading to dissociation, disintegration of consciousness and disintegration of personality.

Yet Jung was no mere ingenious word-spinner who popularized the term 'complex' when describing something that Janet had already worked on. Part of the young Carl Gustav's high talent was an astonishing fertility of ideas and an eclecticism of inspiration. It was not enough for him to sharpen up Bleuer's and Janet's notions, he wanted to make a distinctive contribution of his own. In the field of schizophrenia he broke new ground in two main ways: he demonstrated that the 'complex' was no mere metaphysical idea but could be verified empirically, and he looked forward to his own late theories by investigating the 'archaic residues' in the dreams of his schizophrenic patients.

Jung was always fascinated by what he called 'big dreams' – that is, dreams that did not seem to derive from the circumstances of the dreamer's life but to be concerned with metaphysical or cosmological issues: matters that in classical times were important enough for the dreamer to report to the Greek Areopagus or the Roman Senate. Jung detected 'big dreams' occurring at five main points in a person's life: between the ages of three and six (obviously this related to his own phallus dreams); between fourteen and sixteen (roughly the time of the Basel cathedral fantasy); between twenty and twenty-five; at mid-life between thirty-five and forty; and just before death. Later in his career he would link the 'big dreams' of schizophrenics to an immense harvest of collective symbols, arguing that the schizophrenic had access to a wider universe than the neurotic, who was restricted to the world of his own personal psychology. In the Burghölzli period he struggled to make sense of the abundance of archaic material in the dreams of his schizophrenic patients, and suggested a form of atavism or arrested development in which a primitive psychology remained intact and did not adapt to modern conditions. Another possibility he toyed with was that in dementia praecox a normal consciousness was confronted with an unusually strong unconscious. Given that a patient's weak consciousness might be unable to deal with the inrush of unconscious material, Jung suggested there might actually be two kinds of schizophrenia: one where there was a weak consciousness and a normal unconscious, and the other where there was a normal consciousness but a very strong unconscious.[35]

Yet Jung's major contribution to psychology in his pre-Freudian period – and one that marked a huge advance on Janet – was his demonstration that the existence of a complex could be scientifically demonstrated. First, however, he had to jettison some of his nineteeth-century lumber, and this meant turning his back on hypnosis. Jung gave up hypnotism in 1905, for a number of reasons: he did not understand how the technique worked; he wanted a dialogue between doctor and patient, not simply a master-slave relationship; he could never be certain how long a 'cure' affected by hypnotism would last; and he found that 'the unconscious resented it'.

Matters came to a head when he was demonstrating hypnotic techniques to students at Zürich University. His subject was a paralysed fifty-eight-year-old woman. When Jung announced that he was going to hypnotize her, the woman at once fell into a self-induced trance and poured out the contents of her dreams and unconscious. Jung grew alarmed when he found he could neither control his subject nor bring her out of the trance, but the woman came round herself, declared that she was cured and threw away her crutches. To save face Jung pretended to students that he had effected this miracle cure, but checked with the woman a few weeks later and found that the cure had held. The following summer she returned to the lecture hall, complaining of pains in her back, which she claimed had started as soon as she heard of Jung's new course of lectures. Once again she fell into an auto-induced trance and once again emerged cured. This time Jung asked her to wait behind after the lecture and began to probe her life. It turned out that she had married twice and had a feeble-minded son in a junior job (as a janitor) in the Burghölzli. Yearning for a brilliant son, she had projected her fantasy of a miracle worker onto Jung and then made sure the miracle was performed – by curing herself. Having thus made Jung her 'son', she proclaimed his qualities as thaumaturge far and wide and was responsible for Jung obtaining his first private patients.[36]

Jung's opportunity to put his ideas on a scientific footing came as a result of his rapid ascent up the Burghölzli hierarchy. In 1903 he became First *Obersarzt* (Clinical Director) at the hospital, then in 1905 deputy director under Bleuler. He was given the coveted title of *PrivatDocent* (lecturer) in Psychiatry at Zürich University and became senior physician at the psychiatric clinic at the hospital, where he also took over direction of the Outpatients Department. In 1905 he set up a laboratory for Experimental Psychopathology with Franz Riklin, who had pioneered word-association tests at the Rheinau Hospital, as chief collaborator and the brilliant graduate Ludwig Binswanger as junior assistant.

Serious work now began on establishing the reality of complexes by means of word-association tests. The idea of association of ideas went back to the eighteenth century but became most famous in psychology through the Russian Ivan Pavlov's work on the 'conditioned reflex'. Dogs who were trained to associate the ringing of a bell with food would eventually salivate when the bell was rung even when no food was produced. In word-association tests a list of, say, a hundred words is read out to subjects, who are asked to respond by saying the word that first occurs to them; the interval between stimulus and response is timed by a stopwatch. The more unpleasant the association of the word, the longer will be the response time. A subject will respond rapidly to a stimulus word with no emotional associations, but if there is an emotional significance in the word, the subject will hesitate, make mistakes, stammer, fail to respond, make involuntary movements or show other signs of agitation. In one early case Jung noticed that a male subject showed disturbance in his response to five words: knife, lance, beat, pointed, bottle. Jung deduced that the man had been in a drunken brawl and faced the subject with his conclusions. The man admitted that he had knifed someone in a tavern fracas and had spent a year in jail as a result. He was quite unaware that he had hesitated in response to the five words.[37]

Previous experimenters like Ziehan and Wilhelm Wundt had used the test to probe conscious associations, but Jung and his collaborators aimed to reach the unconscious with the method and in particular to 'touch' complexes. The best indication of a split-off section of the mind or 'complex' was when a subject, without realizing it, delayed significantly his response to certain words; another was the production of an unusual reaction word. Jung and Riklin found that they got better results from uneducated than educated people, and that there was a remarkable similarity between the associations of members of the same family. The large number of identical responses to stimulus words between mothers and daughters was particularly noteworthy; husbands and wives generally did less well, but even then there was evidence of empathy or what Jung, in a favourite phrase, liked to call *participation mystique*. The experiments also convinced Jung that free will was an illusion and that if the association tests were valid, then this clinched the case for determinism; if thoughts really were random, adventitious or voluntaristic, no association could ever be formed.[38]

What Jung and Riklin found time and again was that emotionally charged material had been banished from consciousness and that thoughts, feelings and memories associated with the trigger words grouped themselves into dynamic clusters, which functioned like sub-personalities or Janet's 'fixed ideas'. Jung proceeded to dub these split-off emotional fragments, which were old wounds that still rankled, 'feeling-toned-complexes'.

A feeling-toned-complex was an emotionally driven small secondary mind which deliberately (though unknown to consciousness) drove at certain intentions which were contrary to the conscious intentions of the individual. Jung also demonstrated that the presence of a complex was indicated by the subject's inability to remember previous answers when retested; when a complex was touched by a stimulus word, the subject would often forget the answer given. Riklin and Binswanger built on the word-association test with the 'galvanometer' – a machine which recorded a subject's respiration counts, pulse rate and the amount of blood in the finger and thus anticipated the polygraph; the key idea was the 'psychogalvanic effect' – the increased electrical resistance in the skin caused by an overproduction of sweat glands through excitement.[39]

It was characteristic of Jung's thinking, even at this early stage, to reach out into the wider world to find analogies and comparisons, and he soon found a way to illustrate the feeling-toned-complex by likening it to the *leitmotif* used as the 'signature tune' for characters, themes or ideas in Wagner's *Ring* cycle.[40]

Soon there was dramatic proof of the existence of the feeling-toned-complex or what Freud, using entirely different methods, called repressions. Using the word-association tests, Jung was able to demonstrate the existence of three separate complexes in the case of a dressmaker who had been admitted to the Burghölzli in 1887 at the age of forty-two. Diagnosed as suffering from dementia praecox, the woman heard voices, 'like invisible telephones', telling her that she was of dubious virtue, and imagined that her bed was stuck full of needles and that her spinal marrow was being sucked out at night. She spoke of torture, of wanting to commit suicide by drowning, and had delusions of inheriting millions. When she was given the word test, the most striking association were pupil/Socrates and ink/nutcracker, which had a much longer reaction time, making it clear that these words were highly charged with emotional blocks. Jung uncovered sexual complexes, complaints of suffering injustice and dreams of happiness, which he interpreted as incoherent attempts to express a systematic wish-fulfilment, compensating for a life of toil and deprivation.[41] Once again Jung strengthened his conviction that every schizophrenic has a meaningful story to tell if only it can be deciphered.

Jung also solved an even more intractable case of apparent schizophrenia in a female patient, which had baffled Bleuler. By use of word associations and dream analysis he discovered that the woman was suffering from an acute guilt-complex, which left her clinically depressed rather than schizophrenic. The woman was from a modest background and had been in love with a wealthy industrialist's son. Despairing of winning him, she married someone else and bore him two children. Five years later a friend told her that the man she really loved had been devastated when she married. Cast down by this revelation, the woman did not intervene when she was bathing her children and the girl sucked the impure water from a sponge. The woman then proceeded to give her son bath water to drink. The girl, her favourite, contracted typhoid fever and died; the boy survived. Once she had made a clean breast of it, the woman no longer exhibited schizophrenic symptoms and was released into the community. Jung kept the facts to himself lest the woman be arraigned for murder; he thought that her remorse was punishment enough.[42]

The ultimate significance of Jung's work on the association experiments at the Burghölzli was that it moved his world-view even closer to Freud's. It has been well said that Freud discovered the unconscious through studies of repression via psychoanalysis whereas Jung discovered it through studying schizophrenics via the word-association experiment. The most striking thing about Jung's work was the way it confirmed the hypothesis of repression, which

Freud derived largely from dream analysis, using an entirely different method. It is fascinating to see how the two methods dovetail. A key element in Jung's location of a complex was when the subject, when retested, failed to remember the answer he had given to the key trigger words on the previous occasion. In the *Interpretation of Dreams* Freud had asked his patients to repeat complex dreams: parts of the dream described in different terms were then revealed as the weak spot in the dream's 'disguise', with which it masked the latent content.[43]

Jung for his part, when writing up his studies of hysteria and schizophrenia, paid extended tribute to Freud's analysis of paranoia, which showed how trivial ideas could be accompanied by an intense feeling-tone, taken over from a repressed idea; in this way Freud opened the way to understanding the inadequate feeling-tone in schizophrenia.[44] In June 1905, at the very time he published his work suggesting that the word-association test could be used to solve criminal cases, Jung emerged with his most lavish praise to date for Freud – all the more valuable as Freud was then embroiled in controversy over his famous 'Dora' case.[45] Just before this, Jung had started experimenting with Freudian psychoanalysis, giving a female patient an association test first, then 'topping up' with three weeks of psychoanalysis, two hours a day. The woman was troubled by insomnia and obsessive ponderings about death, and Jung used Freudian 'free association' to get at the sexual roots of the neurosis. The case is almost textbook Freudian, with resistance, revelation and 'abreaction'. It featured an unmarried woman of high libido but strict upbringing, tortured by sexual fantasies which she had repressed and displaced as anxieties about her professionalism as a governess. Jung was forced to discharge the patient without cure, but in November 1905 she returned and presented herself as fully healed.[46]

Despite his many sour later remarks, Jung did not find the Burghölzli regime as great an ordeal as most of his peers. He was proud of his stamina, and, as Anthony Storr has remarked, to be a pioneer in the psychotherapy of the psychoses required extraordinary toughness – not just powers of physical endurance to persevere through what sometimes turned out to be a sixteen-hour day, but also the mental doughtiness to withstand the unconscious of psychotics and not be swept up in the whirlpool of their delusional systems.[47]

Jung liked to show visitors around the wards and chuckle to himself as they quailed at what they encountered. There were 'old soldiers' of the wards to gawp at, like the patient who used to spend a couple of hours every day combing his hair in a robotic manner to remove 'the plaster that had been rubbed into it during the night'. Jung would point out how over the years the comb had moved farther from his head: combing his head in 1900 had given way to raking the chest in 1903 and by 1906 the patient was scratching his thigh.[48] One layman who went with Jung on his rounds remarked that the hospital was like Zürich in miniature and contained a quintessence of the population.[49] Particularly disturbing to visitors was the level of violence, an inevitable concomitant of the liberal Bleuler regime, in which patients were encouraged to live in conditions as normal as possible in their own private space. Jung once took his old school friend Albert Oeri with him on his rounds. They were examining a bedridden patient when Oeri felt a sudden rush of air past his ear. He looked around to see that another patient had aimed a pile-driving blow at him with his fist but fortunately had just missed. Jung simply laughed and said that Oeri was lucky, as the man packed a wallop.[50]

None of the patients tangled with Jung himself. He was tall, square-shouldered and massively built and had a reputation for pugnacity which the inmates respected. Jung did not believe in indulging patients' whims, especially if they involved violence. A six-foot-tall aristocratic woman, suffering from a compulsion neurosis, used to slap her analysts if they said anything that annoyed her. She was consequently handed on like a hot potato from doctor to doctor until she came under Jung's aegis. The inevitable moment arrived when, furious, she sprang to her feet and made to slap him. Jung jumped up menacingly to meet her. 'Very well, you are the lady. You hit first – ladies first! But then I hit back!' The woman sensed the violence in Jung, knew that he meant it, and subsided in her chair, deflated. From that moment the therapy began to succeed and it emerged that she had a compulsion neurosis because she could not impose moral restraint on herself.[51]

By 1905 Jung could take pride in a tough job courageously performed. In addition to the testimony of the 'miracle cure' woman, his American colleagues on the association experiment, Charles Ricksher and Carl Petersen, wrote papers in American learned journals which made Jung's name known abroad. Soon he was developing an impressive roster of private patients, most of them American. In one of the first such consultations he put his knowledge of alcoholism to good use. He successfully treated a dipsomaniac with a 'mother-complex', whose problem was that he worked for his mother in the family firm, did not really want to leave the nest and take responsibility, and therefore drank to forget his humiliating position. Jung warned the man not to return to his job but he did so, and there was a relapse. Since his mother said that she would do anything to help her son, Jung arranged to interview her in Switzerland. He saw at once how dominant she was – 'a real power devil' – and therefore wrote a medical certificate for the mother, stating that her son's alcoholism made him unfit to carry out his duties. She dismissed him. He was initially furious with Jung for 'meddling', but soon struck out on his own and made a successful independent career.[52]

Jung's own career was already attracting the epithet 'brilliant'.[53] His private life was not so successful, for even as he became the toast of the Burghölzli and also solved all his financial problems, he began the turbulent married life that is one of the most problematical aspects of his biography.

Chapter Five

SEX AND MARRIAGE

In his memoirs Jung overplayed his hermit-like existence in the Burghölzli, for it was less than two years after entering the alleged anchorite's cell that the period of austerity came to an end. Some of Jung's admirers have, justifiably, trimmed the period of self-denial down to a mere six months: Van der Post, typically, compares these six months to the long night of the esquire's initiation into knighthood in the Arthurian legends.[1] Indeed Jung does not mention that, even in 1901, he had his annual leave plus the period of compulsory service in the Swiss army. This was the year when he completed his officer's training and was promoted to first lieutenant. As an Army medical officer Jung was depressed by the physical calibre of the young Swiss he examined. At an enlistment he attended in Lucerne, only 30 per cent of the draftees were physically fit and many of the recruits were mentally subnormal; of 506 men examined, forty-seven were certified as imbecile. Jung wondered whether this physical and mental degeneracy was attributable to the benighted ignorance of the rural peasantry, who were well known for their habit of sending all their milk and cheese to market, dosing their children instead with coffee and brandy –

which would also account for the high levels of alcoholism in the drafted men.[2]

There can be no denying that in the years 1900–02 money continued to be a major worry for Jung, who also had his mother and his sister to support. His mother repaid her son's generosity with more of her unhelpful eerie behaviour. On one occasion, when he was first starting work on the word-association tests, Emilie Jung paid one of her phantom-like visits to the Burghölzli. She looked disdainfully around his room, the walls of which were covered in flow charts showing the correlations of reaction times and complexes, and said, 'Do those things really mean anything?' Jung was devastated and confessed that if he had been a weak person he would have been utterly crushed. After she left he had a terrific fit of anger, enraged that any mother could use such a 'demonic mode' on her son.[3]

The year 1902 was a decisive one for Jung, for it was then that he re-encountered a young girl glimpsed just once before in a Hardyesque fleeting moment. In 1896, when he was a medical student, Jung had first seen Emma Rauschenbach, then aged fourteen, standing at the top of a staircase in the Rauschenbach family house in Schaffhausen, and claimed to have told a friend he had a deep intuition that some day he would marry her. Apparently it was his old 'aunt' Bertha Schenk, who used to take him for walks when he was a child, who introduced him to the Rauschenbachs, since she had married into the family.[4] Since the documentation dealing with Jung's private life during his early years has never been released, we can only guess at the circumstances in which he reacquainted himself with Emma, now twenty, in 1902, but we do know that the romance did not go well at first.

Emma was an attractive, educated young woman, quiet, warm, independent, charming and gracious. The personality that emerges from her letters and other writings is delightful: no nasty or malicious rumours have ever surfaced about her, and Jungians who remember her speak, in the inevitable jargon, of a 'fine balance of creative animus and feminine functioning'.[5] Her reactions to Jung's rapid courtship and proposal of marriage reveal a mixture of naïvety and shrewdness. He had no money or property, worked in an unglamorous profession, and was prickly and hypersensitive to the point where some of his colleagues at the Burghölzli referred to him as the 'prince with the pea'. At his first proposal Emma turned him down flat. Two additional reasons have been given for the rejection. One is that the ingenuous Emma believed herself already 'engaged' to a young man she had allowed to kiss her a few times, and before considering a fresh suitor had to get her parents to dissolve the 'engagement'.[6] The other, more plausible, explanation is that she sensed the commitment to psychiatry needed for a young man as ambitious as Carl and did not want to marry 'a slave to an ideology'.[7] Whatever the true circumstances, when Jung proposed a second time she accepted him. To marry into the fabulously wealthy Rauschenbach family would solve all Jung's financial problems. It was agreed that the couple would marry as soon as Jung finished an imminent sabbatical in Paris.

In the winter of 1902–03 Bleuler granted his young assistant study leave to attend Janet's lectures and seminars on hysteria at the Collège de France; it was the director's hope that permanent links could be established between the Paris and Zürich schools of depth psychology. Evidence is thin as to what exactly Jung got up to in the fleshpots of Paris while he cut most of Janet's classes, but one significant event was a reunion with Hélène Preiswerk. Jung had now established to his own satisfaction that the two Helens fitted neatly into his hysteria/schizophrenia model. Thus his cousin suffered merely from hysteria, but Flournoy's Helen Smith was a genuine schizophrenic, as was evident from her letters.[8] Moreover, as he later told J.B. Rhine, Jung was now convinced that the 'occult' events of the table-splitting and the shivered bread knife in 1898 were caused by Hélène Preiswerk's 'actions at a distance', since she told him that she had been thinking vividly of the seances at the exact time both 'explosions' in the Jung household had taken place.[9]

Hélène Preiswerk and her elder sister Emmy were working as seamstresses near to the Madeleine, and it was there that Jung sought her out. He took her on an excursion to Versailles, drove with her in a two-horse carriage and, on her twenty-first birthday, took her and her sister to the theatre. A letter from Jung, written from the Hôtel des Balcons in rue Casimir Delavigne on 2 January 1903, informed her that he was going to London for a short trip on 19 January and from there would cross to Ostend and then straight home for the wedding with Emma on 14 February.[10] Seeing again the man with whom she was secretly in love seems to have stirred in Hélène Preiswerk a yearning for the scenes of her youth – or perhaps she thought that by now the scandal would have died down – for she almost immediately relocated to her native city and in autumn 1903 opened a dress shop on Basel's Aschenplatz. But if she was hoping for interest from Carl she was disappointed, for the only Jung who came to her shop was the newly-wed and intrigued Emma, who called by for a fitting.[11]

Whether through flirtation with Hélène Preiswerk or some other form of hedonism, Jung seriously neglected the commission given him by Bleuler. He did meet the psychologist Alfred Binet, who was keen on the idea of cooperation with the Burghölzli on the word-association experiment, but unfortunately the projected collaboration foundered when Binet made it a point of understanding that all joint protocols be written in French, and Jung felt his mastery of the language was not up to such a task.[12] To cover his tracks, on his return to Zürich, Jung turned in a highly negative report on Janet and his school, and he always spoke dismissively of his contacts with the French in 1902–03.

The wedding with Emma was duly celebrated on 14 February 1903, after which the couple departed for their honeymoon on Lake Como. The wedding photograph shows Jung looking every inch the portly young Swiss burgher, dressed in white waistcoat, watch chain, drainpipe collar, bow-tie and stiffly correct cufflinks, with a solemn expression on his face. Emma in long skirt and blouse stands close to him looking demure and almost fearful. According to Jung's later account, he and Emma spent most of the honeymoon arguing about the rights and wrongs of distributing money between husbands and wives.[13]

With his new-found wealth, Jung decided that the Como sojourn was not enough. He and Emma then departed on a cruise to Madeira and the Canary Islands.[14] In the light of Jung's many complaints about the austere years at the Burghölzli, it is worth noting that, between the Paris interlude and the extended honeymoon, he had a continuous period of six months away from his duties, and this *before* he had completed two years' full service at the hospital. That is generous sabbatical leave by any standards.

Moreover, on his return to the Burghölzli, when Emma moved into married quarters with him, Jung decided on a more lavish and expansive lifestyle. He bought expensive clothes and went to theatres and nightspots with Emma. He no longer took institutional meals at the Burghölzli but had his own personal chef to prepare his food. There was little Bleuler could do about it, even had he wanted to, for Jung resumed his punishing workload and let it be known that he intended having a new house built for himself and his bride. Since Jung was proving his worth as a psychiatrist every week that passed, Bleuler had to accept that Jung was now in the Burghölzli on special terms.

At the beginning of 1904 Jung took another two months' leave and went to London to improve his English.[15] His sight of the dreadful slum quarters of Whitechapel, Stepney and Bermondsey may have been among the experiences in Jung's mind when he wrote that a good psychologist needed a knowledge of brothels, suburban pubs and gambling halls just as much as a knowledge of hospitals and lunatic asylums; the experience could potentially furnish wisdom no textbook could supply.[16] The two-month sojourn did, however, confirm Jung as a lifelong Anglophile and devotee of the English language and he found in England the 'rugged individualism' usually associated with the USA.

Jung returned to resume luxurious married life in his flat in the Burghölzli. Emma was soon pregnant, and at the end of the year bore Jung the first of five children, Agatha (born 26 December 1904). Jung started to widen the circle of contacts he entertained, and among the 'catches' he trawled in was Albert Einstein, then based in Berne, who in 1905 became famous when he published his Special Theory of Relativity when only twenty-six. At this stage the two young men got on well, though Jung soured on Einstein later, as he did with almost all his male friends and acquaintances. In 1905 Einstein was often at the Jungs as a dinner guest and impressed Carl with the simplicity and directness of his genius as a thinker. In later years Jung would sometimes claim Einstein as a great influence on his own increasingly odd views of time, but in those days he was flustered and embarrassed when Einstein tried to explain relativity by means of differential equations. A mathematical dunce had no chance of following tensors and partial differentials, but Jung liked to get his own back by working the conversation round to the mysteries of the human psyche, where he had the advantage.[17]

By the time of Emma's pregnancy it was already clear that all was not well with the marriage. It soon became apparent that Jung was a compulsive womanizer. Everyone agrees that he had a mesmeric effect on women, though it is not clear from his photographs why this should be. Tall, broad-shouldered, high cheekboned, prematurely balding, with small blue eyes, firm jaw, aquiline nose and short clipped moustache, he often gave the impression of a peasant rather than a doctor. He was also extremely strong, lumbering and bear-like.[18] But there was something else: one hesitates to call it charisma, but clearly he conveyed a sense of power – sexual power – which women responded to, and this was coupled with an uncanny, quasi-occult ability to 'read' people. One of his 'conquests' reported, 'Given a summer's evening, a private place looking out on the lake and he would quote something in that deep, resonant voice of his and look at a woman like a young girl he had just fallen in love with on a spring day.' Another wrote, 'He gave the impression of great power and insight, and I was altogether shattered at the idea that he would see right through me, even into the sexual fantasies that were tormenting me.'[19]

Why did Jung chafe so fretfully under the yoke of monogamy? The key must be sought in his relationship with his mother. Not only was she a 'dual' person, making an integrated response to a single woman difficult for her son, but she had been absent at a critical time in his life and important 'imprinting' had been done by the maid whose beauty Jung always remembered. To use Jungian terms, his fantasy woman tended to be invoked by an 'anima', but his anima was split as between his early perceptions of his mother and the maid.

Since it was a perennial failing of Jung's to generalize wildly from his own experience, we can get important clues to the dynamic of his marriage from his many pronouncements about the role of mothers vis-à-vis sons. A man with a mother as powerful as his had but two choices, he opined: homosexuality or Don Juanism, and the woman married to such a man was doomed either to meek submission or overbearing tyranny. Jung thought that where the bond between mother and son persisted into adulthood, there was a 'secret conspiracy' between the two, whereby each helped the other to 'betray life'.[20] To break out of the coils of such determinism was impossible, and a clear choice had to be made. Homosexuality occurred when the boy's heterosexual libido remained fixated on the mother and was therefore unavailable for any other woman. Don Juanism was the other possibility. Here the quest is for an ideal woman who is all mother, but since this role is already filled and by definition no 'normal' woman can fit the job description, the man must forever be dropping his mistresses and moving on to the next one. Some have seen the early phallus dream as a clue to mother fixation in Jung, pointing out that the masculine principle (the phallic god) was entombed in the feminine (the womb of the earth).[21]

However, it is a cardinal principle of Jungian thought that every phenomenon has its compensating aspect, and in delineating the character traits of the typical sufferer from philandering syndrome Jung paints a shrewd self-portrait. His idea was that what was Don Juanism in its negative aspect was in its positive manifestation what Nietzsche would call the 'morality of strenuousness' – connoting ambition, self-sacrifice, heroism, intellectual curiosity and toughness of will.

Because of his 'mother-complex' Jung placed any woman he married in an impossible position, as he himself realized. A 'mother's boy', if he avoided homosexuality, would almost inevitably marry a girl obviously inferior to his mother or a female tyrant who would tear him away from his mother.[22]

To sum up, Jung regarded himself as doomed to promiscuity because of his mother, but at the same time some part of him despised his wife for not being strong enough to destroy Emilie Jung's hold over him. He consistently argued for free love; to Freud he put it more bluntly, stating unequivocally that the prescription for a happy marriage was a licence to be unfaithful.[23] Emma's impossible position can be gauged when it is realized that Jung added the further requirement that the wife should bear all without jealousy, under pain of incurring overt contempt, for it was a dogma of Jung's that jealous women did not really love their husbands.[24]

That Jung's theories were in themselves a recipe for an unhappy marriage can be seen when we analyse his view of a relationship between a couple as that between 'container' and 'contained'. Jung's theory is that marriage is inevitably a conflict between a complex personality that he calls the 'container' and a simple personality, the 'contained'. Both partners will be unhappy because the container will flounder in the relationship, since 'simplicity always has the advantage over complexity' and the container will 'constellate his complexities with her everlasting insistence on simple answers'.[25] Meanwhile the contained lives entirely inside the marriage, but in an unsatisfactory way; her simple nature will not allow the complex container enough space, but the complex container gives *her* too much space, so that she is bewildered.

Jung thought that the more the 'contained' clung, the more the 'container' felt shut out of the relationship and therefore inclined to stray and be unfaithful. In the end the container becomes aware that marriage cannot provide everything he needs and therefore seeks completion elsewhere.[26]

One might conclude that anyone entering a marriage with such views, tricked out with the notion that he was a 'many-faceted gem' while Emma was a 'simple cube', would be doomed to fail, and indeed it has been suggested that the only reason Jung's marriage survived was that, though he thought he was the 'container', it was really Emma who had that role.[27] What is clear is that Jung did not, in any significant sense of the word, love Emma. This fact might be inferred, as Anthony Storr suggests, from the simple fact that Emma is mentioned just twice, in entirely trivial contexts, in *Memories*, Jung's testament to the world.[28] This is true enough, but one purpose of *Memories* was obviously to excise any mention of sexuality in Jung's personal world. As Walter Kaufman remarked on the oddest of all autobiographies, 'It is a story of a man who, like so many Victorian gentlemen, had a mistress but found sex an unsavoury subject that it was better not to talk about; a man who was remarkably self-indulgent and self-righteous and who felt a great need at the end of his life to engage in a lengthy exercise in self-justification.'[29]

Overwhelmingly, the evidence suggests that Jung married Emma for money, and that he had a 'money-complex'.[30] Since neither money nor economics is discussed much in Jung's social thought, we might infer that this is yet another Jungian 'compensation', but there is better evidence to hand. In January 1907 Jung, very creditably, agreed to be a subject for Ludwig Binswanger's experiment for his medical dissertation, in which he combined the methods of the word-association test and the galvanometer. Binswanger detected eleven dissociations, of which the most important was the 'Goethe-complex'. Among the others were a money-complex, a travel-complex, a philosophical-complex, the wish to have a son, guilt about his father's death, hypochondriacal feelings relating to his own death, restlessness with his life and a detestation of the idea of fidelity to his wife.[31] Furthermore, towards the end of his life Jung told his adoring disciple Barbara Hannah that the influence of his father and his brand of Christianity had given him taboo feelings not just about sex but also about money, because of his father's excessive interest in spirituality, and for this reason he had found the financial support of his mother after 1896 particularly burdensome.[32]

Jung's story about a *coup de foudre* when he saw the fourteen-year old Emma not withstanding, there are grounds for doubting that Emma was even one of those women who 'constellated the anima' and, even if she was, she was a long way behind other Jung fantasy women.[33] Moreover, Jung hated her natural philoprogenitive urges, and was intensely irritated by her many pregnancies, even though they imposed no financial burden on him. He wrote to Freud in 1911 about his unsuccessful attempts at contraception: 'One tries every conceivable trick to stem the tide of these little blessings but without much confidence. One scrapes along one might say from one menstruation to the next. The life of the civilised man certainly does have its quaint side.'[34] Emma knew, or sensed, that her pregnancies made Carl depressed and angry and in 1905, pregnant again months after giving birth to Agatha, she evinced her fear that he was losing interest in her. The occasion was when her husband was looking round for guinea pigs for his experiment on reaction times in the word-association test and she revealed a complex about being unloved.[35]

Finally, in 1909, Jung decided to deal with the problem of Emma by analysing her and converting her to the idea of a polygamous husband, but the analysis foundered on her (natural) resistance to such an idea. Yet the venture had beneficial indirect results, since Emma decided to become a Jungian analyst and, in a classic example of sublimation, having failed to give Carl what he wanted in life, tried to succeed in his work. There are occasional passages in her published work which hint at her marital woes and her valiant attempts to surmount them.[36]

Apart from the mountain of circumstantial evidence that Jung's marriage to Emma soon came very close to the rocks, there is direct testimony in the form of Jung's dreams and his own and Freud's analyses of them. On 8 February 1906 Jung's second daughter, Anna, was born, and the event increased Jung's feelings of disenchantment. Later that year he had an important dream. Horses were being hoisted by thick cables to a great height. Jung was particularly struck by a powerful brown horse, but suddenly the cable snapped and the horse crashed to the street. Thinking it must be dead, Jung was surprised when it leapt up and started galloping away, dragging a heavy log. Then a rider came up on a little horse and rode slowly in front of the frightened horse. Just when Jung thought the two mounts would collide, a cab came along, drove in front of the rider, and brought the frightened horse to a dead slow and safe gait.[37]

For public consumption Jung remarked that the dream was recorded by a friend whose circumstances were well known to him, though to Freud, with whom he started corresponding in 1906, he eventually admitted the truth: it was his own dream. Jung's interpretation of the dream was fourfold. The dreamer was personally ambitious and wished to travel to the USA to advance his career but was prevented by his wife's pregnancy; the horse stood for the dreamer who was being hoisted to the top of his profession but preferred to gallop off alone; the log referred to his nickname at university – a variant of Barrel; the little horse with the rider was his pregnant wife, but the cab was full of children, which meant that the prospect of too many offspring was reining in the dreamer's sexual impetuosity.[38]

Jung divulged the details of the dream to Freud without at first revealing that he was the dreamer, but he was soon forced from cover. In a letter that does not survive, Freud evidently spoke of 'the failure of a rich marriage' for Jung felt nettled by the charge and wrote back admitting his wife was rich, claiming to be 'really' happy and suggesting the 'failure' was social not sexual.[39] Without explaining how to be happy 'in every way' squared with the likelihood that there had been a social failure in the marriage, Jung went on to reinterpret some of the features of the dream. Perhaps the rider on the little horse was Bleuler, who after a long bachelorhood had married and sired two sons, and this touched on Jung's undoubted desire to have a son. Next Jung admitted that he had been disingenuous in his earlier analysis and that the abstract notion of sexual restraint disguised the detail of a current affair he did not wish to divulge.[40]

Freud diplomatically replied that although he had guessed the identity of the dreamer, he had not wanted to give offence by making his hunch explicit, and gently suggested to Jung that he ponder the equation log = penis. Jung's response merely obfuscated matters. It was quite clear that Jung wished to keep Freud in the dark about the details of his current affair.[41]

Jung's polygamous instincts and the numerous infidelities they engendered raise many questions about his life which are resolved partly by chronology, but some issues are worth raising at this point. It is clear that Jung was proud of his ability to seduce women. He once told Lewis Mumford that when he died nobody would realize that the old man in the coffin was once a great lover.[42] There is much other testimony to the same effect. Paul Stern reported: 'He considered himself a great lover, even experienced concern that this fact might escape future biographers.'[43] Yet some of his women whispered that he was not particularly skillful or passionate as a bedmate; his associate Jolande Jacobi maintained that he was undersexed, though this was generally held to be sour grapes on her part. The truth is probably that Jung when young had a considerable appetite for 'straight' non-adventurous sex and was perhaps more interested in quantity than quality.[44]

Dramatic events soon demonstrated that Jung's polygamous instincts were no mere theoretician's day-dream. In 1904 he was writing about a case of hysterical reenactment by a seventeen-year-old girl, consequent on reading Clemens Brentano's life of a bogus 'saint', Katharine Emmerich (in reality a cataleptic).[45] Jung noticed that the codename given the hysterical girl in Carl Furstner's 1888 account was 'Sabina S'.[46] A few months later, in August 1904, a real life Sabina S arrived at the Burghölzli as a patient. Jung thought that this was more than coincidence and that supernatural forces were at work: not only did it sow the seed of his later idea of 'synchronicity' but the new patient seemed an uncanny simulacrum of Hélène Preiswerk.

The new patient's name was Sabina Spielrein. Born in Rostov in Russia in 1885 into a wealthy Jewish merchant family, she had suffered grievously through being the child (one of five) of a loveless marriage. Her mother was a flighty coquette who liked to drift around the spas and watering holes of Western Europe – where her husband owned extensive property – with young Sabina in tow. Sabina proved to be an intellectually precocious and brilliant girl, and in 1904 she came to Zürich to enrol in the medical school.[47] It has been pointed out that Spielrein enjoyed privileges unavailable to intelligent Swiss girls, since liberal Tsarist educational policies permitted females a mainstream education; Sabina held a *gymnasium* diploma and so could enter a Swiss university, unlike Swiss girls of her class, who were inevitably educated at home.[48] But on arrival in Switzerland she suffered a severe nervous breakdown with psychotic episodes and was admitted to the Burghölzli.

Spielrein was an intriguing addition to the roster of Burghölzli patients: she was rich, she was educated, she was Russian, she was

Jewish and on admission she was classified as an hysteric. In 1904 less than 5 per cent of new admissions to the Burghörzli were listed as hysteric, there were only five Russians out of 276 in the new intake, and only three patients could be regarded as rich. Spielrein therefore stood out among the new admissions and, supernatural *diablerie* apart, it was not surprising that Jung was attracted to her case. Nevertheless, some modern observers have expressed surprise that she should have been hospitalized for hysteria, which, as was well known, was at epidemic proportions at the turn of the century.[49] The answer is certainly a cultural one – in the sense that one hundred years ago hospitalization was routine for cases that would today be treated by drugs like Valium. Also not to be discounted are the then influential theories of Janet, who proposed that institutionalization was necessary both to ratify the patient's sense of being ill, and to separate him/her from parents.

For two months – and some say that the period of treatment was even shorter[50] – Jung devoted himself to cracking the enigma presented by the new patient. The going was tough, and Jung later referred to the sessions with Spielrein as his proving ground in psychoanalysis.[51] It is interesting to observe the ways in which he was and was not a Freudian at this stage of his career. He did not believe in full 'abreaction', or trying to release the entire body of repressed material from the unconscious, but in bringing to light those images that the patient's consciousness found particularly intolerable.[52] In a word, he was attempting a fusion of the Freudian method of confronting patients with reality with the Janet method of raising their energy level. He did not use a couch but had Spielrein sit in a chair while he sat behind her.

The raw material presented by Spielrein in her sessions with Jung revealed traumas going back to the age of three. That was when she saw her father spanking her brother on the bare bottom, and immediately afterwards felt as though she had defecated on her father's hand. From the age of four to seven she veered between trying to retain her stool – on one occasion she went two weeks without a bowel movement – and attempting to defecate on her own feet: she used to sit on the floor with one foot behind her and press her heel against her anus. She had no idea how she hit upon the idea, which she described as accompanied by 'blissfully shuddersome' feelings, and thought it completely instinctive. From the age of seven she switched to masturbation, but was caught at it and (allegedly) beaten on the buttocks by her father, and was sexually excited by the experience. From then on, whenever her father beat her brothers, she had the same sense of excitement.[53]

As she grew up, she was unable to sit at table without bursting into hysterical laughter at the thought of the assembled company defecating. At fifteen her sexual fantasies proper began, but were confused by the continuing obsession about defecation. By the time she was admitted to the Burghölzli she was in deep depression, alternating between tears and hysterical laughter, and sticking her tongue out with loathing if anyone touched her.[54]

The Spielrein case enables us to gauge Jung's talents as an analyst at this point in his career. He saw that masochism was a key element, since the fantasies of beating produced both sexual pleasure and disgust. Whether the beating by the father actually took place remains open, and this issue is clouded by the entire debate about infantile seduction: nine-tenths reality as in the fashionable contemporary view, or nine-tenths fantasy as in Freud's view? Kerr suggests that Sabina's father might have beaten her to instil a sense of reality into her, since her mother insisted on keeping her locked in a dream world, and argues that, in that case, Sabina might have sensed her father's sexual frustration as a subtext to the beating, as the Spielrein parents echoed Jung's parents in their preference for separate bedrooms.

However, Jung failed to identify a key element in Spielrein's background. She was totally ignorant about sex and reproduction, having been kept in deliberate ignorance by her mother, who felt that all women were victims and that in some obscure sense to bring up a sexually ignorant girl was a form of revenge against men. Kerr suggests that Jung failed to uncover this because he was using a faulty methodology, setting the agenda himself and not letting the patient set the pace (as in Freudian association). Spielrein quite naturally then would have supposed that since the doctor did not question her directly about sex this was not important.[55]

The sessions between Jung and Sabina seem to have been classics of 'transference' and 'countertransference' – the curious but well-known psychoanalytic phenomena whereby undischarged sexual fantasies from the past are visited by patient on doctor ('transference') and by doctor on patient ('countertransference'). Excited by his patient, Jung became carried away and, in obvious defiance of his experience with Hélène Preiswerk, declared that Sabina was the woman who first revealed the 'anima' to him.[56] Sabina's besotment was of a deeper kind, as we shall see.

However, Jung's extremely brief treatment worked to the point where Spielrein enrolled as a medical student at Zürich University in April 1905 and was discharged from the Burghölzli at the beginning of June. Some embarrassment was caused at the university by her giving (masochistically) the Burghölzli as her home address.[57] But there was now no impediment to her making good her great intellectual promise. As Bruno Bettelheim commented, 'The most significant event in Sabina's young life was that, whatever happened to her during her treatment by Jung at the Burghölzli, it cured her. However questionable Jung's behaviour was from a moral point of view . . . somehow it met the prime obligation of the therapist towards his patient: to cure her.'[58]

After Spielrein left hospital, she and Jung started meeting in secret, in his office, in her flat or in the countryside. There is little doubt that they became lovers but some Jungians have found this hard to stomach and have tried to argue that physical contact between the two went no farther than kissing and touching.[59] Certain Jungians argue that the word Spielrein uses to describe her intimate moments with Jung, 'poetry', is sometimes used by her in contexts that do not connote intercourse. This is true, but it is also true that 'poetry' is more often used in contexts where any other reference than 'intercourse' makes no sense.

Three further points might be made to clinch the argument that Jung and Spielrein were lovers. Jung uses the German word *hingabe* ('sexual surrender') to refer to this relationship, hinting strongly that he and Spielrein were lovers.[60] Spielrein herself later introduced herself to the psychoanalyst Arthur Muthmann as Jung's mistress.[61] And it strains credibility to imagine that the promiscuous Jung would have spent so much time and energy on a 'platonic' affair. The common-sense view would seem to be that 'poetry' was Sabina's favourite 'feeling-toned' word and that she used it in *all* contexts where her emotions were highly engaged. It is surely a simple-minded view of female sexuality that assumes that all erotically charged references must refer to the sex act itself, or that 'poetry' commits one to an either–or scenario.[62]

One of Jung and Sabina's forays into the countryside ended badly. Spielrein dropped her cloak in the dust and Jung picked it up and tried to beat the dust off it with his stick. Sabina suddenly became violent, threw herself on him, tore the cloak from his hands and said that she could not bear the sight of it. It was not difficult for Jung to guess that the beating with the stick triggered the fantasy/memory of the beating by her father.[63]

Yet if Spielrein still had serious relapses into a quasi-psychotic state, Jung for his part became aware of a neurosis in himself which he termed a 'Jewish complex'.[64] It will be remembered that one of the ploys Hélène Preiswerk used to make herself more attractive to him was to pretend to have Jewish ancestry, almost as though she uncannily intuited this peculiarity in Jung's psyche. Using the Jungian theory of compensation, one might be tempted to interpret the 'Jewess-complex' as compensation for Jung's perennial unconscious antagonism towards Jewish males. Whatever the explanation, there can be no doubting that the young Carl Gustav was preternaturally attracted to Jewish women. Not only was there to be another infatuation in 1907,[65] but Riklin, in one of his association tests on Jung, uncovered such a 'complex', and Jung himself wrote up the story of the love of a Christian doctor for a Jewish girl – a disguised narrative of his own experience with Spielrein.[66]

Jung was Sabina's first love, and she never really got over him. At first she idealized him yet feared that the anal fixation she had revealed might disgust him. As part of the idealization she expressed an ambition to be a psychoanalyst once she had graduated from medical school – an ambition Jung interpreted both as a wish to identify with him and a desire to sublimate and thus fulfil otherwise unfulfillable sexual wishes.[67] Jung was always the cooler one in this troubled relationship, even though at the height of the romance he left notes in her pigeonhole at the university with such comments as 'you have taken my unconscious into your hands with your saucy letters'.[68] These notes, ostensibly concerned with the time and place of the next rendezvous – for Jung and Spielrein varied their movements as if they were secret agents – were full of praise for Sabina's free spirit and absence of banality.

In order to be nearer to her at other times without suspicion, Jung made her his research assistant on the reaction-time ratio experiment in the word-association tests. But the problem of Jung's wife was looming, as it tended to with all his mistresses, no matter how 'liberal' they claimed to be. Looking back in 1909 Spielrein summed up her liaison with Jung up to 1907 and claimed that in that year he openly preached polygamy, and claimed that his wife had no objections.[69]

Spielrein was only half convinced, as her dreams showed. In one of them Emma complained to her about her difficulties in living with the tyrannical Jung.[70] By 1908 the affair had moved on a notch, with Jung and Spielrein fantasizing about having the perfect child, which they named Siegfried. But by this time the entire relationship had moved into another dimension, becoming entangled in the wider world of psychoanalytical politics. Spielrein's significance in Jung's life was, to use a Freudian term, 'overdetermined', for it was as a result of his liaison with her that Jung made the momentous decision to enter into correspondence with Sigmund Freud.

Chapter Six

FIRST CONTACTS WITH FREUD

The first contact between Freud and Jung came in April 1906 when Jung sent the great Viennese pioneer his work on the connection between psychoanalysis and the word-association test. Freud wrote back to thank him for his overture.[1] In fact Jung was able to back him up the very next month, at a conference in Baden-Baden, when Freud's theories came under attack from Gustav Aschaffenburg, professor of Psychiatry and Neurology at Heidelberg. Although Jung had reservations about Freud's emphasis on sexuality, he pointed out that the ideas of repression, resistance and transference, and Freud's work on dreams and parapraxes (slips of the tongue) easily survived Aschaffenburg's facile criticisms of Freudianism as an 'evil method'. Jung's approach was to modify Freudian theory so that very many, but not *all* cases of hysteria derived from sexual roots: only hunger, after all, rivalled sex as a basic drive.[2]

Even though Freudians like Ernest Jones later claimed that Jung's defence was 'weak,'[3] doubtless because hedged around with so many cavils, it was a courageous and disinterested stance for Jung to take. By the end of 1906 he and Freud were in sustained correspondence. Why did the two men forge this alliance, and why then?

There were at least four different reasons. In the first place, there was Jung's passionate interest in Freud's ideas. Although Jung later recanted, at this point in his career he was prepared to credit Freud with being, so to speak, the Captain Cook of the unconscious, the true discoverer of its scope and dimensions. Cook was not the first person to discover Australia – others, like Abel Tasman, had been there before him – but he was the first person to put the southern continent on the map in the full sense. So it was with Freud, or so Jung claimed in this period of his life. Historians and antiquarians could trace the idea of an 'unconscious' at least as far back as St Augustine, but it was Freud who first provided a systematic 'cosmology' of the unconscious.

Jung's feeling was that Freud's ideas were too important to be left to the pedantic mercies of orthodox psychiatry. His position is well summed up by a paper written in July 1906. Although he did not attribute to infantile sexual trauma the exclusive importance Freud gave it, he declared that Freudianism could be refuted only by someone who had made repeated use of psychoanalytical methodology; otherwise, they were like the 'scientists' who disdained to look through Galileo's telescope. He endorsed Freud's methods on dream interpretation and hysteria, admitting that his few reservations were nugatory.

The most significant of Jung's doubts and cavils concerned sexuality, which he did not wish to place so firmly in the foreground or to endow with a psychological universality.

Secondly, Jung was caught up in the entire process of psychoanalytical politics, designed to build bridges between the Vienna and Zürich 'schools'. Bleuler and his associates wanted to make use of the exciting new techniques emanating from Vienna and to incorporate them in a synoptic psychiatry. Freud, for his part, wanted the scientific respectability the prestigious Burghölzli could confer on his fledgling discipline and wished to take the Jewish 'gospel' of psychoanalysis to the gentiles. Having heard a garbled version of Jung's treatment of Sabina Spielrein (though no names were mentioned), he was disturbed to learn that 'unqualified' people were practising psychoanalysis.[4]

However, Freud was not blind to the extraordinary array of talent working at the Burghölzli. Apart from Jung and Bleuler there were Max Eitingon, Hermann Nunberg, Ludwig Binswanger, Karl Abraham and Franz Riklin, all of whom would feature as major names in the history of psychiatry. In time Freud would win over Eitingon, Binswanger and Abraham to his cause. At this stage the most promising young man, Jung apart, seemed to be Franz Riklin, three years Jung's junior, bound to him both by kinship (he had married Jung's cousin) and their common interest in the word-association test.[5]

Bleuler had groomed Riklin as his clinical right-hand man and sent him to study the word-association experiments in Emil Kraepelin's laboratory. When he returned and set up the Burghölzli laboratory, it was Riklin, not Jung, who had the inside track as the leading empirical psychologist at the hospital. Yet Riklin was an ambitious malcontent and departed soon afterwards to take up Bleuler's old post as director of the Rheinau asylum. This was an unwise career move on two fronts. Henceforth all the word-association experiments at the Burghölzli were conducted by Jung, who put his name to the publications, so that soon the experiments were indelibly associated with Jung and Riklin's pioneering contribution forgotten. Then Riklin himself turned out to be an unstable, henpecked dreamer. On the one hand he allowed himself to be convinced by Sabina Spielrein that his true vocation was as an artist, with disastrous later effects. On the other, he was persuaded to return to the Burghölzli at the end of the decade, to occupy a position junior to Jung's. The persuasion came from his wife, who, like so many of Jung's cousins, was smitten with him, wanted to be near him, and held him up as a model to her husband.[6]

Bleuler's first ambassador to the court of Vienna was the brilliant and controversial Max Eitingon, later in life to be accused of being a secret agent for the NKVD.[7] Eitingon, who arrived in Vienna in January 1907, was a young Swiss psychiatrist with a junior position at the Burghölzli; he was also a rich Jew with a reputation as a ladies' man. John Kerr claims that Eitingon did not get on well with the Viennese, and it was this experience that made Freud think of bypassing Bleuler and dealing directly with Jung.[8] This thesis does not, however, seem borne out by the close rapport that developed between Freud and Eitingon – in 1909 he moved from Zürich to Berlin to associate himself more closely with 'the master' – and which never faded.[9]

The third reason for this early alliance between the two men is that Jung badly wanted advice from Freud on the increasing problem of 'transference to the doctor' – increasing in part because of his undoubted physical attraction in the eyes of his female analysands. In late 1905 there was a serious transference problem with a patient who fantasized an *alter ego* known as 'Miss L' (this was not Sabina Spielrein). The patient had a 'crush' on Jung, which was actually a transference from an overdeveloped relationship with her mother. Jung dealt with this by pointing out that he was already married. Predictably, the woman responded to this brush-off by breaking off the treatment and complaining that Jung had tried to make 'morally dangerous' conversation with her. Jung was perplexed, since the woman could find no therapeutic rapport with him, only a sexual one[10].

In this instance he almost immediately got the reassurance he needed, for Freud analysed the case as one of hysteria and pointed out that transference took place most readily with such an illness. For Freud this was clear proof that neuroses were determined by the individual's love life.[11]

Freud's further wisdom on transference, in which he insists that the analyst show a female patient manifesting transference love that the 'love' is a form of resistance,[12] has a direct bearing on Jung's liaison with Sabina Spielrein.

Finally, and perhaps most importantly, Jung felt that he was getting into deep waters with Sabina Spielrein and needed guidance from a master pilot.[13] Apparently Jung composed a letter to Freud about Spielrein a full nine months before they began to correspond, but never sent it.[14] In only his second letter to Freud, in October 1906, he discussed the Spielrein case, without naming names or mentioning his own erotic involvement.[15] Then he dropped the matter abruptly and did not take it up again for another eight months. It may be that John Kerr is right when he interprets this as Jung's disappointment that Freud analysed the case as one of anal eroticism, and his feeling that Freud had not done justice to the flesh-and-blood woman he knew.[16] If so, he only had himself to blame, for without the full erotic context of the affair Freud was necessarily working in the dark.

The early epistolary contacts saw Freud trying to put Jung's mind at rest about psychoanalysis and the doubts he entertained. Jung resisted the idea that hysteria was exclusively sexual, though he conceded it might be predominantly so. He was adamant that some other basic drives (perhaps hunger) were involved in neurosis. Jung mentioned three other reservations: first, that most uneducated hysterics were not suitable subjects for psychoanalysis; secondly, that if psychoanalytic techniques became widely known, it would attract charlatans who would debase the coinage; thirdly, that the very concept of hysteria was still too unclear. However, he sugared the pill of his grudging acceptance by talking overconfidently of the progress Freudian theory was making in Switzerland. As likely adherents he mentioned Dr Ludwig Frank, follower of Auguste Forel and formerly director of the Munsterlingen Asylum, and Dr Dumeng Bezzola, head physician at the Schloss Hard Sanatorium in Canton Thurgau. He also (disingenuously) claimed that Bleuler was converted, although this was far from being the case.[17]

Freud, for his part, assumed the persona of the much-misunderstood man. Congratulating Jung (and Bleuler) for their work, he expressed the hope that Jung would one day come round to the sexual aetiology of neuroses, although he insisted he had no theoretical objection to the dethronement of sexuality from its prime position as monarch of the instincts. All he claimed was that psychoanalysis was superior to any other technique for probing the unconscious, not that it was a panacea, and he stressed how lonely it was to be accused of being a crank; if he was resistant to ideas other than his own, this was the natural consequence of self-reliance and the lack of wider contacts necessitated by the ten-hour day he spent on his patients. While praising Jung's publications on schizophrenia, he begged to differ on the 'toxin' theory and suggested that such an hypothesis offended against Occam's razor, since the domain of sexuality had not been exhausted. The two men sparred warily on the subject of schizophrenia, accepting that their backgrounds, milieux, training and experience had been very different, though Jung was keen on seeing neurosis and psychosis as existing on a continuous spectrum.[18]

The single case they got down to before meeting in person concerned a twenty-six-year-old woman patient of Freud's, who had just given birth. A depressive, she was unable to obtain sexual satisfaction from her husband, because of childhood practices when she used to retain her urine to experience a sexual frisson. Convinced that she was a freak and would not be able to give birth normally, the woman gloated in an 'I told you so' manner when there was a forceps delivery. Some megalomania was in evidence, since the woman was convinced she was a unique case, but she was also certain that there was imbecility in her blood and therefore that her child would be an imbecile.[19]

Freud asked Jung if in his opinion this was a case of schizophrenia. Jung wrote back with the surprising verdict that the problem lay in the marriage: the woman did not love her husband. In his view women loved the husband in the children and if the husband didn't suit, the children didn't either.[20]

The bonds between the two men were tightened by a mutual exchange of intellectual gifts. Jung sent Freud a copy of *Diagnostic Association Studies* containing his seminal article on word association – a paper that Freud's disciple Ernest Jones called 'great . . . perhaps his most original contribution to science.'[21] Freud assured Jung he liked his paper by far the best and in return sent him a recently edited collection of papers on the theory of neurosis.'[22] Freud was brutally frank and open in his early letters with Jung, but he flavoured candour with diplomacy and tact. As Peter Gay has pointed out, 'When it came to throwing graceful compliments at correspondents, Freud could at times rival the suavest of courtiers.'[23]

By now both men were intrigued enough to want a face-to-face meeting. Jung indeed was so keen on an encounter with Freud that Binswanger, while using Jung as a guinea pig on the word-association tests, recorded the following replies to questions 98 and 100 : 'Vienna. Paris. Soon. Yes.' Soon the joke around the Burghölzli was that this was Jung's 'Vienna-complex'.[24] At the end of February Carl and Emma Jung set out for a tour of Eastern Europe, in company with Binswanger. Their first stop was Vienna.

On Sunday 3 March 1907 at 1 p.m. the Jungs called at Freud's house at Berggasse 19 in Vienna. There followed thirteen hours of virtually continuous talk, which went on right through mealtimes. Freud's son Martin, who was present with the other Freud children, remembered Jung talking non-stop while his father listened. Jung 'never made the slightest attempt to make polite conversation with mother or us children but pursued the debate which had been interrupted by the call to dinner.' Martin Freud noted Jung's 'commanding presence. He was very tall and broadshouldered, holding himself more like a soldier than a man of science and medicine. His head was purely Teutonic with a strong chin, a small moustache, blue eyes and thin close-cropped hair.' Martin Freud found Jung's most outstanding characteristics to be vitality, the ability to project his personality and to control those who listened to him.[25]

This account of the first meeting is largely confirmed by Jung's own version, as told to Ernest Jones three months later. Jung poured out a torrent of words and ideas for three hours while Freud listened. Then Freud interrupted to suggest it would be better if the conversation was conducted more systematically; he then drew up a list of topics that had arisen in Jung's harangue and he and Freud worked through them in order and, as Jung conceded, more profitably.[26] At one point there was a pause in the conversation, and Freud suddenly asked Jung, out of the blue, what he thought about transference. Jung replied that it was the alpha and omega of analytical method. Freud beamed with pleasure: 'Then you have grasped the main thing.'[27]

It was 2 a.m. on Monday before this first session broke up. Both were deeply impressed. Freud later told Ernest Jones that Jung had the most sophisticated grasp of the neuroses of any man he had ever met.[28] Jung too was bowled over. Later he wrote that Freud was the first man of real importance he had encountered. With the benefit of hindsight, he added that he had never been totally convinced by the Freudian theory of sexuality.[29]

Next day Jung returned with the twenty-six-year-old Binswanger and Freud interpreted their dreams of the night before. Binswanger, who had been hugely impressed with Jung when he employed him as his assistant at the Burghölzli, was even more taken with Freud and the singular atmosphere of cordial intellectuality he fostered at Berggasse 19. He admired and was awestruck by Freud, but did not find him intimidating or frightening. He took it well when Freud interpreted one of his dreams as expressing an interest in Freud's eldest daughter, and did not note the ominous undertone to one of Jung's dreams, which Freud interpreted as a wish to dethrone him and take his place.[30]

Sightseeing in Vienna followed, and this threw up an interesting sidelight on Jung's personality. Freud's daughter Mathilde was accompanying Carl and Emma on a shopping expedition when they suddenly found one of the main streets lined with soldiers. Hearing that this was because the emperor was passing, Jung ran off into the crowd of onlookers like an excited boy.[31]

On Wednesday night Jung and Binswanger attended a meeting of the Viennese Psychology Club, presided over by Alfred Adler, to hear a presentation on anal eroticism laid on especially for their benefit. The two Swiss visitors kept a low profile, on the grounds that they were still trying to absorb a plethora of new ideas, but it was obvious to everyone that Freud was inordinately fond of them.[32] Perhaps he was more fond of them than discretion warranted, for he allowed himself to make depreciatory remarks about his Viennese followers such as Adler and Wilhelm Stekel – adverse opinions which were shared by Jung who later spoke disparagingly to Jones of an allegedly 'bohemian' Viennese group.[33]

On the surface, Jung's first meeting with Freud was a glowing success. Once back in Zürich Jung wrote to say that his resistance to Freud's conception of sexuality was crumbling and that the visit had been an event in the fullest sense of the word.[34] Freud in turn confirmed the impression made on Binswanger that he had already decided on Jung as his son and heir.[35]

Yet, according to Jung's testimony later in life, something happened on this visit to Vienna so startling as to throw an entirely new light on the founder of psychoanalysis. In 1957 he told John Billinsky, an American psychology professor, that Freud's relationship with his wife was non-existent both professionally and sexually. Whether this relates to the strange phenomenon observed by Martin Freud, whereby Freud was charming and courteous to Emma Jung, while Jung barely exchanged a single word with Mrs Freud, is unclear. Jung told Billinsky further that Freud's true 'wife' – in the sense that she, unlike his actual wife, understood all about his work – was his sister-in-law, Minna Bernays. Most dramatically of all, Jung claimed that Freud had been carrying on a sexual relationship with Minna.[36]

Jung made this sensational claim to at least half a dozen other people, including the journalist Hugo Charteris, though his account seems to suggest that by then Jung's mental faculties were failing. 'I don't know what happened. Once I think . . . I think he slept with her once, he told me,' said Jung.[37] According to Jung, he learned about the affair from Minna herself who, a few days after the Jungs' arrival in Vienna, asked for a few private words with him and poured out her confession. She claimed to be guilty about her physical relationship with Freud. Jung related the encounter to Billinsky as follows: 'Soon I met Freud's wife's younger sister. She was very good-looking and she not only knew enough about psychoanalysis but also about everything that Freud was doing. When, a few days later, I was visiting Freud's laboratory, Freud's sister-in-law asked if she could talk with me. She was very much bothered by her relationship with Freud and felt guilty about it. From her I learned that Freud was in love with her and that their relationship was indeed very intimate. It was a shocking discovery to me, and even now I can recall the agony I felt at the time.'[38]

Anti-Freudians have seized on the story with relish. Peter Swales has constructed an ingenious web of circumstantial evidence, linking the Billinsky story with certain items in Freud's writings that could be read to suggest that Freud and Minna had an affair in August–September 1900 and that he was worried she might be pregnant.[39] It has to be conceded that the custodians of the Freud archives have done themselves no favours by withholding the portion of the Freud–Minna letters written during the exact period of the alleged affair.

Yet the idea of an affair between Freud and Minna Bernays strains credulity to snapping point, which is not to say that the story might not still be true. All the dispassionate observer can do is to draw up a balance sheet of probabilities. Against the story first of all are the internal inconsistencies and implausibilities in Jung's narrative. Freud had no 'laboratory', the existing photographs certainly do not sustain the judgement that Minna was 'good-looking', and the idea of a private interview between her and Jung at Berggasse 19 seems far-fetched, if we remember the strict protocol governing formal behaviour between the sexes at this historical juncture. If Jung was visiting Freud's consulting rooms, presumably Freud was with him. What attitude did he take to Minna's extraordinary request for a private interview with a man she had just met? And presumably if he had been having an affair with Minna, Freud would have moved to head off the confession. And where were Emma Jung, Mrs Freud and even Binswanger betimes? If we nevertheless assume that Jung and Minna somehow had the house to themselves, is it plausible that she would have confided such a dire secret to a complete stranger and a gentile to boot? Much has been made of Jung's uncanny fascination for women, but his influence would need to have been mesmeric to draw such a confession from Minna Bernays.

Moreover Jung and those who believe his story seem unable to agree on the details. According to Charteris, Freud and Minna made love just once, and Freud told Jung about it. According to Billinsky, it was Minna who told him about it. According to Swales, the affair was a sustained one that went on for most of the autumn of 1900 – which makes us wonder why it took Minna nearly seven years before she decided to tell a third party about it.

Late in 1900 Freud had to pay for Minna to spend six weeks at a spa in Merano, and Swales conjectures that she went there to have an abortion. However, it has been shown that she went to Merano because of lung trouble, though it is still just possible that she could have combined this treatment with another purpose.[40]

Two things are certain. There were frequent rumours during Freud's life that he was unconscionably attached to his sister-in-law and, in an era of chaperones when it was believed that a man and a woman could not be alone together in the same room without sexual 'impropriety' taking place, the time he spent alone in Minna Bernays's company inevitably led to whispers of an affair. Yet all three of Freud's main biographers, all of them highly talented practitioners of the art, have investigated the rumours and the Billinsky/Swales allegations and found them without substance.[41] Secondly, it is quite clear that Jung did come away from his first meeting with Freud with ambivalent feelings, which may have been reciprocated. Freud's interpretation of Jung's dream as a desire to replace him may have increased the irritation he undoubtedly felt that, at five-feet-seven, he seemed a dwarf alongside the six-foot-one Jung.[42] Jung, unhappy about Freud's 'pansexualism', seems himself to have been in a state of some confusion, for he made up a total fairy story about being strongly attracted to Freud's daughter Sophie.[43]

Beyond that, all is turbid and the waters are further muddied by the retrospective nature of Jung's claim and its role in the continuing propaganda battle between Freudians and Jungians. It is highly significant that the most ardent believers in an affair between Freud and Minna Bernays (Kerr and Swales) are also the most committed to the view that the affair between Jung and Sabina Spielrein did not go beyond kissing and some light petting. Clearly there are four views one can take on all this. First, that Jung and Spielrein had an affair, but that Freud and Minna did not. Second, that both men had the said affairs. Third, that neither did. Fourth, that Freud and Minna were lovers but Jung and Spielrein were not. The first is overwhelmingly the most probable, but Kerr and Swales opt for the fourth possibility, easily the least likely scenario of all. In a word, the entire discussion has become subsumed in infighting between the rival psychological cults.

Jung, we know, was a womanizer, and after his break with Freud in 1913 was concerned to show his old mentor in the worst possible light on all occasions. Jung wanted the high moral ground, and in this context Freud's well-known monogamy was an irritant. Since Freud knew about the affair with Spielrein, the best way for Jung to hit back was to insinuate that Freud himself was common clay and not resistant to the tugs of the flesh; it was also important that the alleged affair had to be one that involved a breach of trust – in this case with Freud's wife, Minna's sister. Since there was literally no other candidate available than Minna – because of Freud's well-known sexual abstinence – Minna it had to be.

Only the most dedicated anti-Freudian would entertain the Freud–Minna allegations in the same breath as the Jung–Spielrein liaison, for the simple reason that the former rests purely on Jung's say-so, made long after Freud's death, while the latter is confirmed in unimpeachable contemporary documentation. The thesis of mutual blackmail, producing a stand-off in the struggle for mastery of the psychoanalytical movement, as in Kerr's recent book, will not hold for the simple reason that nowhere in the Freud–Jung correspondence is there the slightest sign of any attempted blackmail by Jung. Jung was not the sort of man who bowed his head when engaged in conflict, as his letters show clearly. If he had evidence of a shameful liaison by Freud he would certainly have used it when the exchanges between the two became heated.

The evidence for an affair between Freud and Minna does not stand up to scholarly scrutiny, predicated as it is on a farrago of inference, innuendo, circumstantial evidence and ingenious speculation. As Peter Gay, who has made a careful study of the allegations, concludes, sometimes the dog does not bark in the night because there is no dog.[44] Yet Jung's accusations are evidence of another kind – evidence of the violent hatred he later entertained towards Freud. The most charitable interpretation would be to suggest that when Jung made these allegations, at eighty-one, his faculties were impaired and his memory failing. Kerr, adamantly committed to denying that this is the explanation, makes a perhaps revealing slip when he says that Jung was only *seventy-one* when he made the allegation,[45] indicating too great an eagerness to believe the truth of Jung's claim.

After saying goodbye to the Freuds, the Jungs proceeded to Budapest, leaving Binswanger to spend a second week in Vienna. From Budapest they proceeded to the Adriatic town of Rijeka (then Fiume) and spent a couple of weeks at the seaside resort of Opatija (then Abbazia). Here Jung became violently attracted to a young Jewish woman; whether the liaison developed into an affair in the full sense, or remained at the level of heavy flirtation, is uncertain (probably the latter), but Jung referred to 'compulsive infatuation' and cited the episode as further evidence of his 'Jewish-complex'.[46]

Once back in Zürich, Jung renewed with gusto the correspondence with Freud. For the next two and a half months Freud and Jung discussed technical matters relating to the aetiology of paranoia and schizophrenia. Two questions in particular gnawed away at Jung. Why was it that schizophrenia, psychoanalysis and the word-association test seemed to pull in opposite directions? And if auto-erotism was the answer – implying regression and infantilism – what distinguished schizophrenia from hysterical infantilism?[47]

Freud cautioned against the idea that hysteria could *develop into* dementia praecox and suggested that the more correct proposition was to say that hysteria was broken and replaced by schizophrenia. In the correspondence between the two, it is everywhere apparent that Freud is the superior literary stylist, and some of his formulations have a pleasing lucid economy. Jung's letters, on the other hand, tend to bog down in technical arcana.

Jung, himself never much interested in child psychology, took the opportunity to pick the brains of the theoretician of infantile sexuality. He was treating a six-year-old girl for excessive masturbation and lying, and the girl told him she had been seduced by her foster-father. Jung found it hard to believe the story but in that case wondered where the child got the sexual detail from. Freud reassured him that the case-history overwhelmingly indicated fantasy.[48]

A more difficult nut to crack was one of Jung's schizophrenic patients with the most complex anamnesis (case history). At the age of nine she became sexually excited when she saw traces of her mother's menstrual period. When her own periods commenced, at the age of twelve, she became a rabid reader of sex manuals and had fantasies about her brothers' genitals. At sixteen she wept all day when the Alpinist fiancé of an older girlfriend was in danger on the mountain slopes. At eighteen she was violently excited all day when her sister got married, and spent most of the wedding celebrations masturbating and feeling guilty. When she was twenty her elder brother got married, which led her to compare herself unfavourably with the bride. Finally, when she was twenty-one, a man expressed interest in her and she was attracted because he looked like her brother; but then immediately felt guilty, depressive and suicidal and ended by being admitted to the Burghölzli. There she began having delusions of grandeur, claimed to be related to all kinds of distinguished people, and told the doctors she suspected them of elaborate sexual liaisons. Here was a test case in the twilight area between hysteria and schizophrenia, but Freud, disappointingly, hedged his bets: it was probably dementia rather than hysteria, he thought, but it was a partial case, probably not yet concluded or fully understood.[49]

Freud did better with another of Jung's cases, this time a thirty-six-year-old woman in a state of catatonic depression. Having grown up with a bullying father, she developed an over-close friendship with her mother. Although uninterested in sex, at twenty-eight she married a man younger and less intelligent than she but was sexually frigid. When her mother died she said she would go mad and pitched into an ever-deepening depression that ended with institutionalization. Freud analysed auto-erotism deriving from revulsion towards her father.[50]

Another borderline case, again a woman, came to Jung as an outpatient. The particular symptoms were that the woman could not finish her coffee without vomiting if there was a crumb in it, and went into spitting fits lasting days if she saw a corpse. Freud suggested that the coffee symptoms pointed to urine and faeces and the root cause was probably disgust with her mother's corpse, which in turn related to the disgust the woman felt when her mother told her the facts of life – since, according to Freud, in neurotic fantasies menstrual blood could feature as faeces.[51]

All of these cases show Jung and Freud working happily together as dedicated professionals, Jung enjoying the favour and confidence of a respected mentor. Freud, though, was impatient to 'make over' the talents of the Burghölzli to the cause of psychoanalysis, and here Jung's bulletins were disappointing, hinting at one moment that Bleuler was on the point of coming over, then correcting the impression in the following letter. Having assured Freud in December 1906 that Bleuler was now won over to the new dispensation, on his first letter after the return from the Adriatic Jung entered a caveat that Bleuler was putting up vigorous 'resistance'.[52] By mid-April Jung was backtracking furiously on his earlier grandiose claims.

Gradually Jung let his latent hostility towards Bleuler surface more and more. When Bleuler took three weeks' convalescent leave at a spa, Jung complained bitterly about the administrative load he had to assume as acting director.[53] As soon as Bleuler returned, Jung himself departed on a two-week study leave.

He went first to Geneva to talk to Edouard Claparède, friend of Flournoy and Janet and leader of the Francophone Swiss psychiatric school. Unlike Freud, who was accused of pan-sexualism, though he always advocated a dualistic tug between libido (the sexual instinct) and the ego instinct, Claparede really did believe in a single sexual instinct.[54] Next Jung went to Paris to meet Janet, intending to proceed to London. But the Jung of 1907 was not the young man who had come to hear Janet lecture five years earlier, and he found his erstwhile hero a great disappointment.

Jung was so disillusioned that he gave up the idea of going on to London and stayed in Paris for a brief affair with an unhappily married thirty-five-year old German–American woman, before returning to Switzerland via a sightseeing tour of the Loire châteaux.[55] Referring to the word-association test which had linked 'Paris' with 'Vienna', he told Freud triumphantly that there was no question of a Paris-complex.

Jung barely had time to check in at the Burghölzli when he was off again, this time on his compulsory three weeks' military service in Lausanne. The workload as military doctor was gruelling; Jung stated that he had to get up at 5 a.m. and work through until 8 p.m., with not a single moment for himself. However, these periods away from the Burghölzli were valuable, as they introduced him to a range of neurotics he rarely met in the hospital, concerned as it was with psychoses and severe traumatic neuroses. Jung found that these cases were quite easily solved by the 'anamnestic' method – where the doctor simply trawls through the patient's *conscious* case-history.

When Jung returned to the Burghölzli in August, he was again inundated with paperwork as both Bleuler and his first assistant physician, Karl Abraham, were on holiday for a month. On top of these administrative chores and the usual rounds at the hospital, Jung had to prepare a paper for the First International Congress of Psychiatry and Neurology at Amsterdam in September. He departed for the Congress on 1 September, with a heavy burden on his shoulders, for it was his task to carry the Freudian banner into battle. It had been widely expected that Freud, the theorist of the 'unconscious', would debate with Janet, the apostle of the 'subconscious', but Freud had no stomach for public acrimonious debate and stayed away. In this he emulated Darwin, who absented himself from the famous Oxford meeting in 1860, leaving Thomas Huxley to do the streetfighting for him.

The Amsterdam Congress was notable for the hostility evinced towards Freud. Janet criticized him for generalizing wildly from insufficient instances and referred to the Freudian theory of hysteria as a joke.[56] The Munich neurologist Max Isserlin attacked Jung's book on schizophrenia, saying that there was no demonstrable connection between the test word and the answer in the association test and, further, that he doubted that the answers really revealed dissociated complexes.[57] Jung answered vociferously that only those who had practised psychoanalysis were in a position to criticize Freud, but this stance was attacked by critics who said that the obvious response to this was to treat hysterical patients without psychoanalysis.

But Freud's young champion unfortunately bungled things badly. Jung was the third speaker but had not timed his paper properly, so that it overran; he then refused to heed the chairman, who signalled repeatedly to him to make an end. When he was finally forced to yield the floor, he strode angrily from the room, flushed and scowling, thus losing the audience's sympathy.[58] Almost the only solid achievement Jung brought back from Amsterdam was the link with a group of American doctors led by the noted psychiatrist Smith Ely Jelliffe; Jung and Jelliffe got on well together, and later in September the American visited Jung in Zürich, where he was introduced to Maeder and Riklin.[59]

Feeling guilty that he had left his young associate to bear the brunt at Amsterdam, Freud wrote him the most fulsome letter to date, in which he told him how important he was to him. Such a letter merely reinforced the feelings of 'transference' Jung self-confessedly felt towards Freud, and he admitted that his admiration for him contained elements of a quasi-religious 'crush', which, however, made him apprehensive, since the last person he had so admired sexually assaulted him when he was eighteen. For this reason he hated it if Freud or Bleuler ever gave him personal confidences.

It did not bother Jung, as it did Freud, that there was a kind of disguised homosexuality, which he recognized, at work in the relationship. Yet his intense feelings towards Freud had two undesirable consequences. One was an intense jealousy for anyone of his own age about whom Freud said a favourable word, or about whom Jung thought Freud might comment favourably. Jung dealt with this by systematic denigration of anyone he suspected Freud had a soft spot for. His first target was Otto Rank, the twenty-three-year-old secretary of the Wednesday Society, whom Freud had taken under his wing. Rank came from a poverty-stricken Jewish family. The product of an unhappy marriage, he had been obliged by financial pressure to train as a machinist, even though he was a youth of phenomenal intelligence. An omnivorous reader and dedicated autodidact, he was introduced to Freud's writings by Alfred Adler, the family physician. With his dazzling intellectual gifts Rank was soon able to apply psychoanalytical theory to the time-honoured problem of the creative artist. Having presented Freud with a short monograph on the subject when he was just twenty-one, Rank became in effect Freud's adopted son. Freud smoothed his way through the acquiring of a Gymnasium certificate and a university degree, which the phenomenal Rank acquired in record time, then made the young man his secretary and research assistant.

Here was an obvious target for Jung's jealousy. In March 1907 he contrasted his enthusiasm for Freud's empirical methods with the 'apriorism' of Rank. Freud took the hint and reassured Jung that he did not put Rank in the same class, though it is noteworthy that he did not provide the kind of ringing dismissal Jung wanted to hear.

The next target was Max Eitingon, whom Freud met in Rome in September 1907. When Freud casually mentioned the fact, there was the predictable explosion from Jung: he told Freud that Eitingon was merely a gasbag, an intellectual nonentity whose 'impotence' was belied only by his sexual promiscuity.[60]

But Jung's greatest outburst of jealous anger was reserved for Karl Abraham, two years his junior, a Bremen Jew who had joined the Burghölzli in 1904 as Bleuler's assistant.[61] Even by the energetic standards of the Burghölzli, Abraham was a dynamo: afflicted with asthma and a frail constitution, he had made himself super-fit by tennis, swimming and, especially, mountain-climbing – a sport well known to be a favourite of psychoanalysts. A bouncy, optimistic personality, Abraham disliked Jung, and the feeling was reciprocated. Jung accused him of being a hyena, snapping up odd ideas dropped by him and Bleuler and rushing into print with them as original insights. Jung was affronted when Abraham declined his suggestion that they collaborate, and thereafter took to insinuating that Abraham short-changed his colleagues on the main work at the Burghölzli, but loved to step into the limelight with a paper he had cobbled together by filching the ideas of others. For good measure, Jung threw in the accusation that he had no rapport with the patients and was unpopular with them. However, he admitted what it was that was really grating on him when he confessed that he was jealous of Abraham's status as Freud's confidant.[62]

Once again Freud reassured him and wrote conspiratorially about Abraham, 'Your picture of his character seems so apt that I am inclined to accept it without further examination. Nothing objectionable, yet something that precludes intimacy. You make him out to be something of an "uninspired plodder," which is bound to clash with your open, winning nature.'[63]

Jung became alarmed again in October when Abraham resigned and spoke of opening a private practice in Berlin[64]; clearly he would be in contact with Freud, and Jung would no longer be able to monitor the correspondence in the old way. Jung claimed that Abraham had mild feelings of persecution about him, encouraged by his Berliner wife. From then on Jung lost no occasion to ram home his message that Abraham was beneath Freud's attention, but Freud did not agree and, once he entered into regular correspondence with Abraham, became the unenviable man in the middle, having to listen to rancorous denunciations from either side. Freud made clear his dissent from Jung's animadversions after Abraham went to see him in December 1907. But he did tell Jung that he found Abraham lacking in dash.

Abraham's place at the Burghölzli was taken by the American A.A. Brill, who was amazed and impressed by the commitment and dedication of the staff, and the extent to which Freudianism, under Jung's influence, had already become orthodoxy:

> *In the hospital the spirit of Freud hovered over everything. Our conversation at meals was frequently punctuated with the word 'complex', the special meaning of which was created at that time. No one could make a slip of any kind without immediately being called upon to evoke free associations to explain it. It did not matter that women were present –*

> *wives and female voluntary interns – who might have curbed the frankness usually produced by free associations. The women were just as keen to discover the concealed mechanisms as their husbands. There was also a Psychoanalytical Circle, which met every month. Some of those who attended were far from agreeing with our views; but despite Jung's occasional impulsive intolerance, the meetings were very fruitful and successful in disseminating Freud's theories . . . Jung was at that time the most ardent Freudian . . . Jung brooked no disagreement with Freud's views; impulsive and bright, he refused to see the other side. Anyone who dared doubt what was certainly then new and revolutionary immediately aroused his anger.*[65]

One young talent about whom Jung had no major reservations at this time was Ernest Jones, the Welsh doctor he first met at the Amsterdam Conference. In the second half of November 1907 Jones spent a week with Jung in Zürich, and attended some sessions of the Freudian Society of Physicians in Zürich, a twenty-five-strong body that formed the nucleus of what was later called the 'Zurich school'.[66] Jones was impressed with Jung's toughness and with the 'streetfighter' qualities evinced by him in the frequent clashes with the Russian–Swiss neurologist Constantin von Monakow, but found him a chameleon, a man hard to know intimately or to fathom. He also reported on the palpable tension between Jung and his wife, and on Jung's continuing unease with what he took to be Freudian 'monosexuality'.[67]

This unease was clear in the correspondence with Freud. In August Jung asked plaintively if sexuality was the mother of all feelings; Freud, all diplomacy, and not wanting such a promising professional relationship to go sour on a technical matter of doctrine, conceded that hunger was clearly another important instinctual urge.[68]

However, the issue of sexuality and its role in psychoanalysis was one that simply would not go away, and would continually return to haunt the relationship.[69] John Kerr suggests that Jung's acceptance of a half-hearted Freudianism, committed to defend publicly theories he only half believed in – to say nothing of using as case material his own affair with Sabina Spielrein – was taking him dangerously close to the youthful split between No. 1 and No. 2 personalities:

'Jung's Freudianism was dividing into a public and private version. Psychologically, Jung was nearly back to where he had started, with an outer and inner self, and no easy way to reconcile the two.'[70] Yet in 1908 all abstract discussion of libido had to go into abeyance, for the dormant erotic volcano that was Jung's relationship with Sabina Spielrein went active once again.

Chapter Seven

SABINA SPIELREIN

All this time the bizarre on-off relationship between Jung and Sabina Spielrein, by now making significant progress as a medical student at Zürich University, was continuing. With hindsight, traces of it can be discerned in Jung's letters to Freud. On 10 October 1907 he referred to a lady who was making him the object of her sexual fantasies. And on 15 February 1908 Jung broke a three-week silence to apologize for being a bad correspondent, pleading a recent attack of the 'flu and a 'complex' connected with his family.[1]

This complex may well have been the 'Siegfried complex' that so exercised Jung and Spielrein in 1907–08 at their various trysts – in his office, her flat, out in the countryside. By 1908 Spielrein was obsessed with 'having a child' by Jung, a heroic male offspring to be named Siegfried.[2] The problem was that neither of them could decide whether they meant an actual flesh-and-blood child or a creature of fantasy – the mythical 'offspring' of an idealized intimacy. Jung was sure that what Spielrein wanted was a real child, but Sabina inclined at this stage to see 'Siegfried' as simply a metaphor for her own heroic destiny. Sometimes she wobbled and saw herself as a sacrificial victim destined to create a real-life hero, but she would then swing back to a symbolic interpretation. A paper she published in 1911 analysing the Siegfried motif seemed to suggest that she and Jung were cast in the role of the incestuous Sieglinde and Siegmund.[3]

The confused and superheated state of Spielrein's mind emerges from diary entries at this time.[4] The degree of agonizing and indecision that marked Spielrein's relationship with Jung can hardly be overstated, and the 1908 letters to Jung make painful reading.[5] The details of the relationship are, as ever, difficult to fathom, partly because of Spielrein's maddeningly obscurantist style.

Spielrein's constant vacillation and prevarication seems to have had three main causes. In the first place, she could not decide whether her ultimate desires were physical or symbolic. Secondly, she was uncertain how much reliance to place on Jung, for she was by no means his only mistress. Her letters and diaries are full of details of young women patients and students clustering admiringly around Jung and vying for his favours. After meeting a particular Jung favourite in his informal harem, one Fräulein Aptekmann, while she and Jung were walking in the countryside together, Spielrein's patience seems momentarily to have snapped but Jung talked her round and said it was as if he had a necklace in which all his other admirers were pearls and she the medallion.[6]

Thirdly, Spielrein, who later anticipated some aspects of Freud's late 'death drive' (*todestrieb*) theory, sincerely believed that in sex the man wished to annihilate himself and the woman wished to be annihilated.[7]

The turbulent relationship with Spielrein sometimes drove Jung to a near-psychotic state, and his anxieties were increased in 1908, for in that year his wife Emma became pregnant again. However, it would be a mistake to think that Jung simply wanted to be rid of Sabina. As he later acknowledged, the Siegfried fantasy was a joint fantasy, not just a product of her diseased mind. It seems that he simultaneously needed her and feared her effect on him. When she went back to her native Russia in August 1908 for a holiday and did not write for a week, Jung became fretful and, when she did at last write, he admitted his anxiety. The letters that passed between the two lovers in September were as odd as any in the bizarre correspondence. Spielrein announced her intention of becoming more sophisticated and lady-like and said she would give up wearing the peasant dresses she favoured; Jung for his part warned her about meeting a Fräulein Gincburg, one of his patients and also a Russian, who had moved to an address near Spielrein's in Zürich.[8] Presumably she was yet another of Jung's mistresses whose revelations could be embarrassing.

The emotional crisis with Spielrein was the deep context in which Jung's see-saw relationship with Freud was played out. A reference Freud made to his one-time collaborator but now bitter enemy Wilhelm Fliess at the beginning of 1908 led Jung to write to ask that their relationship be that between father and son.[9] This was something of a left-handed act of deference, given Jung's disastrous relations with his own father and his unsatisfactory dealings with Eugen Bleuler, the only previous father surrogate. Since Freud knew about the relationship with Jung's father, one wonders how he felt about this 'father transference'.

An uneasy relationship with Freud also seems indicated by Sabina Spielrein's later cryptic remarks when writing to Freud, which appear to suggest that she and Jung had discussed Freud's character and she had not liked the tone of what she had heard.[10] Certainly, the theoretical differences between the two men seemed as far as ever from resolution. It is notable that Freud and Jung praised and reinforced each other in generalities, but could never quite agree when it came to specifics. Detailed case studies provoked disagreements. Freud posited that obsessional neurosis rested on two basic instincts: the instinct to see and know and the possessive (sadistic) instinct, whereas hysteria involved direct repression of genital impulses. Jung, however, clung to his belief that there must be *some* organic cases of schizophrenia, possibly involving a toxin, and that Freud's 'psychologizing' of all mental illness was too pat; he remarked that one would have to be a spiritualist to believe in an exclusively psychogenic aetiology. This implied acceptance of eclecticism – always a capital crime in the Freudian book – drew a stern reproof from Freud.[11]

However, in these early days of the psychoanalytic movement it was more important to make common cause against enemies than to labour the minute particulars of Freudian theory. Having accepted Jung as his 'son and heir', Freud asked him to organize the first international conference for psychoanalytical studies and suggested Salzburg as the venue. Jung, always reluctant to undertake administrative chores, wrote back to ask Freud to book the hotel accommodation, as he knew nothing about Salzburg.[12] Nevertheless, he was dragooned into being the planning supremo for the enterprise and came up with the title of Congress for Freudian Psychology. This was greeted with widespread protest, Jones among others pointing out that the title offended the ideals of scientific objectivity.[13]

This was not the only sign that Jung was not really the right person to organize such a conference. Freud was sure that making Bleuler chairman of the congress would force him finally to come down off the fence and declare for psychoanalysis.[14] But Jung was equally determined that Bleuler, for whom he increasingly entertained hostile feelings, should not have the place of honour. In a masterly example of disingenuousness, he claimed there was no point in offering Bleuler the position as he would refuse.[15] The upshot was that Bleuler was not offered the chairmanship but, contrary to Jung's predictions, attended the Congress; to avoid embarrassment, the position of master of ceremonies was not offered to anyone else, so that the Congress took place without a chairman.

Whenever Jung had to perform administrative chores, he tended to go down with some malady; it had happened in 1907 when he returned to the Burghölzli (while Bleuler was on holiday) and found a mountain of paperwork.[16] In April, just before the conference, it happened again. Jung went down with 'flu and took sick leave, going first to the thermal baths at Baden-Baden and then on to Baneno on Italy's Lake Maggiore to recuperate.[17] The omens were not propitious for a successful conference even before Jung, the so-called organizer, arrived in Salzburg for the two-day symposium on 26–27 April 1908.

Freud himself opened proceedings with a five-hour lecture (from 8 a.m. to 1 p.m.) on the case that later became famous as 'The Rat Man'.[18] In succeeding sessions, Jung argued powerfully against the Bleuler thesis that dementia praecox was caused by a toxin by proposing instead his thesis that the unidentified toxin was produced by a severe complex. This was strong stuff, for Jung was placing himself as the 'man in the middle', between Bleuler's theory of organic causation of schizophrenia and Freud's hypothesis that it was merely a severe form of the repressive behaviour seen in neurosis.[19] The strangeness of Jung's position was noted for, as John Kerr has remarked, 'This amounted to saying that certain thoughts, or at least certain feelings were metabolically dangerous.'[20]

Jung was responsible for making some important introductions at the conference, principally of Bleuler and Jones to Freud. Jones, who had been told by Jung in Zürich that Freud's Viennese followers were all a degenerate and bohemian crowd, had been inclined to regard the remark as an instance of the anti-Semitism he always suspected of lurking in the Swiss, but after he had met Adler, Stekel, Rank and the others he was prepared to concede that Jung had a point.[21] Jung claimed, a trifle unconvincingly, that his own paper had won Bleuler over to the view that there were no organic primary symptoms in schizophrenia, and, more convincingly, that Bleuler had been mightily impressed by Freud, who, by contrast, merely commented that the Burghölzli director was a very strange man.[22]

But no two views were possible for Jung concerning the behaviour of his old enemy Karl Abraham. First Abraham delivered a paper on auto-eroticism which drew heavily on the ideas of Jung and Bleuler, without acknowledging their work.[23] Even worse, Jung got a hint that Abraham had already informed Freud that the casework on anal eroticism which Abraham presented was based on Jung's experience with Sabina Spielrein; Abraham knew about Jung's liaison with Spielrein from his Burghölzli days.[24] The experience set Jung off on a year-long vendetta against his old but unlamented colleague.

On the practical side, some important decisions were taken at Salzburg. Over the protests of the Viennese, who complained to Freud that he was too trusting towards Jung, and that the Swiss was bound in the end to desert the cause of psychoanalysis, it was decided to found a biennial learned journal, with Jung as editor and Freud and Bleuler as co-directors. Freud's Viennese followers were effectively marginalized, and all the glittering prizes given to the Zürich school. Jung, though, was not entirely happy at the outcome of the conference as he saw little of Freud himself; unfortunately for him, Freud's half-brother Emmanuel, aged seventy-four, arrived unexpectedly at the closing banquet and monopolized Freud's attention that evening and the whole of the following morning.[25]

Once back in Zürich, Jung opened his campaign against Abraham. Freud had asked him not to make an issue of Abraham's behaviour at Salzburg, since psychoanalysis needed every man it could get.[26] But at the beginning of May Jung stirred the pot again by accusing Abraham of plagiarism and implying that Abraham was not a gentleman. Freud was determined to heal the rift and now put his foot down in his next letter to Jung, stating categorically that he was too hard on Abraham.[27]

But the quarrel could not be patched up. Jung, who had corresponded in a friendly professional manner with Abraham early in

1908,[28] never wrote a personal letter to him again. Abraham, for his part, was quite happy that between him and Jung there should be *guerre à outrance* and began working on Freud to persuade him that Jung would never accept the sexual theory of libido.[29] Freud, whose personal sympathies were with Abraham, but who valued Jung more in terms of the politics of psychoanalysis, tried to pour oil on troubled waters by tacitly admitting that Jung was motivated by anti-Semitism.[30]

Freud frequently made the charge of anti-Semitism against Jung. He told the American psychologist James Jackson Putnam in 1915 that the psychoanalytic movement badly needed gentile adherents, which was why he tolerated Jung, but in return he had had to put up with Jung's 'anti-Semitic condescension towards me'.[31] Two years earlier he noted in his short history of the psychoanalytic movement that Jung had seemed ready to enter into a friendly relationship with him and for his sake to give up certain racial prejudices he had previously permitted himself.[32] Later in 1908 he again mollified Abraham by tacit acceptance of his charge of anti-Semitism on Jung's part: 'I nurse a suspicion that the suppressed anti-Semitism of the Swiss that spares me is deflected in reinforced form upon you.'[33]

For the time being Abraham was prepared to do the master's bidding. He wrote an apologetic note to Jung, but admitted to Freud that he had deliberately omitted from his Salzburg speech a sentence which would have placated Jung and Bleuler.[34] But he would not accept that Jung was a mere puppet manipulated by Bleuler, and inclined rather to the contrary view. And he kept plugging away at the theme that Jung would in the end revert to 'his former spiritualistic inclinations' and that 'at the Burghölzli Freud seems to be an idea that has been superseded.'[35]

Freud often metaphorically tore his hair out with frustration over this feud and rhetorically asked why he could not harness the two of them together, Abraham with his precision, Jung with his élan.[36] After his visit to Jung in Zürich in September 1908 Freud was confident that he had healed the breach, but the truce thus effected lasted just two months. In November Abraham delivered a paper to the Berlin Association of Psychiatrists and Nerve Specialists, arguing that neurosis was the cause of intermarriage between close relatives, not its effect.[37] Although Jung, as editor of the new *Jahrbuch* agreed to take this important paper, he postponed publishing it in the first number and instead included a paper of his own. Abraham was angry about this, and so the rift was reopened. Exasperated, Freud wrote to Abraham that Jung was entirely within his rights as an editor, and followed this up with a reassuring letter to Jung.[38]

Yet if the Salzburg conference set off a long-running vendetta between Jung and Abraham, it also brought solace, albeit shortlived, in the form of a 'soul mate', the thirty-year-old psychoanalyst Otto Gross (1877–1919). Jung knew something of Gross already, for in 1902 Gross adumbrated a theory of clinical types which Jung had read and made use of.[39] Gross, an opium and cocaine addict, was already a notorious figure in Munich, where he divided his time between being an assistant at the Kraepelin clinic and frequenting the cafés in the bohemian Schnabing district. A man of great intellect and charm, Gross had the abiding ambition of using Freudianism to abolish monogamy and patriarchy and introduce a communal form of society.[40] Among the many scandals he had been involved in were a harebrained scheme to sue Kraepelin for not offering psychoanalysis at his clinic, and for providing a patient with the means to commit suicide. Yet it was his sexual profile that most of all attracted attention. He conducted group psychotherapy, which he used as an excuse for sexual orgies; one of his mistresses had been hospitalized by her parents in order to get her out of Gross's clutches; and in 1907 his wife and his mistress Else Jaffe, a married woman, gave birth to Gross's sons almost simultaneously.[41] In the same year Gross was also carrying on an affair with Frieda von Richtofen, later to marry D.H. Lawrence.[42]

Gross's father, Hans, professor of sociology at Graz, alarmed at his son's wild behaviour, had written to Freud and Jung to ask them to help rehabilitate his son.[43] They agreed and originally planned to have Gross escorted back from Salzburg to Zürich, where he would be committed to the Burghölzli. But Jung ducked the responsibility, pleading urgent business with his architect in Munich (he was having a new house built on the shores of Lake Zürich).

Freud's original diagnosis had been that Gross was probably in the early phase of a toxic cocaine paranoia, but Jung pointed out that he was also addicted to opium, so opted for obsessional neurosis as the cause of his problems. He began by curing his obsessional need to have lights around him at night, then moved on to his latent homosexuality. Whenever Jung got stuck in his analysis, Gross took it in turn to analyse *him*. Jung began by giving him the full ration of opium so as not to upset the analysis by feelings of privation. Then, suddenly, Gross voluntarily cut his daily dose from six grams to three. Jung began to be hopeful. He finished his first bout of analysis on 24 May and reported his progress to Freud.

Freud did his best to encourage Jung and candidly admitted that he had foisted Gross onto Jung because he did not have the time or energy to deal with him. He tempered the confession with flattery, suggesting that both Jung and Gross could learn from each other, and that the analysis might be the beginning of a fruitful professional partnership. The letter contained a sting in the tail, for Freud expressed amazement that Jung had been able to accomplish so much in a mere two weeks.

The last words were a coded warning that Jung had completed the analysis too fast and had not taken into account the 'masking' effect of the drugs, especially cocaine.[44] But for a while Jung was euphoric: he liked and identified with Gross, especially his desire to kick over the traces of monogamy, and referred to him as his twin brother. He was now prepared to subscribe to Jones's opinion that Gross was comparable to Byron and was the nearest approach to a romantic genius he had ever met.[45] Sabina Spielrein left a revealing glimpse of the impact of Gross on Jung: 'Now he arrives, beaming with pleasure, and tells me with strong emotion about Gross, about the great insight he has just received (i.e. about polygamy); he no longer wants to suppress his feeling for me, he admitted that I was his first, dearest woman friend, etc (his wife of course excepted), and that he wanted to tell me everything about himself.'[46]

Jung assured Freud that only 'mopping-up' operations were now required, but quickly found himself in a quagmire. Having made an initial diagnosis of obsessive neurosis, he soon became obsessive himself, and sacrificed his days and nights to the analysis of Gross, who cooperated by giving up all medication. For three weeks they worked intensively on material from his early childhood; on one occasion they worked for twenty-four hours at a stretch, at the end of which both men were exhausted. Jung soon discovered that Freud was right, that he had been too hasty.

His revised diagnosis was schizophrenia – a thesis confirmed by association tests, by partial psychoanalysis, by the case history, and by what Gross's wife told him. Gross finally found the pressure of non-stop analysis too much to take and cut the Gordian knot by climbing over a garden wall in the Burghölzli and escaping. Next day he sent a note asking Jung to pay his hotel bill and decamped to Munich. Frau Gross meanwhile wrote to Bleuler with further details. In his flat in Munich Gross heard knockings on the walls and upper floors and a voice enquiring, 'Is the doctor at home?' His one night in the Zürich hotel ended disastrously when he expressed a paranoid fear that he was being spied on. Frau Gross ended by telling Bleuler that her husband was driving her to breakdown.[47]

After hearing the bad news, Freud hastened to thank Jung for his dedication and admitted that he should have taken the case himself and would have done had it not been for his egotism and self-defence mechanisms. He added later that he had consulted Jones and now regarded Gross as a hopeless case, whose adherence to psychoanalysis could do the movement incalculable harm.[48] Jung put the best possible face on his failure, despite being secretly devastated: he claimed that in Gross he had discerned his own 'shadow' and perceived the road he himself might have travelled on had he been afflicted by schizophrenia (the dread of which was one of Jung's secret fears). The case had also stretched him to the limit and provided a model study of the application of psychoanalysis to the severe psychoses.

Jung added that Gross was a very fine man with an unusual mind. Unfortunately Gross had no idea of the revenge which reality was sure to take on him; Gross was one of those whom life was bound to reject and with whom nobody could live in the long run.[49]

While Gross returned to Munich and sexual orgies, embraced anarchism and formed a circle of admirers around him, Jung continued to reiterate that the experience with him had done him a world of good; Freud meanwhile publicly credited the gruelling experience with Gross as being *the* factor that finally converted Jung to psychoanalysis.[50] Jung himself praised Gross's book *On Psychopathic Inferiorities*, later wrote admiringly of Gross's work on the 'primary function' and admitted his influence on his 1911 paper 'The Significance of the Father', in which he argued that the neurotic is one who fails life's tasks since he approaches them with emotional baggage from his father rather than relying on his own spontaneous emotions.[51] However, the appearance of Jung's paper enraged Gross, then on one of his 'drying-out' periods in the Steinhof sanatorium near Vienna, and he wrote to Freud branding the 'Zürich school' as wholesale plagiarists: on the one hand Bleuler had filched all his best ideas on schizophrenia and on the other Jung's 'The

Significance of the Father' was simply a rehash of statements Gross had made to him during the ill-fated analysis in the Burghölzli. Stung by this, Jung forgot the tributes he had paid to his 'twin brother' and wrote back angrily, that Gross was a demented parasite.[52] Yet Jung's forecast of Gross's likely end was correct. After a wretched life of drug addiction and financial hardship, Gross died miserably at forty-two in mysterious circumstances, sometimes described as starvation, sometimes as suicide.

Jung's preoccupation with Gross in the early summer of 1908 seems to have brought to a head Bleuler's growing feeling that his second-in-command was a prima donna, prepared to work hard at cases that interested him, and only those cases. There was considerable tension between the two men, as Jung's letters to Freud indicate.[53] Given the crisis with Bleuler, the fiasco with Gross and his consequent perplexity about the correct way to draw up a differential taxonomy of hysteria and schizophrenia, Jung now badly needed another long face-to-face session with Freud. Freud was willing enough, but the Burghölzli timetable was as inflexible as ever, with Bleuler due to go on a month's leave in August (leaving Jung chained perforce to the hospital), Jung due two weeks' holiday at the beginning of September and another month's military service looming at the end of that month. In the end it was settled that Freud would come and stay at the Jungs' flat at the Burghölzli between 17 and 21 September.

After a month of the administrative chores he so hated, Jung took a two-week vacation at the Alpine retreat of Appenzell, forty miles east of Zürich. Freud meanwhile left Berchtesgaden on 1 September and set out via Holland for England, which he had visited just once before, at the age of nineteen. He spent a week visiting his half-brother Emmanuel in Manchester and Blackpool, then had a week alone in London before doubling back to Berlin with Emmanuel. He arrived in Zürich on 18 September for a three-day visit to the Jungs. During his time at the Burghölzli he and Jung spent up to eight hours each day walking and talking: Jung discussed Gross, Bleuler, his wife's pregnancy and the so-called 'star-complex' (the wish to have a son) revealed by Binswanger's experiment. Freud got on particularly well with Emma, who subsequently wrote him two thank-you letters even though she was the hostess. Emma described him as 'a delightful man – on the gloomy side perhaps – I talked to him once about my own troubles.'[54]

Freud showed himself a loyal friend to his 'son and heir' by taking his side in the dispute with Bleuler in the most pointed way. Even though he was staying in the Jungs' flat, and Bleuler's was directly beneath, Freud did not make so much as a courtesy call on Bleuler. The slight seems to have affected Bleuler, whose quarrel was purely with Jung, and he and his wife went to Vienna a few weeks later to call on the Freuds. This visit in turn went well enough.[55]

Freud departed for a short holiday in Italy while Jung spent October in the barracks at Yuerdon in Vaud canton. There now ensued a veritable honeymoon period between Jung and Freud. Binswanger remembered Freud saying: 'When the empire I founded is orphaned, no one but Jung must inherit the whole thing.'[56] Fritz Wittels recalled Freud beaming when he spoke of Jung and quoting, 'This is my beloved son, in whom I am well pleased.'[57]

The entente was sealed by an exchange of views over the continuing conundrum of the difference between hysteria and schizophrenia. Jung introduced one of his favourite ideas, 'compensation' as the key concept, suggesting that in hysteria compensation was successful but in schizophrenia it was a failure. He cited the case of a recent Burghölzli internee, a forty-year-old anaemic woman who had to be hospitalized because she solicited every man she met in the street. She had lost all desire for her husband, but in proportion as her libido decreased, she increasingly suspected him of having affairs. She therefore forced the husband to make love to her four times a night in order to drain him; she would act passionately right to the point of his orgasm, then go limp; she would then demand intercourse again. Things reached a pass where she tried to climb into bed with her brother-in-law while he was sleeping with his wife, suggested coitus to her own brother, and finally went out onto the streets soliciting.

Freud responded by working the idea of compensation into his framework of auto-erotism and suggesting a threefold classification: there was successful auto-erotism, as in schizophrenia; unsuccessful, with full recovery of libido after projection and transformation, as in the typical paranoia; and partial failure (partial auto-erotism), with attempted compensation, as in hysteria, which could perhaps be seen as the midway point between paranoia and schizophrenia.[58]

However, for Jung sexual neurosis was rearing its head closer to home as a result of some disastrous dabbling in child psychology, inspired by Freud's celebrated 'Little Hans' case.[59] On 28 November

Emma gave birth to a son, Franz. Jung wrote delightedly to Freud that he felt like a peasant, at peace, now that he had a son.[60] Just before the birth Jung asked his four-year-old daughter Agatha what she would do if she got a little brother. 'Kill him,' she replied. When Franz was born, Agatha, devoted to her mother, began acting strangely and finally asked whether her mother really had to die. Jung's questioning of her revealed that Agatha thought that mothers must inevitably die after childbirth, that they became angels and were then reborn as children. It then transpired that the child was hopelessly confused about the processes of procreation and birth, and that she realized that her parents had lied to her by fobbing her off with the old story about the stork.

She became insistent on knowing exactly which aperture the baby emerged from: was it the mouth, or a hole in the chest. And when Jung took to his bed one day with mild 'flu, Agatha came into his room and said, 'Why are you in bed? Have you got a plant in your inside too?' Jung was then forced to tell the child the full facts about sexual intercourse; Emma was too prudish to undertake the task. Although Agatha then felt superior to her mother by virtue of possessing these 'unknown' facts, she had many disturbing dreams about childbirth and coitus. Jung realized he had failed the child badly, and by not explaining the facts of life had led her to believe that every birth must be purchased with a death. For a long time Agatha continued very disturbed, and conflated the story of the earthquake at Messina, then the talk of the household, with the idea of losing her mother's love and being displaced by the infant Franz.[61]

Even while he soothed Agatha's fears, Jung had to confront the final crisis with Bleuler. What caused the showdown is still not entirely clear; some say the antagonism was largely in Jung's mind.[62] Probably Jung had been itching to resign for some time, and the approaching completion of the house he was having built at Küsnacht provided both motive and opportunity. But the appearance of Bleuler's mentor, Auguste Forel, under arms as an anti-Freudian, did not help matters. In November Forel went public with his misgivings about the new bearings at the Burghölzli; by singling out as the most reprehensible aspect of the 'Young Turks' the obsessive quest for sexual complexes he seemed to imply that Jung was the major culprit.[63] Not only did Bleuler fail to disavow Forel, but he seemed to react with inertia or impotence when

Jung's old enemy von Monakow, Zürich's professor of neurology, set up, in obvious rivalry to the Zürich Freudian Society, his own Swiss Association for Neurology, a backward-looking body whose inaugural conference, according to Jung, was attended by 'every last hillbilly in our fair land.' Speaking of one of the invitees, the Zürich experimental psychologist Otto Veragath, Jung remarked scathingly that 'the only thing he understood was the menu.'[64] When it is recalled that at this very time Abraham was clashing in Berlin with anti-Freudians at the Berlin Association of Psychiatrists, events at the end of 1908 seemed to suggest a general crisis for the psychoanalytic movement.

Bleuler in any case forced Jung's hand. At the beginning of 1909 a prestigious lectureship in 'Mental Hygiene' at the university came up; since this invariably went to a senior member of the Burghölzli, Jung was the obvious favourite. Yet, without consulting Jung, Bleuler gave the post to Franz Riklin, who resigned his position at the Rheinau Hospital to take up the new appointment. This was the last straw for Jung. He submitted his resignation in January 1909 but agreed to stay on until the end of March to ease the crushing workload at the hospital. He was angry about his treatment but managed to appear reasonably insouciant when writing to Freud about the affair.[65]

The birth of Franz finally decided Jung that his liaison with Spielrein must end. At a stormy meeting in early December 1908 he informed her that from then on they should be 'just good friends'. On 4 December Jung wrote to her to say that he was feeling wretched and desperate, pleaded with her not to seek revenge, and asked for her understanding. He asked her to return, in this his moment of need, some of the love and altruism he had given her at the time of her illness.

Even as Sabina Spielrein pondered her next move, Emma Jung's patience with her husband's polygamy snapped, for she wrote anonymously to Mrs Spielrein about the affair, suggesting her daughter was in moral danger and should be detached from Jung. Mrs Spielrein then wrote to Jung to tax him with unprofessional conduct. Jung's shocking reply has proved too much even for the ingenuity of his most devoted followers; even Kerr admits it was the action of a weak man.[66]

I moved from being her doctor to being her friend when I ceased to push my own feelings into the background. I

> *could drop my role as doctor the more easily because I did not feel professionally obligated, for I never charged a fee. This latter clearly establishes the limits imposed upon a doctor. You do understand, of course, that a man and a girl cannot possibly continue indefinitely to have friendly feelings with one another without the likelihood that something more may enter the relationship. For what would restrain the two from drawing the consequences of their love? A* doctor *and his* patient, *on the other hand, can talk of the most intimate matters for as long as they like, and the patient may expect her doctor to give her all the love and concern she requires. But the doctor knows his limits and will never cross them, for he is* paid *for his troubles. That imposes the necessary restraints on him . . . I would suggest that if you wish me to adhere strictly to my role as doctor, you should pay me a fee as suitable recompense for my trouble. In that way you may be* absolutely certain *that I will respect my duty as a doctor* under all circumstances. *As a friend of your daughter, on the other hand, one would have to leave certain matters to Fate. For no one can prevent two friends from doing as they wish.*[67]

Jung wound up this astonishingly impudent attempt to brazen things out by mentioning that his fees were ten francs an hour; the message was hammered home that if Mrs Spielrein did not like the situation existing between Jung and her daughter, he would be glad to have matters put on a doctor–patient footing, but this would require Mrs Spielrein to make out a cheque for 'back pay'. In a word, his behaviour was entirely justified because he had not taken a fee. Some die-hard Jungians have tried to enter the plea that Jung was concerned for the political impact on the psychoanalytic movement if he was exposed. This does not square with the overall character of Jung, and in any case someone genuinely concerned for the credibility of psychoanalysis would not have put his name to such a crass letter.

Jung was still visiting Spielrein in her apartment and she was still visiting his office for consultations, but, following the exchange of two further letters between him and Mrs Spielrein, he suddenly broke off his visits, without explaining to her that he was in correspondence with her mother. Spielrein retaliated by staying away from her weekly appointments, keeping this up for three weeks on the trot. But a conversation with another patient (probably another Russian woman) convinced her that her experience at Jung's hands was simply the way he treated all his women: first lead them on, then rebuff them. On 26 February 1909 she stormed into his office for a tempestuous conversation. Jung accused her of pushing him into a sexual liaison which he had never wanted. Once again Jung tried to turn the tables by suggesting, as he had with Mrs Spielrein, that *she* was in the wrong, that such behaviour was a poor recompense for all the time and care he had lavished on her. Sabina responded by a physical attack, with a knife, and fled.[68] This time Jung was convinced she would make trouble and feared the scandal. It was not so much that he was Switzerland's most eminent Freudian and editor of the *Jahrbuch* as that his private practice would be ruined and it would be said that he had left the Burghölzli under a cloud because of the Spielrein affair. If his letters to Mrs Spielrein became public, it would be assumed that he beat Bleuler to the punch by putting in his resignation, since the director would have had to dismiss him for unprofessional behaviour had the correspondence become known.

The first half of the annual volume of the *Jahrbuch* appeared in February 1909, containing articles by Freud on 'Little Hans', and by Jung on 'The Significance of the Father', a paper on epilepsy and hysteria by Alphonse Maeder and a case study by Binswanger; Freud's paper apart, all contributions were written by Swiss psychiatrists – the point that had so angered Abraham. Freud assured Jung he had avenged himself brilliantly for Amsterdam.[69]

Yet Freud was again concerned about the 'crown prince', for Jung suddenly dropped out of regular correspondence, and postponed for a week a visit to Vienna, due to have taken place on 19 March, and allegedly deferred because of pressure of work at the Burghölzli.[70] This seemed more than a little unconvincing as an excuse when Jung barefacedly admitted that he had been out of Zürich visiting Paul Haberlin, his old college friend. This may have been the occasion when Haberlin joshed him by comparing the bombast of philosophers and psychologists with the bragging of loudmouthed hunters he met in the Swiss mountains, and Jung, admitting that there *was* such an element in his own writings, added cynically that the world liked being deceived.[71]

In some alarm at the eccentric behaviour of his protégé, Freud cabled Jung, who finally broke the silence and admitted the truth about the Spielrein affair in general terms, though without naming her. According to Jung, it was all a question of a neurotic woman causing trouble because he had refused to father a child on her.

Freud replied reassuringly that he had heard of one of Jung's mistresses from Arthur Muthmann, but made light of such entanglements; they were simply an operational hazard of psychoanalysis. Jung in turn hastened to assure Freud that there was nothing personal in his unwonted silence. He told Freud that nothing 'Fliess-like' was going to happen, which had rather the sound of a man protesting too much; he then disingenuously declared that he had never 'really' had a mistress.

The best way to reassure Freud was finally to have the long-promised meeting in Vienna. Yet at the last moment Jung had to postpone his trip once again, and instead hastened to Berlin, in response to an urgent cable from the wife of one of his patients. The hurried trip proved to be very much a false alarm, so that Jung finally arrived in Vienna on 25 March to link up with his wife; he and Emma were in the Imperial capital until 30 March.

This was not such a successful trip as the one two years before. Freud invited Jung into his study for a private chat and told him he had decided to adopt him openly as 'crown prince', but almost immediately after telling him this got embroiled in an argument about the occult. Jung found Freud's attitude to parapsychology excessively sceptical and his resentment found expression in a curious sensation as if his diaphragm was made of iron and was becoming red-hot. At that moment there was a loud report in the bookcase. Jung claimed the 'detonation' was an example of what he called a 'catalytic exteriorisation phenomenon'. Freud snorted with derision but Jung insisted that he was right and prophesied a second explosion. Sure enough, a second detonation occurred. Freud looked suspiciously at Jung, who became convinced that from that moment things were never the same between then.[72] Certainly there is distinct uneasiness in the letters exchanged between the two after they parted.

Jung suggested they both felt uncomfortable because the 'spookery' had analogues with the Fliess débâcle and suggested that 'psychosynthesis' was needed to explain the strange events.[73]

That was the second reference to Fliess in a short space of time and that, plus the defiant rivalry exhibited both by Jung's firm belief in the occult and by 'psychosynthesis', must have left Freud wondering what was really going on in the Jungian unconscious. There is both sadness and steely rebuke in his reply. Jung, he said, on the very evening he was adopted as successor and crown prince, managed both to divest him of his authority and to take pleasure in so doing. He went on to say that he had conducted experiments and was convinced he could explain the 'magical' noise from the bookshelf by purely natural causes. He spoke of his own lifelong battle to ward off superstition, the insidious influence of numerology, and the consequent conviction that he would die between sixty-one and sixty-two.[74]

Jung received the letter on his return from a holiday in Italy and dealt with it emolliently, on the surface at least.[75] Yet that the 'occult experience' caused great tension between the two men is clear from Jung's later rationalizations. In *Memories* he recalled that on his last visit to Freud in Vienna (so it must have been in 1909, as there is no record of a later visit), Freud asked him never to abandon the sexual theory, and that it was necessary to make of it a dogma, an unshakeable bulwark. 'He said that to me with great emotion, in the tone of a father saying, "And promise me this one thing, my dear son: that you will go to church every Sunday." In some astonishment I asked him, "A bulwark – against what?" To which he replied, "Against the black tide of mud," – and here he hesitated for a moment, then added – "of occultism."'[76]

Jung claimed that Freud closed his mind to the occult, because he wanted to build an adamantine structure of sexual ideology. Yet it is clear that Freud's remarks were spoken in the context of the specific 'exploding bookcase' phenomenon and were meant as a purely personal exhortation to the man he had just appointed his crown prince.

This is the only interpretation of Freud's remarks which makes sense, for throughout the Freud *oeuvre* there is a deep and abiding interest in the paranormal and preternatural. Freud was always interested in telepathy but feared it could be used for reactionary and superstitious purposes rather than to advance the understanding of the unconscious.[77] It was for purely prudential reasons that he did not publish until late in his career the many strange cases of thought-transference he had come across;[78] he simply feared that until psychoanalysis was established beyond risk of destruction by ridicule, to exhibit open-mindedness was to hand enemies a weapon. In 1932 he wrote that he used to fear that science might be overwhelmed by spiritualism or mysticism if parts of the occultist canon were proved true, but he no longer felt like that and was, indeed, convinced that thought-transference was a fact.[79]

What Freud disliked was the charlatanry of mediums and spiritualists, but, though a sceptic, in 1911 he became a member of the Society for Psychical Research. Although he himself, conscious of his position as founding father of psychoanalysis, always kept the occult at arm's length, he privately encouraged his disciples to write on the subject.[80] Freud's open-mindedness had been reinforced by an experience on his fiftieth birthday in 1906, when his followers struck a medallion for him, bearing a motto from Sophocles's *Oedipus Tyrannus*: 'Who divined the famed riddle [of the Sphinx] and was a man most mighty'. This struck Freud as an uncanny coincidence, since the words were identical to the inscription he had placed on an imaginary bust when fantasizing about himself as a great man while a student at the University of Vienna. Ernest Jones relates that when Freud saw the medallion's legend, he became pale and agitated and asked in a strangulated voice who had thought of it.[81]

Most of all, Freud alienated his own supporters by the tolerance he evinced towards the 'superstition' of Jung and the Zürich school.[82] And finally, there is a triptych of observations on the occult made in the last years of his life. He told Cornelius Tabori that he thought parapsychology could throw light on the phenomenon of transference and vice versa; to Romain Rolland he wrote, 'I am not an out and out sceptic. Of one thing I am absolutely positive; there are certain things we cannot know now,'; and to Ernest Jones he remarked, 'If I had my life to live over again, I would devote myself to psychical research rather than to psychoanalysis.'[83]

This diversion into Freudian thought has been necessary to rebut the popular and widely believed notion that Freud had no time for the occult or paranormal, and closed his mind to vistas that the more adventurous Jung chose to explore. It is abundantly clear that the strictures on the supernatural made to Jung were purely personal, dictated as much by fear for the fate of the psychoanalytic movement as by anxiety about the real attitude to him of his 'son and heir'.

That Freud was right to worry about a certain ambivalence in

Jung's attitude was demonstrated when Jung departed from Vienna for a bicycle trip to Italy, for during his tour Jung had two deeply revealing dreams.

In the first of these dreams Freud appeared to him as a disgruntled customs official of the Austrian Hapsburg empire. The Imperial customs official appeared as 'one of those who would not die', of which the obvious meaning was that Jung could not wait for Freud to die so that he could inherit his kingdom.

In the second dream Jung found himself walking at noon in a city (which was a kind of conflation of Basel and Bergamo) where, among the midday crowd, he met a questing medieval knight in the uniform of a crusader.[84] Jung analysed the dream symbolically, as relating to the twelfth century, to alchemy and the Holy Grail – meaning that there was a part of himself that wanted to go on a quest for the Grail – but it can be clearly taken to refer also to Freud. The twelfth century might well denote an era when the Jews (i.e. Freud) were kept in their place. And the red cross on the crusader's uniform could well signify a crusading doctor (Freud), since the red cross also connotes the world of the medical.[85] This would not be the last time Jung dreamed dreams, whether medieval or modern, in which a wish for the death of Freud was a significant element.

The city which conflated Bergamo and Basel could well hint also at the ambivalence Jung felt about Italy, also now associated with Freud since his successful overcoming of 'Rome-complex' (see below pp. 163–4). Jung was always simultaneously attracted to and repelled by Italy. The Italian peasants themselves irritated him. When he was cycling he asked what the road was like farther ahead after he had sustained a puncture on a dreadful stretch of track. A peasant told him it was a beautiful stretch of paved road, but it turned out to be so pitted and rutted that Jung had to get off his bicycle and walk. Jung consoled himself with the thought that he had enjoyed ten minutes in a fool's paradise, whereas a Swiss would have told him the unpleasant truth at once.[86] He was always fascinated by the tension of opposites – Latin southern Europe against Teutonic northern Europe – which he saw as the conflict of a northern nomadic and polydaimonistic culture with a settled polytheism.[87]

However, in travelling to Italy from Vienna, Jung was aware that he was crossing the Rubicon in more senses than one. Almost his first action on returning to Zürich was to write to Freud to tell him that the last evening in Vienna, during which the dispute on the occult had taken place, had freed him from the oppressive sense of his paternal authority.[88] There followed another two-month lacuna in which nothing significant was discussed.

Then at the beginning of June the Spielrein affair took its most serious turn yet. For three months a distraught Spielrein, self-confessedly beside herself, pondered her next step. After the violent knife scene with Jung she interrupted her medical studies and left Zürich for the countryside to recover. Her parents came to Zürich to watch over her, and Mrs Spielrein tried to get a private meeting with Jung, who countered by insisting that any meeting should be in the Burghölzli in office hours (Jung was now in the curious position of being still resident in the hospital despite having resigned, as his new house was not ready until 25 May). Sabina herself could not raise the energy to return to her medical studies. In May she attempted to face her tormentor and stood at the back of the hall during one of his lectures, intending to accost him afterwards; but her nerve failed and she fled. Finally she hit on the idea of laying her case before the only man Jung accepted as his superior: Sigmund Freud himself.

At the end of May she wrote to Freud to ask for a private consultation on a matter of some urgency, and mentioned that she was a patient of Dr Jung's. Bemused, Freud sent a copy of her letter to Jung with a query asking who she was; whether busybody, chatterbox or paranoiac.[89]

Jung's reply did not do him much credit, as even his champions acknowledge. He admitted that Spielrein was the person in question, claimed she had been systematically planning his seduction and had capped it all by spreading the rumour that he was about to divorce Emma and marry one of his students.[90] Freud in reply was very forgiving and simply put the whole experience down to the occupational hazard of countertransference.[91]

Jung was thankful to get away so lightly, as he had been expecting a dressing down.[92] Freud meanwhile wrote to Spielrein to say that he could not really act as a judge, since he had to listen to the other side as well. He suggested trying to solve things without third parties.[93] Spielrein, naturally, realized that Freud was trying to protect his 'crown prince' and wrote, 'when I received your last letter, unfavourable though it was to me, tears came into my eyes: "he loves him. What if he could understand this?"'[94]

Taking Freud's advice, on 10 June Spielrein started writing down the history of her relationship with Jung. Meanwhile she sent a sheaf of love letters to Freud, as well as the correspondence between Jung and Mrs Spielrein. Freud, honourably, kept Jung informed of developments. He did not tell Spielrein how much he knew but led her to infer that he had a Sherlock Holmes gift for sifting clues.[95]

Writing out her story acted for Spielrein as a form of therapy, to the point where she felt strong enough to collar Jung after one of his lectures on 19 June and thrash things out with him. Jung was astonished to learn that she was not, after all, the source of the rumours about his impending divorce from Emma. He threw out a smokescreen to the effect that his initial attraction to her was a 'transference' of the inexpressible feelings he had entertained for Freud's daughter, Sophie. A truce was then cobbled together, which had the effect of demolishing Jung's earlier protestations that there was no problem except Spielrein's neurosis. Spielrein's conditions were that Jung must apologize to her parents, confess everything to Freud, and ask Freud to write to her to acknowledge the confession. Jung accepted but then had the hard task of admitting to Freud that he had written the incriminating letter to Mrs Spielrein, which even he now had to concede was a piece of staggering moral impertinence: as he put it, it was 'a piece of knavery which I very reluctantly confess to you as my father.'[96]

Freud then wrote to Spielrein to apologize for not having understood the situation properly: he thought it was a doctor – patient transference relationship, not an affair between a man and a woman.[97]

Yet although Jung had assured Freud that Spielrein now accepted that the affair was over and had suffered no relapse apart from a paroxysm of weeping, it was not easy for her to come to terms with the loss of her beloved. Confident that Freud was now on her side, she continued to write about the relationship, and sent Freud a huge letter containing her day-to-day thoughts on the liaison as it developed, along with material on Hélène Preiswerk, Gross, Binswanger, Siegfried, dream analysis and references to herself and Jung and their 'poetry' together. If she had presented it all in a lucid manner, instead of in stream of consciousness form, Freud might have been able to work out how far from the psychoanalytical fold Jung had already strayed. But he found hacking through the thickets of obfuscated and disconnected thoughts a trial and wrote to Jung that he was bemused.[98]

Sabina Spielrein was by no means destined to disappear from the history of psychoanalysis, but the sexual side of her relationship with Jung was now over, as was her successful attempt to make Freud the third side of a triangle. Neither man emerges entirely with credit from this story, but Freud was at least actuated by a desire to protect the 'crown prince'. If he can be faulted, it is for too readily assuming in the beginning that Spielrein's narrative was a neurotic fantasy, and perhaps this ties in with recent criticism that he was always too prepared to opt for fantasy rather than reality in any seduction story. He was also obsessed with the dangers of amorous pursuit by women in transference: 'an incomparable magic emanates from a woman of high principles who confesses her passions.'[99]

Jung, on the other hand, acted shabbily. Even John Kerr, usually disposed to give Jung the benefit of doubts, says, 'Jung had proved himself a coward.'[100] But Kerr goes too far in his thesis that Freud now had a weapon of counterstrike to use against Jung, who knew about Minna Bernays. In the first place, as we have seen, it is doubtful if there is anything in the Minna story. More importantly, if Jung and Sabina were not lovers, as Kerr maintains, – though how one can maintain this after a close reading of the letter from Jung to Freud dated 21 June is a moot point – his own thesis falls down. He argues that Jung was worried that Freud had Spielrein's letter, that it was sinister that Freud did not return this (a private letter from Spielrein to Freud) to *Jung* (which would have been a breach of professional courtesy) and that Jung remained worried and uncertain about how much Freud really knew. But if there was nothing to know anyway, why should Jung have been worried? Clearly, he was worried because he and Spielrein *had* been lovers. It is interesting that those who cling to the consoling theory that Sabina never had intercourse with Jung base their argument on the idea that, as a neurotic, she might have been unable to distinguish fantasy from reality – exactly the argument in fact that Jung used, and was later forced to retract.

The denouement of the Spielrein affair had also forced Jung back into a filial relationship vis-à-vis Freud – precisely what he thought he had thrown off after the trip to Vienna. It was not surprising that by July 1909 Jung should have entertained violently ambivalent feelings towards the 'father'. This is what lies behind the bizarre circumstances of the next meeting of 'father' and 'son', in Bremen.

Chapter Eight

VOYAGE TO AMERICA

By 1909 the Freudian movement, despite its adherents in Vienna, Zürich, Berlin, Budapest and London, still lacked academic respectability. That defect was remedied when Freud was invited to receive an honorary doctorate during the twentieth anniversary celebrations of Clark University in Massachusetts.[1] The invitation came from the colourful and controversial first president of Clark, Stanley Hall, who, with the help of liberal endowments, had built the university up to a position of prestige rivalling Harvard and Johns Hopkins. Hall, an eccentric character with a passion for new ideas, also had a flair for publicity, and sensed the kudos that could attach to Clark if he put it in the vanguard of modern thought by making it a haven for the leading practitioners of the intellectual avant-garde. Always interested in psychoanalysis, in 1899 he had brought Auguste Forel over from Europe as a visiting lecturer on the new bearings in psychiatry, including Freud and Breuer's work on hysteria. In his two-volume work *Adolescence* (1904) Hall made a number of favourable references to Freud, and brought his long-running flirtation to a head by a formal invitation to Freud to be among a galaxy of intellectual talent he intended to have on hand for Clark's twentieth birthday celebrations.[2]

Freud was flattered and intrigued by the invitation from a man who had the reputation of being 'something of a kingmaker'.[3] Yet at first he was not at all keen on taking up Hall's offer. There were a number of reasons, financial and ideological. The celebrations had been originally scheduled for June 1909, but this would have made significant inroads on Freud's analytic year and thus cut down his income; and in his own way Freud was just as anxious about money as Jung. He told the Hungarian psychoanalyst Sandor Ferenczi, who was rapidly becoming his most trusted confidant, that sacrificing money in order to lecture in the USA was just a bit too 'American' for his taste: 'America should bring in money, not cost money.'[4] Yet, money apart, he feared that the Americans would round on him and his colleagues once they discovered the sexual bedrock of Freudian psychology.[5]

However, some part of Freud always wanted to accept the invitation, and his dog-in-the-mangerism led him to keep Stanley Hall dangling awhile. When the letters from a frustrated Hall started to dry up, Freud became anxious and began to think he had overplayed his hand with the many objections he had made. However, Hall came through triumphantly and acceded to all Freud's demands: not only would the travel allowance be raised substantially, so that no financial loss would be involved, but the celebrations had been moved to September, expressly to fit in with Freud's schedule.[6]

Hall meanwhile invited Jung and Ferenczi, as Freud's leading European disciples. Writing about this many years later, Jung managed to give the impression that he had been invited entirely in his own right as Europe's leading expert on schizophrenia. If that had been the case, Clark would almost certainly have invited Bleuler instead.

Gradually Freud allowed himself to become excited by the American trip, began honing his English and buying books about the New World. Jung was if anything even more excited, for one of the elements uncovered in his analysis of his own dreams was a passionate desire to visit the USA.[7] He took Freud's advice and booked passage alongside him on the steamer *George Washington* of the Norddeutsche Lloyd line out of Bremen; Freud explained that this would enable them to spend a week sightseeing before arriving at Clark. On 11 August Jung set out on a five-day tour of

Lake Geneva on his sailboat; on the 18th he was in Basel for the day, and from therc took the train to Bremen.

In Bremen Jung met up with Freud and Ferenczi, and the three of them had lunch together while waiting to board the liner. Jung, as he admitted, was still smarting at the humiliation from the Spielrein affair.[8] The feelings of humiliation found expression in a barely concealed manifestation of hostility towards Freud during the lunch. Freud ordered a bottle of wine and persuaded Jung to take a glass and thus renounce his Burghölzli-inculcated teetotalism. Jung raised the topic of the corpses of 'peat-bog men' – drowned men from prehistoric times found in a state of mummification – recently discovered in north Germany. Freud showed increasing irritation at Jung's continual harping on the theme, became agitated, and finally fainted at the lunch table. Later he accused Jung of harbouring a death-wish against him, signified by his obsession with the peat-bog men.[9]

This was not the last time Freud would faint in Jung's presence, and the incident has always invited speculation. There are three main lines of interpretation, in ascending order of probability. Ronald Clark argues that Freud often fainted and that he later explained to Binswanger that he was then suffering from sleeplessness and his perennial low tolerance for alcohol; the fainting fit is thus, for Clark, a 'psychic penalty' for the minor triumph in persuading Jung to take a drink.[10] Alternatively, one could view the faint as an act of deference or appeasement by a Freud anxious that the Spielrein affair had driven a wedge between them.

Yet what Clark does not make clear is that Freud's propensity to fainting was not an organic deficiency, but something that occurred in extremely stressful situations. He had had fainting fits before, when he did not want to criticize Fliess, his one-time friend and later bitter enemy: once over the incident when Fliess left a piece of gauze in the patient Emma Eckstein's nose; and again in Munich after a dispute with Fliess, when he fainted in the selfsame room where he would later swoon in Jung's presence.[11]

The second explanation is that Freud fainted because he suddenly discerned the murderous hate towards him lurking in the crown prince's unconscious. The faint would then either have been spontaneous shock or a therapeutic gesture, designed to show Jung the latent content of his apparently harmless story and its homicidal implications – as in the fainting fits Freud analysed in his essay 'Dostoevsky and Parricide'.[12] To swoon would have been a particularly appropriate response, since Jung had already confided his own fainting fits at the age of twelve when trying to avoid school. The trouble with this explanation is that it is too simple. As Bruno Bettelheim has remarked: 'Oedipal situations that bring about death-wishes are so frequent that if the reaction to them was fainting, people would be fainting right and left.'[13]

The third and most likely interpretation of Freud's faint was that *he* found Jung unpalatable face-to-face, that Jung's puzzlement about why his 'father' had let him off so lightly over the Spielrein business had substance, that Freud had exercised considerable powers of repression to prevent his moral repugnance at Jung's behaviour from seeping out but that, finally, he could not control the anger he felt when the response from Jung was this barely concealed death-wish. This interpretation receives support from Freud's later statement to Binswanger that repressed feelings towards Jung had played the major part in the incident.[14] It is well-known that fainting fits occur when the swooning person is unable, for one reason or another, to say or do something important. In this instance the faint was an obvious escape route from the otherwise compelling necessity to engage in face-to-face conflict with Jung.

It was Saturday 21 August 1909 when Jung, Freud and Ferenczi left Bremen, New York-bound in the *George Washington*. The crossing was an easy one, for although they encountered mists in mid-Atlantic there was the compensation of calm seas as the invariable concomitant; Jung thought the liner resembled a prehistoric monster gliding through primeval slime as it nosed forward into the gloom. Freud was ill for much of the crossing, suffering from indigestion, urinary difficulties and intestinal complaints.[15] Jung was unhappy on other counts. He had looked forward to finding some of his friends and American contacts on board, but instead ran into the very man, the psychologist William Stern, who had so severely criticized the association experiment in 1905.

On the eight-day crossing Jung, Freud and Ferenczi practised dream interpretation on each other, and this led to yet another conflict between Freud and Jung. Freud related a dream which Jung thought he understood but, just to be sure, asked Freud for some associations drawn from his private life. According to Jung, Freud then looked at him suspiciously and said, 'I cannot risk my authority.' Telling the story many years later, Jung commented, 'At that moment he lost it altogether. That sentence burned itself into my memory; and in it the end of our relationship was already foreshadowed. Freud was placing personal authority above truth.'[16]

Here we encounter a perennial problem about *Memories*, from which this comment comes. Almost everything said in that book emerges differently in the more direct sources for Jung's life, and so it proves with this story. Here we have a man putting dogma and authority before truth and inquiry, as if he were a Pope claiming infallibility. But Jung elsewhere portrays Freud's reluctance to open up on this occasion as connected with the 'affair' with Minna Bernays. In the famous interview with Billinsky, Jung puts a rather different gloss on Freud's reluctance to speak freely: 'Freud had no idea that I knew about the triangle and his intimate relationship with his sister-in-law. And so, when Freud told me the important parts, I asked Freud to tell me some of his personal associations with the dream. He looked at me with bitterness and said, "I could tell you more, but I cannot risk my authority."'[17] In this version the 'authority' referred to is not that of papal head of the psychoanalytic movement but the authority of father over errant son – a very different matter. Besides, even if we accept Jung's 'papal' version of the story, if it is true that Freud 'lost it altogether' at that point, why did Jung continue to be the obedient 'son' in correspondence, at least until 1911? If his first version of the encounter on the liner is correct, we could hardly fail to convict him of humbug thereafter.

Further problems arose when Freud, in turn, analysed Jung's dreams. The most striking was a dream about descending through a large house, storey by storey, from the seventh floor to the basement. Under the cellar, in the basement, was a cave containing two human skulls. Jung later interpreted this dream as a vision of the psyche, collectively considered, with the lowest level in the cellar being like that of the animals. The 'message' of the dream was that consciousness was arranged according to cultural and racial history, not an individual's personal past. As Jung told it, it was this dream that first made him realize that there were contents of an impersonal, collective nature in the psyche.[18]

Freud, however, insisted that the dream was a classic of manifest content masking latent content and pressed Jung to say whose skulls they were. Jung understood that Freud interpreted the dream as a death-wish and, not wishing to bring on a major breach with him on the brink of triumph in America, lied casually and said that they were the skulls of his wife and sister-in-law (perhaps a hint at Martha and Minna Bernays?). Freud seemed disappointed and simply smiled without comment.

Why did Jung lie? His own explanation was that Freud would have resisted any interpretation other than the obvious 'death-wish' one, that he (Jung) did not want to quarrel with Freud or lose his friendship, but at the same time he wanted to see the reaction to his answer. However, Jung seemed unaware that on this occasion he had shown the truth of the old saying that the best way to lie is to tell the truth. Why, after all, should he have opted for his wife and sister-in-law as owners of the skulls, unless it was an obscure sideswipe at Freud? Did this answer not denote that he did find his wife Emma a burden? Besides, Jung's account is self-contradictory. He says 'I wanted to know what he would make of my answer,' but on the previous page of *Memories* he has already said: 'I knew perfectly well, of course, what he was driving at: that secret death-wishes were concealed in the dream.'[19]

Clearly both answers cannot be correct and that Jung was involved in some obscure psychic game becomes clear with a further utterance, 'I was quite aware that my conduct was not above reproach, but *à la guerre, comme à la guerre!*' But no-one had declared war at this stage, so the remark looks like an intrusion from a later era when war *had* been declared. The main point of the story, as told in *Memories*, is to argue that Freudian dream theory is false – and this is a preoccupation of Jung's later career. What the obscure psychic game might be is suggested by Winnicott, who speculates that Freud may unwittingly have played a therapeutic role during the Atlantic crossing. Jung the youth could keep secrets only at the cost of a split personality, but the adult attempt at integration seemed to imply an end of secretiveness; here for the first time was an instance of 'integrated lying': 'When Jung deliberately lied to Freud he became a unit with a capacity to hide secrets instead of a split personality with no place for hiding anything.'[20]

Shipboard proximity seemed to exacerbate the latent tensions. As the skyline of New York City came into view on 29 August, there was another testy exchange. Freud stood at the rails with Jung and said that America was in for a surprise. Jung accused him of being ambitious. 'Me?' said Freud, 'I am the most humble of men and the only one who isn't ambitious.' 'That's a big thing to be – the only one,' Jung replied sardonically.[21]

Neither Freud nor Jung was world famous as yet, and from the passenger list of psychological notables disembarking from the *George Washington* the Manhattan newspapers singled out William Stern as the most noteworthy.[22] In New York the trio of psychoanalysts were met by their colleagues Ernest Jones and A.A. Brill. Jones came down from Toronto, where he was currently working, while Brill, late of the Burghölzli but now back in New York, his home since 1889, was already the self-appointed proselytizer for Freudianism in the USA.[23]

Although the weather in New York was dreary and Freud, Jung and Ferenczi were all afflicted with stomach aches and diarrhoea from the strange new American food, they set out on an earnest programme of sightseeing. On 30 August Jung and Freud took a long walk in Central Park discussing the difference between Jews and Aryans; Jung wrote to Emma that the walk and discussion did him a lot of good, though he lamented that the noise and bustle of Manhattan made it impossible to concentrate and have a deep-delving conversation. They followed with a car drive through Chinatown and visited a joss-house, where Jung claimed to be able to smell a murder at every corner, a traditional Chinese tea house, and an 'Apache music hall'. Jung reported that the quarter thronged with white prostitutes, since in Chinatown there were 9,000 men but just twenty-eight Chinese women. The tourists rounded off the first day with dinner at the Brills' home.[29]

Next day came a visit to a New York State insane asylum, to the Metropolitan Museum of Art, where Freud lingered over the Grecian antiquities, and to Coney Island. Subsequent days saw the travellers riding from 42nd Street to the pier on the elevated railway, visiting the museum of palaeontology, shopping in Tiffanys and touring Columbia University. In a Manhattan cinema Freud and Ferenczi saw their first movie – a Keystone Cops-style slapstick chase – and later joined Jung for dinner at Hammerstein's roof garden.[25]

Soon it was time to set out for Massachusetts. On Saturday 4 September the five psychoanalysts (Freud, Jung, Ferenczi, Brill and Jones) boarded a five-decked steamer which made landfall at the Massachusetts city of Fall River early the next morning. From there Jung and party took the fifty-mile train ride to Boston and thence to Worcester, where they arrived in the early afternoon and checked into the Standish Hotel – all except Freud, who as the senior invitee was to be the house guest of Stanley Hall himself.[26]

Jung was impressed with Worcester, then a city of about 180,000 people and largely set in a forest. After a rest, at about 6 p.m., the Standish Hotel party called on Stanley Hall for dinner, at which Jung was fascinated to be waited on by black servants in evening dress.

The lecture programme commenced next morning. Freud and Jung lectured in German, but their discourses were eagerly received by a large audience and widely reported in the local press.[27] Freud, scheduled to speak at 11 a.m. each morning, began with an account of his early work on hysteria and paid handsome tribute to his one-time collaborator Josef Breuer.[28] His skill as a public speaker served him well, as did his meticulous preparation, for early every morning he went for a long stroll with Ferenczi and rehearsed what he would say. He provided a rapidly drawn thumbnail sketch of his ideas and techniques and cautioned against regarding psychoanalysis as a miracle cure. By the end of the third lecture his audience was in possession of the essential facts about repression, resistance and dream interpretation. In the fourth lecture he moved on to the tricky subject of sexuality, including infantile sexuality, but neutralized any objections by citing the work of Sanford Bell, a Clark University fellow and thus as American as apple pie, to support the notion. In the final lecture Freud demonstrated how psychoanalysis could be used in literary and cultural criticism.[29]

Jung meanwhile gave three lectures, starting on Wednesday 10 September. He began with a splash, keeping his audience spellbound with the dramatic tale of how the word-association tests had been used to detect crime.[30] His second address concentrated on the 'family constellation', showing how complexes and reaction types tended to run in families. His final lecture, on 'Psychic conflicts in a child' was a rehash of his experiences with his daughter 'Agathli' and her reactions to the birth of a baby brother.[31]

All the lectures were a great success, but even more so was the kudos gained by Freud and Jung in informal seminars and discussions. Two distinguished Harvard professors, James Jackson Putnam and William James, had come to Clark for this gathering of the notables, and the Europeans soon demonstrated that in many areas of psychological understanding they were far ahead of the Americans. Putnam and James, both interested in abnormal psychology, brought along a medium who had puzzled them for months. It took Jung and Freud next to no time to extract a confession from the medium that her manifestations were fraudulent and designed to attract the attentions of a young man. The medium was not the only woman to enliven proceedings, for at one stage the anarchist Emma Goldman interrupted a lecture and had to be escorted from the hall; always a witty man, Freud then amusingly compared her antics to the 'interloper' role of dissociated ideas seeking to enter consciousness.[32] Then there were the social events: lunches, dinners, garden parties. Jung wrote to Emma about the experience of being the centre of attention for no less than five women simultaneously.[33]

Finally, on Friday evening came the award of the honorary doctorates in law. Freud spoke off the cuff, hailing the invitation to Clark as a breakthrough for psychoanalysis and calling the award 'the first official recognition of our endeavours'.[34] Five years later, with justifiable hyperbole, Freud referred to the Clark University lectures as 'the first time I was permitted to speak publicly about psychoanalysis . . . In prudish America one could, at least in academic circles, freely discuss and scientifically treat everything that is regarded as improper in ordinary life.'[35]

Jung, who celebrated the award of his doctorate on Monday 13 September by driving out to a remote lake and having lunch at an idyllic spot, confirmed Freud's euphoria: 'Freud is in seventh heaven and I am glad with all my heart to see him so.'[36] The two of them often seemed in competition for the favours of William James. Freud went for a long walk with him, but James was already ill with the heart disease that would carry him off a year later. On the walk James suddenly stopped, handed Freud his briefcase and asked him to walk on, saying he would catch up with him later. He explained that he had just sustained an acute attack of angina pectoris; Freud was deeply impressed by James's stoicism and wished that when the time came he would be able to face death with James's courage.[37]

Jung managed to spend the whole of two evenings with James alone and was enormously impressed by his clarity of mind and absence of intellectual prejudice. He and Jung shared a deep interest in mediumship and the paranormal and Jung was irritated by Stanley Hall's occasional hints that James was an intellectual lightweight because of his interest in such matters. But James was more than capable of dealing with Hall, as Jung soon discovered, to his great delight. Hall invited James round to his house one evening so that Jung and Freud could investigate some of his material. James entered the Hall residence at the appointed time and told Hall that he had brought the papers in which he was particularly interested. With that he put his hand to his breast pocket and drew out a wad of dollar bills. He then apologised profusely and produced the real papers from his other pocket. Jung thought this a particularly felicitous rejoinder.[38]

James himself was ambivalent about Freud and his disciples. Ernest Jones remembered James saying to the Freudian group 'the future of psychology belongs to your work.'[39] But a few days later he wrote to Professor Mary Calkins, 'I strongly suspect Freud, with his dream theory, of being a regular *halluciné*. But I hope that he and his disciples will push it to its limits as undoubtedly it covers some facts and will add to our understanding of "functional" psychology, which is the real psychology.'[40]

These, however, were private reservations. Publicly the Clark University twentieth anniversary celebrations broke up in an orgy of mutual congratulation. Finding that the Europeans had some free time before embarking from New York for the trip home, Putnam invited them to his family summer camp in the Adirondack mountains near Lake Placid. Freud and Jung first visited the Niagara falls, then headed for Keene, New York, where the Putnam camp was located.[41] This turned out to be a sylvan oasis, a bewildering mixture of luxury and austerity. In a forest clearing Putnam had built a number of log cabins hard by a fast-flowing stream. The camp reminded Jung of the Wild West as described in the travels of Friedrich Gerstäcker, the celebrated German globetrotter, whose adventures he had read as a boy. With his perennial fear of snakes, he was glad to be assured by Putnam that this was not rattlesnake country.[42]

For four days Jung sampled the pleasures of the wilderness. He scaled a 5,600-foot mountain peak and gazed triumphantly over a vast virgin forest. In the evenings after supper another of Putnam's guests accompanied him on the piano while he sang German songs. Jung was torn between enthusiasm for American life and a perception of its deficiencies.[43]

From Putnam's camp the travellers made their way to the state capital, Albany, and thence to New York for embarkation on 21 September on the liner *Wilhelm der Grösse*. The steamer cleared from New York at 10 a.m., leaving Jung to ponder his impressions of the New World. He had been astonished to see that there were no barriers at the railway crossings and no protective hedges alongside the track; even more amazing was to find that in remoter areas the railway line was actually used as a footpath. When he expressed his amazement to Americans, he was informed curtly that only an idiot could be unaware that trains travelled between 40 and 100 mph and that the country people knew all the schedules and the signs of approaching locomotives.

Another thing that struck him was that in the USA nothing seemed to be *verboten*: instead, people were politely requested not to do such-and-such. He concluded that in North America civil life was designed to appeal to the intelligence, not, as in Europe, to stupidity.[44]

As the homeward voyage progressed, Jung increasingly found that he had developed a taste for champagne, and decided that on return to Switzerland he would withdraw from his various teetotal societies. Standing by the ship's rail, sipping champagne and gazing out onto a tranquil ocean, he felt at peace with himself. But the North Atlantic crossing did not have its dreadful reputation for nothing, and on 24 September Jung saw the other face of the sea. The wind and waves increased from moderate gale force through severe gale to outright storm conditions, and a ferocious tempest raged all day and through to midnight, causing the ship to roll fearfully. For most of the day Jung stood towards the aft, in a covered but elevated spot near the bridge, watching the spectacle as mountainous waves whipped up a whirling cloud of foam over the ship. In his cabin everything that was not fixed was crashing about frighteningly, but Jung climbed into bed and slept like a top.[45]

The travellers disembarked at Bremen on 29 September. Freud spent a few days in Hamburg and Berlin before returning to Vienna, but Jung sped home to his new house in Küsnacht, full of a new plan to psychoanalyse his wife. Although he would later recall the analytic sessions he had with Freud during the homeward shipboard journey with great bitterness, at the time he claimed to Freud that the encounters had done him a lot of good.[46]

The most important long-term result of the American trip for Freud was that it made a life-long convert out of Putnam, even though in the short-term Freud was angry that Putnam had described him as an 'old man'. For Jung the consequences were more attenuated, but the deepest imprint left was that made on him by William James. Whenever Jung returned to the United States, he would mention

James in his lectures, notably at Fordham in 1912 and at Harvard in 1936.[47]

Yet it was no mere American association of ideas that caused Jung's long love affair with Jamesian thought. The two psychologists, superficially so different, had an astonishing number of points of similarity and convergence. Both were lapsed Protestants, caught between doubt and belief, attracted to both science and religion and committed to finding a new synthesis of the two.[48] Both – Jung ultimately, James immediately – took exception to what they saw as Freud's sexual monocausalism.[49] Both were much exercised by the 'problem of the father', suffered identity crises in youth and had breakdowns in middle life; as Erik Erikson put it; 'James's later philosophy became at once a continuation and an abrogation of his father's philosophy.'[50] Both were fascinated by the occult: Leonora Piper, James's famous medium, was the analogue to Jung's Hélène Preiswerk. Beyond this, at a philosophical level, both men embraced the viewpoint of radical empiricism – that the duality of subject/object was misconceived, and that too rigid a distinction had been drawn between mind and matter.

The view that the mind/matter dichotomy is a crude oversimplification of reality, that both are simply manifestations of a more primal 'stuff' – a view that some philosophers, though not James, have called 'neutral monism' – was the most fundamental core idea shared by the two men. The notion that there is no necessary hard and fast distinction between events in the external world and events 'in the mind' would underlie much of the later doctrine of Jung – especially his theory of synchronicity – and is the fundamental starting point of the Jamesian philosophy.

There is the same scepticism with regard to the existence of God and the role of religion. 'The attempt to demonstrate by purely intellectual processes the truth of the deliverance of direct religious experience is absolutely hopeless,' James wrote, but went on to say that this does not imply that God does not exist.[51] Both Jung and James stressed that the existence of God was impossible to prove but that *belief* in a deity might be desirable for social or utilitarian reasons. They also shared the view that the outright sceptic had obeyed the sane injunction to shun error without the concomitant obligation to embrace the residual truth.

James's pragmatism attracted Jung, particularly in its 'prospective' view, stressing consequences of phenomena rather than causes.

James's notorious phrase, the 'cash value' of an idea, was likely to appeal to a man with a money complex, and he quoted it approvingly in the introduction to his 1912 Fordham lectures. Jung's relish for Jamesian pragmatism, in the sense that he wanted to make psychoanalysis more pleasant and acceptable and therefore more workable, if necessary by ditching the theory of sexuality, was noticed by Ernest Jones, who explicitly drew to Freud's attention the influence of James.[52]

It is possible to detect three main lines of James's influence on Jung. The first is the domain of the unconscious, where assimilated ideas are absorbed and later breach the surface in transmogrified form. It has been noted that the most typical Jungian theory of the later period, that of the collective unconscious, was heavily influenced by James.[53] And one can see archetypal images foreshadowed in William James's reaction to the 1906 San Francisco earthquake, which provided the flash of intuition enabling him to understand primitive man's mythological view of such tragedies.[54] Moreover James's 'abandoned' or 'murdered' selves can be seen as the germ of the idea for Jung's 'shadow'.

Secondly, there are the areas where Jamesian thought is a palpable influence on Jung's work. *Varieties of Religious Experience* is the obvious source, much quoted by Jung, especially as an influence on his late work *Job*. In his Tavistock Lectures (1935), Jung cited James's famous theory of emotions which, typically, reverses the sequence of cause/consequence: emotions are the perceptions of physiological consequences rather than the reverse, so that we are frightened *because* we run.[55] The convergence of Jung and James on psychological types is so obvious as scarcely to need stressing: where Jung divided personalities into extravert and introvert, James classified according to 'tough-' and 'tender-'minded individuals. One of James's phrases in *Pragmatism*, where he described the tough-minded person as being characterized by a 'nothing but' attitude,[56] particularly took Jung's fancy. He took it over for his own theory of types and described the 'extraverted thinking type' as being the 'nothing but' type.[57] It was characteristic of Jung, once he fastened on a good idea, to do it to death, and so it proved with 'nothing but'; Jung's German version *nicht als* thereafter became an habitual and, it must be said, monotonous part of his polemical repertoire.[58]

Thirdly, James and Jung were united by their common and abiding interest in the occult. One obvious link was Théodore Flournoy, a devoted friend of James, who wrote an introduction to Jamesian thought.[59] Jung, after his experience with Hélène Preiswerk, was particularly fascinated by the experiments James and his friend James Hyslop had carried out with the American medium Mrs Leonora Piper.[60] To support his later theory of the 'animus', Jung cited the 'masculine control' on Leonora Piper, known to her as 'Imperator'.[61] To his credit, Jung did not give the James/Hyslop experiments more weight than they deserved – a caution not always exercised by his more perfervid disciples.

In some ways even more striking than the intellectual influence of James is the way his imagery and symbols touched a chord in Jung's unconscious. One would be lucky to come across a couple of references to crocodiles in Freud's *oeuvre*, but in Jung's work they make appearances in the most unexpected places, and Jung tells us that if a crocodile turns up in a dream, it represents the archaic residues of the cold-blooded things human beings once were.[62] It is more than likely that the ultimate inspiration for the excessive interest in saurians is the following striking passage in James's *Varieties of Religious Experience*:

> *Crocodiles and rattlesnakes and pythons are at this moment vessels of life as real as we are; their loathsome existence fills every minute of every day that drags its length along; and whenever they or other wild beasts clutch their living prey, the deadly horror which an agitated melancholic feels is literally the right reaction on the situation. It may indeed be that no religious reconciliation with the totality of things is possible. Some evils, indeed, are ministerial to higher forms of good but it may be that there are forms of evil so extreme as to enter into no good system whatsoever, and that in respect of such evil, dumb submission or neglect to notice is the only practical recourse.*[63]

The mention of pythons may be the cue to stress that Jung, despite his fascination for the symbolization of serpents in myths, had an acute fear of actual snakes. He liked to tell his students that zoologists maintained that rapport with any animal was possible until it came to reptiles, at which point one attempted a relationship at one's peril.

He cited the case of a man who reared a python and used to feed it by hand until one day, without warning, the constrictor wrapped itself around him and nearly killed him; it loosened its coils only when hacked to death with a hatchet by the man's friend.[64]

Chapter Nine

STORMCLOUDS GATHER

Once back in his new home at Küsnacht after the travails of the American trip, Jung started on a fresh work programme. First, he began analysing his wife, but the sessions soon broke up in turmoil when it became clear how little stomach Emma had for his polygamous activities. Next he consolidated the US connection by running a private seminar on psychoanalysis at his home – this was quite distinct from his formal lecturing and analytic hours with private patients. Among the participants were his new friend Trigant Burrow, with whom he often went sailing, and August Hoch, designated as Adolph Meyer's successor as head of the New York Psychiatric Institute.[1]

Another concern was psychoanalytical politics in Switzerland. During Jung's absence in the United States, Forel had written to ask him and other Freudians to join a Swiss psychiatric society which would be a 'broad church'. Jung stalled until he got Freud's approval, then, at a meeting of the society in Zürich, cleverly conciliated Forel so that the 'Grand Old Man' of Swiss psychiatry ended by attacking the rival neurologists' society of von Monakow and Paul Dubois for unnecessary factionalism.[2]

Yet Jung's central concern was always the relationship with Freud, and here there were worrying signs that all was not well. Freud had just published his famous essay on the 'Rat Man'[3] and, although Jung praised this, he confessed that his central preoccupation from now on would be archaeology and mythology. Jung began his studies by reading Friedrich Creuzer's four-volume work on symbolism and mythology, and Richard Payne Knight's *A Discourse on the Worship of Priapus*. He proceeded to devour Herodotus and was amazed at the 'Victorian' prudery of his history.[4]

Something about Jung's new bearing was vaguely disquieting to both men, and the unease found expression in two classic Freudian slips, deriving from the distinction between the German words *ihnen* ('them') and *Ihnen* ('you'). In a letter of 8 November Jung wrote, 'I have to fight like mad . . . until I have dinned it into you/them that psychoanalysis is a scientific method and not just guesswork.' Needless to say, Freud noticed the slip and, whether consciously or unconsciously, returned the compliment: three days later he wrote back, paraphrasing the emperor Caligula, 'I sometimes get so angry with my Viennese that I wish them a single rear end, so that I could thrash them all with one stick,' but used the *Ihnen* form, implying that it was Jung's backside that needed a caning. Earlier in the letter he had expressed irritation that Jung's communication of 8 November was the first for twenty-five days.[5]

'*Pater, peccavi*' ('Father, I have sinned') were Jung's words of apology in his next letter, but he continued to worry Freud with his obsession with the cultural, historical and mythical roots of the psyche, and with the fact that his long letters were full of little other than displays of erudition on mythology. Things came to a head when Jung wrote (on 30 November) that he had not so far found a satisfactory definition of libido. Freud's reply was icy. For a definition of libido he suggested consulting the first sentence of his *Three Essays on the Theory of Sexuality* and showed his displeasure by a sarcastic reference to Jung's spooks; he suggested that the two of them needed to get together and reproached Jung for seeming to follow in Adler's footsteps by concentrating too much on the repressor, not the repressed. Jung was stung by these criticisms, and his reply, written on Christmas Day 1909, contains some ominous rumblings, particularly the aside, 'It is a hard lot to have to work alongside the father creator.'[6]

Freud wrote back soothingly, but Jung appeared to be sulking in his tent for, apart from a postcard sent from the secluded mountain resort of Unterwasser in Canton St Gallen, east of Zürich, where he went in early January for a winter break, and another perfunctory communication on 10 January, there was a thirty-five-day silence. Freud, who had complained about the earlier twenty-five-day gap, was understandably concerned, especially as he had written with detailed queries about the proposed Second International Psychoanalytic Congress scheduled to be held in Nuremberg in March. When Jung finally broke silence, on 30 January 1910, he explained that he was in a disturbed state of mind because of domestic upheaval, that he was consequently plagued by 'complexes' but hated writing 'wailing' letters; the long and the short of it was that there had been a tremendous row with Emma over his sexual infidelities. In one of his most outspoken letters, he frankly announced to Freud that the prerequisite for a good marriage was a licence to be unfaithful; he ended the letter with a sheepish postscript, to the effect that Emma was pregnant again.[7]

Jung then finally got down to the administrative chore of organizing the conference, admitting that he was lazy about writing letters but claiming this was because of the heavy demands on his time of the editorship of the *Jahrbuch*. But his letters continued to trouble Freud. On 11 February Jung argued for a fusion of psychoanalysis and Christianity so as to conserve the best features of that religion. Arguing that 2,000 years of Christianity could be replaced only by something spiritually equivalent, he said that his wish was to change Christ back into a pagan god of the vine.[8]

Nor was his next letter, written on 20 February, much to Freud's liking. Jung argued that homosexuality should be viewed as the principal form of 'resistance' in men, whereas with women resistance took the form of perversion or the desire for sexual variation. He put forward three arguments for homosexuality: that it was a form of 'contraception'; that it was a release for the 'inferior'; and that it was an escape from enforced marriage. Moreover, he argued, homosexuals actually performed a useful biological function and should therefore be credited with monklike sanctity.[9]

It has been suggested that these commendatory words on homosexual seducers represent Jung's attempt to come to terms with his own seduction at eighteen. More likely, it is a bitterly ironical reflection on the 'misfortune' of being heterosexual, such as married men sometimes indulge in after a serious passage of arms with a wife objecting to 'open marriage'. Jung's dreams from this period lend credence to the idea for, having injured his thumb one day, the next night he dreamed that his wife had her right arm chopped off. Yet, whatever the provenance of the notion, this idea that homosexuals qualified for sainthood seems to have upset Freud. There is a missing letter in the series, but on 2 March Jung was complaining about 'all sorts of misunderstandings'.[10]

Once again Freud poured oil on troubled waters and said that Jung would in the future play the role of Alexander the Great to his own Philip of Macedon.[11] That this was a perfectly honest response from Freud is clear from his correspondence with Ferenczi: 'Jung has again emerged from his personal perplexities. I was quickly reconciled with him, for I was not angry, only concerned.'[12]

The response to this generous effusion was the worst blow Freud had so far received. Suddenly a letter arrived from Emma Jung to say that her husband had been summoned to America by Harold Fowler McCormick for an urgent consultation. McCormick and his wife Edith, who was a Rockefeller, were the first of what would be a long line of American millionaires to fall for Jung's charisma. In Europe in the early summer of 1909 the thirty-seven-year-old Chicago industrialist came under the Jungian spell and now, hypochondriacal like so many millionaires, had sent out an SOS to Küsnacht. From Paris Jung wrote a few lines to Freud, presenting him with a *fait accompli* but assuring him he would be back in time for the Nuremberg conference.[13]

Understandably, this made Freud nervous, for here was the chief organizer of the conference suddenly decamping so as to be incommunicado for the three weeks immediately preceding it. His claim that everything was in safe hands, since he had left full instructions with Emma and his new assistant Johann Jakob Honegger, was scarcely reassuring. Freud faced the prospect that the second world gathering of psychoanalysts would be a shambles. He had counted on a sizeable contingent from Zürich to counterbalance his Viennese, with whom he was increasingly disillusioned, but now the disappointments began to rain in. First Bleuler announced that he would not be coming, then Oscar Pfister, the highly intelligent Swiss Protestant pastor and zealot for psychoanalysis, also dropped out. Pfister, who had made contact with Freud in 1909 and followed up with a notably successful visit to Berggasse 19 in April 1909, was the one Swiss who never wavered over the years in his support for Freud,[14] so his defection at this stage was a blow. Added to the prospect that Jung would not return from the USA in time for the conference, Pfister's abstention was almost the last straw for Freud.

Jung meanwhile boarded the *Kronprinzessin Cäcilie* at Cherbourg on 9 March and arrived in New York on 15 March. He sped to Chicago, reassured McCormick, returned to New York and sailed for Cherbourg on the 22nd. Arriving in Cherbourg on 28 March, he travelled via Paris and Cologne to Nuremberg, arriving on the 29th, just in time for the conference the next day. Jung had cut it fine, but an even worse aspect of his handling of the conference was that he had managed to alienate both the Viennese and Kraepelin in the Munich clinic simultaneously; this was singularly ironical in view of the frequently expressed proposition in the Jung–Freud correspondence in the six months following the Clark visit that Freudians were employing poor tactics while charting a course through the minefields of medical politics.

However, the 'crown prince' managed once again to reaffirm his position as heir apparent. Even his enemies conceded that he made a first-class contribution to the symposium.[15] Freud got matters off to a smooth start on the 30th with his keynote address on 'The Future Prospects of Psychoanalytic Therapy',[16] and any residual feeling of pique towards Jung for his organizational irresponsibility was soon subsumed in a monumental row with his Viennese colleagues. Freud had decided that the way to improve the image of psychoanalysis and get a better class of contributions for the journal was to move the centre of gravity to Zürich and to appoint Swiss analysts to the positions of president and secretary of a new International Psychoanalytic Association. However, when Ferenczi presented Freud's detailed proposals, both their content and the Hungarian's tactless way of handling things gave grave offence. When Ferenczi said that Freud had stood alone until the coming of Jung and the Zürichers, the Viennese felt they were in the position of the workers in the parable of the vineyard, who had laboured all day only to be supplanted by eleventh-hour johnny-come-latelies.[17]

Even greater offence was provided by the absolute 'papal' powers Freud proposed to give Jung, who was to be made president for life with full control over the organization of the association and untramelled right to hire, fire and disbar. Jung, in effect, was given a licence to indulge his dislike of the Viennese. As Freud's early biographer Fritz Wittels remarked, 'Freud behaved like the Old Man of the primitive horde – was simultaneously ruthless and simpleminded.'[18]

In dismay at the attempted *coup d'état*, the Viennese under Adler and Stekel held a private breakaway meeting at the Grand Hotel to discuss what to do. This strategy was thwarted when Freud got wind of the meeting and put in a sudden personal appearance himself. He harangued the Viennese at length, making the point he had stressed repeatedly to Abraham two years earlier, that as Jews they could not take the gospel of psychoanalysis to the gentiles, and that this could be done only by Jung and the Swiss.[19] He spoke of his many enemies and, melodramatically tugging at his coat by the lapels, said, 'They won't even leave me a coat to my back. The Swiss will save us – will save me, and all you as well.'[20]

A compromise was hammered out. Jung was made president, though not for life but only for two years, while Riklin was appointed secretary; the official seat was to be where the president was, which in this case meant Zürich for the next two years; and Freud withdrew from presidency of the Vienna Society in favour of Adler. To counterbalance Jung's editorship of the *Jahrbuch*, Freud announced the founding of a monthly journal, the *Zentralblatt für Psychoanalyse*, to be edited by Adler and Stekel; each of the journals had the absolute power of veto over contributors. But by clever manoeuvring, Freud ended up as the director of the *Zentralblatt*, thus neutralizing its potential importance as a forum for Viennese dissidents like Adler and Stekel. He had cunningly insinuated that without his name on the masthead, the journal would not find a publisher.

The compromise decision forced on Freud turned out to be a stroke of luck for him in view of his later conflict with Jung. As Ronald Clark has remarked, 'Since Freud himself was to play the leading part in eventually driving Jung from the movement, the compromise forced on him in Nuremberg was an example, albeit unwitting, of a man's friends saving him from himself. But for them, Jung might have ruled supreme for more than half a century until his death in 1961.'[21]

All that lay in the future. For the moment Freud could see only his victory over Adler and Stekel. The one cloud over Freud's achievement was the singular rancour evinced by the Viennese towards Jung. Freud was well pleased with his labours and later told Ferenczi that the success of the Nuremberg conference was 'unquestionable'.[22] Jung returned to Zürich suffused with the spirit of Freudianism. He wrote to an unknown confidant to repudiate his praise for Christianity written to Freud in February.[23]

Back in Küsnacht Jung spent an uncomfortable nine months mired in psychoanalytical politics. His main anxiety was that he could persuade almost nobody to join the International Psychoanalytic Association. Part of the problem was that he was the worst conceivable choice to head such an organization, being deficient in organizational and administrative skills and primarily interested in his own research. He tended to pass the buck of day-to-day correspondence to Riklin, but Riklin was even more hopeless as an administrator and 'solved' the Association's problems by simply not answering letters. The general perception arose that the Association was a sectarian shambles, thus detaching it even further from the general scientific community. Meanwhile the movement's rivals were making significant progress, as when Edouard Claparède and Pierre Janet persuaded the Sixth International Congress of Psychology in 1909 that it was necessary to distinguish the subconscious – a clinical concept – from the unconscious – a philosophical concept.[24]

To his lack of organizational skills Jung added a bull-like stubbornness when what was most needed was a fine hand in diplomacy. The disastrous consequences of Jung's rift with Bleuler now became apparent, though, in fairness to Jung, it must be stressed that the psychoanalytic movement's problems with the Burghölzli director were overdetermined. In the first place there was Bleuler's almost visceral antipathy for Stekel – a quality shared by Jung himself. Instead of building bridges to the wider scientific community, psychoanalysis was tearing itself apart with the rift between Swiss and Viennese, symbolized by the fact that Jung, Bleuler, Maeder and Binswanger all refused to publish in the *Zentralblatt*.[25]

Yet not all the blame for the alienation of the Swiss could be piled on Stekel and Adler. Jung and Freud themselves were partly to blame for their own willingness to indulge in scapegoating. Not wishing to upset the crown prince, Freud backed Jung in his vendetta against the Munich school of Emil Kraepelin and particularly *his* crown prince, Max Isserlin, an old enemy and the man who in 1906 had ridiculed the word-association test. Jung proposed, and Freud agreed, that Isserlin be barred from membership of the International Association.

Kraepelin then got on to Bleuler and so bent his ear that he and the

Burghölzli staff in retaliation held the Association at arm's length. Jung came to suspect that Bleuler would never join an association of which he was president. His successor at the Burghölzli, Hans Maier (who would eventually succeed Bleuler as director in 1927), informed him that he and his ideas were right out of favour in the hospital. Jung intuited that the real reason for Bleuler's displeasure was not so much Jung's resignation from the Burghölzli, or even Freud's failure to visit him during his stay at the hospital, as Jung's abandonment of teetotalism following the trip to the USA in 1909.[26]

Jung's frustration would have been compounded had he known that other Freudians were sniping at him behind his back, encouraged no doubt by the gloom Freud expressed about the 'rebels' in Zürich – a curious way to describe Bleuler, Binswanger and the other Burghölzli staff.[27] Ferenczi suggested to Freud that Jung was secretly annoyed that he had consented to the foundation of the rival journal *Zentralblatt*.[28] Ernest Jones, whose relations with Jung, initially friendly, were becoming more and more strained, hinted to Freud that, after his sudden abscondment to Chicago just before the Nuremberg conference, Jung was not really someone who could be fully relied on.[29] In some perplexity Freud wrote to the one Swiss he could fully trust, Oscar Pfister, asking for his help in rallying allies in Zürich: 'I hope you agree with the Nuremberg decisions and will stand loyally by our Jung. I want him to acquire an authority that will later qualify him for leadership of the whole movement.'[30]

Perhaps Jung intuited or otherwise became aware of Freud's unease, for on 17 June he wrote to ask for his 'forgiveness' and 'patience'. Freud wrote back at once to say these were inappropriate words to describe their relationship.[31] Matters scarcely improved that summer. At a meeting of Forel's International Society for Medical Psychology and Psychotherapy in August the bumptious Freudians merely succeeded in getting backs up. Jung confided to Freud that the Association seemed to frighten people and Freud acknowledged in reply that its foundation had been a mistake attributable to his own impatience.[32] By autumn Jung was blustering again, his letters full of bile about Bleuler. The word 'ambivalence' had recently been coined by Bleuler, and Jung remarked that this was no accident, since it described the man perfectly. A little later he implied that negotiating with Bleuler was like swimming through treacle, though he thought the contents of a Bleuler dream, recently divulged to him, held the key to his behaviour.[33]

Freud gently suggested that it was worth a sacrifice to net Bleuler for the Association and advocated 'wait and see' policies rather than the full frontal Jungian aggression.[34] But he was beginning to appreciate that real ideological and doctrinal problems were giving Bleuler pause; it was not just the farrago of peevish personal points alleged by Jung.[35] Direct correspondence with Bleuler confirmed the Burghölzli director's doubts and hesitations. Bleuler told Freud that for him psychoanalysis was simply one theory among many, that it was not a matter of life or death for him (as it was for Freud) whether it survived, and therefore he was not prepared to sacrifice everything for its advancement.[36]

There were a few moments of consolation for Jung during this summer and autumn of discontent. He continued to work away diligently on his mythological studies, often neglecting his presidential duties in the process, and his interest in the occult received a fillip from two different directions. In 1910 the French painter Cornillier read Jung's thesis on Hélène Preiswerk and was thus able to make sense of strange occurrences featuring his nineteen-year-old model Reine. The girl began to pour out Preiswerk-like mediumistic utterances and Cornillier, armed with his knowledge of Jung, understood at once that this masked Reine's secret passion for him. Years later Henri Lenormand put the episode to good effect in his play *L'Amour Magicien*.[37]

Jung also came across more fantasy material of the Helen Smith/Hélène Preiswerk type in the fantasies of Miss Frank Miller, a young American woman who in trances and visions poured out utterances that seemed to contain archaic residues crucial for the interpretation of myths.[38] He lectured on Miss Miller in May 1910 in the Swiss city of Herisau, and predicted that she would soon suffer schizophrenic breakdown (he was wrong as it turned out, for although she was hospitalized for a short while she avoided breakdown). Although his presentation won great applause from the audience at Herisau, it was a different story when he confided his findings to Freud. While Jung, himself in an almost trance-like state, waxed lyrical about the role of the hero in mythology and his self-sacrificial role, Freud's rejoinders were harsh: in particular he scouted Jung's idea that modern dreams were the residue of ancient modes of thought, making the simple but effective point that the Ancients, who lived among the everyday reality of this 'mythology', had dreams themselves.[39]

But Freud tempered his severe criticism of Jung's theories with many flattering personal observations, proving the truth of Homans's theory that at this stage of the relationship Freud was in 'narcissistic transference', that he saw in Jung an idealized version of himself.[40] And there were other compensations for Jung. As the work of the Association piled up, he took more and more to his sailing boat on Lake Zürich. Eventually a reluctant Ludwig Binswanger joined the Association, so that Jung was able to report a complement of fifteen members.[41] Additionally, in August he wrote one of his typically sarcastic and hyperbolic letters, suggesting that it would take 1,500 years for psychoanalysis to be launched, because of people's stupidity.[42] This completely charmed Freud and was enough to convince him that Jung was finally proving himself worthy of his mantle[43]; he wrote to Binswanger, 'I wish I lived closer to Jung in order to support him in his youthful authority on which much of the future seems to depend.'[44]

Jung's greatest source of consolation in 1910 came from his brilliant young assistant Johann Jakob Honegger, whom he regarded as his 'son', in the same way that Freud was his 'father'; the generational tie was made explicit when Jung sometimes referred to Freud as Honegger's 'grandfather'. Honegger came to the Burghölzli at the beginning of 1909, just as Jung was on the way out, but made such an impression that Jung immediately adopted him as a protégé. The twenty-four-year-old Honegger had a good pedigree for psychiatric work since his father, also a psychiatrist, had been Adolf Meyer's teacher.[45] However, there was an ominous side to this illustrious parentage, since Honegger senior had died at forty-five of brain disease in 1896. His son, born in Zürich, had been a leading light in the Zofingia fraternity ten years after Jung's heyday and in the course of his university career met his fiancée Hélène Widmer, a pretty and musically gifted girl from a highly respected bourgeois family.[46]

In mid-June 1909 Honegger sent Freud an unsolicited letter containing a lengthy psychoanalysis of the master. Freud took this in good part and told Oskar Pfister, 'Honegger has fathomed me well; the sample shows that the young man has a gift for psychoanalysis.'[47] It has been convincingly demonstrated from documentary evidence that the analysis of Freud was really Jung's work, since he discussed meticulously with Honegger the details of the psyche of his 'grandfather'.[48] Later in 1909 Jung referred twice to his brilliant young aide when writing to Freud. Freud was impressed by everything he heard about Honegger; he stressed how important it was that Jung bring this precocious talent to Nuremberg with him.[49]

While Jung was on his controversial flying visit to Chicago in March, Honegger and Emma Jung carried the administrative load for the Nuremberg conference preparations. Honegger was keen to be taken on as Jung's personal assistant on a regular basis but Jung, pleading the expense of paying his salary, secured him a junior position instead in the sanatorium at Territet, east of Montreux. Freud thought this a great mistake.[50]

There is a mystery about Jung's behaviour towards Honegger, which has never been satisfactorily cleared up. The usual explanation is that in the course of his analysis of the young man Jung found himself in the grip of a virulent 'counter-transference', and that he wished to get rid of Honegger, his 'son', since the unconscious wish of parents to destroy their children can be just as strong as the Oedipal rage of children towards parents.[51] A milder version of this thesis – and one espoused by Freud himself – was that because of the countertransference Jung saw his own deficiencies in Honegger with such limpid clarity that he treated him with especial harshness, nagged him for laziness and exhorted him to work harder. But in view of Jung's notorious promiscuity, it is legitimate to ask whether the solution may not be simpler. Why did he initially oppose Honegger's engagement to Hélène Widmer and why the sudden *volte-face* as evinced in his letter to Freud in May 1910, just after he had banished Honegger to the Territet sanatorium: 'Honegger's fiancée is doing valuable work as my secretary. I judged her much too unfavourably, she is an excellent worker . . .'?[52]

Jung now felt called upon to give a more extended explanation for his banishment of Honegger. He explained to Freud that he wanted to keep the young man in Territet until he had completed his doctoral dissertation simply because he was too inclined to work by flashes of inspiration and therefore neglected the hard reading and sheer studious slog needed to become a first-class analyst. This explanation proved inadequate for Freud, who reproved Jung sternly for his harsh treatment of Honegger. Freud followed up ten days later with a scarcely veiled reproof of Jung's 'money-complex', dismissing as bogus Jung's selfish motive for despatching Honegger to Territet. He suggested that Jung could have been more generous and less concerned with expense since he was both independently wealthy and had made a lot of money on his recent trip to America.[53] This was tactful: the obvious point to make was that Jung was married to an immensely rich woman.

Jung conceded that Freud was right, and entered the lame excuse that Honegger had already accepted the appointment at Territet before Freud suggested that he be taken on as a permanent assistant. He then invited Honegger to go into private practice with him as partner in Zürich; Honegger immediately asked his close university friend Walter Gut (later professor of theology and rector of Zürich University) to help him find a three-roomed unfurnished flat with telephone in Zürich. Why this plan fell through is unclear, but it is known that Honegger deputized for Jung in his practice during his fortnight's military service from 14–29 August.

There is a gap in the evidence between August and November 1910, but something serious evidently happened to sour the relationship between Jung and Honegger, for on 7 November Jung wrote to Freud with a lament about the young man's worries, mentioning that his engagement to Hélène Widmer had been broken off.[54] Again the trail goes cold, but it is clear that the plan to take Honegger into partnership did not work out, for on 1 February Honegger took up a junior post at the Rheinau Hospital. Apparently, he felt a wretched failure who had not been deemed worthy to be Jung's assistant, and his mood darkened perceptibly and extraordinarily when he learned that he was about to be called up for military service. His Rheinau colleague Karl Gehry pointed out that for a doctor military duties were easy and that, in any case, Jung could sign a certificate of exemption for him. Honegger did not act on this suggestion and as 29 March, the day of his military induction, neared he became more and more depressed. On 28 March Honegger injected himself with a fatal dose of concentrated morphine solution.

Jung's initial reaction was brutally glib. He suggested that Honegger's motive was to avoid psychosis and that he could not live except by the pleasure principle.[55] Freud was deeply sympathetic and refrained from blaming Jung in any way.[56] When Jung continued to brood on his failure to see what was wrong with Honegger, Freud reassured him that Honegger could not have been saved, whatever discoveries Jung had managed to make about his paranoid delusions.[57]

What is the truth about Honegger? It is clear that he had severe mental problems and that he did consult Jung about a seven-day loss of reality. The Jungian analyst Aldo Carotenuto alleges that Honegger was psychotic and could not have been saved by Jung.[58] An excellent and balanced witness, the Burghölzli analyst Herman Nunberg, confirmed the quasi-psychotic delusions and pointed out that it was from Honegger's delusions that Jung got his later much-touted idea about the 'solar phallus'.[59] Yet not all critics are so charitable. Hans Walser says firmly, 'We can discard as unlikely the hypothesis of evading an incipient psychosis, which was Jung's first reaction.' Walser is even harsher on Jung's letter to Freud dated 19 April 1911, his apologia for the Honegger affair: 'At first in this letter Jung shows himself as a loving father who wishes his son to survive under all circumstances; then, in the following phrases, we see the demanding father who, although he loves his son, intends such greatness for him that he would rather see him dead than failed.'[60]

Freud's restraint needs stressing, for this was the third time in successive years, to his knowledge, that a Jung protégé had come to grief: first there was Gross, then Spielrein, and now Honegger. The Gross and Honegger cases seemed to bear out an unsavoury pattern: in the first case it was Jung failing with a 'brother' and in the second with a 'son'. It seems clear that Freud, his reassuring words notwithstanding, felt that Jung had failed Honegger badly, both in his analysis and by not taking him into partnership, and it is surely no accident that, after pondering the early failures in the Jung–Honegger relationship (but before the final Rheinau episode and suicide), Freud wrote a seminal paper on the dangers of 'wild analysis';[61] from this germ came the idea that it was necessary for all analysts to go through a training analysis.

In fairness to Jung, one must also place the Honegger tragedy in the context Freud referred to when he wrote that psychoanalysis wore out quite a few men (and, he could have added, women). The early years of the movement were notable for the high rate of suicide among analysts: apart from the two best-known examples, Honegger and Stekel, all the following highly talented individuals died by their own hand: Paul Federn, Viktor Tausk, Herbert Silberer, Karl Schroffer, Monroe Meyer, Martin Peck, Max Kahane, Karin Stephen, Eugenia Sokolnicka and Tatiana Rosenthal.

Nevertheless, it is abundantly clear that the full story of the Honegger tragedy has not yet been told, and in particular one would like to know the details of the three-way relationship between Jung, Honegger and Hélène Widmer. Jung's dealings with Honegger's fiancée seem particularly germane, for in 1910 Jung's polygamous career reached its apogee; at one time he was in concurrent contact with no less than five present or former mistresses.

First there was the Fräulein Aptekmann about whom Jung had earlier warned Sabina Spielrein. Then there was Martha Boddinghaus of Munich, an enthusiast for Jungian psychology, who later attended conferences and published papers in her own right. Most long-lasting of this crop of mistresses was Maria Moltzer, a year older than Jung, the daughter of the owner of the Dutch distillery Bols, who became a nurse at the Burghölzli in protest against alcoholic abuse. Jung had a particularly high opinion of Maria Moltzer and trained her as a lay psychotherapist. In the summer of 1910 the two mistresses staged a struggle for power to see who would assume the position of 'first hetaira'. Moltzer won and Boddinghaus took a private post with a rich American woman in Zürich. Jung later 'squared' her by introducing her to his close friend, the Zürich businessman Hermann Sigg, whom she married.[62]

Yet even while Jung juggled these competing claims for his favours, Sabina Spielrein reentered his life. During 1909 and the first half of 1910 Bleuler had been supervizing Spielrein's doctoral thesis on schizophrenia but, because of the direction in which her ideas were taking her, he handed over to Jung in the summer of 1910 after Spielrein complained to Jung that he (Bleuler) was seriously deficient as an analyst. The carnal relationship had by now changed into intellectual partnership, with the increasingly confident Spielrein now seeing herself as Jung's rival and competitor. Her ideas on the relationship of sexuality to death (sometimes wrongly said to be similar to Freud's 'death instinct') were certainly original, and she fretted suspiciously that Jung, whom she knew to be an opportunist, might steal them.[63]

Jung managed to schedule a reunion between a two-week sailing holiday on Lake Constance from 24 July to 6 August and his military service from 14 to 29 August.[64] Jung then departed for military service and continued his travels at the end of the fortnight. He went to Paris and then crossed via Calais–Dover to London for a quick consultation. He suggested returning via the Hook of Holland so as to meet Freud, then also on the road, Paris-bound, in the

Netherlands. He did in fact cross to the Hook, but his letter to Freud, dated 31 August, arrived too late, for on that very day Freud set out with Ferenczi for an extended trip to Paris, Rome and Sicily.[65]

Spielrein's state of mind when separated from the man with whom she was infatuated becomes clear from an examination of the diary entries during August and September when she was with her parents in Berlin and Kolberg. She confessed to 'gruesome loneliness', 'yearning for love', and 'fear of emotional atrophy', and took to looking at herself naked to the waist in the mirror, with the curtains left slightly open. Her diary records that she still wanted to be Jung's guardian angel and spirit of inspiration.[66]

When Jung got down to reading Spielrein's thesis he got something of a shock, for the main subject on whom Spielrein had based her data on schizophrenia – her patient – was a mentally deranged but highly educated Protestant woman whose husband was a compulsive philanderer. According to Spielrein, in a surely diaphanous piece of transference, her 'patient' could not stop talking about Dr Jung and dropped such asides as 'Dr Jung, who has prostituted me, is a friend of the Mormons – he wants to get divorced once a year.'[67] Not surprisingly, Jung had mixed feelings about the thesis. In one letter he said that Spielrein's work had thrown him into raptures, but in a second missive he complained grumpily that Spielrein did not cite his works enough and seemed to be trying to make fun of him.[68]

Yet when the two of them were reunited on 20 September, everything went well. Jung suggested that they work through the dissertation together with a view to publishing it in the *Jahrbuch* and, seeing at last the chance of a recruit for the International Psychoanalytic Association, suggested that she join. She agreed, but continued in a state of rare emotional turmoil.[69] Jung and Spielrein next met on 24 September. She had arrived late for the ferry to Küsnacht and, running to catch it, had skinned her knee, torn her skirt and bent her umbrella. Jung laughed with her about this mishap and urged her not to go about fulfilling 'anxiety desires'. But the encounter turned sour when Spielrein said something that wounded Jung in his vanity.

But there was worse in store. Three days later, on Tuesday 27 September, Spielrein was turned away from the door of Jung's house with no explanation. Only in the evening did she discover that Emma Jung had given birth to a daughter, Marianne. Jung telephoned her to set the appointment back to the 29th, and the two-day postponement proved worthwhile for Spielrein, for her diary entries once more speak of Jung as a lover. She went on to say that their talk on the link between sex and death had drawn them closer and closer together until it was clear to Spielrein that Jung was her true soul mate.[70]

Jung wrote to Freud on 29 September to express his enthusiasm for Spielrein's work, confirming as it did his own present work on the redemptive role of the sun-hero in the fantasies of Miss Frank Miller; curiously, Jung said nothing about the birth of his daughter, leading one to speculate that it was Sabina not Emma who was uppermost in his mind at the time and, possibly, knowing his dislike of the increase in 'brats', that he even felt a certain distaste for Emma.[71] Certainly it was passing strange that he should have chosen the exact moment of the birth of a daughter to decamp for another bicycle tour of northern Italy with his friend Wolf Stockmayer, a Zürich physician. Before he left he must have had second thoughts about the last session with Spielrein, for he sent her a message that they could never be lovers again. A distraught Spielrein wrote in her diary of finding some other father for 'Siegfried' or, if that was impossible, taking cyanide.[72]

The bicycle tour of northern Italy was a curious affair, inspired in the first place by Freud's trip to Sicily and Rome. Like Freud, Jung began with a deep 'complex' about Rome but, unlike him, never mastered it. A major running motif in Freud's *The Interpretation of Dreams* (written before he had visited Rome) is the idea of Rome as supreme prize, at once impossibly distant and vaguely menacing; Freud was simultaneously dying to see the Eternal City and strangely paralysed by feelings of inhibition and foreboding.[73] In his early forays into Italy he got no farther south than Lake Trasimene, scene of the great victory by Hannibal, Freud's schoolboy hero. It was Hannibal's fate to glimpse Rome from a distance, like Moses's view of the Promised Land from the Pisgah. Hannibal, like Freud, was a Semite; the conquest of Rome therefore symbolized the triumph over anti-Semitism; it also represented other Oedipal wishes, adumbrated, Freud thought, by the ancient oracle given to the Tarquins that whoever first kissed the mother would be ruler of Rome. In a word Rome was a potent symbol, representing both erotic and aggressive wishes.[74]

In 1901 Freud finally conquered his deep psychic inhibition about

Rome, and was rewarded by finding it a 'divine city', by far his favourite city in the world; he revisited it four times later in his career. Jung, however, was stranded in his Rome-fearing limbo for life. In August, hearing of Freud's trip there with Ferenczi, he wrote that his unconscious did not yet permit him to visit Rome.[75] In fact Jung never did go to Rome, though he did manage, in 1913, to visit Pompeii and the Naples area. He always protested that he could not understand how people could visit the Eternal City as casually as they would visit London or Paris. Even the trip to Pompeii taxed his unconscious.[76]

Yet though Jung limited his 1910 trip to northern Italy, where he would be safe from the occult emanations of Rome, he soon found himself in the grip of the uncanny. In Verona he found a statue of Priapus that had a powerful appeal for him, and he got Stockmayer to take a number of photographs of it. A snake bites Priapus's penis while Priapus smiles and points to the snake – one libido symbol attacking another – thus confirming the Jung–Spielrein view of 'sexuality destroying itself' which had aroused Freud's ire in June.[77] Jung also found some ancient mystic inscriptions which he felt he could decode with the help of his recent theories, and began to grow confident that he was getting to the heart of ancient paganism.

The cycling itinerary was to have taken Jung and Stockmayer from Verona to Lake Maggiore, where they would pedal along the lake through Tessin as far as Faido before taking the train for Zürich. But when they reached Arona on Lake Maggiore Jung had a dream so disturbing that he at once abandoned his tour and took the train home. He seemed to be in the company of a number of distinguished spirits from earlier ages, and was asked questions in Latin which he could not answer. Feelings of humiliation woke him up, and he felt so gloomy about the questions he could not answer – and thus by implication all the unanswered questions in his proposed book on mythology – that he felt compelled to return to his studies at once.[78]

What particularly disturbed Jung was that the dream suggested there might be survival after death, and he connected it with the recurring dreams he had had after 1896, when his father appeared to him, asked to return home and seemed not to know that he was dead. A further worrying hint from the dream was that he might have been unwarrantably neglecting the occult for psychoanalysis.

Later he concluded that the distinguished spirits were his forefathers asking him a question that could not be answered in their time but only in the twentieth century. Moreover, all the evidence suggested that the souls of the dead knew only what they knew at death; so far from bringing back superior wisdom from the 'other side', they came back to the living to find things out.

Jung arrived back in Zürich on 16 October and three days later had another session with Spielrein; the occasion was notable for a failure to communicate, since Spielrein was trying to resolve her 'Siegfried-complex', while Jung's preoccupation now was his own 'Jewish-complex'. Her diary shows Jung in mystical vein following his Italian experiences.[79]

In line with his new-found wisdom about mythology, Jung on his return from Italy tried to get Spielrein to think of 'Siegfried' as a pointer to ancient spiritual wisdom, not frustrated sexual longing. Spielrein's diary entries chart the success of this manoeuvre. Jung told her that he loved her both because her thoughts mystically paralleled his and for her magnificent, proud character, but said he could not marry her because he was essentially a typically Swiss philistine.[80] Spielrein's last meeting with Jung was on 23 November 1910 and in a huge diary entry three days later she wrote *finis* to the relationship. She took her finals on 16–19 January 1911, received top honours in psychiatry, and quit Zürich on the evening of her last exam. Her envoi was optimistic and she expressed confidence that she had put Jung behind her.[81] But a month later her diary entries were recording great pain and sacrifice. Jung's strategy of trying out his new spiritual perspective on Spielrein's 'Siegfried complex' had appeared to work brilliantly, but the truth was that it worked as long as she could be in his company; when this was no longer the case, she began to grow seriously depressed again.

Spielrein had heroically accepted that she and Jung would henceforth have to be soul mates alone, being fully aware of his carnal affair with Maria Moltzer, which was still going strong in 1912.[82] She might not have bowed her head with such equanimity if she had known that Jung had already bestowed the mantle of *femme inspiratrice* elsewhere.

In 1910 he acquired a new patient – a young woman of twenty-two suffering near-schizophrenic breakdown after the death of her beloved father. Antonia Wolff was born in Berne, the daughter of an aristocratic and successful businessman who had married a woman twenty years his junior. He had an affinity for Japan and had lived there for twenty years, but Antonia had read literature at Zürich University. In Jungian terms, she had unfinished business involving the need to encounter aspects of paternity her real father had been unable to provide.[83] She was introduced by Oscar Pfister, from whom she had taken religious instruction, and Jung once again proved that he was an inspired short-term healer of the feminine psyche though, as with Spielrein, he was unable to provide consolation in the long run.

Reconstructing the details of the affair between Jung and Antonia Wolff is very difficult, for Jung later burned all his correspondence with her; it is unlikely that a cache of documents to rival the Spielrein papers will ever surface. Yet it is probable that the liaison followed on logically from the treatment, as was often the case with Jung's female patients, and was well under way by late 1910; certainly by the time of the Weimar Conference in September 1911 it was widely known that Jung and Wolff were lovers of long standing. Antonia was a very different type of woman from Jung's conquests hitherto. In the first place she was very conscious of being a patrician, an *haute Suisse* from a family that could trace its origins to the Middle Ages.

In addition to feeling patrician, Antonia Wolff looked the part. She was always immaculately dressed, something that was to be particularly noticeable in the Jungian gatherings of the 1930s when a slovenly sartorial appearance was the norm. First impressions of her invariably put people off, for she seemed stern, aloof, reserved and forbidding; she was all of those things, but also genuinely and immensely shy. There was something exotic in her dark, brooding beauty, so that someone once described her as a black pearl; she had wide dark eyes that looked as though they could see in the dark and delicate bone structure.[84] Highly intelligent and erudite, like most of Jung's serious mistresses, she eventually became an analyst herself, and her oracular utterances were said to be only slightly less labyrinthine than those of Jung. She had a younger sister who married the psychoanalyst Hans Trub, at one time a member of the circle round Jung.

By the end of 1910, then, Jung's life was again in turmoil. He had intimate relations with some half dozen women, had failed signally as president of the International Association and as mentor to Honegger, was riddled by Italian complexes and dreams, and was engaged in a study of mythology that seemed to presage a head-on clash with Freud. Having told Freud that he intended to publish his work on the Miller fantasies in successive half-issues of the *Jahrbuch*, he lectured on the material in Zürich on 16 December, reporting to Freud that the lecture was a great success.

By now Freud had decided that the bruiser tactics of the 'crown prince' would never persuade Bleuler to join the International Association and that he would have to lend a hand himself. He arranged a meeting with Bleuler on Christmas Day at the Park Hotel, Munich, and, killing two birds with one stone, suggested that Jung arrive at the same hotel the following day to discuss these negotiations. Freud was prepared for a bumpy ride with Bleuler, for the Burghölzli director had told him in October how much he deplored the intolerance and witchfinding mentality of the Association.[85] But the two men got on extremely well personally – they always did – and as a result of the meeting Bleuler promised to join the Association two weeks later, and did so.[85]

There was now a slight change in plans, for Bleuler stayed overnight and had another talk with Freud in the morning. He eventually left at twelve-fifty and Freud, who had had a disturbed night, caught up on his sleep until five-fifteen when Jung arrived at the hotel for a briefing. Freud coached him on how to behave towards Bleuler and, to soften the blow, asked Jung's advice on how to proceed with Adler, whose deviant views of psychoanalysis were threatening a 'Reformation' within the movement. Jung's view was that Bleuler and Adler were both nuisances who did not understand the implications of libido theory; Freud, however, reiterated his view that Adler was simply another Fliess, and that both men exhibited the same paranoia.[87]

Freud was not in good health when he met Jung, complaining of headaches and memory lapses – the result, it later transpired, of a gas leak in his study.[88] Fearing that his general health might be in decline, Freud gave Jung fatherly advice on his conduct as president of the Association. Jung deferred to the father and made a number of shrewd observations that delighted Freud, for he wrote to Ferenczi in euphoria: 'Jung was again magnificent and did me a lot of good . . . Now, don't be jealous, but take Jung into your calculations. I am convinced more than ever that he is the man of the future.'[89] 1910 had been a tough year, but Jung was still clearly the crown prince of the psychoanalytic movement.

Chapter Ten

THE RIFT DEEPENS

During the early months of 1911 Jung, as president of the Association and the supposed administrator, devoted himself almost entirely to the studies which would eventually be published in English as *Symbols of Transformation*, while Freud was taken up with further serious episodes of psychoanalytical politics. The problem this time was Adler and Stekel. Freud's concern was that Adler and Stekel were backsliding so far in their wild theories that they would soon be denying the existence of the unconscious altogether. Stekel was small beer: although a talented, erudite and ingenious critic and polymath, he had revolting intellectual habits. If he could not find the evidence he needed to buttress one of his ideas, he invented it, and the cohorts of his imaginary patients exhibiting whatever symptom was relevant to the particular matter under discussion became legendary. It was not surprising that in the end Freud was referring to Stekel to his intimates as a 'pig' and a 'swine'.[1]

Adler was a more serious figure altogether, and Freud's invariable bracketing of him with Stekel was not entirely fair. But it was true that he was developing theories in which the unconscious, and indeed sexuality itself, seemed to play no part. A key Adlerian idea was that of 'compensation' or 'organ inferiority'. When a human body possesses, say, a defective kidney, the other, sound, kidney takes over most of the work and compensates. A similar process of compensation went on with other organs: at the limit the 'inferiority complex' triggered by being substandard in some physical department would transfer into the psyche; hence the well-known correlation, observable in the case of Napoleon, Stalin, Hitler, Mussolini, Franco and others, between being short of stature and the exercise of dictatorial power. In the end Adler came to see the will to power, activated by 'organ inferiority', as the key human instinct; sexual libido, on this view, was a mere sub-species of this general lust to dominate.

As Adler's statements on this subject became more and more overt, an increasingly troubled Freud confided his anxieties to Jung and his fear that Adler would turn out to be another Fliess.[2] The tone of the correspondence between Jung and Freud in January 1911 is instructive. While Jung, immersed in his mythological speculations, wanted to talk about the implications of Part Two of Goethe's *Faust*, Freud was preoccupied with Adler.[3] Not until 8 March did Jung seriously address any of the 'political' issues raised in Freud's letters, and when he did so the irritation at having to suspend his work on mythology showed itself in a characteristic explosion of violent sentiment.[4]

The resolution of the crisis with Adler was the work of Freud and his acolytes in Vienna; Jung played no part. In February 1911 Adler gave up his post as presiding officer of the Vienna Psychoanalytic Society, and Stekel, the vice-president, resigned in sympathy. By June Freud had managed to secure Adler's departure from the editorship of the *Zentralblatt* (Stekel stayed on as editor) and later effected his resignation from the Society. He still had some way to go before he saw the last of Adler and Stekel but by mid-1911 he clearly had the whip hand.

Isolated from the mainstream of psychoanalytic politics by his preference for the study and the library over the committee and the smoke-filled rooms, Jung was also being challenged in his own backyard, and on a number of fronts simultaneously. In Zürich Bleuler's accession to the Association had not brought in the expected troop of acolytes and junior doctors from the Burghölzli – it was almost as though Bleuler were saying that he had joined as a personal mark of his regard for Freud, not for the ideals of the general movement. In 1911 Bleuler brought out his definitive book on schizophrenia, in which he redefined schizophrenia so as to encompass not just the old dementia praecox but other symptoms hitherto thought distinct. Declaring that schizophrenia was not incurable but could be halted or made to retreat, he showed himself a Freudian in his interpretation of the contents of schizophrenic delusions and a Jungian in his 'dynamic' understanding of the illness, with a distinction into primary and secondary symptoms.[5] Since leaving the Burghölzli Jung had lost touch with schizophrenia – his private patients were mainly neurotics – and Bleuler appeared to have stolen a decisive march on him.

But Jung hit back in two ways. Taking Bleuler's key concepts of ambivalence and schizophrenic negativism, he showed that they lent even more weight to Freudianism, since the source of schizophrenic negativism was resistance, and the aetiology of resistance, both in neurosis and schizophrenia, was sexual.[6] Even more original was the brilliant notion derived from his mythological studies – which Freud hailed as a breakthrough idea – that there was a similarity, amounting to correspondence, between the cosmogonies of primitive races and the fantasies of schizophrenics.[7]

To understand how Jung arrived at this idea we need to examine some of the ideas in *Symbols of Transformation*, on which Jung worked so assiduously in the first half of 1911, breaking off only for a research trip to Friedrich Kraus's clinic in Berlin in April, the two-day annual meeting of the German Society for Psychiatry in Stuttgart (21–22 April) and a week's motoring trip with Emma in the south of France. *Symbols* takes as its starting point a situation very like that of Hélène Preiswerk and Helen Smith, but ends by espousing positions totally incompatible with Freudianism.

Once again the spur to Jung's investigations was Théodore Flournoy, for it was Flournoy who first drew attention to the fantasies of Miss Frank Miller and published them.[8] Miss Miller, a young American girl, greatly prone to auto-suggestion, produced three main fantasies, triggered by what Jung would later call 'active imagination' – the technique of allowing the mind to follow whatever fantastic course it takes. While daydreaming during a Mediterranean cruise, Frank Miller 'heard' a poem of three stanzas called 'Glory to God'. Later, while travelling on a train one night, she made up a set of ten verses called 'The Moth and the Sun'. Finally, after an anxiety-filled evening, her active imagination produced a fantasy of an Aztec hero, Chiwantopel. When recording these fantasies, Miss Miller tried to trace their source in her early life or in her reading.[9] It may seem odd that Jung should have erected an entire mythological foundation around the Miller fantasies, but he thought her utterances a vital piece of evidence in a chain linking schizophrenic delusions with mythical motifs. Because she was an introvert, Jung thought, she was able to turn her psychic energy inwards to tap into an archaic residue of motifs and images.

When Jung was publishing papers on schizophrenia at the Burghölzli, the key idea he used was that schizophrenics suffer from regression of the libido. Bearing in mind the delusions of schizophrenics, he now hypothesized that the regressing libido released a kind of symbolic thinking from the archaic level of the mind. Whereas regression was usually thought to lead back into childhood and the realm of the parents (especially the mother), Jung thought it could lead back farther still into an area of archetypal images, no longer connected with the individual's memory but belonging to a stock of inherited ideas, born anew in each individual. These images would typically be of gods, heroes, animals and all the rest of the farrago of typical myth-systems. The guise in which these symbolic figures appeared would depend on the attitude of the conscious mind.[10]

If regression took one into a *symbolic* realm, it followed that the regression of libido might also be symbolic, that an incest-wish denoted, not a literal desire for sexual intercourse with the mother, but a desire for spiritual rebirth. Jung stressed the incest taboo as the key to the transformation of libido into many other symbolic forms. Sexuality as the key notion in the psyche was now under attack from two directions, since not only did regression take one into a symbolic sphere, but the original libido drive itself, it seemed, was not primarily sexual.[11] Jung compared his new conception of libido to Schopenhauer's Will as thing-in-itself, distinct from all concrete manifestations of Will. He also said that it could be conceived as roughly the equivalent of Henri Bergson's *élan vital*, provided one understood it as primarily psychological rather than biological.[12]

Yet there was a two-way traffic with this new libido since, as well as regressing to the 'historical' level, it could also serve a progressive and purposive function. If regression explained schizophrenia, progression could explain neurosis, in that it was the libido's attempt at healing.[13] If this were true, it would make the subjective and symbolic approach of paramount importance, implying that collective symbols (what would later be called archetypal images) could transform libido from a 'lower' into a 'higher' form. 'Canalisation' – a process in some respects similar to Freudian sublimation – became a key notion in understanding the process.[14]

Since the symbols of mythology represent the quest of the psyche, either in failure, regression and schizophrenia, or in 'success', progression and neurosis, it follows that these symbols in turn yield important information about the crucial tasks in life. In the typical myth, the devouring monster that the hero has to slay in order to win the maiden is a metaphor for breaking free from the parental orbit. The knight who kills the dragon is symbolically slaying the father, while the hero's triumph over the she-monster represents the final cutting of the umbilical cord – the cutting adrift from the mother which will enable him to win a bride. This is the symbolic meaning of the treasure motif ('the treasure hard to attain') that underlies so many myths. The converse situation is that of the *puer aeternus* or eternal child (the best known example from modern times is Peter Pan), who shirks life's task and never accepts adulthood. According to Jung, a 'mother-complex' is typically to be found in writers who specialize in fantasies of childhood, and he in later years singled out Saint-Exupéry's *Little Prince* as a classic instance.[15]

It is worth following Jung through his discussion of the three Miller fantasies to see how these ideas work out more concretely. First he demonstrated the analogy between modern fantasies and ancient myths, arguing that they came from the same source. Some of Miss Miller's ideas could have come from books, but others were clearly from sources other than her own experience. To buttress this point, Jung mentioned one of his schizophrenic patients who had a fantasy that the sun possessed a phallus and it was this that caused the winds. Shortly after encountering this fantasy in the Burghölzli, Jung came across a discussion of the cult of Mithras in a book by Albrecht Diederich and encountered the selfsame notion of the phallic sun; both the Mithraists and Jung's patient swore up and down that if you looked closely at the sun, you could see a tube hanging down from the disc. Since Jung's patient was an uneducated Zürich clerk who never read serious books, and Diederich's book was anyway published after the patient had been institutionalized, Jung thought it certain that he had not got the idea from the book, but rather that the Mithraists and the clerk had energized the same archetypal image.[16]

Jung further demonstrated how mythology could shed light on child psychology. His starting point was the well-known similarity between children's fantasies about where babies come from and the magical appearance of babies in fairytales and myths. The usual view was that fairytales were simply childish fantasies transmogrified but Jung argued that children, trying to solve the riddle of the origin of babies, fell into a reverie in which unconscious race memories from the dawn of time floated to the surface.

Jung also argued that Miss Miller, plunging deeper into her introverted state, would encounter a symbol analogous to Flournoy's 'teleological hallucinations' – revelations to people about to commit suicide that life did after all have a meaning. This was the prospective aspect of libido in operation.

This part of the book, first published in the 1911–12 number of *Jahrbuch*, raised no particular Freudian hackles. Ernest Jones, indeed, thought it Jung's best work to date and reported to Freud, 'Jung sweeps over the canvas like a Rubens, you draw with the accuracy and close feeling of a Del Sarto.'[17]

The second and third parts, published in the 1912–13 number, were far more controversial. Here Jung piled Ossa on Pelion of raw erudition and wild speculation. There were learned (or merely would-be learned, said the critics) excursuses on an amazing variety of subjects: classical literature, Longfellow's *Hiawatha*, Rostand's *Cyrano de Bergerac*, *Faust*, the work of Poe and Byron, Shakespeare and Nietzsche, Sanskrit, Hindu and Egyptian myths, Greek and Norse legends, the Bible, the Church Fathers, Mithraism, Gnosticism and Aztec mythology. In the second part of the book Jung used the Miller fantasies and libido theory as the stimulus (or excuse) for a madcap foray into the myths, symbols and practices of Judaic, Hellenic, Eastern and primitive cultures. This was emphatically not scholarship, which requires discipline as well as erudition, but a method of free association allowing us to glimpse Jung's fantasies.

Ostensibly explicating the Miller fantasies, Jung overwhelmed them with his own preconceptions, to the point where a paragraph of the Miller fantasies generates fifty pages of speculations and the entire set of fantasies, a mere fifteen pages long, produces a book of more than five hundred pages. For example, Miss Miller imagined a city of dreams. This would provoke Jung to a discourse on cities in ancient culture and mythology – biblical and Egyptian. Then he noted that cities and women were related but women also represented the 'Mother Earth' principle, and that in turn led him to reflect on the movement of the sun over 'maternal waters'. This triggered a reference to Leo Frobenius's notion of the night-sea journey, which in turn led to Noah's voyage in the Ark; but then, reflecting that journeys were also an expression for the wish to be reborn, he would move on to the Book of Revelation, and so on.[18] Even a sympathetic critic like John Kerr is appalled by the long, rambling, inconsequential twenty-page-long footnotes-in-all-but-name, some of them totally impenetrable.[19]

In the third Miller fantasy the Aztec Chiwantopel, searching for his soul mate, was attacked by a snake which bit him and killed his horse, after which a volcano erupted and an earthquake engulfed him. Snakes in Jungian thought tend to be signs of a mother-complex; both serpents and their near-relations, dragons, are symbolic representations of the fear of the consequences of breaking the incest taboo.[20] But at this point in *Symbols* Jung introduces material that by no stretch of the imagination could be considered to arise organically from the Miller fantasies. He was heavily influenced by the theories of Frobenius concerning sun worship and the stories of mythical heroes swallowed by monsters, who journey through the beast's interior before emerging to start a new life.

In Jungian terms the sun-hero motif depicts the descent of the ego into the well-springs of the libido through the incest barrier. The figure of the hero is central, since the hero is a symbol of the dynamics of the libido. Always the hero is involved in primal conflict with the mother, who tries to devour him, and his heroism consists of breaking free from the regressive libidinal bond between them; for Jung, the drama of the hero symbolizes the renunciation of mankind's universal infantile wish to return to the mother. In Miss Miller's case the fantasy of Chiwantopel had a personal meaning, in that his death symbolized her own failure to separate from her mother. Jung predicted, wrongly as it turned out, that the conflict between Miller's unconscious need to separate from her mother and her inability to do so indicated that, like Chiwantopel, she too would be engulfed by a landslide.

The night-sea journey or *Nekyia* would become one of the most central organizing myths in Jung's entire *oeuvre*.[21] To achieve psychic wholeness, Jung thought, each individual should go on a night sea journey, a symbolic re-enactment of the waxing and waning of the sun, famously achieved in mythology by Jonah in the belly of the whale or Odysseus descending into the Underworld in Book Eleven of the *Odyssey*. Such a journey is necessary, for only through re-entering the mother (in the form of the belly of the whale or whatever is the context of the appropriate myth) can the hero be born again and achieve spiritual rebirth.

In this work Jung broke decisively with Freudianism and its biological notion of libido. For Jung psychosis could be explained as withdrawal from the outer world only if libido meant general psychic energy, which expressed itself through symbols. Sexuality as the explanation for incest-wishes and neurosis was jettisoned. Where Adler had thrown out the unconscious to concentrate on the ego's will to power, Jung appeared to reinforce the notion of the unconscious but at the cost of making it a purely symbolic realm.

It is clear enough that, in writing *Symbols*, Jung was unconsciously exorcising demons. He insisted that Miss Miller took over his own fantasies and became their stage director.[22] Yet the plethora of references, especially in Parts Two and Three, to the 'destructive mother' alert us to the fact that the important woman here is his own mother, not Frank Miller. The incestuous mother who keeps the hero imprisoned in the Underworld recalled all too clearly Emilie Preiswerk and her 'uncanny' powers. By extension, since his mother represented his No. 2 personality, the book was an attempt to come to terms with that personality, but since the 'stage director' was Frank Miller, an inadequate vessel for such a task, the attempt was unsuccessful.

More interesting is the struggle with the father – Freud – and the concern with Judas in *Symbols* is highly significant.[23] However, it is pure myth (in another sense) to suggest that Freud read the work solely as 'Oedipal' rage. Legend has it that when Jung sent Freud his copy of *Symbols*, it came back by return post, unread and with the pages uncut, with the words *Widerstand gegen den Vater* (Resistance to the Father), scrawled across the fly leaf, whereat Jung turned to his wife and said, 'I feel as though I had been thrown out of my father's house.'[24] The sober truth is that Freud read the work very carefully when it was published in two parts in the *Jahrbuch* and kept a copy of the book with Jung's inscription.[25]

All this is to anticipate by a year, but it is necessary to evaluate the book and the responses to it in order to gauge what was going on while Jung was writing so cagily to Freud in the first six months of 1911. He presumably knew where his intellectual journey was headed, and that the destination would make a break with Freud inevitable. Was he hesitating before committing himself to the final break, or was he genuinely uncertain whether an irreparable breach would be the outcome?

As his work on *Symbols* progressed, Jung threw out many a hint that Freud might not entirely like the finished product.[26] But as publication time for the first part approached, his tone in the correspondence became more affable. He confided to Freud that a recent difficult experience with a schizophrenic patient made him aware of his deficiencies when dealing with Honegger. In the same letter there is a mysterious comment thanking Freud for advice (in a missing letter) on his tangled private life.[27]

Yet the most considerable lifeline Jung threw to his relationship with Freud was the offer to help in conquering the kingdom of occultism for psychoanalysis; he confided that he had made a start by plunging into the jungle of astrology.[28] Since Ferenczi was the other analyst most interested in the occult, Freud at once got in touch with him: 'Jung writes that we must also conquer occultism, and requests permission to undertake a campaign in the realm of mysticism. I see that the both of you can't be restrained. You should at least proceed in harmony with each other; these are dangerous expeditions, and I can't go along there.'[29] Ferenczi replied that he thought the fight against occultism premature. He would be willing to collaborate with Jung on the project, but he declined to make the requisite overtures; instead he complained to Freud that it was depressing that two of the leading lights of psychoanalysis could not work together.[30]

That Freud by now shared some of Ferenczi's ambivalence seems indicated by a curious slip Freud made in June when informing Jung that Adler had resigned as editor of the *Zentralblatt*: 'I have got rid of Adler at last,' he announced, a trifle prematurely, but instead of writing *endlich* (at last), he wrote *endlos* (endless), perhaps indicating that all he could expect from his followers was endless trouble, and that the defection of Adler was merely one episode in a long-running saga.[31]

Freud's pessimistic feelings seemed confirmed when Adler triumphantly produced a statement from Jung which expressed regret at his resignation from the editorship. Adler had written to Jung, casually announcing the fact, and Jung had made polite noises of regret, which Freud feared could be used as a wedge to open up further fissures in the movement. He wrote a tart letter to Jung, recommending that he exercise more caution in future. Annoyed both at being gulled and at the reprimand, Jung nevertheless penned an emollient reply, doubtless reckoning that if he had to fall out with Freud it should be on matters of substance, not the picayune matter of Adler's career. He threw in as an excuse tiredness and overwork: he laboured through a six-day week and could then no longer enjoy his day of rest, since he had to spend Sundays recuperating.[32]

Appeased by Jung's apology, Freud wrote a placatory letter which, however, contained a sting in the tail about Jung's taste for money and concomitant liking for America. Jung accepted the reproach meekly and explained his 'money-complex' as overcompensation for the sensation of inferiority he felt whenever he measured himself against Freud.

Although most of his energies were spent on *Symbols*, some portion had necessarily to be spent on his presidential responsibilities, including the organization of the annual conference in the autumn. This administrative duty turned into a nightmare, for no sooner had Jung chosen a venue and made tentative hotel bookings than some section of the movement would find the proposed location impossible for one reason or another: it was too far away, it was too expensive, there were too many tourists there in September, there were no cut-price rail fares, it was not in a sufficiently neutral situation as between Zürich and Vienna, etc. Locarno (on Lake Maggiore), Lugano, Vienna, Nuremberg and Munich were all suggested and vetoed before, finally, a consensus emerged in favour of Weimar.

Having made the final arrangements, Jung set off on 9 August to lecture on psychoanalysis at Claparède's International Congress of Pedagogy in Brussels, where he went, in his own words, 'with a guarantee of safe conduct, like Luther to the Diet of Worms'.[33] In Brussels from 11 to 16 August Jung found the proceedings 'idiotic' and the papers of such low calibre that he played truant from most of the conference and went sightseeing. When the time came for him to speak, he insisted on addressing the conference for an hour instead of the twenty minutes agreed, and successfully appealed for an extension to the audience, over the head of the irate chairman, who made repeated interventions to try to bring the lecture to an end. He then departed for a holiday with Emma in the Bernese Oberland, where he found time to answer Freud's latest letter, expressing eagerness to read the completed work on mythology. Jung's reply, however, was as enigmatic as some of his excursuses in *Symbols*. He even managed to blame his own turbidity on an alleged lack of clarity in Freud's letter.[34]

Once again, as so often in the past, uneasiness expressed in letters was temporarily resolved by face-to-face contact. Freud, who was holidaying in the Dolomites with his wife and Ferenczi, travelled alone from Bolzano to Zürich to meet Jung, and then spent four days as the Jungs' guest at Küsnacht.[35] Also a guest of the Jungs' was James Jackson Putnam from the USA, and Freud, although in depressed mood, spent six hours analysing him: he told Putnam that he was a potential murderer.[36] This was the time Emma Jung first sensed that all was not well between Freud and her husband, for they seemed to make a point of avoiding discussion of their respective mythological projects; Freud was by now well into the study that would eventually see the light of day as *Totem and Taboo*.[37]

On 19 and 20 September parties from Zürich began making the long rail journey to Weimar. Freud, Putnam, and the Jungs travelled up together; Bleuler and eight other Zürichers made their way separately; finally there was Jung's harem, about whose attendance *en bloc* he had boasted to Freud: principally Toni Wolff and Maria Moltzer but also the forty-nine-year-old Beatrice Moses Hinkle, described by Jung as 'an American charmer', married to an Eastwick heir and later to be a leading Jungian analyst in Connecticut. Sabina Spielrein was also supposed to attend, but cried off at the last moment.

The Third Psychoanalytic Congress was held at the Erbprinz Hotel, the best in Weimar; proceedings began at 8 a.m. on 21 September and continued through the next day. Fifty-five persons attended, of whom forty-six posed for a group photograph, Jung considerately crouching so as not to overshadow Freud. Jung and Riklin were re-elected as president and secretary respectively, and the proceedings ran smoothly. According to Jones, the twelve papers read were of a high order and included several classics of psychoanalytic literature.[38] Bleuler delivered a well-received paper on autism. Jung spoke on the similarities between the crucifixion myth and the delusions of a patient at the Burghölzli; Putnam argued that psychoanalysis needed more bolstering from philosophy but backed Jung in the proposition that the myth of the sun-god was an appropriate metaphor for a person's progress through psychoanalysis. Freud spoke briefly to summarize his already published work on the noted English jurist, also an extraordinary paranoiac, Daniel Paul Schreber. He made a favourable reference to Jung's current work: 'Jung had excellent grounds for his assertion that the mythopoeic forces of mankind are not extinct, but that to this very day they give rise in the neuroses to the same psychical products as in the remotest dark ages.'[39]

All now seemed sweetness and light between Jung and Freud, and when someone ventured a criticism that Jung's jokes were coarse, Freud replied, 'It's a healthy coarseness.'[40] Freud's euphoria was doubtless attributable to the final victory won over the Adler–Stekel faction, already foreshadowed at Weimar but actually implemented at Vienna in October. At the first session of the Vienna Psychoanalytic Society for 1911–12, Freud announced that since Adler and three of his supporters had formed an Adlerian group since resigning, this constituted 'hostile competition' and, therefore, that the Adlerians were to be anathematized. Freud's determination to have it explicitly understood that membership of the Adlerian group was incompatible with that of the Vienna Psychoanalytic Society led to six more resignations, but he carried the day.[41] Henceforth there was bitter feuding between the two societies; long-standing friendships came to an end, wives stopped speaking to each other, and couples from opposing camps made a fuss about being seated next to each other at Viennese dinner parties.[42] Some of Freud's critics felt that the way he had removed Adler smacked of the early Church's way with heretics and that his intention was to found a religious sect with strict rules and dogmas, perhaps with a catechism and guidelines for excommunication.[43]

Shortly before leaving for Weimar Jung had again been in touch with Sabina Spielrein. She had by now graduated as a physician and her medical thesis was published in the *Jahrbuch*. She sent her original work on sex and death to Jung as editor and could not refrain from describing it as the product of their love.[44] Jung replied that since the ideas in it were so good, she ought to approach Freud with a view to having the work published as a book.[45] His real motive in passing her onto Freud may have been to keep at arm's length a woman he had had some trouble in jettisoning. But her ideas intrigued him, perhaps, as Kerr suggests, because her work, with its multiple exegeses on death, destruction, sexuality and incest, provides the missing key that made sense of the two unintegrated halves of *Symbols*: 'the two texts, his and hers, adjoin each other like severed halves of a forgotten conversation.'[46]

Immediately after the Weimar conference Jung had to report for a month's military service in the eastern canton of St Gallen, while Freud tarried a while in Weimar, talking to Abraham. Just before he left for the barracks, Jung wrote a long but inconsequential letter to Spielrein.[47] Jung did not heed her request to send an 'open reference' or letter of recommendation, but simply stated that she would be welcome in Freud's Vienna circle, since the master liked her dissertation.

Since Jung had already broken with Spielrein, the reason for his long letter seems elusive. Kerr suggests that the letter indicates Jung's continuing fear that Spielrein might 'spill the beans', but on his own theory there were no beans to spill. If Kerr's thesis of a 'platonic' relationship were to be taken seriously, the very worst that could happen to Jung was that he might be ridiculed for an adolescent 'calf-love' pre-sexual infatuation, in which he and Spielrein played at being mother and father to 'Siegfried'. Kerr is right to suggest that Jung feared Spielrein's indiscretion, but the clear logical inference is that there was something to be indiscreet about.

At the barracks in St Gallen Jung, fresh from his mythological lucubrations, was brought abruptly face-to-face with what he called 'odious corporeality'. He did not mind so much being a medical jack of all trades, treating soldiers for athlete's foot, cutting out their corns and bunions, prescribing for their diarrhoea, colds and insomnia, but he did not relish being a factotum for urino-genital complaints. On one 'phallic parade', known in Army slang as the 'short-arm inspection', he had to pass in review 500 penises. Nonetheless for the first twenty days of his military service Jung had sufficient leisure to reflect even on matters that rarely drew his attention, such as world affairs; he told Freud he heartily approved of the neutrality of the European powers in the war then raging between Italy and Turkey. However, the last ten days of his tour of duty were a different matter entirely: Jung was detailed for a mountain exercise in remote valleys, which left him exhausted.[48]

Freud, meanwhile, now also launched on mythological studies, made soothing noises and reported an insight from his examination of famous couples like Gilgamesh and Enkidu, Romulus and Remus and Quixote and Panza. Pointing to the recurrent motif that one of the 'twins' is always weaker and dies first, he suggested that this might be primitive man's transmogrification of the placenta, for in Sir James Frazer's *The Golden Bough* it was reported that primitives often called the afterbirth brother, sister or twin, and even fed it and took care of it for a while. He ended with an obvious sop, when he conceded there might be such a thing as a phylogenetic memory in the individual, which would help to explain in part the phenomenon of the uncanny.[49] Jung, unfortunately, chose to be tactless in reply by stating baldly that the so-called early memories of childhood were not individual memories but phylogenetic ones. Freud ignored this, and steered the conversation round to the safe topic of the detested Viennese, this time mentioning a feud Stekel was conducting with Viktor Tausk.[50] That he was secretly angry with Jung is clear. In October Magnus Hirschfeld, a German sexologist and an original member of the Berlin Psychoanalytic Society, resigned from the Association. To Jung Freud wrote that this was no great loss.[51] But to Karl Abraham he complained that it was Jung's blustering manner and uncomplimentary remarks about Hirschfeld which were to blame.[52]

At this stage, entirely unknown to Jung, his wife Emma wrote to Ferenczi to say that she was sure there was something wrong between her husband and Freud, partly, she thought, about libido theory but also partly about Jung's impatience with Freud's 'authority'. She asked Ferenczi for advice and requested him not to mention the matter to Freud.[53] Ferenczi, naturally, did just what she had asked him not to, saying that he thought any disillusionment on Jung's part was merely a temporary blip, like the irritation *he* felt with Freud in Sicily in 1910 when they were discussing paranoia and could not agree. Freud advised him to get Emma to write directly to him and wondered whether the letter indicated a rift with Jung or collusion with him.[54] Yet it was somehow typical of the world of Freudian slips that Ferenczi, having consciously ignored Emma Jung's request, should then have compounded this by unconsciously disobeying Freud also. Freud requested that in his reply to Emma Ferenczi should strike all references to libido and occultism. Ferenczi, though, misread 'strike' (*streichen*) as 'touch on' (*streifen*), and so raised the forbidden topics with Emma.[55]

Emma then wrote directly to Freud, reiterating her concern that his relationship with Carl was not all it might be, and stressing that she was willing to do all in her power to put matters right.[56] Freud, who liked Emma, sent her a reassuring letter, but this prompted Emma into a highly indiscreet reply. First she suggested that Freud treat her husband more like an equal than a son, mentioning how anxious Jung was about Freud's likely reaction to the completed work on mythology. Then she went on to suggest that some cynical remarks Freud had made to her on the morning of his arrival at Küsnacht on 16 September were really meant as a coded reference to *her* marriage. Finally, she criticized Freud's general approach to Jung, suggesting that a loosening of the bond might be in everybody's interest.[57]

Although this was well-meaning, Freud bridled at Emma's 'impertinence'. In a lost letter he apparently accused her of megalomania – of overstepping her bounds – and of encouraging Jung to set no store by his (Freud's) opinions. He was also very angry about what he took to be her meddling in the family affairs of the Freud household and her uncalled-for remarks on his children, which he took to mean that they were doomed to degeneracy. Emma apologized abjectly and added a significant sentence, 'Please write nothing of this to Carl; things are going badly enough with me as it is.'[58]

Content with her grovelling, Freud once again sent an emollient letter. Emma replied with fawning gratitude and revealed that Jung now knew about the correspondence, since he had been surprised to see the familiar handwriting on a letter addressed to her; she added that he knew little of its content. The final letter of the series showed Emma seriously depressed about her marriage. She complained that she had no friends, that all visitors to Küsnacht wanted to see Carl and not her, that men ignored her while women, especially the young ones, clustered round her husband.[59]

The references to problems in the marriage and the plethora of women in love with Jung constituted the tip of an iceberg, for in late 1911 there were violent rows between Carl and Emma about his latest mistress, Toni Wolff. One of Jung's other mistresses in a fit of jealousy tipped off Emma that Jung was sleeping with Toni. Taxed with this latest infidelity, Jung admitted it and brazened things out. He explained to Emma, by now well conditioned in Jungspeak, that he needed Toni because of his fragmented 'anima' – which he blamed on his disastrous relationship with his mother. Since Emma alone could not compensate for the emotional scars of his childhood, he had to have Toni as well, so that Emma could play the role of consort while Toni played that of *hetaira*. Naturally Emma kicked against the idea and began by getting Toni dismissed as Jung's research assistant. But Jung was adamant that he had to have his own way, and counter-attacked by insisting that Emma accept a *ménage à trois*. He had earlier threatened to introduce Spielrein into his household but this time, with Toni, he made good his threat. Emma stormed and raged but in the end she had to concede defeat.

The situation was an impossible one for both women; as Paul Stern remarked: 'Jung's affair with Toni might have been less troublesome if he had not insisted on having her as a regular guest for Sunday dinner.'[60] Humiliated in her home, Emma hit back by encouraging her children to be openly rude to Toni, who, shy and reserved as she was, had no defence against their cruel asides. Emma's bitterness turned eventually to stoicism as she realized that Toni was different in kind from all Carl's earlier mistresses, that Jung preferred Toni to her both as bedmate and as intellectual companion; he even compared her poetry to Goethe's. The irony of the *ménage à trois* was that even that form of 'open marriage' did not solve Jung's problems. Not being able to make sexual lover and mother coincide in one woman is a common enough fate for the neurotic male in marriage, but in Jung's case the division of roles did not enable him to achieve integration, and he continued to need other women as well. Neither Toni nor Emma was able to be happy. Caught in a rivalry not of their making, they tried to rationalize it by having regular meetings with Carl Meier, in which each tried to analyse the other – a 'resolution' encouraged by Jung.

Both now and later Toni made sporadic attempts to get Jung to divorce Emma and marry her. Jung always resisted, and with good reason. Part of him was a homeloving Swiss bourgeois, and Emma was in this sense the model wife and mother. Moreover, he knew very well that Toni would never give him the polygamous freedoms Emma allowed him. Most crucially, of course, Emma was rich, and Jung could not live without her fortune. Toni was doomed to be the eternal 'other woman'; a wiser person would have cut and run but Toni seemed forever in Jung's spell, unable either to achieve what she wanted in life or to break out of his orbit.

Even as the crisis with Emma and Toni passed its climax, Jung still continued to have problems with his old love, Sabina Spielrein. Toni Wolff and Emma Jung were both highly intelligent women, but they lacked the spark of genius possessed by Spielrein, and it was this, most of all, beyond any prudential reasons, that made it so hard for Jung to shake loose of her. In Vienna, after the initial contact with Freud, she attended two of the famous Wednesday night meetings but disappointed Freud by saying not a word. To coax her out of her shell Freud asked her to present a short paper at a future meeting, so she wrote to Jung to get the manuscript of her dissertation back. Jung acted badly in not returning the manuscript as requested, absurdly claiming that he had lost her address. He finally sent it off on 13 November, asking for its return as soon as possible.

On 29 November, now armed with her full manuscript, Spielrein addressed the Vienna Society on her thesis that death and destruction were contained in the sexual instinct. Freud in reply launched a very strong attack on Jung's methods, accusing him of using whatever mythological material suited his book, and of a careless and uncritical attitude to sources. In particular he stressed that mythological material could be used as evidence only when it appeared in pure form, not after being sieved and winnowed through other cultural influences. This was the first occasion when Spielrein realized how great was the tension between Vienna and Zürich.[61]

What had happened since Weimar to produce this remarkable downturn in relations? It seems that some time in November, possibly once he discovered that Emma had been writing to Freud, Jung decided to throw off the mask and make clear the ways in which he was no longer a follower of the true faith. In some ways this was merely making manifest what had anyway been latent in the letters from St Gallen, for when Freud stated that children's dreams were exempt from the complex symbolism of adult dreams, Jung by return post reported his daughter's dreams about foreskins. In the same letter he all but threw down the gauntlet by repeating that the early memories of childhood were not individual but phylogenetic.[62]

'The tone of Freud's letters during this period is that of a man fighting desperately against his own and Jung's rage.'[63] This, from Paul Stern, is an accurate summary of the acidulous correspondence during November–December 1911. The first to escalate the conflict was Jung, for in reply to Freud's conciliatory letter of 12 November, he wrote describing him as a dangerous rival.[64] For the time being, Freud ignored the implications of all this, taking a deep breath, as he thought, for the greater good of the psychoanalytic movement. But then came a development that made him think he was merely being foolish in his restraint. The more diplomatically he dealt with Jung, the more assertive, confident and aggressive Jung became. Perhaps that was just bearable, as long as Jung was doing a good job as president of the Association, but news coming in from Zürich made it certain that he had neglected his official duties expressly to spare time for the research that so irritated Freud. On 28 November Freud received a letter from Bleuler to say that he was resigning from the Zürich Psychoanalytic Society because of the fundamentalist 'all or nothing' attitude of psychoanalysis; nevertheless he hoped he and Freud could still be friends.[65]

On the same day a letter arrived from Jung, apologizing for his own mishandling of the situation in Zürich which had led to Bleuler's resignation. In a pre-echo of the later debate over 'lay analysis', Bleuler and Binswanger had objected to the gung-ho enthusiasm of Oscar Pfister and other non-doctors for psychoanalysis, arguing that this brought the dispensation into disrepute. Instead of conciliating the parties in this quarrel, Jung tried to force the Burghölzli assistants, led by Hans Maier, into finally joining the Association by threats of barring all non-members from meetings. Maier complained to Bleuler and Bleuler, exasperated by Jung, sent in his resignation; the plea to Freud to remain personal friends was a pretty broad hint that it was Jung who stuck in his craw. The implication of Bleuler's resignation was that henceforth Binswanger would be sending assistants to train at the Burghölzli without routing them through Jung and the Association.

Even worse was the fact that Jung, bored with committee meetings and keen to get back to his research, had left a meeting of the Zürich Society early, thus enabling a hostile motion to be tabled, to the effect that the Society should hold a meeting of Swiss psychiatrists jointly with Forel's International Society for Medical Psychology and Psychotherapy.[66]

A disappointed Freud wrote to Jung that he was determined to fight on in Zürich even though the Zürich Society had collapsed. Turning to theoretical matters, he took Jung to task for saying that libido equalled any kind of desire, whereas he (Freud) had always made it clear that there were two drives, and only the power behind the sexual one could be called libido. And what did Jung mean by an extension of libido to make it applicable to schizophrenia? Bracketing Jung and Spielrein, he wrote that Fräulein Spielrein's chief defect was that she wanted to subordinate psychology to biology.[67] Jung replied by distancing himself from Spielrein while digging in on libido theory.[68] He also asked for some examples of derivative mythology as opposed to the pure form mentioned by Freud.

Freud replied with an analysis of the Genesis myth. According to him, the Genesis story as it appears in the Bible is a reversal of an original incest myth with Eve as Adam's mother, which would then make sense of the eating of the fruit, connecting it as a marriage rite with the Greek myth of Pluto and Proserpine. The Genesis story we have, claimed Freud, is almost certainly 'a wretched tendentious distortion devised by an apprentice priest.'[69] John Kerr has ingeniously, and convincingly, suggested an allegorical reading for this letter: the wretched priest who wove together two entirely different strands was Jung the apprentice weaving together two different instincts.[70] Moreover, in reality, it was not the woman who had seduced the man, but the man (Jung) the woman (Spielrein). This Freud now knew, since Spielrein had been having analytic sessions with him and had revealed all about 'Siegfried'.[71]

The reasons for anger on both sides are clear. Jung resented Freud's correspondence with Emma and, even more, the fact, increasingly apparent, that Spielrein was now in the Viennese camp. As Bruno Bettelheim pointed out, the letter of 14 November 1911 in which he calls Freud a 'dangerous rival' is classically overdetermined: Freud was a rival for his wife's confidences, a rival in theoretical matters and finally a rival for Spielrein's affections.[72] This last was more clearly the case than Jung realized. Just before Christmas Spielrein left Vienna for a two-week trip to her native Rostov and on her return on 7 January 1912, noted, 'Professor Freud, of whom I have become very fond, thinks highly of me and tells everyone about my "magnificent article" and he is also very sweet to me personally.'[73]

Jung had reason to fear the effect of Spielrein's revelations to Freud. The sexual side of it was a bagatelle, for Freud was surrounded by compulsive womanizers – Gross, Eitingon, Jones, Stekel. Even Pfister had succumbed to one of his charges, while Ferenczi capped all by taking into analysis the daughter of his mistress and then falling in love with the girl – a mess that Freud, in late 1911, was trying to sort out along with all his other concerns. What probably worried Freud more, having heard what Spielrein had to say, was that Jung clearly interpreted 'Siegfried' as a symbol of spiritual yearning, conjuring visions of a 'Christianized' form of psychoanalysis. As John Kerr puts it, 'it smacked of what, from Freud's point of view, was the worst sort of hypocrisy, sexual hypocrisy masked by religious claptrap.'[74]

Although Freud had not yet been able to digest the full horror (from his point of view) of *Symbols*, some of the material he had read in Part One was disturbing enough, especially on religion.[75]

Moreover, from Freud's point of view, Jung had gone beyond mere intellectual disagreement with a colleague and into professional discourtesy, by going back over Freud's Schreber essay and using material in it to come to entirely different conclusions. The Schreber essay was widely acknowledged to be a *tour de force* in the analysis of paranoia, showing how the mind mobilizes its defences, revealing the itinerary of regression and the role of ambivalence.[76] Jung, indeed, earlier in 1911 had praised its brilliance but now he saw how strongly it buttressed the Freudian view of sexuality and was thus an implicit criticism of his own work. He therefore worked back over the material, especially the part where Schreber talks of the sun as a symbol for his father, and reinterpreted it in the light of his own theories in *Symbols*.[77] This was much as if Lenin, say, had trawled over Engels's raw data to argue that Marx's conclusions were systematically misguided.

All in all, we are justified in regarding December 1911 as a turning point, the moment when Freud finally lost patience and ceased to entertain friendly feelings for his 'crown prince'. Freud confessed that he had been a 'sentimental donkey' in his dealings with Jung, but still hoped that their mutual interests would allow them to make common cause.[78] Yet two further events at the end of the year widened the breach between them.

One of Freud's female patients, about whom he had often complained to Jung, secretly went to Zürich for consultations with Jung late in 1911, but Jung 'forgot' to inform Freud of the fact, even though this was hard on the heels of Freud's 'seal of the confessional' pledge regarding Sabina Spielrein. The patient, codenamed Frau C, told Jung that Freud was remote and uncaring, and Jung made sympathetic noises. The patient then went back to Vienna in triumph, spreading tittle-tattle around the psychoanalytic salons. At this further instance of unprofessional behaviour Freud exploded. In a highly intemperate letter he accused Jung of allowing himself to be imposed upon by plausible neurotics and thus of lacking the necessary objectivity for analysis.[79]

Jung replied that he had sensed a trap and informed Frau C that Freud's 'cold' approach might be more efficacious in the long run, but in the end her emotionality and wretchedness drew from him an expression of sympathy which he instantly regretted; most of all, he was furious at having been dragged into the affair in the first place. Since that letter was posted in the Engadine, where Jung went for a winter holiday in January, it was delayed in the mail and it was two weeks before Freud heard from him. Unmoved by the apology, Freud reproached him for his long silence, but in the meantime two more letters had arrived from Freud, in tones that made Jung regret his earlier apology.[80] Jung followed up by not communicating for another two weeks. This was a significant departure and showed that the quarrel had entered a new phase, for in the past whenever Freud wrote irritably or peevishly, Jung had sent him soothing and conciliatory letters.

Freud's increasing impatience with the crown prince was evinced by another of his ingenious essays written in December and published in the *Zentralblatt* in January 1912. In the course of a discussion on dream interpretation he brought up the 'Great is Diana of Ephesus' episode from the Acts of the Apostles, when St Paul's preaching in Ephesus led to a riot of the silversmiths. Freud mentioned that after the riot the Christians in Ephesus swung away from St Paul and over to St John, who promoted the cult of the Virgin Mary.[81] It has been convincingly argued that the subtext is that Freud was St Paul and Jung the new St John, and that the story has no point at all unless we read the treachery of John towards Paul at Ephesus as symbolic of Jung's treachery towards Freud.[82]

Clearly Freud was beginning to see that all his earlier hopes and dreams were in vain. Jung had been appointed as the son and heir and as the apostle to the gentiles, precisely to ensure that psychoanalysis did not fall foul of anti-Semitism and instead became a 'world religion', but here was Jung threatening to undo all his work by producing a Christianized version of the faith. By the end of 1911, and for the first time, Freud saw Jung as an alien, an Aryan, someone who would not save psychoanalysis but would more likely destroy it.

Chapter Eleven

THE KREUZLINGEN GESTURE

Early in January 1912, having completed three-quarters of *Symbols*, Jung took a break in the Engadine and did some sightseeing. After a few days in St Moritz, he spent about a week 'whistlestopping' towns in Germany that contained important art galleries. Still smarting from the dressing down from Freud over 'Frau C', Jung wrote the brief letter referred to at the end of the previous chapter, closing his remarks by saying that he did not claim any validity for his views.[1]

Any hopes of a rapprochement were dashed by two further incidents. First, Jung was bitten by a dog and was in considerable pain for some days, yet he did not think it worthwhile to inform Freud, who learned of the mishap at second hand, from Pfister. Much more seriously, there was an acrimonious and long-running debate about psychoanalysis in the Zürich press, and again not a word of this passed from Jung to Freud, who heard about it from one of his patients.

The controversy began with a routine attack on Freudianism made in a series of articles in the *Neue Zurcher Zeitung* by Dr Max Kesselring, a specialist in nerve diseases; he included a sideswipe at

Jung as the most 'vulgar' of contemporary Freudians.[2] Jung replied in his already familiar intellectual bruiser mode, asking rhetorically if it was now the fashion to bring technical subjects before an uninformed lay audience: if psychoanalysis could be rationally discussed by the man in the Zürich street, did that also apply to other branches of medicine, such as gynaecology?[3] Kesselring hit back by accusing Freudians and their allies of being the pioneers of this particular custom, to which Jung replied that this argument depended on a bird-brained confusion of the vulgar sense of 'sexuality' with the broader definition of libido used in psychoanalysis.[4]

At this point Auguste Forel, now living in retirement on Lake Geneva, decided to enter the fray, and began by castigating Kesselring and other critics of psychoanalysis, such as Fritz Marti, for ignorance and philistinism in their remarks. Jung, however, could not leave well alone, and, in a joint remonstrance written with Alphonse Maeder, deploring the spate of psychologically illiterate and pig-ignorant articles on psychoanalysis in the *Zeitung*, he managed to imply that Forel was almost as addle-pated as Kesselring and Marti. Forel, in a last word before the editor declared the correspondence closed, emerged as a *tertius gaudens*, on the one hand berating the Kesselring school for its philistinism and defending the essence of psychoanalysis considered as methodology, and on the other attacking Freudianism as a secular religion for its 'one-sidedness . . . its sanctifying sexual church, its infant sexuality, its Talmudic-exegetic-theological interpretation.'[5]

The debate, though seldom rising above abuse and name-calling, did underline the huge 'resistance' in Switzerland to sexuality as a key aetiological notion. In Vienna men such as Otto Weininger, Krafft-Ebing and Arthur Schnitzler had, through their voluminous writings on sex, conditioned the Austrian intellectual public to accept Freud's ideas. In Switzerland, as Forel's remarks indicated, the thrust was all towards making psychoanalysis a general methodology in the service of religious and educational problems. The irony was that this tendency was by now clearly discernible in Jung himself, and that he was increasingly having to defend in public a sexualized version of the doctrine in which he himself no longer believed.

However, one could legitimately have expected that details of such a protracted discussion, carried on in the pages of Zürich's leading daily, might have been relayed to Vienna by the so-called president of the International Association. Certainly Freud thought so, and he was even more irritated when Jung brought the subject up purely in the context of his inability to sue Kesselring, since he had defamed an *idea* and not named individuals. Jung compounded his tactlessness by lamenting that having to answer Kesselring meant he could not get on with his mythological work.

That Freud was by now losing patience with Jung is clear. Two papers he published in the *Zentralblatt* early in 1912 contained implicit criticisms of Jung. In 'The Dynamics of Transference', where Freud argued that whereas a patient's conscious love for an analyst helped treatment, unconscious love merely prolonged it,[6] hints of Jung's liaison with Spielrein could be picked up. And in 'Recommendations to Physicians Practising Psychoanalysis' Freud seemed to be hinting at the 'Frau C' imbroglio when he stated that analysts should not volunteer information about themselves to patients or give them books on psychoanalysis to read[7] – exactly what Jung had done. But there was more explicit criticism still in Freud's letters, for in one barbed epistle on 18 February he virtually accused Jung of neglecting his official duties in favour of his private interests.[8]

This went far beyond the usual 'wink and nod' by which Freud usually evinced his displeasure. This time Jung was forced to sit up and take notice. He wrote to Freud to say that all his energies had gone into his important work on libido and mother-incest, and that was why he had neglected both his official duties and his correspondence.[9] But since Freud already had an inkling of the sorts of things Jung was bringing back from 'the realm of Mothers', this reply scarcely mollified him. He wrote back to say that he had always looked forward to Jung's letters with eagerness but, when Jung started to appear reluctant to write, he (Freud) simply turned off his 'excess libido'. He then went on, implicitly, to castigate Jung for the shambles in Zürich and in the International Association in general.[10]

Jung shrugged off the charge of organizational incompetence, and implied that he was doing Freud a favour in writing at all, since correspondence – any correspondence – interfered with his work on mythology. He was obviously stung by Freud's accusation that the journals emanating from Zürich were being upstaged by the Viennese productions; in particular there was a problem about a new *Bulletin*, which was supposed to complement the *Jahrbuch* but which had appeared only once. Jung's way with this criticism was brisk: the non-appearance of the next *Bulletin* was all Riklin's fault. As for the *Zentralblatt*, which, Jung alleged, contained only dilettante articles, this would soon be eclipsed when a new 300-page edition of the *Jahrbuch* appeared. Moreover, the only reason he had not set a date for the next international congress was that the Swiss military authorities would not confirm the dates of his military service. In a word, Jung was completely blameless on all fronts.[13]

Freud was unimpressed. He replied that he said nothing but the plain facts: the Association could not prosper if its president lost all interest in it, especially if the unreliable Riklin was secretary; despite all this, he had still respected Jung's wish not to be bothered with letters. He ended by saying he was surprised Jung accused him of intellectual tyranny, since that was the precise charge Adler had made. Jung got out of this by a brief statement that he had no wish to imitate Adler, thus sidestepping the substance of Freud's complaints.[12]

A diversion was afforded both men by the reappearance of Sabina Spielrein – for the last time – as a factor in their lives. In response to Jung's request, Spielrein sent back her manuscript (once she had filleted it for the triumphant presentation to the Vienna Society on 29 November 1911) and for her pains received merely a curt reply. She wrote back angrily and got another brusque reply, this time an arrogant note pointing out the parallels between her work and his.[13]

Once again Jung had behaved foolishly, for if he was to stand any chance in the battle between himself and Freud for hearts and minds, he had to go out of his way to be conciliatory to Spielrein. The signs are that any such attempt would anyway have been in vain, for Spielrein's diary for February 1912 shows her as already a dedicated Freudian.[14] At the very moment Jung was arguing that infantile sexual fantasies had to be interpreted symbolically, not literally, and as the manifestation of an ancient racial heritage, Spielrein was becoming more and more Freudian in her thinking. Her latest work, 'Contribution to the Understanding of a Child's Soul', dealt with the sexual fantasies of childhood in an orthodox manner. This was a blow for Jung, who seems to have taken it for granted that Spielrein would be his unofficial ambassador at the court of Vienna.[15] In this connection it is worth remarking that Jung's new bearing, in which he interpreted sexuality symbolically, marked the extreme point of the psychoanalytical retreat from the physical world. Freud's early belief in the existence of widespread actual infantile seduction was transmuted into the fantasy of such seduction, while in Jung's latest work even sexual fantasy had to be interpreted as symbolic of some even deeper force.

By now relations between Freud and Jung had deteriorated to the point where even routine administrative matters caused Freud to be angry. He was already convinced that no more disastrous choice as president of the International Association could have been imagined, since Jung invariably put his private concerns and predilections miles ahead of his official duties. Out of the blue Jung announced that he had been invited to lecture at Fordham University in New York in September. Since he had been informed around the same time as the invitation that his Swiss military service would run from 22 August to 6 September, the only practicable time for a conference would be on 19/20 August, preferably in Munich. Angry that Jung seemed to expect everyone else in the psychoanalytic movement to fit in with his personal timetable, Freud snapped back that since the proposed dates were not convenient for *him*, and too little had happened in the movement during the past twelve months (another jibe at Jung), the best plan was to postpone the 1912 conference to the following year.[16]

Another lacuna in the tense and troubled relationship (and correspondence) between Jung and Freud was provided by the extensive holiday Jung took in Italy in April. First he spent some days in Lugano on his own, thinking over a variety of matters while incommunicado. Then he continued into Italy by bicycle with his friend Hans Schmid-Guisau, heading for Ravenna. The bicycle trip was one long discussion, 'which lasted from coffee in the morning, all through the dust of the Lombardy roads, to the round-bellied bottle of Chianti in the evening.'[17] At Ravenna they rode along the sands and through the shallow waves, heading for the ancient mosaics. At this stage, thinking her a forerunner of Spielrein, Jung was obsessed with the Roman empress Galla Placidia, who lived in the fifth century AD. He visited her tomb and meditated on the stained-glass windows of the chapel.[18] Then Jung continued to Florence, where he met Emma and completed the second half of his Italian tour, taking in Pisa and Genoa as well. The fascination for statuary and stonework was again to the fore as Jung contemplated the gargoyles in Florence's Boboli gardens.[19]

The holiday seems to have inspired Jung to throw off the mask for, resuming correspondence with Freud on 27 April, he made plain how far he had already departed from orthodoxy with his statement that incest was overwhelmingly a symbolic and mythological issue, not a real biological one. He went on in successive letters to expand his heretical views on the incest taboo, concentrating on the anthropological aspects; Freud simply replied that Jung's conception of incest was unclear.[20] Once again, Freud was showing restraint, for some of Jung's arguments were bizarre. He argued that a literal fear of incest was absurd, since in early ages by the time a son was in a position to lust after his mother she would already be an old crone with sagging belly and varicose veins.[21] As Paul Stern justly remarks, 'This argument sounds so incredibly hollow and superficial in its literal commitment to physical attributes that it points to what must have been a very sore spot in Jung's personal history.'[22]

The differential tone of the combatants in May 1912 is interesting. Freud, despite his intense irritation with Jung, still appeared to be fighting desperately to avoid the inevitable rift that loomed; Jung, though, was already reconciled to the break and was, consciously or unconsciously, looking for an excuse for the final rupture. The pretext came with the Kreuzlingen affair. Ludwig Binswanger, a key figure in Swiss psychoanalysis, who veered more and more to Freud's side and away from Jung's, had recently been appointed director of the sanatorium at Kreuzlingen on Lake Constance. He went into hospital for a routine appendectomy operation, but the surgeon, while operating, discovered a cancerous tumour. Convinced that his days were numbered, Binswanger confided in Freud but asked him to keep the news a secret. He also wanted to write a farewell testament on his life's work in psychoanalysis, and Freud agreed to visit him at Kreuzlingen to discuss the contents of this valedictory work.[23]

Freud wrote to both Jung and Binswanger to say that he would be at Kreuzlingen for forty-eight hours as from Saturday 25 May. The letter to Binswanger was dated 16 May and that to Jung 23 May, leaving it open to suspicion that there might have been another, earlier, letter from Freud to Jung with this information (which, if it ever existed, has not survived). The letter to Jung arrived at Küsnacht on the morning of 25 May. Since Küsnacht was just over forty miles from Kreuzlingen, and since Freud had just forty-eight hours to spare and the return trip from Vienna occupied another forty-eight hours, it was reasonable to suppose that if it was important for Jung and Freud to meet in Switzerland, it was for Jung to travel up to Lake

Constance.[24] Jung, though, thought that Freud should travel to meet *him* and claimed that Freud had deliberately sent the letter late so that by the time it came into his hands (allegedly on Monday 27th), Freud was already setting out on his homeward journey.

Ever since, the 'Kreuzlingen gesture', as Jung referred to this contretemps, has divided partisans in the rival camps. Freudians, convinced that Jung was an habitual and accomplished liar, maintain that Jung received a letter, which was allegedly posted on 16 May, in plenty of time to make the trip; that he did not care to do so shows how deep was the antagonism he already felt towards Freud.[25] Jungians argue that since Jung was to be one of the principal subjects in the confidential discussion between Freud and Binswanger, it was clear he was not welcome there. They are also on firm ground in being able to point to an extant letter, dated 23 May, in which Freud informs Jung of his visit to Kreuzlingen in terms which certainly suggest this is the first mention of the matter. Moreover, as John Kerr has pointed out, Freud's mention of the trip to Kreuzlingen comes at the end of a letter, highly critical of Jungian theoretical innovations, that was virtually 'a psychoanalytic declaration of war'.[26]

What is the truth of all this? Probably the battle lines between the factions have been drawn too tightly. By sending the letter to Jung on 23 May, Freud made it unlikely, but not impossible, that Jung would meet him, and no doubt he thought that in the existing climate a meeting would serve no useful purpose. However, he did not close the door entirely, since he knew the letter would arrive most probably on Saturday morning, giving Jung the option as to whether he wanted to make a swift forty-mile dash northwards. Perhaps at some level he even intended the information to be a kind of psychological test, just to see how Jung would respond when put on the spot and asked to react quickly and under pressure – for the inability to respond to events except in a slothful fashion was one of the key points in Freud's criticism of Jung as Association president.

What actually happened, as Jung later conceded, was that the letter *did* arrive on the morning of Saturday 25 May – in time for Jung to make the trip, had he been at home. But he was not at home. He had departed on Friday evening for a weekend's sailing trip and did not return until Monday morning.[27] Playing on the ambiguity of the word 'receive', Jung stated, correctly, that he had received the letter on Monday morning, meaning that Emma handed it to him then, but omitted to mention that it had *arrived* on Saturday while he was away.

It was a classic illustration of the old axiom that the best way to tell a lie is to tell the truth. In any case, the imbroglio over the letter clearly suggests that deeper currents were at work and that the letter was subsumed in some wider psychic drama for, as Ronald Clark says, 'Whatever the truth about the contretemps, it seems that it could readily have been removed by either man picking up the telephone.'[28]

Another delay in correspondence was occasioned by an additional spell of military duty by Jung – another mountain manoeuvre – about which he did not notify Freud until it was over. It was not until 8 June that he came bounding back into the fray, eager to rebut Freud's two main criticisms of his new incest theory. Freud said, first, that psychoanalysis had explained anxiety in terms of the prohibition of incest, but Jung now reversed cause and effect; and, secondly, that Jung had fallen into the Adlerian fallacy, whereby the neurotic has no desire at all for his mother but wants to provide himself with a motive for scaring himself away from his libido, and therefore pretends to himself that his libido is so omnivorous that it does not even spare his mother.

Jung's reply was notable for addressing the man and not the argument. He accused Freud of 'mobilising affects' against the new interpretation of incest; he was not cowed by the comparison with Adler; and he expressed great bitterness that Freud had not called on him when he visited Binswanger at Kreuzlingen – a fact he attributed to Freud's displeasure at his (Jung's) new theoretical bearings.[29]

Freud then carefully explained the circumstances of his visit to Binswanger, said how pressed for time he was, and reassured Jung that he would have been pleased to see him had he come to Kreuzlingen. To reinforce the point, he divulged the secret of Binswanger's cancer, then revealed it to others, seeing that the matter was now in the public domain.[30] Binswanger's desire for confidentiality was thus destroyed by Jung's prima donna-ish injured innocence about the 'Kreuzlingen gesture'. (Fortunately for Binswanger, he made a full recovery and lived another fifty-four years.)

Freud also made a final effort to prevent scientific differences from ending his personal relationship with Jung. He reminded Jung that in 1908 the canard was abroad that Freudianism was out of vogue at the Burghölzli but this had not stopped him from visiting Jung in Zürich; it could therefore be seen how foolish was Jung's grievance over the 'Kreuzlingen gesture'. But Jung was having none of it. His reply to this, on 18 July, was laconic brusqueness itself: 'Now I can only say: I understand the Kreuzlingen gesture.'[31]

This was the last correspondence between the two on other than routine business until November. The split caused an 'agonizing reappraisal' in Freudian ranks. Apparently Sabina Spielrein wrote to Jung in a futile effort to compose the quarrel, for Freud, thanking her for her intercession, remarked that henceforth she and Abraham would receive the favour previously enjoyed by Jung.[32] Freud told Oscar Pfister he was indifferent if Jung developed theories wildly different from his.[33]

Yet it was, predictably, to Ferenczi that Freud turned to confide his deepest thoughts on the split with Jung. Sending on to him a copy of the brusque letter of 18 July, which he termed an open declaration of war, Freud wrote, 'This letter seems to be a flat refusal, despite some incomprehensible things – for what does he mean by the Kreuzlingen gesture? What is the policy supposed to be that will be proven by the success of his work? Binswanger, to whom I sent a copy because he alone has been oriented towards the "Kreuzlingen gesture", has the same impression. I will not reply straight away; I can also give myself weeks' time and do absolutely nothing, which will facilitate a formal break . . . Jung must now be in florid neurosis. However this turns out, my intention of amalgamating Jews and goyim in the service of psychoanalysis seems now to have gone astray. They are separating like oil and water.'[34]

Ferenczi enthusiastically took up the 'Jews and goyim' motif arguing that the 'Kreuzlingen gesture' was obviously a fantasy enabling Jung to justify his actions and appease his conscience. He ended by voicing his suspicion that all the Swiss were a secret band of anti-Semites.[35]

Since Jung was about to go to the USA to spread his dissident creed there, Freud felt it necessary to warn his American followers of what was afoot. In August he wrote to James Jackson Putnam, 'After the disgraceful defection of Adler, a gifted thinker but a malicious paranoic, I am now in trouble with our friend Jung, who apparently has not outgrown his own neurosis. And yet I hope that Jung will remain loyal to our cause in its entirety; nor has my feeling for him been greatly diminished. Solely our personal intimacy has suffered.'[36]

The displacement of Jung as crown prince gave other ambitious Freudians their chance. Abraham in particular felt vindicated in his dislike of Jung and his attribution of anti-Semitism. Yet the clearest beneficiary from Freud's disinheritance of the crown prince was Ernest Jones, who now inveigled himself into the inner circle, partly by keeping up the anti-Jung momentum. Jones made all the right noises, assuring Freud that the theoretical divergencies to be expected in the Fordham lectures would not be too serious, reporting Bleuler's (largely favourable) reaction to *Symbols*, and writing three times to Brill in America to put him on his guard. Most of all, he organized a secret committee to defend Freudian doctrine, expressly committed to excluding Jung and the elected presidents in favour of a directing cabal consisting of himself, Rank, Abraham, Ferenczi and Hans Sachs.[37] To clinch the deal Freud gave each member of the secret committee an antique Greek intaglio which the recipient wore in a gold ring.

Ferenczi, who had been collaborating with Jones, meanwhile gave him such a glowing testimonial to Freud that by autumn he was almost as trusted a confidant as the Hungarian himself. The changed nature of the relationship between Freud and Jones, which began with the master's amused condescension but was now approaching genuine friendship, is evident from a letter Freud wrote to him in September, while revisiting his beloved Rome with Ferenczi. After accusing Jung of intellectual arrogance and incompetence as president, Freud confided to Jones his present thoughts on Jung the thinker and the man:

> *The fact is he stumbled a first time in the application of libido theory on paraphrenia and now he is stumbling again to the opposite direction, but he might [continue] to do so and continue to be my friend as he was during the first of his errors . . . I am not angry with him and am sure enough that my former feelings for him cannot be restored. I am quite sure his friends are mistaken about my provoking his sensitivity in some points. I never but spoiled him and he behaved in details, which are not known to you, quite odiously against me. He wanted a dissension and he produced it.*[38]

Jung meanwhile did another stint of Army service in August, then spent just one day at home before departing for the USA on 7 September. By now he had numerous American contacts, including the rich American woman Fanny Bowditch, who had come to him for analysis early in 1912 on Putnam's recommendation.[39] Additionally there was the McCormick clan: not just Harold Fowler and Edith Rockefeller McCormick, the rich patrons, but also Harold's younger brother Medill, who consulted Jung in 1908 about his alcoholism, and his wife Ruth.[40] But the most important professional contact was the man he had met at the 1907 Amsterdam Conference: Smith Elly Jelliffe.[41] Already in May Jung had persuaded Jelliffe to let him stay at his house during the Fordham lectures because he found hotel life in New York 'somewhat disagreeable'.[42]

Jung always enjoyed transatlantic crossings, for they provided him with an opportunity to indulge his perennial fascination with Americans. He liked to draw out the wealthy passengers and learn from them the secrets of the New World's unconscious. He very soon gained the insight, hailed by later cultural critics as their own special original idea, that American pragmatism means a distinct liking for translating questions of ethical and political theory into points of law: a problem that cannot be disentangled by abstract reasoning can be 'solved' by a legal judgement. One American he met on a transatlantic liner produced the *reductio ad absurdum* of this approach. He told Jung he was going to divorce his wife, who had borne him five children, and marry a much younger woman. Surely, queried Jung, it would not be ethical simply to turn your wife and children out into the street? 'Why not?' said the American. 'The law's the law. I married her under the law and I can divorce her under the law.'[43]

Jung arrived in New York on the *Kaiser Wilhelm II* on 18 September. Although the centrepiece of his tour was to be the Fordham lectures, he spent a lot of time on other ventures. He lectured in Chicago and Baltimore, where he visited his friend and disciple Trigant Burrow.[44] In New York, apart from the Fordham programme, he addressed the New York Academy of Medicine, gave two clinical lectures on schizophrenia in the Bellevue hospital and one at the New York State Psychiatric Institute on Ward's Island.[45] An attempt at a more popular presentation, however, flopped badly: Jung lectured with audio-visual aids at the Plaza Hotel, but his volunteer slide projectionist ruined the occasion by projecting everything wrongly – out of order, back to front and upside down.[46]

In Washington DC Jung fared better. Here he was the guest of William Alanson White, superintendent of St Elizabeth's mental hospital, whom he had met with Jelliffe at the Amsterdam Conference in 1907. White took him on a tour of St Elizabeth's and Jung used the occasion for some informal analysis of black schizophrenics.[47] Jung found that 'Negroes' (as they were then called) did not differ in any essential way from whites in their psychoses, but evinced three traits that were consequences of their culture: they were ignorant, they were unable to introspect, and they were extraordinarily religious.[48] Jung was amused to see how often black people co-opted 'the Lord' into their schizophrenic fantasies: one woman told him, 'Yes, the Lord is working in me like a clock, funny and serious.'[49] But much more important were the pointers that the schizophrenic fantasies used material found in the great myths of the world. Jung would later cite the St Elizabeth's experience as a turning point, when he first began to grasp the reality of archetypal images and their common origin in a collective unconscious. The uneducated black man who told him of a dream of a man crucified on a wheel suggested links with myths like Ixion's wheel and Tibetan mandalas.[50]

However, it was the nine lectures to an audience of some ninety psychiatrists and psychologists, and a daily two-hour seminar for nine professors, given in English at the Extension Course at Fordham University in the Bronx, New York, during the last fortnight of September 1912, that were of most importance in the history of psychoanalysis, for here Jung broke decisively with Freud. Some of the points at issue had already been raised with him in the course of the debate over *Symbols* and the incest taboo, but some of them expressly contradicted assurances Jung had already given him – over Adler for instance.

In adumbrating his scheme for an entirely new approach to psychoanalysis, Jung told his audience that the first essential was to abandon the Freudian conception of libido. According to Freud, hunger was a manifestation of sexual desire, but it could just as easily be the other way round. Such chicken-and-egg arguments were decisively dealt with if we simply regarded libido as psychic energy.[51] Moreover, Jung suggested, if we take libido simply to be the overall energy system of sexuality, this explains why sexuality itself can take the different forms of heterosexuality, homosexuality and bisexuality.

Jung went on to argue that many things that were connected with the reproductive function in primitive times have ceased to be so in the course of evolution.[52] Jung therefore wanted to break down the distinction between the instinct for the preservation of the species and the instinct for self-preservation, and to make the conception of libido like Schopenhauer's Will or Bergson's *élan vital*. The schizophrenic would then be seen, not as one who suffered lack of libido, but simply as one who has withdrawn libido from the outer world and thus suffered a loss of reality compensated for by an increase in fantasy activity.

According to Jung, the first manifestation of this general Bergsonian energy is in the nutritive instinct of the infant, which is not sexual. So, having jettisoned Freudian libido, Jung went on to abandon the core idea of infantile sexuality. Instead, he substituted a threefold model of child development: in the first stage, between the ages of three and five, libido was at the service of growth and nutrition; in the second stage, between the ages of five and thirteen, there were germs only of sexuality; finally came sexuality proper. In sum, infantile sexuality was not so much an error of empirical observation, but *a priori* conceptually erroneous.[53]

Part of the problem, Jung thought, was that Freud's definition of sexuality was impossibly wide, and he had also made the egregious mistake of thinking that pleasure was synonymous with sexuality. He criticized Freud for not seeing the nutritive element in sucking. Freud postulated that the nutritive act of sucking was itself a sexual act, to which Jung retorted that obtaining pleasure is by no means identical with sexuality.[54]

Since the basic energy powering human beings is not sexual, and since infantile sexuality is false, it follows that the cause of neurosis cannot be a sexual trauma experienced in childhood. It was known that childhood trauma was universal – Rank even postulated that the mere fact of being born was the most basic and most important trauma. It was also known that many patients invented stories of infantile seduction, and even when it could be decisively proved that a childhood trauma had taken place, this could not be responsible for the whole of the neurosis, since in that case there would be millions of neurotics. Freud concluded that the morbid fantasies of neurotics derived from bad habits formed in childhood – what he called infantile fixations. As the neurotic appeared to be dependent on his infantile past, the main task of analytic treatment was to resolve the infantile fixation, conceived of as an unconscious attachment of the sexual libido to certain infantile fantasies and habits.

Why did the libido fix on these old infantile habits? The reason seemed to be that most fantasies of the infantile past were grouped around the so-called 'nuclear complex' and the neurotic was far more influenced by this complex than the normal person. Jung acknowledged the presence of the Oedipus-complex in men and coined the term 'Electra-complex' for the similar disposition in women. What was important about a trauma was not the thing itself but the predisposition in a person that made the trauma effective. The original trauma might not be of aetiological significance and the cause of the neurosis might have to be sought in what Jung called 'the retardation of affective development'. The cause of this retardation was the parental complex, Oedipus or Electra. Jung's theory was that the libido became introverted and that it then inverted to a greater or less extent large areas of memory, with the result that these reminiscences acquired a vitality that was no longer appropriate to them.[55] The patients then lived more or less entirely in the past.

It is clear that emotions towards parents particularly fit into this category, either as Oedipus and Electra complexes or, when the parents are dead, as the 'imago' or distorted image of them still exerting a potent force in the patient's mind. Jung conceded that the damage caused to children by parents was often the 'nuclear complex' or master trauma, but was inclined to interpret this in common-sense terms, pointing out that a striking number of neurotics were spoiled as children. But what was certain was that the 'nuclear complex' of infantile sexuality could not be the 'open sesame', since neurosis could occur when children first went to school, when they had to choose between love of parents and other duties, or, in adult life, when they had to navigate between the competing tugs of the comforts of bourgeois existence and the strenuous demands of professional life. Moreover, a 'fixation', conceived of in Freudian terms, would surely be everlasting and not amenable to analytic treatment.

With these preparatory remarks Jung was building up to his most signal departure from Freudianism: the theory that the key to neurosis lies not in the past but in the present.[56]

It would appear, then, that complexes about parents did not derive from painful childhood experiences but from present difficulties that reactivated ancient conflicts, in a word, to that 'regression of the libido' which featured so largely in Jung's work in *Symbols of Transformation*. Since Jung accepted that Oedipus, Electra and incest-complexes existed in everyone, even people with foster-parents, it followed that their significance was not as things-in-themselves but as agencies triggered by regression;

so the incest-complex was not a reality but a purely regressive fantasy formation.

The next obvious question is why the libido becomes regressive. Jung answered that this happened when we refused to accept that the obstacles blocking our progress are in ourselves and instead pretend they are in the external world. The libido is constantly adapting to new challenges, but if some obstacle seems insurmountable the libido will abandon the task and regress; instead of harnessing its forces for an increased effort, the libido gives up its present task and reverts to an earlier and more primitive mode of adaptation. So in cases of hysteria a disappointment in love can precipitate a neurosis, and symptoms like loss of appetite show the regressive libido taking over the nutritive function; fantasies such as the Oedipus complex are also reactivated. But always regression is the key explanatory factor.[57]

All this brought Jung to the crux of his argument, when he ringingly endorsed Adler's view that the cause of neurosis lies in the present. The questions we should ask about a neurotic patient are: which task does he/she wish to avoid, and which difficulty in life is he trying to avoid? It is no good asking whether a patient has a father-complex or a mother-complex, for we all do. Much more fruitful is to ask what is it that the patient shirks and does not want to fulfil.[58] As for what causes the shirking, Jung suggested a twin-track approach: partly it was an innate oversensitivity on the part of the neurotic, and partly it was the general law of inertia, in terms of which human beings seek the line of least resistance.

Neurosis, then, is an act of adaptation that has failed. But the picture is not wholly black, for the dreams and fantasies of the neurotic have a teleological or prospective function, and represent inchoate attempts to find new ways of adapting. The analyst's task is to bring the unconscious libido under the control of the will. Seen in this light, psychoanalysis would no longer appear as a reduction of the individual to sexuality but as a moral task of great educational importance.[59]

It is worth summarizing what exactly Jung's departures from Freudianism were in the Fordham lectures and what were their implications. The redefinition of libido as general life-energy and the denial of infantile sexuality subverted the very foundations of Freud's theory. Endorsing Adler's idea of neurosis as rooted in the present rather than the past seemed to play down the role of the unconscious, certainly as conceived hitherto, and it is not surprising that soon afterwards Jung found it necessary to substitute a collective unconscious for Freud's dynamic personal unconscious. On the Oedipus complex, which he saw as consequence, not cause of regression, it is true, Jung was formally ambivalent, but, again, he seemed to want to downplay the role of the unconscious and to interpret the complex in commonsensical terms.[60] As Ronald Clark remarked, this reduced one of Freud's key ideas to 'cosy nursery normality'.[61]

A certain personal animus towards Freud is also evident in the Fordham lectures. Acknowledging grudgingly that past events often did lie at the root of a neurosis, he added dismissively, 'This truth was already known to the older physicians.'[62] And, while conceding that Freud's experience of neurosis was wider than his own, he added that his formulations fitted the facts better than Freud's.[63] He also implicitly accused Freud of selective interpretation of the evidence by stating that the apparent aetiology of neurosis uncovered by psychoanalysis was merely an inventory of carefully selected fantasies masking a failure of adaptation to reality; the vicious circle of flight from reality and regression into fantasy can, and obviously had managed to, seduce analysts into drawing unwarranted causal relationships. Finally, in his first appearance as enhancer of hopes and allayer of fears, Jung stressed the future where Freud stressed the past and contrasted the optimism of his doctrine with the pessimism inherent in Freudianism.[64]

Since Jung was all but preaching schism from the Freudian flock, it is not surprising that Freudians began counting American heads and trying to calculate what the impact of Jung's new doctrine would be in the USA. Putnam, who met Jung in New York and attended some of the Fordham lectures, immediately nailed his colours to the Freudian mast, accusing Jung of having jettisoned the most valuable part of psychoanalysis.[65] Jones, with his knowledge of the New World, told Freud he was sure Brill and Trigant Burrow could be squared and counted on Meyer's personal dislike of Jung to help the cause; there were, however, others, like Pierce Clark, made of intellectually weaker stuff and suffused with American pragmatism, who 'bought' the Jung line that the abandonment of sexuality would make psychoanalysis more popular.[66]

Flushed with the enthusiastic reception of his Fordham lectures, Jung continued with his travel plans, which he had designed to bring him home via the West Indies. Yet this time even the vainglorious lover of Atlantic storms met his Waterloo. Jung confessed to Jelliffe that the seas were so huge on the homeward run that he was unable to get any work done at all.[67] Finally a chastened and battered Jung disembarked at Amsterdam. He returned to find the International Association again in disarray. In his absence Freud had been corresponding with Alphonse Maeder, but the correspondence had become acrimonious, to the point where Freud ended by accusing Maeder of anti-Semitism.[68]

Jung's first actions on returning home were scarcely tactful. In a spirit of triumphalism he wrote to Freud that his new version of psychoanalysis had won over many people previously put off by the problem of sexuality in neurosis. Unable to let well alone, he added that the 'Kreuzlingen gesture' had dealt him a lasting wound but he was still prepared to maintain friendly relations.[69]

Freud replied by dropping the 'Dear Friend' mode of address he had adopted hitherto and substituting the coldly formal 'Dear Dr Jung'. In a witheringly ironical letter of 'welcome back', he advised Jung not to preen himself on his success in the USA, since the farther one retreated from psychoanalysis the less resistance one would encounter and therefore the more applause.[70] He reproached Jung for harping on the Kreuzlingen gesture, which he found both incomprehensible and insulting and for encouraging Adler, who was going around Vienna claiming that the Zürichers were now in full flight from sexuality.

There were a few more inconsequential exchanges, but the relationship took a significant turn when Jung and Freud met face-to-face in Munich on 24 November, on the occasion of an extraordinary conference called at the Park Hotel to deal with the problem of Stekel and the *Zentralblatt*. As a result of Stekel's poisonous vendetta with Tausk, Freud's patience had finally snapped and he now wanted to have Stekel removed as the journal's editor. The problem was that the original compromise terms hammered out for the direction of the journal, which allowed all three principals the right of veto, made this impossible. Freud tried to persuade the publisher, J.F. Bergmann, to waive this rule, and when Bergmann refused he interpreted this as a plot or secret protocol between Bergmann and Stekel.[71]

After an angry confrontation with Freud in his editorial office, Stekel agreed to resign from the Vienna Society but not from the *Zentralblatt*.[72] Freud's response to this was to get his followers to boycott the journal and instead take their contributions to a new journal, the *Zeitschrift*, which would begin publication in January 1913.[73] But there was still a snag in that the International Association was committed to subsidizing the *Zentralblatt* for the next twelve months, conjuring visions of anti-Freudian outpourings being financed by Freudian money. Freud had appealed to Jung as president to find a way round this, and the extraordinary conference in Munich was the result.

Invitations were sent out to Abraham, Leonhard Seif, leader of the Freudian group in Munich (and, ironically, later to defect to the Adlerians), and Ernest Jones. From Zürich came Jung, Riklin and Johan van Ophuijsen, a young Dutch analyst currently serving a four-year term at the Burghölzli. Relations between Jung and Jones were by now at their nadir, and Jones arrived late for the meeting because Jung 'accidentally on purpose' misdated the invitation. Jones, having by chance found out that the correct date was 24 November, not 25 November as on Jung's notification, arrived on the correct day, and thought he detected an astonished look on Jung's face. When Jones complained to Freud, who had already had experience (over the Kreuzlingen affair) of Jung's cavalier way with dates, Freud replied wittily, 'A gentleman should not do such things, even unconsciously.'[74]

From 9 to 11 a.m. Freud's colleagues heard his proposals for dealing with Stekel and gave him their unequivocal backing. They also agreed that the next Congress would be held in Munich in September 1913 on the theme of the function of the dream. At 11 a.m. Freud suggested to Jung that they take a walk and talk over their differences. Once they were on their own Freud asked what was the matter with him and what he meant by harping on about the Kreuzlingen gesture. Jung told him that he regarded Binswanger as an enemy and he took particular exception to the fact that his old rival Paul Häberlin had been with them at Kreuzlingen. Freud firmly reiterated all the points he had made by letter, asked him to check the postmark of the letter with his wife and reproached him for launching into sensational accusations on such slender evidence. Jung became quiet and subdued and mumbled something about his father-complex. Freud, unwilling to let him off the hook so easily, pointed out that it was not just a question of the 'father', since he had problems with other men as well. Jung promised to mend his ways, but Freud was only half convinced. He reported to Ferenczi that Jung was like a drunkard who swore up and down that he was not drunk. 'Neurotic', 'immature', 'dishonest' and 'mendacious' were the epithets Freud used to characterize the erstwhile crown prince. Jung had promised to mend his ways, but Freud did not believe a word of it since he now saw his Swiss colleague as a pathological liar.[75]

Yet Freud himself was being disingenuous in this letter, for he ended by saying that Jung took his leave at 5 p.m., pledging loyalty to the cause, but he said *nothing* about the extraordinary events over lunch. Tension was already evident when Freud asked Jung and Riklin why his name had not been mentioned in any of the recently published articles by the Zürich school. Jung replied blandly that Freud's name was so well known that it was unnecessary to remind readers who the founding father of psychoanalysis was. Freud, apparently, was not convinced by this reassurance, and his suspicions of Jung's disloyalty hardened to certainty when they got into a heated discussion about the Pharaohs. Freud was talking about the Pharaoh Akhenaton (Amenophis IV), the 18th dynasty ruler who renounced the old gods and introduced a monotheistic and universalized solar cult. He suggested that Akhenaton's negative attitude towards his father – evinced by scratching out his father's name on monuments and substituting his own – was the key element in his religious conversion, that behind Egyptian monotheism lay a father-complex. This line of argument annoyed Jung – 'this derogatory way of judging Amenophis IV got my goat' – and he expressed forcefully his contempt for Freud's 'simplistic' analysis, pointing out that all Pharaohs before Akhenaton had also scratched out the names of their predecessors.[76]

At this point Freud slid off his chair in a faint. Jung picked him up, carried him into the next room and laid him on a sofa. As Jung was carrying him, Freud came to. Jung reported, 'I shall never forget the look he cast at me. In his weakness he looked at me as if I were his father.'[77] Freud later claimed that alcohol and sleeplessness had played their part, but he knew very well that his disciples would not accept this explanation, if only because they were so well primed in his own theories. He therefore admitted to Binswanger that the true cause of this faint, as of the one in Bremen, was repressed feelings towards Jung.[78] He also mentioned to Binswanger that he felt distinct intimations of mortality as a result of the incident, reinforced by the awareness that enemies like Stekel could hardly wait for his demise. His first words on regaining consciousness were very significant, 'How sweet it must be to die.'[79]

The fainting incident was an almost exact carbon copy of the swooning in Bremen three years earlier, also in Jung's presence. Here in Munich the faint seemed overdetermined, for it was in this selfsame room that Freud had fainted many years before in Fliess's presence. Much the same explanation as at Bremen holds good. On the face of it, Freud could not bear the fact that Jung was a traitor and blotted the fact out with unconsciousness; also he registered Jung's breakaway moves as a death-wish against him and so underwent a *petite mort*.[80] Yet beyond this was a hot spring of anger, a gushing geyser of rage, towards Jung himself. Seif, who was an eyewitness, told Jones that the faint was a kind of backhanded compliment from Freud to Jung, in a curious sense giving him the due recognition which the Jewish patriarchal tradition had earlier choked off.[81]

Since the Bremen fainting fit had followed discussion of the 'peat-bog men' and the Munich one a discussion of the Pharaoh Akhenaton, the theme of mummification was another subtext, suggesting perhaps that Jung's likely defection threatened an ossification of the psychoanalytic movement. Certainly the discussions that triggered both fainting fits concerned mankind in its infancy, and it may be that the theme of phylogenetic inheritance and the legacy from early man, so vociferously promoted by Jung, were as much a red rag on this occasion as the associations of death. Yet, whatever the depth psychology explanation, Freud felt that he had lost caste as a result. He wrote to Jones, 'Unfortunately by my last attack I have lost a portion of my authority . . . There is some piece of unruly homosexual feeling at the root of the matter.'[82]

Jung's first letter to Freud once he got home to Zürich was an odd affair. Freud told Abraham it was 'very kind'[83] but, with hindsight, it can be read in a very different way. Jung spoke of the profound insight he had gained into Freud's character in Munich and how he would not make the same mistakes again. Ostensibly, this was a placatory letter, but its ambiguous irony is also palpable.[84]

The brilliant Freudian disciple Lou-Andreas Salomé, who had earlier analysed *Symbols of Transformation* as 'a premature and hence quite sterile synthesis', was not far wrong when she noted in her journal: 'We are all supposed to behave "diplomatically" on the Jung affair; but actually Munich was already a rupture.'[85]

Whether or not Freud read the ambiguities in Jung's letter as veiled hostility – in a letter to Ferenczi he took them at face value but added 'but you know it won't last'[86] – his letter in turn is equally curious. He began by saying that he hoped Munich got them both to an equilibrium point in their relationship for, whereas before 1912 he had expected too much from Jung, since then the pendulum had swung too far. Then he threw down the gauntlet: 'You seem to have solved the riddle of all mysticism, showing it to be based on the symbolic utilisation of complexes that have outlived their function.'[87]

Interpretation of this sentence has divided critics. Paul Stern thinks it was the criticism of *Symbols* that so angered Jung; John Kerr thinks it was an implicit threat to use Sabina Spielrein's revelations about 'Siegfried' to demonstrate that all mysticism has a neurotic core that enraged him – though it is a nice question how such a complex interpretation can be spun from such a brief statement.[88] Yet enraged Jung certainly was, and his reply, on 3 December, was blistering. Referring to the 'bit of neurosis', he launched a heavy attack. First, he pointed out that in *Interpretation of Dreams* he had admitted his own neurosis. Then he reminded Freud that they had stopped their mutual analysis because Freud saw it as a threat to his authority. Finally, he made the charge that critics of psychoanalysis have since returned to again and again: that analysts systematically misuse their position to devalue others and insinuate that they are suffering from this or that 'complex'.[89]

This outpouring has also divided the critics; Kerr, unaccountably, thinks it an attempt by Jung to hint at the 'affair' with Minna Bernays, though how this reading can be extracted from the above would baffle cryptanalysts, let alone psychoanalysts. Kaufman is on firmer ground in viewing it as an explosion of rage, a realization that the fainting fit at Munich was not serious and that Freud was not going to die.[90]

Freud, as so often, moved to defuse the crisis by assuring him that he did not take amiss what Jung called his 'new style' of writing. Jung replied by saying that as Freud had reacted so badly he would for the present tune his lyre a few tones lower. There is no sign on the surface that Freud had reacted badly, but perhaps Jung's antennae were as 'supernaturally' acute as ever on this occasion, for Freud's letter to Jones, written three days after the emollient letter to Jung, tells a different story, and one in line with Jung's intuitions: 'He [Jung] behaves like a perfect fool, he seems to be Christ himself, and in particular things he says there is always something of the *lausbub* [rascal] . . . The letters I get from him are remarkable, changing from tenderness to overbearing insolence. He wants treatment . . . After all I think we have to be kind and patient with Jung and, as old Oliver said, keep our powder dry. I restricted myself to the remark against Jung, that I do not think *he* has been a sufferer by my neurosis. In any case, there is a suspicious amount of dishonesty, want of simplicity and frankness, I mean in his constitution.'[91] A letter to Ferenczi endorses this: 'Jung is crazy; his letters are vacillating between tenderness and arrogant presumption.'[92]

Ironically, in view of Jung's oft-asserted assurance that he despised the Adlerians, it was the issue of Adler which brought Jung and Freud to the final break. Jung had promised to review Adler's complete work in the *Jahrbuch* (he never did), and Freud looked forward to this, for it would rebut rumours that Jung was swinging over to Adler's side. However, he nudged Jung that it was Adler's unacceptable innovation regarding libido that was the real problem.[93] The implicit criticism was perhaps just too obvious; as Peter Gay has put it, 'This was too much for Jung's unconscious.'[94] Jung wrote back to reassure Freud, but now made the slip to end all slips. 'Even Adler's cronies do not regard me as one of theirs,' he wrote, but, by writing *Ihrigen* (yours) instead of *ihrigen* (theirs), he showed the way the unconscious was working.[95]

It may have been tactless for Freud to point out the slip, but he had suffered too much from Jung's twists and turns to be able to resist this opportunity of pointing out that his (Jung's) every action bespoke the hostility that his tongue denied. With heavy irony he asked whether Jung could summon enough 'objectivity' (one of Jung's favourite buzz words) to consider the slip without anger.[96]

It was a forlorn hope. Jung's reaction established beyond any doubt that the relationship with Freud was mortally wounded and required only the *coup de grâce*. One can almost perceive the anger spilling onto the page as he wrote:

> *May I say a few words to you in earnest? I admit the ambivalence of my feelings towards you, but am inclined to take an honest and absolutely straightforward view of the situation . . . I would, however, point out that your technique of treating your pupils like patients is a* blunder. *In that way you produce either slavish sons or impudent puppies . . . I am objective enough to see through your little trick.*

> *You go around sniffing out all the symptomatic actions in your vicinity, thus reducing everyone to the level of sons and daughters who blushingly admit the existence of their faults. Meanwhile you remain on the top as the father, sitting pretty. For sheer obsequiousness nobody dares to pluck the prophet by the beard . . .*
>
> *If ever you should rid yourself entirely of your complexes and stop playing the father to your sons, and instead of aiming continually at their weak spots took a good look at your own for a change, then I will mend my ways and at one stroke uproot the vice of being in two minds about you.*[97]

The only epithet that covers all the facets of this extraordinary letter is: amazing. It is amazing for its intemperateness, for the mental anguish it reveals, and for what it discloses in the mode of the 'lady protesting too much'. As Peter Gay has pointed out, analysing each other's slips and dreams, bandying around terms like 'paranoid', 'complex', and 'homosexual' and in general carelessly using among themselves a popular form of technical terms, as a relief from the stresses of analysis, was part of the common currency of the psychoanalytic movement in the early years.[98] To react with such ferocity, even to a 'joking but serious' leg-pull, was a massive over-reaction. Freud expressed his dilemma in a letter to Ferenczi: if he responded vehemently, Jung would say that the father of analysis could not tolerate analysis; if he responded calmly, that would merely invite Jung to launch even more vociferous attacks. 'He is behaving like a florid fool and the brutal fellow that he is. The master who analysed him could only have been Fräulein Moltzer, and he is so foolish as to be proud of this work of a woman with whom he is having an affair.'[99]

It is symptomatic of the increasingly important role Jones was taking in the psychoanalytic movement that Freud leaned on him most of all in this crisis and took his advice. 'As regards Jung,' he wrote to him, 'he seems all out of his wits, he is behaving quite crazy.' Accusing Jung of being a second Adler, Freud confessed that the receipt of such an intemperate letter produced in him a feeling of shame. He had decided not to send the mild answer he originally composed as Jung would take that as a sign of weakness.

On the other hand, for the sake of the wider movement he could not allow himself to be provoked to the degree the letter merited. So he had decided to make no reply whatsoever and to hold himself in readiness for a complete severance of personal relations.[100]

After ten days without an answer to his bombshell, the tension became too much for Jung, so he wrote offering not to send any more letters. The letter he received from Freud made it clear that the feeling was mutual. Freud wrote, 'In building your construction on this foundation you have made matters as easy for yourself as with your famous "Kreuzlingen gesture". Otherwise your letter cannot be answered. It creates a situation that would be difficult to deal with in a personal talk and totally impossible in correspondence. It is a convention among us analysts that none of us need feel ashamed of his own bit of neurosis. But one who while behaving abnormally keeps shouting that he is normal gives ground for the suspicion that he lacks insight into his illness. Accordingly I propose that we abandon our personal relations entirely.'[101]

Jung accepted this without demur: 'the rest is silence,' he wrote, somewhat pretentiously.[102] It had come to this: the relationship that had begun so promisingly and with such high hopes six years earlier had now ended. The road to Vienna, which Jung at first thought would be his version of the road to Damascus, had finished up in a cul-de-sac of hatreds that would never die.

Chapter Twelve

GUERRE A OUTRANCE

By the beginning of 1913, having severed personal relations with Freud, Jung was groping his way towards a new theory radically different from Freudianism. The essence of this new theory was a stress on the future rather than the past, consequences rather than causes, the world of symbols rather than sexuality. Where Freudianism interpreted symbols as a sign of something repressed or concealed, Jung saw them as an attempt to point the way to further psychological development of the individual. Disregarding the intense suspicion of teleology in the social sciences, Jung stressed the notions of function and adaptation and declared that his work was the synthesis of which the 'one-sided' views of Freud (stressing the pleasure principle) and Adler (stressing the will to power) were merely thesis and anti-thesis.

Embryonic forms of the mature Jungian doctrine are already discernible in the new interpretations of transference and the stages of life. For Jung transference was no longer just the projection of infantile-erotic fantasies onto the analyst but a process of empathy and adaptation. The sexual character of transference, on this view, was merely the first stage in the process – a bridge leading one to the realm of empathy, whereby the patient becomes aware of the inadequacy of his own attitude through recognition of the normal, adapted and integrated attitude of the analyst.[1]

Jung was to become a major interpreter of the meaning of middle age, and this aspect of his work first emerges in correspondence with a new disciple, Dr R. Loy, in early 1913. The thrust of Jung's argument was that middle age was the time when the value of human personality was discovered, and that the exaggerated longing of an older person for the sexual life of youth was a cowardly evasion of a duty – one of life's essential tasks.[2]

A further aspect of the new Jung doctrine that the neurotic's problems lie in the present, not the past, was the way neurosis linked with culture, for one of Jung's tenets was that the fragmented culture of the twentieth century was to society what schizophrenia was to the individual. The neurotic could not really be blamed for confusion about life's tasks, for the collapse of the old nineteenth-century certainties and the 'organic' moral code left him uncertain what those tasks really were. So the real reason for neurosis was not lack of sexual satisfaction but failure to recognize the individual's 'cultural task'.[3]

Yet if Jung was making great strides as a theoretician in early 1913, he was falling down badly as a practical therapist. His international reputation was spreading and among the patients referred to him at this time was the forty-two-year-old English banker Montagu Norman, later (1920–44) to be governor of the Bank of England. Norman was suffering from interludes of hypermania, including delusions of grandeur, at first thought to be paranoia, and travelled to Küsnacht with his brother Ronald for consultations. Jung diagnosed Norman as suffering from General Paralysis of the Insane (GPI), the tertiary stage of syphilis, extrapolating largely from the delusions of grandeur which were at that time thought to be an infallible pointer to GPI, and predicted that Montagu would be dead in a few months. The Normans were deeply shocked when Jung pronounced his verdict and Montagu's brother, in particular, was unconvinced. Had Norman in fact been suffering from GPI his days would indeed have been numbered, but he lived on until 1950. The Normans sought a second opinion in Switzerland and Dr Vittoz of Lausanne came up with the (correct) diagnosis of manic-depression. Why did Jung get this case so spectacularly wrong? His defenders say that he based his diagnosis too strongly on the physical evidence – blood serum and spinal fluid report – but on any analysis it was a serious error. The most charitable explanation is that Jung was already beginning the descent into psychic turmoil that would take him close to madness in 1914–16 and therefore should not have been seeing patients at all.[4]

On 4 March 1913 Jung set out for another long lecturing trip to the USA, revisiting many of the places where he had spoken four months earlier.[5] A lover of travel, Jung always liked to organize his itineraries so that he visited different places, and this time he arranged to sail to New York on an Italian steamer. He boarded at Genoa and cruised down to the first port of call at Naples. At the latitude of Rome he stood at the ship's railing, hoping he might catch a glimpse of the 'forbidden' city, but saw nothing; he was secretly glad, as he still feared the tremendous impact of the Eternal City on the unconscious. Pompeii, visited from Naples, was overwhelming enough.[6]

The next stop was Malta, where Jung visited churches and temples,[7] then the liner threaded its way through the Straits of Gibraltar and out onto the open Atlantic for the 3,000 mile run to New York. In a packed programme in New York Jung lectured to the Liberal Club in Grammercy Park and revisited the asylum on Ward's Island where, if Jones can be believed, he made an unfavourable impression on his professional colleagues. The oft-repeated motif of Jung's revisionist lectures was that psychoanalysis was a religion not a science, but that he was interested in empirical data, not dogma.[8] As ever, Jung observed Americans and their idiosyncracies closely and told many amusing stories about their conformity and lack of real individualism. He wore his usual Swiss burgher's hat in New York but a friend took him aside and advised him that this would not do: he should wear a bowler hat as all men did in the United States.[9]

Jones accused Jung of making these transatlantic trips just to draw vast fees from wealthy fulltime hypochondriacs like the Fowler McCormicks. Jones had his own furrow to plough in so speaking, but it does seem odd that Jung should have spent so much energy in visiting America only to be back at Küsnacht five weeks later, in mid-April.[10] He found the battle with the Freudians hotting up, as Freud's secret committee made strenuous efforts to win over those to whom the final break between Jung and Freud had come as a shock, or who were uncertain which way to jump. At this stage Freud's intention was to marginalize Jung as an eccentric figure within the

International Association without bringing on a schism; he made a clear distinction between terminating his personal relationship with Jung and ending the *professional* association with the Zürich school for, as he put it to Abraham, 'Jung is crazy but I have no desire for separation and should like to let him wreck himself first.'[11]

Freud cleverly put all the major players in international psychoanalysis in the picture very early, making it difficult for Jungian canards about his dogmatism and autocracy to take root. Pfister at first felt divided loyalties, as between his fellow Swiss and the international movement itself, but Freud's early explanations did much to assist in winning him over eventually.[12] Binswanger and Haberlin, having already experienced the irrational side of Jung over Kreuzlingen, and being further apprised that he regarded them as his enemies, made a point of journeying to Vienna to show where their sympathies lay.[13]

The Americans were more difficult to square, especially as Jung had been back to the USA three times since his Clark visit with Freud in 1909, and obviously had better contacts. Here Freud relied on a combination of his own personal touch and Jones's North American know-how. Freud stressed to Putnam that, contrary to Jungian rumour, he did not mind theoretical disagreements in good faith; Jung's deviations, however, took him out of the orbit of psychoanalysis altogether and were anyway inspired by his frightening personal ambition.[14] To Stanley Hall, Freud wrote, 'Jung, who was with me, is my friend no longer, and our work together is approaching a rupture. Such changes are very disagreeable but they cannot be helped.'[15]

Jung meanwhile continued honing his new ideas ready for a fresh foray at the 17th Congress of Medicine in London on 7–12 August 1913. However, Pierre Janet bade fair to steal his thunder by launching his own attack on Freudian doctrine. Janet argued that whatever was good in Freud's work had been plagiarized from him, and the rest was worthless; he tricked out his paper with a few patronizing references to Freud's work, described as 'some previous studies'. He did *not* say, however, as in the legend, 'Psychoanalysis could arise only in such an immoral place as Vienna.'[16]

Jung then stood up and did a masterly impersonation of Mark Antony defending Brutus. Speaking in English, in his usual combative heavyweight bruiser style, he began by pitching into Janet, a man he admired. His sarcasm was withering: 'Unfortunately it is often the case that people believe themselves entitled to judge psychoanalysis when they are not even able to read German.' But Jung soon showed that this brutal way with Janet was a smokescreen from behind which he launched an even more vociferous attack on Freud. He began, as in New York, by 'liberating' libido from sexuality and redefining it as something like Bergson's *élan vital*. Then he moved on to the idea of neurosis as failed adaptation that dammed up energies.

Jung went on to give offence to all Freudians in the audience by saying that Freud's stress on sexuality and Adler's emphasis on the will to power were simply different but equally partial and one-sided ways of looking at the same phenomena; if anything, certainly when it came to interpreting dreams, the Adlerian perspective was to be preferred.[17] Jungian thought transcended these limited categories by being pluralistic where they were monistic; moreover, Tomorrow was more important than Yesterday and Whither than Whence. Since neurosis was holding the wrong attitude *now*, it made no sense to rummage around in the early period of infancy.

Moving on to the subject of dreams, Jung scouted the reduction of dreams to personal factors, as in Freudianism, and suggested instead that they be compared with mythology and the secrets of religion. He gave as an example the dream of a neurotic young man going up a flight of stairs with his mother and sister and finding when he reached the top that his sister was going to have a child. According to Freud, this was an incestuous dream, but Jung objected that to distinguish, à la Freud, between manifest and latent content in the dream was to take an eclectic approach to symbolism. If the stairs are interpreted as the sexual act, where is the logic or justification in regarding the mother and the sister as just that and not symbols of something else? To analyse the dream as the failure of the neurotic to attend to life's tasks, on the other hand, made perfect sense. The young man was one who had just finished his studies and could not face going into his profession; therefore, said Jung, the dream was not so much about repressed, infantile, incestuous wishes as about shirking duties the dreamer was called on to fulfil.

To avoid Freudian pessimism, spirituality must be emphasized, for otherwise there is no way out for the pent-up energy: 'a vicious circle is set up, and this is in fact what Freudian psychology appears to do. It points no way that leads beyond the inexorable cycle of biological events . . . As for Freud's concept of the "superego", it is a furtive attempt to smuggle in the time-honoured image of

Jehovah in the dress of psychological theory.'[18] With that peroration Jung concluded. It is reported that there were no questions after his speech, but not whether this was because the audience was bowled over by his arguments or merely stupefied by the vehemence with which he put them over.

The next stage in the battle was more serious, for on 7–8 September Jung and Freud were due to come face-to-face at the Fourth International Congress in Munich. As president Jung had considerable powers to set the agenda, and he stipulated that the balance between time for the delivery of formal papers and time for discussion should be weighted in favour of the latter – a manoeuvre that worried Freud, who foresaw the Association breaking up in a chaos of public acrimony.[19] Things did not quite reach that stage at Munich, but the atmosphere was tense and unpleasant. Eighty-seven people attended the Congress at the Hotel Bayerischer Hof, including Théodore Flournoy (as Jung's guest) and the Austrian lyric poet Rainer Maria Rilke, guest of his former mistress Lou-Andreas Salomé. The beautiful and brilliant Lou noted in her diary that where Jung was aggressive and dogmatic, Freud was defensive and constrained by emotion at the loss of his 'son'. She noted with distaste that Jung and his supporters sat down at a table opposite Freud in open confrontation, pretending that they were defending the master against his own errors: 'If Freud takes up the lance to defend himself, it is misconstrued to mean that he cannot show scientific tolerance, is dogmatic, and so forth. One glance at the two of them tells which is more dogmatic, the more in love with power. Two years ago Jung's booming laughter gave voice to a kind of robust gaiety and exuberant vitality, but now his earnestness is composed of pure aggression, ambition and intellectual brutality.'[20]

Jung fulfilled all Freud's worst fears about his presidential performance: he bullied the Congress, arbitrarily shortened the time for papers and went back on undertakings given. As Freud said later, the conference was from the organizational point of view a disaster, being 'conducted by Jung in a disagreeable and incorrect manner; the speakers were restricted in time and the discussions overwhelmed the papers.'[21] Neither Jung nor Freud entered into open ideological confrontation: Jung read a brief paper, the germ of his later work on psychological types, and Freud lectured on 'The Disposition to Obsessional Neurosis'.[22] While Jung sheltered behind his presidential office and Freud maintained an Olympian detachment, the streetfighting went on among subordinates: Maeder attacked Freud on dream interpretation, to which the Freudians replied that what Maeder was doing was not psychoanalysis; and Ferenczi adumbrated a new theory of neurosis and transference, critical of Jung, which he called 'the psychology of conviction'.[23]

Occasionally attempts were made to lighten the atmosphere with jokes. 'The yung no longer believe in Freud,' was Ferenczi's contribution. Another joke was as follows: 'Why do certain women go to Freud, others to Jung? Because the former are *freudenmädchen* (harlots) and the latter are *jungfrauen* (virgins).'[24] But all such feeble attempts to generate a more genial ambience faltered on the second afternoon – the last time Freud and Jung were ever in the same room together – when Jung was up for re-election as president. Abraham suggested that all who disapproved of Jung should abstain and simply hand in blank ballot papers. Many, including Jones did so, and the result was fifty-two votes cast for Jung with twenty-two abstentions. Jung was furious at this implicit vote of no confidence by the Freudians. He collared Jones and taxed him with duplicity: 'I thought you had ethical principles,' he yelled. This was quite the wrong thing to do with the slippery Jones. He simply reported the remark back to Freud as 'I thought you were a Christian,' with the clear implication of anti-Semitism and the hint that Jones, as a gentile, should have made common cause against the Jewish enemy.[25]

While Freud departed for another visit to his beloved Rome, Jung brooded on the insult that had been offered him by the twenty-two abstentions. He wrote to ask Ferenczi what he meant by joining the ranks of the abstainers, and Ferenczi replied forthrightly, 'It was only the absolutely improper way in which you as Chairman of the Congress dealt with the suggestions we put forward, the quite one-sided and partial comments on the part of your group that caused us to protest by voting with blank cards.'[26] The upshot of this was a letter from Jung to Freud stating that since he had heard that Freud doubted his good faith, he was resigning as editor of the *Jahrbuch*.[27]

This move caused consternation on both sides. Maeder warned Jung that by resigning he had fallen into Freud's trap, but Jung waved the objection aside.[28] Jones told Freud the resignation was too good to be true, and counselled against trusting the Greeks when bearing gifts; Freud agreed and added that Jung's Machiavellian ploy was that he hoped Freud and Bleuler would fall out so that he would then be invited to take up the editorship again.[29] There was also the distinct possibility that Jung might negotiate directly with the *Jahrbuch*'s publisher Franz Deuticke, so Freud summoned Ferenczi urgently to Vienna for a meeting.[30]

Yet despite the manna from heaven in the form of the editorial resignation, Jung was still president of the International Association, and that was where the real power lay. At first Freud toyed with the idea of dissolving the Association or getting the Vienna, Berlin and Budapest groups to secede, but in the end he was persuaded by Jones and Abraham to let things lie, for otherwise Jung would be left in possession of the field. Freud wrote mournfully to Abraham, 'You know that in these matters I gladly let myself be advised by my friends, as since being taken in by Jung my confidence in my political judgement has greatly declined.'[31]

At the same time Jung was being urged by his friends to secede from the International Association, raising the prospect that what the Freudians wanted might be achieved for them by the other side. Jung declined to oblige, so Freud was forced to face the prospect of a long, hard struggle, in which Jones's influence in Britain and the United States would be crucial in determining the attitude of the Anglo-Saxons.[32]

Jung's self-destructive behaviour – linked to the mental crisis he was undergoing at this time – helped Freud. Although Franz Deuticke strongly sympathized with Jung, and Jung would have been willing to decamp with the *Jahrbuch* had the statutes permitted it, he made the mistake of resigning as editor and agreeing to bring out a rival journal before Deuticke had thought through the commercial consequences of having two journals under his aegis competing for a single market. When Jung realized his error, he lashed out at Jones and sent him an angry letter in English. Jones wrote to Freud gleefully, chuckling that Jung had not made sure of Deuticke in his haste.[33]

Deuticke, however, eventually decided he would risk the publication of both journals, clearly having it in mind that he would dump the *Jahrbuch* in favour of Jung once his contractual obligation ceased. Jones therefore urged Freud to transfer publication of the journal to Hugo Heller of Leipzig, on the ground that Deuticke would favour the rival Jungian journal by attending to it with despatch, while going slow on the *Jahrbuch* and by providing Jung with the best printers, proofreaders and so on. Yet Freud saw the mileage to be got out of keeping the journal with Deuticke and thus maintaining the psychological screws tightly fixed on Jung and the commercial pressures on Deuticke. In the end his judgement was proved right, for Jung abandoned his attempt to set up a rival journal and agreed to write a number of books for Deuticke instead.[34]

The next stage in exerting pressure on Jung to quit the Association was an ideological campaign to discredit the new Jungian theories. While his disciples prepared papers on detailed aspects of the new Jungian theory, Freud composed, in his 'Short History of the Psychoanalytic Movement', a devastating polemic against the man who was once his 'crown prince'.

Freud began by turning the tables on Jung. In his Fordham lectures and in subsequent addresses, Jung had continually stressed that the theories of Freud and Adler were both partial and one-sided versions of the truth. Freud repaid the compliment by stressing that it was the Adlerian and Jungian heresies that could be characterized by such epithets and, beyond that, their theories represented a truckling to bourgeois morality. Adler deferred to conventional opinion by throwing out the unconscious, Jung retained a bogus 'unconscious' while jettisoning sexuality: 'One of them explained that what is sexual does not mean sexuality at all, but something else, something abstract and mystical. And another actually declared that sexual life is merely one of the spheres in which human beings seek to put in action their driving need for power and domination.'[35]

Freud referred scornfully to Jung's boast in the USA in 1912 that he had overcome popular resistance by modifying sexuality and made again the point he had made to Jung in 1912: that the more he sacrificed the hard-won truths of psychoanalysis, the more he would see resistances vanishing.[36] Reproaching himself for not having spotted that analysts, as well as patients, could become resistant to psychoanalysis – precisely what had happened to Jung and Adler – Freud later went on to condemn the myopia of Jung's insistence that he was battling against 'sexual monocausality' when Freud had all along made it clear that in his (Freud's) system there was an ongoing duality as between the ego instincts and the libido or sexual instincts; it was Jung's psychic energy or *élan vital* that was the true monism.[37]

Jung and Adler were both guilty of taking the part for the whole: where Jung picked out actuality and regression, Adler fastened on egoistic motives.[38]

For Freud the basic fallacy in Adlerism was its relativism; with Jung the cardinal error was the fallacy that all knowledge is upwards and onwards and that youthful rebellion is always on the side of progress. Adler's ideas, though, were at least marked by coherence; Jung's were so unintelligible that almost anything (or nothing) could be made of them. On the one hand Jungian thought posed as a mild deviation, and on the other as a message of salvation and a world-view, leading one to wonder how much in Jungianism was simple lack of clarity and how much lack of sincerity.[39] This charge of turbidity was frequently brought against Jung by the Freudians. Lou-Andreas Salomé remarked, 'In Jung's hands it becomes purely a mystery how libido turns against itself and is transformed into culture and, so to speak, devours itself in the living body.'[40]

Freud accused Jung of lacking moral courage, of not being able to take the storm of disapproval he saw ahead if he pursued psychoanalysis to its conclusions; that was why he diverted into bogus religiosity and appealed to people – precisely because he appeared to free them from the 'repellent' findings of psychoanalysis.[41] Because Jung could not bear to admit that ethics and social norms derived ultimately from the Oedipus-complex, he had to claim that the complexes themselves bore a higher 'anagogic' meaning that could be dissolved in religious mysticism. Freud likened the process to that of someone who had his 'Family Romance' challenged by people who knew his actual parents, and countered this by producing a phony genealogy, thus 'proving' that his parents really were descended from royalty. The Oedipus-complex was thus dissolved in religious symbolism to create a new religious-ethical system.[42]

For Freud the most preposterous aspect of Jung's demolition of the Oedipus-complex was his assertion that it was not a specific enough idea for the aetiology of the neuroses, followed by the attribution of this specific quality to the concept of inertia, 'the most universal characteristic of all matter, animate and inanimate'.[43] Freud frequently poked fun at Jung for trying to explain neurosis through inertia, and pointed out that it was merely another word for his own, better, term 'fixation', which had been in widespread use during the years Jung was the 'crown prince'.[44] He also decisively rejected the idea that the neurotic's problems lie in the present and accused Jung of confusing the secondary gain from neurotic illness (the avoidance of a life task) with the primary source (the travails of the instinctual life).

One of Jung's strongest arguments was that withdrawal of libido would not in itself bring about the loss of the normal function of reality such as is found in schizophrenia. Of this Freud remarked that it 'is no argument but a dictum. It "begs the question" and saves discussion; for whether and how this is possible was precisely the point that should have been under investigation.'[45] Freud argued that it was Jung's own investigations on schizophrenia which established the presence in it of complexes also found in neurotic and healthy subjects, but since leaving the Burghölzli he had been content to point to the similarities between myths and schizophrenic fantasies without throwing any further light on the mechanism of the disease. This all tied in with the general consideration that all Jung's best work had been done while he still embraced psychoanalysis; his work had gone downhill only when he conceived the ambition of becoming a prophet.[46]

By concentrating on Jung's wild analogies (his analogies were always the weakest part of his argumentation), Freud was able to rebut the idea that libido theory could not explain schizophrenia and therefore could not explain the neuroses. Jung glibly observed that libido theory would result in the psychology of an anchorite, not a schizophrenic.

By his 'varicose veins' remark, Jung left himself wide open to counter-attack on the grounds of simple-mindedness. To use so-called common sense to unseat the Oedipus-complex by saying that a young man would be bound to prefer a young and pretty woman to a hag is as absurd as the notorious attempt made by Oxford 'ordinary language' philosophy to say that, because we can ascertain that a bridegroom is at a wedding of his own free will, the general problem of free will does not exist. Freud thought that a similar simplistic confusion of dream-images with latent dream-thoughts vitiated the allegedly 'new' Jungian theory of dreams: 'The view that sexual representation of "higher" thoughts in dreams and neurosis is nothing but an archaic mode of expression is of course irreconcilable with the fact that in neuroses these sexual complexes prove to be the bearers of quantities of libido which have been withdrawn from utilisation in real life.'[47]

Freud wound up his polemic with a flourish as fine as Jung's anti-Freudian rhetoric: 'It may be said lastly that by his "modification" of psychoanalysis Jung has given us a counterpart to the famous Lichtenberg knife. He has changed the hilt and he has put a new blade into it, yet because the same name is engraved on it we are expected to regard the instrument as the original one.'[48]

Freud's lead was followed by his disciples. Ferenczi objected that Jung had got rid of repression, abandoned the individual unconscious, and reduced the incest-complex to the purely symbolic. Inertia or laziness as the real cause of neurosis was absurd, as was the hypothesis that the erotic impulses uncovered in analysis were 'symbolic', not real. Worst of all errors was to direct the patient's attention away from the past and to surrender the vital part of analysis – the patient's reliving of traumatic infantile experiences; one could not deal with complexes by directing the patient away from them and urging him to sublimate, but only by exhaustive examination of the complexes.[49]

Freudians combed through their work to winnow out any expressions that might have heretical connotations. Freud detested the term 'subconscious' when used instead of 'unconscious', for it had resonances of Janet's 'subconscious' and hence of Jung.[50] Even when talking of the death-drive in 'Beyond the Pleasure Principle' Freud made a point of avoiding the popular tag 'Thanatos' (as the opposing instinct to Eros), since this was a term too closely associated with Stekel.[51] But the most important term to be excised from the Freudian vocabulary after 1913 was 'complex'.[52]

Freud took especial delight in engaging Jung on his own chosen ground. A source of particular satisfaction was the publication in late 1913 of *Totem and Taboo*, in which he explained that Jung's speculations had inspired him, but he had come to radically different conclusions.[53]

In some ways even more richly satisfying was the emergence of Sabina Spielrein as a fully-fledged Freudian and Freud confidante. Although Freud never had any personal affection for Spielrein, as, for example, he had in abundance for Lou-Andreas Salomé – possibly because Spielrein and Jung had been lovers – she was useful to him as another glaring example of Jung's perfidy. Freud notified her of the final break with Jung, and was alarmed to hear that Spielrein, though married and pregnant, still nursed a passion for him.[54] Freud was now increasingly inclined to see the split with Jung in racial/cultural terms, as the incompatibility of Jew with Aryan. Writing to enquire about the progress of her pregnancy just before he departed for the tension-laden Munich conference in September 1913, Freud told her, 'I am, as you know, cured of the last shred of my predilection for the

Aryan cause, and would like to take it that if the child turns out to be a boy he will develop into a stalwart Zionist. We are and remain Jews. The others will only exploit us and will never understand or appreciate us.' When Spielrein gave birth to a daughter, Renate, in September, Freud wrote, 'Well now, my heartiest congratulations. It is far better that the child should be a "she". Now we can think again about the blond Siegfried and smash that idol before his time comes.'[55]

Meanwhile the organizational battle with Jung continued into 1914, for Jung, though no longer editor of the *Jahrbuch*, was still very much president of the International Association. Jones, who directed the Freudian campaign, was determined that Jung should not be permitted to manoeuvre the Freudians into staying away from the next conference, possibly by choosing a difficult venue, and was in favour of dissolving the Association rather than submit to that tactic. Freud and Jones tried to pre-empt any such manoeuvre by building up a head of steam for a conference in Dresden, hoping to create a runaway bandwaggon that Jung could not resist.[56] Clever politicking by Jones and other Freudians coupled with errors by the Zürichers forced Jung into a corner where he either had to accept being a figurehead president, at the beck and call of the Freudians, or assert his independence. Jung chose the latter course, and on 20 April 1914 he resigned from the presidency. Although Jung was still a member of the Association, Freud was ecstatic, as is clear from his correspondence with Abraham.[57]

Elated by the resignation of Jung, Freud turned on the heat to force out the rest of the Zürich school. His correspondence showed a new mental spring in his step, evidenced by some striking shafts at Jung's expense: 'Anyone who promises mankind liberation from the hardships of sex will be hailed as a hero, let him talk whatever nonsense he chooses.' Remarking that Jung was now showing open adherence to Bergson, he quipped, 'So you see he has found another Jew for his father complex. I am no more jealous.'[58]

What finally broke the spirits of the Zürich school was the publication of the swingeing polemic in Freud's 'History of the Psychoanalytic Movement'. Freud toned down just one reference to Jung which had appeared in his original draft. On Jones's advice he excised a passage which read, 'One characteristic trait of Jung's was . . . his tendency to push aside ruthlessly someone else who is in the way.'[59] Yet what remained was powerful enough. Jung could not tolerate what he read as a public insult, and on 22 July 1914 he resigned as a member of the Association. On the same day the Zürich group voted 15–1 to withdraw. This ended three months of uncertainty as to Jung's ultimate intentions.[60] Freud wrote in euphoria to Abraham, 'So we are at last rid of them, the brutal sanctimonious Jung and his disciples.'

As Jones had feared, Jung's new tactic was to take his gospel to the Anglo-Saxons and, with this in mind, he accepted an invitation to lecture to the British Medical Association in July 1914. Jones was in favour of sending Freudians to each lecture for the purpose of heckling, but Freud advised against this, saying that such a demonstration, if used, should be reserved for a single occasion and the most important lecture. Jones kept nagging away at the precarious state of the psychoanalytical movement in Britain, mentioning that three had already defected to Jung, including Dr Constance Long, his hostess in July. Jones responded by a three-line whip, ordering all British Freudians to have no contact at all with Jung, on pain of excommunication.[61] Freud's particular worry was that his favourite among British Freudians, Dr Montague David Eder, might declare for Jung. Jones advised him that his fears were well grounded, since Eder had told him that Freud's treatment of Jung was undignified and unworthy; also Eder sympathized with Jung on religious grounds and had more than a dash of anti-Semitism in his makeup.[62]

Preoccupied with a battle against insanity, of which more in the next chapter, and of which the Freudians knew nothing, Jung lacked the surplus energy for the Machiavellian ploys imagined by Jones. In April 1914, at the same time as his resignation as president of the Association, he resigned in disgust as lecturer (*Privatdozent*) when the University of Zürich refused to promote him to full professor.[63] His wife's fifth pregnancy scarcely impinged on him, nor did the birth of his fifth child, Emma, on 18 March 1914. Buoyed up by a eulogy in the *British Medical Journal* in January 1914, which spoke of Jung's new bearing in psychology as a return to 'a saner view of life', Jung was keen to accept the invitation to address the BMA's annual conference in Aberdeen in July. His first stop was London where, in Bedford College, Regents Park, he attended a joint session of the Aristotelian Society, the Mind Association and the British Psychological Society, who were holding a symposium on 'Are Individual Minds Contained in God or Not?' Jung found the proceedings intellectually shallow and disappointing and listened in astonishment to arguments that would not have been out of place in a thirteenth-century monastery.[64]

Then he continued north to Aberdeen. His lecture, on the importance of the unconscious in psychopathology, was a great success. Once again he stressed the wider definition of libido and substituted the term 'prospective psychology' for psychoanalysis. The psychologist W. McDougall was so impressed that he arranged to be analysed by Jung, and Jones's hopes for British Freudians suffered a setback when Constance Long and Eder announced that Jung's 'deviation' from orthodoxy was a legitimate development of psychoanalysis.[65]

While Jung was in Aberdeen in the summer of 1914 the international crisis boiled over. The Great Powers mobilized, and the exigencies of railway timetables did the rest. In Jung's precarious mental state, to be stranded in Scotland while a world war broke out was not a consummation devoutly to be wished. It took him a month to get back home to Switzerland, proceeding tortuously at every stage of the journey, first back to England, then to Holland, thence to Germany and finally down the Rhine to Basel. The continental part of the journey was particularly painful: he spent several nights standing in train corridors while the train was shunted into sidings to let express troop transports through.[66] From his experience of Germany gripped by war fever Jung derived many of his later ideas about the group unconscious of nations. Everyone in Germany was in a state of ecstasy, with food being given away and nobody bothering to take payment for anything. Jung began to form the theory that Germans had a lower threshold between consciousness and unconsciousness than other nationalities, which was why they had a tendency to succumb to ideas that appeal to the masses. The relief when he crossed the Swiss frontier into normality was indescribable.

1914, that fateful year which doomed the old Europe of the Central Powers, Prussia and the Austro-Hungarian Empire, also closed the door for ever on the relationship between Freud and Jung. Why did their friendship come to an end? Was it doomed from the very beginning? How far was the rift primarily ideological and how far did ideology act as camouflage for deep personal incompatibilities?

We may dismiss at the outset any reductive explanation for the breach. John Kerr, taking the oldest route of them all, *cherchez la femme*, has suggested that just as it was Sabina Spielrein who was instrumental in bringing the two men together, so she was the catalyst that eventually drove them apart. On this view, what each man knew about the other's private life created a tension that was in the end unsustainable.[67] This highly speculative view depends on too many unverifiables and is not borne out by the portion of the evidence that is verifiable.

Another simplistic view is that Freud was a dogmatist who could not bear to have his cherished views questioned, who made sexuality into a kind of secular religion, and therefore had to cast into anathema all heretics who deviated from the 'party line'. Freud made his position clear on many occasions: that although he was not distressed by disagreements on points of detail, there was simply no point in trying to work together within a single movement with people whose views diverged so widely from orthodoxy that there was no agreement on first principles or basic methodology. A.A. Brill summed this up well: 'As I have been in the thick of the movement I can definitely state that Jung would have preferred to have remained in the psychoanalytic fold but his views differed so much from those of Freud that it was best for both parties to separate.'[68] Another dispassionate observer, Hermann Nunberg, who, like Brill, had worked with Jung at the Burghölzli, stated that Jung's new bearing in 1912–13 was in effect an abandonment of psychoanalysis and was therefore not so much a deviation as a desertion.[69]

At one level, of course, the Jung–Freud rift was merely another in a long line of notorious intellectual quarrels between individuals of supreme talent, drawn together by the attractions of genius but finally separated by incompatible ways of viewing the world. The obvious examples are the quarrels between Hume and Rousseau, D.H. Lawrence and Bertrand Russell, Wagner and Nietzsche.[70] It would be absurd to deny that ideological differences played a part in the split, but seismic cracks like this do not appear simply because of technical disputes on the origin of the incest taboo. Freud himself was inclined to believe his problems with Jung typified a general incompatibility between Jew and gentile, that Jung hated the 'Jewishness' of psychoanalysis and wanted to substitute a Christianized version. Here was irony indeed. Freud had wanted Jung to be his apostle to the gentiles, to prevent psychoanalysis from becoming a Jewish sect. But Jung played the role of St Paul in a quite other sense. Just as Paul had substituted neo-Platonic

'Christology' for the original teachings of Jesus, so Jung proposed a psychoanalysis purged of the elements that had kept Freudianism ghettoized as a construct of Viennese Jews.

Jung's 'Christ complex', the view that he was a deliverer and, like the Messiah, must suffer at the hands of the Father, together with the desire to Christianize psychoanalysis, suggests that the deep drive in his relationship with Freud was the desire to solve the problems left undone in his youth, principally those of religion and his father. The father/son motif in the relationship was explicitly recognized by both parties – indeed Emma Jung protested about it in her epistolary interventions in late 1911 – but the inevitable result of replaying the Oedipal struggle would have to be that Jung 'killed' the father. The extent to which Jung conflated his real father and Freud has been widely recognized. As Homans has remarked, Jung's portrait of Freud as a dogmatic 'is identical to the view he repeatedly expressed about his father, whom he pitied for being hopelessly trapped in dogmatism, not of psychoanalysis but of Christian theology.'[71]

No-one reading the Jung–Freud correspondence closely can be unaware of Jung's death-wishes towards Freud – about which the master complained so often, and which triggered his two separate fainting fits; for one thing, the evidence is clearly there in Jung's dreams. Parricide was often on Freud's mind, and never more so than when he wrote *Totem and Taboo* at the height of the crisis with Jung. One of the key notions in this work was the idea of the father of the 'primal horde', who possessed all the women in the tribe, being slain by his sons. Just as the father's harem was then shared between the sons, so it was the fate of the unified and synoptic psychoanalytic doctrine to be apportioned by Freud's 'sons'. This was why, in his view, each of the Freudian successors fastened on part only of his teachings and made that part the centre of a world-view: so Adler opted for the will to power, Jung ethical conflict, Rank birth trauma and the Mother, and Reich genitality.[72]

That Jung was an unwilling son was noted by Freud, who, particularly during the tension filled years of 1912–13, often referred to him as *L'Aiglon*. This was typical of Freud's complex cast of mind. *Aiglon*, French for 'young eagle', was originally a reference to Jung as emulator of Adler, whose name means 'eagle' in German ('jung' means 'young'). The 'eagle' therefore meant a deserter, but it had a further layer of meaning when applied to Jung, for Napoleon's son (Napoleon II) had also been called *L'Aiglon*, and he had not lived to fulfil his father's mission. Freud's love of word-play emerges in his letter to Ferenczi just before the 1913 Munich Conference when he hoped that the two eagles would rend each other: 'It would be quite right if Adler and Aiglon tore each other up a bit with their beaks.'[73]

Alongside the father–son, 'Oedipal' conflict there was an element in the relationship between Jung and Freud, especially in the early years, that was bound to lead to disillusionment and disappointment. Homans has identified this as a kind of transference, which involved narcissism and hence (by transference) an idealization of the other, complete with feelings of empathy and psychic merger.[74] The early letters are full of this kind of thing, most notably the occasion after the return from the USA in 1909 when Freud wrote, 'The day after we separated an incredible number of people looked incredibly like you; wherever I went in Hamburg, your light hat with the dark band kept turning up. And the same in Berlin.'[75] Another striking example of Freud's indulgence of Jung was the way he dropped everything to read a novel Jung recommended in 1907 – Thomas Jensen's *Gradiva* – and then wrote an essay on the book.[76] This was no mere one-way traffic: the compliment was amply repaid by Jung on a number of occasions.[77]

On this aspect of the relationship two comments are pertinent. On Freud the judgement comes from Paul Roazen: 'He sometimes extended himself to people too enthusiastically and tended to idealise them. He then later blamed them for not having qualities which he himself had imputed to them, for having failed to live up to his fantasied conception of them.'[78] As for the Jungian side of the equation, Homans comments, 'Jung's need to idealise Freud became so strong that he idealised Freud's psychoanalytic ideas into the dimension of a religion. Jung tried to endow Freud and psychoanalysis with religious powers. Freud repudiated these idealisations, provoking responses of narcissistic rage from Jung, and it was Jung's disappointment that . . . led to the break between the two men . . . it seems inevitable that Jung's many unresolved childhood and adolescent religious experiences would emerge under the impact of a regressive relationship such as he had established with Freud.'[79]

Some observers have taken an Occam's razor approach to the Jung–Freud relationship and suggested that the whole thing was a case of mistaken identity. On the one hand was Jung, a man who was the exact opposite of a team player, hated belonging to any form of organization and, as his later career showed, was only happy when functioning as a solitary oracle. On the other hand was Freud, foolishly imagining that such a man would work assiduously to promote a great movement rather than his own career. Freud's poor judgement of men was often commented on, even by his friends and disciples. Jones wrote that the choice of Jung as 'crown prince' was the first indication he had that Freud, despite being a genius, was not a connoisseur of men.[80] Abraham took great delight in pointing out to Freud that he had been right about Jung from the very beginning, only to be over-ruled by the Master, and Freud reluctantly conceded the truth of this.[81]

A variant of this view is that Freud had an unconscious need to quarrel with his collaborators, and the names of Fliess, Breuer, Adler, Stekel, Rank and Ferenczi are mentioned, alongside Jung's, as proof of this. As early as 1900 Freud noticed that his friends often became enemies.[82] He was not able to shrug this off and in 1913 spoke darkly of the 'tragedy of ingratitude'.[83] Some critics, using the central Freudian notion of 'repetition compulsion' – which brought him to the idea of the 'death-drive' in 1920 in *Beyond the Pleasure Principle* – have argued that this notion was a rationalization of Freud's own 'compulsion to repeat' as evinced in the many breakdowns of friendships. Certainly in his 1920 work Freud did speak of patterns of human relationships which had the same outcome and gave as an example 'the benefactor who is abandoned in anger after a time by each of his protégés, however much they may otherwise differ from one another, and who thus seems doomed to taste all the bitterness of ingratitude.'[84]

However, the idea of Freud as doomed to fall out with his friends and co-workers does not really survive critical scrutiny. Apart from his many enduring friendships outside his own field, Freud retained the friendship and partnership of many leading figures in psychoanalysis, with some of whom he had major arguments and disagreements. Aware of the canard that he could not keep friends, Freud near the end of his life pointed out that he had never broken with Abraham, Jones, Eitingon, Brill, Reik and van Emden, to mention just a few of the luminaries of the psychoanalytic movement.[85] Most significantly of all, he maintained a close professional and personal relationship with Swiss Aryans like Pfister and Binswanger. Even Bleuler, who broke with psychoanalysis, always remained on friendly terms with Freud, but after 1913 had nothing to do with Jung. Jung, by contrast, quarrelled with *all* his important male friends and associates, so that his 'court' came to be composed solely of admiring females.

It is probably necessary to take the long view before coming to any final judgement on the Freud–Jung split. Sifting through the correspondence between the two during 1907–12 yields some clues, but the letters can be read selectively so as to yield diametrically opposite conclusions, a Freudian seeing only Jung's faults, and vice versa.[86] Perhaps the most salient consideration is that Jung could never co-operate properly with others or treat them as equals. Binswanger's comment, when asked why so many of Freud's most talented followers broke away, is shrewd, 'Precisely because they too wanted to be Popes.'[87] But a Pope can ascend to the throne of Peter only when the old Pope is dead. St Paul could amend Jesus's teachings radically, and Lenin Marx's, precisely because the founders in whose name they purported to speak were dead. Even Plato, who transmogrified Socrates's ethical teachings into metaphysics, cosmology and epistemology while claiming that this was all the work of 'Socrates', could begin his work only when his master had taken hemlock. Here, then, we see the significance both of Jung's death-wishes for Freud and of his own *ex cathedra* pronouncements once he became an independent prophet.

Whether Jung could have elaborated a satisfactory general theory of the world if he had stayed within the psychoanalytic movement and waited patiently for Freud's death, or whether Freud could have deepened his individual-based critique of the world in *Civilisation and Its Discontents* by incorporating the insights of Jung's vast erudition, must remain unanswerable and, ultimately, meaningless questions, for had they been capable of such partnership, Jung would not have been Jung and Freud would not have been Freud. One thing can, however, be asserted with certainty. The impact of Jung's desertion rocked Freud and he had, so to speak, to take a count of nine before getting to his feet again. But for Jung the effect of the break with Freud was to take him to the very edge of incurable insanity.

Chapter Thirteen

THE DESCENT INTO THE UNDERWORLD

During 1913–14, when the break with Freud was becoming absolute, Jung became ever more agitated and unbalanced in his mind, to the point where he eventually accused Freud of being the Devil.[1] This was part of a general process of mental disintegration which took him to the edge of the abyss. Jung realized he was suffering from psychic disturbance after a number of dreams and fantasies involving corpses and death. First came a puzzling dream of a white male dove and twelve dead people: the dove had a human voice and declared that only when the male dove was absorbed with the twelve dead could the female convert herself into a human. Christian imagery suggested that the dove was the Holy Ghost and the twelve dead the twelve apostles, but in that case what did the dream mean? Jung began to think he was on the wrong track and that the significant twelve might be the signs of the zodiac or the months of the year. Next came a dream in which he was in a necropolis like the one at Cerveteri or the Alyscamps in Arles. In the necropolis dream he found himself among rows of tombs – stone slabs on which lay the mummified dead. He found one dead figure from the 1830s, another from the eighteenth century, and finally a twelfth-century crusader.[2]

It does not take exceptional insight to see that in his dreams Jung was trying to come to terms with the loss of Freud. The link between the crusader and Freud has already been made, as have images of the mummified dead (peat-bog men and Pharaohs) with Jung's wish for Freud's death. Moreover, if the twelve dead people in the first dream were taken to refer to the Apostles, this would conjure associations of betrayal of the Master – Judas and Peter's denying thrice – again making a link with Freud.

Realizing that if a patient had come to him with these symptoms he would have diagnosed nervous breakdown, Jung determined to engage with his visions and at first tried self-analysis, going over his childhood memories with an analytical fine-tooth comb. His first strong childhood memory was as a child playing with stones as building blocks in order to create castles, temples and houses. to begin with he resisted the idea of 'regression' to childhood by playing infantile games, but then thought that the strength of his resistance might itself indicate neurosis. He began by walking along the shore of Lake Zürich, gathering suitable stones for the construction of cottages. Then he built cottages, a castle, a church and finally an entire village, reproducing accurately his childhood habits. As he thus 'abreacted' his childhood, he reactivated the childhood dream of the underground chamber with the giant phallus, assisted by the finding on the lake shore of a red pyramidal stone.[3]

These building games served as a conduit for a stream of fantasies: whenever he suffered from 'analyst's block' he painted a picture or hewed a stone and this released a creative torrent. He built up a daily routine, whereby he would play with his village in the morning, break off to see patients in the afternoon, and then return to the stones in the evening. His secret fear was that he was tainted with the madness of his maternal great grandmother and that what he was experiencing was incipient schizophrenia. By the late summer of 1913 he had resisted the temptation to turn inwards sufficiently to be able to deal with life in the external world, and it was in this mental state that he attended the Munich conference.

Yet the return to the 'normal' world did not reassure him as much as he had hoped. This world too seemed darker than he had remembered it before his first disturbing dream, and he began to be convinced that what was oppressing him was 'out there' and not in his mind. The conviction hardened after a bizarre experience in early October 1913 while travelling by train between Zürich and Schaffhausen. As the train entered a tunnel, Jung went into a trance, lost all consciousness of time and place, and came to an hour later only when the conductor announced the arrival at Schaffhausen. During his hallucination he saw all the countries of Europe gradually sink into the sea, overwhelmed by a monstrous flood with huge yellow waves which drowned people and bore away the rubble of civilization. Switzerland was like a high mountain, completely safe, and he himself was perched on the highest peak; but when he looked into the sea, it was red with blood, and corpses and houses were floating in the water. Three months later, at the end of December, on the very same train and when entering the selfsame tunnel he again went into a trance and saw the same vision.[4]

During April–July he had another alarming vision in which he found himself in Sumatra with a friend. They learned that a dreadful cold wave was sweeping Europe, so Jung decided to go to Jakarta to take a ship for home. When he arrived, Europe was in the grip of an Arctic chill; he remembered seeing the canals of Lorraine frozen and blighted. Switzerland was covered in snow and he came upon a tree in the polar landscape. The tree was covered with sweet grapes, full of healing juices, and he found himself feeding grapes to a throng of hungry people. This hallucination in turn was repeated three times, the last when he was in Aberdeen in July 1914. The declaration of war in Europe came as a relief to him, for he was then able to interpret his visions as having cosmic rather than merely individual significance. It was also in his mind confirmation that there really was a collective unconscious, from which the prophetic dreams had come.[5]

However, parts at least of this vision seem to refer to Jung's personal experiences. The cold, ice and frost of the Arctic dream suggest a sense of abandonment and vulnerability, of Siberian exile after the years of solidarity with Freud. In February 1910 he had told Freud that what excited him about psychoanalysis was the possibility that it might transform Christianity.[6] Giving grapes to the crowd at the end of the 'Arctic' vision seems to indicate that he now thought of himself as the 'god of the vine', and it is fascinating to see in the light of this vision Jones's charge that Jung wanted to be a redeemer and Freud's that he wanted to be a prophet.

At various times Jung felt that his unconscious was on the point of overwhelming and subduing his conscious, which would make him like the poor creatures he had tended in the Burghölzli. He decided to carry the fight over into the enemy's territory by plunging into the 'dark continent' of the unconscious. He noted the exact date when he 'let himself go': it was 12 December 1913.

At first panic overtook Jung when he plunged down into the dark depths and let the hallucinations from the unconscious take over. He feared he might have dived into a bottomless pit but in the end his fall was checked by 'a soft sticky mess'. He found himself at the entrance of a cave, blocked by a mummified dwarf. He forced his way past the dwarf and waded through cold water to the other end of the cave, where he found a crystal glowing red. He lifted a stone supporting the crystal and found a smaller cave underneath, through which water ran. In the water floated the corpse of a youth with a wound in his head. A huge black scarab then appeared, followed by a blood-red sun rising out of the depths of the second cave. A brilliant light blinded him, he tried to replace the stone over the corpse, the water and the sun, but a thick jet of blood spouted upwards and poured crimson over everything.[7]

He interpreted this as a drama of death, reversal and rebirth, symbolized by the scarab, but was at a loss to understand the blood. Clearly the blood linked with the blood in his vision on the train, but the mummified dwarf is an unmistakable reference to Freud, not just because of the already noted mummy theme, but because of the difference in height (Freud was five-foot-seven, Jung six-foot-one) he had frequently commented on. The dead dwarf was the man with the defunct doctrines blocking his passage to rebirth, new values, aims and ideals.

On 18 December 1913 Jung recorded an even more significant dream featuring Freud. Just before he went to sleep, an inner voice told him that if he could not understand the dream he was about to have, he would have no choice but to shoot himself; obedient to his voices, Jung loaded his service revolver and placed it on the bedside table. In the dream that ensued he saw two men, one a dusky savage, the other himself, in a rocky landscape; the pair had been given a mission to kill Siegfried. Then Siegfried appeared in a chariot and the two men shot him down. The murderers then ran away full of remorse, the landscape darkened, and it began to rain. When he awoke Jung interpreted this as a message that life should go on, so he did not use the revolver. Consciously he explained away Siegfried as the Kaiser's Germany with its expansionist desires, while the brown-skinned savage who had accompanied him and taken the initiative in the slaying was the embodiment of his own primitive shadow or possibly his No. 2 self.[8]

Once again Jung shied away from the obvious meaning. It is a commonplace of Jungian hermeneutics that Siegfried stands for Freud and that the murder and guilt represent Jung's 'parricide'. It is also entirely plausible that the brown-skinned savage who 'took the initiative' in the murder could be Adler, the first to defect.[9]

Following this dream, which seemed to hold out some hope that the tension between conscious and unconscious might be resolvable, Jung decided to make a determined effort in his next fantasy to reach the bottom of the abyss. This time he found himself in the land of the dead and met an old man, whom he identified as Elijah, in company with a beautiful blind girl, whom he named Salome. Jung hypothesized that in dreams one encounters archetypal figures and archetypal pairings. Salome and Elijah fitted easily into a mythical tradition that an old man is frequently accompanied by a young girl; he cited the Gnostic tradition of Simon Magus and his young girl companion Helen, Klingsor and Kundry in the Teutonic myths and Lao-tzu and the dancing girl in the Chinese stories. At another level Elijah and Salome represented the principles of, respectively, Logos and Eros.[10]

Jung's explanation for Elijah and Salome is of the kind that, while purporting to explain something, actually ends by making it more mysterious than ever. So what did they really mean? At one level they represented Jung's experience of the female principle. Elijah was Jung's No. 2 personality reified, while Salome was a transmogrification of Toni Wolff. To put it another way, Elijah and Salome were inner symbolizations of the 'real' relationship between Jung and Toni, and the symbols worked particularly well since Jung, approaching forty, looked much older while Toni looked much younger.[11] But, as Jung was constantly to stress, no one interpretation exhausts the significance of the symbols encountered in dreams and visions. It may be, as Walter Kaufman suggests, that Salome as female image was only partly Toni Wolff, and that there was an added component in the form of Jung's remembrances from the Munich conference of the beautiful Lou-Andreas Salomé.[12]

Salome is also significant as one of the first images of the feminine (what Jung called the *anima*) to appear in his dreams. Her blindness can be read as a warning: that unless she was made to see, Jung's own future was doomed. As Van der Post puts it, 'For him to say that Salome was blind because the anima is incapable of seeing, is really the unconscious way of confessing that he himself could not see the meaning of Salome.'[13] Moreover, in the course of 'amplification' of the symbol, we should not forget the biblical significance of Salome: she it was who, in pursuit of an incestuous affair with her stepfather, had John the Baptist beheaded. And the motif of destroying female gains extra resonance from the old Hebrew legend that Elijah had been seduced by the witch Lilith, in some traditions Adam's first wife.

From the therapeutic point of view the most important thing about Elijah and Salome as fantasy figures was that Jung controlled them; they did not become his masters as would have been the case in full-blown schizophrenia. To put it another way, they remained as characters in his drama, where in madness he would have been a character in theirs.

The next fantasy figure to emerge from the unconscious was Philemon, a sort of fusion of Elijah and Salome. Where Elijah and Salome were wholly human, Philemon was a composite being, a mythological creature recalling centaurs, mermaids and the Minotaur. One aspect of him was an old man 'of Egypto-Hellenistic atmosphere with Gnostic colourations.' But he also had the wings of a kingfisher, the horns of a bull, and was lame in one foot. He first appeared to Jung while in flight, holding a bunch of four keys, one ready to open a lock.

Jung used to talk to Philemon in his garden at Küsnacht as if he were a real person. Whole dialogues were transcribed into notebooks which came to be known as the Black Book and the Red Book: the Black Book consisted of six black-bound, smallish leather notebooks in which the original jottings were scribbled, while the Red Book – a folio volume bound in red leather – contained the same fantasies couched in elaborately literary form and language, set down in calligraphic Gothic script in the manner of medieval manuscripts, and embellished with drawings. As part of his therapy Jung painted a picture of Philemon, complete with kingfisher wings; in an amazing example of what he would later call 'synchronicity' or significant coincidence, while he was painting he found in his lakeshore garden a dead kingfisher – a bird that was extremely rare in Zürich and environs. The experience with Philemon reinforced Jung's growing belief that elements in the psyche could arise from sources independent of personal experience, for Philemon uttered thoughts that were alien to Jung's consciousness.

From the psychiatric viewpoint Jung was talking to himself, and the entire Philemon experience was a schizophrenic episode, a psychotic symptom in no essential way different from the delusions and voices perceived by the Burghölzli patients. But from Jung's point of view he experienced in the Philemon period the core of what he would later call the 'individuation process', in which the conscious ego encountered the archetypes of mother, father and self. In his 'conversations' Jung asked Philemon if he was real, and he replied enigmatically.[14] In terms of Jung's later theories, Philemon was an 'archetypal image of the spirit', one of the plethora of unconscious images which can overwhelm and destroy the people we call 'mad'. Jung regarded Philemon as proof of what he called 'the objectivity of the psyche' and also the sign of the 'mythopoeic imagination' or old wisdom forced underground in a modern, technological society. Philemon represented forces that were both scoffed at and feared in the West, but in the East they had an honoured place, and a Hindu would have no trouble in regarding him as a spirit guru. Many years later a friend of Gandhi's told Jung that gurus could be living or ghostly, and while most people had live gurus to guide them, some special souls had spirits as teachers.[15]

Bracketing the 'objectivity' of Philemon, we may still ask what he means in symbolic terms. Jung always saw him in purely mythological terms and later syncretized him with the Egyptian *ka* as a kind of earth demon or spirit of nature.[16] Critics have suggested that Philemon has three possible sources or is perhaps a conflation of three elements. There is, first, the winged bull of Mithras, a recurrent motif in alchemy – this is plausible, for Jung always stressed the importance of alchemy for understanding Philemon. Secondly, there is the Greek comic poet Philemon, who was Menander's contemporary. Thirdly, there is the Philemon who, with Baucis, appears in mythology as the only humans to offer hospitality to Zeus and Hermes when they came down to earth in human form to test Man's piety, and was rewarded by being made high priest of the temple of Zeus.[17] Clearly, given that Philemon and Baucis appear in Goethe's *Faust* (Jung's favourite book), where they are murdered by the eponymous hero, it is this Philemon that Jung had at least partly in mind, and he explicitly confirmed this.[18]

Jung admitted that he felt an irrational sense of guilt when he read how Faust murdered Philemon, and later chiselled into the stone wall of his second home at Bollingen the expiatory words PHILEMON SACRUM – FAUSTI POENITENTIA (Philemon's shrine – Faust's penitence).[19] On the face of it, the guilt about Philemon suggests murderous feelings towards his parents, but it may be that, once again, the true focus of parricide is Freud – for one thing, Jung's painting of Philemon actually looks like Freud. The 'safe' reading of Philemon is to view him as a Janus figure: at once a sign of Jung's regaining his own authority (by a process of inwardness) after destroying Freud/Siegfried and a prefiguring of his emphasis on the tasks of the second half of life, when gurus and wise old men come into their own.[20]

We know that Jung had a particular interest in St Paul, and the New Testament contains Paul's epistle to Philemon, in which Paul asks Philemon, a Christian convert, to take back his thieving runaway slave and forgive him. It is not entirely implausible that the true conflation in Jung's mind was between this Philemon and the one in *Faust* who caused him so much guilt. If Jung's No. 1 and No. 2 personalities were split as between Philemon and Faust, victim and murderer, in Goethe's work, he may also have been split as between Paul, the apostle to the gentiles (the role he was supposed to have played on Freud's behalf), and the thieving runaway slave (with Freud as Philemon) in the New Testament. The Faust/Philemon pairing could then take on the resonance of all the other legendary pairings featuring a betrayer and a betrayed – Judas/Jesus, Hagen/Siegfried, Brutus/Caesar and, at the limit, Freud and Jung.

If Jung's theory of neurosis were correct, his own attitude to Philemon would make perfect sense. Jung had stressed the prospective function of neurosis, which enabled feelings of anxiety and guilt to be transmuted positively so that the neurotic could face life's tasks. Philemon might well have played a therapeutic, 'individuating' role for Jung, enabling him to break through into the second half of life without going mad, but this 'prospective' function would have been matched by the backward-looking elements of Philemon which referred to Freud.

How are we to interpret Jung's mental illness during these years? Those hostile to Jung have suggested that he was certifiably schizophrenic from 1913–18, and we can therefore discount his post-Freudian ideas, as they are the product of madness and thus no more significant than the ravings of his Burghölzli patients. All experts are agreed that Jung's skirmish with insanity was a 'near miss', but disagree on the diagnostic model that would explain his plight.

Perhaps the safest, if perhaps overly timid, diagnosis is to make Jung a sufferer from the 'mid-life crisis' famously analysed by Elliott Jacques.[21] Jacques demonstrated that creative people often go through a profound crisis in their late thirties, leading either to death or significant renewal. Jung, who was obsessed (not too strong a word) with Nietzsche, was perfectly well aware how closely his own experience resembled that of the great German who had died in an insane asylum in the year Jung graduated from Zürich. It was this fate that he feared above all and, having survived madness by the skin of his teeth, he was often to say that the experience gave him a unique insight into the forces that carried off Nietzsche.

Jung sometimes wrote later as if his 'spirit guide' Philemon virtually guaranteed that he would emerge from the valley of shadows, but a close reading of the evidence shows that for a long time it was touch and go. For at least four years he lived in a state of constant tension and near-breakdown, and he often reflected, with justifiable pride, that it was only his immense toughness that pulled him through. As one mental storm succeeded another, he frequently had to force himself to do yoga exercises to keep his emotions in check. But he made it clear that his motivation was very different from that of the Indian yogi, who exercised in order to obliterate the multitude of psychic images and contents: Jung practised yoga simply to give himself the strength to *return* to the fearsome world of the unconscious. Whenever he was able to translate his emotions into images he was overjoyed, for that way he navigated between the Scylla of leaving the images hidden within his emotions – with the danger that he would be torn to pieces by them – and the Charybdis of 'splitting', which would have sucked him into the vortex of 'autonomous complexes'.

Permanently afraid of losing command of himself and becoming prey to his fantasies, he reasoned that he had to take the chance, for how could he expect his patients to do what he could not do himself? From these experiences as much as from the discussions with Freud he came to the absolute conviction that every analyst, to be any use to his patient, should have submitted to a training analysis himself. But he never pretended that any part of his journey through the realm of the unconscious was anything but painful. He admitted that he was writing down fantasies which struck him as nonsense and found it a singular irony that, himself a psychiatrist, he had run into material which usually appeared in the dreams and images of his psychotic patients. The germs of the 'collective unconscious' were born here.[22]

By 1916 Jung had experienced three years of conversations with Philemon and thought it was time to write down his thoughts and make sense of them. There was immediately a strange atmosphere in the house: his eldest daughter saw a white figure in her room and his second daughter reported that twice during the night her blankets had been snatched away. His nine-year-old son had a nightmare the same night, and in the morning asked for crayons (normally he never drew) and sketched an alarming picture of a fisherman over whom an angel and a devil struggled. That was on a Saturday morning. On Sunday afternoon, about 5 p.m., the front door bell began ringing insistently, but when the maid opened it, there was nobody there. It seemed to Jung that the house was filled with a crowd of spirits, so tightly packed inside the house that he could scarcely breathe. Slipping into one of his trances, Jung asked the 'spirits' what it all meant. The answer came, 'We have come back from Jerusalem where we found not what we sought.'[23]

Jung immediately sat down at his desk and began writing furiously; as soon as he started, the hauntings ceased. Within three days he had completed the essay later published as *Septem Sermones ad Mortuos*. He claimed that the process was a form of automatic writing, whereby through Philemon's mediumship he transcribed the thoughts of the Alexandrian Gnostic Basilides (117–61 AD). From 1916 dates Jung's intense interest in Gnosticism – the secret, dualistic, pansexualist sect which fused neo-Platonism and Pauline Christianity.[24]

This bizarre incident calls for further comment. In the first place, it convinced Jung that highly charged emotional states could produce parapsychological phenomena, and that this was probably the root explanation for ghosts and poltergeists.[25] This theory made sense of the other puzzling occult events he had witnessed, such as the cracking of Freud's bookcase in Vienna and the splitting of the table and the knife when he was involved with Hélène Preiswerk in 1898. Secondly, the sensation of being 'forced' to write by the throng of spirits unlocked his writer's block. For three years, while in the eye of the psychic hurricane, he had written nothing, but 1916 was a turning point: after writing *Septem Sermones* he wrote essays on 'the Structure of the Unconscious', 'On the Psychology of the Unconscious', and 'The Transcendent Function'.[26] Thirdly, the imagery of the 'haunting' hallucinations seems highly significant. The angel and the devil fighting over the fisherman suggests the battle within Jung about how to integrate Christianity into his emerging world-view, for the fish was the symbol of the early Christians and of Peter the 'Big Fisherman'. The spirits returning from Jerusalem express disappointment with the existing state of Christianity, but 'Jerusalem' also suggests Judaism and hence, inevitably, Freud. The dual symbolism of Jerusalem hints that neither Freudianism nor Christianity is adequate to sustain the human spirit.

In short, this episode in 1916 suggests that Jung reached crisis point in that year, surmounted the perils and then proceeded through dangerous, though no longer calamitous, psychic seas to safe anchorage some time in 1918. Much of this must be attributed to his own mental toughness, but he was able to draw on valuable human assistance and he did not make many major mistakes. Nietzsche had been overwhelmed by madness because he did not retain a strong enough impression of the difference between the external world and his own fantasies. Jung insisted on seeing patients right through 1913–16, even though the therapeutic process was presumably more from them to him than vice versa. He carried on a normal academic correspondence with Professor Hans Schmid on the subject of psychological types.[27] And he took great comfort from his family: he repeated over and to himself, 'I have a medical diploma from a Swiss university. I have a wife and five children. I live at 228 Seestrasse, Küsnacht.'

Most of all, it was the dedication and commitment of his mistress Toni Wolff that pulled him through. Apparently, when Jung first took the fall into the land of the dead and was engulfed by near-madness, a number of his mistresses vied with each other to help him.[28] But only Toni Wolff was successful, at great cost to herself. When she saw that she alone, not Emma, not Maria Moltzer or any of the others, could comfort Jung when he was in the slough of despond, there was a huge temptation to move in for the kill and insist that Jung divorce Emma and marry her. Jung begged her not to take what he described as the natural route of all women, and Toni acquiesced. The price she paid was everlasting sadness: those who knew Toni Wolff when she travelled outside Switzerland spoke of finding her often in considerable overt distress. One such was Van der Post who wrote, 'I doubt whether any man is capable of a full comprehension of what she was called on to endure, let alone measure her achievements.'[29]

By 1916 Jung finally managed to persuade Emma to accept Toni as part of a permanent *ménage à trois*. Emma had been unmoved by Jung's previous pleading that he needed other women, as a natural polygamist. She may not even have been particularly swayed by Jung's other favourite argument for his philandering: that if a married man does not live out the full meaning of his erotic imagination, he will cause problems for his daughters by unconsciously displacing his unlived life onto them. Pointing out that the daughters of outstanding personalities usually did not marry young, because their famous fathers had, through creative sublimation, ruined their daughters' Eros, he argued for the necessity of obeying the dictates of the unconscious, which in his case prescribed promiscuity. Yet what really swayed Emma was the simple fact that Toni's ministrations worked where her own did not. 'I shall always be grateful to Toni for doing for my husband what I or anyone else could not have done for him at a most critical time,' she said, and added later, in explanation for her lack of jealousy, 'You see, he never took anything from me to give to Toni, but the more he gave her, the more he seemed able to give me.'[30]

Jung's problems with women were not confined to the external world, for his female 'voices' were telling him things he did not want to hear. For some time he had been formulating in his mind the idea that part of his psychic problems might arise from the overdevelopment of the No. 1 personality, stressing science and empiricism, and the downplaying of No. 2, representing art, religion and mystery. He became convinced that there was a 'woman within him', a kind of internalization of the feminine principle that he called the 'anima'. Every evening he wrote down what the anima had told him, hoping thereby to keep 'her' at arm's length from his fantasies.[31]

One day the anima whispered to him that his new ideas were art, not science. Jung reacted angrily to this, on the grounds that there would then be no moral imperative in his fantasies, they would have no more importance than if he was watching a movie. He would thus be a member of the banal class of 'misunderstood artists'. He also suspected the anima of playing games, that if he acquiesced in her suggestion, she would then taunt him for naïvety.[32] It has been suggested that the 'anima' was really Toni Wolff 'speaking' to him from the unconscious because of his guilt about their affair. This is not only unlikely *a priori*, given that Jung never felt guilt about adultery, but contradicts the internal evidence which points, instead, unmistakably at Sabina Spielrein.[33]

By the beginning of the First World War Spielrein, now married with a child, had become dissatisfied with her treatment by Freud and wrote to tell him so. Freud replied that she was emulating her 'Germanic hero' and was going mad herself. Spielrein settled in Switzerland and continued to write about Jung to a palpably bored Freud, who asked her to write no more on the subject, since she would always find excuses for her hero.[34] In 1917 Spielrein resumed correspondence with Jung about his new theories, but received a demented letter in reply, in which he announced he would be divulging no more of his secrets: 'Round this garden there is now a thick high wall, I can assure you.'[35] However, the correspondence continued: between November 1917 and October 1919 there are extant eight letters from Spielrein (in which she attempted a synthesis of Freud, Jung and Adler) and ten from Jung. When Spielrein told him that the Jungian method worked only for special cases and that in general the Freudian method was better, Jung snapped back that her trouble was that she lived between two worlds, the Russian and the German; her mistake had always been to think of 'Siegfried' as a reality rather than a symbolic bridge between two worlds.[36]

But Spielrein, now a dedicated Freudian, was having none of this and replied that she now realized her desire for 'Siegfried' had been a desire for a flesh-and-blood child;the realization that she had missed her life's goal nearly made her miscarry: 'Siegfried almost took my daughter's life.'[37] Once again, as so often, the two of them had reached an impasse, with Jung trying to wean her away from Freud, and Sabina scouting his method of spiriting away everything into the ether of generalized spiritual symbols.[38]

The correspondence petered out in disillusionment on both sides. Jung's parting shot was to tell her that he would have gone mad if he had continued the relationship with her.[39] Spielrein seems finally to have got Jung out of her system. She bore another child and, in 1922, published a disguised autobiographical dream wherein Jung features as a 'syphilitic Don Juan' whom she has finally learned to despise.[40] Jung, meanwhile, clearly identified his 'anima' with Spielrein, for the words 'this is art' came to him after Spielrein had written to say that although she could never accept that 'Siegfried' had a purely symbolic meaning, it might just relate to the artist in her that she had never succeeded in expressing (she was a talented amateur musician).[41] Nettled by her refusal to accept his symbolic doctrines, Jung in one of his last letters to her complained of the 'frivolity' and 'tyrannical self-glorification' of the female psyche and said there was an inherent feminine tendency to reduce everything to the level of the banal.[42] Jung later said that he mastered the 'anima' once he broke with a female correspondent and further added that he recognized the voice from the unconscious that told him his theories were art rather than a description of reality as that of 'the voice of a patient, a talented psychopath who had a strong transference to me.'[43]

It was a constant refrain of Jung's that psychic health consisted in finding the equilibrium point between the conscious and the unconscious. At the conscious level women were of immense importance to Jung during these crisis years for, with the exception of Spielrein, whom he had virtually expelled from his circle anyway, all the members of his 'harem' rallied round and vied to give him sustenance. In the battle for the hearts and minds of *men*, by contrast, Jung was a spectacular loser. Of the so-called Zürich school, the only ones to stick with him through his crisis years were Franz Riklin and Alphonse Maeder. Riklin, a divided character who could never decide whether he wanted to be a creative artist or a psychoanalyst, had already become notorious in Freudian circles on two counts: he was an even more useless administrator than Jung and his tenure as secretary of the International Asociation had been an unmitigated disaster; and he was the henpecked husband of one of Jung's cousins, who constantly held the sage of Küsnacht up as a model for her husband.[44] Additionally, Riklin was a spendthrift with permanent money worries. He used to ask Jung to refer patients to him, but was sometimes overcome with 'creative spells' during which he would not turn up to appointments or kept his analysands waiting; the consequence, with paying clients, was predictable. In the end Riklin would get hopelessly into debt, blame Jung for not helping him enough, break with him irrevocably and die in poverty and misery in the 1930s.

Some tension with Jung was evident even in these years. Around 1915–16 Riklin had an intellectual circle of which Toni Wolff, her sister, and her husband, the psychiatrist Hans Trub, were members. When the mists of schizophrenia cleared sufficiently, Jung would make occasional visits to this club, where he liked to play the iconoclast. On one occasion the talk turned to Abraham Lincoln. Jung declared that Lincoln was not a great humanitarian and that his freeing of the slaves had been dictated by crude economic and political interests.[45] This was true enough, but it was an odd argument for Jung to advance, for he was usually heavily scornful of any interpretation of history in socio-economic terms.

Even closer to Jung was Alphonse Maeder (Fliess to his Freud), and similarly the only person he knew professionally with whom he used the 'du' form of address. A diminutive, graceful Francophone Swiss, universally popular for his wit, charm and generosity, a great raconteur and in great demand by patients, Maeder was at one with Jung in stressing the future-directed function of dreams and their 'subjective level', which related the dreams to the dreamer rather than to the external world, as in Freudianism.[46] During the First World War Jung was especially close to Maeder, and wrote him an elegant letter of condolence when his mother died in 1918.[47] Yet the inevitable break occurred in the 1920s, after which Jung liked to ridicule Maeder to his family at mealtimes and jeer at his method of encouraging his patients to pray or even praying with them.

Other sources of external sustenance for Jung in his crisis period were his wealthy American friends, especially Edith Rockefeller McCormick, daughter of John D. Rockefeller, the dynasty's founding father.[48] She had first made contact with him in 1908–09 about her husband Harold Fowler's manic-depression. In 1915, in the midst of a world war, she travelled from the neutral USA to neutral Switzerland and entered analysis with Jung. Edith was a difficult customer: endowed with a private fortune of one hundred million dollars, she liked to keep people twitching on the end of her line, doling out largesse and then suddenly withdrawing it on a whim. Jung, being a man of independent fortune, was immune to her whims and, as often happens in such cases, having discovered he did not need her money, she decided to give it to him anyway. In 1916 she made $75,000 available for the establishment of the so-called Jungian Psychological Club.

On 24 February 1916, while Jung was still wrestling with his demons, he attended an inauguration ceremony in Zürich, attended by forty of his close associates. Emma Jung was appointed president, Toni Wolff became head of the lecture committee and Edith took a seat on the board; her husband Harold Fowler was given the job of heading up the 'entertainment committee' (roughly the equivalent of a 'wine fellow' in an Oxbridge college). The idea was to attract celebrities to address the club by dangling Edith's money before them. One who took the bait was the composer Ermanno Wolf-Ferrari (1876–1948), best known for his operas *Susanna's Secret* and *The Jewels of the Madonna*.[49] However, material support from Edith Rockefeller had the effect of making Wolf-Ferrari down tools and enjoy a sybaritic existence. Jung promptly advised Edith to stop his subsidy, whereupon, not surprisingly the composer began composing again. This would not be the last time Jung advised La Rockefeller to deal roughly with her artistic clients.

The Jungian Psychological Club did not prosper. First came a scandal in 1918 when the club's accountant, one Irma Oczeret, suddenly left under a cloud. It turned out that she had been diverting funds so that her husband, a Jungian analyst, could set up his female patients as mistresses. In Jungian terms he had lived out the fantasies of his mentor's unconscious. Then in 1921 Edith Rockefeller returned to the USA to divorce Harold; she later married the Polish singer Ganna Walska. Harold too remarried and spent a fortune (he had his own money, inherited from his father who invented the combine harvester), trying to rejuvenate himself with monkey serum. He died in 1941 at sixty-nine, having failed to discover the elixir of youth.[50]

With the McCormicks gone, some of the club members who had chafed under Jung's autocracy felt freer to protest. In the early 1920s Hans Trub was club president and, finally tiring of Jung's irrelevant iconoclastic incursions into the club proceedings, tabled a motion of censure, drawing attention to Jung's invariable habit of using whatever subject was under discussion as an excuse to ride his own hobby horse. Jung, it was alleged, wandered off the point and behaved like a prima donna, turning authoritarian if anyone disagreed with him. Jung, stung by the fact that Alphonse Maeder seconded the censure motion, underlined its point by stalking angrily from the room, taking Emma and Toni with him. History had indeed repeated itself, the second time as farce, for Jung, divorced from his own club, was now in the exact position Freud had been in 1913 vis-à-vis the International Association. The situation was not rectified until the late 1920s, when Trub resigned and the entire governing body was replaced.[51]

However, these were later developments, and during 1916–18 Edith Rockefeller's club gave Jung the perfect platform for sounding off on a variety of matters. He also met Herman Hesse, the great German writer, for the first time in 1916, while Hesse was consulting the analyst J.B. Lang at Sonnmat, a private clinic near Lucerne. Lang had been one of Jung's students and through him Hesse made the acquaintance of the master himself. Hesse later admitted that his *Demian* (1919) was a story of 'individuation' in the Jungian manner, and that from 1916–18 he was heavily influenced by Jung, before reverting to Freudianism.[52]

The First World War had a devastating impact on Europe's intellectuals. Everywhere there was the feeling that the old organic certainties of the pre-war period were gone for ever. Freud, who lamented the passing of Austria–Hungary while admitting that perhaps his 'beloved country' had never existed outside his own imagination, did important work on war neuroses and penned significant reflections on the slaughter in the trenches and thus on death in general. His work on shell-shock and war psychotics was seminal, and in his essays *Mourning and Melancholia* and *Thoughts on Death* he engaged fully with the horrors of the Western Front.[53] Jung, though, for the most part was too caught up in his private war to have much time to ponder the external conflict: by and large he shut his eyes to it, in what the unkind would say was a typically Swiss response to the world.

Whereas in the Second World War the Swiss were largely on the side of the Allies, in the first global conflict opinion was divided and in the German-speaking areas there was strong sympathy for Germany and the Central Powers. On the rare occasions when Jung did comment on the war, it tended to be along the lines of 'a plague on both your houses'. He always insisted that the war was an outbreak of mass madness and could not be understood in any other terms.[54] In a sense, then, the near-madness he was suffering from was merely a subclass of a general madness – again evidence of a collective unconscious. It was typical of Jung that the boundaries between internal and external worlds should become blurred, and that he should correlate the catastrophe in Europe with his own psychic convulsions. In a series of dreams in 1916 he functioned as a shaman and tried to persuade the Kaiser to make peace, on the assumption that he was a dynamic part of the collective unconscious.[55]

Jung's most worthwhile observations on the First World War date from ten years later. Writing to his old friend Albert Oeri, he pointed out how people who are insignificant in peacetime can become heroes in wartime. The classic example was General Grant, a failed storekeeper when the American Civil War broke out and a national monument when it ended four years later, but Jung instanced the opposing generals Joffre and Hindenburg as good exemplars of his theme. Such people, he suggested, were usually peasant-like by nature and could act as 'accumulators' or 'condensers' of the expectations of an entire people.[56]

If Jung's normal disposition was to run the events in his private world and those in the external world together, the boundaries could not always be blurred for, short of certifying himself as insane, he had no option but to continue his military service with the Swiss Army.[57] By 1917 the authorities had found him something more significant than overseeing sick parades and treating syphilitics. He was appointed commandant of the prisoner-of-war camp at the town of Château d'Oex, halfway between Lausanne and the Bernese Oberland. This was a camp where escaped British POWs and other military personnel who had strayed across the Swiss border were held in benign confinement, in accordance with the Geneva Convention, so that they could not return and fight against the Germans.

There were already 131 British prisoners quartered at Château d'Oex by May 1916 and by 1918 the number held in all Swiss camps exceeded 10,000. All expenses for the prisoners' upkeep were borne by the British government – the costs were charged to Army funds – and once the status of a prisoner was verified from London and the appropriate moneys paid over, the regime was lax. Officers were allowed to live in hotels and *pensions* in the town provided they reported twice a week to the commandant, and were permitted to have their wives with them. However, the administration of the British prisoners engendered a number of tricky problems. In the first place, bored and disgruntled officers would often hold drunken parties in their hotel rooms and proceed to smash up the furniture; the War Office in London then had to be applied to for compensation. Moreover, unmarried officers were resentful that London would pay for wives to go out to Switzerland to be with their husbands but would not do the same for other relatives. Dysentery and tuberculosis were also at times rampant in the camp, and there was a notorious lack of discipline, because the troops were not under the direct authority of British officers. Finally, of course, there was the notorious injustice that officers and seamen of the Merchant Navy who had escaped from German POW camps into Switzerland were regarded as non-combatants and therefore received no pay.[58]

By the time of Jung's appointment as camp commandant, there was an urgent need for administrative reform. The Swiss authorities had agreed to repatriate invalids and the seriously ill, so it made sense for the local commandant to be both a doctor and a psychiatrist. Jung took steps to prevent the outbreak of disease, and tried to combat boredom by encouraging both officers and men to attend university courses, in Geneva, Lausanne and Neuchâtel. He also tried to remedy outstanding complaints from the British about conditions at Château d'Oex. But when he drew the attention of the British government to the plight of the penniless merchant seamen, he received a cold answer, refusing to put them on the same footing as the accredited servicemen.

It was while he was at Château d'Oex that Jung began the habit of drawing mandalas in his notebook each morning.[59] The Sanskrit word *mandala* means circle, and the typical mandala features a quaternity, with a circle containing a cross, a star, a square, or an octagon. Mandalas feature in ancient religions, Tibetan Buddhism, dreams and the fantasies of schizophrenics; in the case of psychiatric patients their appearance is supposed to denote that psychic healing is taking place. They occur in conditions of psychic dissociation or disorientation:

typical examples would be children aged between eight and eleven whose parents are about to divorce; neurotic adults confronted with the problem of opposites in human nature, or schizophrenics whose view of the world has become confused as a result of the invasion of incomprehensible contents from the unconscious. The idea is that the mandala is part of Nature's self-healing and compensates for the confusion. So, in later Jungian language, the squaring of the circle is an archetype of wholeness, whose symbol is invariably the quaternity, as in the three Synoptic Gospels being 'compensated' by John's Gnostic one.[60]

Typical mandala symbols appearing in dreams are a blue flower, a red ball, a globe and a snake. The snake motif particularly interested Jung, for it opened up a new dimension for his perennial fascination with reptiles. During his time as commandant at Château d'Oex he became friendly with the wife of one of the interned officers. This woman, who had clairvoyant gifts, told Jung that whenever she dreamed of a snake, it meant illness. A few days after she told Jung of a dream of a huge sea serpent, the epidemic of Spanish 'flu, which accounted for more dead in 1918–19 than the entire battle casualties of the First World War, swept over Switzerland.[61] This confirmed Jung in his equation reptile = evil. He wrote that whenever you encountered a crisis in life and things were getting serious, you would find a saurian in the way.[62] It also convinced him of the truth of another of his favourite theories: that everything exists in fantasy before it exists in reality: thus the world war had come about because of 'opinion' – the opinion that war should be declared on Serbia.[63]

Jung thus returned in effect to his original thesis of 1913 – that there was a convergence or 'synchronicity' between disturbances in his own psyche and events in the external world. So a problem that was at root personal and subjective would often coincide with problems in the external world.[64] Yet Jung's interpretation of this 'phenomenon' was always selective. There is not a mention anywhere in his work of the most dramatic event in Switzerland in 1918: the three-day general strike that paralysed the country and which, though a defeat for unionism, nevertheless convinced the Swiss political élite that in future relations between capital and labour would have to be harmonized. Jung's notorious undervaluing of socio-economic factors in favour of the purely psychological sometimes left him looking like not so much a prophet as an ostrich with its head in the sand.

Chapter Fourteen

THE PSYCHOLOGY OF TYPES

Jung's experiences with the British officers at Château d'Oex confirmed an already strong Anglophilia. There were many signs of this in 1919. First he took on as his principal assistant in Zürich the young English therapist Peter Baynes.[1] Then he made a point of strengthening his British links. Almost his first public engagement when the war ended was a trip to London to lecture to the Royal Society of Medicine and to the Society for Psychical Research. In his address to the latter body he explained ghostly manifestations and apparitions as unconscious projections.[2] There is considerable dramatic irony in these remarks in the light of his experiences the following year.

While in London during the first two weeks of July 1919 Jung found time to write to his nine-year-old daughter about the city's sights. He mentioned the Horse Guards, the Tower of London, the Crown Jewels and the 5,000 cars that drove past his hotel each day.[3] The years 1917–20 show Jung taking more interest in his large family than at any time before or after. It has often been alleged that he was a domestic tyrant, that his children went in fear and trembling of him. He could be cruel and cutting and insisted on certain modes of behaviour at mealtimes – no shop talk, for example – but he was not noticeably illiberal by the standards of the times. Mindful of his own juvenile misery, he allowed his son Franz to decide for himself his attitude to Christianity; Franz chose not to attend Sunday school and not to be confirmed. The truth seems to be that Jung was an inconsistent parent: sometimes gloomy and authoritarian and at others spontaneous, eccentric and even bohemian. It was Emma who had to provide the uniformity and consistency that kept the children on a tight rein.

The summer holidays of 1919 and 1920 Jung spent with his family in the Engadine, near the Italian border. He liked to teach them his own skills of wood and stone carving, and on one occasion helped them to build and embellish a totem pole. In the Engadine they played in brooks with sand and stones and constructed canals. Jung showed them how to build model ships and houses, harbours and forts; his games were always connected with the art of war. On one occasion in the Engadine he overcame his fear of snakes sufficiently to kill an adder. Even when not on holiday, he would sometimes spend Sundays taking his children on hikes through the beautiful Bernese Oberland.[4]

Once he had recovered fully from the psychotic interlude of 1913–18, Jung began the routine that would characterize his days in Küsnacht during the 1920s, starting work with his patients at 7.30 a.m., analysing eight or nine a day, and usually seeing them three times a week. Already he was attracting the rich and famous as analysands, but in 1919 the 'one that got away' was the novelist James Joyce, then a financial protégé of Mrs McCormick. She suddenly took a notion that Joyce should go to Jung to be analysed, at her expense. Joyce, however, had no great opinion of psychologists of any stripe, as one of his utterances showed clearly: 'We grisly old Sykos who have done our unsmiling bit on alices when they were young and easily freudened . . . the law of the jungerl.'[5] He refused to comply, but soon learned what a stern taskmistress Edith Rockefeller McCormick was. On 1 October 1919 he called at his bank in Zürich to draw his monthly allowance, only to be told that Mrs McCormick had stopped it. Joyce at first thought his one time friend Ottocaro Weiss had put her up to it, but he eventually came to suspect that Jung was the villain of the piece. Jung, who at this stage suspected Joyce of charlatanry, was piqued at the writer's refusal to be analysed by him, so when Mrs McCormick asked him the best way to get more work out of her unproductive protégé, he suggested giving Joyce the Wolf-Ferrari treatment. She took the hint with alacrity.[6]

By March 1920 Jung was feeling stale and overworked, so he was delighted to receive an invitation from his friend the Swiss businessman Hermann Sigg to accompany him on a trip to North Africa. They sailed from Marseilles to Algiers, where they arrived on 15 March after cold and heavy weather all the way across the Mediterranean. Algiers presented its best face on a sunlit, sparkling morning, and Jung got his first impressions of North Africa from a stroll in the Botanical Gardens. Sigg's main business was in Tunis, so they made their base there, after travelling along the coast in a gruelling twenty-hour train journey. In Tunis Jung spent many days in Arab coffee houses, particularly one frequented by the local business community, simply absorbing the atmosphere. He knew no Arabic, having taken a deliberate decision not to learn any, since the language was so closely associated in his mind with his father. But although he understood nothing of the animated conversations, he picked up a lot from close observation of the gestures, body language and emotions, and most of all from the Arabs' subtle change in behaviour when they spoke to Europeans. He began to intuit what it would be like to experience the white man outside his natural environment. As for the fabled oriental calm and apathy, this seemed to him a mask behind which he sensed restlessness and agitation.[7]

Sitting in the Tunis coffee house, Jung first learned the truth about the Greek merchant's love of trade. Everyday such a man would come up to him and whisper in his ear that the price of wheat had gone down, or some such. Jung protested that he was not a businessman but the Greek took this as the claim of the card-sharp that he does not understand the rules of poker; he redoubled his efforts and gave him more and more information each day. Jung explained that for the Greek it seemed inconceivable that there could be any point to existence other than business.[8]

Tunis seemed to Jung a mixture of Granada, classical antiquity and the Baghdad of the *Arabian Nights* and he was assailed by a kind of sensuous overload. He thought North Africa actually had a queer smell and that its soil seemed soaked in the blood of the Romans, Carthaginians and Christians who had lived, fought and died there. The sky became something of an obsession with Jung during his

North African trip and one night he was delighted to see clearly the nearest equivalent in the northern hemisphere to the Southern Cross – the intersection of the Milky Way with the zodiacal line.[9]

While Sigg pursued his business contacts, Jung continued his rovings into other parts of Tunisia. At Sousse he was bowled over by the Roman remains and was amused to be told by an Arab through an interpeter that he was so big and strong he could carry the sky. He proceeded south along the coast to Sfax then cut inland, south west to Tozeur, an oasis town on the present-day border with Algeria. Here he checked into the Grand Hotel Sousse and set out to explore a town that was a notorious hotbed of homosexuality. Jung found the open and unashamed display of homosexuality a perfect complement to the bold colours of the oasis town and fantasized that he was back in the Athens of the fifth century BC. He loved the cacophony of early dawn, camels grunting, donkeys braying, dogs barking as a vast caravan arrived from the depths of the Sahara.[10] It seemed to him that the Arabs, menaced as they were by the incursion of western technology, were like game unaware of the approach of the hunter. With his growing love of the primitive, Jung was impressed that the Arab way of life had not changed in a thousand years; this gave the people a kind of detached nobility unavailable to the Westerner, who had to compensate the lack with aeroplanes and other machines.

From Tozeur Jung, accompanied by a guide, ventured into the northern Sahara as far as the oasis of Nefta, fifteen miles away, travelling in shimmering heat between vast sand dunes. He got a unique insight into the culture of Tunisia by glimpsing the power of the *marabout* – a saintly tribal elder, whose task was to see that the poor were fed. The *marabout* was entrusted with communal land for agricultural purposes, which had to be cultivated by voluntary labour. Villages in need which supplied the labour got the benefits in a rotating system, one year village X, the next village Y, and so on. At Nefta Jung saw such a labour system at work. Hundreds of people converged on a spot with camels and streaming banners early in the morning. A wild drumming and singing commenced, then the whole crowd began to dance. With baskets, sacks and hoes the work force worked to a dancing step, and by midday had constructed a large dam, though half-dead with fatigue in the broiling heat. Such was the power of religious inspiration, for Jung reported himself certain that if he had hired such a tired and exhausted crowd, they would scarcely have moved for any money.[11]

He returned to Tunis via Sfax and Sousse and, while waiting for the steamer to Marseilles, had a dream in which he fought with an Arab prince in the casbah of an eastern city and then, in a large vaulted octagonal room, forced the Arab to read a book written in an oriental script. Two things most impressed Jung about the dream: the casbah was like a perfect mandala and his fight with the Arab was a clear echo of Jacob's biblical struggle with the angel. He concluded that the dream was a parable of his encounter with Arab culture and that his fight with the prince expressed a side of himself that lay hidden; in other words, the Arabs' emotional and unreflective nature suggested those historical layers in Europeans that they would like to have left behind and overcome.[12]

In travelling to North Africa it seemed to Jung that he had unconsciously wanted to find the part of his personality which was submerged or invisible because he was European, and the dream showed him that there was a danger that his European consciousness might be overwhelmed by an unexpectedly violent assault from the unconscious psyche, that if the Arab was his 'shadow', the unconscious might, so to speak, collude with the primitive. What could be construed in Freudian terms as a struggle of id and ego, or in D.H. Lawrence's language as a conflict between the white mental consciousness and the deep red 'blood self' was in Jungian terms a collision between European consciousness and primal African instincts and affects. The fact that archetypal memories had been awakened by the trip to North Africa Jung took as further evidence for a collective unconscious. It also reinforced his growing conviction of the importance of the feminine principle. On his new theory, Islam was based on Eros, the feminine principle of relationship, whereas Christianity and most of the other world-religions were based on Logos, the masculine principle of relationship. Jung also stressed the greater subtlety of the Moon (feminine) over the Sun (masculine): in the bright light of the Sun everything could be seen and discriminated, but in the mild light of the Moon things were merged and fused rather than separated.

Moreover, Jung thought that the insights of the traveller could often be superior to those of the anthropologist, for it was only possible to understand cultures and nations from the outside, not from inside observation, which would at best breed a sterile relativism. 'I understand England only when I see where I, as a Swiss, do not fit in,' he declared.[13] He had a good opportunity to observe England in 1920, for in that year he spent the longest period ever in the country as visiting psychologist, to the point where he found himself thinking and dreaming in English.[14]

It was on this trip that Jung first got to know England's West Country and, although the record is confused, it was almost certainly on this trip that he visited Glastonbury, Tintagel and other Arthurian places. In September he held a two-week seminar for twelve disciples at Sennen Cove in Cornwall; the subject was dream analysis via controlled association, not the Freudian free association. By this time Jung's English was near perfect, fluent, vigorous, full of humour and often spiced with English and American slang and neologisms. Each time he came to England he noted an improvement in his command of the language, but by 1920 at Sennen Cove he was good enough to win word games, involving a complex knowledge of English idiom and nuance, against native speakers.[15] Later in London he read drafts of his new work on psychological types to his students, expounding difficult ideas in English. He would walk up and down the lecture room, smoking his pipe and looking vaguely displeased with his own formulation of an idea. On one occasion he was heard to utter, 'But this is difficult!'[16]

The 1920 visit to London was valuable for Jung, for it increased his perplexity on the subject of ghosts and other manifestations. Jung disliked staying in hotels if he could avoid it, and so his English colleagues rented a farmhouse cottage in Buckinghamshire so that he could get away from London at weekends. Jung retired there with two colleagues every Friday night during his London lectures, but the experience was not a happy one. He slept badly at the cottage and awoke each morning irritable and unrefreshed, for every night, even with the windows open, a sickly smell, identified by him as from a carcinoma, pervaded his room; there was also a persistent sound of dripping water, though there was no tap in the room and it was not raining outside.

Next weekend Jung had the same experience, but this time there was something else. The furniture in his room creaked every now and then, there were rustlings in the corners, and something seemed to brush along the walls. As long as the light was on, the air in the room was fresh and there was no noise; as soon as he turned it off, the assault on his senses began. The noise got worse every night until, on the Sunday night of the second weekend, he fancied he saw an animal about the size of a dog rushing round the room. However, the hubbub always ceased at the first light of dawn.

On the third weekend the cacophony increased, and this time there was the sound of knocking from outside. By the fourth weekend, with no improvement, Jung put it to his colleagues that the house might be haunted: he pointed out additional suspicious circumstances, such as the surprisingly low rent asked for the cottage, and the fact that the two young women who did the cooking and cleaning always made a point of decamping before dark. He decided to question one of the girls, and from her he learned that local opinion held that the house was indeed haunted.[17]

On the Friday night of the fifth weekend, after the usual knockings and bangings, Jung was just starting to doze off when he suddenly saw, next to him on the pillow, the hideous face of an old woman. He just had time before he leapt out of bed to notice that the left half of the face was missing below the eye while the wide open right eye was glaring at him. He spent the rest of the night in an armchair with the light on, then moved to another room for the rest of the weekend, where he slept soundly and was never disturbed. Annoyed by the sceptical and superior attitude of one of the colleagues who had rented the cottage, Jung challenged him to spend a night in the haunted room. The man went to the cottage alone the following weekend but was so terrified by his experiences that he spent the night with his bed in the garden and a loaded shotgun at his side. He wrote a letter to Jung recounting his experiences and vowing never to sleep at the cottage again. Shortly afterwards the owner of the property had it demolished as unsaleable.[18]

Jung speculated that the knocking and rustling could have been hypnoid catalepsy and the vision of the old woman hypnagogic hallucination, but he could find no explanation for the dripping water. In any case, why catalepsy and hallucination then and there, at that particular place and time? One possibility was that the unconscious, with its more powerful perceptions, could pick up traces of past events and project a visionary picture of the psychic situation that excited it. Yet Jung never provided a consistent and coherent explanation of ghosts, and this has irritated believers in the reality of such phenomena, such as Colin Wilson, who think that it is implausible to explain them as manifestations of the unconscious and so conclude they must in some sense exist 'out there'.[19]

Jung hedged and dithered in his attitude to ghosts. His fundamental stance was the Kantian one of doubting any single ghost story while having a certain faith in the body of such stories taken together.[20] One of his favourite tales also came from England. A rich woman had a fantasy about a house she wanted to buy and tried to find somewhere answering the description. In the meantime a haunted house was put on the market at a knockdown price. The rich woman bought it, but when she arrived at her new property the housekeeper fled in terror. It turned out that the ghost that had been seen repeatedly in the house was the image of the new owner, who had 'haunted' it because it lived so vividly in her imagination.[21]

Jung's fundamental idea on spirits and spooks was that in the early stages of psychic evolution those fragments that are within us as complexes somehow existed outside as arbitrary powers with intentions of their own, but over time were absorbed within us.[22] But not only does Jung not explain the physics of this curious statement, he does not explain how fragments continue to exist 'out there'. The truth is that most of the time Jung was more interested in the *effects* of a belief in ghosts than in the manifestations themselves. 'The fear of ghosts means, psychologically speaking, the overpowering of consciousness by the autonomous contents of the unconscious. This is equivalent to mental derangement,' is a typical utterance.[23] The farthest Jung was prepared to go was his statement in 1947 that he could no longer be so certain as in 1920 that an exclusively psychological approach could explain psychic phenomena.[24]

Jung had completed his massive work on *Psychological Types* before going to England, and it was published in 1921. Here was a work that demonstrated at once how far Jung had moved away from Freudianism, for the principal influence was William James's conscious psychology and, especially, his famous distinction between 'tough-minded' and 'tender-minded'. For James the fundamental divide between individuals was between the rationalist ('tender-minded') who approached the world with a set of principles or organizing ideas, and the empiricist ('tough-minded') who was governed by what James called 'stubborn and irreducible facts'. So tender-minded individuals were intellectualistic, religious and monistic, philosophically idealistic, dogmatic, optimistic and believers in free will; tough-minded characters were irreligious, sceptical, sensationalistic, materialistic, pluralistic, pessimistic and fatalistic.

Jung embraced James's dualistic methods but cut the cake up in a different way. For him the fundamental division was between extraverts and introverts, terms that have now become household words. The extraverted type was defined by the object; such people were full of self-expression and self-confidence, looked for themselves in other people, flourished in the regard of others and were exhibitionistic (in the non-sexual sense) and gregarious, turning events to their own purposes and acting on first impulses and thoughts. The introverted type was subjective: such people were inhibited in self-expression and self-confidence; detached in attitude and seemingly indifferent to the concerns of others, lone wolves, making heavy weather of external responsibilities, acting on reflection or second thoughts, solitary and forever on the defence against the external world.

It is likely that Jung got the idea from his observations in the Burghölzli, when he noted the differential patterns of hysterical and schizophrenic patients. Hysterics tended to find significance in the outer world and its objects (what Jung called a centrifugal movement of libido) whereas schizophrenics found meaning in the inner world and its artefacts (dreams, fantasies, archetypes), which seemed to Jung to exemplify a centripetal tendency of libido. Those finding significance in the outer world Jung labelled 'extravert', those in the inner 'introvert'. Jung also thought it interesting that Freud and Adler interpreted exactly the same data in diametrically opposite ways: what for Freud was a manifestation of sexuality was for Adler the will to power. The entire idea of the pleasure principle in Freudian thought rested ultimately on the existence of objects which either promoted or impaired the subject's desire for pleasure, whereas in Adlerian thought the emphasis was placed on a subject who, regardless of objects, sought his own security and supremacy. Freud, then, on this perception of the world, was an extravert and Adler an introvert.[25]

Before developing his detailed typology of character, Jung first sought to show that throughout history significant pairs of thinkers or artists had been differentiated by the extravert–introvert divide. The poet Heine had identified Plato and Aristotle as being two distinct psychological types, and Jung endorsed the judgement. The respective traditions of Platonism (the disclosure of ideas and symbols from the fathomless depths of the soul) and Aristotelianism (the organization of ideas and symbols into a fixed system) were carried into Christianity, where the Aristotelian tradition manifested itself in cults and dogmas and the orderly, practical lives of priests, while the other-worldly Platonism found expression in monasticism.

Jung claimed that in the history of Christian theology there was a perennial conflict between the abstract standpoint that hates any contamination by the concrete, and the concrete that despises the abstract and looks to the object. But it was typical of him that, having found a good idea, he should confuse it with a quite unnecessary sub-idea, in this case the recurring Jungian motif of compensation. So, not content with remarking that it was entirely logical and characteristic that Tertullian should have sacrificed his intellect and Origen his genitals, Jung adds that the two men eventually became the opposite of their former selves: Tertullian, the acute thinker, became the fanatic and man of feeling while Origen, the devotee of the flesh, became a scholar and lost himself in intellectuality.

Jung proceeded to give numerous other examples of the extravert–introvert divide: the extravert Luther, for example, clashing with the introvert Zwingli over the real or symbolic presence of Christ's body at Communion, or the introvert Schiller contrasted with the extravert Goethe. Mention of Schiller brings Jung by association of ideas to Schiller's distinction of naïve poets (the poet as nature) and sentimental ones (the poet seeking nature), which Jung correlates with introversion and extraversion. Other pairs of opposites are then brought forward for inspection: Nietzsche's polarity of Apollonian (introvert) and Dionysian (extravert); and Carl Spitteler's dichotomy between Prometheus (introvert) and Epimetheus (extravert). Soon Jung was in full flow, citing examples of the bifurcation into two types of character in Blake (the 'prolific' and the 'devouring'), and in Eastern religion.[26]

The really original aspect of *Psychological Types* was the way Jung layered the basic extravert/introvert distinction with categories drawn from the Gnostics, whom he had been reading since 1916. The Gnostics made a threefold typology of the functions of thinking, feeling and sensation; Jung, ever in search of the 'completion' of the quaternity, added the faculty of intuition. More correctly, what he did was to correlate the functions of sensation and intuition with, respectively, the object-entranced extravert and the subjective introvert, and then derive thinking and feeling from intuition and sensation, with consequent problems for the alleged quaternity. Introversion and extraversion could thus be paired with each of the four functions to produce eight basic psychological types, and it was to the investigation of each of these eight that Jung devoted the second half of *Psychological Types*.

The extravert–thinking type typically attempts to discover the objective and universal laws of the cosmos. This type, according to Jung, is a worshipper of facts, which he loves to build into theories, and is intolerant, fanatical and given to proselytizing. Jung displayed particular animus towards this type: 'Its habitual mode is best described by the two words "nothing but".' Goethe personified this in the figure of Mephistopheles. Above all, it shows a distinct tendency to trace the object of its judgement back to some banality or other, thus stripping it of any significance in its own right. The trick is to make it appear dependent on something quite commonplace. Whenever a conflict arises between two men over something apparently objective and impersonal, negative thinking mutters "*cherchez la femme*".[27]

The extravert–feeling type, by contrast, is usually a woman and is always ready to identify with others on a conventional basis, tends to exhaust the emotions in external relations, is readily suggestible, quick to overvalue and inhibited in the capacity for real thought. The essential epithet here is 'conventional': such people never feel they are born in the wrong place or time, but slip easily into a given milieu or society and embrace ephemeral values. Relationships based on feeling tend to be short-lived, so people of this type are drawn to the *mariage de raison* as an anchor against their own fickle, moody and volatile personalities.[28] Were Jung writing in the 1990s he would identify the world of showbusiness, the movies, rock music and television as a natural home for the feeling extraverts.

The extraverted–sensation type, usually men, throws up architects, bankers and sexual adventurers of the Casanova type. Such people are hard-headed, practical and imaginative and never contrast the world as it is with the world as it could be or ought to be. They are hungry for external stimuli which need to be frequently changed to head off boredom or impatience, are refined in external values, well-meaning but fundamentally inconsiderate and selfish. Hedonists one and all, they are particularly susceptible to sexual jealousy and the sensual lust for life that characterizes them can lead to sexual perversions, drug addictions, alcoholism and other neurotic compulsions. This type is the polar opposite from the intuitive–introvert and notoriously finds marriage difficult.[29]

The extravert–intuitive type also works on sheer intensity of perception rather than rational judgement but is more solid than the sensation type, being particularly good in an emergency. Nevertheless this type is unstable, changeable, impulsive, positive, superficially optimistic, and subject to error in long-term relationships. Explorers, adventurers, big-game hunters, gamblers, politicians and Stock-Exchange speculators are typically found in this group. H.M. Stanley and Sir Richard Burton would belong in this group.[30]

The introverted–thinking type classically produces scholars and philosophers, particularly those concerned with questions of epistemology and metaphysics. Jung mentions Kant, but he could just as well have included Hume or Descartes. Such people are more interested in concepts than facts, are often dogmatic, addicted to theoretical perspectives and intellectually arrogant; lacking in feeling and intuition and devoid of sensation, but sensitive to criticism, this type is the most likely of the eight to throw up misogynists and misfits.[31]

The introvert–feeling type, of which monks, nuns, poets and musicians are obvious examples, is in Jungian terms one of the obviously 'feminine' categories. They react with strong likes and dislikes which they are often incapable of expressing. Tactless and incompetent in personal relations, they are much misunderstood, and prone to irritate because of their peculiar mixture of inaccessibility and apparent harmony and self-sufficiency. Mysterious and enigmatic, they tend to attract powerful extraverts of the opposite sex. Jung was inclined to think that this group overwhelmingly comprised women and that it produced females notorious for their unscrupulous ambition and mischievous cruelty. He spent a lot of time on the analysis of this group because of their high propensity to neurosis, which he thought neurasthenic in origin rather than hysterical; he found such people often had severe physical complications, such as anaemia.[32]

The introvert–intuitive type Jung found the most interesting of all, not least because he placed himself in this category. These characters have little concern for external circumstances, are unstable and undependable in personal relations, obtuse in point of understanding and easily misunderstood themselves, to the point where they can appear to others as mere cranks. Mystics, clairvoyants, psychics and simple daydreamers, they often see themselves as misunderstood geniuses and prophets without honour, Cassandras burdened with a unique gift which the world rejects. Jung mentioned William Blake as a person of this type, but the category was by no means limited to males. Jung cited a female patient of his who was so innocent that she took a room in a brothel without realizing where she was.[33] The intuitive–introvert has the most difficult life of all, but in compensation is also the most interesting. Jung, when linking his four functions to general notions of quaternity, said that sensation was a one-dimensional classification, thought was two-dimensional, feeling three-dimensional and intuition four-dimensional. By analogy with Einsteinian space–time, therefore, intuition was like the dimension of time, the key element.[34]

Finally, there is the introvert–sensation type, classically producing painters and aesthetes. Irrational and incalculable, they feed on sense impressions and react through subjective sensations. Often externally unassuming but with difficulty in making normal communication, this type is a sensualist who projects unconscious fears onto the world, which in turn he senses archetypically. Jung often mentioned Van Gogh as belonging in this group.[35]

Jung likened his psychological types to a group of people who have to cross a broad brook which stands in their way. One jumps over it for the sheer joy of doing so, another because there is no alternative, a third because he likes to overcome every obstacle. Another will refuse to jump because he dislikes useless effort, a fifth will turn round because he has no urgent need to get to the other side, and so on.[36]

Jung further subdivided his groups by assigning each one an ancillary co-function or *inferior function* – one different from rather than the polar opposite of the superior function and serving it rather than being antagonistic to it. This inferior function may belong to the opposite type: for example an introverted–sensation type may also contain aspects of the opposite–attitudinal type – extraverted–thinking – so that the ultimate number of variables in the typology is very great. What is the role of this inferior function? Jung's explanation was that 'the inferior function is always associated with an archaic personality in ourselves.'[37] Jung further hypothesized that when different types intermarried, each was unconsciously relying on the other to take care of his or her inferior types, but that this was in principle (though, clearly, not always in practice) a bad mistake. On the other hand, playing safe through opting for a same-type marriage could double up on the superior function and thus increase the negative and destructive power of the inferior function.

Jung was extremely pleased with his theory of types and considered it a work of great complexity: he wrote condescendingly to a Frau Vetter in 1932 that she might understand one or two chapters.[38] He was especially pleased with the way he had, to his own satisfaction at least, seen off Freud by describing him as an object-obsessed extravert. He described transference as the *pièce de résistance* of object theory and added that with Freud 'the subject remains remarkably insignificant.'[39]

Though there is a wide consensus among psychologists that a division into extravert and introvert is a seminal idea, Jung's detailed differentiation of psychological types has found favour only among dedicated Jungians. His eight-fold categorization has been assailed from a number of directions. In the first place, he unwisely toyed with a correlation between feeling, thinking, intuition and sensation and Hippocrates's ancient idea of the four temperaments – choleric, sanguine, melancholic and phlegmatic.[40] Then he further muddied the waters by writing that thinking and feeling *derived* from sensation and intuition, since sensation, telling you that something exists, is logically prior to thinking, which tells you what it is; similarly intuition tells you where something is coming from and whither bound, but feeling establishes the value of the something, whether it is good or bad. Since intuition and sensation are visceral and pre-mental, Jung's views on their primacy constitute a curious kind of Freudian throwback.

On points of detail Jung was especially vulnerable. Walter Kaufman pointed out that in common-sense terms it was surely Adler who was the extravert and Freud the introvert, and that Jung's special definition of the types affronted normal usage. He was especially scornful that two very different philosophers, Kant and Nietzsche, were both lumped together as 'introverted–thinking types' and remarked, 'A typology that has no place for the immense differences between these two types surely leaves much to be desired . . . For every one of his observations that is insightful there are many others that are appalling.'[41] Jung was also accused of introducing the four functions as an a priori quaternity, to fit his obsession with the mystical qualities of the number four.[42]

Even more misguided, according to some critics, was the attempt to derive general propositions of cultural history from the extravert/introvert typology and the four functions. Jung argued that the transition from the Ancient to the Christian world was essentially a crossover from the extravert viewpoint to the introvert; for objective slavery, guaranteeing privilege for a tiny élite, in the Ancient World there was substituted the subjective slavery of the soul, which made slaves of the body and the instincts. The rights of man were really, according to Jung, purchased by the transfer of slavery to the sphere of individual psychology; collective culture was thereby enhanced, but individual culture was degraded.[43] Jung also argued that the implication of his theory of types ruled out schemes for social improvement like socialism, since these would always involve injustice for one or other of his psychological types; Rousseau's Legislator, for instance, 'would have to give at least twice as much money to the one man as to the other.'[44] Such an argument might have had more bite if Jung had been able to demonstrate that the status quo was notably predicated on justice and fairness.

The most sustained attack on Jung's theory of psychological types was mounted by the English Freudian Edward Glover. He argued that Jung concentrated on end-products (the 'intuitive–introvert', for example) and did not explain how people came to be a particular type: it is just a datum that people do or do not relate to objects. Freud, with his anal, oral and genital stages of development, had at least sketched the primary mechanism by which characters came about, whereas for Jung the eight types appear fully-formed with no explanation as to causality. 'In short, the vicissitudes of object relations and of the instincts directed towards objects, give rise to an infinite variety of character reactions which, when shoehorned into the descriptive categories of extraversion and introversion, lose thereby whatever *specific* characteristics they may possess . . . Having made the cardinal blunder of confusing conscious end-products with two out of many primary tendencies in libido (whether Jungian or Freudian), Jung proceeded unabashed to rectify this blunder by multiplying it by four . . . We are left with a definition that would place the paranoid lunatic with his delusions of persecution in the same category as the man with a hunch.'[45]

Other critics suggested that it might be more fruitful to classify types by mental disorder, since neurosis was almost universal: so there would be hysterical, obsessional, depressive, alcoholic, hypochondriacal, paranoid, schizoid and pyschopathic types. Or a 'Theophrastian' typology might be better, based on an outstanding characteristic: the miser, the gambler, the misanthrope, the misogynist, the prig, the bully, the moaner, the improvident, the hypocrite, the optimist, the scapegoat, the seducer, the gold-digger, the braggart, the egoist, and so on.

Jung tried to meet many of these criticisms but in so doing retreated farther and farther from his original conception and hedged his eightfold typology around with so many cavils that it was finally useless as a hermeneutic device. At first he argued that since introverts and extraverts were found in the same family, and transcended class and sex, the type differentiation must be innate and the types must perform some biological function.[46] Later he backtracked and admitted that his eight types did not exhaust all possibilities, since further points of difference such as age, sex, activity, emotionality and level of development had to be taken into account.[47] Finally, he evaded the difficulties by means of his favourite notions of compensation and enantiodromia, whereby every phenomenon engenders its opposite. He cited the introverted intellectual who after a good dinner and a bottle of wine seemed to be a 'feeling extravert'. 'Before dinner I am a Kantian but after dinner a Nietzschean,' this man said, apparently ignorant that Jung had assigned Kant and Nietszche to the same type anyway. In the end Jung came close to admitting that his taxonomy of types was virtually useless.[48]

Freud and his followers were in no doubt that by publishing *Psychological Types* Jung had scored a spectacular own goal. Freud wrote to Ernest Jones in May 1921, 'A new production by Jung of enormous size, seven hundred pages thick, inscribed "Psychological Types", the work of a snob and a mystic, no new idea in it. He clings to that escape he had detected in 1913, denying objective truths in psychology on account of personal differences in the observer's constitution. No great harm to be expected from this quarter.'[49] Lou-Andreas Salomé, by this time very close to Freud professionally, considered that Jung had given up the attempt to be a scientist and was now an out-and-out mystic. She thought the 'haunting' experience of 1916, of which Freudians learned at the end of the First World War, had turned his mind; speaking of a friend who had started believing in demons, she said, 'Poor Jung, somewhat tragicomically, seems to have fallen victim to something similar.'[50]

The greatest triumph for the Freudians was that Jung's new bearing finally forced Oscar Pfister to declare unequivocally for Freud and against his countryman. Even those whom Jung might have expected to understand his work gave it short shrift. Jung had made a great deal of use of *Prometheus and Epimetheus* by the Nobel-prize winning author Carl Spitteler (1845–1924), and sent a copy of his book on psychological types to him. Spitteler did not reply, but soon afterwards referred to the book during a lecture and said that it meant nothing.[51] Perhaps the single most significant thing about *Psychological Types* was that it was written at all, reinforcing the view of his acolyte Aniela Jaffé that the period as commandant at the Château d'Oex really was a turning point, when Jung finally emerged from the valley of the shadow of psychosis.[52]

Chapter Fifteen

THE GLOBETROTTER

Since 1916 Jung had been reading the Gnostics, but in 1920 he added another arrow to his mystical quiver when he began studying the famous Chinese book of hexagrams, the *I Ching*.[1] He spent much of his spare time that year casting reed sticks in the manner prescribed in that book, and claimed to find many parallels between the message of the reeds and external events. A man came to him for advice on whether he should marry a girl with 'a strong mother-complex'. Jung separated the bundles of forty-nine stalks at random, then consulted the relevant hexagram. The answer was clear: 'The maiden is powerful. One should not marry such a maiden.' This idea of a 'pre-established harmony' between mental events and external reality would lead him years later to his notion of synchronicity or meaningful coincidences, though the first mention of 'synchronicity' as such does not occur in the Jung *oeuvre* until 1928.

Jung's interest in the *I Ching* quickened in 1922 when he met the greatest living European expert on the subject during a meeting with his friend Count Hermann Keyserling's 'School of Wisdom' in Darmstadt. The purpose of the school was to achieve a synthesis of eastern and western thought, and it was there that Jung encountered

Richard Wilhelm, an ex-missionary to China who was besotted with all things Chinese and had translated the *I Ching* into German. Jung invited him to lecture at the Psychology Club in Zürich in 1923, and a close friendship resulted.[2]

Another attempt at a new friendship did not fare so well. Herman Hesse, who had met Jung in 1916 and consulted his pupil J.B. Lang at Sonnmatt, a private clinic near Lucerne, had been through a Jungian stage during 1916–18, when he wrote *Demian* but had afterwards reverted to a belief in orthodox Freudianism. It seems strange, then, that in 1921 he decided to enter analysis with Jung himself, but the explanation was that Hesse was bowled over by *Psychological Types*, the only one of Jung's publications to which he always gave unqualified praise and a palpable influence on later Hesse masterpieces such as *Narziss und Goldmund*.

Hesse took lodgings at Zürichsberg in May 1921 and every day for a week made the long walk to Küsnacht for the sessions. Then, suddenly, for reasons unexplained, he cancelled the analysis. Thereafter, Hesse remained polite in his dealings with Jung but always took the line that he was merely one of Freud's most gifted pupils and not to be mentioned in the same breath as the Master.[3]

In addition to his other mystical leanings Jung was, in 1921–23, much taken up with mediumistic experiments in Zürich, sometimes in collaboration with Bleuler and his colleague Von Schrenk-Notzing. In experiments with the Austrian medium Rudi Schneider they were said to have experienced puzzling examples of materialization and psychokinesis. The fact that Jung's assistant Aniela Jaffé mentioned this episode in Jung's career only after his death has led some to accuse Jung of wilful suppression, on the ground that he liked to keep his distance from the supernatural or the occult.[4]

In 1923 Jung returned to England accompanied by Emma and Toni Wolff, both of whom by now seemed to accept the *ménage à trois* as a fact of life. He held a seminar at Polzeath in Cornwall, organized by Peter Baynes and his assistant Esther Harding, for about thirty students, mostly British but with a sprinkling of Swiss and Americans. The subject was 'active imagination' and its differences from Freudian 'free association', which Jung criticized for keeping the patient imprisoned inside his own circle of complexes. The thirty invitees packed the only hotel in the village and met in the community hall for lectures and seminars. This was all part of

Jung's growing reputation and influence in his favourite foreign country. Increasingly fascinated by everything to do with stones, he loved to visit Penzance and contemplate the nearby menhir named Menetol.[5]

Yet undoubtedly the most significant event for Jung himself in the years 1923–24 was the building of a private tower at Bollingen on the upper Lake Zürich. At first he was interested in buying the island of Schmerikon, at the end of the lake, intending to build a kind of stone temple that would be adorned with fragments of his thoughts and other sayings, both lapidary and inspirational. The proposed purchase fell through, so Jung turned his attention to a large slab of land near Bollingen with lake frontage, a mile away from a railway station; the railway track in effect fenced it off. Investigation of the title deeds for the parish of St Meinrad revealed that the land had once belonged to the monastery of St Gall. This seemed a good omen to Jung, who wanted to use the site as a retreat, so he bought the land and started building on it, doing a lot of the work with his own hands. At first he envisaged a rude one-storey building like an African hut, then abandoned the idea as too primitive and proceeded with a two-storey tower which would represent the 'maternal hearth'.[6]

Four years later, in 1927, he added another structure, with a tower-like annexe, which became the centrepiece of the complex. Still not satisfied, in 1931 he extended the tower-like annexe. In 1935 he decided he needed a piece of fenced-in land, and added a courtyard and loggia by the lake. This delighted him as, separated from the trinity of main buildings, it completed the quaternity in his preferred 3+1 fashion. The finishing touches were added in 1955, after his wife's death, when an upper storey was added to the central section of the house.

Jung's Bollingen tower has always attracted extreme interest, since it seems a multi-layered focus for various Jungian motifs and almost an 'objective correlative' of the Jungian Self. In the first place it represented death, for Jung's mother died aged seventy-five in January 1923 just as he began work on the first tower. The night before her death he was in the Tessin, and had a bizarre dream that he was in a dark forest when suddenly a gigantic wolfhound burst out of the undergrowth. He realized that the 'Wild Huntsman' had commanded it to carry away a human soul and that the Wild Huntsman was Wotan, who was gathering his mother to her ancestors. He at once set off for home but was not mournful or sad, for during the entire journey he continually heard dance music, laughter and jollity, as though a wedding was being celebrated.[7]

Death also manifested itself in another form at Bollingen. In 1923 his eldest daughter Agathli came out to look at the site and told him she sensed the presence of corpses; she had already given signs of psychic powers which Jung thought she had inherited from her maternal grandmother. When Jung and his workers were excavating the annexe in 1927, they came upon a skeleton, which seemed to have been thrown into a grave when in an advanced state of decay. Further research revealed that the body was one of dozens of French soldiers who were drowned in the Linth in 1799 and later washed up on the shores of the upper lake. The soldiers were drowned when the Austrians blew up Grynau bridge, which the French were storming. After noting the date of the discovery – 22 August 1927 – Jung arranged a proper reburial and fired a gun three times over the grave.[8]

Since his mother connoted Jung's No. 2 personality, it was not surprising that the Bollingen Tower, which felt to him like a maternal womb and gave him the feeling of being reborn in stone, in turn came to represent this aspect of his personality, with Küsnacht playing the role of No. 1. This was expressed in concrete form, since Toni Wolff was his constant companion at the tower, while his wife remained in Küsnacht.[9]

Bollingen answered Jung's recipe for a place where he could be completely alone and exist solely for himself. The tower-like annexe functioned as a 'withdrawal room', like the arcane area in an Indian house to which the master could withdraw. Jung regarded his retreat as a place of spiritual concentration, where he could paint, carve in stone or meditate: he loved painting onto the walls messages received straight from his unconscious. The retreat to the tower bore an obvious analogy with the withdrawal to the loft when he was eleven and can be seen on one level as a regression to infancy. Nobody was allowed there without his permission and nobody could visit Bollingen unless he went there with them, lest they bring an alien aura. Jung also regarded the tower and its many later annexes as a symbol of psychic wholeness. The original round tower he saw as a perfect mandala, symbolizing the self, and over its door he chiselled into stone the legend, 'Sanctuary of Philemon, Penitence of Faust'.

Jung's Bollingen tower recalls the even more famous tower of

W.B. Yeats, a man in many ways not dissimilar to Jung, down to the right-wing politics and the interest in the occult. The difference, though, was that Yeats's tower was a refuge *for* his family, but Jung's tower was a retreat *from* his family.[10] Normally the only person he allowed there was Toni Wolff or, in later years, a housekeeper. There was no electricity or gas, and all light, heating and cooking derived from oil and oil-lamps. He and Toni did all their own cooking and cleaning, cut their own wood for the fire and drew their own water. At first they filtered lake water but in 1931, through a water diviner, Jung discovered his own spring. The tower was suitably remote, for it could be reached only by boat or by a long hike up from the railway station. Until 1929 Jung did not drive a car, so he preferred to travel from Küsnacht to Bollingen by sailboat. Not that the rail journey bothered him, for he had such intense powers of concentration that he could switch off the outer world. This concentration seemed to increase at Bollingen and when, at a later period, his housekeeper summoned him for meals, she said it was like trying to raise the dead. Often he would be wrestling with some conundrum from the unconscious but equally often he sat, Socrates-like, in a kind of cataleptic trance, explaining that he was composing symphonies from the noise of a kettle singing or water boiling.[11]

The tower was a spooky place even during the day, and at night the atmosphere in and around the tower could be positively eerie. On one occasion in the late winter of 1923 Jung seemed to hear footsteps going all round the tower and found it hard to convince himself that he was dreaming and not waking. He went back to sleep and this time dreamed of several hundred dark-clad peasant boys laughing and prancing around the tower. Recurrent dreams on the same subject lasted until spring 1924. Since the experience was much more like the waking state than dreams, Jung concluded that he had experienced another haunting.

After 1924 he never experienced the visitation again, but later he came upon a seventeenth-century chronicle of Lucerne by Rennard Cysat, which told how the author had climbed Mount Pilatus and had been disturbed in exactly the same way by a crowd who poured past his hut singing and playing music. The next day a herdsman told Cysat that the rioters were Wotan's army of departed souls, that Pilatus was notorious for apparitions and it was well known that Wotan still practised his arts there. The obvious explanation for Jung's experience is the well-known phenomenon of hermit hallucination but, typically, Jung chose to believe that he had been a witness to a supernatural event. Later Jung reinterpreted the experience as a synchronistic happening. In the Middle Ages there were gatherings of young Swiss mercenaries who usually assembled in the spring, marched from central Switzerland to Locarno, met up at Casa di Ferro in Minusio, and then marched to Milan where they took service with foreign princes. Jung therefore interpreted his vision as an actual experience of one of these gatherings.[12]

In the mid-1920s Jung entered a restless period of globetrotting which took him back to Africa and the United States. Some have speculated that by now he was getting tired of his 'harem', and especially of Toni Wolff; that he needed an excuse to get away from his 'Valkyries'. Jung himself explained his journeys as a desire to acquaint himself at first hand with the psychic life of primitives: he wanted to travel to 'backward' areas since the more primitive the locality, the more likely it was that the archetype would manifest itself.[13] As with the working-class schizophrenics of the Burghölzli, there was likely to be less cultural overlay between the individual and the collective unconscious.

Jung's decision to depart for the USA over the Christmas period in 1924 was apparently taken at very short notice. At the time there was something of a craze for the Santa Fé and Taos area of New Mexico, stimulated by the novels of Willa Cather and D.H. Lawrence. Mary Austin's *The Land of Journeys' Ending* (1924), describing an extended motor tour of Arizona and New Mexico, had a great vogue in its year of publication[14] and may have influenced Jung in his decision. At all events, he departed from Zürich on 10 December 1924, heading for Bremen where, fifteen years earlier, he had embarked for the New World with Freud. On 13 December he boarded the North German Lloyd steamer *Columbus*, but the liner soon ran into the full fury of a North Atlantic winter, with severe storms and wave heights of fifty feet reported. The battered *Columbus* limped into New York a day late on 22 December, looking like a ghost ship, its deck covered in ice.[15]

Jung was in New York until Christmas Eve, then boarded the overnight train for the eighteen-hour journey to Chicago. Accompanying him were his old friend Fowler McCormick and George Porter. In Chicago Jung spent the rest of the Christmas period alternately with Fowler's divorced parents Harold and Edith Rockefeller McCormick, then entrained at Dearborn station at 8 p.m. on the nightly Santa Fé Railway's 'California Ltd', bound for the Grand Canyon. After a transfer at Williams, Arizona, the travellers reached the Grand Canyon on New Year's Day 1925. They checked into El Tovar, a hotel perched on the rim of the canyon, where two more old friends, Professor Chauncey Goodrich of Berkeley and his wife, were there to meet him: it was Goodrich's sister, Elizabeth Whitney, who had pioneered Jungian analysis in the San Francisco Bay area. Another Berkeley professor, Jaime de Angulo, a Spanish speaker, joined the party at the Grand Canyon.

After a day's sightseeing Jung, with Fowler McCormick, Porter and Angulo set off for Taos. William McGuire, who has made a close study of this trip, thinks they either motored the six hundred miles on second- or third-class roads or went by train from Williams to Lany, New Mexico, hired a car in Santa Fé and then drove the sixty-four miles north to Taos.[16] Jung, with his customary disdain for the details of the external world, simply records the journey impressionistically as bowling through New Mexico in a Chevrolet.

In Taos, where they spent 5–6 January 1925, Jaime de Angulo, an authority on American Indian languages, came into his own. He had the most perfect credentials as Jung's guide to the Indian pueblo since, after meeting Jung in Zürich in 1923, he had met D.H. Lawrence in Taos the following year. The paths of Lawrence and Jung were not destined to cross, since DHL and Frieda had left Taos in October 1924 and did not return until April 1925.[17] However, even if the two had met, it is unlikely that they would have got on, since Jung regarded Lawrence as a Freudian in all but name and later spoke most unflatteringly of him: 'D.H. Lawrence exaggerated the importance of sex because he was excessively influenced by his mother; he over-emphasised women because he was still a child and was unable to integrate himself with the world. People like him frequently suffer from respiratory illnesses which are primarily adolescent.'[18]

It was in Taos that Jung had his celebrated meeting with the Pueblo Indian sage Mountain Lake, allegedly introduced to him by one of his American female enthusiasts, Frances Wickes.[19] Jung spent hours talking to Mountain Lake, and his work is studded with references to this man and his tribe's sun-worship, to the point where some sceptics have suspected Jung of having been gulled by a charlatan. Jung scarcely helped matters by referring to

Mountain Lake as a 'chief' and a shaman, which has led iconoclasts to downgrade him to the status of a gas-station attendant. Careful research has established that Mountain Lake, alias Ochwiay Biano, aka Antonio Mirabal (c. 1891–1975) was a kind of spokesman for the council of the Taos Pueblo tribe, since he spoke the best English in the tribe, even though he had progressed only as far as the third grade in school.[20]

His nebulous status notwithstanding, Mountain Lake provided Jung with much food for thought and an abundance of quotable (and much-quoted) remarks, which make him sound like a forerunner of the later sage of the South-West, Carlos Castaneda. In the 1920s there was no trace of the cultural relativism of the post-1960s era, which has reclassified the American Indians as 'Native Americans' and insinuated the superiority of an animistic, non-technological culture. In the 1920s official policy was designed to civilize the Indians on the reservation and make them shed their primitive superstitions. Jung's conversations with Mountain Lake uncovered the Indians' deep anger on this score. Mountain Lake told him the whites looked cruel and they were always restlessly seeking something. Their restlessness made the Indians think they were mad.[21]

Jung pressed Mountain Lake to expound on this thesis. The explanation given by Biano/Mirabal made whites sound exactly like people who were possessed by demons. He went on to say that if the whites did not stop interfering with the Pueblos' religion, they would soon see something that would make them regret their actions bitterly. When pressed, he explained that he and the Pueblos might simply stop helping Father Sun on his daily journey across the sky. An absurd idea, perhaps, said Jung, but no more absurd than to think that you could communicate with a Supreme Being through prayer or that the bread and wine of Communion could be changed into the body and blood of Christ.[22]

Jung decided to press Mountain Lake hard on the subject of his sun-worship. He tried St Augustine's tack against the Mithraists and quoted the tag, 'Not this Sun is Our Lord, but he who made the Sun.' Mountain Lake became indignant and pointed to the sun animatedly. He described it not as a star but as a god and a father, the source of light, the source of fire, and the source of all life.[23]

This exchange apart, Jung by his own account achieved a remarkable rapport with Mountain Lake, and claimed that communication between them was immediate and non-verbal – what Jung called 'the primitive language of inward vision'.[24] Biano told him that Pueblos and other Indians thought with their hearts, but the white men with their heads, which was further proof that they were mad. He also pointed out that mountains formed an important part of the imagery in Pueblo belief, which set Jung's mind racing on comparative examples of the role of mountains in the lives of visionaries, Moses on Sinai and Nietzsche in the Engadine among them.[25]

But when attempting to probe deeper into Pueblo beliefs, Jung ran up against a brick wall. The Pueblos guarded the secrets of their religion closely and their taste for the esoteric reminded Jung of the Eleusinian mysteries. He noticed that the Pueblos moved rapidly from self-control to excitement whenever essential items of their religion, like sun-worship, were touched on, and was able to put into practice the expertise learned twenty years before at the Burghölzli in the word-association tests. He knew he had touched a sensitive point in the Pueblo religious sensibility from the length of time they took to respond to certain penetrating questions. Again and again the Pueblos insisted that by helping the sun they were universal benefactors. Jung found their mixture of sincerity and naïvety deeply touching and declared later that the white man's feeling of superiority when he listened to the 'superstitions' of these 'benighted savages' simply masked his unconscious envy and deep-down realization of his own spiritual impoverishment.[26]

The visit to New Mexico left Jung with two firm convictions. One was an abiding interest in North American Indian culture, not just that of the Pueblos, but of the Navajos, the Sioux and others.[27] The other was a deep hatred of colonialism, whether of the formal type practised in the British empire, or the informal 'internal' type practised in the USA, where whites subdued and bullied Native Americans.[28]

Jung packed a lot into his visit to New Mexico. After witnessing the buffalo dance at Taos pueblo on 6 January 1925 he and his party visited some more remote tribes in the Canyon de los Frijoles near pueblo San Idefonso, between Taos and Santa Fé.[29] Then he departed, probably by train, for New Orleans, where he arrived on 9 January. With his continuing interest in American blacks, Jung mentioned that he wanted to see them in a more or less natural environment. Fowler McCormick knew just the place near New Orleans where gangs of blacks felled trees.

In Washington DC he saw Jelliffe's colleague Dr William White and relaxed a little before setting off for a final hectic two days in New York, where he arrived on the 13th.[30] There he called on his disciple Dr Kristine Mann at her apartment on 59th Street and to a small band of admirers gave an informal talk on some American characteristics, including ruthlessness and lack of regard for ancestors.[31] Then he embarked on SS *France* for the homeward trip.

Jung arrived home feeling the worse for wear, but this was to be a curious aftermath of all his trips, prompting the conclusion that the illnesses induced by his foreign travels were largely, and mysteriously, psychosomatic. Once recovered, he plunged into his workaholic routine again, and from 23 March to 6 July he gave his first long seminar in the English language, on Nietzsche.[32] Almost without pausing, he then travelled to England, where he gave a seminar at Swanage in Dorset from late July to 7 August, talking two hours a day on dream analysis. Every time Jung went back to England the number of his adherents had swollen, and this time he was faced with an audience of between fifty and a hundred people, something that he, with his 'small is beautiful' approach, found distressing. Furthermore, the weather was atrocious, and since the meetings were held in a tent in the middle of a hayfield, his voice was accompanied by a constant pitter-patter of rain on the canvas roof.[33]

In London Jung visited the British Empire exhibition at Wembley and, seeing the material from East Africa on display, was seized with a sudden desire to go there. He spent most of the rest of the summer and the autumn of 1925 making preparations for the trip of a lifetime and arranging it so that he could be away from his practice for a long time. Matters did not proceed smoothly, so Jung consulted the *I Ching* and deduced from the oracular utterance of the hexagram that he might not return from Africa. He decided to press on anyway, and even began learning Swahili, even though at his age acquiring new languages was difficult.[34]

Accompanying him on this trip were the forty-three-year-old Helton Godwin ('Peter') Baynes and a young American named George Beckwith, who was killed soon afterwards in a car crash. According to Jung, Beckwith had consulted him and Jung had learned from an analysis of his dreams that the young man had not long to live. Beckwith decided he would live life to the full and at once signed up as amanuensis on the African trip. Jung travelled to England, from where he took ship to Mombasa on 15 October.

The itinerary took him to Lisbon, Malaga (where he was joined by Baynes and Beckwith), Marseilles and Genoa, and they were at the Suez Canal and Port Said by 7 November. Five days later, after a passage through the Red Sea, they arrived at Mombasa.[35] The ship was full of young Englishmen going out to Colonial Office posts in East Africa. At table Jung got into conversation with a number of them and took contact addresses, but was later appalled to find that many of them had died within the first few years from tropical diseases: amoebic dysentery, malaria and aggravated pneumonia.

After two days in Mombasa the travellers departed for Nairobi on the narrow gauge railway leading into the Kenya Highlands. Waking at dawn on the train, Jung looked out and saw a Masai warrior outlined against a steep cliff which gave him a sensation of *déjà vu*.[36] Jung intuited from this one incident that Africa was going to be important to him, since his only previous experience of *déjà vu* had been during the parapsychological experiments with Bleuler involving the medium Rudi Schneider.

He arrived in Nairobi at noon, in a blinding light that reminded him of the Engadine when ascending from the lowlands. After buying guns and cartridges and hiring servants and a cook, he relaxed in the New Stanley Hotel, where a young woman named Ruth Bailey, aged twenty-five, who had been visiting her sister and brother-in-law, introduced herself to him. Jung liked her and talked expansively of his forthcoming trip to the Mount Elgon region. Next day they breakfasted together and went shopping, after which Jung invited her to join them on the expedition; with his mystical belief in quaternity, he thought that having a fourth person along would bring good luck. Bailey's sister and brother-in-law were dead set against the idea, especially as she would have to travel alone to the final rendezvous point because her immediate plans and Jung's diverged, but an engineer agreed to escort her.[37]

While in Nairobi Jung hired a small Ford jeep to visit the Athai Plains, still the scene of pasturage by countless herds of antelope, zebra, wildebeeste and giraffe. On the plains he had his second mystical experience – this time a kind of god-like vision of himself, a sensation that he had in a way created the world, that he was therefore a special, divinely blessed being, favoured with unique insights. As he observed the animals from a low hill, it suddenly came to him that their 'reality' was guaranteed by our observation of them – a point like the one made by the philosopher

Berkeley in the eighteenth century. This meant, Jung thought, that consciousness had a cosmic purpose and that Man was indispensable for the completion of creation. It occurred to him, further, that such knowledge could provide a humanist 'myth' to replace the discredited 'certainties' of Christianity, and so it would be possible to imbue modern life with the meaning it so signally lacked.

From Nairobi Jung and party travelled to Station 64 on the Uganda railway, then the end of the line. Once the baggage had been transferred into their two cars, the eight-strong party headed for the village of Kakamegas (Kapsabet), an important administrative centre, boasting a District Commissioner, a company of the King's African Rifles, a hospital and also – to Jung's amazement – a mental asylum. The travellers expected a short and easy run, but their trip soon turned into a nightmare. While they were trying to cross a stream, the wooden bridge collapsed under one of their Fords, precipitating the car into the water. With ropes and Herculean efforts they got it out again, but then almost immediately a tropical storm blew up. It was midnight before they reached their destination, thoroughly drenched.[38]

The commissioner for the Nandi district of Kenya was Francis Daniel Hyslop, who welcomed them with whisky in his drawing room. A splendid blaze was burning in the fireplace, and Jung was reminded of nothing so much as a country house in Sussex. However, his capacity for taking impressions was limited, for the day in the monsoon rains had prostrated him with fever. He was ill for two days and had to stay in bed for twenty-four hours with acute laryngitis. As he lay there, his powers of concentration failed him, for he felt irritated by the atonal singing of the tropical birds.

Once he was up and about he tried to take the measure of Hyslop, who seems to have enjoyed 'coming the old soldier' with his eccentric visitors. He expressed astonishment at the general amateurishness of the expedition and the fact that they had no bearers with them. 'I noticed that they had no African servants with them,' he wrote afterwards, 'and it occurred to me later that perhaps this explained young Douglas's [sc. Beckwith's] gloom.' With practised Colonial Office hauteur, Hyslop went on, 'I cannot help wondering what kind of field work you will find to do on Elgon.'[39]

Jung explained his interest in the primitive, but Hyslop asked him how he would communicate. Jung explained that he had learned the rudiments of Swahili on the ship out and had a good dictionary with him, but Hyslop scouted this in short order. He pointed out that Swahili's status as lingua franca meant merely that in every area there would be someone who spoke it, but the more primitive the region (as among the Elgonyi people), the less easy it would be to find that someone. No doubt chafing at Hyslop's relentless 'wetblanketry' Jung then tried to turn the conversation by asking if the commissioner had ever been inside any of the caves on Mount Elgon. Hyslop replied that he had been in one and found it full of fleas. At this Jung was able to break the ice with one of his full-throated bellows of laughter. It was often observed that Jung laughed uproariously at remarks and jokes that were not all that good, and it may be that the true explanation is that his bull-like laughter was overcompensation, masking the anger he really felt.

With Hyslop's help the expedition started taking a more professional shape. By the time they set out on the trek to the 14,000-foot Mount Elgon, whose crater wall was visible on the horizon, they had acquired forty-eight bearers, three Askaris as escorts, four servants and a cook for the five-day march. Once beyond Kakamegas they were truly in the wilds. Every night lions, leopards and hyenas roared around their encampment, and Jung sometimes detached a few of the bearers from the main column so that he could follow the clear footprints of rhino and hippo some way into the bush.[40] At first he found the marching rhythms of his porters hard to adjust to, for the bearers never walked straight ahead, as a European would, but followed a curving route. After a while, Jung realized that this method of swinging around curves at a steady six kilometres an hour on the flat was exactly the motion that matched the terrain, so he relaxed.[41]

The days spent trekking through the bush, though rigorous and demanding for a man of fifty, always stayed in Jung's mind as an idyll, and he made light of the dangers from wildlife. On one occasion he used his 9mm Mannlicher rifle to disperse a pack of hyenas which had gathered menacingly after the cook slaughtered a sheep. True to their traditional custom, the bearers gave names to their employers. Jung was *mzee* (old man – because of his grey hair), Baynes 'Red Neck' and Beckwith *bwana maredadi* (the dapper gentleman). They were full of shrewd insights into all manner of things, were excellent judges of character and had astounding gifts as mimics. Jung enjoyed their company and especially that of the headman, a Somali who had been brought up in the Muslim faith.[42]

Mount Elgon lies just over the Kenya border in Uganda and, to Jung's amusement, as they reached the rest-house at the foot of the mountain he received a letter from the governor of Uganda asking him to take an English lady under his expedition's protection. The 'English lady' turned out to be none other than Ruth Bailey, who at once proved her worth as a trained nurse by looking after Beckwith when he went down with malaria.

The chief of the Elgonyi came to meet Jung and told him, with commendable exaggeration, that he and his people had never seen a white man before. However, this was exactly the news Jung wanted to hear, and he settled in with great gusto for a three-week sojourn with the Elgonyi. Although Jung liked to exaggerate the extent of pioneering involved in safaris in East Africa in the 1920s, it is worth remembering that the Lake Rudolph region of Kenya in the north had not been explored under Count Teleki's expedition until just thirty-seven years before, and although the Elgonyi country was not exactly *terra incognita*, it was a remote and little travelled area.

Speaking his halting Swahili, and using the services of his Somali headman, Jung made reasonable progress in penetrating the mental and emotional world of the Elgonyi peoples. Not surprisingly, he found their world-view Manichean, with sharp differentiations between the realms of light and darkness, often literally so. He found that a kind of pantheistic optimism was the rule during the day but this went rapidly into abeyance between 6 p.m. and 6 a.m., when fear of ghosts and demons took over. In the morning the Elgonyi would stretch out their hands for joy that the night had passed.[43] Although Jung found penetrating the secrets of the local religion as hard as among the Pueblos in New Mexico, he soon worked out that, similarly, the Elgonyi were actuated by a kind of primitive sun-worship. He noticed another morning custom, whereby the locals spat on their hands and stretched them out to the first rays of the sun – offering their spirits to the great spirit or *mungu* – not the sun itself, but rather the spirit symbolized by the moment of sunrise.[44]

Another link with the New Mexico Indians was the belief that thoughts do not come from the head or the brain. The locals assured Jung that the seat of thinking was in the belly because, Jung surmised, they were conscious only of emotional thoughts or those that actually disturbed the liver, intestines or stomach.[45] Yet the Elgonyi peoples lacked any notion of an afterlife comparable with that of the Pueblos.

Jung's porters told him they had no idea what would happen to them after death, and they even seemed to have little idea of what a normal life-span was. Although Jung encountered very few old people, judged in calendar terms, he thought they all seemed old, through having 'assimilated their age'.[46] Moreover, most of them had no idea how old they actually were: a girl of seventeen told him she was four and, because of his grey hair, judged that he was one hundred years old.[47] The Elgonyi seemed to fear, not death itself, but the spirits of the returning dead, and Jung once caused consternation by uttering the dread word *selelteni* (ghost), causing a tribal assembly to break up in disarray because a taboo had been broken.[48]

Hopes of breaking new ground by analysing the dreams of primitives were soon dashed when the Elgonyi told him flatly that they never dreamed. Even the witch-doctor, who traditionally dreamed the tribes' 'big dreams', was reduced to faith healing and voodoo-style suggestion therapy, because, as he and others told Jung, the District Commissioner now did all their dreaming for them. According to the Elgonyi, power works with power, so that God now spoke in dreams to the British, who had the power.[49]

One aspect of Elgonyi folkways of which Jung approved thoroughly was the rigid division of labour between the sexes and the doctrine of 'separate spheres' for men and women. He found that, as in southern Europe, it was customary for men to speak to men and women to women; anything else was construed as lovemaking. White men who breached this taboo, and especially those who slept with black women, were despised. With his Germanic belief in the essential deep differences between the sexes, Jung found this wholly admirable. It tied in with his conviction that equal rights for women in Europe meant that women had become masculinized and the European man feminized.[50]

Jung was deeply amused by the primitive African reaction to the sending and receiving of letters. Whenever he was brought a letter, the Elgonyi crowded round excitedly while he opened it. First they inspected the letter from above and below; then they listened as he read aloud, open-mouthed in the belief that the paper was talking to the white man. They could not get beyond the idea that a message by definition must be by word of mouth, and that anything else was magic.[51] On another occasion he wanted a letter delivered to Station 64, two and a half days' journey away by fast trot. He gave orders to the messenger, who stood there uncomprehendingly. Then one of his Somalis took him aside and told him that the orders had to be given in a set formulaic ritual. Once this was done the messenger smiled contentedly and set off on the first lap of the journey – seventy-four miles covered in thirty-six hours non-stop.[52]

Jung often marvelled at the native people's astonishing powers of endurance. Apart from the marathon running abilities of the letter couriers, the thing that astounded Jung most was when a woman in her sixth month of pregnancy, with a baby on her back and a long pipe in her mouth, danced all night long round a blazing fire where the temperature was 95°F. Yet paradoxically Jung could never engage them in a palaver for more than two hours, for after that they claimed to be exhausted.[53]

Another amusing motif for Jung was the 'thin veneer'. His hosts would often try to act sophisticated then give the game away by some piece of atavistic behaviour. His female water carrier fell ill with a high fever, probably the result of a septic abortion. The witch-doctor was summoned and said the illness was caused by the ghosts of the woman's parents. He proceeded to 'catch' the ghosts, whereupon the woman made a swift and seemingly miraculous recovery.[54] Another of the Elgonyi swore up and down to Jung that he had outgrown all primitive supersititions. While walking the two of them came to a fork in the path near his hut and there Jung found a brand new 'ghost trap', perfectly got up like a little hut. Seeing Jung smile, the man denied with all the signs of extreme agitation that he was responsible for the contraption, asserting that only children would make such a 'ju-ju'. He gave the 'ghost trap' a kick and the whole thing fell to pieces. The moral Jung took away was that the need to save face in the presence of the white man overrode the man's deep fear of ghosts.[55]

Not all Jung's time in the environs of Mount Elgon was spent in amateur anthropology. He went on a number of short expeditions into the impenetrable forests on the slopes of the extinct volcano and recorded altitudes for his two camps at 2,900 metres and 2,100 metres. He claimed to have encountered an (unnamed) tribe on the western slopes who ate their dead. More authentic was an occasion when he genuinely did encounter a savannah community who had not seen white men before. Using three different languages to make any sense of the peculiar dialect, his Somali interpreters suddenly doubled up with laughter. Jung asked what the joke was. The Somalis explained that when asked who they were, the people had all replied with their given names. When pressed for the name of the tribe, the people looked puzzled then came out with the answer that so tickled the Somalis. '*Bwana*,' said the head man, 'these people are so stupid they don't even know what they are called. When we asked them, they said they were "the people who were there".'[56] This was to become one of Jung's favourite after-dinner stories.

Most of the African explorers in the classical period brought back hair-raising stories of encounters with wild animals, and Jung learned for himself that this aspect of things was a living reality in tropical Africa. One of his expeditions took him into the Kabras forest in the Kitoshi region of Mount Elgon. In the thick grass he nearly stepped on a puff-adder, which was poised to strike when he managed to jump clear. Amazingly, when he returned to camp he learned that George Beckwith had had an even narrower escape, for while he was out hunting, an eight-foot black mamba, the most deadly snake in Africa, came hurtling down a hill towards him with aggressive intent. Fortunately Beckwith was an excellent shot and managed to kill the serpent, but the shock of his near encounter with death hit him later and he returned to camp pale and trembling.[57]

The foray into the Kabras provided the party with virtually non-stop encounters with animals dangerous to man. They shot a further three venomous snakes, including a green mamba, and at various times had buffalo and leopards in their sights. One night a pack of hyenas surprised a sentry who had fallen asleep at his post and tore him to pieces; next evening at 9 p.m. they attacked the camp and swarmed into the cook's hut, sending him screaming over the stockade before the predators were routed out by gunfire. Other adventures for Jung included finding himself on a rhino trail and suddenly realizing he had forgotten to load his rifle; and walking over a crocodile-infested river on a slippery tree trunk.[58]

Beckwith's close encounter with the black mamba set Jung thinking about the warnings he and Beckwith had received in Europe that death was stalking them. The evening after the mamba incident Jung reminded Beckwith of a dream he (Beckwith) had related in Zürich shortly before they left for Africa. Beckwith had actually dreamed he was attacked by a large mamba and awoke in terror; Jung took the dream seriously for, snake symbolism apart, he had a terror of the actual reptiles and was learned enough on the subject to know that the only three snakes that attack man unprovoked are the black mamba, the Indian cobra and the fer-de-lance of South America.[59] After talking the dream over, Beckwith became convinced that his mamba dream portended Jung's death, but Jung was struck by the fact that shortly after the snake attack Beckwith fell seriously ill with malaria and was critical for a few days. He continued to think of himself and Beckwith as marked men right to the very end of the African trip.

After completing their northward trek round the southern foot of the mountain and spending three memorable weeks among the Elgonyi, the travellers set out for the Bugishu territory in Uganda, and spent the New Year at the rest-house of Bunambale, with a splendid view of the broad Nile valley. To compensate for his lack of success in eliciting any dreams from the Elgonyi, Jung turned to dream analysis with his Somalis. This was also fruitless ground, since his bearers carried with them a book of Arabic alchemy as large as the Koran, which usually gave them satisfactory interpretations; only in the case of extremely obscure dreams did they consult Jung. Nevertheless, he learned enough to convince him that the basic store of archetypal images was common to all human beings: 'I analysed dreams of Somali Negroes as if they were people of Zürich, with the exception of certain differences of languages and images. Where the primitives dream of crocodiles, pythons, buffaloes and rhinoceroses, we dream of being run over by trains and automobiles. Both have the same voice, really; our modern cities sound like a primeval forest. What we express by the banker the Somali expresses by the python.'[60]

From Bugishu the travellers proceeded to Mbala, where two Ford trucks took them to Jinja, on Lake Victoria. With his dread fascination with saurians, Jung was intrigued to find that a huge crocodile basked contentedly near the town. When he asked the locals why they did not kill such a dangerous predator, they explained that they fed it like a pet, as it chased all other crocodiles away so that no humans were ever taken at the lake shore.[61] The real menace at Jinja, Jung felt, were the people. He found the Buganda people frightening and prophesied that one day they would rise up and massacre all Europeans and, especially, the Indian merchants and moneylenders whom they loathed.[62] The second half of Jung's prophecy, at least, came true many years later.

At Jinja they loaded the baggage onto the narrow-gauge railway for the trip to Masindi, situated on the plateau that separates Lake

Kioga and Lake Albert. Now came the most gruelling part of the expedition, for it was 250 miles north to Rejâf in Equatoria province of the Sudan, where they could take the paddle-steamer down the Nile. For two days, escorted by three Askaris, they started at 5.30 a.m. and trekked twenty miles a day; Jung noted that he had already lost twenty pounds since the beginning of the trip. On the first night of the trek they were involved in a nasty incident with the villagers among whom they had sought shelter. In honour of his guests the chief called on his warriors to display their dancing prowess, which they did fully armed. Jung knew enough about Africa to recognize that things could suddenly turn ugly in such a situation, for 'in war-dances primitives can become so excited that they may even shed blood.'[63]

Apprehension increased when the travellers found themselves at the centre of an ever-narrowing circle of sixty armed and apparently berserk warriors, who were being egged on to ever great feats of unbridled gymnastics by the chief. Jung and Peter Baynes sprang up and joined in the dance. Jung had a huge *sjambok* or rhino-whip which he cracked like a lion-tamer, bellowing and swearing at them in German. Eventually Jung brought the proceedings to a halt by ignoring the chief's exhortations for 'just one more dance' and distributing cigarettes while making sleeping gestures. The warriors took the hint and dispersed, but all four European witnesses reported that the atmosphere was very tense indeed and the dance could have ended tragically. Jung was scarcely reassured later when a district commissioner told him that the selfsame tribe had recently murdered two white men, but he explained that he had acted in such a spontaneous and unexpected way because he was 'seized by the force of the archetype'.[64]

Nevertheless, the incident seems to have convinced him that trekking was just too dangerous for, in circumstances unexplained, the party commandeered jeeps for the last part of the journey to Rejâf. Here they took passage down the Nile in a paddlesteamer, but Jung made a bad impression on his travelling companions by selfishly booking the best cabin and showing an unchivalrous lack of concern about the arrangements for Ruth Bailey.[65] However, he had an uncanny knack for conciliating women to whom he had behaved badly, so that the next we hear of Ruth Bailey is that near the junction of the Blue Nile he disguised her as a man so that she could visit a Coptic monastery.

On the trip down the Nile Jung made a special study of snakecharmers and their art, once again trying to come to terms with phenomena that he most feared.[66] Until they reached Khartoum the paddlesteamer was able to draw very little water and had barges alongside to stabilize it. An Arab on one of the barges was suffering from malaria, and all through the night Jung heard him call out at uniform intervals, 'Allah! Allah!', calling on his god for a cure. It is typical of Jung that he does not tell us the outcome.[67]

In Khartoum Jung lectured at the university, then the travellers proceeded on the classic descent of the lower Nile. Jung revelled in the ruins at Aswan and Luxor – far more than his comrades, for Barbara Hannah says that he 'bullied' Beckwith and Ruth Bailey into viewing the pyramids of Saqqara.[68] The sculptured baboons in the temple of Abu Simbel reinforced his theory that the light/darkness motif among the Elgonyi was the Horus/Set principle taken down the Nile into Black Africa. He loved the fact that he was approaching Cairo from Africa and not from Greece, as he was less interested in the Asiatic elements in Egyptian culture than the Hamitic, and more enthused by Islam than by Hellenism. Jung fancifully interpreted his journey from the heart of Africa to Egypt as a metaphor for the birth of spiritual illumination.[69] In Cairo Jung did the usual sightseeing rounds – the Pyramids, the Valley of the Kings, the tombs of the caliphs.

Jung arrived back in Küsnacht in April 1926, having been six months away, his longest ever foreign trip. His African journey made a profound impression on him, suggested dozens of different lines of analytical enquiry, was a fertile sourcebook for his later theories, and provided a fund of illuminating anecdotes. No bald summary can exhaust the significance of Africa in 1925–26 for the Jungian unconscious, but three conscious reflections are of special importance for the light they throw on Jung's attitudes and development.

Although his time among primitive peoples had not yielded the treasury of 'big dreams' he had been hoping for, Africa crystallized many of his inchoate theories about dreaming. He had long toyed with the key tenet that dreams represent a form of compensation, with the unconscious compensating the conscious. He had been much struck by the fact that in the First World War soldiers at the front usually dreamed of home; if a man started to dream about the war, this was a sign of psychic overload and it was time to pull him out.

On the basis of his experience in Africa he was ready to widen this to include the proposition that normally one does not dream about the situation one is in, and if one does, psychic disaster looms. In Africa he never once dreamed about Africa and the only time a black man appeared in his dreams, it was a man who had cut his hair in Chatanooga in 1913. In his dream the barber was holding very hot curling tongs, intending to kink Jung's hair in negroid fashion. Jung read this as a warning from the unconscious that the primitive was a danger to him. His interpretation was that at the deepest level he had gone to Africa to escape from Europe and its problems but by staying too long in the Dark Continent he had run into the danger of being overwhelmed by his unconscious.

On the particular subject of Africa, Jung speculated that white men who lived there too long 'went native': not in the sense of Richard Burton or Kipling's Strickland, in which a white master of disguise could take on protective camouflage when he chose, but in a more profound sense of loss of identity.

'Going black under the skin,' as Jung expressed it, could mean either that the white man succumbed to savagery himself or that he would develop an irrational hatred of the blacks who had elicited such tensions. Conrad's Kurtz in *Heart of Darkness* had, of course, undergone both processes.

In the light of his experiences in Central Africa Jung also reinterpreted his time in Northern Africa in 1920 and in particular the puzzling dream of his fight with the Arab prince. The Arab, as well as being his 'shadow', also represented the danger that his European consciousness would be overwhelmed by a violent assault on the psyche by the unconscious, colluding, so to speak with the primitive. From this it was but a short step to the theory that there were dangers in any form of cultural or racial uprooting.

Another implication of this viewpoint was Jung's firmly held tenet that the modern-day consciousness hankered after the primitive as a compensation for the modern machine age; this particularly struck a chord after his time in Cairo. The 'Tutankhamen craze' after Howard Carter discovered the Pharaoh's tomb in 1922 seemed to back this up; forty years earlier the discovery would have been of interest only to scholars and Egyptologists.

Jung also pondered deeply the two ideologies he had seen at work in British East Africa: Christianity and imperialism, the twin pillars supporting 'the white man's burden'. He was cynical about how far beneath the soil Christianity had really sunk its roots, and said the Africans accepted it from the British just as the Ancient Britons had from the Romans: at the point of a lance. He considered that the missionaries had made a thorough mess of things, unwittingly producing a nest of anarchists, which was why the British were so jumpy about any sign of unrest in their domains. He had seen how easy it would be to connect Uganda and the Anglo-Egyptian condominium in the Sudan with a network of good roads, but the British had deliberately left the no-man's land through which he had had to trek to prevent 'infection' reaching Uganda from Egypt via the Nile.[70]

Jung was particularly disdainful of the mission-educated African boys, who had evolved beyond the unsophisticated locals only in point of being consummate thieves, liars and cheats. The typical mission boy was an animal speaking a meaningless Christian argot: 'I am a good Christian like you, I know all those fellows, Johnny and Marky and Lukey.'[71]

For imperialism Jung always had a genuine loathing. The white man in Africa seemed to him a worse animal than the man-eating beasts in the jungle, and the very worst products of colonialism were the corrupt, venal and cynical missionaries.[72] The return home via the Mediterranean strengthened the 'reverse culture shock' of approaching Europe from Africa. For the first time he saw Europeans from the viewpoint of what would now be called the Third World and he came to see why the Chinese referred to 'foreign devils' and the Japanese to 'barbarians'. Even the approach to the coast of Europe, with its bays and snowcapped peaks, made him feel he was entering the land of the pirates.[73]

If his relationship with Freud was the most significant interpersonal event of Jung's life, the six-month trip to Africa was his most important contact with the external world. The experience convinced him he was on the right track in interpreting myth as the product of universal archetypes in a collective unconscious and validated and legitimated the primitive, uncanny, No. 2 personality that had given him so much trouble in his youth. Though very far from an orthodox believer, Jung, in his contact with sun-worshippers in New Mexico and Africa, had integrated the Christian imagery of light into a new synthesis.

The cynical Jung of the Second World War period sometimes tried to rewrite history and downplay the significance of his African safari. In 1942 he remarked sardonically that he could have found what he was looking for just as readily in the remote areas of the Lietschental in the Bernese Alps, where the people still preserved archaic customs.[74] But, as Van der Post pointed out, the African adventure was the one occasion when Jung successfully integrated his inner realm with the outside world, and the relevant quotation was from Sir Thomas Browne: 'We carry within us the wonders we seek without us: there is all Africa and her prodigies in us.'[75]

Chapter Sixteen

THE DOCTRINE

Jung paid two more quick visits to the USA in 1926 and 1927 but in the main, after his African trip, his peregrinations came to an end. From the late 1920s to the early 1930s he was largely engaged in perfecting his general view of the psyche and in seeing patients. Like the academic who loves research but hates teaching, Jung was increasingly irritated that he could not devote all his time to writing, but he was in a trap of his own devising. Had he been content to be a prophet pure and simple, Jung could have retired to Bollingen and cut down his human contacts. But because of his insistence that he was a scientist, that his findings were 'empirical' and not pure speculation, he was forced to take on patients to provide him with the empirical base.

Jung elaborated a theory of the 'stages of life' – that the second half of life, from the age of thirty-five on, had a radically different purpose and meaning from life until then. The idea certainly applied well to his own life, for until middle age he was involved in psychoanalysis and the problems of psychotic patients. Thereafter his patients were people who had very little wrong with them at all, except what he called 'individuation' problems. Freud, by contrast, began and ended with the seriously neurotic as analysands. By 1926 Jung consciously avoided the kind of cases that had so exercised him during the Burghölzli years, claimed that he was no longer an expert on schizophrenia and declared that he did not have the strength for that kind of work.[1]

Certainly the Jung of his fifties and sixties was a notably erratic and explosive therapist, who often lost his temper with his patients or lost interest in them if their cases did not exemplify one of his pet theories. His attraction for women and his uncanny mediumistic ability to read other people's characters and problems were qualities offset by darker ones: a love of practical jokes at inappropriate moments and directed against undeserving targets; a pronounced dislike of any authority except his own; and violent mood swings which would fling him between geniality and anger in a single therapeutic session and make him oscillate between bragging arrogance and secretiveness.

Many stories and sayings testify to his ill-concealed hostility towards patients who did not interest him. 'I'm sometimes driven to the conclusion that boring people need treatment more urgently than mad people,' was one of his *obiter dicta*. 'If I get another perfectly normal adult malingering as a sick patient, I'll certify him,' he declared, forgetting that his own method of 'individuation' encouraged just such behaviour. And, in Groucho Marx mood, he once said, 'Show me a sane person and I'll cure him for you.'[2]

More serious were the occasions when he rounded angrily on his patients. His vocabulary of foul-mouthed abuse included 'slimy bastard', 'empty gasbag', and 'a pisspot of unconscious devils,' while his volcanic rage is well conveyed by 'I would have softened up his guttersnipe complex with a sound Swiss thrashing.' Among his recorded sayings are the following, to a patient, 'Stop buggering about and wasting my time.' He interrupted the confessions of a woman patient with this impatient outburst, 'You want to fuck this priest, don't you? Come on, be frank about it. Tell me the real truth of the matter.' Another female patient brought him her dreams written on dirty scraps of paper, and Jung warned her that in future she must write on clean paper. When she arrived next time with the same dirty paper, Jung threw her out. Another woman tormented by a syphilis phobia consulted him, but he turned on her, accused her of being a 'filthy swine' who sullied him with her presence, and ordered her from the house forthwith.[3]

On one notorious occasion a long-standing patient arrived for his appointment to find that Jung had gone sailing on Lake Zürich. In a towering rage the patient hired a boat, set off in pursuit and, once he caught up with him, used a loud-hailer to upbraid him. 'Where the hell are you? I've been waiting at your house.' Jung then zigzagged away, with the patient in hot pursuit. When they again came within hailing distance, Jung cried out, 'Go away – you bore me!'[4]

There was a bullying, authoritarian side to Jung which even his disciples found wearying. Dr Michael Fordham found him thoughtless, insensitive, inconsiderate and tactless, with a tendency to ride roughshod over people and a conviction that the ultimate test of the value of any person or thing was whether or not it bored him. Jung was well known to have walked out of dinner parties because he did not find the company congenial. At home he would get his way by sullen and silent disapproval until the 'offender' reformed; in this way he gradually steered his children away from orthodox Christianity. Fordham reports that Jung could often fly into a towering rage about trivia – for example, if his wife had failed to give him a key – but then moments later would be laughing and joking as if nothing had happened. People who were not used to this aspect of him were seriously alienated and he made many enemies, especially among men.[5]

These unpleasant aspects of Jung have always worried his disciples, who have sought to exculpate him or explain his faults away. They concede he could be unpredictable and lose his temper violently and frighteningly, but argue that this was 'compensated' by his great sense of humour.[6] Less sympathetic observers have queried how genuine his sense of humour was. Much is made of his booming laughter, but its very exaggerated quality makes one suspect that he was, as it were, protesting too much. Walter Kaufman, who made a detailed study of Jung's humour, found that it was mainly sarcasm and hyperbole of the *reductio ad absurdum* kind, and suggested that the booming laughter might be the mark of an introverted sick soul.[7]

By and large, Jung's disciples dealt with the problem of his brutality, foul language and volcanic anger by pretending that it hurt him more than it hurt others, and by insinuating a therapeutic effect. The disgraceful treatment of the woman with the syphilis phobia was brushed aside by one Jungian as 'masterful cruelty', which, 'by playing along with the patient's masochism, jolts her out of it.' A faithful female Jungian duly reported that Jung's 'apparent cruelty' towards her promoted her inner growth. The method of *reductio ad absurdum* which he so favoured was unwittingly used by Frances Wickes in one of her unguarded comments. She said she had been worried by the abnormally large number of suicides and premature deaths among people analysed by Jungians but cheered up once she realized that 'integration alone matters, even if it does not come about in this life.'[8]

It is worth conceding, however, that few analysts or psychotherapists are saints and that even the most patient and stoical can be taxed to the limit by certain analysands. Moreover, Jung had a remarkable breadth of interests and sympathies which enabled him to take seriously certain patients who might have been shown the door by more orthodox therapists. On one occasion he had a woman patient who complained that she was forever being attacked by black birds, rather in the manner of the Hitchcock film. Instead of assuming that this was a transmogrified sexual trauma, Jung went for a walk with her in the countryside and found that crows did indeed cluster round her and one even nipped her in the neck, yet they left him completely alone.[9]

Jung's therapy was designed for people in the second half of life and was a process of inner development. In this it contrasted strongly with Freudian analysis, which was at that stage largely preoccupied with the problems of neurotics up to the age of thirty-five. The overriding principle in Freudian therapy was the achievement of 'genitality' or a satisfactory heterosexual relationship: Freud indeed stated that the goals of the normal male were 'honour, power, wealth, fame and the love of women'.[10] In Jungian therapy, to reach the stage of psychic wholeness did not require the participation of another person. Jung's patients tended to be rich Protestant Swiss bourgeois who had attained all life's glittering prizes but felt a sense of dissatisfaction, a feeling of 'is this all?' He found that about a third of his patients were not suffering from any clinically definable neurosis, but from the sense of pointlessness and aimlessness in their lives.[11] Jung interpreted this to mean that they were in search of a satisfying form of religious belief.[12]

The point that most of Jung's patients were middle-class Protestants (hundreds of them, as against a couple of Jews and half a dozen Catholics) is worth stressing, on two grounds. First, it helps to explain the contradictory reports on Jung's fees as an analyst. Some say that his charges were steep, others that they were reasonable and were varied according to his estimate of the patient's means. It seems likely that the fees were predicated on the income of a prosperous member of the bourgeoisie and therefore high, objectively considered – which would be in line with Jung's previously considered 'money-complex'. On the other hand, it is probable that he did take under his wing certain patients whose cases were unusually interesting, and here he may well have modified his fee. The reason most of his patients were Protestant in the first place was that, as his researches showed over and over again, when in trouble Protestants opted for the doctor over the clergyman every time, whereas the reverse was true for Catholics; the celibacy of their clergy and the institution of Confession were the principal reasons.[13]

By the 1920s the techniques of psychoanalysis were well developed. Analysts saw patients five times a week, and the patient lay on a couch with the analyst out of sight. Jung disliked the couch as it prohibited face-to-face contact with the patient, and he spaced out contact with his analysands: four times a week was the maximum, but often he saw people only once or twice a week and encouraged breaks in the analysis. Again in contrast to Freudian methods, Jung was an active, interventionist therapist, who did not shrink from admonishing and instructing his patients and making suggestions.[14] This led to charges from the Freudian camp that Jungians simply 'led the witness', to which they replied that the Freudian fear of transference led to excessive coldness, reserve and remoteness on the part of the analyst. Freud's daughter, Anna, herself a noted analyst, came to feel that the early Freudian emphasis on detachment had been overdone, and that there was no possible harm done if the patient knew where the analyst went for his holidays or his handicap at golf. A notable post-Freudian, Heinz Kohut, sided with Jung on this point: 'To remain silent when one is asked a question is not neutral but rude.'[15] Ferenczi, too, disagreed violently with Freud on this issue, believed in giving emotional gratification to the patient, even with hugs and kisses, and went some way to sympathizing with Jung on the need for 'psychosynthesis'.[16]

Jung acknowledged that the analytic method was all that was required for some patients. If a woman had a problem with sexuality, Freudian psychoanalysis was a perfectly valid way of dealing with it; if a man had a complex over the 'will to power', Adlerian 'individual psychology' was equally useful. Generally, the pleasure principle was a better way of accounting for neurotics who had achieved a successful *social* adaptation and the lust for power a better way of accounting for social inadequates.[17]

But Jung thought that both these were 'partial' views of the human psyche, which overemphasized the pathological aspects of life and interpreted human beings exclusively in the light of their defects.[18] Besides, most people with obviously Freudian and Adlerian problems would seek out analysts of the relevant persuasion. What Jung's own 'analytical psychology' had to offer was what he called the 'synthetic-hermeneutic method', specially tailored for those in the second half of life with moral, philosophical or religious problems. Jung linked what he called the 'analytic-causal-reductive' approach with extraversion, since the extravert is concerned with his relationship to the world of objects, and Freudian dream therapy equated dream images with real objects; the 'synthetic-hermeneutic' interpretation, on the other hand, referred every part of the dream back to the dreamers themselves.[19]

Why the emphasis on the second half of life? Jung thought that people went wrong by making youth and young adulthood the ideal-type matrix of human life and consigning the second half to the dustbin. There had to be a biological reason why people lived until eighty, well beyond their reproductive capacity, especially since Nature was normally so cruel and careless of individual life so long as the species survived. On his view, the first half of life was devoted to activities explicitly sanctioned by Nature – money making, success in a career, marriage, the rearing of a family – but evolution had given human beings a second, 'cultural' phase of life.[20]

Jung lamented that in the West there was no cult of the elders or reverence for grey-haired wisdom; on the contrary the old tried to compete with the young, especially in the USA, where Jung found it almost mandatory for a father to be a brother to his sons and the mother to be, if possible, the younger sister of her daughter.[21] Yet he recognized that people fought tooth and nail against the transition into middle age and that women, in particular, felt they had no meaning apart from their children and would sink into a vacuum once they had flown the nest. Again and again he underlined his doctrine of the stages of life. It was particularly important for women to realize they were not 'finished' after the menopause.[22] Some people tried to face the changed situation by a radical swing in the opposite direction – changing their profession, getting divorced, becoming converted to a religion or apostatizing from an old one.

The snag with this was that repression of one's former life was no better than the repression of its opposite in the first stage of life.

The key notion in Jungian therapy – as indeed, by definition, in any depth psychology – was the unconscious. Jung thought that the only way forward towards psychic health was to engage in a dangerous fight with the unconscious's contents. This was the symbolic meaning of the hero's fight with the monsters he had analysed in *Symbols of Transformation*, and true human value lay in 'victory' over the collective psyche. No other approach was possible. To try to repress the unconscious via reductive analysis was impossible as its contents simply could not be reduced to inactivity; on the other hand to be submerged by them meant schizophrenia.

So the typical patient of Jung's would start by coming in twice a week for an hour, with the aim of cutting down to once-a-week sessions as soon as possible. The patient would sit on a chair facing the master, and at the end of the session would be assigned tasks to carry out and given books to read; it was stressed that collaboration with the therapist was crucial. The emphasis of the analysis was placed on the present life situation, so that the patient did not fall into infantile regression or become alienated from his surroundings. Moreover, the treatment, with fewer weekly sessions, was less expensive than Freudian analysis, and the therapist could treat more people.[23]

Although Jung changed his view, and the emphases within his view, many times on the phenomenon of transference, in general he did not assign it anything like the importance Freud did, arguing that it was a marginal affair which could prolong or vitiate treatment. In the 1920s Jung took the somewhat simplified view – which he amended later – that transference was simply a desperate attempt by the patient to compensate his faulty attitude towards reality and mainly showed that the analyst in question was deficient in basic skills. Transference in any case, being composed of power drives and fears and sexual neuroses, was mostly encountered in patients for whom the Freud–Adler 'analytic' method was most suitable. Potentially dangerous, since it could destroy an analysis, transference could be headed off if therapy, as in the Jungian method, was collaborative not conflictual.

The first stage in treatment was to make the patient face reality. It was a favourite tenet of Jung's that most people led an inauthentic life, with some waking up to reality early in life, some in middle age, others late in life and others again only on their deathbed. It was vital that people realized the moral implications of what they were doing. Jung cited the case of a spinster schoolteacher, besotted with a handsome but worthless young man, who saved from her tiny salary to send her 'beloved' on expensive trips to Monte Carlo and other watering places. When the young man had a breakdown and came to Jung for treatment, Jung discovered to his horror that his patient had no idea of the moral dimensions to the case, nor any conception of the extent to which he had exploited the poor teacher.[24]

The second stage was the uncovering of the pathogenic secret that was sapping the psychic energies of the patient. The classic instance was the Burghölzli case of the woman who had allowed her daughter to suck polluted water from a bath sponge.[25] This was the stage when Jung always persuaded lapsed Christians to return to their religions, as a coldly pragmatic act of policy, since in his view religious crisis was really what ailed most neurotics over the age of thirty-five. For the reasons given, this was more difficult for Protestants than Catholics, but was feasible in the context of a revivalist spirit of the age, as with the Oxford Movement. Next Jung decided whether the Freud/Adler-based analytic-reductive therapy was all that was required, or whether the synthetic-hermeneutic approach was called for. Usually he decided it was, if only because the good results achieved with his patients from the analytic-reductive method turned out to be merely temporary.

At this point doctor and patient entered the truly Jungian territory. Gradually the patient had to be led forward on the path to individuation via the 'transcendent function' – the progressive synthesis of conscious and unconscious material. The role of the therapist was to stimulate a weak or inhibited unconscious and to help confront the conscious life situation. The best way to get the contents of the unconscious to emerge was through paintings, dream analysis and active imagination – a method of directed day dream; clay modelling, automatic writing and mandala drawing were other methods used. The essential task of Jung and other Jungian therapists was to put the patient in touch with the unconscious so that archetypes could emerge and be assimilated by the conscious mind, but not allow them to gush out with such force that they overwhelmed consciousness.

Jung's therapy usually lasted about three years. The fact that it was a process of self-development seduced some of the unwary into thinking it was a kind of do-it-yourself analysis, but Jung always emphasized that frightening material came out of the unconscious and that it could overwhelm and destroy the conscious if a patient undertook it without a guide or therapist. The key was partnership: as psychotherapy was at bottom a dialectical relationship between doctor and patient.[26] Again in contrast to Freudianism, Jung specified re-education of the patient as a goal of his therapy. If the analysand begins responding to everyday life more rationally, psychological projection will fade away and spouses, children, parents and friends will cease to be victims of intrigues from the unconscious.

Jung never disguised how difficult the art of psychotherapy was. Unlike in normal medicine, the diagnosis had to come at the end, not the beginning of treatment, since a neurosis would yield up its meaning only gradually in the course of the analysis. Moreover, again in contrast to the situation encountered by the physician, the anamnesis or case history was always suspect. Jung often referred to psychotherapy as a process of navigating between Scylla and Charybdis and stressed the extreme difficulty of the therapist's position: he was in danger either of getting caught up in his patient's neurosis or robbing himself of therapeutic efficacy by keeping his distance.[27]

Such a thumbnail sketch cannot begin to do justice to the complexity of Jungian therapy, for this in turn depends on the elaborate cosmology of the psyche that Jung began to chart in the 1920s. Jung criticized Freud for believing that psychoanalysis was, like Marxism, a praxis, in that it embodied a unity of theory and practice: in Freud's words: 'Psychoanalysis is unique in that it embodies both a method of treatment and an explanation of the psyche.'[28] But Jungian therapy involved a similar fusion of thought and action, since his day-to-day therapy rested on a mapping of the human mind as complex as a mariner's chart of the Tuamotu archipelago. Any attempt to explain Jung's theories is bound to result in charges of misunderstanding, similar to those which legendarily bedevil biblical exegesis, but no-one who seeks to explain Jung's life can shirk the task, if only because for Jung the archetypes and the collective unconscious were living, everyday realities.

From his study of dreams, the fantasies of schizophrenics, the beliefs of primitive peoples and the recurring motifs in the myths of civilization after civilization, Jung came to the conclusion that there existed something very like what Plato called in the *Timaeus* the 'world-soul'. Jung's term for this core of actual and potential human mental dispositions he called 'the psyche', though he sometimes muddied the waters by using 'psyche' in the normal sense, referring to the totality of an *individual*'s psychic make-up.[29] If the psyche was the 'world-mind' – in the sense that at the deepest level, as in Walt Whitman's poetry, every individual self was identical to all other selves – the true task of psychotherapy and all other Jung-inspired inner journeys was to find the Self – that level of the unconscious where the individual consciousness merged with the psyche, as a river flowing into a mighty ocean.

The unconscious, then, was collective, and because of its collective nature the human mind was predisposed to respond to situations through fixed behaviour patterns Jung called archetypes – a concept which he claimed could be traced back to St Augustine.[30] These archetypes manifested themselves in images and symbols, found in dreams, fantasies and myths. The recurrent and universal motifs found in all the world's mythologies pointed to their common origin in archetypes in the collective unconscious. Many anthropologists had speculated that cultures and their attendant myths had been spread from one society to another. In the most extreme form of such 'diffusionist' theory, adventurers like Thor Heyerdahl actually set out to demonstrate the mechanics of the diffusion by sailing rafts across the great oceans. In Jung's view Heyerdahl's journeys were unnecessary, since the only relevant ocean was the ocean of the unconscious on which the individual ego floated like a log.

Although Jung was an indifferent philosopher, he was deeply influenced by philosophical ideas. In the case of the archetypes the obvious influences are Plato and Kant, but it is possible to see in his notion of the 'objective psyche' an echo of German idealism and, in particular, of Hegel's *Phenomenology of Mind*.[31] Individuation – the penetration to the level of the Self by an individual person – is, as in Hegel's system, the self-actualization of the ultimate world principle, which in Jung's terms is the objective psyche. Jung's system is thus a psychological version of Hegel's objectification in history, just as Marx's is a materialist version. For the Marxist materialistic conception of history Jung substituted the objective psyche; for the dialectic revealed in class struggle he substituted the dialectical interpenetration of opposites in the psyche.[32] The dominant theme in Jung's thought is the unfolding of the objective psyche or collective unconscious in the lives of individuals and in art and culture. Hence the at first sight startling propositions, enunciated by Jung, that the so-called great events in human history were profoundly unimportant and that in the last analysis the only true history was the life of the individual.[33]

We can now understand better Jung's notion of 'stages of life' and his insistence that the second stage of life commences at thirty-five or thereabouts. His argument was that the individual human psyche, precisely because it was linked to the objective psyche of the cosmos, was programmed to trigger a consciousness detached from the world at middle age. This was why statistics showed a rise in the frequency of depression in men around the age of forty and in women somewhat earlier. The conventional view was that this was linked with career success or failure with men and with emotional, sexual or child-related problems with women. Jung was impatient with such 'simpleminded views' and stressed that the human organism was simply preparing itself for death. Determinism was not rigid, and people's move into the second stage of life could be delayed until their fifties if, for example, they were the son or daughter of a long-lived parent. But essentially it was an internal dynamic in the psyche, which could be traced in dreams and fantasies, that triggered the 'life crisis', not success or failure, war, revolution or religious conversion or even trauma and illness. The *pièce de résistance* of Jung's system was the suggestion that the detached consciousness which appeared at middle age might even survive death.

Jung's system was centripetal, aimed at the still point where ego merged with Self, and the mid-life transition showed the process in action. But in a well-balanced individual, moving towards this fusion with the Absolute – or what Buddhists call *Atman* – a second process took place, that of homeostasis or self-regulation. Just as the Earth orbits round the Sun but also rotates on its axis as it does so, so the journey into the collective unconscious in 'individuation' is accompanied by a self-regulating process, particularly observable in dreams, whereby the conscious and the unconscious compensate each other. It is a commonplace of physiology that such a process takes place in the body: the kidneys balance the secretion of alkalis and acids; the pituitary and the endocrine glands balance their secretions of hormones; the hypothalamus at the base of the brain regulates temperature; and all the many other examples known in cybernetic language as 'negative feedback'. As the individual descended into the unconscious in individuation, it was essential that the analyst kept the patient's conscious and unconscious balanced, rather as a pilot adjusts trim and ailerons when bringing an aeroplane in to land.

The analysand's descent into the unconsciousness, probing deeper and deeper levels until the final encounter with the Self, has been compared to the epic descent in Jules Verne's *A Journey to the Centre of the Earth*, often hailed by Jungians as a metaphor for the individuation process.[34] Once the analyst has decided that the patient is a suitable case for the 'synthetic-hermeneutic' treatment, the first stage is to guide him (or her) through the personal unconscious. Basically, Jung took over the notion of Freud's dynamic unconscious and repartitioned its area, consigning some of it to what he called the 'personal unconscious' but regarding most of it as being in the domain of the collective unconscious.

In the first stage of treatment, the principal features of the personal unconscious are encountered. These are the 'shadow' and the 'persona'. A patient who dreams of a repulsive figure resembling himself in some respects will gradually come to learn that this is his shadow, which must be assimilated. Making the shadow harmless resembles the action of St Francis of Assissi when he tamed the wolf of Gubbio.[35]

The shadow is the sum of those characteristics we wish to conceal not only from the world but from ourselves; the classic example comes in Robert Louis Stevenson's *Dr Jekyll and Mr Hyde*. Mostly the shadow is projected, so that we see our own dark side in others; hence scapegoatism.[36] Also, Jung thought that under the influence of drink or drugs the shadow could take over completely. He stressed that the 'shadow' was not the equivalent of Freud's id, as the former was mere unawareness whereas the id was the repressed unconscious (technically, the distinction between, respectively *die unbewusstheit* and *das unbewusste*). Unawareness referred to the aspects of a person he could see if he had a mind to and which others can see clearly enough; the id, on the other hand, is the repressed and the unconscious. By making this distinction, and at the same time insisting that all the really important elements of the unconscious were collective, Jung laid himself open to the charge that he did not really believe in a dynamic unconscious susceptible to treatment by psychiatry.

The other principal element of the personal unconscious is the persona, which mediates between the ego and the outer world. The persona (from the Latin word meaning 'mask') is a compromise between the individual and society as to what that person should be and takes us straight into the arena of role-playing.[37] Neurosis occurs if we put on the wrong mask or if we *identify* with the persona, in which case stereotypical attitudes such as racial, social and national prejudice are likely to result. Clearly, social pressure can drive the ego into identification with the persona, and there are people who really do believe they are what they pretend to be. But there is a price to pay in terms of subsequent neurosis.[38]

The persona makes its appearance in dreams involving clothing or the lack of it, as when we dream of attending meetings in our underwear or going into examinations naked. The persona is an obstacle to individuation because it is associated with just *one* psychological function, whether thinking, feeling or intuition.[39] There was also a danger of what Jung called 'regressive restoration of the persona'. He gave as an example the businessman who gambled on a venture and failed. The correct procedure was to 'try, try and try again' rather than to regress to an earlier, safer stage of existence and pretend all was as it was before the disastrous experience. Whereas the entrepreneurial gamble might have been a case of exceeding one's abilities, the correct response was not to descend to a level *below* them.[40]

The other aspect of the persona is that it is supposed to be in compensatory relationship with the shadow. If the balance between the two breaks down, the typical outcome is either someone obsessed with 'what people think' or someone who recognizes no law save his own instant gratification (a psychopath). Jungian therapy aims at making both shadow and persona conscious so that they can be integrated, but Jung warned that there would be as much resistance to this as there would be to admitting that your opponent might be right.[41]

It has to be conceded that Jung's discussion of the shadow and persona is far from lucid. He states that the ego has arisen out of the Self in psychic evolution just as the Moon detached itself from the Earth aeons ago, and that the personal unconscious is the result of interaction between the collective unconscious and the environment. So far, so good. But then he confuses things by referring to the units of the personal unconscious as 'complexes', adding a new connotation to the word, since in his early work complexes denoted the split-off fragments of the unhealthy mind.[42] Further confusion is added by the statement that the 'complex' is to the personal unconscious what the archetype is to the collective unconscious. Another layer of turbidity is added by the gnomic statement that the persona, a compromise between the individual and society as to appearances, is merely a segment of the collective psyche.[43] There is also confusion as to whether the 'shadow' relates only to the personal unconscious or can sometimes operate in the collective sphere; the later discussion of the 'trickster' archetype seems to suggest the latter.

The next stage of the individuation process involves pressing into the marches of the collective unconscious to encounter the contrasexual images of *animus* and *anima*.[44] As a man, Jung spent more time on the analysis of the anima, man's archetypal image of woman, than on the animus, woman's image of man. The anima is an innate image of the opposite sex projected on, and therefore distorting our perception of, an individual man or woman. Jung's favourite examples were taken from literature – Rider Haggard's *She*, John Erskine's *Private Life of Helen of Troy*, Hermann Hesse's *Steppenwolf*, Benoît's *L'Atlantide* – but he claimed to have found hundreds of cases in his patients' dreams.[45]

Jung explained that every man carried within him an unconscious archetypal image of woman, which was then unconsciously projected onto the person of flesh-and-blood women, producing either passionate attraction or revulsion.[46]

The animus and the anima were what Jung called 'archetypes of the soul' and he warned eloquently of the danger that they could irrupt into the conscious, causing schizophrenia or other psychoses.[47]

In line with his pervasive theory of compensation, Jung suggested that not only were the shadow and the persona ideally in a state of mutual equilibrium but a similar 'compensating' relationship existed between anima and persona.[48] Jung was uncertain of the exact place of the animus and the anima in his orrery of the mental planetary system, but suggested that just as the persona was midway between the external world and the individual, so the anima probably acted in a similar capacity midway between the individual and the heartland of the collective unconscious. He also suggested that the anima will always react to the persona in compensatory terms. This could lead, for example, to a man's being dominated by his wife.[49]

Having persuaded the patient to see women (or men) as they are, without projection of the animus or the anima, the analyst then takes the patient ever closer to the centre, to the next stage, that of archetypes of the spirit. These usually appear in critical life situations and in dreams typically manifest themselves as ancestral figures, divinities, helpful animals or the wind. Most common of all archetypes of the spirit is the 'Wise Old Man', supposedly a psychic personification of objective psyche, neo-Platonic Logos or Hegelian Spirit: ancient sages in the form of priests, medicine-men, monks, even analysts and psychotherapists.[50] The Wise Old Man is a familiar motif of mythology – Arthur's Merlin and Nestor among the Greeks besieging Troy are examples, as is Jung's spirit-companion from the 1913–16 period, Philemon. As with all archetypes, those of the spirit can take an evil shape, for example as a wizard, and this archetype can be projected onto a real human being, as when the patient visualizes his doctor as a magician. To identify with the Wise Old Man means to run the danger of what Jung called 'psychic inflation', as when Nietszche identified with Zarathustra, thus producing delusions of grandeur and psychosis.[51]

The Wise Old Man can appear to women, though more rarely, for they tend to experience the archetype of the 'Wise Old Woman' or Magna Mater, which likewise can sometimes appear to men. This maternal archetype can be projected onto mother, grandmother, nanny, nurse, headmistress, etc and appears as saint, female ancestor, the Virgin Mary, Sophia or divine wisdom, and even Holy Mother Church, university (alma mater) or mother country. Negatively, the archetype can manifest itself as a witch or a dragon.[52] The patient is now at a stage which, according to Jung, can be reached only by the individuation process and certainly not by psychoanalysis.

The theory of archetypes is one of the most confused and controversial aspects of Jung's doctrines. He was often accused of believing in the discredited theory of Lamarckianism, the inheritance of acquired characteristics but, as the above passage makes clear, he always insisted that the archetype was determined as to its form and not its content.[53] This was the famous distinction between the archetype and the archetypal image which Jung insisted on, but it was a distinction he himself frequently blurred in his writings. He denied that the archetype was an inherited idea or common image but likened it to a psychic mould into which individual and collective experiences were poured.[54] He sometimes drew an analogy between the archetypes and philosophical concepts like Plato's Forms, arguing that the image of a cat we have in dreams is not any particular cat but neither is it the pure Platonic Form of a cat. Another favourite analogy for the archetypes was with Kantian thought, though here again Jung was less than convincing, suggesting at some times that the archetypes were a priori predispositions like Kant's categories, and at others that the archetypal image was to be thought of as a Kantian phenomenon (available to sense-perception) while the archetype proper was the noumenon or thing in itself, an object of thought but not of knowledge.[55]

At other times Jung suggested that the correct analogy for the archetypes was to be found in biology, that the archetype was something like an instinct or behaviour-pattern.[56] His favourite examples were the common structure of the human brain, irrespective of race or culture, the behaviour of sticklebacks, and the nest-building instinct of birds.[57]

Jung argued that the existence of archetypes had been demonstrated in ethnology by Lévy-Bruhl in his *représentations collectives*, in biology by Alverdes, in history by Toynbee and, above all, in comparative mythology, as in the studies by Kerenyi, Tucci, Wilhelm and Zimmer on, respectively, ancient Greece, Tibet, China and India. Jung even managed to patronize Freud by crediting him with the discovery of the first archetype – the Oedipus-complex, the archetype of the son's relationship to his parents.

Jung was confident that he had discovered a master matrix explaining human behaviour and informing the various intellectual disciplines. He particularly liked tacking between philosophy and biology, which was satisfying for two main reasons. In the first place, this was in itself a process of integration, since it united the No. 1 personality (the doctor, the student of biology) with the No. 2 (the visionary, the student of philosophy). Secondly, moving to and from the philosophical and biological domains was Jung's equivalent of the three-card trick, since it pre-empted the criticisms which would arise if he based the theory of archetypes too closely on models drawn from either discipline. If he concentrated too much on biological analogies, he was in danger of the accusation of Lamarckianism. If he concentrated too much on philosophical ones, he could be dismissed as a mere metaphysician, an abstract German system-builder. Once again we can see the analogy with Marx. Marx always insisted that his a priori view of reality and human nature, heavily dependent on German idealism, was simply how the world operated. Jung insisted that his ideas, which seemed metaphysical and too dependent on Plato, Kant and Hegel, were no more than 'empiricism'.

Jung's archetypes covered a lot of ground for, besides the behaviour pattern ideas, there were a number of functional and situational motifs – motifs of ascent and descent, of crossing a ford or strait, of tension and suspension between opposites, of the world of darkness, of the creation of fire, of dangerous animals, of invasion or breakthrough. The archetype makes you behave in an unforeseen way once it is constellated.[58]

This was why Jung encountered an archetypal situation during the war dance on the borders of the Sudan, since a spontaneous archetypal situation analogous to 'God's will' occurred whenever there was illness or danger to life. The archetype could not be activated by human will, but it was activated independently of the will by a psychic situation crying out for compensation. People who are not religious may utter a silent prayer, and then the archetype of a 'helpful divine being' would be 'constellated' by their submission to the numinous and would be likely to intervene, engendering an influx of strength or saving impulse which is then felt to be miraculous. Hence the appearance in dreams of so many helpful figures: friendly animals, guardian spirits, good angels, saints, saviours, helpers.[59]

Apart from the 'Wise Old Man' and the 'Magna Mater', one of Jung's favourite archetypal images was what he called 'the Trickster'. This was supposed to be a collective shadow figure, a summation of all the inferior character traits in the individual.[60] Jung suggested that the Trickster was linked to disturbances in the psyche, just as poltergeists were associated with adolescent girls. He also hinted that certain medieval cardinals could also be considered as avatars of this archetype, but in the main referred to figures in Greek, Norse and Red Indian mythology. The Pau-puk-Keewis of the Hiawatha cycle is one such figure, as is Loki in Norse mythology and, Jung's favourite figure from mythology, Hermes or Mercury. Although such figures often seemed evil, Jung stressed that they were simply the shadow side of the archetype of God, an adumbration or forerunner of deity, systematically ambiguous, both subhuman and superhuman.[61] Jung also hypothesized that the archetypal antics of the Trickster figure were most clearly seen in political life, where 'botching' characterized every single political culture.[62]

Just as Jung sometimes seemed to identify himself with the Wise Old Man, so he fancied himself as the Trickster personified; he liked practical jokes, getting people drunk or persuading them to play wild party games so that their true nature would emerge.[63] There was a particular empathy with Hermes/Mercury as he was the god of interpretation and travel and the guide through the Underworld. Hermes was also the patron of the kinds of household duties Jung liked to perform – chopping wood, lighting fires and preparing meals – and some have speculated that his phallic god from childhood was really the spirit Mercury.[64]

Such, then, was the world of the archetypes. Once the archetypes of the spirit had been encountered, all that remained was the final stage of the journey, confronting the archetype of archetypes: the Self. The patient on the journey of individuation knew he was approaching the centre of the maze when his dreams, fantasies or active imagination were characterized by mandalas, universal religious symbols such as Christ, Buddha, Anthropos and Adam, and increasing experience of the deity as the 'God-image'.[65] It was the paradox of individuation that a person was most himself or herself after fusion with the world-mind or objective psyche. Again and again Jung stressed that the Self had nothing to do with 'self' as used in ordinary language; for this he always used the word 'ego'. Jung's Self can be roughly approximated to the Buddhist 'Atman'.[66]

Much confusion on Jung's notion of the Self was caused by his own careless use of expressions like 'selfhood' or 'self-realization' which had a clear meaning in every day usage utterly at odds with his purpose.[67] By stressing that individuation was a process whereby the individual became perfectly differentiated, he seemed to suggest that his interest lay along the lines of Gerard Manley Hopkins's 'inscape'. Nothing could be farther from the truth.[68]

On reaching the level of the Self in this psychological *Pilgrim's Progress*, we come to understand the full significance of Jung's remark that most of his patients were struggling with religious problems, for we find the closest possible identification of the Self with God.[69] Jung states that the God-image is a symbol of the Self and of psychic wholeness. He wrestled with the conundrum of whether the God-image and the unconscious were two separate entities but concluded that it was most likely that the God-image did not coincide with the unconscious as such but with a special content of it, the archetype of the Self. The God-image is a reflection of the Self, and the Self in turn is an *imago Dei* in Man.[70]

Jung often slipped (unconsciously?) between the terms 'God' and 'Christ', perhaps naturally enough for one brought up the son of a Christian pastor. For a while he dithered over the symbol of Christ, uncertain whether the Self was a symbol of Christ, or Christ a symbol for the Self. In the end he opted for the latter explanation.[71]

Having described all the stages of the journey to the heart of the Self, Jung felt confident enough to give a general analysis of the nature of the unconscious. Once we understand that the collective unconscious is a sea upon which the ego rides like a ship, we can understand what is going on in mental illness. The unconscious was like the sea. Mental illness was analogous to a tidal wave overwhelming an oceanic island, and neurosis was like the bursting of dykes in Holland.[72]

For psychic health the ego must be in touch with the Self but in a balanced way, just as a ship must be careful not to 'broach to' before the waves and be overwhelmed. If the ego is too closely linked with the Self, drawing too much power from its colossal collective reservoir, the result is 'psychic inflation' – a sense of omnipotence, omniscience and invulnerability, the characteristics of the egotist and egomaniac.[73] When becoming aware of the unconscious, patients tended to respond in one of two ways: either with optimism and self-confidence or with depression and a feeling of powerlessness. In extreme forms 'psychic inflation' could topple into schizophrenia. One of Jung's favourite anecdotes concerned a locksmith's apprentice who thought the world was his picturebook, the pages of which he could turn at will. When asked about this, he replied that the proof was quite simple: he had only to turn round and there was a new page for him to see.

When dealing with the 'nature and deeds' of the unconscious, Jung showed his deterministic slant by making it the primary engine of the psyche; the ego, he said, evolved from the Self and acquired a distinct identity in the way that children emerge from their parents and become separate persons. To use again the analogy with Marxism, we might say that in the Jungian system the unconscious is the 'base' and the consciousness the 'superstructure'. It would be a good thing, Jung declared, if the unconscious were in thrall to consciousness, but the opposite is the case.[74] The autonomy of the unconscious does not reveal itself only in cases of insanity, since this tendency to autonomy is a general feature of the unconscious; mental illness is therefore a special case of a general predisposition.[75]

However, for all the reasons stated, it was destructive for a person to deliver himself up entirely to the unconscious. If that were the right procedure, Nature would never have invented consciousness and animals would be the ideal vessel for the collective unconscious.[76] Properly treated, the unconscious was as necessary for mental health as the heart for physical well-being, and Jung often rounded on those artists, influenced by Freud, who regarded the unconscious as a monster. In the Jungian system there could never be 'monsters from the id' as in the film *The Forbidden Planet*. The unconscious, like the ocean, was neither good nor evil but neutral and ambiguous. A typical personification of the unconscious, Hermes/Mercury, was essentially dual, at once fiend, monster, beast and panacea, philosopher's stone, God's wisdom and the home of the Holy Spirit.[77]

Repeatedly Jung stressed that the unconscious could be understood only by paradox.[78] For those who remained puzzled by all the abstract talk of balance and imbalance between ego and Self, consciousness and the unconscious, he suggested, for guidance on the invasion of the conscious by the unconscious, the reading of H.G. Wells's *Christina Alberta's Father*, Léon Daudet's *L'Hérédo* and William James's *The Varieties of Religious Experience*.[79]

The staggering ingenuity with which Jung linked up his new cosmology of the mind, as set out in the theories of individuation, the Self and the unconscious, with all his earlier work, commands admiration. The link with his Burghölzli work was provided by his theory that the archetypes were to the collective unconscious what the complexes were to the personal unconscious. A close relationship was posited between complexes and archetypes, and it was sometimes suggested that complexes were in some sense 'personifications' of archetypes, or the means through which archetypes manifested themselves in the personal psyche.[80] A similar complementary relationship was assumed between the 'shadow' and the 'Trickster' figure, and between the image (imago) a child forms of its father and the archetypal figure of the Wise Old Man.[81] Jung even suggested there might be a figurative association between the Oedipus-complex and the general relations of conscious to unconscious.[82]

Many other links with his earlier work are discernible. At one time Jung toyed with the idea that the archetypes might be localized subcortically in the brain stem, just as Descartes speculated that the seat of the mind might be in the pineal gland. This reopened the possibility of treating schizophrenics with an as yet unidentified drug.[83] As for the theory of psychological types, this helped to explain differential reactions once the nature of the unconscious was revealed to patients: introverts became depressed while extraverts became elated and suffered 'psychic inflation'.[84] Jung stressed the continuity of his theories and mocked those who claimed that he invented a new crackpot theory every year. Because he encouraged patients to draw mandalas as the symbol of the Self, the canard arose that his treatment simply consisted in getting his patients to paint, whereas previously it had consisted in telling people that they were living as extraverts when they were really introverts, and vice versa.[85]

Moreover, Jung was able to show that his entire cosmology of the psyche was implied and latent in the work that brought on the break with Freud: *Symbols of Transformation*. To dissolve oneself in the mass of the collective psyche is in other terms 'the longing for the mother'.[86]

The Hegelian tendency to link up every aspect of his theories with every other did not end there. The theory of the self-regulating psyche was neatly dovetailed with the individuation process by means of Jung's notion of enantiodromia – the tendency of all phenomena to return to their opposite, an idea he took over from the pre-Socratic philosopher Heraclitus. The encounter with the Self, on this view, sparked an enantiodromia or return to the normal world, similar to the process whereby the travellers in Jules Verne's *Journey to the Centre of the Earth* were blasted to the surface by the fireball, thus emphasizing the homeostatic role of the psyche.

The individuation process also meant coming to terms with death, and so it could be demonstrated that there was an intimate connection between the encounter with the Self and the theory of stages of life. Shrinking from death robbed the second half of life of its significance, for an old man who could not bid farewell to life was as pathetic as a young man who could not embrace it.[87] And since life's script was already written, and we are living a life determined by the archetypes, with psychological changes programmed into the human system just as much as biological ones, it made perfect sense to talk about the stages of life.

Jung's system was very far from being intellectually coherent; ever since, critics have attacked his ideas across a very wide front. The archetypes and the collective unconscious were the most controversial notions. The most fundamental criticism of the archetypes was that they were an unnecessary metaphysical postulate, like phlogiston or the nineteenth-century idea of the ether, which added nothing to knowledge and simply provided a layer of obfuscation.

Since everything that the archetypes purported to explain could be explained more simply by far more plausible hypotheses, the notion of archetypes fell foul of the principle of Occam's razor ('entities should not be multiplied beyond necessity'), which states that there is no need for a complex explanation when a simple one will do just as well. Which, after all was more likely: that a two-year-old child was influenced by its mother, or by the collective archetype of the eternally feminine?

Jung insisted that his experience with patients proved the truth of the archetype, but his notions of 'proof' were eccentric, and his letters are full of wrangles with correspondents about what constitutes evidence.[88] He seemed unable or unwilling to understand that because a set of data is compatible with hypothesis X, it does not thereby prove X. The same set of data could just as well be compatible with dozens of other hypotheses, and what is needed to clinch the case for archetypes is a set of repeatable phenomena incompatible with *any other* hypothesis. Needless to say, no such candidates were forthcoming.

That the notion of the archetype was at best unproved becomes clear when we examine the uses to which Jung put it. As an explanation for myth, fairytale and legend, it is vulnerable to the obvious objection that the similarity of motif observable in culture after culture could easily have been the result of diffusion.[89] Alternatively, and more likely, the existential situation of mankind in itself determined the similarity, since birth, copulation, death, victory in battle, the winning of a fair maiden – all the staples of such stories – are common to all races and cultures. A similar argument can be deployed against the collective unconscious: that the content of the unconscious of mankind is common because of its common experience of life.[90]

Even if we accept the reality of archetypes for the sake of argument, the difficulties do not end, for Jung was notoriously careless in defining the word: sometimes it seems equivalent to a Platonic form, sometimes to a Kantian noumenon, sometimes to a biological instinct.[91] Archetypes are as protean as the Old Man of the Sea in mythology and take on as many forms: primordial images; thought-dispositions; reaction-dispositions; contentless psychic forms; potentialities actualized by an image system; organs of a pre-rational psyche. Apart from the perennial confusion between archetypes and archetypal ideas – which themselves run the gamut from fantasy images to recurring motifs in mythology – the archetypes seem to function too as a kind of psychic fire alarm, along the lines of sixth sense and second sight. Also, they are at once too general (in form) and too specific (as regards the content of their images) to be analogous to biological instinct. He suggested that the idea of archetypes was directly analogous to the migrating instinct in birds.[92] This shows Jung's hopeless way with analogies. Unlike the theory of archetypes, a theory that birds migrate can be verified by sense-experience. Moreover, just one migrating species proves the truth of the proposition. By contrast, the theory of archetypes could never be proved no matter how many favourable compatible *instances* were adduced. Since the archetypes are meant to be universal, we would have to identify a migrating instinct common to all animals before making analogical progress.

Linguistic philosophers, too, have joined the fray with conceptual analysis of favourite Jungian terms like 'old', pointing out that he confuses 'old' in the sense of mature with 'old' in the sense of ancient and primitive. The primitive, who is closer to the unconscious, has a 'younger' mind in developmental terms than modern man, leading to the conclusion that he is both wiser and less wise than modern man.

The individuation process itself has attracted probably more criticism than any other part of Jung's system. Whereas discussion about archetypes seems no more than medieval scholasticism updated, down-to-earth issues of healing and mental health are at stake in the search for the Self. The most common criticism is that the entire 'Pilgrim's Progress' is simply a generalization from the peculiar circumstances of Jung's own life. Even if it had a more general validity, there are many who say that it is irremediably 'élitist'. As one by no means unsympathetic critic has pointed out, 'To benefit fully from Jungian analysis . . . one should be relatively affluent, well-read and familiar with Greek mythology, articulate and good at visualisation of images, and have a relatively strong ego to be able to confront the instincts and images of the unconscious. In other words, Jung's procedure is designed particularly for a leisured, cultivated, creative élite.'[93]

The emphasis on individual development and the neglect of relationships with other people is a serious defect in any theory of psychotherapy. It may well be that Freud's prescription of 'honour, power, wealth, fame and the love of women' does not exhaust the sum of human aspirations, but they surely come closer to it than the individuation process which, whatever its ostensible aims, is bound to take the patient in the direction of solipsism. Moreover, without extreme mental toughness, many analysands would be unlikely to come back from the journey Jung prescribes, and this is undoubtedly the reason for the high number of suicides among Jung's patients in the early years.

There is no necessary path leading back from the encounter with the Self to the real world. Jung's specious answer to this – that our relationship to the world is contained in our experience of the Self – has been widely regarded as a piece of sophistry.[94]

Neglect of personal relationships is bad enough, but is compounded by an insouciance on Jung's part about the role played in an adult's development and in his or her dreams and fantasies by the experience of work and career. As Homans has said, 'For the Jungian – be he patient, therapist or teacher – the problem of social order ceases to exist at all: it has been replaced by the problem of the inner, psychological order.'[95] Only the very privileged can allow themselves the degree of introversion Jung allowed himself, and it has been suggested, surely rightly, that Jung's lack of money worries led him to see the world from a very peculiar viewpoint.

Perhaps the most serious defect in Jung's psychology is the lack of any theory or analysis of childhood. Anyone seriously wishing to dethrone Freudianism would have had to confront it at its strongest point, the theory of infantile sexuality and early trauma, but Jung never rose to the challenge. Edward Glover has colourfully referred to Jung's deficiency here as 'the cloven hoof of the conscious psychologist, namely an obsession with the adult'.[96]

Predictably, the Freudian critique of Jung's system is lengthy and detailed. It includes the following charges: that by his self-regulating system, establishing a reciprocal relationship between conscious and unconscious, Jung obliterated the dynamic distinction between the two systems, and effectively destroyed the unconscious as a useful concept; that his system was far more deterministic than Freud's and was bound to plunge his patients into despair; that he abandoned Freud's sophisticated dualistic model of instinctual conflict for a monistic theory of mental energy.

Jung always played fast and loose with data. When scientific facts supported his theories, he took them at face value; when they did not, he argued that, since the unconscious was compensating the conscious, the opposite was the case; when all else failed, he could always refer back to the notion of enantiodromia. Jung always insisted that he was not a visionary but a scientist, not a prophet but an empiricist, yet he often used the word 'empiricism' in a way that suggested he did not understand its meaning. Instead of defining empiricism as 'based on sense-experience' he seemed to think it was permissible to call yourself an empiricist if you held views *theoretically compatible* with sense experience.

The hallmark of empiricism is the belief that the human mind is a *tabula rasa* – a blank tablet on which are written life's impressions. Jung consistently denied this (how could he not, given the theory of archetypes?), often explicitly mocking the mere idea of a *tabula rasa*. Many thinkers from Plato to Hegel and beyond have disdained empiricism and referred loftily to 'fact worship', but their brisk way with facts could not be taken by Jung who, visionary and seer as he was, insisted he was no more than a working scientist. He dealt with the difficulty in a number of ways. Sometimes he declared that 'psychic facts' were a sufficient condition of empiricism – not a definition many would subscribe to. At others he equated empiricism with 'common sense'. Common sense, however, tells us that you cannot substitute the religious impulse for the sexual, as Jung tried to do. And since he himself often objected to Freudianism on the ground that hunger was just as important an instinct as sex, he was vulnerable to the counter-argument from common sense that economic motives must be at least as important as religious ones.

Moreover, it was not really open to a man who operated in the realms of mysticism, alchemy and recondite theology to appeal to common sense. Jung's understanding of 'common sense' seems to have been that he could tack in and out of disciplines as he pleased, disregarding the fact that every intellectual discourse had its own internal logic and set of rules. So at one moment he would appeal to academic psychology, at another to Kant, and at another to Buddhism. He was like a man ostensibly playing soccer who reserved to himself the right also to use the rules of rugby, cricket, hockey and American football, if it happened to suit his book. In fairness, Jung is by no means alone in the 'pick and mix', eclectic approach to empiricism, accepting it when it endorses a favourite theory, rejecting it otherwise. This is the well-known intellectual phenomenon the social philosopher Ernest Gellner has referred to as the 'self-service' approach to thought.

Paul Kline, a notable critic of Freud's, dealt harshly with Jung on this score.

Sometimes Jung's apologists tried to rescue him from this quagmire by saying that he did adhere to scientific method but went beyond it.[97] Talk of 'scientism' and 'transcending scientific method' is, again, the eclectic approach to empiricism. If you are 'picking and mixing', and you deny the overall validity of scientific findings by 'going beyond', how do you know that the findings you do accept are true and the ones you reject false? On your own premises, it could equally well be that the ones you reject are true and the ones you accept false. How could Jung accept scientific notions of probability in the word-association test yet abandon them in other areas in favour of 'synchronicity'?

In sum, one cannot be half in and half out of science. The best approach for those who claim to 'go beyond' is to embrace metaphysics or mysticism wholeheartedly. Acres of print could have been saved if Jung had come clean and admitted that he was a prophet. But such an admission would have made him vulnerable to certain aspects of his own theories, namely the danger of confusing the individual with the collective psyche. As he himself wrote, this peril was particularly acute for the man of great achievement, with universal prestige, for the man is then in danger of becoming a collective truth.[98] In a classic boomerang statement, Jung warned solemnly that prophets were likely to be psychically disturbed and that to be the disciple of a prophet was the escape route for the mentally lazy.[99] It was a favourite saying of his that 'only the wounded physician heals.' Even if his cure rate remained uncertain, there could be no doubt that he qualified as the wounded physician.

Chapter Seventeen

VALKYRIES AND OTHER WOMEN

From 1927–35 Jung gave up his hitherto frequent visits to the English-speaking world where, particularly in the USA, his popularity went into a temporary decline as his new mystical doctrines alienated many supporters.[1] His physical existence was limited to the yin and yang of Küsnacht and Bollingen, attendance at conferences in the German-speaking countries, and summer holidays in the Engadine. By now his children were growing up, so the summer idylls he had spent with them during 1918–23 were a thing of the past. Those were the years, before the building of the Bollingen tower, when he and his family spent the summer holidays on an island at the mouth of the Linth canal, at the upper end of Lake Zürich. The children would play at pirates and Indians, in the manner of J.M. Barrie's lost boys, and Jung would act as the un-Hooklike captain. Jung was always a hearty exponent of the Swiss cult of the great outdoors, and encouraged his children to live in tents and to master sailboats, row boats and canoes. The family would buy their provisions in Schnerkon, twenty minutes away by row boat and, lacking refrigerators, would bury perishables in the ground to keep them cool. Water came from the lake, firewood could be collected in the forest. Only if the children were ill would Jung allow the 'luxury' of an overnight stay in the cabin of his beloved sailboat *The Pelican*.[2]

Such things were sentimental memories by the late 1920s. Jung withdrew more and more into the isolation of Bollingen, where he took to running up a flag as a sign that he was on no account to be disturbed.[3] A glimpse of the prophet in splendid isolation comes in a letter to an American admirer on 19 December 1927, when Jung reports that he is marooned in his tower, 'actually buried in the snow of a fierce attack of winter, unusually cold for our climate.'[4] As mentioned before, 1927 was the year of the building of the Bollingen annexe, when the French soldier's body was discovered, and the year when Jung perfected his mastery of the stone-mason's art, to the point where he needed just two workmen to help him on the extensions.[5]

Jung usually holidayed in the Engadine in August, following a mandatory period of Army service in July – for until the age of fifty-five he was still subject to call up for the reserve as a military doctor.[6] He was a familiar figure at psychological conferences in Germany and Austria, where he frequently clashed with Freud's supporters, though he never again met the Master himself. He was invited to lecture at the prestigious though highly conservative Kulturbund in Vienna on 21–22 February 1928 and thereafter was frequently invited back.[7] Freud was annoyed to find the enemy holding forth in *his* city.

In 1929 Jung learned to drive and by 1930 he could often be seen driving like Mr Toad through the twisting streets of Zürich in his new red two-seater Chrysler.[8] The burghers of Zürich did not seem to mind, for in 1932 they awarded him the city's prize for literature. Jung also bought a large Dodge limousine as the family car, perhaps as a nod to acknowledge the fact that his wife Emma and third daughter Marianne dealt with all his correspondence and accounts. However, they were not altogether competent in this department and in 1932 Jung had to take on a full-time secretary, Marie-Jeanne Schmid.[9]

By the early 1930s some of the zest for foreign travel was obviously returning, for Jung made a long trip to Italy with Toni Wolff and revisited Ravenna. In the Church of San Giovanni he visited the tomb of the empress Galla Placidia, who died in AD 450, a woman who always fascinated him to the point where he considered her an archetypal image of the anima. He proceeded from the tomb to the Baptistery and there saw 'four great mosaic frescoes of incredible beauty' which he did not remember from his 1913 visit. He later recalled that one represented the baptism in the Jordan, another the crossing of the Red Sea by the Israelites, and the third, vaguely remembered, probably concerned the healing of a leper. The fourth mosaic was the most impressive and showed Christ holding out his hands to Peter, who was sinking beneath the waves. He and Toni Wolff discussed the four mosaics and, once back in Zürich, asked a friend who was visiting Ravenna to buy some reproductions of them. The friend reported back that no such mosaics existed, and further enquiries confirmed this. Jung concluded that he and Toni must have had a vision of some long-perished mosaics as a result of the depth of his concentration on Galla Placidia.[10]

Sceptics have queried whether this incident ever took place or have suggested that perhaps Jung and Toni Wolff were experimenting with drugs at the time. The general feeling is that the 'vision' was just a bit too convenient, seeming as it did, to endorse Jung's conclusion that interior and exterior were both part of the same reality.[11] Since the account given in *Memories* – and particularly the details of the mosaics – differs both from that given in Jung's seminar on Tantric Yoga in 1932 and the description he gave Esther Harding in 1948, it has been speculated that Jung coloured the 1932 experience – whatever it was – with his later reading about Galla Placidia.[12]

In March 1933 Jung went with his friend Professor Markus Fierz on a lengthy Mediterranean cruise, taking in Athens, the Greek Islands (there was a long stopover at Rhodes), Cyprus, Egypt (including Alexandria and Cairo) and Palestine.[13] There was already a steady influx of Jewish refugees from Europe into Palestine, and Jung predicted trouble ahead as more arrived to displace the Arabs (this just three months after Hitler came to power in Germany).

The late 1920s and early 1930s, then, were a relatively uneventful period in Jung's outer life, but also the years of his original thinking. They, furthermore, exemplified a running theme in his life: that he could not sustain male friendships, and that women clustered round him to an abnormal degree. Some of the men who were close to him Jung simply alienated; but an alarming number died young in tragic or unexpected circumstances, giving rise to a rumour at the time that there was something uncanny about him, that he was a Jonah or an angel of death. Hermann Sigg, his companion in Tunisia, died early in 1927 and Beckwith, his comrade on the African trip, was killed in a motor accident. Most grievous of all losses for Jung was the death of his close friend Richard Wilhelm, who had introduced him to the wonders of the *I Ching* and whom Aniela Jaffé credited with triggering Jung's most creative phase in the 1920s.[14] Wilhelm was for Jung the epitome of the feminine intellect, and Jung considered that such a sensibility was almost never found in experts, who almost invariably had 'masculine' minds; it was this rare combination that made Wilhelm unparalleled in his ability to get inside the oriental idiom and the 'inscrutable' Chinese mind.[15]

Wilhelm later translated the Chinese work *The Secret of the Golden Flower*, which seemed to Jung to offer conclusive proof that mandala symbolism was indicative of the Self.[16] Jung was forever picking Wilhelm's brains about aspects of Chinese literature and culture that would lend credence to the theories of individuation. A typical letter shows Jung identifying five meanings of the elusive term *Tao*: whereas Wilhelm had translated it as 'meaning', Arthur Waley proposed 'way', while Jesuit missionaries in the Orient had opted for Logos or God; Jung, however, suggested that its fundamental meaning might be bringing what is unconscious to the light of consciousness.[17]

Wilhelm had gone out to China originally as a missionary and fallen in love with the culture. However, Jung was worried about his friend's state of mind on his return to Europe. He felt on the one hand that Wilhelm had been not so much influenced as overwhelmed by China, and on the other that he had been too quickly reassimilated in Europe, leading to an unconscious conflict that would damage his health. 'His dreams were filled with memories of China, but the images were always sad and gloomy, a clear proof that the Chinese contents of his mind had become negative.'[18] In his rather brutal way, Jung chided Wilhelm with being unfaithful to his mission of transmitting the wisdom of the East to the West. Wilhelm agreed gloomily but said he did not see what he could do.

In 1930 Wilhelm was taken ill in Frankfurt, where he lived. The official diagnosis was a recrudescence of the amoebic dysentery he had picked up in China, but Jung, typically, chose to see his friend's illness as an invasion from the unconscious. Jung visited him in hospital and claimed to have sinister forebodings as soon as Wilhelm told him his dreams. Jung's idea was that he was being torn apart because he would not acknowledge the endemic unconscious conflict between East and West. When Jung dreamed that a Chinaman was standing at the end of his bed, he concluded that Wilhelm had not long to live, and so it proved.[19] The essay 'Richard Wilhelm. In Memoriam', which Jung wrote in 1930, was full of praise for his friend's intellect, but suggested that he had been overwhelmed by the very forces that Jung himself overcame in 1913–16. The impression of a certain callousness was not absent from the essay – an impression reinforced by the story that Jung said that Wilhelm's death was not such a disaster, as his life's work was complete with the publication of *The Secret of the Golden Flower*.[20]

The next friend to be lost was the charismatic Alphonse Maeder, who had stood by him during the darkest days after the break with Freud. Gradually during the 1920s Jung became estranged from him, possibly because Jung's new psychological bearing seemed to Maeder impossibly introverted. Matters came to a head in 1933 when Jung invited Maeder to head the Swiss subgroup of the 'General Medical Society for Psychotherapy'. Maeder declined and announced that he was joining the Oxford Group instead.[21] From then on Jung ridiculed Maeder at the dinner-table and scoffed at his practice of encouraging his patients to pray and of praying with them. He liked to tell the story of how Maeder had confessed the sin of vanity to the Oxford Group, on the grounds that he had worn a stand-up collar for sartorial reasons even though it chafed his neck. It was, said Jung, typical of the nugatory dilettantism of Maeder that he could not find anything more substantial to confess to.[22]

Jung resembled his early mentor Freud in that he had no taste for 'popular front' tactics in psychology, stressing points of similarity with other schools; indeed he shared the besetting sin of the political factionalist, which is to attack far more vehemently than the common enemy those putative allies who differ only on points of doctrine. It was often suggested to Jung that he and Rudolph Steiner (1861–1925), the founder of 'anthroposophy' had many features in common. Both had had parapsychological experiences, both worked out their own form of self-training for exploring the unconscious, both emerged from spiritual journeys with new personalities. Steiner was like Freud and Jung in that he suffered a 'creative illness' in middle age, from which he emerged convinced, like Jung, that life was a series of metamorphoses, with a crucial turning point being the mid-life threshold at thirty-five. Also in Steiner's work, albeit not with the same phraseology, were the 'shadow' and the projected subpersonalities. Most Jungian of all was Steiner's idea that Mephistopheles was simply an aspect of Faust's personality. The essential difference between the two prophets was that where Jung spoke of projected contents of the unconscious, Steiner postulated independent spiritual beings.[23]

However, visitors to Küsnacht who mentioned Steiner usually left with the proverbial flea in the ear.[24] Jung told one of his correspondents that he had read a few of Steiner's books but found nothing worthwhile in them at all.[25] This pot-and-black-kettle situation is very reminiscent of devotees of one religion (Catholicism, say), who are required by their faith to believe in miracles, nevertheless finding incredible and incomprehensible the views of another set of people (spiritualists, say), who believe in miracles of a different kind.

As well as Maeder and those swept away by death, Jung also lost his chief assistant, Peter Baynes, this time to marriage. Jung liked Baynes's wife, Cary, but on the basis of his knowledge of both of them predicted that the marriage would not last. He was convinced Cary was not Peter's 'anima' type and was also struck by the fact that the pair, both strong swimmers, had got engaged while breasting the flood far out at sea. Needless to say, Jung thought this symbolic of their having been too far out in the sea of the unconscious to be fully aware of what they were doing. His famous mediumistic intuition was proved right once again: Peter Baynes soon met a girl twenty years his junior, left Cary and married her.[26]

Perhaps the most sustained relationship with a male friend, which inevitably also ended badly, was with Hermann Keyserling, founder of the Darmstadt 'School of Wisdom'. Keyserling was a Russian aristocrat, born in the now vanished province of Livonia to the north of Lithuania. After the 1917 Revolution Keyserling fled to the West, became a German citizen and also began a notable career as a globetrotter; his fatherland of Livonia meanwhile disappeared, being swallowed up by the new national creations of Latvia and Estonia. After meeting Jung at Darmstadt in the early 1920s, Keyserling corresponded regularly with him. Realizing that for Jung the dream was more important than waking life, Keyserling deluged the sage of Küsnacht with his dreams, which Jung dutifully interpreted.[27]

Jung's advice to Keyserling in the 1920s provides a classic illustration of the fault for which his enemies criticized him – slotting patient's dreams and fantasies into an a priori structure determined by his theories. So when Keyserling in 1928 reported on his negative attitude to his mother in contrast to the great love he felt for his father reaching the point where he dreamed his father was not really dead – Jung replied that he was suffering from 'psychic inflation' or identification with an archetype.

Keyserling gradually took the view that Jung's advice was either too abstract to be useful or just plain wrong. Keyserling finally lost patience, stopped writing and told friends that the mind-body problem as posited by Jung did not exist, and that the sage's attempt to decode a universal language of symbols was fundamentally flawed. He said that Jung was one of those people with little talent for improving the human lot but with an uncanny instinct for an individual's weak spot, which convinced people of his wisdom. Even if his action was unwitting, the net effect of Jung on patients was likely to be that he would 'injure them as fatally as the sting of the digger-wasp, stinging the ganglia of a caterpillar.'[28] When these comments got back to Jung, he in turn started jibing at Keyserling, and soon the friendship petered out altogether.

Jung's difficulties with other males extended to the famous men he came in contact with. A superficial acquaintance could produce a friendly enough response, but once mutual knowledge deepened, disillusionment usually set in. A good example of the superficial was Jung's meeting with the popular English novelist Hugh Walpole, who was at the height of his fame in the 1920s as a prolific writer of second-rate novels. On 30 July 1930 Walpole lectured on literature in Zürich. Jung was in the audience and later dined with Walpole, who recorded in his diary, 'He's like a large genial English cricketer. We sat together at supper after and he delighted me with his hatred of hysterics.'[29] Jung was sufficiently intrigued to read Walpole's books and in mid-August sent him a fan letter, typically singling out a lesser production, *The Prelude to Adventure*, for special praise.[30] Jung was convinced, possibly correctly, that lesser works of literature held the greatest interest for the psychologist, and mentioned in this respect the works of Rider Haggard and the detective fiction of Conan Doyle.[31]

A more sustained contact, that with H.G. Wells, left both men wary and ambivalent. Wells visited Jung at Küsnacht in 1928 and they had a long conversation. Unfortunately a full record of their talk does not survive; it would be of peculiar interest since both men held themselves forward as prophets. Both agreed that Christianity was on the wane and would have to be replaced by a new religion: Wells still inclined towards the worship of science and a belief in a quasi-socialist technological revolution, while Jung stressed the religion of individuation and the Self. Jung remembered that Wells rubbed his nose with his finger, seeming to indicate that with the decline of Christianity mankind ought to be able to sense – or smell – what to do next.[32] Wells recalled an abstruse discussion about the 'Wise Old Man', which seemed to him to be the old God reintroduced in a new disguise. However, he was much struck by Jung's observation that neither Nietzsche's *Ubermensch* nor Shaw's Superman should be thought of as individual persons, since both were the race in progress.[33] Wells told the Swiss press that he found Jung a great inspiration.[34] Jung responded with some lavish praise for Wells's work, especially *God the Invisible King*.[35] Later, however, Jung revised his opinion of Wells downwards.

Jung's growing fame as a therapist and guru brought him into contact with many international celebrities or their families. In 1919 Romola Nijinsky had consulted him about the schizophrenia of her husband, the famous dancer Vaslav Nijinsky, who became incurably insane in Switzerland in 1917.[36] In the 1930s Alexander Woollcott, the waspish American columnist and critic came for a consultation; the apocryphal story disseminated by Edmund Wilson was that Jung had concluded Woollcott was in love with Harpo Marx.[37] Yet the most famous of all Jung's contacts was with James Joyce and his daughter Lucia.

Lucia Joyce was schizophrenic and in September 1934, after she had nearly burned down her room, Joyce had her hospitalized in the Burghölzli. After a week in which she made no progress at all, Joyce took her to Jung for consultation, telling him that he was the twentieth doctor who had investigated her case. Joyce's decision to consult Jung was a courageous one, and speaks volumes for his love of his daughter, for there was bad blood between Jung and Joyce. Joyce's animosity dated back to the incident in 1919 when Jung persuaded Edith McCormick to stop subsidizing the Irish writer. But Jung had compounded the offence by writing a notably hostile analysis of Joyce's *Ulysses* for the Zürich magazine *Rhein-Verlag*.[38]

Jung said that the stream-of-consciousness and interior monologue 'ramblings' in the book reminded him of the ravings of a schizophrenic, and concluded that the only explanation for the book's genesis was that 'medieval Catholic Ireland' must have a greater grip on its people than he had realized and therefore the people needed rebels like Joyce to struggle free.

Joyce got wind of this attack, and his initial response was to persuade Dr Daniel Brody, owner and manager of the *Rhein-Verlag*, to publish the piece and show Jung up in a bad light. However, Joyce's friends thought it was better if the article did not see the light of day, and persuaded Brody to this effect. Yet Jung's attack rankled with Joyce and he commented scathingly, 'He seems to have read *Ulysses* from first to last without one smile. The only thing to do in such a case is to change one's drink.' When he met Brody, Joyce again expostulated, 'Why is Jung so rude to me? He doesn't even know me. People want to put me out of the church to which I don't belong. I have nothing to do with psychoanalysis.' Brody replied disarmingly, 'There can only be one explanation. Translate your name into German.'[39] Jung made partial amends by writing an emollient letter to Joyce in 1932, saying he found *Ulysses* a hard nut to crack and that he was 'a perfect stranger who went astray in the labyrinth of your Ulysses and happened to get out of it again by sheer luck.'[40]

Such was the background when Joyce brought Lucia to see Jung. She was in a catatonic trance, which the Burghölzli doctors had been unable to penetrate. Jung succeeded in breaking through Lucia's defences; she spoke freely, gained weight, and the prognosis seemed hopeful. But the initial positive transference was followed by a severe backlash. Jung's estimate was that Lucia's schizophrenia was ultimately traceable to her relationship with her father, who was himself, according to Jung, a latent schizoid who used alcohol to control his schizoid tendencies. When Jung suggested that Joyce leave Switzerland and let Lucia develop an independent life, she reacted dementedly. From then on the rapport between doctor and patient ceased, and Jung was soon obliged to report that her madness was incurable.[41]

Was Jung right about Joyce? There is some support for him from an unlikely source, since Ernest Jones described Joyce as a highly pathological case.[42] But Joyce's biographer Richard Ellmann thinks that Jung profoundly misunderstood the role played by alcohol in Joyce's life; Joyce, says Ellmann, was no dipsomaniac, abstained during the day, and drank only at night with 'a nice combination of purpose and relaxation'.[43] There is the further point that Jung, heavily influenced as a young man by the teetotal culture of Bleuler in the Burghölzli, may not have understood the role played by drink in Irish culture, and indeed knew little about Ireland at all; on his own admission, his one and only glimpse of the island was at Cobh when returning from the USA on a transatlantic liner.[44]

The next, painful stage in the treatment was to call Joyce in and talk to him about the gloomy conclusions. Jung told Joyce flatly that his daughter was incurable, but Joyce insisted that the evidence he adduced for her schizophrenia was merely a sign of Celtic 'clairvoyance'. Jung then pointed out the schizoid elements in Lucia's poetry but Joyce, mindful of the criticism of *Ulysses*, insisted that Lucia was merely a creative artist ahead of her time.

Jung, however, insisted that her neologisms and portmanteau words were random, and not the inspirations of creativity; comparing father and daughter, he said they were like two people going to the bottom of a river, one diving, the other falling.[45]

Joyce took Jung's advice that Lucia be placed in a private *pension* in Zürich under the care of a nurse, but he was left bitter and angry at Jung's analysis of his daughter. Later he wrote witheringly of 'the Rev. Dr Jung' and wrote to the art-critic Dr Carola Gielion-Walker about Jung 'your friend, my enemy'. In *Finnegan's Wake* Joyce alluded with bitterness to Jung's charge that *Ulysses* could be read backwards or forwards. He included among a joking list of schoolboy essay subjects 'Is the Co-education of Animus and Anima desirable?' referred to 'the law of the jungerl,' and coined the word salad 'anama anamaba anamabapa'. However, it was a weakness in Joyce's burlesqueing of the sage of Küsnacht that he seemed unaware how radically different Freudianism was from the Jungian doctrine, as when he spoke of 'the Swiss Tweedledum who is not to be confused with the Viennese Tweedledee, Dr Freud.'[46] For her part, Lucia commented scathingly, 'To think that such a big fat materialistic Swiss man should try to get hold of my soul!'[47]

The incident with Lucia hardened Jung in his resolve to have no more to do with schizophrenic patients, which was why he narrowly missed an encounter with Scott Fitzgerald, who includes several mentions of Jung in *Tender is the Night*. Zelda Fitzgerald was treated by Bleuler for schizophrenia in the late 1930s; Scott had wanted Jung, but his decision to take no more psychotic patients put paid to that.[48]

If Jung's relationships with men were on the whole failures, with women the situation was entirely different. Jung seemed to have had an attraction for the fair sex that was entirely unaffected by his generally bad treatment of them. The evidence is murky, but the indications are that after the 'schizophrenic interlude' of 1913–18 he largely abandoned his promiscuous past and settled down in a cosy *ménage à trois* with Emma and Toni Wolff. He encouraged his wife to become a Jungian therapist and eventually, though grudgingly, acquiesced when Toni took up the same profession. He continued to state that having Toni as an analyst was a waste, since he regarded her as a poet equal to Goethe, but in the end he came to see that she had a creative block about writing and publication and might after all be better off as a therapist. There is a suspicion, too, that by the late 1920s Jung liked her in smaller and smaller doses and frequently expressed irritation: 'Toni behaved this morning as if she really were a reincarnated goddess,' was one of his irascible asides.

One view is that Toni Wolff was the single crucial factor enabling Jung to re-emerge into sanity in 1918 but, precisely because he had conquered the demons of his unconscious with her help, she was thereafter redundant. Certainly she was deeply unpopular in the Jungian inner circles. All observers agreed that she was beautiful and intelligent, but few had a good word to say for her; the conventional opinion was that she disliked other women and tried to lord it over them, while being charming and deferential to men. Any woman arriving in Zürich to consult Jung was regarded as a potential rival for the master's affections and treated accordingly.[49]

The only woman friend Toni Wolff was known to have had was Linda Fierz-David (1891–1964), a Basler and daughter of a politician. She came to Jung originally because she was consumptive and had heard of his theory that half of all cases of tuberculosis were psychosomatic: people with a complex tended to breathe less deeply.[50] She consulted Jung again when the strain of living in a *ménage à trois* with her husband and an Italian cousin became too much for her – it was plain why she and Toni Wolff saw eye to eye. As with all the women Jung was interested in for whatever reason, he encouraged her to become a therapist. Linda, or 'Sieglinde' as Jung called her, declined, though her son did become a Jungian analyst, and instead worked on an 'archetypal-influenced' book on the mysteries of Pompeii.[51]

Besides his wife, Toni, the *femme inspiratrice*, and his mistresses, Jung gathered around him a close circle of women utterly devoted to his cause and teachings, often referred to as the 'maenads', 'the Valkyries' or the *jungfrauen*. Usually these women had psychological problems of their own which they sublimated by becoming Jungian analysts or acolytes. The American author Thornton Wilder visited Zürich soon after the success of his Pulitzer Prize-winning novel *The Bridge of San Luis Rey* and noted that hovering around Jung was a particular kind of grass-widow, 'whose melancholy gentleness seems to allude to the fact that life has been unjust and unkind.'[52]

Undoubtedly two of the women Wilder referred to were Esther Harding and Jolande Jacobi. Esther Harding, a Shropshire county doctor, saw the light when she attended Jung's first English seminar at Sennen Cove in Cornwall and followed him to Zürich before eventually making a career in the USA. Jung very soon spotted that she was a lesbian and teamed her up with another of his Valkyries of similar persuasion, Dr Eleanor Bertine, also a Sennen Cove recruit.[53] Bertine and Harding founded the Jung Institute in New York, engendering controversy about whether homosexual analysts could really help heterosexual patients. The author of *Women's Mysteries*, a book about matriarchy sometimes said to be a forerunner of Robert Graves's *The White Goddess*, Harding repelled Jung by her aggressive feminism, and he was glad when she departed for America. She had the reputation in Zürich of being a martinet who would interrupt guest lecturers or insist on delivering a speech of 'refutation' at the end. However, she was influential in spreading the Jungian gospel in the USA and when she died at eighty-three left a fortune of over one million dollars to the New York Institute. Despite their British origins, Harding and Bertine were often referred to, along with Dr Kristine Mann, as the 'three American musketeers.'[54]

Another martinet was the wealthy Hungarian Jewess Jolande Jacobi, later a convert to Catholicism, who first met Jung at the Kulturbund in Vienna in 1927. She made an immediate impression on him by being able to write down all sixty-four hexagrams from the *I Ching* from memory. In 1934, at the age of forty-four, she completed her training as a Jungian analyst and impressed everyone with her erudition, stamina and dauntless, extravert energy. However, she soon developed an unfortunate reputation as a disturber of the peace and became notably unpopular in Jungian circles. Aggressive, pushy and dynamic, an achiever who got things done, and who was very good at getting her own way on committees, Jacobi, as an extravert, was strongly disliked by the mainly introvert Valkyries. Critics said she was like Toni Wolff, in that she had no time for other women and gave them the sharp edge of her tongue, while wheedling and cajoling men. Perhaps this was the reason why the one woman Jacobi got on well with was Toni Wolff, for whom she had genuine respect. With Jung himself she had a famously fraught relationship: on one occasion he lost his temper with her and actually threw her down a flight of stairs. Jacobi was the subject of many amusing stories. She used to conduct her analytic sessions pacing the floor, and it was said that the owner of the apartment block where she lived got tired of the constant tramp-tramp and took her to court for noise pollution; the judge Solomonically declared that she could pace between the hours of 8 a.m. and 10 p.m. but not at night.[55]

Jung's circle of female followers widened perceptibly after the inauguration of what came to be called the 'Eranos conferences' held at Ascona on Lake Maggiore, close to the Italian border. In 1930, while Jung was still friendly with Keyserling he attended the Darmstadt 'School of Wisdom', where he met a wealthy woman named Olga Fröbe-Kapteyn. Highly intuitive and with mediumistic skills, she impressed Jung with her psychological 'green fingers', and he accepted readily when she proposed an annual conference for Jungian studies to be held in the grounds of her estate at Ascona. In the grounds of her extensive residence at the northern end of Lake Maggiore she built a conference hall, separated from her 'villa' by a terraced garden with a splendid view of the lake and mountains. This was the seat of the Eranos conferences which, like the Darmstadt school, were designed to bridge the gap between eastern and western philosophy. (Eranos in Greek referred to a banquet at which the guests proved themselves worthy of invitation by offering a spiritual gift.) Jung's idea during the early years was to soft-pedal on psychology proper so as to leave the field clear for Sinologists and Indologists.[56]

The first lectures at Ascona were on the occult, though Olga Fröbe-Kapteyn's close friend Alice Bailey advised her that this was a bad omen, since the Lake Maggiore area had at one time been the European centre for the celebration of the Black Mass.[57] Other visitors disliked Ascona because of the *föhn* wind and the cult of personality which the 'maenads' built up around Jung himself. During the half-hour intervals between lectures, the mainly female audience would ignore the guest speakers and cluster around Jung as he sat on a wall. E.A. Bennet, an authority on Jung, recalled that Eranos resembled a Chinese court, with the great man surrounded by courtiers, while Anthony Storr remembered that when Jung came down to breakfast in the morning his followers listened spellbound to his dreams of the night before.[58]

In the early days of the Eranos conferences Jung stayed at Casa Semiramis, a villa on the nearby Monte Veritá, but in later years, when the walk became tiring for a man in his seventies, Olga Fröbe-Kapteyn provided him with a flat above the lecture-hall. In the evenings at such gatherings Jung liked to let his hair down: the German psychologist Ernst Kretschmer related that at the parties following meetings of the German Medical Association for Psychotherapy Jung liked to take his jacket off and dance and yodel until late.[59] One notoriously noisy party at Eranos found Jung running around in a high state of inebriation, making toasts, embracing the women, laughing and whooping with his Homeric bellow and baptizing people with libations of wine. Although there was no music, neighbours complained of the noise and the police were called. Olga Fröbe-Kapteyn played the outraged *grande dame* when the hapless constabulary arrived, but no such party was ever held again, so that the 'night of the Maenads' went down in Eranos legend as an episode of the 'good old days'.[60]

There was always a tense and uneasy relationship between Jung and Olga, caused, according to Aniela Jaffé, because she projected onto Jung the archetypes of a powerful, evil and unjust demon.[61] Yet although Jung and his hostess did not really get on, the Eranos conferences were the occasion for a significant widening in recruitment to the 'Valkyries'. In later years Jung would surround himself with pretty young women, especially Americans. One such was Mary Bancroft, married to a Swiss banker. Beautiful, intelligent, twenty-eight years younger than Jung and with an independent career as a journalist, she found him physically attractive and witty – a quality she claimed never to have found before in erudite people. Jung relieved her of sneezing fits once he got her to see that they were merely a reaction to the feeling that she could not say no to people, for fear they would not love her.[62]

Other recruits to the maenads included the German Jewess Hilde Kirsch and the Americans Alice Crowley, Frances Wickes and Mary Foote. Kirsch came to know Jung in a singular way. She shared an apartment with a woman who was in analysis with Jung and her flatmate asked her to telephone Küsnacht to cancel an appointment. Kirsch, who had wanted to get into analysis with Jung but had been turned down by letter, insisted on speaking to Jung personally and boldly told him that the *I Ching* had told her to take the vacant appointment. Jung roared with laughter and told her to come.[63] Significant American women, often in Zürich, were Alice Lewisholm Crowley, the director of the Neighbourhood Playhouse in New York, Frances Wickes, who imported Jungianism into the world of American dance and ballet, and the shadowy Mary Foote.[64]

The most prolific female authors among the Valkyries were Jung's long-time chief assistant Aniela Jaffé, Jolande Jacobi, Cornelia Brunner, author of a huge work on Rider Haggard, Barbara Hannah and Marie-Louise von Franz. Hannah and von Franz merit further comment. Barbara Hannah, the daughter of an Anglican bishop, first met Jung in 1929 when she was thirty-eight. At fifty-four Jung was grey-almost-white haired but otherwise looked youthful and vigorous, with no spare flesh. When he took off his gold-rimmed spectacles, she noticed that his eyes were dark-brown and on the small side. The nose and chin were prominent and the high forehead 'expressive'; he had a small 'salt and pepper' moustache but was otherwise clean-shaven. From his mouth hung the inevitable pipe and at his side was a large grey bulldog called Joggi, to whom he was so devoted that when it died, during the Second World War, he carved a replica of his childhood mannikin on its grave.

The first meeting was inauspicious and a sign of things to come. Hannah patted the dog, at which Jung bridled and said, 'Did you come from Paris to see the dog or me?'[65] He agreed to take her as a patient but almost immediately passed her over to Emma, who in turn passed her on to Toni. In the end Hannah managed to inveigle her way back as one of Jung's patients, but he spent most of the sessions raging at her for being a 'hellcat' and an 'animus hound'. He told her she had got him into a ditch and he could keep her on as a patient only if she promised to get him out of the next ditch she plunged him into. When Hannah protested at his unkindness, Jung excused himself: 'I never do it on purpose – the unconscious does it through me.'[66]

Hannah repaid his brutal treatment with a kind of dumb adoration, to the point where he later boasted that healing her 'animus possession' had been his greatest miracle cure. Hannah was interested only in Jung and cold-shouldered anyone else who tried to get close to her. Mary Bancroft described her as, 'a large English spinster of indeterminate age with a prominent nose that curved down to a chin that curved up to meet it . . . she reminded me of a witch I had seen as a child in a production of Hansel and Gretel at the Boston Opera House. She was always making "in" jokes about arcane matters and laughing uproariously at certain obscure connections that puzzled me.'[67]

All of Jung's 'Valkyries' seemed to have problems relating to other women similar to those Jung experienced towards men. Just as Toni Wolff, Esther Harding and Jolande Jacobi found one other woman with whom they could establish a rapport, so the one woman in Hannah's case was Marie-Louise von Franz, also unmarried, twenty-four years her junior, the daughter of an Austrian nobleman. Allegedly the most introverted of all the Jung women, she lived outside Zürich with Barbara Hannah and poured out a stream of books on numerology, alchemy, myths and fairytales. She had the reputation of being the most intellectually brilliant of all Jung's disciples but even the faithful found her books obscure and esoteric. She clung tenaciously to the original dogma of the master and was criticized by some for wishing to set Jungian theory in tablets of stone. As a reward for her absolute fidelity, in the last decade of Jung's life she was closer to him than any other human being outside his family.[68]

Despite the plethora of women in his circle, his fondness for being surrounded by pretty American students, and his many formulaic references to the importance of the feminine principle in psychology, there has always been a suspicion that Jung only truly engaged at a serious level with men and that his attitude to women was misogynistic. Certainly there were many incidents in his life in which he displayed reactions best described by the phrase 'amused contempt'. On one occasion a patient fell in love with him and proposed marriage. Jung pointed out that he was already married but this did not seem to sink in, so he decided to play along with the 'positive transference'. It got to the point where the patient actually issued printed invitation cards to the wedding, and the day was named. Gambling that 'the unconscious would find a solution,' Jung played a waiting game. Sure enough, the day before the 'wedding' an express letter arrived at Küsnacht, saying that God had revealed to her that the marriage could never be consummated.[69]

The issue of Jung's alleged misogyny is a complex one and calls for a close examination of his many pronouncements on female psychology and the 'animus-anima' split. Unfortunately, Jung was in the habit of giving reasonably clear definitions of his ideas, and then qualifying and 'amplifying' them so that all clarity was lost. He says at one time that most men can give an accurate picture of the anima but elsewhere declares that although they can understand the shadow it costs them enormous difficulties to understand what the anima is.[70]

Some of the difficulties of the concept, even in principle, will already be apparent. It makes sense to say that a man's image of woman is unconsciously formed by ideas and impressions formed about his mother, but this is too 'Freudian' for Jung, who, typically, resists the simple explanation in favour of a convoluted one. If every man has a primordial image of woman, it seems odd that there should be such variety in sexual attraction. If the anima is an archetype, and therefore analogous to an instinct, what sort of instinct is it that leads millions of men to seek millions of different kinds of mate? If the animus and anima are facts of biology, one would have to conclude that animals too possessed these primordial images. If, on the other hand, the animus and the anima are the products of *consciousness*, what is it about them that is 'emergent', given that typical manifestations, such as falling in love, are not strictly necessary for the propagation of the human race?

Although Jung admits the importance of 'maternal imagos', he is at pains to distinguish the anima from them.[71] So the anima is ambivalent: sometimes it is projected from the unconscious to produce infatuation or love at first sight; sometimes it can be a source of wisdom, inspiration and creativity.

The anima, it would seem, connotes both narcissism and bisexuality: narcissism in that a man projects his own unconscious feminine aspect onto a woman; and bisexuality since in falling in love we are falling in love with our complementary personality. It is fair to say that Jung never cleared up all the logical incongruities that flowed from these theses. But some recurring propositions do seem to stand out from his many remarks on the anima. The first is that the *coup de foudre* is the work of the anima.[72]

Another characteristic Jung idea is that an early love can be transferred from one woman to another via the anima, and Thomas Hardy's *The Well-Beloved* is often cited in this regard. Indeed, it is literature that gives us the best clues to what Jung means by the anima, for another of his favourite motifs was that of the *femme fatale* with an 'anima gestalt' such that she attracts the projection of the anima in men. But Jung, ever concerned to thread ambivalence and ambiguity into everything he touched, also provided examples of the 'positive' anima, mentioning the girl Helen who always accompanied Simon Magus on his travels in thc Gnostic legend; like Rider Haggard's *She*, she was perfect for Jung's purposes, being immortal also and a reincarnation of Helen of Troy. He added a further refinement by mentioning that anima and animus were never projected totally onto a member of the opposite sex, however beloved, but occurred in dreams of active imagination as autonomous figures, gods and demons.[73]

The anima is of the greatest importance in the emotional life of the male.[74] As always in Jungian theory and psychotherapy, the aim is to achieve the equilibrium point between conscious and unconscious. Those who in childhood have experienced an intense identification with the parent of the opposite sex may confuse this imago with animus or anima and suffer psychic 'inflation', producing a man who is too feminine or a woman who is too masculine. Jung sometimes explained this condition as the emergence in the role of primary function of the inferior function – feeling in the male and thinking in the female. On the other hand, banishment of the anima altogether in a man produces a warped individual in the shadowlands of psychosis.[75] The correct balance between unconscious anima and conscious thought was crucial for a man, because according to Jung's compensation theory the unconscious in a healthy individual always balanced the conscious: the more masculine a man was at the conscious level, the more feminine he would be at the unconscious level – an obvious explanation, thought Jung, for the higher suicide rate among men.[76]

Jung initially thought his anima/animus theory was wholly original, but later had his attention drawn to the passage in *Tristram Shandy* where Sterne talks of 'the two souls in every man living – the one . . . being called the ANIMUS, the other, the ANIMA.' Further research suggested that Sterne had got his ideas from the Rosicrucians, thus reinforcing Jung's conviction that he was dealing with an eternal archetype. He also brought in the similar ideas of *hun* (animus) and *p'o* (anima) from the Wilhelm translation of *The Secret of the Golden Flower*.[77]

It was typical of Jung, having introduced a complex and challenging idea, to compound the difficulty by adding further layers which shed further darkness rather than light on the notion. Having adumbrated the idea of the anima, he attempted to fuse with it both his theory of psychological types and his mystical ideas about the number four. Toni Wolff worked out a four-fold typology of women, which won Jung's approval. First there was the wife and mother, then the *hetaira* or mistress, thirdly the 'Amazon' with a calling of her own, and fourthly the seeress, the woman with mediumistic ability who could mediate between conscious and unconscious; Toni obligingly described herself as a mixture of mistress and seeress, with Emma as type one, and most of the 'Valkyries' as type two.[78]

Jung, however, thought that a general typology of women overwhelmingly placed them as either the 'married mother' type or the 'friend and concubine'; he thought prostitution was a normal and honourable phenomenon, taken for granted in primitive tribes, and mentioned the case of a tribal woman who had had intercourse outside the approved group and then infected 400 tribesmen with syphilis. It need hardly be said that this has drawn the ire of feminists, because it defines women purely in terms of men, because it legitimatises prostitution and because, by 'archetypalizing' the role of women, it gives a cosmic sanction to existing social arrangements.[79]

Yet Jung could never leave well alone, and even Toni Wolff's quaternity did not entirely satisfy him. After tinkering with the idea of the anima, he came up with his own variations on a theme by Wolff.

This time the anima quaternity featured first, Eve, as the symbol of instinctual relations – woman as mother; secondly Helen, woman as 'sex object' but with value as an individual; thirdly, Mary, the Blessed Virgin of Catholicism, representing Eros transformed into spiritual motherhood; and fourthly the female Logos of Sapientia – the eternal feminine, the ancient wisdom that transcends purity 'presumably only by virtue of the truth that less sometimes means more.'[80]

If the notion of the anima in men is controversial, that of the animus in women has launched a thousand feminist polemics. Jung sometimes admitted he was on tricky ground here, but forged ahead nevertheless with his customary aplomb.[81]

Jung's key idea about the animus was that it constituted a plurality: represented by such figures as tenors, boxing champions or famous men in distant cities.[82] To explain the animus Jung cited the literary examples of Marie Hay's *The Evil Vineyard* and H.G. Wells's *Christina Alberta's Father* but was unhappy that he could not find a single treasure hoard for the animus comparable to the Rider Haggard *oeuvre* for the anima.[83] But the recurrent literary theme of the attraction for women of the mysterious stranger could be cited in support, and it has been suggested that in Ibsen's *Lady from the Sea* Ellida's animus is projected on the demon lover.

Why was the anima singular and the animus plural? Jung advanced two different explanations. One was that since man was consciously polygamous and woman monogamous, the unconscious contrasexual archetype compensated for this. The other was that woman's conscious attitude concentrated on persons – it was a world of fathers, mothers, brothers, sisters, children – whereas a man's concentrated on things or abstractions – the State, the nation, the business.[84] To those who objected that the whole structure of monogamy/plurality, polygamy/ singularity was simply a fanciful a priori notion or *jeu d'esprit*, Jung liked to cite the plurality of male controls codenamed 'Imperator' who instructed the famous American medium Mrs Leonora Piper – the woman William James and James Hyslop had studied so closely at the turn of the century.[85]

According to Jung, women were liable to suffer more than men if there was imbalance between conscious and unconscious. Where an excess of anima in a man produced moodiness, depression and other 'old maid' symptoms, excess of animus in a woman produced a wholesale perversion of her true being and turned her into what Jung called an 'animus hound'. Jung wrote extensively, and intemperately, on the 'animus woman' who represented 'irrational thinking' just as the anima-invaded man represented 'irrational' feeling. Since the animus liked to project itself on 'heroes', especially creative artists and intellectuals, the 'bluestocking' was a particular target for Jung's – well – animus, in the normal sense.

Jung argued that the animus was rather like an assembly of Church elders or dignitaries who laid down incontestable and 'rational' *ex cathedra* judgements, which on closer inspection turn out to be a collection of clichés, and Christmas-cracker mottoes, sometimes based on 'common sense', sometimes on appeal to custom along the lines of 'People have always done it like that,' or 'Everyone says it's like that.' The animus, in a word, is a projected omniscient, a conservative collective conscience with a taste for clichés which serve as a substitute for reflection.[86]

Jung traced the phenomenon of a woman's being over-masculine, an 'animus hound', to an overidentification with the father and a poor relationship with the mother. American women, he thought, were particularly prone to be *filles à papa*, and this misplaced empathy with masculine values was reinforced in the USA by the large numbers of women attending traditional courses in subjects like philosophy and sociology. He described American universities as 'animus incubators'.[87] The search for 'animus hounds' in literature became a favourite Jungian sport: Chaucer's Wife of Bath was the most obvious candidate.[88]

Jung was utterly confident in his pronouncements on the differential psychology of men and women. In this he was well within the Germanic tradition that saw the sexes as totally different and diverse, as opposed to the modern feminist thinking that reduces all differences to social conditioning and the socialization in 'roles'. He frequently asserted that Logos (reason and thought) was *the* denoting feature of Man, and Eros (relations and feelings) of Woman, and even declared that for most women sexual intercourse was a 'meta-activity' concerned not so much with immediacy of sensation as with *feelings about the act of coitus*. He was of the opinion that many women were frigid, and that female orgasm, so far from being a physical sensation resulting from a skilful partner, was connected either with feelings about conception or with a general feeling about the relationship.[89]

Logos and Eros tended to confine men and women rigidly to their respective spheres, and the split between two entirely different principles was the principal reason for lack of understanding between the sexes. This, in his view, endowed women with peculiar strengths and weaknesses. Psychology was a natural arena for them, for obvious reasons.[90] On the other hand, their concentration on the minutiae of the personal made women natural intriguers. Jung disliked women in politics for this reason and referred to Madame Pompadour and Madame de Maintenon as 'power devils'.[91] Women, he thought, had an irrestible tendency to seek out a man's weak spots, to fasten on them and exasperate him.[92]

Yet women, for all their acute observation, were blind to certain aspects of men, and could never understand why they were moody after a day's work: 'A man comes home in the evening wanting to bang someone over the head. Instead he is expected to continue the torture by being nice to his wife.'[93] And Jung had no time for the sentimental view of women as helpless creatures in need of protection. 'To call women the weaker sex is sheer nonsense. Beware those angel-faced types who always appear weak and helpless and talk in a high-pitched voice. They are the toughest of them all.'[94]

There were many, then as now, who took the line that Jung's view of women was simply that of the prosperous middle-class Swiss burgher, tricked out with a few quasi-psychological refinements. Certainly the rigid division into spheres of influence denoted as Logos and Eros troubled even some of his disciples, and an exchange recorded at one of his seminars on 7 November 1928 is revealing. After reiterating his usual view on the sexual apartheid between Logos and Eros, Jung stated that women can be analysed only through their emotions: 'One can only talk to her so-called mind as if to a library, perfectly dry. Her real feeling is Eros.' At this point a female voice from the audience called out, 'Don't make us feel inferior because we really feel superior!' 'That's right, get emotional about it!' Jung flashed back.[95] It is, however, supremely interesting that Jung devoted far more attention in his writings to the problems of women than to those of men. This can be read either as masculine bias – indicating that women as 'the Dark Continent' (Freud's phrase) need more exploration – or feministically, as a sign that he actually thought the female psyche more rewarding. Jung's comments on male homosexuality, for instance, were perfunctory and nowhere near as intriguing as his analyses of women possessed by a 'mother-complex' or overwhelmed by a 'same-sex archetype'. Jung was hostile to male homosexuals and largely indifferent to their problems. There is not the same richness of analysis as in Freud's work and Jung limits himself to saying that the principal cause of homosexuality in men is identification with the anima. This is a form of infantile relationship with the feminine, which Jung sometimes loosely calls a 'mother-complex' and sometimes 'unconscious matriarchal psychology'.[96]

It is otherwise when he deals with women with 'gender problems', for then his interest is immediately caught. He explains that because in men the mother-complex is never pure but always mixed with the anima, it was easier to examine the effects of the mother-archetype in women.[97] The mother-complex, however, in Jung's view, is far from simple and can take one of four (naturally!) manifestations: maternal hypertrophy, Eros hypertrophy, identification with the mother or resistance to the mother.

Maternal hypertrophy means reifying the mother or regarding her simply as a breeding machine. Women suffering from this are driven by a ruthless will to power and a fanatical insistence on their maternal rights.[98]

Eros hypertrophy or overdevelopment of the sexual instinct most typically leads a woman to have affairs with married men; once the relevant marriage is wrecked, such a woman then moves on to her next victim. Identification with the mother, on the other hand, results in a woman becoming a cipher. Such women, suggests Jung, are often highly sought after in marriage as they are so empty that a man is free to impute to them anything he fancies.[99]

Finally comes the woman who resists and is antagonistic to her mother. This type of woman, if she does marry, either does so for the sole purpose of escaping her mother or else ends up marrying someone who shares all her mother's traits. The problem here is that stubborn resistance to the mother as the symbol of life-giving can mean that everything is pointless – sexuality, married life, children – and such a woman may become a bluestocking simply in order to have a sphere where there is no question of her mother being able to compete. However, bearing in mind his doctrine about the stages of life, Jung then suggests that the anti-mother woman has probably the best chance of making an outstanding success of marriage *during the second half of life*. Women, then, were in danger of four kinds of mother-complex from overconcentration on the female parent, and of becoming 'animus hounds' from too close an identification with the father. There remained a further peril, of being overwhelmed by the female archetype or anima itself.

Jung attempted to dovetail his extensive reflections on women with his general theory of the human personality. He linked animus and anima with the stages of life by stating categorically that they should be encountered as a task for the second half of life. This was both cause and consequence of the fact that a successful encounter with the contrasexual archetype made falling in love less likely. Jung argued that you could live without anima and animus until the age of thirty- five, but after that came the inevitable diminution of vitality, flexibility and kindness. Typical 'confirmed' bachelors and spinsters tended to be rigid, crusty, stereotypical, sloppy, irresponsible and with a tendency to alcohol.[100]

The other aspect of the stages of life was that the older men got the more feminine they became, and the older women, the more masculine. Jung claimed that in a man his 90 per cent of masculinity was all but exhausted by the age of fifty, so that he had to keep going on the remaining, feminine, 10 per cent; while women at fifty, having used up their 90 per cent femininity had to power themselves on with their 10 per cent of masculinity. The more rigidly separate the spheres of the sexes were kept in a given culture, the more pronounced this phenomenon would be, which was why it was so observable among the Latin peoples.[101]

Jung also linked his anima/animus theory with the general ideas of individuation and the Self. The fundamental notion was that when the archetype of the anima was assimilated, an autonomous complex was thereby transformed into a function of the general relations between conscious and unconscious. By falling in love a person gets in touch with underdeveloped aspects of the Self. By attaching oneself to the beloved through the constellation of the anima, one entered a state of *participation mystique*. By repetition of the cycle of projection and integration, neglected aspects of the human personality become available to consciousness, showing that the phenomenon of 'falling in love' could actually be an aid to individuation.

The ultimate purpose of both anima and animus is to be fused in the totality of the Self. Mary Magdalen and the other women around Jesus have been interpreted as helping him on his mission, which on a Jungian reading was not to save mankind but to reconcile anima and animus in the process of wholeness or individuation.[102] Jung sometimes referred to the fusion of the anima and animus as 'syzygy' – a process in which anima and animus in turn generate masculine and feminine archetypal images.

It can be seen that Jung eventually came to view his theory of the Self as a master key that might unlock the secrets of all disciplines: politics, sociology, anthropology, philosophy. Many scattered remarks attest to this, as when Jung suggests that the anima/animus stage of individuation represents the polytheistic stage in the history of religion, while the Self represents monotheism.[103] He further hinted that Christian dogma was merely a metaphor for the individuation process. The anima as *femme inspiratrice* derives wisdom from the Father, just as the Blessed Virgin Mary derives hers from God the Father.[104]

Thus Jung on women and animus/anima. In the light of his comments, it has always seemed odd that Jung should have been taken as pro-woman, as opposed to the allegedly anti-woman Freud. The psychologist Clare Thompson summed up an attitude that was and is widely prevalent: 'As a woman, I both resented intellectually and found sterile emotionally the Freudian definition of a woman in terms of what she is not, that woman is a non-man. Jung respected my right to be a woman and defined me in terms of what I am.'[105] In the early days of feminism, Freud was identified as a 'misogynist' and Jung the champion of the feminine. More thoughtful work by feminists[106] has rehabilitated Freud as an essential basis for a theory of women, while there are clear signs that a backlash against Jung may be starting.[107]

The question of Jung's relationship to feminism and his possible misogyny bears further examination. Numerous aspects of his thought have given offence to doyennes of the women's movement: his apparent willingness to define a woman's identity in terms of her value to men; his statement that there was merit in the old patristic conundrum about whether women had souls; his likening the feminine principle to *yin* or emptiness; and, most of all, his fulminations against 'animus hounds'.

Since the theory of anima and animus is claimed by some as Jung's most original contribution to psychology and since, at the same time, Jung's intellectual heirs are concerned to sustain the widely accepted image of Jung as pro-woman, it is not surprising that many ingenious attempts have been made to rescue the founding father from the allegedly 'sexist' hook on which he had impaled himself. The most simple approach to the problem is to stress the positive features of the animus.

More radical revisionism has aimed at jettisoning the distinction between Logos and Eros, detaching the notions 'masculine' and 'feminine' from gender, and stressing that animus and anima are archetypal components found in both men and women. This sort of thing has become a growth industry among post-Jungians.[108] Another approach has been to 'tidy up' Jung by postulating bisexuality as the human norm and then applying animus and anima to a basic substratum of androgyny. The *reductio ad absurdum* is reached by those theorists who try to integrate the anima/animus split at source, so as to make the resulting 'anima-animus' a composite at the unconscious level.[109]

However interesting and ingenious such ideas are, it must be stressed that they have nothing whatever to do with the thoughts of Jung himself, and such 'heresies' founder on the solid rock of the master's own writings. Jung always rejected the idea of separating psychology from biology, which is what the feminist divorce of sex from gender amounts to, and frequently cited anthropological and palaeontological evidence that showed the exact opposite. A sex/gender bifurcation implies the kind of Cartesian dualism Jung so often excoriated and denies his fundamental proposition that body and mind were aspects of the same archetypal reality. Above all, the idea of androgyny effectively puts paid to the archetypes – the cornerstone of Jung's theory. Again and again he emphasized that animus and anima were fundamental components of human nature, *contrasexual* archetypes that were irreducible.[110]

To rename the unconscious part of a man anima and the unconscious part of a woman animus, and then make animus/anima a dialectical interplay between elements of conscious and unconscious *in the same sex* is a departure from Jung's teachings as radical as his own departure from Freudianism with the incest theory in *Symbols of Transformation.* And if any doubt remains on this score, we should remember Jung's reverence for alchemy and bear in mind the fundamental alchemical principle that only what is properly separated can be properly joined.[111]

The concern of post-Jungians to make the founder appear 'politically correct' would not have been shared by Jung himself. He had firm views about the very different nature of men and women and found many female disciples to develop and advance those views, many of whom have expressly stated that Jung described the very considerable differences between the sexes correctly.[112] Whereas the first wave of Jungian women – the 'Valkyries' and those he trained himself – accepted his views as gospel, a newer generation has tried to accommodate his teachings with some of the prescriptions of feminism. A common view is that the strident anti-male rhetoric of the early years of the women's movement marked a kind of 'enantiodromia', which must sooner or later yield to an integrated view of relations between the sexes, stressing the archetypal feminine.[113]

However, there are still radical feminists who object violently to their representation as 'animus hounds'. For them, the countless women who see merit in Jung's theories on the sexes are suffering from what is described as 'internalised oppression' – a form of false consciousness engendered by 'patriarchy'. The feminist critic Demaris Wehr has remarked, 'Many female Jungians have corroborated Jung's devaluation of women because their own internalised oppression is reassuringly in tune with his opinions.'[114] Such a view is as much an adamantine a priori as the animus theory of Jung's which is being objected to, and cynics may derive wry amusement from the collision of two ironclad, hermetically sealed systems of thought. Radical feminists, according to Jungian theory, are 'animus hounds'; female Jungians who believe in the animus are, according to the radical feminists, victims of 'internal oppression'. It is the irresistible force against the immovable object – a result inevitable when both sides start from the premise of vague, unverifiable ideas.

Jung's misogynism – if such it is – is better established by his treatment of actual flesh-and-blood women than by an appeal to abstractions, and the aspect of animus/anima which is of more interest to the biographer is the extent to which the entire theory is a mere rationalization of his own idiosyncratic and highly unusual experiences.

The idea of the 'feminizing' of men after the age of fifty may be connected with the many dreams about his father Jung had in the 1920s when he was elaborating his theories about the sexes. Yet it is undoubtedly his mother who stands out as the figure behind the whole animus/anima structure and the many remarks on the nature of women. That she was a split personality resulted in the splitting of the anima between Emma and Toni Wolff, with Emma getting the role of wife, mother and companion, while Toni got the (superficially at least) more desirable roles of mistress and seeress. Jung also suggested that the twin impetus of his anima and mother-complex was towards Don Juanism for, having analysed exhaustively the effects of the mother-complex on women, he added that in a son it led either to sexual promiscuity, with the man seeking his mother in every woman he met, or to homosexuality, where the son's entire heterosexuality was tied to the mother in an unconscious form.[115]

Jung also justified his many adulteries in terms of his theory of the sexes, interestingly insinuating that the precipitants towards adultery lay both in the psyche and in the external world. There were two aspects of the external world that led to a breakdown in marital fidelity. One was the contingent fact that in Europe between the wars the surplus of females resulted in pressure on married men by unmarried women, which triggered adulteries; the divorce rate was high because married women, instead of accepting male polygamous instincts as a fact of life, instantly became cynical about marriage if their husbands were guilty of even a single peccadillo.[116] The other was simply that the institution of marriage was quite different from the way it was presented in bourgeois propaganda. The official myth was that marriage was a partnership of equals but, as Jung never ceased to insist, in fact one partner always 'contained' the other.[117] Such considerations led him finally to a full-blooded diatribe against a legal and cultural system that exposed men to financial ruin via alimony and child support payments for the utterly venial and unimportant sin of marital infidelity.[118]

The many ironies in Jung's view on sexuality and the sexes hardly need emphasizing. That his immediate circle of 'Valkyries' was composed almost entirely of 'animus hounds' was the most striking, but even that anomaly fades besides the breathtaking audacity with which Jung, in the passage just cited, manages to project his own anarchic views on marriage onto women, so that they, not he, are supposed to be the ones chafing at the restrictions imposed by bourgeois institutions. One is tempted to paraphrase the famous letter Jung sent to Freud on 18 December 1912 and ask, 'Who's the whited sepulchre now?'

Chapter Eighteen

THE SHADOW OF THE NAZIS

In January 1933 Adolf Hitler came to power in Germany. For the next six years Jung spoke and acted in a way that was, at best, highly ambivalent and, at worst, openly supportive of the Nazis. The issue of Jung's real or alleged fascist sympathies is one of the most contentious issues in a far from uncontroversial life, but has usually been discussed in a self-contained way. His attitudes make more sense when placed in the context of his general political and social sensibility.

Jung was a man of extreme right-wing political views, even though he supported no particular party line. Like many men of the Right, some of them in today's headlines, he combined ferociously reactionary and Social Darwinist views with liberal and permissive attitudes in the area of sexuality. He frequently stated that although as a Swiss he had to pay lip service to democracy, Nature itself was aristocratic, and that social inequality was a consequence of the natural inequalities existing among mankind – inequalities of intellect, ability, temperament and money (though Jung, typically, never mentioned that last aspect). He believed, with his hero Nietzsche, that different rules applied to 'beasts' and 'supermen' and one of his favourite tags was *quod licet Jovi non licet bovi* (what is allowed to Zeus is not allowed to an ox). Jung's objection to the hyper-inflation that devastated Germany in 1923 was not the chaos and misery caused to ordinary people but the threat to the savings of 'the better sort': 'Since nature is aristocratic, the valuable part of the population is reduced to the level of misery.'[1]

Jung shared the Swiss petite-bourgeoisie's fanatical hatred of communism. His hatred for communism centred on three aspects: its elevation of 'mass man' and the lowest common denominator; its lack of spirituality and its attempt to create a secular religion; and its function as a dark, anarchic force emanating from the collective unconscious. Under communism, Jung thought, all Man's lowest desires were activated; oddly, he includes among these greed and avariciousness[2] – oddly, because it is generally acknowledged that these are the very qualities stimulated by *capitalism* and that communism went wrong in thinking these elements could be purged from human nature. In any case, the destruction of all tradition could lead only to barbarism.[3] Jung also thought that there were two kinds of leadership, one aiming at human improvement through the suppression of the individual (Lenin and other communist leaders), the other aiming to enhance the individual (clearly he had himself in mind).[4]

Jung also considered that communism, in its misguided attempt to abolish religion – 'the Bolshevist delusion that "god" can be educated out of existence'[5] – had been forced to internalize and absorb the numinous: hence the many similarities between communism and Christianity – the emphasis on salvation, the classless society as the 'second coming', and so on. The fallacy of this approach was that the numinous can only be achieved through the spirituality of individuals composing a society: if you multiply zero by a million, the answer is still zero.[6] But human beings were not rational, and Jung made his point by once again yoking together Christianity and communism: even though the literal truth of the Resurrection had been refuted over and over again, the faithful still clung to it, just as the refutation of Marxist theory made no difference to the hundreds of millions who subscribed to it.[7]

For Jung there had to be a psychological explanation for communism; it answered a deep need in the soul of man. Characteristically, Jung explained the process in terms of archetypes: communism was a primitive archetype accepted in its primitive form, through misunderstanding, because of its numinous fascination for the underdeveloped mind. Thus communism was a primal numinous force that had burst its bonds when the Russian cultural mould could no longer contain it – an example of the Jungian adage that the old gods had not ceased to exist but now rhymed with *ism*.[8]

However, these sophisticated explanations of Jung's dislike of communism do not explain why he never displayed equal ferocity towards the other 'isms' that arose in the same way, especially fascism, nor does he explain the pre-established harmony or 'synchronicity' between psyche and the external world that makes Swiss capitalism the peak of social achievement yet reached by Man. Moreover, some of his less cautious remarks about communism and the Soviet Union display a prejudice shorn of all rationalisation, as when he remarks that the Soviet five-rayed star, blood red in colour and recalling the pentagram, is 'an intensely evil sign'.[9]

A closer insight into Jung's right-wing sensibility is afforded by his ferocious remarks on crime and punishment, which bespeak the authoritarian conservative's belief in original sin and the necessity for firm action to arrest the threatening tide of chaos. Jung was fascinated by the criminal mind and once investigated a case in Germany where a man committed eight motiveless murders. He found that the murderer was a weak man, but that his wife was a dominant personality and a member of a fanatical religious sect: Jung's inference was that the woman was a sort of devil and had projected the evil into him.[10] However, he was prepared to listen to no excuses for criminals when it came to punishment. Institutionalizing murderers was a farce, for the State was then feeding and keeping their own dark selves, much as if a psychiatrist deliberately kept a patient's autonomous complexes unintegrated. Jung added, self-contradictorily, that life in prison was anyway so hellish that it was more humane to dispatch criminals via the noose or guillotine.[11] He argued strongly for capital punishment, saying that in such a case if one did not exact the supreme penalty, one was not facing up to the criminal in oneself.

Part of individuation involved integrating every part of the individual, even the criminal part, which, if left alone, worked evil. A humane approach to capital punishment could only be predicated on the delusion that human beings were improving year by year, and therefore the aggregate improvement was helped by 'rehabilitating' a few criminals. This was nonsense: human beings were not improving and criminals could not be improved; the murderer, for instance, had murdered himself long before we chopped his head off. Jung stressed that his approach was not biological determinism, which would entail weeding out degenerate stock and putting lunatics, imbeciles and the handicapped to death, but was simply a stoical facing up to the irremediable dark side of human nature.[12]

As a devotee of Nietzsche, Jung had ambivalent feelings about capitalism. He believed in inequality, privilege and the aristocratic principle properly so called (rule by the best people), but disliked both money-grubbing, as a pursuit for lesser minds, and the giant capitalist corporations, because they offended against his fundamental tenet of 'small is beautiful'. Nevertheless, at the limit Jung would always come down in favour of capitalism against its critics.

He was under no illusions about the giant corporations. Because of his close personal contacts in the Rockefeller family he knew a good deal about Standard Oil and often referred to their famous interwar rivalry with the Dutch Shell company.[13] On one of his visits to the USA he met the founding father of Standard Oil, John D. Rockefeller, who remarked out of the blue that Austrians were very wicked people. Expecting to find that Rockefeller had an 'Austrian complex' and would reveal some telling fantasies, Jung probed further, but his findings were banal: John D. was simply annoyed that the Austrian government had rebuffed Standard Oil and signed an agreement with Romania instead.[14] Elsewhere Jung argued that Standard Oil had destroyed thousands of decent human beings. Yet such criticisms of American capitalism as Jung made were a kind of left-handed attitude soon corrected by the reflective right hand; aware that his critique of Standard Oil might appear 'socialistic', he backtracked later and said that people cried out for convenient gas stations for their cars, yet did not seem to realize that, but for the economies of scale a giant like Standard Oil practised, such corporations would not be able to provide these facilities for the public.[15]

The core of Jung's social and political ideas forms a traditional cohesive theory of ultra-conservatism. The best way to appreciate his views is to offer them first as a series of propositions. So: the idea of progress is an illusion, and most of the woes of the modern world can be dated from the Enlightenment and the cult of reason; there is no such thing as society; a group ethos destroys the individual and leads to mass man and mass culture; modern technology produces alienation and dissociation; the emphasis on individual rights rather than duties leads to communism; small is beautiful and every large-scale organization including the State is a disaster; the ideal is a stable and geographically fixed small community like the city-states of Ancient Greece; only the individuated man can resist the State.

The Enlightenment and the rule of reason (what Jung liked to refer to contemptuously as *Déesse Raison*) introduced a cult of increased production and improved social conditions to which all modern societies make obeisance, but there was no longer any myth of the individual, the really important thing: the communist utopia could never help the individual back to himself.[16] This linked with Jung's idea of the Enlightenment as 'false consciousness': it simply replaced the incubi, succubi and woodsprites of the Middles Ages with weapons of mass destruction and other effects of technology.[17] Jung's point was that the Englightenment tried to reason such diabolical spirits out of existence but merely disposed of the erroneous way they were *perceived*; the psychic reality inadequately portrayed by the medieval mind as demons and fairies continued to exist within the human personality.

It was one of Jung's favourite ideas that there was no such thing as society, a doctrine which recently reappeared in the mouth of Mrs Thatcher; Van der Post, Jung's disciple and her guru, was presumably the transmission belt.[18] Jung always spoke with venom of the State, describing it as democracy's 'shadow side'. Just as the superstitions supposedly dethroned by the cult of reason in the French Revolution have simply taken other forms, so the State represents the ghosts of the dethroned autocrats returned in another guise; like the Ancien Régime, the State is bound to penalize the most gifted individuals within its domain.[19] The State emphasized collectivity over individuality and a group ethos over independence of thought and self-reliance with disastrous effects: collective man would commit crimes he could not countenance as an individual and peer pressures and the values of reference groups were allowed to overrule reason.[20] Group conformity, paradoxically, even makes so-called 'rebels', the criminal classes, yearn for middle-class respectability.[21]

Jung shared the concern, fashionable in the 1930s and given a wide currency by writers like Ortega y Gassett, about 'mass man' or the insectification of the human species, which he thought produced a mass culture, expressly aimed at the extinction of the individual. The political movements of the twentieth century were thus mass madness, yet the psychoses did not appear out of the blue but were the products of long-standing predispositions which Jung called psychopathic inferiority. Mass man sank to an inferior intellectual level, and the demons that lie dormant in every human being until he is part of a mob were then allowed to emerge. Mass man was not simply dangerous through being mindless, conformist and undifferentiated, but because his abdication of individuality allowed the monsters of the psychic underworld, who were usually chained, to burst their bonds and breach the surface.

Jung also had a kind of Luddite attitude to modern technology. He denounced telephones, radio and air travel as breaking down a sense of reality. On the radio in the 1930s, for example, one could switch from a report of the Japanese invasion of Manchuria to one on civil disobedience by the Congress party in India and then move on once again to another channel relaying reports on the Italian assault on Abyssinia, yet all the time one would be in a room in Zürich.[22] According to the Jungian law of compensation, everything better was always purchased at the price of something worse. This applied particularly to technological advance, which, far from bringing happiness, simply accelerated the tempo of life and left us with less time than before. In this connection he liked to quote the old patristic tag: *Omnis festinatio ex parte diaboli est* (all haste is the work of the devil).[23] Technology, the product of the Goddess Reason, alienated Man from his true nature and produced a dissociation of personality analogous to the splitting of the world into competing ideologies.[24]

Jung was also extraordinarily hostile to what we have come to recognize today as the 'rights-based culture', emphasizing so-called 'absolute rights' with no corresponding duties, and he was convinced that its logical corollary was communism.[25] Size always meant degeneracy. The larger the number of people involved in an action, the greater the propensity towards mindlessness and barbarism.[26] The 'rights-based culture' – expecting from the state what you would not expect from an individual – begins the dangerous slide into mass psychology and eventually into inhumanity.[27] Since mass psychosis was easier in the large, densely populated nation-state, Jung frequently offered a paean of praise to his native land and blessed Fate for making Switzerland a country of six rather than eighty millions. If Switzerland had a population density like Holland's, stupidity would have increased exponentially and morality divided by twenty.[28]

There is much in Jung's fulminations against the state and modern society that suggests anarchism, but Jung, as a conservative, was always concerned to balance order with calls for a less powerful state: the monster of mass man, he often argued, could only be kept in check by an even bigger monster, the state. His ideal was the Greek city-state or, in the modern world, a community of self-sufficient peasant proprietors, and he reserved particular scorn for the American way of life, with its high levels of mobility. Those who speak of Jung as a 'New Age' guru need to understand how little he would have sympathized with today's 'New Age travellers'. He was flatly opposed to an itinerant, gypsying form of life and even to apartment living; his model was the one-family house, the house owned by its inhabitants.[29] How then, to live well? Jung's sole suggestion was that the individuated man or woman was the only bulwark against mass society.[30]

One further aspect of Jung's political and social thought needs to be emphasized. He frequently stated that the most disastrous biological legacy human beings were born with was the imperative to breed. Consequently he had an obsession with the idea of overpopulation, and tended to see this, not economic forces such as the search for markets, the battle for scarce raw materials, and the drive for superprofits, as the trigger precipitating nations towards war. He saw Mussolini's invasion of Abyssinia as a form of Italian purging, getting rid of surplus population through the spilling of blood. In a seminar given on 12 June 1935 he commented that Mussolini's action in sending huge armies to Abyssinia to die in battle or from tropical disease was actually a form of bloodletting. Of course, he added, Mussolini's population aims would be better served by a war with France, but that would be dangerous as it would weaken the economy and infrastructure of Italy; a war with Abyssinia, on the other hand, was risk-free. Jung also thought that the Japanese invasion of Manchuria in 1931, officially undertaken to provide markets for the Greater East Asian Co-Prosperity Sphere, was really motivated by a desire to get rid of Japan's surplus population.[31]

This survey of Jung's views on politics and society explains his unremitting hostility to communism. His ambivalence towards the fascist regimes, which fell foul of his principles almost equally, is explicable in terms of his basic political conservatism. Although both communism and fascism were species of collectivism, fascism had some saving graces which Marxism did not. Fascism endorsed élitism, the cult of the open air, the morality of strenuousness, was not hostile to private property or religion and was, like Jung's own sensibility, backward-looking, nostalgic and reactionary. It is significant that whenever Jung makes a general remark about the horrors of collectivism and mass society, he proceeds to give an example which indicts communism. The messianic and prophetic style of leadership in fascism greatly appealed to him, and this was clearly an organic aspect of the ideology, whereas the personal rule of Stalin in Russia was denounced by many Marxists and Trotskyists as an aberration. Another important aspect of fascism was the way it incorporated tribalism within the modern nation-state. Since, on the 'small is beautiful' principle, Jung preferred tribal society to what Weber called the 'rational-legal' modern form of government, it followed that fascism was Janus-faced as communism was not: fascism was both modern and tribal, whereas the Soviet Union was merely modern.

It is worth investigating Jung's attitude to the fascist leaders and contrasting it with his view of Stalin. His sympathy for Franco and the Nationalists in the Spanish Civil War was apparent from a number of utterances. The egregious cruelty of the Francoists he excused on the grounds that the Spanish temperament only permitted civilized behaviour if it was balanced by atrocities, just as in normal life in Spain decency was balanced by bullfights.[32] In 1932 he expressed stupefaction at the embrace by Spain of the Second Republic – overthrown by Franco in 1936.[33] And at the beginning of the civil war he quoted enthusiastically the claim of Spain's elder statesman of the arts, Miguel de Unamuno, in a speech on 3 October 1936, that Spanish civilization was represented by Franco's armies.[34] But Jung remained silent about Unamuno's sensational recantation at Salamanca on 12 October, which led to his being placed under house arrest by the Francoists; he died of a broken heart on the last day of 1936.[35] Finally, as Franco's forces closed in on beleaguered Madrid to deliver the *coup de grâce* in early 1939, Jung cheered them on with another statement (15 February 1939) expressing distaste for the Left.[36]

This complaisant view of Franco was 'balanced' by a rare loathing of Stalin, whom Jung often liked to compare and contrast with

Hitler and Mussolini. He described Stalin as a brute, a Siberian sabre-toothed tiger, a lineal descendant of Genghis Khan.[37] Jung thought Stalin the least interesting of the three principal dictators of the 1930s, since he was not a creator but a mere conquistador, and even Lenin had been 'creatively destructive'. Stalin's autocracy was understandable on Jungian principles since we all tend to become the thing we most fight against and, moreover, the West should be grateful to him for the wonderful example he had given the world of the axiomatic truth that communism always leads to dictatorship. Nonetheless, there was some grudging admiration in Jung's attitude to Stalin: he admired his matchless instinct for power and said that if Hitler, Mussolini and Stalin were locked in a room with limited food and water, Stalin would emerge triumphant.[38]

In contrast with his view of Stalin, Jung admired Mussolini hugely and never recanted or withdrew his adulatory remarks. He jeered at the popular view that Mussolini had a 'power-complex' and claimed instead that Il Duce was an archetypal religious figure.[39]

Jung was in Berlin on 28 September 1937 when Mussolini visited Hitler in the German capital and was just a few yards behind the two leaders at a parade at which they reviewed troops. He was impressed by Mussolini – 'a certain style, a certain format of an original man with good taste in certain matters' – and gave as examples of his good taste his keeping on Victor Emmanuel as king and his taking the title Duce instead of Doge or Duca. He observed Mussolini getting a childish pleasure out of the goose step, which he introduced into Italy, but Hitler behaved robotically and throughout the entire performance never laughed but appeared to be in a sullen bad mood. Jung admitted he could not help liking Mussolini, who seemed a real human being; Hitler by contrast, was sinister as he seemed not an individual at all but the avatar of a nation.[40]

Jung drew a distinction between the 'chieftain' type of dictator (Stalin and Mussolini) and the medicine-man type (Hitler), who derived his strength from the power the people projected onto him. Of all the dictators, it was Hitler who most fascinated him. Jung wrote that as thaumaturge or medicine man nothing like Hitler had been seen in the world since Mohammed. It was his mediumistic ability in part that enabled him so perfectly to act as the avatar of the State and to fulfil the true meaning of Louis XIV's boast *l'état c'est moi*.

All the symbols of the Third Reich seemed to Jung to point to a mass movement sweeping the German people on in a hurricane of unreasoning emotion towards an unknown destiny. Hitler was the mirror of every German's unconscious, which was different from that of other Europeans; he appealed to the typical German inferiority complex, which accounted for the curious fact that Hitler made no impression on non-Germans, who saw only a comic figure. There is no disguising the admiration in Jung's writings on the Führer in the 1930s: in the way he describes the Führer's dreamy, seer-like expression and in his acknowledgement that Hitler's unconscious had exceptional access to his consciousness.[41]

Hitler plugged into the collective unconscious of seventy-eight million Germans, but his psychic powers were not limited to Teutons. The reason why his brinkmanship during the 1930s was so successful was, Jung thought, his ability to read his opponents like a book; when he met Chamberlain at Berchtesgaden during the 1938 Munich crisis, his unconscious picked up at once that Britain would not risk a war. Hitler's 'magical' aspect explained why he could not turn into a normal human being and why he would die in the job. It also explained why he could not marry. Unlike Stalin and Mussolini, he had sacrificed his sex life for the cause, which is what all medicine men do. Finally, Jung suggested that the key to Hitler the individual was a 'tremendous mother-complex', on the curious grounds that Hitler was a monomaniac in the grip of an idea, and ideas and the brain were always female.[42]

There were aspects of Hitler's Germany that Jung found unpalatable even in the 1930s. He read *Mein Kampf* and found it an eclectic farrago, with one set of ideas drawing on socialism and another set coming from the Catholic Church.[43] Naturally, with his dislike of state power and government intervention in the economy, he had reservations about Nazi social and economic policy, though in his simultaneous dislike of what would later be recognized as Keynesianism in the western economies and his desire to place communism as an 'egregious' evil, he ironically came close to the Trotskyite view of fascism and social democracy as two horns on a single capitalist ram. He disliked President Roosevelt's New Deal economics in the USA and Lloyd George's very similar ideas for regenerating the British economy.[44] He also thought that Britain went wrong in jettisoning the aristocratic principle.[45]

In short, whatever Jung disliked about Nazi Germany he disliked just as much in the western democracies. This links with another issue, which is that he could never quite decide whether Nazism was a phenomenon peculiar to Germany or whether it was part of a general trend, anchored in social structure and the *zeitgeist* of 'mass man' and modern technology. This uncertainty manifested itself even in the 'New Age' gloss Jung sometimes put on events: on the one hand he claimed that the general trend towards collectivism was caused by the approach to the age of Aquarius; on the other, he alleged that the prophecies of Nostradamus (in which Jung believed wholeheartedly) foretold the rise of Hitler.[46]

According to Jung, the twentieth century faced a general crisis as a result of precisely the things liberals and progressives took so much pride in. The rise of mass man was caused by technology, but technology in turn can only achieve 'take-off' when Man has repressed the irrational psychic factors in his make-up. So there is the double jeopardy of repression both of the individual and of spirituality. The repressed elements will find some outlet; hence the peculiar mixture of advanced science and technology and primitive superstition in the collectivist societies. There was an unresolved conflict between the large-scale nature of society and the modern-nation state and the tribalism inherent in fascism.

It was the ambiguity of fascism, both progressive and reactionary, forward-looking and nostalgic, torn between reason and unreason, that so fascinated Jung.[47]

The horrors of the twentieth century, though in part caused by technology, also represented the residues of bygone ages, and in a sense Germany in the 1930s was merely an updating of Europe four centuries earlier under the heel of the Inquisition: barbed wire and concentration camps and the miseries inflicted on coloured races by colonialism replaced the martyrs burned at the stake by the Holy Office, the horrors and atrocities of the Crusades, and the other barbarities and bloodbaths perpetrated by Christianity.[48]

Sometimes Jung tried to unite his general European and particular German perspectives by making the latter merely an extreme case of the former. He linked facism with modern painting, atonal music and modernist literature like James Joyce's *Ulysses*.[49] The swastika, too, was a general wheel-like rotating motif in mandalas, which Jung interpreted as a projection of an unconscious collective attempt at the formation of a compensatory unified personality; but the *Nazi* black swastika, turning to the left, expressed the German preference for a regression into the archaism of the dark unconscious.[50]

Yet most of the time Jung located Nazism firmly within a specific German cultural experience. Occasionally he took the line, not dissimilar from that in Thomas Mann's *Doktor Faustus*, that the rottenness in the state of Germany dated back to 1871 and unification, with all the arrogance and megalomania that followed.[51] But most often he spoke of the Nazi phenomenon as an example of the dark pagan gods rising up from the unconscious, with Hitler as an incarnation of the pagan deity Wotan. Jung's fundamental idea was that Christianity had originally been forced on Germany at the point of a sword, and that therefore the Christian veneer was thinner and the pagan gods nearer the surface; the rise to power of Hitler was simply Wotan waking from his sleep in the Teutonic unconscious.[52] Christianity had also split the German barbarian in two, forcing him to repress the dark side which awaited redemption. The more Christianity lost its authority, the more likely it was that the 'blonde beast' would break the bonds of its underground prison and breach the surface.[53]

Jung thought that the Germanic peoples had never developed organically out of primitive polydemonism to polytheism and its philosophical subtleties, and had accepted Christian monotheism and its doctrine of redemption only when overwhelmed by the might of the Roman legions; he often drew the comparison between the Roman policy of 'convert or die' and the introduction of Christianity into Africa from behind the protective bulwark of the Maxim gun.[54]

Wotan, then, had come to life in a modern civilized country thought to be well past the Middle Ages, and this was what was so impressive about Nietzsche, as he had heard the first rustlings of the savage god in the primeval forests of the unconscious. This was why it was so ludicrous to trace the ideology of the Nazis back to Nietzsche, for this would be an example of 'shooting the messenger': because Nietzsche sensed what was going to happen and the form it might take, he was now being accused of having willed it on Germany. Nietzsche's big mistake was to publish *Zarathusthra* in the first place, as his highly complex thought could be understood only by experts in the psychology of the unconscious.[55]

Wotan was an archetype that had disappeared for a thousand years, but archetypes were like river beds which dry up when the water deserts them yet can well up again at any time. Wotan was the *furor Germanicus* that had the German nation in its grip, and it was Hitler's genius to have infected the entire German people with this madness.[56]

Jung was very proud of his Wotan insight and took it very seriously indeed. He asserted that the Wotan thesis explained more about National Socialism than economic, political and psychoanalytic explanations put together.[57] Wotan also explained certain otherwise puzzling aspects of German culture, in particular the relative absence of the anima in German literature, as contrasted with its omnipresence in that of France and the Anglo-Saxon nations. As Jung pointed out, in German culture women – as opposed to their roles as Frau Doktor, Frau Professor, daughter, sister, etc – did not really exist.[58] He also thought that Wotan explained the primitive and adolescent nature of German psychology, as manifested in the extraordinary prevalence of homosexuality, and in German sentimentality (*Gemütlichkeit*), which was really another 'nothing but' apparition, masking hardness of heart, unfeelingness, soul-lessness. Wotan also explained why Germany time out of mind had been the land of psychic catastrophes – the Reformation, the peasant wars, the Thirty Years War – and why Goebbels was able to make such infantile projections of evil upon the Russians.[59]

To put it more in the terms of analytical psychology, Jung sometimes said that Hitler was a reflected image of collective German hysteria; the German nation was mentally ill but could go about its instrumental tasks perfectly well, just as the individual hysteric could appear completely normal much of the time. The lack of any real opposition in Hitler's Germany was the outcome of a peculiar state of mind, which in an individual would be called hysteria. Jung's analysis of Nazism shows many of the diverse strands in his thinking coming together. Germany, like a sick and unintegrated individual, was a series of fragments. This is why the myth of *Faust* is so indicative: Faust is split and sets up an evil outside himself (Mephistopheles), to serve as an alibi in case of need; he likewise 'knows nothing of what happened', knows nothing of what the devil did to Baucis and Philemon.[60]

Because he thought his theory of Wotan was triumphantly borne out by Hitler and Nazism and therefore vindicated his defence of archetypes against the sceptics and scoffers, Jung sometimes wrote about the upsurge of Wotan from the unconscious in triumphalist terms. This, coupled with his many admiring remarks about Hitler as medicine man and seer, seemed to some to clinch the case for Jung as Nazi sympathizer.

However, Jung was always ambivalent about the Nazis. Insofar as they represented dark, unconscious forces, previously unacknowledged, which lent support to his own theories, he spoke of them with grudging admiration. He referred to 'the formidable phenomenon of National Socialism' and mocked those who were sceptical about the unconscious: 'Has the tremendous phenomenon of National Socialism, which a whole world contemplates with amazement, taught them better?'[61] After the Second World War, when he spent a lot of time 'compensating' his earlier ambivalence by furious denunciations of Hitler and his acolytes, he was still honest enough to admit that Hitler had done a lot of good for Germany in the early years.[62] He also defended his posture in the 1930s by arguing that 'wait and see' was the only sane policy: since Nazism was Wotanism, an archetypal movement, and every archetype contains both good and evil, it was impossible at first to know whether National Socialism would turn out positively or negatively.[63]

Jung's unwise attitude to the Nazis *in general* was composed of two main strands. He was a man of the extreme Right, a vehement anti-communist who saw Hitler as a bulwark against 'godless Bolshevism'. In the 1930s such attitudes did not seem so reprehensible as they do now with hindsight. D.H. Lawrence, T.S. Eliot, Ezra Pound, W.B. Yeats, Wyndham Lewis and Roy Campbell were only some of the leading literary figures who flirted with fascism, to put it no more strongly. In Germany itself Richard Strauss, Furtwängler and, especially, Heidegger, attracted criticism for their initial enthusiasm for National Socialism. Secondly, he was delighted that the Nazis seemed to bear out his Wotan theories and thus, implicitly, the notion of archetypes. Moreover, after the war Jung to some extent tried to rewrite history by doctoring articles and talks he had given on Hitler during the 1930s. The original transcript of the interview he gave to Dr Weizsacher of Radio Berlin in July 1933, in which he used words and phrases with a strong Nazi echo and connotation, is even more inflammatory than the favourable references to Nazism in his published works.

Jung and his followers attempted many defences of his attitude to Hitler and the Nazis. Jung himself tried to counter the unfavourable impression made by his 1933 radio broadcast by claiming that on the same visit he formed an extremely adverse opinion of the Party functionaries and of Goebbels in particular.[65] It is true that he did not like Goebbels but his disciples have exaggerated the extent of his opposition to the Propaganda Minister. When he was in Berlin on 28 September 1937, during the famous visit of Mussolini, he received a message that Goebbels wanted to see him; it turned out that wires had been crossed and that Goebbels had made himself available to see Jung, on the understanding that it was Jung who wanted to see *him*.[66] A pointless meeting did follow, which has been worked up by some Jungian acolytes into a story of the Master's brave defiance of the awesome 'Jup'. Van der Post tells a story, said to come from Jung himself, that at the meeting Goebbels lost his temper and ended by banging the desk with his fists.[67]

Other evidence showing Jung holding Nazism at arm's length comes in his denunciation of the racist theories of the virulently anti-Semitic ideologue Alfred Rosenberg.[68] There is, too, the circumstantial pointer that in 1938 he went with Alfred Tomic to see the anti-Nazi play *Glorious Morning*.[69] Moreover, Jung frequently brackets Hitler with Napoleon and Lenin as men who created entire peoples in their image and likeness and imposed a single faith on them – and Jung is consistently hostile in his oeuvre to both Napoleon and Lenin.[70] As for the admiration of Hitler as medicine man and thaumaturge, Aniela Jaffé pointed out that the German resistance poet Carl Zuckmayer also likened Hitler to a medicine man.[71] On the general count of being a Nazi supporter, then, one could enter the Scottish verdict of 'not proven', and the most judicious conclusion would be that Jung was being extremely foolish and naïve in thinking that one could sup with such a devil; this would bracket him as Nazi dupe with the man he most detested, Martin Heidegger.[72]

However, the case for the defence becomes virtually impossible when we move from the *general* count of fascist sympathies to the two specific counts of the indictment against Jung: that he collaborated with the Nazis in the area of psychoanalytical politics; and that he made offensive remarks about Jewish culture and the Jewish mentality that were grist to the Nazis' anti-Semitic mill.

When the Nazis came to power in 1933, one of their first aims was to ensure that education and the media were 'conformed' (*gleichgeschaltet*) to official ideology. Learned societies and their journals were not exempt from the process, and pressure was at once put on the president of the International Society for Psychotherapy, Dr Ernst Kretschmer, editor of the *Zentralblatt für Psychotherapie*, to bring the society and journal into line. Kretschmer resigned, and Jung then accepted the presidency and editorship. To prevent *gleichschaltung*, Jung then used his freedom as a Swiss citizen to redraft the statutes of the society – which was international, though based in Germany and dominated by Germans, who held all the main positions – and make it formally international in character.[73]

Jung was now president both of the international society itself and of the Swiss section. In response, the Germans set up a separate German society in Berlin in September 1933, fully in conformity with Nazi doctrines, and headed by the psychiatrist Professor H.M. Goering, cousin of Reichsmarshal Hermann Goering. Some Jewish psychoanalysts were at once expelled, and all remaining Jewish members of the German society promptly resigned, in order, as they said, to preserve the integrity of psychoanalysis in Germany.[74] Jung recommended that the International Society should acquiesce in the situation in Germany and not try to expel the German section under Goering, lest the position of psychotherapy under the Reich become impossible. Meanwhile all expelled and resigned Jewish doctors should be given a warm welcome as members of the International Society.[75]

Jung's supporters make a number of points in his defence; that in the 1930s many people still believed negotiation and dialogue with the Nazis was possible; that Ernest Jones himself, as Freud's legate, met Professor Goering and other members of the German society in Basel in 1936 and had discussions with them;[76] and that Kretschmer himself, so far from blaming Jung for accepting the presidency, fully exonerated him from wrongdoing and painted a favourable picture of him.[77]

Matters took a more serious turn in early 1934. The German section continued to collaborate with the *Zentralblatt*, and Professor Goering planned to bring out a supplement for circulation in Germany only, in effect a manifesto, calling on German members to conform to the tenets of the Nazi state. Through error, incompetence or design, this manifesto appeared not only in the German supplement but in the December 1933 issue of the *Zentralblatt*. Thinking this had been done with Jung's approval, the Swiss psychiatrist Dr Gustav Bally attacked Jung as a Nazi sympathizer in the Zürich press, pointing out also the intrinsic undesirability of Jung's remaining as president and author of a society and an organ so tainted by association with the Reich.[78]

In a series of letters to the Zürich daily *Neue Zürcher Zeitung* Jung explained that his general motive was to help his Jewish colleagues in Germany and he would persist in this aim even if his motives were misunderstood. He regretted that his name had appeared over a Nazi manifesto 'which to me personally was anything but agreeable,' but insisted he had nothing to apologize for in his general strategy, claiming that psychotherapy was 'above politics', that he had acted in good faith, and that he would have done the same if beleaguered analysts and therapists in the Soviet Union had needed his help.[79]

The *Zentralblatt* affair became a *cause célèbre* in international intellectual circles. The usual opinion was that, whatever might be said *in general* for Jung's dangerous strategy of collaborating with the Nazis, the business about the manifesto showed that Goering was simply manipulating him to make it appear that he was a Nazi sympathizer; unless he really was one, he had no realistic option but to resign as president and editor forthwith and make it clear by forceful action that he entirely dissociated himself from the manifesto that had appeared in the *Zentralblatt*, with his own name on the masthead.[80] Thomas Mann, for one, was disgusted by Jung's attitude, and he wrote in his diary for 14 March 1934: 'C.G. Jung's self-justifying article in the *Neue Zürcher Zeitung* is most unpleasant and disingenuous, even badly written and witless; strikes the wrong pose. He ought to declare his "affiliation" openly.' Almost exactly a year later, on 16 March 1935, he wrote: 'Another one about psychoanalysis in Germany and the revolting conduct of Jung has caused me to reflect on the ambiguousness of human and intellectual phenomena. If a highly intelligent man like Jung takes the wrong stand, there will naturally be traces of truth in his position that will strike a sympathetic note even in his opponents.'[81]

Can anything be said in Jung's defence? The usual tactic of his supporters is to say that the proof of the pudding is in the eating, that psychotherapy did survive under the Third Reich.[82] The case is often cited of a Freudian in 1942 helping Professor Goering analyse a girl sent to him by Heinrich Himmler.[83] Another ploy is to attempt to divorce words from acts and to maintain that whereas the Nazis, all too obviously, operated at the level of brute facts, Jung worked at the level of mere abstract advocacy.[84] Others, in a kind of version of 'politics should have nothing to do with sport', say that it is beyond the competence of a psychotherapist, even one of genius, to decide on what is right and wrong in politics, and that Jung followed the correct therapeutic procedure in trying to remain above the fray.[85] But the issue of the society and the journal will not go away. Jeffrey Masson has pointed out that many of the post-1934 articles in the *Zentralblatt* go far beyond routine Swiss bourgeois anti-Semitism and contain virulent attacks on the Jews coupled with eulogies of Hitler. Masson further argues that the issue about the manifesto in the supplement is a red herring, since Jung knew all about the later articles and did nothing.[86] Since he could not claim ignorance, as these articles were edited in Switzerland, he tried after the Second World War, to shift the blame onto C.A. Maier, claiming that he did all the editing.[87]

Moreover, in 1936 Jung threatened resignation as president when the Dutch tried to prevent Nazi sympathizers joining the society.[88] As a calculated snub to his critics, in the same year he appointed Goering as co-editor of the *Zentralblatt*, though still on the basis that the journal would not be 'conformed' and would continue to publish uncensored articles by Jewish authors. It was not until 1939 that Jung's hand was forced. In that year the Germans tried to flood the Society with large Italian, Hungarian and Japanese groups. Receiving no assurances that Goering would not try to impose 'Aryan regulations' by a majority vote with this new influx of fascist sympathizers, Jung resigned the presidency. Although by statute the vice-president, Dr Hugh Crichton-Miller, should have succeeded him Goering illegally declared that the journal was henceforth 'conformed' and moved the society's headquarters from Zürich to Berlin.[89]

What were Jung's real motives during this unsavoury collaboration with Nazi sympathizers? We may reject the obvious answer – that he was a Nazi himself – although it is true that his obsession during the 1930s with the question of leadership and the attempt to frame a psychology of nations took him dangerously close to Nazi ideology. Nor, in the light of his attitude to the Jews (shortly to be examined), is it really plausible that he was playing a long-term game to help Jewish analysts and therapists.

Three views of Jung's deep motivations, in ascending order of probability, are worth investigating. Henri Ellenberger thought that Jung's experience of the Nazis triggered a kind of 'grandfather-complex'. Influenced by his grandfather's participation in the

German nationalist and democratic movement, crushed after 1848, he may, unconsciously, have identified the incipient Nazi movement with the patriotic upsurge of German youth in 1848.[90] There is support in Jung's work for the notion that he was obsessed with German identity in the same way his grandfather was and that this underlay his actions in the psychotherapeutic politics of the time.[91]

Thomas Mann, though, thought that the key to Jung's attitudes was that, like all true right-wingers, he went wherever the power was and yearned to be on the winning side; on this view, Jung's 'radical' ideas were merely a mask for ultraconformism. Castigating Jung for his pernicious irrationalism at the very time when all good men and true should be fighting hard for reason, Mann wrote, 'Jung's thought and his utterances tend to glorify nazism and its "neurosis." He is an example of the irresistible tendency of people's thinking to bend to the times – a high class example. He is not a loner . . . is not one of those who remain true to the eternal laws of good sense and morality and thereby find themselves to be rebels in their time. He swims with the current.'[92]

Yet by far the most likely motive actuating Jung was the desire to conquer Germany for his own school of analytical psychology, especially since this had been Freud's goal for psychoanalysis. That Freud, even after twenty years, was never very far away from Jung's thoughts becomes clear when we consider the perfervid thoughts on the 'Jewish question' which have most of all blackened Jung's reputation and brought him the unenviable (and in many ways deserved) tag of Jew-hater. Jung was not really an anti-Semite but he allowed his hatred for Freud to poison his mind and invade his thoughts; it is almost always the case that when Jung says 'Jew' he means Freud and when he says 'Jewish' he means Freudian. In an article in the *Zentralblatt* for January 1934, Jung virtually admitted as much.[93]

During the 1930s Jung became obsessed (not too strong a word) with the 'Jewish question'. At the very least such an obsession was tactless at a time when the murderous Nazi regime was similarly preoccupied, and even the most dogmatic Jungians accept the charge of gross indiscretion. But, it may be asked, since Jung had intense feelings of anger towards Freud and could have exercised his 'scientific right' to investigate the psychology of races and nations at any time since 1913, why did he choose the 1930s to do so? This looks like the very worst kind of opportunism, to say the least.

Jung's propositions on the 'Jewish question' can be separated for the purposes of clarity, though he himself tended to run one point into another. He believed that yesterday's persecuted become today's persecutors; that Jews and Germans were in competition for the title of 'chosen race'; that there were inherent differences in the racial psychology of Germans and Jews; and that Freud was a typical Jew and insinuated a Jewish world-view as a universal theory.

Jung believed that the treatment of the Jews by the Nazis was a manifestation of his old favourite, enantiodromia, that it was a kind of compensation for the treatment of Germany by the Allies after the Treaty of Versailles, and that if the Jews achieved a national home in Palestine they too, in accordance with the principle of enantiodromia, would become persecutors. And because the Jews as the 'chosen people' vied with the Germans as 'master race', both Jews and Germans awaited a saviour and thus suffered from an inferiority complex.[94] The key to Germany was its sense of having arrived too late among the family of nations, of thus being like a younger brother who realizes that the older brothers (Britain and France) have taken all the good things; this, for example, would be the Jungian gloss on the nineteenth century 'scramble for Africa'. The key to the Jews, on the other hand, was the diaspora mentality.[95]

This explained the unique Jewish psychology. Jung always insisted on the right, as a scientific investigator, to explore the differential psychology of nations, and liked to probe for the idiosyncracies of the Swiss, the English, the Americans, and so on. In writing about Jewish psychology he claimed to be doing nothing more than he had always done. So he argued that the German psyche split into a Christian upper half, representing the forces of light, and a dark, repressed, pagan side, represented by Wotan, waiting in the unconscious to be released. The Jewish psychology, as a result of the diaspora was very different, for the upper half was German, Swiss, English – the culture of the host, of adaptation and socialization – while the lower half was the old biblical culture of the Ancient World. To put it another way, the Jews had no 'chthonic' quality, while Germans had it in dangerous excess.

Jung reiterated that it was not anti-Semitic to say that Jewish psychology was different: he had stated on many occasions that Chinese psychology was very different, yet no Chinese had ever accused him of being anti-Chinese. Common sense indicated that it made all the difference in the world whether your culture was recent (Christian), 2,000 years older (Jewish) or 4,000 years older (Chinese).[96] However, certain Jews took exception to this statement, claiming that, in making this comparison with the Chinese, Jung was insinuating subliminal ideas of a Mongol horde or the 'yellow peril' and thus conjuring up, by association, the popular Nazi idea of the Jews as vermin overrunning the national living space. Jung protested angrily at this distortion of his views.[97] He replied witheringly that the narrow-minded attitude of his opponents reminded him of the time at the turn of the century when he was told that the French could not accept the idea of schizophrenia because it was a notion that came from Germany.[98]

When talking about Jewish psychology, Jung often confused the issue by using the phrase 'Jewish psychology' to refer both to the alleged general features of Jewish culture and to psychoanalysis specifically. A close reading of his *oeuvre* indicates that the general theory of a specifically Jewish psychology, tricked out with reference to Chinese, Indian and English peculiarities, is tendentious, that he is using the ill-thought-out idea as a trap with which to ensnare psychoanalysis. Jung hoped to demolish psychoanalysis by showing that it was an idiosyncratic, 'partial' view of reality which arose because Freud was a Jew. Since psychoanalysis was the *locus classicus* of 'Jewish psychology', it followed that the theory had no universal validity.

Although warned and advised on all sides that his speculations on Jewish psychology were giving offence in the West and being seized on gleefully inside the Reich, Jung was now convinced he had a master idea that would discredit Freud utterly, so he continued, quite unmoved, in the same vein. At the end of 1936 he wrote to a Jewish correspondent to lecture him on what was and what was not 'typically Jewish' and stated that Freud was a typical Jew in that his tendency to autonomous consciousness cut him off from his instinctive roots, whereas the happy Jew is the one who is reunited with his roots.[99] Jung claimed that the status of psychoanalysis as a peculiarly Jewish affair had been confirmed by Freud himself when he suddenly brought up an accusation of anti-Semitism following Jung's deviations from orthodoxy in *Symbols of Transformation*.[100]

The evidence accumulates that hatred of Freud was the 'hidden agenda' in Jung's programme during the 1930s, and that the Nazi preoccupation with the 'Jewish question' provided him with a context for his own examination of Jewish psychology, which in turn was merely a Trojan horse enabling him to strike at psychoanalysis. The complaisant attitude to Professor Goering in the International Society ties in with this, once we posit that Jung's aim was to supplant psychoanalysis in Germany with his own 'analytical psychology'.

Just as Jung's attitude to the Nazis has usually been considered in a vacuum, divorced from his general right-wing attitudes, so his anti-Semitism has usually been discussed in isolation, and the discussion restricted to whether or not Jung's remarks amount to racism or worse. His defenders make certain points over and over again: that he discussed the Jewish question before the 1930s; that Freud himself admitted there was such a thing as a 'Jewish psychology'; that the charge of anti-Semitism arose purely because of his opposition to psychoanalysis.

It is true that Jung did occasionally raise the issue of a peculiarly Jewish psychology before 1933 – he did so in 1927, for example.[101] But after 1933 he raised the subject frequently and in a virulent form. It is also true that Freud told Jones in 1908 that Jews had an easier time making their way to psychoanalysis than gentiles since there was not the same accretion of mystical elements in Judaism as in Christianity.[102] It is, further, incontestable that Jung exerted himself to save individual Jews from the Nazi maw and that on occasions his remarks about a specific Jewish identity were not so very different from what Theodore Herzl and other Zionists said.[103] But his insistence that there was a racial layer in the collective unconscious has inevitably spawned charges of racism, and this theme has been taken up by scholars tracing a racist tinge in his writings about Africans and American blacks.[104] Most of all, he has rarely been forgiven by Jews themselves. Wilhelm Stekel wrote to Chaim Weizmann in Jerusalem to accuse Jung of being an 'assassin of Jewishness'.[105] The scholar and critic Walter Benjamin studied Jung's work carefully and found that it did support the Aryan myth and that it was 'the devil's work'.[106]

That Benjamin should have used about Jung's writings the exact phrase that Jung himself used about Freud's is an interesting pointer, suggesting that much, if not most, of Jung's anti-Semitic output was simply a transmogrification of his feelings about a particular Jew. Nevertheless, even if Jung's personal vendetta against Freud led him to make incautious remarks about Jewish psychology, we can still question the morality of a man prepared, by his utterances, to put at risk a beleaguered people within Germany just to score points off psychoanalysis. And we should not forget Jung's self-confessed 'Jewish complex'. According to the theory of enantiodromia we could say that his passionate attraction towards Freud and Sabina Spielrein masked a violent anti-Semitism; alternatively, it could be argued that the virulence of the 1930s masked a frustrated love for the Jewish people.

The Freudian tables have been neatly turned by Anthony Samuels, who argues that, by regarding Germany as a patient, Jung suffered 'neurotic countertransference' on the Jewish question.[107] The neurosis also manifested itself in a splitting that the young Jung would have recognized very clearly as a Swiss illness. On the one hand he looked to Germany as the repository of the main culture shared with the Swiss; on the other, his preoccupation with nationhood, deriving from Switzerland's size, precarious geographical position, polyglot culture and tenuous identity, led to overconcentration on the Jews, also a people with a precarious national identity.

Jung's record in the 1930s, particularly during the years 1933–36, was not an inspiring one. He allowed his anger towards Freud to unbalance him so that he produced anti-Jewish observations that could be used as Nazi propaganda. As a politician, navigating the shoals and reefs of the International Society for Psychotherapy, he showed himself singularly inept. His desire to prove the truth of his theory of archetypes led him to a theory of the German unconscious that is widely regarded as inaccurate, simplistic or simply vacuous.[108] Worst of all, he never expressed repentance for his errors in the 1930s but instead tried to rewrite them out of history. In 1946 the Jewish scholar Leo Baeck visited Switzerland and declined to meet Jung when invited to do so. Jung bearded Baeck in his hotel and a lively, vociferous discussion ensued for a couple of hours. When Jung was unable to make any headway in his defence of his conduct, he finally conceded to Baeck: 'Well, I slipped up.'[109] That was the sum total of his repentance, apart from a grudging written statement, intercalated with another, in which he insisted that to talk about the differences between Jewish and Christian psychology was a respectable thing to do.[110]

The Nazis themselves played a double game with Jung. When his unwise utterances could be used as ammunition for their theories, they used them, and in such a way that it appeared that Jung was giving wholehearted endorsement to Hitlerian ideology. Insofar as he was critical of Nazism, his books were banned, his comments censored and he himself was subtly discredited by the pretence that analytical psychology was indistinguishable from psychoanalysis. Freudian psychology was always under heavy suspicion in the Third Reich, both because it was 'Jewish science' and because, unintelligently read, it seemed to postulate a theory of the unconscious at odds with the Nietzschean morality of strenuousness. Black propaganda both from the Nazis and from those in the West hostile to Jung continued to hint that he was some kind of medical adviser to Hitler and had frequently been summoned to Berchtesgaden to attend the Führer. This was a canard that always particularly infuriated him.[111]

Yet in a sense he had only himself to blame for the rumours. He ran too much with the hare and the hounds, sometimes appearing to endorse 'the mighty phenomenon of National Socialism,' at other times mocking it. Paul Stern is probably right when he remarks: 'It may not be quite accurate to say that Jung was anti-Semitic in the company of anti-Semites, and pro-Semitic in the presence of anti-anti-Semites – yet there was something in his make-up that tended in this direction.'[112]

Chapter Nineteen

THE WORLD OF DREAMS

Jung's experience in the early 1930s was the opposite of that of most prophets. Because of his Nazi associations he was without honour save in his own country, where there were increasing signs that he was being treated as a national icon. On 25 November 1932 Zürich City Council awarded him the literary prize from the city of Zürich, worth 8,000 Swiss francs.[1] In 1935 he was appointed titular Professor of Psychology at the Swiss Polytechnical School in Zürich, and shortly afterwards founded the Swiss Society for Practical Psychology. In 1938 he set up a 'curatorium' at Zürich University, directed by nine psychologists, to foster co-operation among the various schools of depth psychology.

These activities show Jung working the exclusively Teutonic vein that engaged him from 1927 to 1935. During these years he turned down many opportunities for foreign travel, ostensibly because of uncertainties in the world situation. In 1934 he passed up an opportunity to visit China, and the year before he refused an invitation to lecture at the Sorbonne, on the grounds that the French intellectual climate was not yet ready for him.[2]

Jung's new colleagues fared no better than Riklin, Maeder,

Keyserling and the others with whom he had fallen out. The leading light of the 'curatorium' was Medard Boss, a Swiss existentialist psychoanalyst and founder of Dasein analysis. At first Jung collaborated well with him, but soon demonstrated the unique Jungian mixture of arrogance, pique and hurt pride. After one colloquium in Zürich, where Jung had held the floor, shouted the opposition down and prevented anyone else from getting a word in edgewise, Boss wrote to Jung with a lengthy critique. Jung was furious and said Boss should have raised these points at the meeting – the very thing Boss claimed he was unable to do.[3] By 1947 Jung was bitterly attacking Boss's ideas, even to the point where he uttered words of praise for Freud.[4] Not surprisingly, the curatorium broke up in disarray in 1948, and Boss in turn wrote bitterly about Jung, saying that he was 'still loaded with the remnants of the old mechanistic exact-scientific way of thinking and with many outdated biological theories.'[5]

In the late 1920s and early 1930s, Jung concentrated his theoretical studies on a detailed analysis of Nietzsche and on dream analysis. It was his work on dreams and symbols which, most of all, won him his international reputation. Freud, who had also made his reputation with the interpretation of dreams, had described them as the royal road to the unconscious, but later Freudians downplayed their importance as compared with transference. For Jung and his school, dreams always took first place in methodology and transference was relegated to the margins.

When a patient came to see him, Jung liked to apply a fourfold (naturally!) procedure. First the patient summed up the problem as he saw it; then his dreams would be analysed to provide the compensating picture from the unconscious; the relational aspect of analyst and analysand would then be brought into the picture; finally integration of these three elements would be attempted. Crudely speaking, one could say that the Freudian school emphasized the third element and the Jungian the second. Yet the difference in methodology did not end there. Jung rejected Freudian 'free association' in favour of 'active imagination' – a form of reverie ancillary to dreaming during sleep. Jung stressed that active imagination was a back-up system, enabling the analyst to elucidate actual dream images. The patient was asked to start with any image in his dream, concentrate on it and watch how it changed by association. There should be no attempt at forcing or making the image into something else; patience was all important. The aim was to bring consciousness and the unconscious into balance, so that the patient could, so to speak, not only analyse his own unconscious but also give the unconscious a chance to analyse him. Jung used direct or controlled associations, making sure the spontaneous ideas arose from a given dream situation and constantly related to it. The problem with Freudian free association, in his view, was that the ideas that occurred to the subject did not necessarily refer to the dream situation.[6]

Jung's method was centripetal, in that his method of controlled or circular association made sure the dream image remained the centre of attention. Freud's method, at least in Jung's gloss on it, was centrifugal, in that free association proceeded at random away from the original image. Jung alleged that by free association you will always reach your complexes, but it does not follow that the complexes are the material dreamt about; complexes could be 'touched' by word-association tests, they did not require dream analysis.[7] Another way of looking at the difference between the two schools was to distinguish between the Freudian 'analytic-causal-reductive' interpretation of dreams, equating dream images with real objects, and the 'synthetic-hermeneutic' Jungian approach, referring every part of a dreamer's dream back to himself (or herself). We are thus back to the old Jungian distinction between Jung as introvert and Freud as extravert.

It followed from Jung's theories of homeostasis and the self-regulating psyche that the dream was performing a biological function of adaptation, that it had a purpose and was teleogical. It usually denoted the struggle of the individual psyche to make sense of life's tasks, which was why Jung often referred approvingly to Adler's views on dreams.[8]

According to Jung, dreams had a structure containing four elements: exposition, development, culmination and solution.[9] However, no one dream could be analysed in isolation, and he would encourage his patients to build up a whole series of dreams before undertaking definitive analysis. Jung's dream analysis would start with the greatest possible aggregation of personal associations on the part of the dreamer, controlled through active imagination. Without knowledge of the personal situation it was impossible to interpret a dream correctly except by a lucky fluke. If a patient dreamed of a table, the analyst would need to know what kind of table, what colour, had the patient ever seen one like it in waking life, and so on. The emphasis was on gathering associations to the dream and its contents from the patient, rather than applying an a priori list of dream images.[10] The second stage was to amplify a dream by exhausting its possible symbolic and archetypal content. This symbol amplification by reference to archetypes seemed flatly contradictory to the first stage, which ruled out general interpretations.[11]

The amplification method in Jungian analysis has drawn a lot of fire from critics who say that the method is tendentious and consists largely in 'leading the witness' towards a preordained conclusion. It is true that the very notion of amplification by reference to mythology and history takes it for granted that a dream can be meaningfully elucidated in this way. Jung was quite happy to interpret the dreams of a Swiss patient in terms of the Tibetan Book of the Dead, on the grounds of universal archetypes. Naturally the method is bound to produce the result desired by the Jungian analyst but the entire system works on *petitio principii*. One of Jung's patients dreamt he was at a social gathering and, on leaving, put on someone else's hat. There are obvious ways to interpret this dream – anxiety about identity, and so on – but Jung offends against Occam's razor by opting for the most far-fetched explanation involving mandalas.[12]

Similarly, a late middle-aged spinster patient related a dream that appears from all the evidence to have been sexual in origin. To admit this would be to concede ground to Freud, so Jung switched to pragmatic reasoning and asked what possible use such an interpretation would be for a woman with declining chances of being sexually active; instead he gave a religious slant to the dream with the aim of consoling her.[13] This is a slippery slope, for it is but a short step from this to telling people what they want to hear.

Although Jung believed that all dreams could be elucidated and amplified by reference to archetypes and the collective unconscious, he did not believe that dreams were all of a single kind. The most commonly reported ones involved flying, falling, being chased by dangerous animals (or in the case of women, by men), being insufficiently or absurdly clothed in public places, being in a hurry or lost in a milling crowd, fighting with useless weapons, being utterly defenceless, running and getting nowhere.[14] A typical child's dream (as in *Alice in Wonderland*) was of growing infinitely small or infinitely big or being transformed from one into the other. These were evidence for the universality of the human experience and the common structure of the brain and, more controversially, for archetypes. Sometimes the interpretation of dreams did not call for amplification: women patients often dreamed of their analyst as a hairdresser because he 'fixes' the head.[15] But the dreams that most interested Jung were the ones in which archetypal material was clearly on view.

In active imagination patients often produced drawings or paintings incorporating symbolism going back to Ancient Egypt. Impressive evidence for a collective unconscious, Jung thought.[16] A professor came to him with a dream so disturbing that he told Jung he thought he was going mad; Jung went to his shelves, took down a 400-year-old book, and showed the professor the identical vision in a woodcut. Even more impressive. Then there was the child – one of a handful Jung treated – whose dreams uncannily echoed and mirrored the books of Ezekiel and Revelations.[17] But what settled any doubts Jung might have had was the persistence in his patients' dreams, in case after case, of mandala symbolism. As we have seen one of his American patients, an uneducated black man, related a dream of a man crucified on a wheel – the mandala form. Mandalas were not merely ubiquitous, occurring in Tibetan Buddhism, ancient religions, dreams and schizophrenia, but very often contained the quaternity or symbol of the Self in the form of a cross, a star, a square or an octagon.[18]

The mandala dreams connected with another favourite Jungian category – the 'big dreams' which drew on collective material. Jung found that these occurred at decisive stages in one's life: from the age of three to six; from fourteen to sixteen; from twenty to twenty-five; from thirty-five to forty; and just before death.[19] Once again we can appreciate the almost Hegelian nature of Jung's system of thought, for dream analysis is found to reinforce the (apparently) quite different theory of the stages of life.

The 'big dreams' that one has between the age of thirty-five and forty alert one to the fact that the time for individuation has arrived. In such dreams we are likely to meet dangerous adventures and ordeals typical of initiations – encounters with dragons, animals, demons, the Wise Old Man, the wishing tree, the hidden treasure, the well, the cave, the walled garden. Big dreams are different in degree but not in kind from the general thrust of dreams, since in the oneiric state we become aware of things we have not experienced in reality, some of them unrealizable in the flesh, some belonging to the past of mankind and some to its future.[20]

What, then, do these different forms, manifestations and kinds of dreams signify? Broadly speaking, Jung thought that dreams did one of two things: they acted as a means by which the unconscious compensated the conscious; and, more rarely, they foretold the future. The golden rule in interpreting a dream was to ask, what conscious attitude does it compensate? Naturally, the law of compensation operating in the case of dreams was part of the general homoeostatic balance of the psyche which manifested itself in all kinds of unexpected places. For example, an analyst who felt violent lust for a woman patient would actually be receiving important information from the unconscious: it meant that his rapport with the patient was poor and that the unconscious was therefore proving a 'bridge' to cover the distance.[21]

Again and again Jung stressed that the principal function of dreams was to allow the unconscious to process material compensating some deficiency in the conscious state.[22] So the contemporary unconscious was likely to hanker after the primitive as compensation for the machine age. In individual cases the compensation can be equally striking. A spoiled child, when it grows to adulthood, will have dreams of witches, ghosts and demons; this is the unconscious tipping the dreamer off to the harmful effects of the spoiling which consciousness neglects. One of Jung's patients was a sixteen-year-old who had vivid dreams of being pursued by the devil. The youth in question was devout, conformist and concerned with clean living and moral existence, yet Jung told him that the message from the unconscious was that he would have to relax his standards and make a pact with the devil if he wanted to stay mentally healthy.[23]

In general there was nothing untoward or abnormal about having frequent dreams, but if someone who dreamed only rarely suddenly started having many dreams, this would mean that the unconscious was becoming overloaded. Dreams of social chaos were often a metaphor for dysfunction in the individual psyche; one of Jung's patients, suffering from inflation of the conscious and suppression of the unconscious, used to dream of the ultimate social breakdown – revolution in Switzerland. The process of compensation was especially important in the case of recurrent dreams.[24]

Yet the most controversial aspect of Jung's dream analysis was his claim that dreams could foretell the future, and it was this which particularly drew the fire of Freudians. Edward Glover remarked savagely, 'Jungian prospective interpretations differ in no way from candid comments on the personality and potentialities of the dreamer such as might be offered him for his own good by any officious friend.'[25] When accused of simply truckling to popular prejudice and superstition with his 'prospective theory of dreams', Jung replied that if this is what he had desired, he would have produced a simple key to dream interpretation. As it was, the analyst's problem was that the most frequent form of 'precognition' was foreknowledge without recognition: knowledge was given in dreams but it was usually extremely difficult to recognize it for what it was.[26]

Jung himself had experience of such 'precognition' very early in his career. He had a vivid dream about Sabina Spielrein the night before he first met her.[27] His patients also had premonitory dreams, but usually ignored Jung's advice to avoid the danger portended in them. One of his patients had a phobia about Paris, similar to his own about Rome, and material in her dreams suggested there might be an objective basis for her fears. Jung advised her never to go to the French capital, but she ignored him, went there, and was killed in a car crash. Another had a phobia about steps which he too ignored. He was caught in a street riot, fighting broke out, and he sought sanctuary in a public building. Rushing up a broad flight of steps, he was mortally wounded by a stray bullet.[28]

Jung was even able, to his own satisfaction, to isolate the images and motifs that warned of danger, which included high vertiginous places, balloons, aeroplanes, flying and falling.[29] One of Jung's women patients had dreams of an explicit sexual nature. Jung warned her that she was in danger, but she brushed the advice aside. A week later she was attacked by a sexual pervert and narrowly escaped with her life. Piqued by her ignoring of his advice, Jung entered one of those brutal judgements for which he was famous: 'Obviously she had a secret longing for some such adventure.'[30]

An even more striking instance of the failure to heed premonitory material in dreams concerned one of Jung's male patients who was a mountaineer. The man told Jung of a dream of climbing where he mounted upwards into empty air and awoke in a state of ecstasy. Jung advised him not to go climbing alone but, as always, the advice was ignored. The mountaineer then had a close brush with death when he was buried by an avalanche and rescued by a military patrol which by sheer luck was manoeuvring on the mountain side. Nothing daunted, he returned to his feats as an alpinist and was killed: a guide reported that he had seen him literally step out into the air while descending a rockface. The death took place six months after Jung had first analysed the dream.[31]

Jung saw nothing strange in regarding certain dreams as an anticipation of the future, for he reasoned that anything that will be happens on the basis of what has been and this, consciously or unconsciously, exists as a memory trace.[32] Jung was always drawn to ideas that subverted the normal notions of time – whether quantum theory, relativity or the time theories of J.W. Dunne – and he espoused the fatalistic notion that the future is prepared long in advance and can therefore be guessed by clairvoyants.[33]

Jung's views on time as a unity, with past and future as categories imposed by consciousness but ignored by the unconscious, led him to an original argument for survival after death. There was no proof of survival, not even ghosts, for if we saw the ghost of a dead man we could still not prove the *identity* of the ghost and the dead man, but dreams from the unconscious did seem to point to a continuation of life after death. It was possible, of course, to regard such dreams as fantasies compensating for the irreducible fact of our mortality, but Jung thought that telepathy, clairvoyance and other paranormal phenomena did provide irrefutable evidence that parts of the psyche were not subject to the laws of space and time.[34]

Jung derived the raw data for his dream theories not only from his patients but from self-analysis, for he always interpreted his own dreams, in defiance of his own general prescription that the dreamer and the analyst should never be one and the same. He had few genuinely prophetic dreams, but the compensation theory seemed borne out by the circumstance that when he was in Africa he dreamed about Switzerland and when in India (in 1937–38) he dreamed about England. It comes as no surprise, though, to learn that Jung had frequent experience of 'big dreams'.

Perhaps the most celebrated of such dreams incorporating archetypal material was Jung's dream of Liverpool. In 1927 he dreamt he was in Liverpool with a number of Swiss comrades. The Liverpool of his dream was not the actual drab, dingy and poverty-stricken Merseyside city of economically depressed Britain between the wars but an imaginary place, whose physical features recalled Basel rather than anywhere else, with the individual quarters of the city arranged radially around a central point. He climbed up cliffs to a plateau which led to the 'city centre'. It was night, winter, dark and raining. His companions spoke with surprise of a certain Swiss of their acquaintance who had settled there, but Jung thought he knew why. When he awoke he understood the dream as a metaphor for the Self. He interpreted Liverpool as meaning 'the pool of life': the liver, according to an old view, was the seat of life, that which 'makes to live'. He concluded that he had experienced the perfect mandala, and therefore gave up drawing or painting them thereafter.[35]

Jung frequently dreamt of mandalas and, particularly in the 1940s, of the spirit Mercurius or Hermes, sometimes in the guise of an eastern prophet and sometimes as a young prince whom he had to push under the water.[36] Most interesting of all his later dreams was one of Philemon as the Wise Old Man, as related to the Catholic priest Father Victor White in 1948.[37]

Yet it was from his patients that Jung got most of his raw material. Only occasionally does Jung lift the veil on what went on in his consulting room, so that we are fortunate to have as evidence the letters he wrote to anxious enquirers, offering tentative interpretations of their dreams. It is interesting to note that in such cases Jung broke all the rules in his own book: in most cases he knew nothing of the 'life situation' of his enquirers, there was no face-to-face contact so that active imagination could expand the dream, and he was prepared to commit himself on the basis of a single dream, not a series.

The consulting room evidence is the most useful for testing the truth of Jung's dream theories, but often he tells us simply that dream analysis led to a negative conclusion. There was the occasion when he analysed a 'boringly normal' physician because the man had expressed an ambition to be an analyst himself. In the course of the analysis, working from the evidence of dreams, Jung realized that his doctor patient was in the grip of a latent psychosis, which was about to become manifest. He found a pretext to end the training and analysis, and the doctor abandoned his plans to change medical disciplines.[38]

All Jung's most successful dream analyses involved women. A woman suffering from pulmonary tuberculosis had a dream about an elephant eaten up by worms so that its bones showed. The obvious interpretation was that the unconscious was trying to make sense of her wasting disease, but Jung interpreted elephant as consciousness and worms as unconscious and suggested that the dream pointed to the crushing weight of the unconscious in her.[39]

A young Greek woman wrote to ask if her dreams could be

influenced by her reading of his books, but Jung assured her that dreams occurred independently of such immediate stimuli. She dreamt that there was a sudden darkness and the beginnings of a storm; she sought refuge in a building with a square room, where she found a huge bas-relief representing two feminine figures in long Grecian robes, one of whom was the goddess Demeter. Jung interpreted this as meaning that the young woman, an only child, was too much under the influence of her mother and, remote from her father, was spiritually starved of the male principle. He analysed it as a typically Greek syndrome, for in Ancient Greece, he alleged, men were over-influenced by their mothers.[40]

An even more sensational case came Jung's way when a Dr C.R. Birnie asked his advice on a recurrent dream of one of his female patients. Aged twenty-three, she dreamt that she had a child by her father; she was always locked in a dark room with her father outside, and she understood the room to be one in which she had been locked since childhood so that her father could coerce her into sex. This raised the much-vexed and perennial issue of the reality behind incest fantasies. Jung thought that the recurrent dream signified that the unconscious was bringing up an incest memory as compensation, intending that it should be introduced into consciousness and remembered. But since incest traumas could not be assimilated by consciousness – Jung knew of no case where an incest trauma was not at least partially repressed – the dream was reduced to bringing it back again and again in the vain hope that it could somehow be assimilated. Assimilation was only possible if consciousness could understand the *symbolic* meaning of incest. Jung therefore recommended getting the patient to reproduce fantasies about incest, using active imagination if the dreams themselves did not produce the necessary material. But he hedged on whether incest had actually taken place.[41]

In all these cases Jung was clearly labouring conscientiously to find the individual roots of the dream. Yet all too often the patients seemed to be optional extras, mere intellectual cannon fodder for the purpose of providing dream material that could be interpreted in an archetypal manner. Professor Eugen Bohler reported that he had had two dreams: in the first, a lake was covered all over by a pattern of opposing fishes; then a revolution took place and the dreamer solved it by letting the fish devour each other. In the second, Bohler found himself on an old battlefield and dug the heart of a fallen soldier out of the mud. Jung's anodyne comment on all this was that when you are in the middle you are in the flow and need the heart of a warrior.[42] One wonders how useful Bohler found this advice.

Another academic, Professor O. Schrenk, reported a dream series which seems to cry out for Freudian interpretation. In the first dream a revered teacher offered to show his daughter sunbathing naked; in the second, Schrenk urinated and the urine was 'highly unaesthetic'; the third featured a colleague, a young French Jew, who had been in a concentration camp and now found himself back there while a mighty eagle circled overhead, which he thought was either Schrenk or Jung. Given the multiple resonances, Jews, eagles (*l'aiglon*) and the urino-genital motifs, this looks like an open-and-shut case for the sleuth of Berggasse 19. Jung's interpretation, on the other hand, could be considered by some to be more than a little eccentric. He states categorically that the eagle is an archetype, recalling Zeus and Ganymede and proceeds to argue that the figure of Sophia splits itself into the 'Wise Old Man' and his daughter.[43]

Sometimes Jung's interpetations are so banal that it is amazing that he thought the recipients of his letters could draw any sustenance from them at all. Aniela Jaffé told of a dream in which she was in a cellar with a boy and an old man; the boy had been given an electrical installation for Christmas, and a large copper pot was suspended from the ceiling with electric wires going in all directions. Instead of querying who the boy and the old man might be, Jung blandly pronounced that the dream symbolized the self as apparatus.[44]

Jung's religious and mythological interpretations of dreams did sometimes convince, but only when the dream imagery pointed unmistakably towards his favourite motifs and were not distorted artificially to fit a preconceived mould. His correspondent Wilhelm Laiblin's dream, in which the sky changed, the stars fell down as in a cloudburst and two or three moons disintegrated into fragments which finally disappeared, fell into the category capable of plausible explanation. Jung interpreted the falling stars as the collapse of an entire world of obsolescent ideas, and the meaning of the dream that when official religion (with the three moons standing for the Trinity) fails the individual, the psyche steps in and provides numinous nourishment.[45]

Another correspondent, Grant Watson, related a dream that was already so far inside the Jungian idiom that as a challenge to interpretation it was a gift. Watson had three dreams. In the first, a magic horse had been killed in battle and the dreamer carried its entrails around for years; then one day he was going down a flight of stairs and met the resuscitated horse coming up; the horse devoured all its own entrails and presented itself for Watson to mount. In the second dream, a curtain went up in a theatre and the people all lay down as if they were dead but still talking to each other. The third was the most complex of all. The dreamer was in the desert with two Hindu guides and his feet were those of an old man. They came to a place where an initiation ceremony was going on; deep cuts were made in Watson's feet and he had to stand in boiling water. He saw his own idealized image in a concave mirror and was told by his guides to continue the desert journey alone. He then met two new Hindu guides who led him to a building where his father, stepfather and mother greeted him with joy. He then proceeded on a long climb ending at the edge of a deep precipice, where a voice commanded him to leap. After baulking several times he did so and found himself swimming 'deliciously into the blue of eternity'.

Jung seized on this material with alacrity. The dream of the horse represented the union with the animal soul. The second and third dreams showed the deadness of the Western outlook and the transmutation to the Eastern realization of Atman, where you go beyond the ego to the Self.[46]

Jung was nothing if not audacious in interpreting these dreams without a full knowledge of the writers, and thus against his own prescriptions, but his mightiest feat of instant dream interpretation occurred on a train. In the dining car he was sitting next to a martinet general of the old school who, unaware of the eminence of his fellow diner, told him, as to a complete stranger, a dream he had had the night before. Though firmly of the 'no nonsense' school, the general was completely bowled over by Jung's exposition and was totally convinced by his interpretation.[47]

It will be abdundantly clear how very different from Freud's interpretation of dreams was the kind of analysis pioneered by Jung. They diverged sharply both on the importance of dreams for the analytic process, Jung becoming ever more of a devotee while Freud backpedalled in the direction of transference, and on the meaning of dreams themselves and how to investigate them. Interpretation via archetypes and the collective unconscious was, for the Freudian school, largely mumbo-jumbo, while even Jung's most cherished principle in analysis of the personal unconscious –

that one can interpret characters in dreams as standing for aspects of the dreamer's ego (so, for example, a man who dreams of a sad girl may be expressing his own sadness) – was roundly condemned. On this subject Freud said, 'I should reject as a meaningless and unjustifiable piece of speculation the notion that *all* figures that appear in a dream are to be regarded as fragmentations and representations of the dreamer's own ego.'[48]

Jung, as we have seen, hit back at both free association and the sexual interpretation of dreams. He thought it was the paradox of free association that, while taking the dreamer too far away from the original dream image, unlike his own circular and controlled association in active imagination, it always led back inevitably to the emotional thoughts or complexes that were unconsciously captivating the mind; free association, in other words, was 'reductive' since it was destined always to bring you back to the same place, wherever you started from.[49]

Reductive too was the idea that all dreams expressed wish fulfilment or were suppressed wishes. He conceded that some of them were, but others were non-fulfilment of wishes and were rather fulfilments of fears or anxieties. Others again, the majority in fact, were compensatory, and a significant minority were prospective. It was therefore nonsense, Jung maintained, that all dreams could be thought to be sexual in origin.[50]

Yet for Jung the most central Freudian fallacy was that the manifest content of dreams masked a latent content.[51] This was a proposition he attacked again and again. Dreams were neither deliberate nor arbitrary fabrications but natural phenomena which were exactly what they appeared to be; they did not disguise, distort or lie.[52]

Jung even tried to suggest why Freud had been misled into making a distinction between manifest and latent content. He argued that Freud's theories were overwhelmingly the product of his female patients, and the dynamic wishes of women were a prime source of error to analysts.[53]

Yet it was typical of Jung's thinking that the idea of dreams as open, ingenuous phenomena, bearing their meaning openly on their faces was often modified to the point where it disappeared altogether. He maintained, in contradiction both to this general theory and to the moral of the 'mountaineer dream', that dreams portending death did not indicate the death of an individual.[54] To a large extent the clash of Freudian and Jungian perspectives on dreams was a conflict over the meaning of symbols. When Jung first broke with Freud, he criticized him for interpreting symbols one-dimensionally: every symbol had at least two meanings so that, for example, a snake in a dream might have a phallic meaning *and* a non-phallic meaning.[55] But in his later writings Jung argued that what Freud called symbols were merely signs; a true symbol was a much more complex affair.

Jung was very proud of the distinction he drew between signs and symbols and often returned to his cherished definition: that a sign denotes something known, whereas a symbol, properly so-called, pointed away towards something as yet unknown.[56] If you employed a sexual interpretation of dreams, you knew in advance what the 'symbols' represented – Jung teasingly suggested that Freud would have interpreted Plato's allegory of the cave as a disguised uterus fantasy – so such things as 'phallic symbols' were not symbols but only signs.[57] Hence the famous dictum 'the penis is merely a phallic symbol.'

Another argument Jung used – and one more redolent of linguistic philosophy than familiar Jungianism – was that a symbol was a *particular* manifestation of something unknown, as opposed to the archetype, which resembled the Platonic form; thus the mandala was a symbol which hinted at the archetype of the Self. And since, on the Platonic analogy, there had to be an archetype that underlay and was logically prior to sexual symbolism, it followed that sexuality could not be a primary category or a first cause.[58]

The battle between Freudian and Jungian perspectives on dreams is once again that, respectively, between the 'extravert' approach making symbols stand for real objects in the external world and the 'introvert' one, referring them to categories in the psyche. In philosophical terms it could be seen as the irreconcilable clash between realism and idealism. The distaste for the external world also comes through in Jung's differentiation between a symbol and an icon: an icon is a mere primitive talisman, but a true symbol denotes a religious experience that can only be expressed obliquely as it transcends understanding.[59]

There is some support for the Jungian theory of symbols. The historian of psychoanalysis Paul Ricoeur criticized Freud for reading symbols back to their ontogenetic and phylogenetic origin and insisted, like Jung, that symbols should be read progressively because 'the truth of a given moment lies in the subsequent moment.'[60] Yet the central problem about Jungian symbols is either that by explaining everything they in effect explain nothing, or that they act simply as the feedback mechanisms in an entirely circular system. So almost every symbol Jung quotes turns out to be a symbol of the Self. Christ is the symbol of the Self, the Holy Grail is the symbol of the Self, the fish is a symbol of the Self, the cross is a symbol of individuation, and so on.[61] Other symbols seem capable of protean mutations. *Pace* his tolerant and open-minded statement about the snake as phallic symbol in 1913, Jung very soon reached the point where a snake *never* functioned as a phallic symbol: a singularly versatile symbol, it was at various times a projection of the saurian within us, the sign of a mother-complex or the sign of an approaching illness.[62] When a snake appeared in a dream together with its enemy, the secretary bird, this was taken to represent a conflict within the collective unconscious between the spiritual and chthonic principles.[63] Similarly aeroplanes functioned as the projection of the repressed barbaric, a warning of danger or a symbol of the Trinity.

In general methodological terms, it was not surprising that so-called sexual symbols such as the phallus turned out to have a non-sexual significance, since on the Jungian compensation theory the conscious could influence the unconscious rather than vice versa. The determination to turn sexual aetiology on its head sometimes reached bizarre proportions as Jung strained to avoid a sexual interpretation ('for naïve minds') even when it stared him in the face. Even when a series of paintings by a fifty-five-year-old woman patient clearly hinted at vaginal symbolism, complete with snake motifs, Jung deliberately avoided anything that smacked of Freudianism and spoke of the paintings as 'the initial stages of the way to individuation'.

In the opinion of many, Jung's work on dreams and symbols was his finest achievement, far ahead of the speculative work on archetypes or the 'empirical' research on psychological types. Yet it suffered from the very reductive, aprioristic flaw of which Jung so often accused Freud. The methods of amplification and assimilation often looked like nothing so much as the therapist putting his finger in the scales, directing patients' associations and thus 'leading the witness'. Whenever a patient had a dream that could be accommodated to the notion of the collective unconscious, Jung fixed on that aspect as the interpretation and filled in the details, often reducing the analysand to a mere cipher. Even Anthony Storr, a judicious and fairminded Jungian was led to remark, 'Jung was . . . inclined to see collective material in dreams which could equally well be looked upon as merely personal. Like every creative person he sometimes oversold his own creative discoveries.'[64]

Chapter Twenty

AMERICA, AMERICA

In July 1935 Jung celebrated his sixtieth birthday and entered a five-year period during which, after a long lay-off, he turned his attention once more to the English-speaking world. He began by going to London to lecture at the Tavistock Clinic. He never lost his love of England; some said he even looked English in his casual clothes. He liked everything about England: the language, which he spoke with a public-school accent, with just a soupçon of Swiss intonation; the English genius for games; and the English channel itself, where he spent many happy days sailing.[1]

Travel to England frequently seemed to involve Jung in encounters with the occult – whether ghosts, standing stones or Arthurian places – and this time he had an experience of *déjà vu* which led him to declare that if reincarnation was true, then in a previous life he had been an Englishman.[2] *Déjà vu* he explained as a sort of memory hallucination. If it occurred habitually, it was likely to be a dream precognition which we have forgotten and then partially remember when the foreseen event occurs, thus triggering the idea of *déjà vu*.[3]

However, Jung's professional experiences in London in 1935 were not quite so happy, partly because the charges of anti-Semitism and

Nazi sympathy had followed him across the Channel. For the first time in England he was greeted not as a prophet but as a possible crank. The transcripts of the Tavistock lectures show Jung getting a rough ride from British doctors, who accused him, variously, of failing to distinguish affect from feeling or, in his word-association tests, the conscious guilt of the criminal from the unconscious guilt of the neurotic. The general complaint at the conference was about lack of clarity.[4]

Jung's next trip to the English-speaking world came about in an odd way. In 1936 Harvard University was due to hold its tercentenary celebrations and the university authorities were determined to make a big splash, especially since a distinguished alumnus, Franklin Delano Roosevelt, was now president of the USA. The tercentenary committee proposed to offer the honorary degree of DSc to Freud, but his pupil Erik Erikson, who had emigrated to the United States, advised that Freud would not accept because of his advanced age and serious illness (he was suffering from cancer). The psychology subcommittee, not wishing the emoluments to pass to the rival department of economics, proposed instead that the degree be awarded to Jung, who accepted with alacrity.[5]

There was some suggestion that Jung should make his way to the USA by the newly opened clipper route from Lisbon to New York via the Azores, but he always detested flying, ostensibly on the grounds that you were bound to leave bits of your psyche behind if you travelled at such speeds: 'Airplanes and such devilish inventions ought to be avoided.'[6] First he spent his summer holidays of 1936 in Switzerland and, with his growing interest in alchemy, was much struck by a synchronicity. While trying to resolve the symbolism of the fish, he found a dead snake with a dead fish sticking out of its mouth. Interpreting this as meaning that the pagan spirit was trying to eat the Christian spirit and that the reconciling spirit sought by alchemists would be born from these opposites, he carved the image of snake with fish on the wall of his courtyard at Bollingen, which he was then having extended.[7]

In August 1936 he set out for New York by ocean liner, this time accompanied by his wife Emma, who hitherto had not travelled much, officially because she was too busy with the children, but really because Jung had not wanted his philandering style cramped. On arrival in New York in early September he was questioned about his political sympathies and his attitude to the Jews. He told reporters: 'I want to emphasise that I despise politics wholeheartedly: thus I am neither a Bolshevik, nor a National Socialist, nor an anti-Semite. I am a neutral Swiss and even in my own country I am uninterested in politics, because I am convinced that 99% of politics are mere symptoms and anything but a cure for social evils. About 50% of politics is definitely obnoxious inasmuch as it poisons the utterly incompetent mind of the masses.'[8]

At Harvard he lectured on his fourfold theory of wholeness, starting with the quartet of thinking, feeling, sensation and intuition and proceeding to more mystical quaternities. Apparently he impressed his hosts as an old-fashioned eccentric, and two stories testify to this. The first, which is based on a number of good independent accounts, tells how Jung, who was staying at the house of the distinguished Harvard neurologist, Stanley Cobb, put his shoes outside his bedroom door at night to be cleaned, in accordance with the practice of Europeans of the time who were used to servants. Cobb, who had no servants, obligingly polished them for him.[9] Whether consciously or unconsciously, Cobb later had his revenge. He had a stammer and, when introducing Jung in the large amphitheatre of the Massachusetts General Hospital, after a number of generous prefatory remarks handed over to – Dr Freud! This was surely one of the great Freudian slips in the history of psychology.[10]

Another story about Jung at Harvard seems more suspect. It is said that the distinguished visitor realized he had not brought with him the correct academic garb to wear at the honorary degree ceremony and therefore went to a theatrical costumier's and rented a southern Senator's regalia – frock coat, string tie, broad-brimmed black hat. On the day of the ceremony it rained in Harvard Yard, and the blacking of the hat ran down onto his clothes, streaking shirt, collar, coat and face. From the facetious punch-line provided by Robert Grinnell, who told the story, we may suspect that it is a 'Yaley' invention: 'Harvard *does* bring out the shadow in a man.'[11] On the other hand, Jung's taste for buffoonery and particularly for large-brimmed hats is well known, so perhaps there is something in the story after all.

After finishing his business at Harvard, Jung lectured on dream analysis at Bailey Island, Maine. He loved the Maine coast as much as the English channel and relished sailing and exploring the bays and inlets.[12] Then he went down to New York for the final part of his trip and checked into the Waldorf Astoria for some leisurely days until embarkation on 3 October, visiting museums and sightseeing. He was pressed hard for his opinion of President Roosevelt, whom he had observed closely during the Harvard celebrations, but declined to express his views until he had berthed in England. The reasons for his circumspection soon became clear. While admiring aspects of Roosevelt's personality, Jung had no affection for him, and tended to bracket him with Hitler and Mussolini as another 1930s dictator/avatar of his country.[13]

Jung was not yet ready to divulge his visceral antipathy for Roosevelt, whom he later called 'the limping messenger of the Apocalypse,' but the hints are already there for the perceptive to see. 'Roosevelt is the stuff all right, only the circumstances are not bad enough,'[14] is a statement that, if it means anything at all, means that Roosevelt had the sensibility of Hitler and Mussolini but without their fragile economies. It was not surprising that Jung, the man of the Right, should have disliked the architect of the New Deal with his Keynesian programmes of government spending.

After the bustle of the Waldorf Astoria Jung opted to make a quiet hotel in Regent's Park his base while in London lecturing at St Bartholomew's Hospital. In these lectures he tried to distance himself from the image of Jung the anti-Semite and Nazi fellow-traveller.[15]

On his return to Switzerland Jung cut down on his analytical and psychotherapeutic work in order to have more time for studying alchemy. In 1937 he visited London again, but the highlight of that year was his invitation to deliver the Terry Lectures at Yale on 'Psychology and Religion'. This time it was arranged that Jung would stay at Jonathan Edwards College at Yale, and the master detailed two or three undergraduates to have regular lunches with him and report back any sign of discontent on the part of Yale's principal guest that year.[16]

The lectures, given at the beginning of October 1937, went well, especially as Jung made a point of placating the many Americans alienated by his remarks on the 'Jewish question'. In the course of an exegesis designed to show that the archetypes were the engine of the religious impulse, and that the quest for the spiritual was as deeply embedded in mankind as the instincts of sex and aggression, Jung managed to work in a number of disparaging references to Nazi ideology.

In a 'God-fearing' milieu Jung's praise for religion found a ready audience, even if the subtler nuances of his heterodoxy were not always picked up. The result was the kind of packed house associated only with the celebrity lecturer. Jung, the devotee of 'small is beautiful', had asked for an intimate lecturing ambience, but the organizers started his lectures in a large theatre, promising they would switch him to a smaller one later. Normally, numbers fall off rapidly at a series of lectures, as the novelty wears off and familiarity and routine take over, but this time the reverse happened. The first lecture was attended by 700 people, but by the end of the series this figure had swollen to 3,000.

Gratifying as this was, Jung's favourite memory of his time at Yale was his one and only meeting with the pioneer parapsychologist J.B. Rhine. Recently appointed professor of psychology at Duke University, Rhine had devised laboratory experiments involving packs of cards which put parapsychology on a statistical basis. Since some of his human guinea pigs achieved considerably higher scores than could be accounted for by the calculus of probability, Rhine seemed to have made a breakthrough and established extrasensory perception as a scientific reality. When Jung and Rhine came together at a lunch party, there was a predictable meeting of minds, and for Jung Rhine became, second only to William James, *the* American psychologist.[17]

After the Terry lectures Jung went down to New York city, where he gave a seminar on dream and symbol interpretation from 16 to 26 October 1937. By this time his reputation was decidedly mixed. On the one hand, there were dedicated Jungian enthusiasts like Dr Henderson, who later made a name for himself as Jackson Pollock's analyst.[18] And there were distinguished Jungian 'fellow travellers', like William McDougall (1871–1938), an American psychiatrist who had submitted his dreams to Jung. Even here, though, Jung once more proved his incapacity for male friendship by making scathing remarks about MacDougall to mutual acquaintances.[19] Most of all, Jung was attracting more and more celebrated and wealthy patients. The poet Robert Lowell's mother, for instance, a friend of Mary Foote's, was referred to Jung by the psychiatrist Merrill Moore in the mid-1930s, and had many sessions pouring out her worries about her disturbed son.[20]

On the other hand, some of Jung's significant early sympathizers now held him at arm's length because of his views on Nazis and Jews.

Dr Hadley Cantril, a young professor of psychology at Princeton who would make his name with an analysis of the panic caused in 1938 by Orson Welles's overconvincing radio version of H.G. Wells's *The War of the Worlds*, showed that he was already a master of the psychology of rumour by bruiting it about that Jung was a confidante of Hitler and a frequent visitor to Berchtesgaden.[21] Smith Ely Jelliffe, the man who had invited Jung to lecture at Fordham in 1912, wrote to him for an explanation of the *Zentralblatt* affair, to which Jung replied with a couple of evasive letters.[22] The friendship dwindled, and by the time of the Terry lectures Jelliffe was completely alienated. He told Ernest Jones in December 1937, 'I saw Jung this fall. He was distinctly his age and gave a very religious preachment to a lot of female admirers. I was not much impressed, quite the reverse. He seems to have reverted to his pastoral ancestor.'[23]

This was Jung's last visit to the United States. It is remarkable that his attitude to North America and Americans scarcely altered from 1909 to 1937, in which time he visited the country nine times. It has often been said that Jung was pro-American, in contrast to the notably anti-American Freud, but the truth is more complex. Because he was a man of the Right and a rabid anti-communist, Jung supported the USA politically, though he had many reservations about the nation as 'mass society'. His basic pro-Americanism was aided by the money and attention lavished on him by American millionaires – the McCormicks, Rockefellers, Mellons and many others. The Svengali-like fascination he had for these plutocrats was puzzling, especially since he repaid their largesse with amused derision. He enjoyed dominating them and told one American (female) millionaire that if she wished to consult him, she would have to leave her Rolls-Royce at her Zürich hotel and travel out to Küsnacht by train. He made another female of the genus sit on the floor during a consultation and pointedly did not offer her a chair.[24]

Yet for much of the rest of American life Jung had nothing but contempt. He affected the kind of disdain for the 'almighty dollar' which is the prerogative only of the already independently rich, and told many stories of the Americans' 'pitiful' worship of Mammon. Once he analysed a well-known American politician who told him all his secrets, then had second thoughts and said, 'My God, you could get a million dollars for what I've told you!' Jung loftily told the politician he was not interested in money and would have forgotten all the 'secrets' within a fortnight.[25]

If he despised US politics, he did not have a much higher opinion of American academe. American universities, with their fanatical insistence on co-education, were simply 'animus incubators' that destroyed the truly feminine in women; as for the faculty, they lacked a thorough grounding in Classics, without which Jung thought no man properly educated, and were thus beyond the pale.[26] He also thought that American education in general neglected the humanities in favour of a narrow drilling in the natural sciences.[27] Nor did he have any great opinion of American academic psychology. Americans made poor patients, for although they were physically in Europe they were always dreaming about the USA and believed everything doctors told them.[28]

Most of all, the combination of matriarchy and promiscuity made the USA, in Jung's opinion, a sexually sick country, where relations between the sexes were more unnatural and far more tense than in Europe. Jung traced promiscuity to the basic lack of privacy in North America, with its total absence of hedges or fences round gardens, which he personally found both disgusting and terrifying. Promiscuity had dire results, most notably and paradoxically that rapport between the sexes declined.[29]

Jung summed up the basic sexual neuroses of the USA in 1912 and never saw any reason to change his opinion. He thought American women had to work harder to attract American men, which was why they liked to marry 'dangerous' foreigners. American women were not happy with their husbands, and this was how matriarchy arose, for American men, who had never learned how to love them, were content to let them rule the roost. 'Momism' was a manifestation of the deeper phenomenon that American men had turned their women into mothers. The basic problem in American marriages was that women were their husbands' mothers, 'yet at the same time there is in turn the old, old, primitive, desire to be possessed, to yield, to surrender.' On the other hand, there was nothing there to surrender to, since the American male had used up all his energies on his business rivals.[30]

Matriarchy engendered prudery, both a barrier to libido and a mask for brutality; if it could eliminate prudery, the USA could be the greatest country in the world. Brutality, Jung thought, was ingrained in the texture of American life.[31] The USA was at once the most emotional and the most self-contained country, but the effort to maintain self-control in the face of brute instinct produced neurasthenia and a suspicion of the intellect such that a man with more than one idea was not to be trusted.[32]

Since Jung revelled in the attribution of specific characteristics to individual nations, it was only to be expected that he had a field day in the USA. It was an abiding interest of his to elaborate some master principle as the key to unlocking national psychology. He put forward various candidates as his master principle: climate, geography, race. In his Freudian period he told Freud that climate was largely responsible for the frequency of neurosis in America, and especially the colossal temperature differences between summer and winter: how else to explain the puzzling fact that the Indians had been unable to populate the continent more densely?[33]

Later he switched his attention to the impact of physical space and worked out the highly eccentric theory that the middle of any landmass is the qualitative point of equilibrium (or Self, one might say). He argued that on the east coast of the USA you got the 'poor white trash', left behind when the people of energy went west. In the mid-West you encountered the most psychologically stable people in the USA and on the west coast the least balanced. Similarly, in Europe, the eccentric Celtic fringes of Wales, Scotland and Ireland formed the west coast, and the most stable countries, France and England, were in the middle. Germany was on the cusp, and beyond.[34]

Also interesting is Jung's distaste for California and west-coast culture, evident in a number of his writings, as in the dismissive comment on Aimée Semple MacPherson, the religious cult leader of the 1930s.[35] He was once asked why he had never visited Los Angeles and replied, 'I don't need to go there, since so many of my patients come from there.'[36] He even suggested that the reason for the higher proportion of patients in asylums in New York was that eastcoasters drew a harder line between normality and madness than westcoasters.[37]

The racism inherent in Jung's disparaging remarks about Slavs and Celts became overt when he attempted to give a racial interpretation of the North American unconscious. He began by drawing a contrast between the English and the German national psychology, so as to throw the American into sharper relief. He thought the fact that the Englishman felt at home everywhere in the world was what made him a careless motorist; the German, on the other hand, who felt a stranger everywhere because he suffered from a national feeling of inferiority, let himself be overimpressed by foreign cultures and mores. The American's problem was having to assimilate primitive cultures in his midst.[38]

Pondering on the aboriginal inhabitants of North America, Jung produced a version of the 'going native' idea he had applied to white colonial rule in Africa.[39] Jung thought that the unconscious of the white American had been invaded from two directions; by the Red man and the Black man. The American imbibed the Red man from the soil and the Black man from the institution of slavery; the consequence was that the American was a 'European with Negro behaviour and an Indian soul'.[40]

In Jung's view Red Indian influence in American culture was all-pervasive. Americans were obsessed with the idea of the heroic ideal, acquired through identification with the Red Man; as a result American sport, the toughest in the world, as evinced by, say, the Indianapolis 500 motor race, was one from which the idea of play had completely disappeared. Jung was in deadly earnest about the 'Heroic Ideal', describing it as the collective attitude or *spiritus loci* of the United States, just as the corresponding *mentalité* in England was the 'gentleman', in Germany the Idea and in France *la gloire*.[41]

Moreover, college initiation ceremonies were like Indian rites of passage, and secret societies like the Ku Klux Klan were like primitive mystery religions. White religious sects had spiritual leaders like the Indian shamans; spiritualism and Christian Science derived from Indian religion; the power of advertising, with its slogans and 'power words' was simply an extension of the magic formulae used by Indian medicine men.[42] Even that quintessential American manifestation, the skyscraper, was a transmogrified Indian form as a comparison of the New York skyline with that of the Taos pueblo would show.[43] This was simply an aspect of the well-known phenomenon whereby conquerors tended to succumb to the spirit of the conquered, the victorious Romans to a Jewish mystery religion, and so on.

Controversial as these ideas were, Jung capped them with the assertion that the 'chthonic' qualities of blood and earth in America crept into the unconscious and eventually manifested themselves physically. On one of his first American visits he observed a stream of workers coming out of a factory at the end of their shift and remarked to his American companion that he never dreamed there was such a high percentage of Indian blood in New York State. His companion answered laughingly that he was willing to bet there was not one drop of Indian blood in the veins of any of these hundreds of men. Jung did not believe him and affected to be stupefied by the extent of the 'Indianization' of the American people. He was convinced that skull measurements, physiognomy and other physical attributes changed over time to meet the 'chthonic' demands of a given land.[44]

Apart from his 'Indianization', the white man in North America was also troubled by a 'Negro-complex'. Jung claimed to have noticed this on his very first visit to the USA in 1909; it was an inevitable consequence of living cheek by jowl with what Jung called 'lower' races and it led to sexual repression.[45]

Utilizing that freedom to generalize that so grates on a modern readership, Jung said there were three main characteristics of American blacks: they were ignorant, they were unable to look into their own thoughts, and they were extraordinarily religious. Yet their influence in the United States was as pervasive as the Red Indian's. The naïvety of Americans could be correlated with Negro childishness; the endless gabbling of Americans was more like the chattering in an African village than everyday life in a German town; the lack of privacy and the mass sociability recalled the communal hut life of Africa.[46]

Jung thought that white Americans had even inherited their loose-jointed way of walking – the swinging hips of women and the swinging gait of the men – from their black ex-slaves. Even in laughter the influence could be detected.[47] What, then, of the 'Negro-complex'? Here Jung utilized his favourite notion of the 'shadow'. The black man functioned as the white man's 'shadow', as was obvious from an analysis of the dreams of his American patients, while the Red Man's image worked at the deeper layer of the collective unconscious.

Jung thought it made a great difference where you were born and that people born out of their 'proper' continent took on the appearance of the peoples of the host continent: so Europeans born in Asia looked Asiatic, Germans born in the USA looked American, and all second- and third-generation Americans acquired Indian features. This complicated the study of American psychology, since at another level the black man and the red man were to the American white what Wotan was to the Germans; in both cases the 'inferior' aspect reminded them of their childhood and prehistory.[48]

There seems little question but that these observations are racist, especially if judged by the strict 'politically correct' criteria of the 1990s, but it is important to be clear that Jung was no Negrophobe. In his patronizing and paternalistic way he was very fond of the American black, though doubtless modern critics would say he liked him in an Uncle Tom posture. He loved Negro spirituals and Roark Bradford's short stories, especially 'Ole Man Adam an' his Chillun', and had a particular fondness for Marc Connelly's play *The Green Pastures*, which featured Old Testament stories seen through the eyes of simple plantation slaves, viewing 'De Lawd' as a sometimes angry, though usually benevolent 'boss' and Heaven as a gigantic fish-fry.[49] Of the Lord Chamberlain's refusal to give *The Green Pastures* a licence in England in 1931, Jung remarked that censors there must be possessed by the devil.[50]

Jung also liked the American black's sense of humour. He recalled the time in 1909 when he was dining with a po-faced New England family and his jokes were greeted with condescending smiles. Finally he told his best joke and there was an avalanche of laughter – from the black servant waiting at table.[51] He was also fond of arguing that, if the Messiah came from the Jews, an insignificant people in the Ancient World, it was entirely consistent to argue that the next 'redeemer' might be a black.[52]

Two further aspects of Jung's attitude to the USA are worth mentioning. First, Freud always felt that American pragmatism was the irreconcilable enemy of psychoanalysis and any other depth psychology, and that the American mania for cutting corners and getting quick results had seduced Jung (in 1912) and Otto Rank (in 1924).[53] Jung often pronounced fearlessly on aspects of American life, using inadequate or misleading facts as his basis. A good example came during one of his ritual denunciations of the machine age, when he asserted (in 1930) that the average life expectancy was only forty in New York as against sixty in Switzerland; this was meant to be part of the proof of his 'small is beautiful' thesis.[54] In fact in 1930 life expectancy was identical in both places, and was at the same point (the low seventies) in 1980. Jung was always unreliable when talking about historical events and he had no real understanding of historical processes as professional scholars would understand them.[55] Moreover, he was frequently unsound on facts. He claimed that Napoleon's *Grande Armée* had been completely wiped out and that Alexander the Great's army was 'crushed' in India (in fact

Alexander turned back after defeating the Indian prince Porus at the Hydaspes).[56]

There were other aspects of American culture, apart from the 'black question', that suggested for Jung the enactment of the ego-shadow conflict, and perhaps the most obvious was the Western movie.[57] Jung was an enthusiastic, though not especially critical, viewer of films, and sometimes mentions ones which have drawn his attention. He was impressed by *Atlantic*, directed by E.A. Dupont – an Anglo-German version of the *Titanic* disaster, which he saw when it was premiéred in Berlin in November 1929.[58] But by far his favourite movie was *The Student of Prague*, a 1920s product of German expressionism. It was not surprising that Jung found the cinema interesting, for here was a unique and unprecedented way of touching the collective and unconscious fantasies of a world audience, he commented.[59]

It has sometimes been alleged that Jung was a philistine in artistic matters, and it is true that his taste in painting was limited, undisciplined and eclectic. He admired the work of Francesco Colonna and Dali's *The Sacrament of the Last Supper*, but could see little more in Van Gogh than schizophrenia.[60] He particularly loathed modern paintings: 'I cannot occupy myself with modern art any more. It is too awful.' Of Dadaism he remarked, 'It's too idiotic to be schizophrenic.'[61]

The one modern painter who did fascinate Jung was Picasso, even though he refused to withdraw his overall critique that modern art was just one long scream, as in the Munch painting, and was therefore a more appropriate subject for psychological research than for art criticism.[62] What he found intriguing about Picasso was that his painting contained archetypal material: the famous 'Blue Period', for instance, demonstrated a *Nekyia* or underworld journey, complete with a series of regressions in the Jungian sense. Jung bracketed Picasso with James Joyce, in the respect that their work indicated that, if subjected to a profound psychic disturbance, they would react with a schizophrenic syndrome rather than neurosis; this was an example of the 'latent psychosis' Jung wrote about so much – meaning that Joyce and Picasso's work was closer to the artefacts produced by schizophrenics than to the scribblings and doodlings of neurotic patients.[63]

Jung deeply resented it if anyone suggested that Picasso was a peerless artist who could not be critizied. One of his classic prima donna performances at the Ascona conferences occurred when Herbert Read was reading a paper on Picasso and seemed to Jung to be overpraising the Spanish master. Jung shuffled uneasily in his seat and became progressively more sullen, rude and bad-tempered. Read sometimes quoted Jung in his paper, but because he did not always make it clear when he was quoting him and when he was using his own words, Jung began interrupting loudly to point out which was a quotation and which was not.[64]

Jung's musical taste was similarly conservative. He liked classical music properly so-called – Bach, Handel, Mozart and the pre-Mozartians. He was once so moved by Schubert's D Minor string quartet that he had to turn the gramophone off. He did not get on so well with Beethoven: the sonatas distressed him and the late quartets exasperated him.[65]

The sole romantic composer who interested him, and to whom he often refers, was Wagner; *Parsifal*, in particular, seemed a metaphor for the individuation process.[66] Modern music left him cold and, although he loved Negro spirituals, he hated jazz, which he found 'silly and stultifying'. He loathed any form of muzak or arrangements of classical themes played as background music or musical wallpaper, and once, annoyed by the playing of a radio in a restaurant in Ticino, he got up and pulled the plug out of the wall. 'I could slay a man who plays Bach in banal surroundings,' was one of his sayings.[67] However, it would probably be fair to say that it was only in the last decade of his life that Jung realized the importance of music from the standpoint of his own psychological theories.

Jung was widely, if not deeply, read in world literature, but preferred to return to the works that either exemplified archetypal themes or were redolent of what Thomas Mann, in his essay on Tolstoy, called 'heroic gigantism'. As an example of the former Jung singled out Melville's *Moby Dick*, which he regarded as incontestably the greatest American novel, and Dostoevsky's *The Brothers Karamazov*, if only because the three brothers and the father formed a quaternity.[68] Examples of the latter included Balzac's *Comédie Humaine* and Zola's *Rougon-Macquart* cycle; Jung knew his Zola well, even the minor works. However, probably his single favourite book was Anatole France's *Penguin Island*, which he frequently cites approvingly.

Jungian interpretation of the great literary classics has proliferated into a massive growth industry, but Jung himself rarely analysed any of the indisputable literary masterpieces at any length. He believed that literary products of dubious merit, or works not really in the first class, were often of much greater interest to the psychologist than the timeless classics; moreover, the resolutely non-psychological novel provided the most fertile soil for psychological elucidation.[69]

For this reason too he enjoyed popular novels and especially detective stories.[70] The Argentine writer Victoria Ocamp, who visited Jung in 1934, found the works of Edgar Wallace on his shelves. Conan Doyle was another favourite, and the Sherlock Holmes stories have become another happy hunting ground for critics of a Freudian or Jungian inclination.[71] But by far Jung's favourite popular novelist was Georges Simenon, whose books were present in his library in far greater numbers than any other fiction.[72]

Many have drawn attention to the role of the unconscious in creativity and the link between the world of art and the world of dreams. Jung thought that art, like dreams, acted in a compensatory way.[73] There was compensation of another sort with artists, as such people must pay dearly for the divine gift of creativity; it was as though each person was born with a limited store of energy, and creativity burnt up most of the artist's.[74]

If Jung's taste in music, painting and literature was conservative, some of his ideas on art are surprisingly modern, even though the 'modernity' is arrived at by very different routes from that of the structuralist or the post-structuralist. Like them, Jung is sceptical about the reality of authors and creators as autonomous subjects, but for the obvious reason in his case that he considered the collective unconscious, not the individual ego, to be the source of art. Hence the surprisingly modern ring of the following: 'It is not Goethe who creates *Faust*, but *Faust* that creates Goethe.'[75] It was typical of Jung to be both a pro-American anti-American and an anti-modernist modernist.

Chapter Twenty-One

THE LURE OF THE ORIENT

On his return from the USA in late autumn 1937, Jung left almost immediately for India.[1] Earlier that year he had been invited by the British government to attend the twenty-fifth anniversary celebrations of the University of Calcutta, where he would be awarded the honorary degree of Doctor of Law, and his desire to visit the subcontinent had been quickened by two visitors from India in the early summer of 1937: Subramanya Iyer, spiritual adviser to the Maharajah of Mysore, and Paul Brunton, an English writer and specialist on India, and a pupil of the famous guru Ramana Maharishi, whose work had so fascinated Somerset Maugham. Jung was therefore motivated to go to India to activate that side of him which responded to the wisdom of the East.[2]

Jung was in any case glad to get away from Europe, where the accusations of Nazi sympathies still dogged him. Thomas Mann had by now gone public with some of his criticisms of Jung, and on Freud's eightieth birthday in 1936 referred to him as 'a bright but somewhat ungrateful offspring'.[3] Even Adler, whose work Jung often praised as the equal of Freud's, had been disgusted by Jung's anti-Semitism and in 1935 referred witheringly to his tolerance for fascism: 'We owe a particular advance in the use of the concept of complex to the not very original psychologist Jung, whose own complex seems to be that of a fellow traveller.'[4]

Jung may also have been in search of new elements to add to his own syncretic personal religion, for he postulated a catastrophic failure of belief in the West: 'Our blight is ideologies – they are the long-expected Antichrist! National Socialism comes as near to being a religious movement as any movement since AD 622. Communism claims to be paradise come to earth again. We are better protected against failing crops, inundations, epidemics and invasions from the Turk than we are against our own deplorable spiritual inferiority, which seems to have little resistance to psychic epidemics.'[5]

Jung travelled out to India by ship, joining it at Marseilles and following the traditional route of the British servants of the Raj, via Suez and Aden to Bombay. On the voyage out he was enraged to find European women wandering around the liner in trousers, and his fury increased later when he contrasted this ugly and unfeminine dress with the traditional garb of the Indian women. This was all part of the unisex hermaphroditism Jung so detested – the attempt to prove the unprovable, that the differences between the sexes were largely the results of culture and conditioning and not, as Jung asserted, immutable and irremediable differences sunk deep in biological soil.

Jung's thoughts on women's dress were reinforced once he was in India, for he thought the sari the perfect female garment; thus attired, even a fat woman was not disparaged, whereas in Europe such a female would have to starve herself to death. Yet although Jung hated to see women in trousers, he detested it equally if they wore clothes that were too sexy.[6] Jung was clearly deeply disturbed by the short skirts and décolletage ushered in by the 1920s, for he said sardonically that whereas fifty years before the sight of a modern woman would have seemed unutterably shocking, it was a fair inference that fifty years in the future it would be the height of elegance for women to go around naked.[7]

Indeed in general Jung's visit to India seems to have brought him out in a rash of sartorial parochialism, for once in the subcontinent he began denouncing the clothes of Indian men as unmasculine and laughed at the idea of a soldier with garlands of cloth between his legs.[8]

Jung arrived in Bombay in December 1937. Overwhelmed by the thought of a vast land mass lying behind the sprawling city, he hired a car and drove out into the countryside. At first, as he drove through jungle and past a clear blue lake, he thought he was truly on the verge of something sensational. But at the first village he came to, he found himself in the middle of an Indian movie and the entire village commandeered by the film crew. Disillusioned, he returned at once to Bombay.

Bombay depressed him with its seemingly meaningless bustle and ant-like existence: it seemed to him that in India everything had 'lived a hundred thousand times before'.[9]

From Bombay Jung travelled north to Delhi, where he noted the Islamic influences. Islam seemed to him a superior, more spiritual and more advanced religion than Hinduism, and he often rated it highly, second only to Buddhism and certain forms of Christianity, though well ahead of the Greek Orthodox Church.[10] In northern India the Hindu element in Indian culture seemed to have succumbed to the over-masculinity of the Sikhs and the Pathans; this manifested itself in architecture but also in the harsher way people in the north spoke to each other.

From Delhi he proceeded south east to Agra, where he found the Taj Mahal a revelation and visited the *stupas* (hill tombs) at the hill of Sanchi, where Buddha delivered his fire sermon. Since Buddhism was his favourite religion, this experience really did strike a chord and made up for the way the India of his imagination had so far failed to match the reality.[11] It seemed to him that the hill of Sanchi was as much the 'secret of India' as the Taj Mahal had been the secret of Islam, and it reinforced his belief that Islam was built on Eros and all other religions on Logos. Meanwhile Hinduism itself continued to have negative impact. He pressed on to Allahabad and the sacred city of Benares (Varanasi), in both of which places he was awarded honorary degrees, but was not impressed by the Hindu temples at Benares.

Things improved at the next stage of the itinerary, which was the far north of India at Darjeeling; Jung later said that the Himalayas were the most impressive thing about northern India just as the Buddhist residues were about the south.[12] At the monastery of Bhutia Busty near Darjeeling he had a long talk about mandalas with a lama called Lingdam Gomchen.[13] Then he visited the Darjeeling observatory, where he had a glowing experience not far short of the mystical transportation on the Athi plains of Kenya. The sun was setting, Sikkim was already in shadow and the mountains appeared blue up to 4,000 feet and then violet to 7,000 feet. In the middle of the ring of mountains was the world's third highest peak, Kanchenjunga, resplendent as a ruby. Jung was watching the sunset with a group of Indian scientists, all of whom, lost in wonder at the spectacle, spontaneously mouthed 'Om' without realizing it.[14]

The next stop was Calcutta, where Jung was duc to be awarded his honorary doctorate on 7 January 1938. Here he stayed with his contact Boshi Sen, in a quiet residence in Bosepara Lane.[15] So far Jung had avoided all contact with Hindu gurus, partly, he claimed, because he did not want to accept wisdom from others that he needed to attain for himself, and partly also because India was itself 'archetypal' and therefore less differentiated.[16] But at the university of Calcutta he did discuss with various Brahmins the idea of the extinction of consciousness. He said that it was impossible to gain the state of being 'not-conscious' while alive and still be able to remember it, as Hindus claimed. Patiently he argued that you could not get rid of the idea of ego even in the deepest state of *samadhi* (profound ecstasy), for the moments of existence would have been non-existent and left no memory trace.[17]

Using Calcutta as a base, Jung travelled south-west to Orissa province to visit the famous temple at Konarak, celebrated for its pagoda adorned with obscene sculptures. The clash of Western and Eastern sensibilities was again evident. Jung was accompanied by a Hindu pandit, and objected to the man's explanation that the *lingam* and *yoni* symbols were purely spiritual. He pointed to a group of leering peasants, obviously getting material for sexual fantasies. The pandit shrugged this off by saying they could not become spiritualized until they had first fulfilled their *karma*, but Jung was sceptical that young men could so easily forget their sexuality.

To an extent Jung was running with the hare and with the hounds. His quasi-Freudian 'recidivism' in the conversation at Konarak was a clear sign of his irritation with many aspects of Hinduism, but later he agreed that the obscenities of the Black Pagoda at Konarak could be studied as a means of self-knowledge. In the West sexuality was regarded as a purely personal biological and psychological affair, and relations between men and women were perceived as of paramount importance. This was a sign both of Western repression and of the failure to view sexuality symbolically, as the reconciliation of opposites. In the East food was more of a problem than sex, which was perceived primarily in holistic, spiritual terms. This was partly a function of the greater primitiveness of the East, since the more primitive a people the less repression and the more sexuality is accepted naturally, but it was also part of an eastern tradition of regarding carnality as a province of the Gods.

Back in Calcutta Jung went down with dysentery and was unable to attend the honorary degree ceremony. He was in hospital for ten days and admitted that he welcomed the breather after such a strenuous schedule across the subcontinent. Yet he had a last, and important, call to make before departing for Europe. He sailed to Ceylon, and here and in the extreme south of India found the Buddhist paradise he had sought. Ceylon struck him as being totally unlike India and nearer, in its touch of paradise, to a Polynesian isle.[18] He did not tarry long in Colombo, but headed for the hilly country of the interior, visiting the old royal city of Kandy and the Dalad-Maligama temple, containing the Holy Tooth of Buddha. Intoxicated by the drumming and singing, Jung realized that it was Buddhism that had made Ceylon and the south come alive for him as Benares, Calcutta and Orissa never had; these temple ceremonies summed up the relationship between the Self as eternal and the ego as bounded by space and time.

The superiority of Buddhism to other religions seemed to be summed up for Jung in one simple incident when two peasants in their carts met in a narrow street and could not pass one another. Whereas in Switzerland this would have led to a flood of vituperation, the two peasants simply bowed politely to each other and said, 'Passing disturbances, no soul,' – meaning that these events were taking place in the ephemeral world of *maya* or illusion and not in true reality.[19] Similarly, on another occasion he saw two boys fighting with their fists, but the fists always stopped in the air, inches away from the face.

Jung thought that what was most valuable about the wisdom of the East was contained in Buddhism. Van der Post has pointed out that when Jung spoke casually about 'the East', he invariably meant China. India was not really 'the East', as both Indians and Europeans had Sanskrit ancestors, which partly accounted for the love/hate relationship between India and Europe; there was an affection for the British even among the leaders of the Congress party that was unthinkable for Chinese, for whom all foreigners are 'devils'.[20] Buddhism, the symbol *par excellence* of the Orient, had disappeared from Indian life more fully than one could ever imagine Christianity disappearing in Europe and had migrated farther east.

It was not surprising that Jung was drawn to Buddhism. He preferred Buddha's mode of overcoming the world, by reason, to that of Christ, by sacrifice. His work is full of admiring remarks for the great sage and religious founder.[21] Another attractive feature of Buddhism for Jung was that, unlike Christianity, it had a genuine feeling for animals; unlike Christianity, too, it did not seek to deny the animal in humans and thus engender repression.[22]

From Ceylon Jung made a trip to Trivanndrum, capital of Travancore, where he met a disciple of Ramana Maharishi.[23] Then he embarked at Colombo for the voyage back to Europe. His Indian journey had provided the missing pieces in the jigsaw puzzle of alchemy with which he had been wrestling during the 1930s. He began writing feverishly and was so absorbed in his new alchemical synthesis that he did not even bother to go ashore when the ship docked at Bombay.[24]

When forced to rub shoulders with his fellow passengers, Jung took time to note the pecularities of the British in India. He had noticed that Indians tended to speak in small twittering voices – an obvious consequence of having large families (twenty-five to thirty persons) living in tiny houses. The servants of the Raj, on the other hand, to a man and woman, had equipped themselves with great booming voices as a compensation to disguise their essential timidity and nullity. Not far beneath the surface in the mind of every Briton in India was the memory of the mutiny of 1857, and Jung saw the booming voices as part of the confidence trick involved in the holding down of 360 million people by a tiny handful of soldiers and administrators.[25]

However, the booming voices and the determination to act at all times as if one were in a London suburb probably acted as a defence against 'going native'. Jung several times pointed out that there was no worse fate for a sensitive child than to be removed from its parents in India and sent to boarding-school in England after the unconscious influence of the subcontinent had moulded its instincts; even more disastrous was the enantiodromia when the young man or young woman was transported back to India, when the development which would have permitted adaptation in India had been interrupted by Western education and crippled by neglect. Reflecting on his Indian experiences, he reiterated the 'American lesson' that onc cannot conquer foreign soil, because the ancestor-spirits who dwell there reincarnate themselves in the new-born; he meant this, of course, not literally but psychologically.[26]

Jung returned to Switzerland at the end of February 1938, still ill. He consulted a specialist in tropical diseases and was advised to rest. The enforced convalescence gave him time to ponder his impressions of India and what it could teach the West. 1937 was the year when the Congress Party, under Jawaharlal Nehru, having previously boycotted British-sponsored elections in India, entered the electoral lists and swept the board. But the India of political struggle, of *swaraj* and the battle for independence, was not the India Jung was interested in, as a telltale remark made twenty years later reveals. At a time when India was not just an independent state but also a republic, Jung referred to its having obtained 'home rule'.[27]

He *did* confer with members of the Congress party but, significantly, not about politics. It was his great obsession, overpopulation, that was the subject of discussion, and he was reminded of his private remarks at the Vienna Kulturbund in 1931 when he said: 'There are few things which have caused as much anxiety, unhappiness and evil as the compulsion to give birth.' He stood by the remarks, maintaining that overpopulation was *the* major threat to the Earth's future and that we would very soon be unable to feed all the mouths on the planet. In India a single bad harvest was enough to precipitate famine while, thanks to modern hygiene and medicine, the death rate was declining.[28] He asked leading lights in the Congress party how they would avoid racial slaughter if and when they ruled India. He picked up from their answers that a considerable loss of life would actually be welcome, since the subcontinent's population increased by 34 million each year. He was delighted to find that there was little humbug in India, that in the East people admitted things that could not be admitted in the West, such as that disasters, natural or man-made, provided an effective safety valve for dealing with surplus population.[29]

The Indian experience confirmed Jung's holistic feelings, that ultimately everything links up with everything else, which was in itself evidence for a collective unconscious. There was a clear parallelism between the ritual mandalas of lamaism which he had discussed at the monastery in Darjeeling and the circular symbols drawn by educated patients undergoing treatment; there was a further organic connection between mandalas and *kundalini* yoga, the views of the Tantrists, classical Chinese philosophy and Chinese yoga; other parallels were in children's paintings, the prehistoric mandalas of Zimbabwe, the sword-paintings from the healing ceremonies of Navajo Indians and the visions and eschatological warnings of mystics like Hildegarde of Bingen and Jacob Boehme.

Moreover, the difference between East and West matched perfectly Jung's favourite theory of introverts and extraverts, since Western man projected meaning into objects whereas Eastern man felt the existence of meaning within himself. The Oriental was prepared to accept a cosmogony with no beginning and no end, but the Occidental was preoccupied with the need to explain and draw causal lines. Furthermore, Jung had by now concluded that the *I Ching* was simply his own theory of dreams expressed in different language.[30]

However, there were many aspects of India that Jung cordially disliked. He was contemptuous of its university philosophy departments and of the informal training institutes of the gurus and maharishis, on the ground that wisdom was the province of a tiny élite and could not be taught; he pointed out that Confucius and Lao-tse and Chuang-tse, the founding fathers of Taoism, never had institutes. On the other hand, the very best gurus understood that each pupil was distinct, that people needed to know different things and not everyone needed to know the same thing; it was the failure of Western universities that there was no such individual relationship of master and pupil.[31]

The Indian manner of thinking, too, was entirely alien to him. For Jung, Indian 'thought' was really perception; Hindus thought mainly in parables and images and were notoriously weak in rational exposition.[32] Jung took issue with the entire Indian project of *nirdandva* or liberation from opposites. The Indian sought in meditation the condition of emptiness, whereas Jung wanted to enjoy Nature and the psychic images. In other words, real liberation is possible only with participation; withdrawal simply amputates the psyche.[33] Besides, on the Jungian theory of compensation, withdrawal from life was a kind of repression which would provoke enantiodromia. Every action, even inaction, provoked an opposite tendency, which was why, in the same century in which Man achieved the age-old dream of being able to fly, he also invented the bombing raid.[34]

Jung has been accused of being unnecessarily severe on Hindu thought simply in order to throw his beloved Buddhism into sharper relief. Irritated by the detachment and otherworldliness of Indian thought and culture, he failed to see how, on his own theory of compensation, self-annihilating rituals might have a function in societies ground down by poverty. Like many rich men, Jung consistently overlooked the economic dimension in life. He frequently returned to the motif he had emphasized in his debates with the Brahmans at the University of Calcutta: 'There can be no consciousness where there is no one to say, "I am conscious."'[35] But those sympathetic to Eastern philosophy reply that to apply the tools of Western linguistic analysis to problems like these is to embrace the peculiar fallacy that all the problems of human existence can be reduced to language.[36]

Jung was very clear-sighted about some aspects of Indian culture. The key to it all was totality, which was why India was so dreamlike. Indian civilization, unlike European, contained every essential trace of primitivity and embraced the whole human being from top to bottom. Mankind in all his aspects, saint and brute, was represented in India's temples, civilization and psychology, providing the kind of kaleidoscopic 'abridgement' of human nature usually encountered only in dreams. This was why psychoanalysis could never flourish in the East, for what Freud sought to unearth was already included in the totalistic thinking of the East.[37]

But there was a price to pay, and 'totality' brought its own burdens. On one occasion Jung had a conversation with the Chinese philosopher and author Hu Shih, then Kuomintang ambassador in Washington and author of such books as *The Chinese Renaissance* and *The Development of Logical Method in Ancient China*. The first shock for Jung was when Hu Shih dismissed the *I Ching* as a book of superstitious necromancy and made it plain that he was more interested in aeroplanes and locomotives than in the Tao.[38] But the second shock came when Jung noticed that Hu Shih was completely exhausted after two hours' conversation, even though Jung had confined himself to a few specific questions. It became clear that the Oriental mind was so weighed down with totality that it could scarcely get hold of any detail.[39]

It can be readily appreciated why Jung was concerned about the facile embrace of the 'wisdom of the East' by many bored, idealistic or not very bright Westerners. He uttered frequent warnings about the folly of simply taking over systems of thought and attitudes to life which had evolved to meet entirely different circumstances, ideologies, cultures and values and declared that it was impossible to take by theft what it has taken China thousands of years to build up.[40]

The dangers were several. Onc was that Westerners would flock to Nepal, Tibet, Sikkim and other havens in search of instant enlightenment, a 'quick fix', thus distorting the meaning of what they purported to understand; Jung pointed out that even a great philosopher like Schopenhauer, who imported Eastern pessimism into his thought, had only a superficial knowledge of the Upanishads, which allegedly inspired him.[41] Another was that the study of Eastern philosophy could simply be used by the neurotic to evade life's tasks.[42] Yet the most serious Western mistake was to be carried away by Eastern occultism, to take over yoga practices word for word and to become pitiable imitators; such, in his view, had been the fate of the theosophy of Madame Blavatsky and Annie Besant.[43] Worst of all mind-sets was the one that regarded 'the wisdom of the East' as a panacea, for this was *maya* or the veil of illusion with a vengeance.[44]

Jung spent a good deal of his correspondence rebutting the facile and simplistic Western idea of salvation through immersion in Eastern thought. To an unnamed German woman, whose twenty-four-year-old son had joined an Indian religious order and changed his name, he wrote contemptuously that one could safely embrace the Pramachari mission if one was a trust-fund child, but that oriental ideas were only really suitable for people who lived in baking heat for ten months of the year.[45] In any case, Eastern philosophy was absurdly overrated in the West. Whereas in the West consciousness was too detached from the unconscious, in the East it merged with it and became identical with it.[46]

Yoga, too, was overrated. It had begun well, centuries before, and in many ways could be considered one of the greatest creations of the human mind, but had ossified into a fixed system with precise rules and fixed images for compensation, and was thus directly comparable to the *Exercitia* of St Ignatius Loyola. Yet Western yoga devotees would throw up their hands in horror if asked to follow Jesuitical rules for meditation.[47] This was why Jung agreed in the main with the debunking articles on yoga and Zen written in 1960 by Arthur Koestler.[48] But he thought Koestler exhibited the same 'all or nothing mentality' as the blinkered Western *bienpensants* who worshipped everything Eastern. It was true that Zen contained a good deal of nonsense, but it also possessed a valuable core of truth which Koestler had ignored.[49] The point that both Koestler and the Western devotees of all things Oriental missed was that there was a racial and cultural element in the Western unconscious that one ignored at one's peril; this was the 'Wotan' argument all over again. To attempt to build an Eastern superstructure on such a Western basis was bound to end in disaster.

Wotan came into the picture in another way. Jung argued that Orientals progressed naturally from the stage of polydemonism to polytheism. Germany, though, was only just emerging from the polydemon stage into polytheism when it was cut off in its prime and had Christianity foisted upon it, much as if a society were propelled from feudalism directly into socialism, omitting the capitalist phase. It would therefore be a grave error for Germans specifically to accept Oriental ideas uncritically and translate them into the mental language of the West, for this would overload an already precarious system. The best thing was to allow the primitive side in European culture to develop, though Jung admitted he was not sure how this could be done without surrendering to horrors like Nazism.

Overall, Jung's greatest quarrel with Indian thought, as with Catholicism later in his career, concerned the problem of evil, which he thought Eastern philosophy tried to spirit away by sleight of hand. Jung was very hard on the facile Indian approach that saw good and evil as merely varying degrees of the same thing. Where the Christian strove for good and feared to succumb to evil, the Indian declared the world to be a mere illusion and sought to be liberated from it. Meditation and yoga were thus used as an *escape*, whereas Jung saw their importance as bringing more of the unconscious into the light of the conscious and thus putting the material to use in our actual day-to-day lives. Real life, to reiterate a frequent Jung theme, enabled the eternal Self to enter the three-dimensional world of the here and now. The Oriental attitude to evil produced a skewed perspective on life, enabling a heightened feeling for beauty to coexist with terrible cruelty, and thus engendering the familiar Western notion that in the East human life was held cheap.[50] On the other hand, the Eastern attempt to solve the problem of evil by withdrawal and detachment simply led to banality. Jung was scathing about the 'serenity' attained by the famous maharishis, gurus and 'perfect masters' and remarked witheringly that he was glad *he* had not achieved such a miracle as living the first sixty-five years of his life in 'perfect balance'.[51]

Notions of reincarnation are common currency in the East, and Jung's visit to India enabled him to clarify his thinking on this elusive subject. He distinguished carefully between reincarnation and metempsychosis or the transmigration of souls in time through bodily sequences. He pointed out that metempsychosis did not imply reincarnation in the usual sense, since it was not certain that the migration of souls guaranteed the continuity of personality; what was involved might be a simple continuity of *karma*. He argued that Buddha famously made no definitive statement on whether there was or was not continuity of personality. Reincarnation, however – rebirth in a human body – implied such continuity and hence memory of previous existences.[52] As to whether there was any truth in the notion of reincarnation, Jung remained staunchly agnostic.[53]

On the related question of whether there is life after death, Jung was divided. He pointed out that from the universal belief in it in all cultures it was clearly an archetypal expectation. There were authentic postmortal phenomena and there was also a possibility that there was an existence outside time which ran parallel with existence inside time.[54] Ever the pragmatist, Jung recommended embracing the Pascalian way of gambling that it was true that there was an after life, since it was always correct to have faith in an archetype.

On the other hand, heaven, or the idea of a world of spirits in celestial bliss, seemed to him implausible because of the fundamental unity of the universe, which meant there must be suffering in the 'other world' too. Rather than reincarnation, Jung inclined to believe in determinism by ancestors, such that in our lives we answer questions and solve problems or assignments set by our forebears. Another possibility was that life itself was an incarnation of an archetype – a temporary projection of a permanent Self. Jung thought it probable that communication did exist between living and dead, but he also noted that in all 'apparitions' of the dead they never revealed anything new but rather seemed to need the living to ask and answer questions. Presumably since these phantoms lived outside space and time they tended to resort to those still in space–time. But he admitted he could do little more than speculate. The fundamental point was that a general belief in survival after death was justified pragmatically, since it enabled us to live better than the contrary belief.[55]

The refreshing aspect of Eastern thought was that it shed light on such concerns without insisting on a rigid distinction between science and religion or between the individual and God. Oriental religions were more congenial to Jung than their Western counterparts as they stressed the inner quality of the deity, what he called the 'God within us' or the 'God-image'. In keeping with the extravert/introvert divide, Western religion stressed objects in the external world and, not surprisingly, arrived at a conception of God as a transcendent being. For Jung, both the Christian with his dogmatic assertion that God made Man, and atheists like Feuerbach who insisted that this was a subject-predicate mistake and that it was Man who had made God, were misguided, for God and Man existed together in a dialectical and symbiotic relationship.[56]

In Jung's view Western religions were astonishingly unsophisticated. One could trace five main stages in the evolution of the idea of God. First there was the animistic view characteristic of Africa, where Nature was ruled by a ragbag assortment of gods and demons. Then there was the Greco-Roman polytheistic notion of a father of Gods ruling in a strict hierarchy. The third stage was when there arose the idea that God shared the human fate, was betrayed, killed or died and then resurrected. Christianity conflated this third stage with the fourth, when God becomes Man in the flesh and is identified with the idea of the Supreme Good. At this stage 'splitting' takes place, the female aspect of deity is relegated to an ancillary position as 'Mother Church', consciousness is given a superior role to the unconscious, spirit and matter bifurcate, so that in the end the result is science, materialism and atheism. The fifth and highest stage of belief in God is when the entire world is understood as a projected psychic structure and the only God the 'God within' or the 'God-image'.[57]

For Jung it was as absurd to question the idea of God as to question the idea that human beings had sexual instincts. The human psyche was programmed with the idea of God, so that atheists who condemned religion as an illusion were themselves victims of the greatest illusion. According to Jung, the human mind was fashioned with an innate, archetypal instinct towards religion. 'God' already had a place in that part of our psyche which pre-existed consciousness and it followed therefore that he could not be considered an invention of consciousness.[58] It was entirely natural, of course, that people should organize their impulses around creeds or dogmas, which acted as a kind of 'necessary fiction'. But to say that the human psyche was naturally religious was light years away from saying that there actually was a being 'out there' called God. It made no more sense to say that God existed in a transcendent way, independent of the human mind, than to say that the Wise Old Man or any of the other archetypes were independent of the psyche.

Over and over again Jung stressed that when he spoke of 'God' he spoke of the 'God-image' or the 'God within'. Whether there was an entity corresponding with God who existed 'out there' was an unanswerable and actually rather pointless question.[59] Jung accused Western religion of being obsessed with the transcendental aspect of deity and ignoring the immanent side; this was why the Greek words *entos homooun*, referring to the kingdom of God, were dishonestly translated as 'among you' instead of 'within you'.[60] Jung scoured the New Testament to find the many references to 'God within you' which showed that the idea of a transcendental deity was a misunderstanding or later theological accretion. There was a good example in Galatians 2:20: 'Yet not I but Christ liveth in me.'[61] He claimed that St Paul's message, truly understood, endorsed his position but that most theologians were too obtuse to see this.[62] It was quite clear that all statements about ultimate reality were anthropomorphisms.[63]

Jung thought that the most useful method intellectually was to equate God with the Self, as long as we always kept it firmly in our minds that we were talking about a psychic image, not an ontological entity. The God-image is a symbol of the Self, and of psychic wholeness. Although it is not really possible to differentiate God from the unconscious, it is most likely that the God-image does not coincide with the unconscious as such, but with a special content of it, namely the archetype of the Self. The God-image is a reflection of the Self or the Self is an *imago dei*.[64] Another way of looking at it is that Jungian psychology simply demystifies the tenets of Christianity. So God = Unconscious, Christ = Self, Incarnation = integration of consciousness, salvation or redemption = individuation, and the crucifixion = the realization of quaternity or wholeness.[65]

The fallacy both of atheism and of traditional belief can now be seen, according to Jung.[66] Since religion is a worldwide phenomenon, it could not be plausibly explained as repressed family desires transmogrified into a cosmic fantasy, and since the idea of God is universal as an archetype, all traditional 'proofs' of the existence of God, like those of St Thomas Aquinas, were superfluous. The irrationality of religious beliefs does not affect their importance as psychic facts, since irrationality is part of the legacy Man is born with. On the other hand, traditional belief has its own absurdities, the worst of which is to think that because the word 'God' exists there must be something in the external world that corresponds with it.[67]

Jung's defence of religion alienated many believers, not just because he 'psychologized' their most cherished tenets, but because his defence of religion validated any and every religion but no particular one. Western Christians were particularly upset. The distinguished theologian Martin Buber was Jung's most persistent opponent and critic. He accused him of founding a new religion of pure psychic immanence, rejecting the traditional transcendental aspects of God and pointed out that the essence of religion was an I–Thou relationship, not I–It, as in Jung. Buber argued that if God is nothing but an archetype in the collective unconscious, then Jung had obliterated the most fundamental aspect of God – his otherness; this made Jungian thought pure Gnosticism, which accelerated the eclipse of God.[68]

Other Christian apologists were irritated by the way Jung appeared to speak of God in the traditional way – 'I know that he exists' – and would then explain that he was merely speaking of the God-image. All the old charges of lack of clarity were levelled at Jung, and he was accused of tacking in and out of different meanings of God without noticing that he was doing so. 'Why do I have to talk about God? Because he is everywhere! I am only the spoon in his kitchen,'[69] seemed to be an utterance to encourage the most pious and devotional; but then Jung would disappoint those who wanted an endorsement from him for traditional beliefs by saying that he was speaking merely of the universality of the collective unconscious. In fact there seemed to be at least three distinct Jungian propositions about God, between which he oscillated at will: that psychology could prove only that humans believed in God, not that the different beliefs were true; that the universality of a concept of God was strong evidence for his existence; and that a belief in God was pragmatically justified, as it made people behave better.[70]

Jung further angered his would-be supporters in the Christian community, who relished his intemperate attacks on Marxian and Freudian atheism, by many scathing and depreciatory remarks about Christianity. For Jung, Christianity was flawed at every level except the sociological. As theology, the idea of an all-good deity was simply incompatible with the truths he had discovered about the unconscious; since the only God was the God-image, it followed that the myth of Christianity had simply served to keep human beings in a state of perpetual guilt. Moreover, Christian dualism was an obstacle to individuation; it aimed at perfection when it should be aiming, instead, at integration.[71]

Christianity was not even true to the precepts of its founder, and Jung agreed with Dostoevsky in the famous 'Grand Inquisitor' chapter of *The Brothers Karamazov* that if Jesus returned to earth, he would be treated with hostility and contempt by the princes of the Church. Did that mean, asked one Jungian disciple, that if Jesus Christ was living today and preached what he did, he would be crucified again? 'No,' answered Jung, but he would be consigned to prison or the lunatic asylum.[72]

However, Christianity had put down strong roots in Western culture and one ignored those at one's peril. Besides it was difficult to see how one could fuse existing religions to make a universal one because Christianity insisted that Jesus Christ was God, whereas for other religions he would simply be an aspect of the deity, for example, as an avatar in Hinduism.[73] In the West the decline of religion – itself an expression of the unconscious – meant that the overflowing banks of the inundated unconscious flooded into the conscious. This accounted for the curious mystical quality in Nietzsche – for he was overwhelmed with material displaced from Christianity – and James Joyce.[74]

What was needed was either a new religion or new ways of looking at the old one, but so far the candidates presented were not encouraging. The success of the Oxford Movement showed the hunger for a new synthesis, though that particular solution, according to Jung, was simply what he called 'a *psychologie des foules*'.[75] In the meantime there remained the pragmatic argument for Christianity. This, however, was a prescription for the West properly so-called. Jung remained vehemently opposed to Christian missionaries in the Third World and declared that it would be more humane to go to Africa and massacre its native peoples than to visit Christianity on them.[76] Jung always insisted, against the cries of the Christian faithful, that what made Christianity valuable was the mythical elements it shared with other religions; Christians, on the other hand, tried to claim that what made it valuable was its role as repository of the unique truth. Jung argued that to insist on the uniqueness of Christianity made it impenetrable.[77]

Although highly sceptical about Christianity in general, Jung was always far more sympathetic to Catholicism than to Protestantism. He disliked the Protestant emphasis both on the patriarchal Old Testament and on the historical Jesus.[78] However, Protestantism was more successful in separating matters of belief from things that were scientifically demonstrable.[79]

One aspect of Catholicism that appealed to Jung was its feminine, 'maternal' side, as opposed to 'paternal' and macho Protestantism; there was no cult of the Virgin or of female saints in Protestantism.[80] Catholicism also seemed to him more human in that it did not place so much emphasis on faith alone.[81] Moreover, it was only Protestant Europeans who had 'the Jew in their unconscious', much as the American had the Black man and the Red man, and there was less colour prejudice in Catholicism because Catholics tended to be in closer touch with their own collective primitivity.[82] In sum, because the Catholic Church codified the memories and lessons of history so much better and conserved so much of classical paganism, it had good claims to be considered *the* Christian church *par excellence*.[83]

Protestantism attempted to rationalize Christianity and cut out the obviously mythological elements in the New Testament, but failed to realize that any religion that was totally compatible with reason would not satisfy the unconscious.[84] In some ways it was this harmony between religion and the unconscious that made Catholics such good patients; their only failing was that the heavy influence of Jesuitical modes of thought made active imagination difficult for them.[85] In all the patients he had, only six were practising Catholics and they took readily to analysis. The reason was not hard to find, since the rituals and beliefs of the Catholic church – the Mass, Baptism, mariolatry and, especially, Confession – co-opted aspects of the older religions and thus answered the deep psychological needs of human beings. Confession in particular produced the result that Catholics were the least neurotic patients, whereas Jews were the most.[86]

Jung's approach to his Catholic patients was to exhort, force and cajole them back into the faith of their fathers.[87] This meant that anyone suffering from a crisis of belief would simply be told by Jung to snap out of it and go back to believing. If the advice did not work, then he considered he could do little for the lapsed Catholic. This was because a Protestant who had turned his back on his church usually followed a sectarian movement, whereas a Catholic in that predicament generally opted for atheism.[88] Jung claimed that Catholic patients were actually better Christians after analysis, as he taught them to confess properly.[89]

Jung was often asked why, given his admiration for Catholicism, he had not become a Catholic himself. In fact the reasons were legion: his disbelief in a transcendent deity as opposed to an internalized God-image; his impatience with the Catholic solution of the problem of evil; Catholicism's failure to understand that the relation of God to Man was as important as that of Man to God; and much else.[90] He added as further considerations the following: that he was interested in the psychological roots of Christianity, not points of dogma; that as he was a doctor confessionalism was alien to him; and that he was a scientist who worked on the basis of empirical knowledge.[91] Moreover, he often disappointed his Catholic friends by saying that Catholicism had little to do with Christianity properly so conceived. It was a religion in itself, just like Buddhism, Confucianism, Taoism and the rest of them.[92]

Jung's insistence that all religion contained part of the truth but no one religion contained the whole truth made him an uncomfortable bedfellow for true believers who would like to have recruited him in the propaganda battle against humanism and atheism. His visit to India in 1937–38 was important, as it confirmed for him that whereas the religious impulse was as deeply rooted in human beings as the sexual instinct, no religion or culture, except perhaps a very sophisticated version of Buddhism, was capable of shading the others. East was East and West was West culturally speaking, but from the viewpoint of totality or the *unus mundus* neither side had a monopoly of truth, insight and wisdom.

Chapter Twenty-Two

FREUD: FINAL ACCOUNTS

On his return from India Jung convalesced mainly at Bollingen, whence the favourite but troublesome Joggi was banished because of his barking.[1] By mid-April his energies were returning. The high-dextrose diet prescribed by his doctor worked well, and he went on long walks lasting between three and six hours; on his return he liked to try his hand at gardening, digging, spreading manure, planting potatoes. As his stamina built up, he went mountaineering and was soon able to clock up 800 metres of ascent in a day, starting at an altitude of nearly 3,000 feet and climbing to more than 5,000; his heart coped well but his legs felt stiff afterwards.[2]

Even as he recovered, on 12 March 1938, came the news that the Nazis had invaded Austria and annexed it with minimal resistance. Even though he had praised National Socialism and denigrated Freud and his religion, he knew well enough the dubious mercies Austrian Jews could expect from the Gestapo. He and Franz Riklin therefore collected $10,000 from well-wishers and their own funds and sent Riklin's son, Franz Junior, to Vienna on a mission to rescue Freud.

Riklin arrived at Berggasse 19, the $10,000 in a moneybelt, and knocked on the door. It was opened by Freud's daughter Anna, now an important figure in the psychoanalytical movement in her own right. Riklin explained his mission. The suspicious Anna would not open the door all the way, refused to let Riklin go inside, and warned that her father would not receive him. Then Freud himself came to the door to see what all the commotion was about. When Riklin explained, Freud waved him away irascibly: 'I refuse to be beholden to my enemies.'[3] Riklin departed for Zürich, his mission unaccomplished.

Yet the dangers for Freud were real enough and powerful sympathizers in the British and American élite pulled strings in Berlin to get him safely into exile. The Nazis allowed Freud and his family to depart, but not before a few tense interviews that led Freud to make his famous ironic comment, 'I can most heartily recommend the Gestapo to everyone.'[4] On 6 June he arrived in London and took up residence in a rented house in Regent's Park.

Little more than a month later Jung himself was in London, having been invited to receive an honorary degree at Oxford University and to take part in a conference there. This was his first and last visit to Oxford. He loved the ancient university buildings and the green of the lawns, and gazed fondly on the Bodleian library while entertaining the fantasy that he would return on a private research trip and immerse himself in the library's unique collection of ancient alchemical manuscripts.[5]

The conference took place from 29 July to 2 August. Despite his Anglophilia and his love of the physical appearance of Oxford University, Jung was not sufficiently sensitive to its susceptibilities or to English idiom, even though he prided himself on his knowledge of the nuances of British culture. His speech of thanks for the honorary D.Sc. was considered flowery and embarrassing, in the way that high Teutonic culture often grates on the Anglo-Saxon empiricist temperament. But he both overplayed and underplayed, especially by the standards of his po-faced Oxford hosts, to whom seriousness always meant earnestness. As he emerged from the Sheldonian theatre with a host of university dignitaries after the degree ceremony, he caught the eye of his colleague C.A. Meier and gave him a broad wink. Meier and the other Swiss laughed aloud, but unfortunately Jung's gesture and the response was also observed by the senior Oxford academics, who construed Jung's levity as a calculated insult to the university. This was not the first time that his misplaced sense of humour had caused problems.[6]

Another of Jung's gestures also backfired. He and his English disciple E.A. Bennet decided to send Freud a formal telegram of welcome. At first the conference secretary misunderstood Jung's instructions and did not send off the cable, which led to a typical Jung tantrum before the situation was rectified.[7] But Freud was unmoved by this token of reconciliation and gave it a dusty reply, as he noted in his diary: 'The Oxford Psychotherapeutic Congress, chaired by Jung, has sent me the obligatory greetings telegram, to which I have responded with a cool answer.'[8]

So there was to be no eleventh-hour reconciliation. The passions and hatreds of the past twenty-five years had gone too deep for that. Those who met Freud in the 1930s found him still angry when Jung's name was mentioned.[9] Yet ironically and unwittingly Freud had moved some way in Jung's direction. His penultimate work *Moses and Monotheism*, while attacking Christianity, also raised the question which had brought so many charges of anti-Semitism against Jung when he raised it: namely, what is the peculiar quality of Jewishness?[10]

Moreover, Freud had long since abandoned the idea that psychoanalysis had to stand as a bulwark against the mudtide of occultism. His attitude to parapsychology, the abnormal and the uncanny became ever more openminded and nuanced. In 1932 he wrote that he used to fear that science would be overwhelmed by spiritualism and mysticism if parts of occultism were proved true but he no longer felt that way and had no problems about accepting the reality of telepathy.[11] He came to have a kind of Jungian superstitiousness about numbers but remarked sardonically that he was also one of those people in whose presence the spirits suspend their activities and melt away.[12] All in all, Freud confessed himself baffled by the occult and in 1938, in his last utterance on the subject, referred delphically to mysticism as 'the obscure self-perception of the realm beyond the Ego, the Id'.[13]

Nonetheless, a few of Freud's barbed asides on the occult seem to refer indirectly to Jung. He declared that man's craving for mysticism was limitless and if not opposed would win back all the territory gained by psychoanalysis; this surely reflected, not concern over spiritualists and necromancers, but the 'false consciousness' of Jung's analytical psychology.[14] And it is not hard to imagine whom

Freud must have had in mind when he diagnosed the typically superstitious person as follows: 'I believe in external (real) chance, it is true, but not in internal (psychical) accidental events. With the superstitious person it is the other way round.'[15] For Freud, the superstitious person was one with obsessive tendencies whose discovery of 'significant coincidences' masked neurotic projections; there was also an element of power fantasy in believing that one's thoughts could be actualized in the external world. 'Superstition derives from suppressed hostile and cruel impulses. Superstition is in large part the expectation of trouble; and a person who has harboured frequent ill wishes against others, but has been brought up to be good and has therefore repressed such wishes into the unconscious, will be especially ready to expect punishment for his unconscious wickedness in the form of trouble threatening him from without.'[16] As a disguised description of an allegedly malevolent pastor's son, this is hard to beat.

The cable of 1 August 1938 was the last occasion when there was any contact, albeit indirect, between Jung and Freud. Jung returned to Switzerland and began lecturing on Indian texts. Buddhism and alchemy began to occupy his thoughts so greatly that in February 1939 he abandoned his practical therapy seminars given in English.[17] But this by no means meant the end of interest in Anglo-Saxon attitudes. In April 1939 he was back in London again, this time at the invitation of the Royal Society of Medicine. He took part in a panel discussion on 'The Symbolic Life' with a bishop and showed both sides of his enigmatic personality. On the platform he was tigerish, uncompromising and witheringly sarcastic; but when the session was over he was all broad smiles and geniality, and marched out of the hall arm-in-arm with the gaitered divine.[18]

Then he and Emma departed for another tour of the West Country. By this time Emma had sublimated her marital unhappiness through scholarship and had become an expert on the legend of the Holy Grail. She was therefore keen to visit Glastonbury, Tintagel, Badbury Rings and all the other places associated with the Arthurian myths. Jung's last visit to England was made memorable by an extensive tour of the old kingdoms of Wessex and Cornwall, with Peter and Anne Baynes acting as their guides.[19]

If Jung the tourist exhibited the sunny aspect of the man, it was the dark side of his personality that was in evidence when Freud died, aged eighty-three, on 23 September 1939, after a long battle with cancer. Perhaps Jung was angered by Freud's dual brush-off the year before, but his essay 'In Memory of Sigmund Freud', written in late 1939, was marked by bitterness and hostility rather than charity and reconciliation, postulating as it did that Freud was in the grip of a 'daemon'.[20] By common consent Jung never got over the trauma of his break with Freud. Where Freud made perhaps half a dozen disparaging comments on his erstwhile 'crown prince' in the twenty-five years after Jung's defection,[21] Jung's writings, both before and after Freud's death, teem with references to his one-time 'father'. These references are perhaps one part personal abuse to two parts doctrinal critique, but they are worth studying if only to show that Freud well and truly stuck in Jung's craw and that he never managed to spit him out.

The 1939 memorial essay is a good starting point. Homans sums up on this as follows: 'This one is a rambling, disorganized essay, in a tone of bitter repudiation that at times borders on the rude and even the abusive. It is reminiscent of the closing months of their relationship as recorded in the *Letters*, before the final break.'[22] It is true that 'In Memory of Sigmund Freud' contains a 'grand slam' of *ad hominem* arguments, but its main significance is that it collects into one essay discrete items of abuse otherwise broadcast throughout the Jungian *oeuvre*.

The main counts of the personal indictment are as follows: Freud was first and foremost a nerve specialist, had no training as a psychologist and was deficient as a philosopher; Charcot, Breuer and Janet, not Freud, were the true pioneers of the unconscious; it was the Freudian attitude to neurosis which itself made patients ill; Freudianism was purely and simply an offshoot of nineteenth-century materialism; Freud's method was fanaticism in action but like every fanaticism it evoked the suspicion of an inner uncertainty; and, naturally, Jungian psychology was the corrective fulfilment of Freud's work.[23]

Jung amplified these comments elsewhere. On the first count he criticized Freud for having had no mental hospital experience.[24] On the second, he 'topped up' the claim that Freud was unoriginal by adding that he, Jung, was not Freud's pupil but Bleuler's.[25] As for neurosis, Jung frequently alleged that Freud's own 'unacknowledged' neurosis was the root of all evil in psychoanalysis. Freud's neurosis was composed of three main strands. His difficulty in relation to desires came about because he was a city-dweller: had he grown up in the countryside like Jung he would have had a more balanced attitude to life and taken for granted so many of the manifestations of human behaviour he regarded as 'unnatural'.[26] Then there was the difficulty that Freud was basically an introverted-feeling type who masqueraded as an extravert-thinker; according to Jung, the giveaway sign of Freud's 'markedly differentiated feeling function' was his love of precious stones like jade and malachite.[27] Finally, there was Freud's bitterness.[28]

Jung was always severely critical of the 'nothing but' attitude, but he evinces clear traces of it himself when speaking of Freud as the quintessential product of nineteenth-century materialism. After sneering at Freud as a lesser version of his contemporary Nietzsche and then bracketing them both as typical reactions to nineteenth-century repression, Jung destroys his own case by describing Freud *on the very same page* as nothing but an eighteenth-century Voltairean rationalist.[29] One is entitled to ask which of these despised breeds Freud really is in Jung's opinion – debased product of the Enlightenment or epigone to the Romantic agony; he clearly cannot be both.

The fanaticism/inner uncertainty argument need not detain us, for this is simply Jung's a priori category of enantiodromia once again: religious zealots are secret atheists, Nazis are secret lovers of the Jews, and so on. Enantiodromia is unfortunately one of those hermeneutic concepts which, by purporting to explain everything, actually explain nothing. As for the rest of Jung's personal attack on Freud, it needs to be pointed out how wildly inaccurate and often self-contradictory it is. Jung claims that a major source of Freud's neurosis was that he was an introverted-feeling type masquerading as an extravert-thinking type. But he has already made the theory of Freud as extravert (and Adler introvert) a cornerstone of *Psychological Types*, on which in turn the interpretation of Freud as neurotic is based.[30] Moreover, it is absurd to say that Freud was unaware of his own neurosis. In a letter to Ferenczi on 17 November 1911 Freud wrote, 'Man should not want to eradicate his complexes but rather live in harmony with them; they are the legitimate directors of his behaviour in the world.'[31]

It is notable how in his personal attacks on Freud Jung lets his feelings run away with him and thus introduces elements into the argument which smack of gross intellectual dishonesty. He quotes Freud as saying, 'This must be correct because I have thought it,'[32] though the remark appears nowhere in Freud's written work and is not recorded by a single other person who knew Freud. He accuses Freud of basing his theories on the tittle-tattle of his neurotic patients, though the current school of anti-Freud revisionists accuses him of the exactly opposite fault: taking as fantasy what was reality, as in child abuse. He also claimed to have proposed to Freud that the ego had a dual aspect, one representing life and the other death, and that Freud had dismissed this but then twenty years later brought out the theory as his own.[33] At this point even the sympathetic editor of Jung's letters was led to protest: 'Jung's memory for dates was at fault if this refers to Freud's hypothesis of life and death instincts, first formulated in *Beyond the Pleasure Principle*.'

The other aspect of Jung's personal criticism of Freud that irks is the harping on the theme of Jewishness and the attempt to make out the entire theory of Freudianism to be a peculiar aspect of a general 'Jewish-complex'.

When comparing Greek and Jewish thought, Jung stated that of the two cardinal sins of *superbia* and *concupiscencia*, the Greek vice was pride while the Jewish was concupiscence: 'We see this very clearly in Freud, namely in his "pleasure principle", this in turn linked with the Jewish "castration-complex", which was a consequence of ritual circumcision.[34] Yet surely the most disgraceful misrepresentation of psychoanalysis was Jung's dishonest attempt to link Freudianism with Nazism.

Even when combatting Freudian theory at the abstract level, Jung found it difficult not to slip into sneering, sarcasm or vulgar abuse. The core of his critique was that Freudianism was dogmatic, materialistic, and reductive or 'nothing but'; that Freud's views on religion were obtuse and that he had made a new religion out of sexuality; and that his theory of neurosis was hopelessly wrong.

For Freud's atheistic views on religion Jung had only contempt. Referring to Freud's devastating attack on religion in *The Future of an Illusion*, he accused him of propagating the destruction of the bond between the human and the numinous which was the basis of all neurosis.[35] The irony was that Freud was caught in a trap, for it is no more possible to deny the religious impulse than to deny the sexual instinct. The obvious way, then, to square the circle was to make libido itself a secular religion and sexuality a *numinosum* – which, according to Jung, was precisely what Freud did.[36]

It is often difficult to regard Jung's arguments as serious attempts to come to terms with Freud, so often does he seem content merely to score debating points or to yield to his talent for sarcasm and derision. A good example is the quite gratuitous description of Freudianism as an inferior version of the *Sidpa Bardo* (the lowest region of the dead) in the Tibetan Book of the Dead.[37] But perhaps we reach firmer ground in the theory of neurosis, for Jung did have the important insight that a neurosis may be creative as well as disabling, enabling the neurotic to buy time or gain new insights before making a radical change of direction in life.

Jung's quarrel with Freud's theory of neurosis can be traced to their very different ways of looking at the world. Freud, a pessimist and determinist, stressed the influence of the past, the parental legacy, the childhood experiences; he sought out causes and origins. Jung, by contrast, was forced by his theory of the collective unconscious into optimism and a kind of facile pragmatism; he stressed consequences, the future, the whither not the whence. So strong was this 'progressive' orientation that at times one detects an impatience with and very real dislike for neurotics on Jung's part. He castigates them for wallowing around in self-pity by rummaging in the past for the explanation for all their failures, and he berates psychoanalysis even more vociferously for encouraging such a cast of mind.[38] There is a harsh side to Jung, and his prescriptions sometimes come perilously close to the modern bromides that neurotics have 'an attitude problem' and should 'pull themselves together'. There was something utilitarian about Jung's mentality, which is why he has been called a moral educator *manqué*. Between him and Freud an irreconcilable conflict raged around the question of which psychological phenomena were primary and which secondary.

The Freudian position is that Jung confuses the secondary gain from a neurosis with its primary cause; adaptation is a mere 'substitute formation' of the neurosis, not its purpose. So, for instance, the neurosis of 'infantilism' could have secondary manifestations which could appear as 'adaptation'. To this Jung made the unconvincing and unsatisfactory answer that 'infantilism' could just as well be a 'substitute formation' of the primary quality of 'adaptation',[39] – ignoring the inherent unlikelihood that an abstract quality would generate such a specific form of neurosis. Since adaptation is such a wide category, on Jung's theory one would have to explain why this particular symptom formation emerged and not another one; no such difficulty arises if the neurosis is primary and the adaptation secondary. Such an argument from general to particular rather than the reverse surely points once more to the huge influence of Platonism on Jung.

In any case, if neurosis is maladaptation, it follows that the present task being attempted by the sufferer is impaired by some legacy from the past; some have even asserted that it is all but definitional of 'neurosis' that the problem must lie in the past. Jung's way with this difficulty is not to meet the objection head-on but to approach it obliquely. Jung at one moment appears to suggest that if the cause of a neurosis lies in the past, one would need to be a time traveller to deal with it. But the most slippery part of his argument is the suggestion that a neurosis somehow reproduces itself newly minted from microsecond to microsecond; he slides over the enormous difficulties in such a 'phenomenological' view by the sleight of hand involved in his use of 'as it were'.

Jung went further and asserted that Freudians cling to theories that put the aetiology of a neurosis in the past so as to put them in a superior position vis-à-vis their patients.[40] This led Jung eventually to doubt the entire validity of the notion of 'resistance'; his idea was that if you let the unconscious take its natural course it will dredge up all the material a patient and doctor could ever need.[41] It was a short step from this to doubting the good faith of Freudian analysts, on the grounds that a theory of neurosis that stressed only the negative side threw out the baby with the bathwater.[42]

Another favourite Jungian ploy was to insinuate that Freud and Adler both had hold of part of the truth but looked at the selfsame phenomena from two different angles; this was a disingenuous tactic roughly equivalent to regarding General de Gaulle and Marshal Pétain as statesmen of equal stature. For Jung, Freud and Adler were two sides of the same coin, both insinuating that their partial view of reality was the whole truth. The name of their intellectual faults was legion. Among them were: the reductive 'nothing but' attitude; their imprisonment in nineteenth-century materialism; the emphasis on childhood as the root cause of neuroses; a morbid delight in the pathological side of life; hostility to religion and spiritual values; and a distorted view of reality arising from an early training exclusively in the treatment of psychoneuroses.[43] Freudian and Adlerian methods were like thesis and anti-thesis, requiring the method of 'individuation' to be added before synthesis could be reached; this was why they were theories only for the first half of life.[44]

Another way to view Freud and Adler was to see them and their basic drives as the two sons of a single father. Since Adler was the younger, he had a power-complex while Freud, the elder, was already successful and therefore interested only in pleasure.[45] This interpretation went a long way towards explaining the dynamic between elder and younger brothers in general.

It was important to Jung to try to discredit or dismantle every single original concept in the Freudian thesaurus. Inevitably 'sublimation' soon came under the Jungian bludgeon, and he claimed that the term as used by Freud was bogus.[46] This drew an indignant reaction from Herman Hesse, who wrote to Jung in 1934 to accuse him of trying to belittle Freud.[47] Jung wrote back pugnaciously, claiming that for Freud sublimation was merely another name for repression and that he did not understand its true significance, which only a study of alchemy would reveal.[48] Not wishing to fall out with Jung, for whom he still had some residual regard, Hesse sent back an emollient reply, but he remained convinced that Freud was a true genius while Jung was merely a talented apostate.[49]

The systematic denigration of Freud's ideas knew no limits. Jung scoffed at Freud as cultural and anthropological critic and called *Totem and Taboo* and *The Future of an Illusion* 'superficial and incompetent'.[50] So Freud's interpretation of dreams was likewise 'trash', as he told Smith Ely Jelliffe.[51] Jung assumed, questionably, that because the phenomena Freud thought of as 'incest-complexes' and 'infantile fantasies' were common to many cultures, it must therefore be incorrect to analyse them in a Freudian manner.[52] As for the 'superego', Jung criticized the concept on two grounds: that it failed to distinguish between conscious ethical decision-making and the unconscious operation of a complex; and that it assumed morality was created by the tyranny of the primal father, whereas in Jung's view conscience was an innate faculty found even in animals.[53]

Two parts of Freudian doctrine especially aroused Jung's ire: the theory of religion and the 'praxis' of theory and methodology. Pointing out that Freud always quoted Voltaire's *écrasez l'infame* enthusiastically, he declared that the fundamental fallacy in Freud's critique of religion was its assumption that the religious impulse, the result of sexual repression, came from the *personal* unconscious, whereas it was the essence of Jung's position that the numinous derived from the *collective* unconscious.[54] On the unity of theory and methodology, Freud was following in the footsteps of that other great Jewish genius, Karl Marx, and he made his position crystal clear: 'Psychoanalysis is a remarkable combination, for it comprises not only a method of research into the neuroses but also a method of treatment based on the aetiology thus discovered.'[55] Jung was quite right to object to this approach, for a correct general methodology no more guarantees reliable consulting-room results than a fruitful Marxist methodology of historical research guarantees the ultimate downfall of capitalism. One's only cavil is the way Jung rewrote history to make it appear that this was the major cause of his rift with Freud in 1912.[56]

Jung jettisoned almost all Freud's ideas as being of limited value when they were not downright erroneous. In only one area did he add a significant extension to the house that Freud built. The core of Freudian theory lies in the three concepts of repression, resistance and transference. Repression interested Jung mainly when it was the contents of a *collective* unconscious that were repressed. As for resistance he stated over and over again that this was a largely superfluous concept.[57] But the phenomenon of transference fascinated him, for it allowed him to build bridges between psychotherapy and his beloved study of alchemy.

Transference – the phenomenon whereby the patient projects onto the doctor emotions originally felt about parents, siblings, lovers and partners – was for Freud an inevitable part of the analytic process, an irrational barrier that had to be worked through and resolved.[58] Although Jung originally accepted this, he gradually came to believe that the importance of transference was relative only, that at times it was natural, unavoidable and helpful and at others it was better for the analytical relationship if it did not exist at all: the transference was rather like those medicines which are a panacea for one and pure poison for another.[59]

The greatest danger of transference occurred when there was a male doctor and female patient, for this immediately produced the risk that the analyst would become father, or lover, or demigod or saviour – or sometimes a mixture of these, thus engendering further confusion, irreconcilable conflict and neurosis. The transference of the analyst into godlike status Jung took as further proof of the universal human desire for God. He evolved various techniques for dealing with transference, not all of them as cynical as that of a colleague who proposed the following 'solution': 'the transference stops automatically when the patient runs out of money.'[60] If the doctor was genuinely perceived as a saviour, Jung found it was often possible to talk the patient out of the delusion by common-sense admonitions. Where this did not work, he found that dream analysis often weaned a patient off transference. But one had to beware of trying to jolt the analysand out of transference too suddenly, or there could be a violent relapse. Another deep-rooted problem came from patients with a long medical history: those with years of analysis behind them had to work through their emotions towards a whole set of authority figures, consultants, previous analysts, and so forth as well as parents and kin.[61]

Freudians, Jung thought, had overrated transference as an analytic phenomenon because their very methodology encouraged it. Transference was a mental phenomenon akin to the crowd psychology famously analysed by Gustav Le Bon: in other words, patients, particularly women, needed analysts with emotions, not disembodied gurus sitting behind them.[62] It was an important insight of Jung's to appreciate that the analyst's couch, with the analyst out of sight and thus an enigma, actually encouraged transference; leading neo-Freudians like Erik Erikson later endorsed this finding.[63] A linked Freudian fallacy was the tendency of some analysts actually to work for a transference, instead of appreciating that transference was abnormal.[64]

Counter-transference, when the analyst projects inappropriate emotions onto the patient, had long been recognized as the bane of the analyst's life.[65] According to Jung, it was counter-transference above all that clinched the case for the necessity of a training analysis. The analyst had to keep in touch with his unconscious so as not to be absorbed by it and he often pointed out, as proof that no analyst, however brilliant, was superhuman, the fact that the Pope himself had to confess to an ordinary priest. Emotions were contagious and counter-transference was most likely to happen when the contents which the patient projected onto the analyst were identical with the contents of the analyst's unconscious, as for example when an analyst was neurotic or when he came to believe in the messianic role projected on him by the patient.[66] In general, though, Jung thought that instances of counter-transference were relatively rare and that most of the stories of an analyst unwilling to let a patient go were delusions of persecution mania on the part of the analysand.[67]

Jung thought that the Freudian and Adlerian models of transference, though they clearly did explain some cases, were much too limited in scope. Freud had oversimplified transference as invariably erotic and Adler as invariably the will to power by a patient suffering from an 'inferiority' complex, but the truth was that it was a phenomenon with more than one meaning.[68] It was true that transference was mainly projection but there was one connection that did not break off if the projection was severed: this was the connection of kinship libido.

Jung thought that because exogamy had triumphed over endogamy we were all as a consequence atomized individuals and strangers and that transference satisfied the primitive need for quasi-kinship connections. He cited the work of anthropologists who regarded endogamy or the incest tendency as a genuine instinct which, if denied realization in the flesh, would realize itself in the spirit. So it was that transference had an anthropological significance.[69] Hence the (at first sight) eccentric proposition Jung advances that transference is ultimately vital for society as well as the individual and for the moral and spiritual progress of mankind; when the therapist was struggling with a difficult transference problem, he was on this view ultimately working for all mankind.[70]

However, even this did not exhaust the meaning of transference, since the process may involve projection not just of personal emotions and kinship feelings but also of archetypal images. Freud had noticed the violent resistance by patients to the rational termination of transference, and Jung interpreted this to mean that some sexual forms of transference concealed contents from the collective unconscious which defied all rational solution. In that case the ending of transference might cut the patient off from the collective unconscious and he would feel this as a loss or deprivation.[71] This meant that working through, say, a patient's transference where he or she saw the analyst as a saviour might still leave the collective saviour-complex untouched. For example, a patient in 1930s Germany might have worked through the *personal* problem of seeing the analyst as messiah but there would still remain the collective German saviour-complex, as evinced in the attitude to the Führer.[72] On the other hand, there seemed no solution to the problem of transference from the collective unconscious. How could archetypal material in transference be resolved, as this would mean making conscious the entire content of the collective unconscious – a manifest impossibility?[73]

It was at this point that Jung hit on something he considered a stroke of genius: the analogy between transference and the alchemical process. The aim of psychotherapy should be to change the base metal of the unexamined, projected material into the gold of integration rather than trying to resolve the transference at the level of the personal unconscious. This involved looking first at the three stages in the work of the classical alchemists.

The work of the alchemists began by finding a substance called the *prima materia*, which some believed to be salt, some mercury, others earth or water. This was then pulverized, mixed with a 'secret fire' and heated in a sealed vessel. The *prima materia* was supposed to contain two elements, male and female, referred to as *sol* (the sun) and *luna* (the moon), alias sulphur and mercury. In the sealed vessel *nigredo* or blackening then commenced, whose purpose was separation. The analogue in Jungian analysis is the initial stage of therapy, differentiating the adult situation from the childhood complexes, ego from the shadow, animus from anima, and so on. Blackness could also be interpreted as the depression (melancholia) leading the patient into analysis.

In the second stage of *albedo*, or whitening, the mass begins to show white flecks and turns white, as the product of *nigredo* is washed; finally it becomes volatile and recrystallizes as a white stone. Figuratively, this can be seen as integration or the 'washing of one's dirty linen' in analysis.[74] The final stage in the process is *rubedo* or reddening. In the original alchemical formula the white stone was added to 'mercury' and 'exaltation' took place; the stone turned green after being dissolved in acid (the so-called 'green lion' of alchemy) and finally turns red. In short, whiteness is united to redness through raising the heat of the fire. In alchemical symbolism the white queen is fused with the red king in the sacred marriage (*hierosgamos*) which produces the union of opposites (*coniunctio oppositorum*). The final red stone in alchemy is the 'philosopher's stone', allegedly possessing the qualities of an elixir of life and capable of turning base metal into gold.

Since as chemistry this is nonsense, it had long been suspected by students of alchemy that the chemical mumbo-jumbo was a blind, and that alchemy, properly understood, was a mystery religion or branch of occultism. Jung's idea was that the 'philosopher's stone', understood psychologically, was the individuation process. Liberating gold from the *massa confusa* meant bringing the Self to consciousness from the dark chaos of the unconscious, and making gold meant creating the Self. Individuation thus functioned as the true key to all mythologies, since the pervasive figure of the hermaphrodite represented the united king and queen. They consummated their sacred marriage by sexual intercourse in a bath and in turn engendered a son, a figure approximating to the Gnostic Anthropos.[75] This act of procreation completed, the king and queen then die – a process Jung likened to the death of the ego during individuation and the birth of the Self.

Jung had several reasons for thinking that alchemy was a symbolic version of transference during psychotherapy. In the first place he was struck by the similarities between alchemical symbols and those produced by patients in dreams and active imagination. His great friend, the Swiss physicist Wolfgang Pauli (1900–58), later a Nobel laureate, had dreams which strikingly matched alchemical motifs.[76] Jung became convinced that the psychology of the unconscious took up the trail lost by the alchemists. Since each individual is unique, with unique problems, it was not easy to give a general explanation of the process of individuation from case studies. Using the symbols of alchemy, however, made it possible to grasp by analogy the sort of transformation that was involved. Treating alchemical symbols much as the analyst treats modern fantasies yields similar meanings, so that in one sense alchemy was merely an early form of 'active imagination'.[77]

Transference came into the picture because the unexplained part of the alchemical process was the role of the mysterious catalytic agent which permitted, say, lead to be reduced to its original elements and then reconstituted as gold. Jung gradually started to feel certain that alchemy involved the externalization of contents from the unconscious, that it was a form of *projection*. He thought that the alchemists took their work so seriously that, unconsciously, they projected their own desires and obsessions into it; he was sure they had undergone experiences similar to his own *Nekyia* in 1913–18. Alchemical texts, therefore, the products of 'active imagination', purported to be about the chemical process itself but were really about religion. This thesis seemed all the more plausible as the alchemists made no real distinction between material objects and mental processes.[78]

Jung found the analogies between alchemy and transference striking.[79] It followed that Freudian methods, using the couch, would make it impossible to work through the transference.[80] Besides, the usual paradigm case of the male analyst and female patient mirrored the alchemist and his mystical sister (*soror mystica*). Needless to say, Jung soon worked this up into a 'marriage quaternity': first, the direct conscious relationship; secondly, that of the man's anima and the woman's animus; thirdly, the relationship between the man and his anima and the woman and her animus; and fourthly, between the woman's animus and the man, and the man's anima and the woman.[81]

In the 'marriage quaternity' the danger for both partners was that they would be absorbed by each other's anima and animus and become identified with it; this must be resisted at all costs in order to preserve the distinction between the real and the projected. Transference was different from normal projection because, whereas projection was a common-or-garden psychological phenomenon, transference could be used for therapy.[82]

It was not long before Jung was using the alchemy/transference analogy as an established item in the science of psychology. He used alchemy to explain the case of a patient with no parents and no religious faith to sustain him, who was stuck at the transference stage and unable to emerge.[83]

Using alchemy as a master key also enabled Jung to unlock other doors that had a psychological significance, especially in mythology and religion. He went on to theorize that the deep purpose of temple prostitution, *droit de seigneur, ius primae noctis* and other ritual ways of deflowering was to sunder for ever the transference between father and husband.[84] And because in the Ancient world there was a fourth stage (yellowing) in alchemy, Jung was able to see alchemy as tying in with universal quaternities, such as the four elements (earth, air, fire and water) and the four qualities (hot, cold, dry, moist).[85]

He also thought that alchemy stood in a compensatory relationship to medieval Christianity. For the Christian, Man needed to be redeemed by God, but for the alchemist it was God who needed to be redeemed by Man.[86] It was the dogmatism of Christianity that had driven these true religious feelings underground into alchemy, which was to Christianity what the unconscious was to consciousness. Alchemy probed deeper into the psyche than Christianity, stressed salvation through individuation rather than a Second Coming, the Quaternity rather than the Trinity, the God-image rather than the transcendent God.[87]

Jung's treatment of alchemy is typical of his later thought.

An apparently technical problem in psychoanalysis or analytical psychology quickly leads to the most abtruse mystical speculation, and it is this very inability to be analytical in the true sense rather than metaphysical that has so alienated many would-be admirers. After reading *Psychology and Alchemy* and *Mysterium Coniunctionis*, Colin Wilson remarked exasperatedly, 'Even the most sympathetic reader feels inclined to believe that Jung could conjure up reasons for anything he wanted to prove.'[88] The American feminist Demaris Wehr felt that the analogy from alchemy, with king and queen having sexual intercourse, in a subtle way legitimated the sexual intercourse Jung himself engaged in with his patients, for the alchemy/transference analogy would enable him to plead that he was 'merely' working through a difficult transference.[89]

Freud died before he could learn how Jung had developed his cardinal idea of transference. His likely reaction, given the scope and resources of his polemical and vitriolic vocabulary, had better be left to the imagination. By and large it was true that everything Jung said about Freud and his theories was distorted, exaggerated or unhelpful. There were, however, three areas with feedback into the Freudian mainstream where Jung had more positive and useful things to say: the training analysis, lay analysis and group therapy.

From the very earliest days Freud had been dismayed by the reckless and ignorant way amateurs and dilettantes, including many physicians, had applied a superficial and bowdlerized 'psychoanalysis' as a crutch for their patients, and in his paper 'Wild Analysis' he inveighed against such charlatanry.[90] In this regard the furious rivalry of Jung and Abraham when both were at Freud's side is in passing interesting, for it was Jung who first suggested the idea of a training analysis, where the analyst would first of all confront his own neuroses and complexes before treating patients, and Abraham who becamc the past master of the training analysis.[91]

If Freud and Jung were at one on this issue, there was a greater distance between them on the question of lay analysis. In brief, did the analysis of the unconscious entail and presuppose a medical qualification, or could it be carried out just as well by those with philosophical and literary backgrounds, provided always they had undergone a training analysis? This became a major battleground in the history of psychoanalysis, with American analysts insisting on a medical degree as a prerequisite while the British were quite content to countenance lay analysts. While conceding the common-sense point that every patient should have a medical examination before undergoing analysis, to make sure that the alleged hysteria, manic depression and so on did not have an organic cause, Freud insisted that non-physicians were often the very best analysts and physicians the very worst.[92] In a word, he was wholeheartedly in favour of lay analysis – a vastly different thing from 'wild analysis'; this was hardly surprising since some of the leading lights of psychoanalysis were 'lay', including Otto Rank, Hanns Sachs, Lou-Andreas Salome, Melanie Klein and Freud's daughter Anna.

Jung was closer to the Americans on this point and insisted that a lay analyst should always operate under the supervision of a medically qualified practitioner.[93] It is possible to detect in Jung's attitude a concealed love of formal qualifications and academic baubles – an attitude that is evident elsewhere. He does not explain why a qualified physician should be any better at dealing with schizophrenia than a lay analyst. He seemed to be making the unwarranted leap from the acknowledged fact that he himself was both a qualified physician and a master in treating schizophrenia to the generalization that all trained physicians would have the same attributes. He did not display the openness of Freud, who saw that better insights into the unconscious could be gained from literature and anthropology than from medicine and that physicians were often the very worst 'doctors' of the mind. He also contradicted his own frequent fulminations about the undesirability of psychotherapy being subordinated to psychiatry, which he himself compared to subjecting immunology to surgery. Moreover, his own work argued against the stance he took on lay analysis. If a medical degree, based on causality and western science, was so valuable, what price Buddhism, the study of world mythology, synchronicity and the *I Ching*?

Even worse, Jung sometimes confused in his own mind 'wild analysis' and lay analysis. In 1934 he wrote to a correspondent to poke fun at Freud's 'medically unqualified daughter'.[94] To this one might reply that Anna Freud had undergone a rigorous training analysis whereas Jung, despite his frequent references to the Pope and his father confessor, had not. His 'training' had consisted of consultations and discussions with Freud which he later declared worthless. If formal qualifications are at issue, one could argue that Jung's degree from the University of Basel was worthless as a credential for the Burghölzli and that it was the 'training' he received from Bleuler that was important. So wherein was Anna Freud's case any different? Naturally, Jung was unique in that he had a touch of genius, but many would be found to argue that Anna Freud and, even more, Melanie Klein, another 'unqualified' analyst who, according to Jung, should have been working under the direction of a physician, were not without talent themselves.

As for group therapy, Jung was inclined to be sceptical on the ground that it destroyed the individual's sense of personal integrity. It was true that groups engendered solidarity, and he remembered a time while on manoeuvres in the Alps when he was caught in thick fog while crossing a glacier; had he been alone, the experience would have been terrifying but in a squad of soldiers the atmosphere was more like that of a carnival. Groups also heightened suggestibility, which explained the behaviour of people in the Army, in the Oxford Movement, at Lourdes and at the Nuremburg rallies. The 'down side' of all this was that the capacity to discriminate and to exercise personal responsibility was injured: one could look for this in the selfsame places – the German Army which abdicated to the Führer and the Oxford Movement which left everything to 'Lord Jesus'.

Group therapy was unobjectionable as social education, and could even accentuate favourable aspects of the ego. But the Self was in danger from all big organizations – armies, unions, nation states, and the Self could be reached only by individual analysis and the dialectic between doctor and patient. To an extent, then, one could say that group therapy and individual therapy complemented each other, enhancing consciousness and the unconscious respectively, but even then there was the danger that the patient undergoing group therapy would be stuck at the collective level of 'mass man', would regard the group as mother and father and so remain just as dependent, insecure and infantile as before.

Jung outlived Freud by more than twenty years, and so naturally had the last word on many of these controversies. The post-Freudians, however, did not remain silent, and the most vociferous reaction came from Erich Fromm. Describing Jung's work as 'the naïve assertions of a reactionary romantic,' Fromm summed up his black view thus: 'With his blend of outmoded superstition, indeterminate heathen idol-worship, and vague talk about God, and with the allegation that he is building a bridge between religion and psychology, Jung has presented exactly the right mix to an age which possesses but little faith and judgement.'[95] Other neo-Freudians tended to agree. Charles Rycroft claimed that Jung's ideas were unintelligible and others accused him of 'downright unreadability'.[96] There was general agreement that Freud was immeasurably superior as literary stylist and lucid writer. Paul Ricoeur commented, 'With Freud I know where I am going; with Jung everything risks being confused: the psychism, the soul, the archetypes, the sacred.'[97]

Yet some post-Freudians have seen merit in Jung's work, and in this regard the investigations of Heinz Kohut into the nature of the self are particularly interesting.[98] Most nuanced of all is the attitude of Erik Erikson. In many ways Erikson was a stern critic of Jung, regarding him as prophet not scientist, and viewing his work as 'ideological regression' characterized (as in the case of his attitude to the Nazis) by 'weakly denied . . . reactionary political acts'.[99] On the other hand, Erikson found much to commend in Jung's work. He agreed that the Oedipus-complex should be interpreted not as a sexual conflict but as a wish to be reborn, was inclined to accept Jung's view of dreams as compensation, and in general deplored Freudians' ignorance of Jung.[100]

The mutual hatred felt by Jung and Freud did very great damage to the progress of depth psychology. It has to be conceded that it was Jung rather than Freud who, over the years, kept the pot boiling. Yet occasionally, as in Riklin's 1938 mission to Vienna, nobler impulses supervened, and one can even detect in Jung's work at times a hint of regret that the animosity had been taken so far. Despite his constant bracketing of Freud and Adler, Jung did eventually concede that a talent like Adler could not be compared to a genius like Freud and wrote revealingly: 'Without Freud's "psychoanalysis" I wouldn't have had a clue.'[101]

Chapter Twenty-Three

WARTIME

As the fatal year of 1939 opened, Jung's pessimism deepened. Plunged into gloom by the Munich crisis, he predicted that Britain and France would not honour the pledges Chamberlain and Daladier had made to Czechoslovakia; when Hitler sent his troops into what remained of that unhappy country in March 1939, his worst fears were confirmed.[1] The invasion also reinforced the message he had been dinning into the ears of his followers since his return from India: that Oriental philosophy had no answer to the problems confronted by the West.

The conventional wisdom of the East stated that the world of politics, including world wars, was simply part of the realm of illusion. Jung thought that the eternal standpoint was of value only if it was reconciled with daily life in the here-and-now. He was fond of the parable of the mountain and the valley. One must ascend the mountain to see the whole picture in perspective, but one must also descend into the valley; as he repeatedly stressed, the obliteration of ego by Self was just as dangerous as vice versa. If the problem with the East was the belief that only the mountain existed, the malaise of the West was the conviction that nothing existed but the valley.

The drift to war seemed to Jung inevitable. The West, as well as the dictatorships, was in the grip of unconscious possession. For Jung it was the unconscious rather than economic motives or *haute politique* that drove nations to war, and one of the functions of the unconscious was to deal with issues towards which the conscious adopted an ostrich-like stance. Nobody wanted war consciously and at this level the desire for war was projected onto the other side: it was all the fault of the aggressive Germans, the barbarous Russians, and so on. But at the unconscious level mankind did want war to find some means of getting rid of our surplus population. Twentieth-century technology had increased the sense of being overcrowded, for populations had not just exploded but also imploded into huge cities. Moreover, the modern media increased psychic stress by bringing the world's disasters – in Spain, China or South America – into our living rooms. The obvious way to ease this never-ending psychic burden was to arrange to kill as many as possible of these foreign nuisances who were annoying us.[2]

Pessimism about the West was balanced by an increasingly jaded cynicism about the 'mighty phenomenon' of National Socialism. By 1939 there were clear signs that Jung regretted he had given so many earlier hostages to fortune. In February he wrote in disillusionment to an American admirer that he was tired of Nazis and dictators and prophesied that the Hitler Youth would soon be thoroughly sick of the stuff that was being preached to them.

Hitler he more and more viewed as a hysteric and pathological liar. He may not have begun as a deceiver but he was the sort of idealist who is always in love with his own ideas and in thrall to wish fantasies, sometimes thinking it is easy to attain what is in fact very hard to attain and sometimes imagining that what is to be attained has already been attained. Hitler's perverted genius was to be able to persuade the German people that his 'wish-system' was socio-political reality, and the result was a psychic epidemic that swelled like an avalanche. The suggestibility of the Germans was explicable for Jung by the German 'national inferiority-complex' exacerbated by their draconian treatment under the Treaty of Versailles. The Germans saw themselves as underdogs who were really the chosen people, which was why they hated the Jews with a special hatred, for the Jews had already preempted this unique status.[3]

What fascinated Jung about the Nazi phenomenon was the

coalescence of disparate elements: the archetypal figure of the Superman; the unconscious 'blond beast' represented by Wotan; Hitler as medicine man and thaumaturge; and the mindlessness of 'mass man'. Hitler drew his strength from repressed archetypes as Antaeus in the Greek myth drew his from Mother Earth, and it was this which enabled him to pose as the personified nation and which was why rational, intelligent people saw nothing wrong in taking a personal oath of loyalty to the Führer. And, like all great spiritual and mystical figures, Hitler was obliged at times to retreat into the 'wilderness' to meditate: Jung pointed out the significance of his three-day 'retreat' just before announcing the decision to quit the League of Nations.

Hypnotic suggestion applied to an entire people was an interesting hypothesis, but Jung warned that suggestion worked only when there was a secret wish to fulfil it. Hitler was able to work on all those who compensated their inferiority complex with social aspirations and secret dreams of power. As a result, he gathered around him an army of social misfits, psychopaths and criminals. Yet at the same time he gripped the unconscious of normal people, whose perennial Achilles heel is the combination of naïvety and unconsciousness. So-called normal people can be persuaded to such maladaptation – which outsiders would see as an entire society in a diseased state – simply because of the peculiar psychological vulnerability of 'mass man'. Mass psychosis, like the embrace of Nazism by the German people, was really a herd phenomenon, like panic; the more people lived together in overcrowded anthills, the more stupid and suggestible they were likely to become.[4]

Yet whatever the complex psychological causes of Nazism, by 1939 Jung was sure that Germany's new bearing must lead her to war. The logic of *lebensraum* necessitated a full-scale military campaign against either the British Empire or the Soviet Union (for in common with most people in 1939, Jung did not imagine that Hitler would ever be foolish enough to fight on two fronts).[5] The only way for the West to save itself was to persuade Hitler to look East and bend his energies against the USSR.

For Jung, 1939 was a black year, but he tried to set aside his forebodings on the international situation by concentrating on the study of alchemy and lecturing on St Ignatius Loyola. It was also a year of significant dreams. One night, while he was giving a seminar on Loyola, he seemed to wake up and see, bathed in light at the foot of his bed, the figure of Christ on the cross. He took the dream or vision to mean that he had overlooked the analogy of Christ with the gold of the alchemists.[6] His friend Erich Neumann consulted him about a puzzling dream in which he was a pilgrim threatened by Nazis; to complicate matters the pilgrim wore the slouch hat usually associated with Wotan.[7] There were to be many dreams of Nazis and Hitler that year.

A much more important patient was Mary Mellon, a Vassar graduate and daughter of a Kansas physician. More significantly, Mary Mellon was wife to Paul, heir to the Mellon fortunes (Paul Mellon's personal wealth was reckoned in hundreds of millions of dollars in the 1940s) and thus another in the long line of American millionaires who beat a path to Küsnacht. The Mellons first met Jung at the Terry lectures at Yale in 1937, invited him to supper and were at once struck by his down-to-earth quality. The three of them had supper in a simple restaurant in New Haven. At their table was a bottle of Chianti. Without waiting for the waiter to open the wine, Jung produced a large Swiss hunting knife from his pocket, levered out the corkscrew, drew out the cork and served the wine. The upshot was that the Mellons attended Jung's seminar on Nietzsche in Zürich in 1938 and then went on to the Eranos conference at Ascona. Here they struck up a notable friendship with Olga Kroebe-Kapteyn, the founder of the conferences. Olga told them things about herself that she had never told Jung – how when she was young she had been a circus rider, and how the Casa Gabriella at Ascona was a personal gift from her father, a former director of the London office of the Westinghouse Brake and Signal Company. She also confided that she had spent a fortune on the Eranos conferences and her patrimony was almost exhausted. Mary Mellon at once stepped into the breach and agreed to take over funding the project.[8]

At Ascona in 1938 Jung gave each of the Mellons a fifteen minute interview. Mary was keen to be taken on as a patient as she suffered from mysterious attacks of asthma, but Jung told Paul the treatment would be difficult, as Mary had 'a terrific animus problem'. Paul Mellon was nothing like so keen on Jungian therapy as Mary, but was something of a classical scholar and liked conversing with Jung. It was therefore agreed that the two of them would return in the autumn of 1939 and begin analysis, each of them having three or four sessions a week. With some reluctance Paul agreed to return for the 1939 Eranos conference, as he found the atmosphere confusing and the participants 90 per cent female, and he was also unable to distinguish pupils, analysands and therapists in the throng of maenads.[9]

International tensions were palpable in the summer of 1939, and when Jung and the Zürich contingent set out for the Eranos conference he was troubled by the 'synchronicity' of the stormy weather. Never one to shirk a 'pathetic fallacy', Jung was convinced Nature was sending him a message. On a hunch he ordered the fleet of cars to drive at top speed through the Gothard pass. His famous intuition was right, for hours later a landslide closed the pass. Down on Lake Maggiore too the omens were inauspicious, for there was flooding and the lake overflowed its banks. The conference itself was an acrimonious affair, with a notable slanging match taking place between Barbara Hannah and a German delegate over who was responsible for the looming crisis over Poland. Jung came down firmly on Hannah's side, especially when the conference heard personal anecdotes from a Red Cross official about Hitler's foul temper. To scowls of hostility from the German participants, Jung announced he was now convinced that Hitler and the whole of Germany were possessed. The Conference broke up in an atmosphere described as being like that of the Last Judgement.[10]

The Nazi–Soviet pact triggered more of Jung's dreams about Hitler. In one of them he learned that Hitler was 'the Devil's Christ', a representative of the left-hand side of God but His instrument nonetheless; this led to the conviction that any theology, such as that of orthodox Christianity, which neglected the dark side of God, was bunk.[11]

In another, much more elaborate, dream about Hitler, Jung revealed the impact of the Molotov–Ribbentrop pact on his unconscious. He dreamt he was in a castle made of dynamite. Hitler entered and was treated as though he were divine. He and Hitler then stood on raised mounds as if to review troops. Then a herd of buffalo and yak trooped by, and there was one sick cow in the herd over which Hitler was very concerned. Finally a company of Cossacks rode in at the back and began to drive the herd off.[12] Jung interpreted this to mean that the German people were in thrall to a herd instinct, and that the sick cow was Hitler's suppression of the feminine instinct. The coming of the Cossacks seemed to suggest that at some time in the future the Russians would break into Germany and overthrow the Reich. Jung's critics claim that there was no contemporary (1939) description of the dream, which, as analysed, is used as an example of Jung's godlike prescience. Others say the true meaning of the sick cow is Jung's own culpable moral neutrality in 1939.[13]

The Polish crisis in the early days of September convinced the Swiss that the cataclysm was about to descend on them. At a joint session of the two chambers of the Swiss Parliament on 30 August 1939 Henri Guisan, a sixty-five-year-old veteran, was appointed commander-in-chief of the national forces, and two days later all Swiss forces were mobilized – some 435,000 men out of a population of 4.2 millions. Guisan, if not quite king for a day, had extraordinary powers while the war lasted but such was the Swiss dislike and suspicion of individual leadership and their preference for communal decision-making that the day the war ended he would be obliged to return to his home, like Cincinnatus.[14]

The German attack on Poland, which brought Britain and France into the conflict and thus inaugurated the six-year conflict known to history as the Second World War, distressed Jung and he was appalled by the aerial bombing of Warsaw, referring to 'the exquisite bestiality of the young German fighters during the Blitzkrieg in Poland.'[15] Well-wishers made many offers to arrange for wartime exile in the USA but he refused absolutely, declaring he had no wish to lose his identity or his roots.[16] The war provoked a kind of organic solidarity in the extended Jung family. Agathli and Marianne, who had married into the Niehus family, Gret, who was now Frau Baumann, and Helene who had married Herr Koerni, formed a kind of defensive psychological laager around Küsnacht, since all but one of the sons-in-law were in the Swiss army (as was Jung's son Franz) and the wives and children stayed with Carl and Emma in the big house.[17]

Jung constantly gave thanks that Switzerland had not been sucked into the fascist maw. He thought there were two main reasons: Switzerland was a small nation and had therefore not succumbed to the madness of 'mass man'; and the very stolidity and pigheadedness of the Swiss prevented them from being seduced by nostrums and ideologies – after all, it was better to be stuck in the past, a hundred years behind the times, than mindlessly to embrace the so-called 'future'.[18]

The strategic problem faced by General Guisan in the event of war was how to prevent encirclement by the Panzer divisions. Guisan began by planning a defensive line, using all available artillery and anti-tank weapons, which would extend along a line of rivers, lakes and mountains running parallel to the German border. As there was no reserve if the defensive line was breached, the Swiss people were exhorted to bring every single firearm out of attic and cellar, and antiquated guns were exhumed from arsenals, all to provide the maximum possible concentrated firepower. Work began at once on the defensive line and continued during the 'phoney war' of 1939–40. The line began at the fortress of Sargans, then followed the lakes of Walensee and Zürichsee, the river Limmat and the Jura mountains before coming to an end at the heights of Gempen, overlooking Basel; the north-east of Switzerland was to be abandoned to the enemy and the emphasis placed on making Zürich a 'Stalingrad *avant la lettre*'.[19]

The tension in Switzerland made it difficult for Jung to concentrate on his studies. Somewhat reluctantly, he was drawn into the public arena. In October he turned down indignantly an approach from one of Hitler's doctors, who telephoned him from Munich to ask if he would come to Berlin to give the Führer an informal psychiatric examination; the doctor explained that he and his colleagues were worried about Hitler's increasing pathological symptoms.[20] But he did accept the invitation to stand for parliament as a candidate for the coalition formation known as the National Group of Independents. He allowed his name to go forward but, no doubt fortunately, he was not elected.[21]

In October Jung went up to Basel to observe the German and French lines and the new fortifications. Though all was quiet and there was no shooting, Jung sensed a heavy pall of menace and felt that a sword of Damocles was hovering just overhead; he spoke of a disturbed atmosphere and a sense of an apocalyptic future, with Satan roaming the earth in the form of blood-crazed Germans. Everything he heard convinced him that Hitler was at least half crazy.[22]

Despite himself, Jung became more and more involved in the detail of the war. His disciple Mary Bancroft came to ask his advice on a ticklish matter. Allen Dulles, head of the fledgling OSS (Office of Strategic Services), could not bring his agents into Switzerland after September 1939 so he had set about recruiting reliable Americans already in the country. He approached Bancroft, who wondered if, as an extravert, she had the ability to keep her mouth shut. After hearing her story, Jung advised her to take up

Dulles's offer, pointing out the number of lives she might be able to save.[23]

Bancroft had not told Jung the whole story of her relations with Dulles. She had begun life as an 'emancipated' débutante in Boston, had had many lovers and a failed American marriage behind her by the time she came to live in Switzerland in 1934.[24] Her second husband, Jean Rufenach, was an accountant who was often away from home on business, leaving the coast clear for Mary to pursue her career as *grande horizontale*. Among her lovers, and for a while the only one, was the doyen of American secret intelligence, Allen Dulles, a cold fish who related to other men only when they could be of use to him and with women only when he could go to bed with them. Mary Bancroft attracted him not just by her physical charms but because she seemed a born secret agent. Her social sophistication, poise, natural curiosity and fluency in French and German made her a valuable asset.

Dulles began by setting her to work on the analysis of the German press, where she brought Jungian insights to bear on the speeches of Hitler, Goering and Goebbels. Bancroft was a familiar figure in Berne, pounding out political analyses on a beaten-up typewriter, a cigarette dangling from her lips. Every so often Dulles would arrive for a rapid bout of sexual intercourse: he claimed he needed such 'quickies' to clear his head. Bancroft eventually became tired of the blatant way Dulles used her. He for his part became irritated by her overuse of Jungian jargon. One night, after reading one of her reports, he blurted out in exasperation: 'I wish you'd stop this nonsense. I don't want to go down in history as a footnote to a case of Jung's.'[25] Although not privy to the full details of the Bancroft/Dulles liaison, Jung met the American spymaster on a number of occasions and quickly sensed something of his ruthlessness. On one occasion Jung said in an aside to Bancroft: 'Your friend Dulles is quite a tough nut, isn't he? I'm glad you've got his ear.'[26]

Jung also had wartime concerns nearer home and petitioned for a fair deal for the 400,000 conscripted Swiss soldiers. Seeing that all the families of these men had lost breadwinners, while foreigners and those ineligible for military service took their jobs, he wrote to the Federal Council to warn of the evident dangers of social strife and disaffection if this process was allowed to continue unchecked. He proposed that all Swiss citizens between the ages of sixteen and sixty be counted as mobilized, whether they were liable for military service or not. Since everyone would then be under conscript regulations, everyone doing a civilian job and earning more than the soldiers should be compulsorily 'equalized': all wages and salaries exceeding military pay would be confiscated and put in a kitty, from which funds would then be made available for the distressed families of conscripts; there would then be no feeling that the country harboured any skrimshankers or people unwilling to pull their weight.[27]

The Council responded with a scheme of its own. In the first place, taking advantage of a more relaxed public opinion during the 'phoney war,' it demobilised more than half the troops called up, so that only about 175,000 remained under arms. Then, on 20 December 1939, the Council brought in legislation which stipulated an allowance to be paid to the family of the conscript, based on the size of the family and the average earnings of the man in peacetime civilian life.[28]

For a notorious trencherman like Jung, the most immediate threat from wartime was rationing. Switzerland had to import food to survive – a shortfall of 1.2 million tons of food a year had to be dealt with by central planning – and in 1938 a law had been passed granting import permits only to those firms which were prepared to stockpile for six months. In April 1939 the Swiss government ordered a two-month stockpile of food and instructed farmers to treble the land available for wheat production. The cultivated surface of agricultural land was doubled and, in addition, football fields, parks and lawns were ploughed over and sown with potatoes. On 30 October 1939 rationing was introduced. From the beginning of 1940 coffee, tea, cocoa, cheese, eggs and meat were on the ration list, and by late 1942 bread, milk, chocolate, potatoes and flour were added and two days of the week were compulsorily meatless. The initial ration was set at 3,000 calories a day, but in 1941 this was cut to 2,400. However, the Swiss proved inept at public relations, since foreign visitors were exempt from the restrictions; neutrals who came to Switzerland found it a land of milk and honey and mistakenly concluded that the Swiss wanted for nothing.[29]

There were fewer patients for Jung to attend to now, with most of the foreigners already departed and the natives under conscription, so the Mary Mellon case tended to loom large. By early 1940 Paul Mellon was bored and irritated both by wartime Switzerland and Jungian analysis, but Mary was still besotted with Jung and all his works. Paul was impatient with the lack of progress with Mary's asthma and was about to serve an ultimatum demanding an early return to the United States when Mary went down with appendicitis and had to be operated on in Zürich. While she convalesced, in April 1940, Paul joined Jung and Emma and members of his family on a walking tour of the mountains near Locarno on Lake Maggiore, stopping at Losone, Intragna and Ponte Brolla, where Jung had a favourite restaurant. Jung talked about Mary's asthma and criticized the cluelessness of American doctors, who thought the illness was organic. He was also interested in all things military and extolled to Mellon the benefits of compulsory military service. Despite some reservations, Mellon enjoyed Jung's company, but as soon as Mary was fully recovered (in May 1940), the Mellons departed for the United States.[30]

Jung's friend the brilliant physicist Wolfgang Pauli departed for the USA at about the same time. Like a later unorthodox theoretical physicist of genius (Richard Feynman), Pauli had a taste for the low life. After a brief first marriage ended in divorce in 1930, he spent many late nights in Zürich in drunken progress from glittering hotels to sordid bars in the rougher parts of town.[31] He was invaluable to Jung, since he was a brilliant student of the theory of relativity who was also prepared to take seriously Jung's ideas on probability, acausality and synchronicity. It was a heavy blow to Jung when Pauli decided, in the light of the sweeping German military successes in the early summer of 1940, that, as a Jew, he was no longer safe anywhere in Europe and departed for the USA. In many ways Pauli was a good match for Jung in personality, being sharp-tongued, supercilious and dogmatic; he did not suffer fools gladly and dealt with most arguments that were put to him with the single word *quatsch*! (rubbish).[32]

In May 1940 the 'phoney war' came to a decisive end as the German panzers invaded France. As Rotterdam was pounded by aerial bombardment, the Swiss realized to their horror that Zürich was virtually defenceless against bombers and in the event of war was threatened with complete destruction. Evacuation from the cities began: Jung's entire family (apart from his son and sons-in-law in the army) went to a mountain refuge near Saanen. Jung still pinned some hopes on Italian neutrality, thinking that Hitler and Mussolini did not trust each other, but his heart went out to Britain and France.[33]

In an amazingly short time Jung's hopes were dashed. By the end of June a defeated France was under the Nazi jackboot and Mussolini had entered the war on Hitler's side. Switzerland now braced itself for a sudden brutal attack without declaration of war. Many in the upper echelons of industry and government felt that Nazi domination was inevitable and that the sensible thing was to come to terms with this. Industry particularly pressed for demobilization, both to increase output and to appease the Germans. With the people confused and demoralized, the defeatist president of the Swiss Confederation, Marcel Pilet-Goaz, addressed the nation on 25 June 1940. In a government broadcast he spoke in gloomy, Pétain-like tones and proposed an accommodation with Germany much along the lines of that just concluded by Vichy France. He announced that the Swiss armed forces would be reduced by two-thirds and said nothing about resisting an enemy. Warning that the free and easy life had come to an end, Pilet-Goaz urged the people to 'discard old attitudes'.[34]

This defeatist and apparently pro-Nazi speech outraged Guisan and the army leaders and threatened to split the country. Pilet-Goaz and Guisan held each other in mutual contempt: the president considered his commander-in-chief a boorish peasant while Guisan regarded Pilet-Goaz as a typical Lausanne intellectual; in Switzerland Lausanne had a bad reputation for fostering a cult of detached Francophone superiority, which in its critics' eyes was simply a provincial mentality masquerading as a cosmopolitan one. Unable to prevent the immediate reduction of the army to 150,000, Guisan nonetheless forced the government to admit that a commitment to defend the country against attack from any quarter still existed. He made it known that it was his intention, if the Swiss Army was forced to abandon the defensive line (finally completed in May 1940) to withdraw into the Alps to make a last stand.[35]

Guisan's next action was a spectacular piece of theatre. On 18 July he summoned his army commanders to a meeting at the meadow of Rutli, near Lucerne – the very spot where in 1291 the Swiss Confederation had been founded. In a stirring speech, which completely eclipsed Pilet-Goaz's government broadcast, he made full use of the symbolism of the venue by pledging to fight on against an invader.[36] He announced a National Redoubt in the Alps. This new plan called for the army to occupy a position at the foot of the mountain chain stretching from the fortress of Sargans in the east to the fortress of St Maurice in the southwest. A southern line, forming an ellipse, was also planned, which would follow the high mountains (including the Matterhorn) on the frontier with Italy. The centre of the ellipse would be at the St Gothard pass and would comprise a number of deep valleys redesigned as industrial cities, together with underground storehouses for fuel and ammunition. It was envisaged that about a quarter of Switzerland's population would be able to live in the redoubt; the other three-quarters, together with half the national territory and all the major cities, including the capital Berne, would be abandoned to the invader. Guisan's strategy was based on convincing Germany that a war with Switzerland would be long, costly and not worth the trouble, since their war aims could be achieved by pacific means.[37]

Did the Swiss fears of an invasion have a realistic basis? On the one hand, European wars always made them extremely jittery: in 1917, with the approaching defeat of Russia, which freed German armies for the Western front, the Swiss were apprehensive that Ludendorff would invade their country to get round the right flank of the French army. The same kinds of fears were expressed in mid-May 1940 when the German advance in northern France seemed stalled and it was thought the Germans might attack through Switzerland to outflank the Maginot line. On the other hand, Hitler did at various times consider plans for taking over the territory of neutrals, especially Sweden, Switzerland and Spain.

However, a German invasion was always unlikely. There did exist a detailed Nazi plan for the occupation of Switzerland, prepared in October 1940 and codenamed 'Operation Tannenbaum', which envisaged the use of twenty-one divisions, including Italian ones. However, there was never any serious intention of implementing the plan, since twenty-one divisions represented an unacceptable drain on Axis strength – by 1941 severely overstretched with major campaigns in Russia, Yugoslavia and North Africa. The German intention was to keep the Swiss on permanent alert, so that they never allowed their defence forces to fall below the 170,000 level – thought to be the minimum number necessary to deter the Allies from a 'soft underbelly' probe through Switzerland from the south – and for this reason they engineered many invasion scares.[38]

Side by side with the plans for a National Redoubt, the Swiss did their best to conciliate Hitler and not try his patience. By a treaty of 1939 it was agreed that all non-military supplies would continue to be transported by Swiss railway through the Simplon and St Gothard passes. This meant that the Brenner pass could be used by the Axis exclusively for military purposes. Switzerland's alleged softness on the Nazis infuriated the Allies and, particularly when the United States entered the war, led to demand for stiff action against them, on the grounds that the Swiss were Franco-style 'non-belligerents' rather than true neutrals.[39]

Another early bone of contention was the war in the air over Switzerland. German planes sometimes violated Swiss airspace, leading to aerial combats with Swiss fighters and the shooting down of aircraft on both sides. Berlin was prepared to turn a blind eye to minor incidents like these but was displeased when the Swiss seemed more obliging towards British planes and was not prepared to take seriously Swiss protestations that they lacked the anti-aircraft equipment to bring down high-flying bombers. This matter came to a head after a heavy RAF raid on Germany in October 1940. Hitler fumed that the British bombers had been guided to their targets by a well-lit Switzerland which served as a beacon in the night sky. Extreme pressure was put on the Federal Council, with the result that a blackout was imposed over Switzerland on 6 November: it would last for nearly four years, being lifted only on 12 September 1944 when German armies were in headlong retreat before the advancing Allies. The enforced blackout had a deep psychological effect on Swiss morale and also led to accidental bombings, as when Allied payloads rained down on Basel and Zürich at the end of 1940.[40]

Jung followed all these events keenly. In August 1940, from an army camp in western Switzerland, where he was working as a volunteer doctor, Jung wrote to his English friend Peter Baynes as the Battle of Britain reached a climax. He told him that he was now convinced 1940 was the fateful year for which he had waited in trepidation for more than twenty-five years: his fear was all the more acute since 1940 was the year when the planet approached the meridian of the first star in Aquarius.

Jung followed the victory of the RAF in the Battle of Britain and the subsequent switch by the Luftwaffe to the bombing of British cities with horrified fascination. Peter Baynes wrote to tell him that he and his family had had a narrow escape when a bomb fell in the next street. Jung made encouraging noises, but his own mood was darkening and he took the classical advice to cultivate his garden, planting vegetables, living as much as possible like a peasant, with an eye open to the next good meal.[41] Switzerland seemed to him like the frozen kingdom in the Sleeping Beauty myth. Cars had all but vanished from the streets though trains still ran as usual; food was still plentiful though by now very expensive; and the army was concentrated in the redoubt in the mountains, ready to abandon the flatlands of Switzerland if the invader came. Jung tended to oscillate uneasily between momentary optimism and a more deep-seated pessimism.

The Jung of wartime still retained all his old ambivalence towards the USA. Writing at the nadir of Allied fortunes in 1941 Jung favourably contrasted British team-spirit, so admirably evinced in the Battle of Britain, with the American 'rugged individualism', which was simply another name for materialism. Pointing up the fallacy of novelty and 'progress' he argued that it was better for people to live in austerity than in affluence, and that aspirations for a 'better future' simply prevented mankind from living well in the present. He deplored America's influence on Switzerland's mass media, and blamed transatlantic culture for the fact that Swiss divorce levels had now reached those of the USA. Yet ambivalence was nothing new for Jung; indeed, he positively throve on it. After criticizing his fellow countrymen for their lack of community spirit and the national vices of obstinacy and mistrustfulness, he pointed out that it was to those very qualities that Switzerland owed its independence from the world.[42]

Jung liked to ruminate in this general way on the soul of Switzerland, as, whenever he looked beyond his study in the here and now, he saw only gloom. In April 1941 he wrote to Mary Mellon about the increasingly irritating shortages in Switzerland. All private vehicles except those belonging to doctors had been immobilized; this meant that Jung escaped the general ban, but it did him little good, for there was almost no petrol to be had anyway. He could not obtain his favourite English tobacco any longer, and central heating was subject to draconian regulations which, however, seemed to have improved the nation's health, especially its children's. Nonetheless he was tired and deeply depressed by the senselessness of this war.[43]

To Peter Baynes he complained that the war had brought him more work rather than less, because he could never finish an analysis with any patient. As soon as he had made a little progress, the patient would be called away on some war work, and Jung would then have to reschedule the latter stages of the treatment; in the meantime there would be returnees from the mountains whose cases he had to take up again.[44] To some extent he tried to make the best of a bad job, for his correspondence in 1941 shows a renewed interest in therapeutic matters. He accepted, somewhat self-preeningly, an accolade from his admirer Robert Loeb, who said that whereas Freud was Newton, Jung was Einstein.[45] With other correspondents he discussed whether neuroses could in any sense be traced to a causative archetype, and ventured the opinion that psoriasis was a psychosomatic disease.[46]

Yet most of all he withdrew into the world of alchemy and its symbolism, working on a grand theory that would embrace yoga, Buddhism, Loyola's *Exercitia Spiritualia* and the work of the great sixteenth century Swiss alchemist Paracelsus. 1941 was the five hundredth anniversary of the death of Paracelsus, and a special festival in his honour had been arranged at the little town of Linsiedeln, where Jung lectured and stayed at the monastery. The lecture, on the connection between transference and alchemy, revealed a deep knowledge of Paracelsus's work.[47]

Hitler's sudden launch of Operation Barbarossa on 22 June 1941 linked with Jung's early life in a way he never realized, for among the first casualties of the Nazi invasion was Sabina Spielrein, who had returned to Soviet Russia to practice as a psychoanalyst in 1923. When the Nazis swept into Rostov on the Don, they herded all Jews in the city into the synagogue and executed them. Among the victims was the fifty-five-year-old Sabina Spielrein and her two daughters.[48]

One part of Jung's 'consummation devoutly to be wished' had now come about, but the other part, that America should remain neutral, was about to be frustrated. On 7 December 1941 Japan made a surprise attack on the American fleet at Pearl Harbor; four days later Hitler declared war on the USA, making the conflict truly global. Jung displayed an amazing lack of interest in the war in the Pacific. He simply remarked that the Japanese leaders had made a great mistake in not consulting the *I Ching* before they went to war![49]

As rationing and wartime restrictions in Switzerland began to bite, Jung turned inwards, seeking to cosset himself as much as possible. He was concerned that the lectures at the Paracelsus festival had left him tired, and he tried to combat failing powers with a strict regime of swimming. He indulged his love of animals as much as possible, but was saddened by an incident at Bollingen in September 1941 when he saw a deer lying a few feet from the gate at seven one evening. Hoping to feed it by hand, he got within six feet of it before the alarmed animal jumped up and bounded away down the lake shore. Jung went for a walk in that direction and an hour later found the deer lying dead, having been knocked down by a train.[50]

1942 was the decisive year of the Second World War. At the end of 1941 the German army was at the gates of Moscow, while the Japanese, following their short-lived triumph at Pearl Harbor, swept all before them in the Far East and South-East Asia humiliating the British Empire in Singapore, at Hong Kong and in Burma. Twelve months later, after the victories of Midway, Stalingrad, El Alamein and the 'Torch' landings in North Africa, the Allies were confident enough of victory to demand unconditional surrender from the Axis at the Casablanca conference. This rapid reversal of fortunes found an echo in Jung's more relaxed tone in 1942. Fears of invasion had largely evaporated, apart from one short-lived scare in August when it was believed the Germans might invade northern Switzerland to seize the national fleet of trucks.[51]

Perhaps as a consequence of the improving situation in the war, Jung worked well that year. Paracelsus apart, his work contains mentions of Rorschach's inkblot tests, Rhine's telepathy experiments, Baudelaire, Gérard de Nerval, Justinus Kerner, the early nineteenth-century pioneer of the paranormal, and a host of alchemical sources.[52] There was renewed interest in Nicolaus of Cusa ('Brother Klaus'), especially when his son, who was an officer in a Catholic infantry regiment told him that his men had experienced a collective vision of brother Klaus holding out his hands towards the Rhine to ward off the German invader.[53]

Jung also made two important personal contacts, partly filling the vacuum left by Pauli and the Mellons. One was the brilliant Hungarian scholar Karl Kerenyi, whose seminal work on labyrinths mightily impressed Jung.[54] The other was Carl Burkhardt, the Geneva-based historian and diplomat. Burkhardt remembered a conversation in 1942 on the Zürich lake front, when Jung went out of his way to make caustic remarks about Hitler, pointing out that Nostradamus had predicted him. This was also the year when Reinhard Heydrich, principal author of the 'Final Solution', was assassinated in Prague. Jung, with his 'green fingers' for egregious evil, had made a study of Heydrich and told Burkhardt that the deputy Reichsprotector of Bohemia was a classic schizoid – something you could discern from his physiognomy. He related an uncheckable story about Heydrich – how in a drunken rage he had shot at his own image in a mirror, shouting, 'At last I've got you, you bastard!' But Jung was in a vicious mood that day, for he also told Burkhardt that President Roosevelt was 'the limping messenger of the apocalypse' and that FDR 'had, of course, like all Americans, a gigantic mother-complex'. Jung argued that, like all people suffering from such a complex, Roosevelt was pulled in two directions: he tried to please his mother by being an idealist but at the same time he enchanted the woman in her by being a super-rogue.[55]

Jung's dream life in 1942 was also peculiarly rich. He had frequent dreams about the spirit Mercurius, also an interest of Kerenyi's.[56] But, as if to prove his point that the outer and inner world worked in pre-established harmony, he also had dreams about the man he took to be Mercury's equivalent in the external world, Winston Churchill. He noted the two occasions when he had vivid dreams about Churchill, then compared them with Churchill's diary after the war. On both occasions it transpired that Churchill was in Switzerland, unknown to Jung. The first time he touched down near Zürich to refuel on his way to North Africa, and the second time he spent a night in Geneva on his way to Russia.[57] Of course, there is no way to verify that Jung actually did dream of Churchill on the nights in question.

Even though the war began to swing decisively in the Allies' favour, Jung was increasingly inclined to take a dark view of life. For one thing he was bowed down by bad news, for his friends Peter Baynes and Heinrich Zimmer died that year. Besides, he was feeling exhausted and in August 1942 ceased lecturing at the Swiss Federal Polytechnic Institute in Zürich. The University of Basel, seeing a chance to honour one of the city's most distinguished sons, offered him a full professorship, to run from 1943. Jung delivered just a couple of lectures before telling the authorities that ill-health made it impossible for him to continue; they insisted that he retain the post on an honorary basis nonetheless. Some have speculated that Jung had no desire to return to the real Basel and preferred the Basel of his imagination and memory.[58]

Perhaps it was the association with academe, but in 1943 Jung was at his most prickly, jaundiced and unreasonable. A sustained correspondence with Arnold Kunzli of the Philosophy Department of Zürich University began badly when Kunzli gently suggested that Jung's romantic ideas about the creative spirit did not square with scientific empiricism. Jung exploded, and in a masterpiece of petulant insecurity listed all his academic honours, honorary degrees and membership of worldwide learned societies; sarcastically he asked how it was that the universities of Oxford, Harvard and Yale were satisfied with his credentials but the University of Zürich was not.[59]

Kunzli smoothed Jung's ruffled feathers with an emollient reply, which encouraged Jung to wax indignant about the state of modern philosophy, Heidegger in particular.[60] Heidegger had become something of an obsession for Jung, to the point where, in the course of a conversation with a visitor to Küsnacht, he made a famous Freudian slip, referring to Heidegger as 'Heydrich'.[61] In his third letter to Kunzli Jung went right over the top, referring to the philosopher's unconscious subjective prejudices which he tried to conceal behind an inflated language and then going on to blast modern philosophy in general.

This intemperate outburst is worth pondering deeply. The critic Walter Kaufman suggested that Jung's wildly emotional overreaction was a sign that in Heidegger he sensed his own shadow.[62] This is shrewd, for a close reading of selected passages of Heidegger's main works reveals a cast of thought very like Jung's, especially the love of Plato, the discussion of nothingness and the concept of the 'uncanny' (*unheimlich*) in Heidegger's *Being and Time*. There is also the obvious point that both men were, at least in the early Hitler years, admirers of National Socialism.[63] But there may be other reasons for Jung's hostility, principally that the implications of Heidegger's thought lent support to Freud, and that he was Jung's chief rival in the German-speaking world as interpreter of Nietzsche.

Heidegger devoted a lot of attention to a phenomenological analysis of anxiety as connected with the authentic self (in the normal, not the Jungian, sense) and its experience of nothingness. No doubt to Jung that sounded suspiciously like Freud's dictum: 'the ego is the seat of anxiety.'[64] But even more threatening was Heidegger's assumption of the mantle of Nietzsche, as evinced in the two volumes of lectures and writings from 1934–46 which he eventually published in 1961 as *Nietzsche*. It was a matter of intellectual pride to Jung to claim that he alone truly understood Nietzsche, and that Nietzsche's work had been illegitimately raided by fascists, communists, capitalists and anticapitalists to bolster their point of view, whereas it could only be truly understood via enantiodromia and the archetypes.[65]

This interpretation of Jung's loathing for Heidegger receives support from his almost equal dislike of Kierkegaard. In the 1940s it was the received wisdom that the aspect of God neglected by Nietzsche – and which some held to be responsible for the world-view that pitched Nietzsche into madness – had already been anticipated and dealt with by Kierkegaard. The coupling of the two names was by then almost an academic cliché, though the two names were bracketed together only as recently as Karl Jaspers's 1919 volume *The Psychology of World-Views*. Certainly a dislike of Kierkegaard frequently surfaces in Jung's work.[66]

While Jung spent a good deal of 1943 in bile-laden reflections on the great philosophers, the war crept closer to him personally in the form of the many secret missions and espionage endeavours now on foot in Switzerland. At one stage that year Hitler decided to put out peace feelers to the Allies to see if the Casablanca terms of unconditional surrender could be abated. A German professor, Wilhelm Bitter, was chosen to go to Switzerland and find a suitable intermediary for the transmission of Nazi terms. He approached Jung who, flattered, set to work. But barely had he begun raising his contacts when Hitler changed his mind and denounced all who were concerned with the peace plan; the luckless Bitter was charged with being a defeatist and had to flee to Switzerland.[67]

Next it was the turn of Jung's new friend Karl Kerenyi to be drawn into the web of secret missions. The Hungarian prime minister Miklós Kállay, who had been an obedient satellite of the Nazis, started to hedge his bets and make contacts with the Allies, against the day of their now almost certain victory. Kállay sent Kerenyi to Berne under diplomatic cover as cultural attaché. His real task was to mend fences with the British and Americans and sound them on their terms for allowing Kállay to stay in power. Jung was delighted to have Kerenyi in Switzerland and looked forward to long evenings spent discussing alchemy. At first the two were very close, but in the end Kerenyi went the way of most of Jung's male friends. A brilliant philologist, classical scholar and polymath, he annoyed Jung by pointing out that the twentieth century abounded in prophets, and that the age boasted a number of people with visionary powers the equal of Jung's: Thomas Mann, von Hofmannsthal, Rilke, D.H. Lawrence. It was when he mentioned the detested Heidegger that Jung could take it no longer; predictably the friendship gradually fizzled out.[68]

Meanwhile, through the agency of Mary Bancroft, Jung was admitted to the outer sanctum of the OSS in Switzerland. Allen Dulles, later director of the CIA, became a close friend and Jung apparently had inside knowledge of a number of Dulles's projects, including the bizarre plan to kidnap the great German theoretical physicist Werner Heisenberg, thought to be working on an atomic bomb for the Nazis.[69] Dulles's wild schemes included one for a hit man to assassinate Heisenberg in mid-lecture, but in his correspondence with Dulles Jung never breathed a word of criticism or let his ambivalence towards the United States show through.[70] Taking Jung on trust so completely was not a particularly judicious decision by the OSS, but he proved remarkably discreet, even when Mary Bancroft blurted out in advance details of the 1944 July plot against Hitler.[71]

Still besotted with Jungian 'solutions' to political problems, Bancroft arranged for Jung to meet Hans Givevius, one of the conspirators in the abortive plot to murder Hitler in July 1944. Jung was unimpressed. He thought Givevius was merely projecting his own feelings onto von Stauffenberg, the man who actually placed the bomb under Hitler's table. When the plot failed, Jung wrote unfeelingly that von Stauffenberg and Givevius were in no way superior to Hitler: both the Nazis and the plotters wanted the same thing – absolute power. For Jung the Nazis and the conspirators of 20 July were simply two of a kind – 'a couple of lions fighting over a hunk of raw meat'. He noted curtly in his diary: 'It is probably just as well that the *putsch* failed.'[72]

The threat of invasion receded by the month, but wartime life in Switzerland was still an affair of shortages, rationing, blackouts and general austerity. The nation was still blockaded by both sets of belligerents, fearful of re-export to the enemy if free trade were allowed. Specially designated goods had to be issued with Allied navicerts or the German equivalent before being allowed into Switzerland. There were almost insuperable difficulties in the way of obtaining coal and oil, but social morale was high, in contrast to the near-revolutionary hardening of class lines that had occurred by the end of the First War. Swiss production of steel actually tripled by 1944. But the penultimate year of the war also brought Switzerland its greatest dangers. The war in the air had always threatened the country, with 250 belligerent planes brought down, crashed or landed (twenty-six of which were shot down by Swiss fighters or anti-aircraft batteries). In April came the worst accidental bombing to date when the United States Army Air Force dropped 400 bombs on the city of Schaffhausen, destroying fifty buildings and killing or wounding 150 people.

Unknown to the leaders of the Federal Council, Switzerland passed its worst moment of risk in October 1944. At the Allied conference in Moscow, Stalin proposed an Allied flank attack on Germany through Switzerland. Churchill, with the backing of the Americans, opposed this on the ground that it would simply add the Swiss Army to total German military strength. But he told Anthony Eden that he had had to fight hard to overcome a peculiar animus and bitterness evinced by 'Uncle Joe' towards the neutral Swiss.[73]

None of this impinged on Jung, for in 1944 he had his closest brush yet with death. On 11 February 1944 he slipped badly on the snow-covered road near Küsnacht and broke his ankle. In great pain, he managed to get to his feet, limp to a nearby house and telephone for his car. The doctor who plastered his ankle recommended several days of complete rest, but forgot the dangers of immobility in the old – Jung was just approaching his sixty-ninth birthday. After ten days in hospital an embolism developed, followed by a severe heart attack. The diagnosis was triple thrombosis in the heart and lungs. For three weeks Jung hovered at death's door and was saved only by the skill of a renowned heart specialist.

While poised between life and death, he had a series of visions or 'out of body' experiences. Many of them involved space travel: in one he had a clear view of the Earth from a height later estimated (from the fact that he could see the Mediterranean at the top left, Ceylon at the bottom right and India, Persia Arabia and the Horn of Africa between) as being one thousand miles out in space[74]; in another he saw a dark black obelisk floating in space – was this the genesis of the monolith in Arthur C. Clarke's *2001: A Space Odyssey*? In another vision he saw himself as the projection of an unidentified flying object, shaped like a magic lantern, and in yet another as a form meditated by a yogi.[75] From all this he drew the conclusion that the Self assumed human shape to enter three-dimensional existence, and found confirmation that our unconscious existence is the real one and the conscious an illusion, thus neatly dovetailing the Hindu idea of *maya* or the veil of illusion and the Freudian tenet that the unconscious knows nothing of death.

All this time he was on the critical list and there was so little hope that his wife Emma moved into the hospital and slept at his bedside. He rejected all food and his will to live was weak, possibly as he told Kristine Mann, because he had tasted such peace, completeness and fulfilment that he did not want to return.[76]

Jung later told Liliane Frey-Rohn that while he floated in the empyrean he had a dream that thirty women were clamouring for his return to earth.[77] This seemed to jolt him earthwards from his space roving, for in his next vision he had a terrifying intuition that the heart specialist who was overseeing his recovery had been marked out to die in his place. In the vision, just as he was about to enter a temple, he saw his doctor coming towards him, having taken on the features of a king of the island of Kos (the homeland of Hippocrates).[78] It was evident that the physician wanted to bring him back to life, but Jung sensed the danger, since in mythology Zeus killed Aesculapius with a thunderbolt for bringing patients back from the dead. On 4 April 1944 Jung passed his crisis and sat up in bed. On that very day his doctor took to his bed with a fever and died a few days later of septicaemia. Jung felt profound guilt that, like Barabbas in the biblical story, he had evaded death by passing it on to another (his saviour), and had to be reassured that the doctor had been ill even before he took over Jung's case. But Jung was full of remorse.[79]

Jung was now out of danger, but this was far from the end of his visions. He had dreams of the 'mystic marriage' of alchemy, others that seemed to confirm synchronicity and a dramatic vision of dismemberment, similar to the process he had read about in shamanistic rituals.[80] There was also a dream about the theological and mystical 'marriage of the lamb' and one about a garden of pomegranates, complete with sense-impressions that made Jung understand why theologians spoke of the odour of sanctity and the 'sweet smell' of the Holy Ghost.[81]

Jung thought it significant that these dramatic encounters with the numinous aspects of the unconscious took place in early June 1944, just as the D-Day landings were taking place in France; inevitably he read the concurrence as synchronicity between inner and outer worlds.[82] But the war was over for Jung, for he could take only a limited interest in Germany's final nightmare between his departure from hospital in early July and being given the 'all clear' in April 1945, just as the Russians opened the final offensive that would take them into Berlin. Only then would his doctors permit him to visit his beloved Bollingen, but the longed-for solitude in his tower was an anticlimax as, with bitter disappointment, he realized how physically reduced he was after the long illness.

Though physically debilitated Jung emerged from his illness with heightened powers of insight, renewed intellectual energies and a new flow of creative juices, which made him almost more prolific as a writer in the last decade or so of his life than in all the years hitherto.[83] This last productive period also convinced him of the truth of his 'stages of life' theory. Old age, it was now clear to him, was not mere decline but a time of wisdom, when one looked back on life and finally accepted it as the only one there ever could have been.

Chapter Twenty-Four

THE THEOLOGIAN

Jung's first letters and writings after recovery from the near-fatal illness were all concerned with his current obsession: alchemy. Only when the last of the Nazis were facing their Götterdämmerung in the rubble of Berlin did he once again begin to address the external world and its problems. Never was the Jungian dictum that fanaticism is compensated doubt more clearly underlined than in his own pronouncements in 'After the Catastrophe', an essay in which he tried to put as much distance as possible between himself and his own ambivalence towards the Nazis in the 1930s. Now that the Nazi behemoth was slain, Jung delivered himself of the forthright sentiments that courage and integrity required of him ten years earlier when he was praising the wonders of National Socialism. His guilty conscience manifested itself in statements as irrational on the one side as his 1930s utterances had been on the other.

The core of Jung's post-1945 *credo* was that the Germans were collectively responsible for the events of the terrible twelve years of the Third Reich. It followed that there was no real distinction to be made between 'good' Germans and the Nazis.

Jung therefore behaved with consummate irrationality when his old German friends started to write to him again after a six-year silence. Naturally the very last thing they would have wanted to talk to him about was the war, but he interpreted this reticence as a refusal to admit their collective guilt for the past twelve years of history. It never seemed to occur to him that a nation that had produced Bonhoffer, Niemoller, von Stauffenberg and the rest of the resistance figures could not be condemned *in toto* and, even if it could be, that a man with Jung's record was the very last person to whom the guilty would feel like making their *mea culpa*.

In any case, Jung was guilty of playing dog in the manger. He got into a particularly vituperative clash with the German writer Bruno Goetz, who asked to visit Küsnacht to discuss the problem of Germany. Jung chose to interpret this request as 'detachment' and said that German individuals daring to exculpate themselves from collective responsibility for the Nazis was spurious and psychopathic since the Nazis had been sustained by a mass movement.[1]

In 'After the Catastrophe' Jung was determined to prove that *all* Germans were collectively responsible for the Nazis and would not brook any pleas in mitigation. But it was typical of his style of argument that he mixed up entirely disparate arguments. He began by dismissing the idea that Nazism was forced on the German people by the Freemasons, the Jews or the English.[2] Here of course Jung was setting up a straw man, for only Nazi propagandists would have attempted to defend the Third Reich along those lines. But he went on to deny that *any* nuanced consideration of the Second World War was possible. So, for example, it has often been said that the stupidity of the Allies in the Treaty of Versailles created the preconditions for the emergence of a dictator in Germany. And while nobody could ever find any plea that would mitigate the Holocaust, it was pointed out, even at the Nuremberg trials, that many German war crimes could be cancelled out by the Allied terror bombing of civilians in the raids on Hamburg, Berlin and Dresden. Yet Jung refused to listen to any of this, and so implied that the churchmen who opposed the policies of 'Bomber' Harris during the war were no better than Goebbels.[3]

One can see what Jung was driving at, but it was typical of him to muddy the waters so that a good argument became dissolved in a bad one. Obviously it was infuriating that immediately after the war no German could be found who admitted supporting Hitler, and that the Allies were supposed to believe that by some kind of pre-established harmony the war dead were identical with NSDAP members. But this was merely prudential psychology on the part of the vanquished, just as all Frenchmen in 1945 claimed to have been members of the resistance, and no members of the British establishment had ever been in favour of a deal with Hitler. With his much-vaunted knowledge of human nature, Jung should not have been surprised by this. Yet by protesting too much he attenuated some valid points and enabled his critics to dismiss his work as a tissue of illogicality.

The inability or refusal to discriminate ran right through Jung's postwar reflections and accounted for the many glaring contradictions and inconsistencies in his position. For example, at one time he maintained that the only one of his students who was a Nazi was also the only one who could not engage in 'active imagination'. Yet, at another, he claimed that the dreams even of Germans with impeccable anti-Nazi credentials showed that the Hitlerite psychology was alive and well.[4] And he spoiled the unexceptionable proposition that the Germans ought to demonstrate overt remorse for what had happened by claiming that all Germans, Nazis or resistance fighters, were collectively and *alike* guilty.

Moreover, having stated that all Germans were collectively responsible for Hitler, and that external factors like the Treaty of Versailles had nothing to do with it, he suddenly introduced the glaringly contradictory idea that 'we are all guilty.' According to this line of argument, all Europeans were besmirched because the waging of aggressive war, the crimes against peace and, especially, the crimes against humanity as in the concentration camps, took place on European soil and were not strongly enough resisted by Christian leaders.[5]

In some ways analogous to this contradiction are Jung's frequent changes of mind about the exact nature of Hitler's 'diabolism'. At one moment Hitler is 'placed' as a classic case of psychopathic dissociation.[6] At another, the 'Wotan' thesis of repression of the old dark gods comes into play and, confusingly, is at times mixed up with 'original sin and Luciferian pride' – an odd but typically Jungian syncretism of the pagan and the Christian.[7] At yet another moment, Hitler's 'devil' is part of a general twentieth-century 'infernality' which includes such things as James Joyce's *Ulysses*.[8]

Jung also upset some of his American friends by his assertion that Americans shared with Germans the fault of having 'shadows' that could not easily be integrated with the ego. Again, this stood in distinct contrast to his earlier praise of the wisdom of General Eisenhower when compared with the ravings of the German propaganda machine.[9]

The vehemence of Jung's rage against the Germans can be seen as having a threefold causation. In the first place, he realized what a very narrow escape Switzerland had had during the war. As with many people who have had a terrifying experience, the real fear hit him only after the event.[10] Secondly, Jung, as a hedonist, heavy-grubber, sybarite and trencherman, resented the continuing rationing in Switzerland after the war and the shortages of vital foodstuffs; his letters in the late 1940s are full of complaints about having to eat peasant fare.[11]

Thirdly, Jung's statements about the Jews in the 1930s were returning to haunt him, particularly as the horrific details of Auschwitz, Treblinka, Dachau and the other death camps gradually seeped out. Jung's way of dealing with this was to say that accusations that he had ever had Nazi sympathies were all part of a Freudian plot to discredit him.[12] He even alleged that Freud's followers had doctored early photographs of him at the various psychoanalytical congresses so that he looked more sinister.

Jung's mood throughout the late 1940s was gloomy. His life followed a pattern of workaholism, interrupted by periods of severe ill-health and somewhat inconsequential encounters with celebrities. Another honorary doctorate, this time from the University of Geneva, came his way in July 1945, by which time he was hard at work on the book which would eventually see the light of day as *Mysterium Coniunctionis*. But progress was seriously delayed at the beginning of 1946 when he was ill with 'flu and intestinal problems'.[13] What he liked best, when not working, was a little gentle sailing on the lake in the morning, enjoying the gentle breeze and the lapping of water against the bow, with mental activity limited to the fantasy elaboration of attractive menus. He liked receiving visits from Catholic monks and priests, with whom he could discuss the Devil and matters of demonology. A French Carmelite monk, learned in patristic literature, filled that role for a while, until Jung made a more long-lasting friendship with the Catholic priest Father Victor White.[14]

Yet always events seemed to supervene to darken the mood. The first was the death by suicide of his friend and confidante Kristine

Mann in November 1945. In some ways even more of a blow for Jung was the sudden death in 1946, at forty-two, of Mary Mellon. She was a major financial benefactress who had recently made a donation to establish a C.G. Jung foundation in Zürich. Jung wrote a sensitive letter of condolence to Paul Mellon, calling Mary a great woman. Paul by this time had washed his hands of Jungian analysis, finding it useful only for those of a mystical or religious turn of mind but utterly useless for the common-or-garden neurotic. He turned instead to the much-maligned Freudians, and underwent a successful Freudian analysis with a female friend of Anna Freud's.[15] But in memory of Mary he allowed the project of the Bollingen Foundation to go ahead, dedicated to translating Jung's work into English.

Jung was now making great strides in the English-speaking world, since a *Journal of Analytical Psychology* was also about to be founded. About the C.G. Jung Institute itself he was deeply sceptical but eventually allowed himself to be persuaded. Under the energetic direction of Jolande Jacobi, the Institute finally opened its doors in 1948, to thirteen full time students, all British or Americans; from that time dated the custom that all lectures and seminars should be in English.[16]

One of Jung's peculiarities, odd in such a hectoring, domineering character, was to say no to something he did not care for the first time he was approached but to give way later if people insisted. Barbara Hannah explained that his first response was what he really thought, felt or wanted and the second was his acceptance of a certain role thrust upon him as guru and prophet.[17] Such was his response to the request to allow a C.G. Jung Foundation, and the division into private and public selves also found expression in an utter insouciance about and lack of interest in the famous people he met: he claimed to remember nothing about the conversations he had had with politicians, film stars and other public figures. His critics alleged that he remembered famous people only if they were interested in him or his work and not otherwise. The year 1946 provided some slight circumstantial support for this view.

On 18 June that year the well-known British novelist and broadcaster J.B. Priestley visited Jung at Küsnacht. Priestley, who had first read Jung in 1936, had a chequered relationship with Jungian thought, being a fervent convert in the 1940s, a sceptic in the 1950s and a second-time convert in the 1960s.[18] In 1946 he was eager to proselytize for Jung and, following a successful interview at Küsnacht, gave a succinct and lucid overview talk on Jung's ideas for the BBC Radio Third Programme.

Priestley had been a household name in Britain during the war on the basis of his broadcast 'fireside chats'. Just three months later Jung met the man who symbolized the entire British wartime spirit. The deposed Prime Minister, Winston Churchill, began a three-week holiday in Switzerland on 23 August 1946, which turned into something of a triumphal tour.[19] In Berne the Swiss government gave him a reception and in Zürich the university laid on a formal dinner. Present on both occasions, Jung was given the honour of being seated next to Churchill at the dinner. Although Jung claimed to find the occasion 'one of the most interesting experiences of my life', there was scarcely a meeting of minds. Both men were ill and tired and both, being intensely interested in food, did not speak to one another until the five courses had been wolfed down. When Churchill did begin to speak, Jung found his delivery overblown, as if he were addressing the House of Commons. Jung feared that he had bored his guest and not done his best for the university.[20]

In November 1946 Jung suffered another serious heart attack, as grave as the near-fatal 1944 embolism, and this time he was convinced the end was near. From a supine position on his bed at Bollingen – for this time he convalesced at home rather than in a hospital – he managed to scribble a few despondent lines to Father Victor White.[21] But he was not afraid to die, remembering the uplifting sensations of the 'out of body' experiences in 1944.[22]

Slowly he clawed his way back to normal health, easing himself into a work routine with a regime of just two hours reading in the morning, one visitor a day and an extended siesta. When he was strong enough he went down to a hotel at Locarno to convalesce, but the weather on Lake Maggiore in the early spring of 1947 was cruel: for ten days it rained without stop, the sun was never seen, and there was snow down to 5,000 feet.[23] Only in mid-April did Jung declare himself cured, informing Eleanor Bertine that his illness had been caused by overwork, principally the conflict between the demands of his patients and his creative work.[24]

His principal visitor the following year was more distinguished and more accommodating. Alberto Moravia, already a famous Italian literary figure, was intrigued to learn more about the sage of Küsnacht, but Jung was wary and indulged in a form of 'lifemanship'. He arranged his study in such a way that when he sat down to talk to Moravia the lamp shone straight in the Italian's face and blinded him; Jung meanwhile was in shadow, giving him the perfect vantage point for studying Moravia without being scrutinized himself. They began to talk in French and Jung was soon sufficiently won over to discard his defence mechanisms and talk spontaneously.[25]

One of the things Jung did to lessen stress was to cut down his commitment to the Eranos conferences, while still ruling the agenda with a rod of iron. After the war Olga Frobe and the Mellons wanted to broaden the scope of the conferences so as to include political speakers like John Foster Dulles, but Jung insisted that the original conception be adhered to. Although he finally gave up going to the conference in 1952, in the late 1940s he started attending every other year instead of annually, pleading the strain on his liver.[26]

But the stress from the outer world in the form of the Cold War could not be easily shrugged off and Jung's pronouncements on world affairs became ever more pessimistic. He was deeply shocked by the detonation of the first atomic bombs on Hiroshima and Nagasaki, not so much by the explosions and casualties themselves as by what they portended. During the war he had comforted himself with the thought that Switzerland was an island of reason, while outside madness raged, but he found himself unable any longer to believe in this consoling myth when he heard several of his fellow-citizens remark, after the atomic bombs had been dropped on Japan, that it would be a good thing if the bomb could blow the earth and everything upon it down to hell for ever.[27]

Jung's political statements in the late 1940s were a mixture of new and old elements in his political credo. So, for example, the detestation of communism and the Soviet Union, the belief that welfare was an illusion and that capital punishment was a humane penalty, were all chapters from the old book of Jungian political philosophy. His new theory of communism was that the human belief in a golden age in the past was ineradicable and that as a consequence two primordial archetypal ideas are always found operating in ideologies of root-and-branch revolution: the common ownership of goods, as in primitive societies, and the unlimited power of a tribal chieftain, also as in primitive societies. This explained the paradox of the Soviet Union under Stalin: in theory all goods were held in common but in fact everything was controlled by Stalin, demonstrating that the chieftain archetype will always prevail over the common ownership archetype.[28]

There was an amusing incident in October 1946 when Fritz Versaz, a campaigner for the abolition of capital punishment, wrote to enlist Jung's support for the cause, apparently unaware of his strong views on the subject. Jung gave four reasons for his belief in capital punishment. One was that events in Germany from 1933–45 had disillusioned him about Man's capacity for improvement; abolitionists, on the other hand, were bound by their credo to believe in the perfectibility of Man. Secondly, in many cases the death penalty was more humane than imprisonment: referring to the recently completed Nuremberg trials, Jung mentioned the case of Admiral Raeder who had asked to be shot but was sentenced to thirty years instead. Unfortunately for Jung, the force of this argument was blunted when Raeder was released in 1955. Thirdly, even a universal agreement never to take human life was useless, since this could be circumvented by 'living death', as experienced by political dissidents consigned to Siberian labour camps or Negroes castrated in the Deep South. Fourthly, the much-proclaimed commitment to the sanctity of human life in the western liberal democracies was anyway humbug, as could be seen by the level of damages paid out by insurance companies after fatal accidents.[29]

It became clearer and clearer to Jung as he grew older that the welfare state and the notion of guaranteeing people fundamental economic rights were an illusion, simply because people could never be satisfied: there was an inevitable revolution of aspirations, whereby today's luxuries become tomorrow's 'necessities' and the more you gave people, the more they demanded.[30]

If these reflections were simply a rehash of long-held beliefs, the changed circumstances of the postwar world also called forth some fresh reactions from the sage of Küsnacht. In a nutshell, Jung's 'new' views were that mankind in possession of atomic bombs was headed for destruction; and that the *pax Americana* was really no peace, since it was impossible to deal with the Soviet Union by normal diplomatic means. Mankind therefore seemed, in a sense, to be doomed if it did use the bomb, and doomed if it did not, and Jung struggled manfully to resolve the conundrum.

That human beings seemed headed for certain destruction was indicated not just by the bomb itself and the feeling of power it engendered, leading to hopeless fantasies about a technological golden age in the future, but by the accompanying atheism and materialism, which to Jung meant that Man was alienated from the essential and most valuable part of his being.[31] Godlessness accompanied by the atom bomb conjured the suspicion in Jung that there might be a transcendent God who was preparing a second deluge for his creatures.[32]

As for the Cold War, the West had to realize that the Soviet Union was its 'shadow', its own dark self, and so proceed with caution. Jung did not push this idea as far as some later Jungians, who saw all divisions between superpowers or between political Right and Left as neurotic dissociations, reflecting on the world stage what was happening in the divided psyche of modern Man.[33] But it did mean that the West was doomed to almost unbearable frustration.

This did *not* mean that Jung advocated using the bomb against Russia. It meant that the West had to realize that destructive powers were in all of us, that we were threatened from within as well as from without, that any attempt to overcome the enemy by force was nonsensical because Russia was, as it were, identical to our unconscious. The only answer was to integrate the unconscious slowly without violence and with due respect for ethical values. Rearmament was essential, we must be prepared for the worst; Europe must accept the suzerainty of the USA and in particular Washington must watch carefully its trigger-happy generals who itched to use their weapons of mass destruction.[34]

Stoicism, though, did not come naturally to Jung, and the depression he felt about the world situation found an outlet in expressions of anger and contempt directed towards other human beings in the limelight. Often, he aimed at easy targets and even, if one shared Jung's political views, deserving ones, as when he fulminated against the 'ape man' John L. Lewis, former president of the United Mineworkers of America and president of the Congress of Industrial Organizations, who in 1948 was locked in a bitter labour dispute with the US government.[35] But sometimes he assailed figures with a worldwide reputation and the suspicion arose of a kind of primitive jealousy of all prophet figures past and present.

One of the first objects of Jung's revisionist anger was Einstein, whom he had known well in the early years of the century. In the late 1940s he began to speak slightingly of Einstein's unimaginative and purely analytical mind.[36] Possibly because Einstein had conducted a famous correspondence with Freud on the causes of war, Jung's comments became increasingly hostile. In the course of a discussion on Galileo and the Inquisition, he sidetracked to make a gratuitous attack on Einstein and remarked sourly that if Galileo were alive today he would be sunning himself on a beach at Los Angeles in company with Einstein.[37]

Einstein could be dismissed as a 'mere' one-dimensional scientist. To dislodge the widely admired Albert Schweitzer from his pedestal required heavier artillery. Jung therefore argued that Schweitzer's withdrawal to medical missionary work at Lambarené in West Africa was a classic evasion of life's tasks, and that monasticism, expressing disgust with civilization, was the moral coward's escape route. Albert Schweitzer was urgently needed in Europe and should be addressing the problems of his fatherland instead of the hygiene of Lambarené.[38]

Jung was inclined to be more generous to rival prophets who were dead. In 1948 he began studying the works of William Blake, a visionary whose cosmology came close to his own at many points: both devoted their lives to the inner world, both had read the same Gnostic texts, and some critics suggest that in terms of the 'individuation process' Blake's view is more thoroughly Jungian than that of Jung himself.[39] After reading the more difficult Blake texts Jung was prepared to accord him a place in the pantheon along with Dante, Goethe, Wagner and Nietzsche as an artist dealing with true archetypalmythological material.

It was not the recondite language and esoteric references in Blake that irritated Jung but any form of modernist obscurantism that seemed not to have an archetypal base and to be written largely from conscious artifice. This was his objection to T.S. Eliot, of whom he knew nothing until Esther Harding wrote with strong recommendations for *The Wasteland* and *Murder in the Cathedral*.[40] Having read Eliot, Jung delivered his negative verdict, complete with a sideswipe at Sartre. The trouble with both of them, according to Jung, was that they talked always of consciousness and never of the objective psyche or of the unconscious.[41]

It was a choice irony that, having been so harsh with Eliot, Jung should have found himself in the dock of anti-Semitism once more for support given to a lesser poet, Eliot's one time collaborator and editor Ezra Pound. In 1949 the Bollingen Foundation put a prize of $1,000 at the disposal of the Fellows in American Letters of the Library of Congress, and the Fellows chose Ezra Pound as the recipient of the Bollingen Prize. Jung had nothing to do with this at all, as the Bollingen Foundation was not under his direction, even though its major task was to publish his work.[42] Nevertheless the popular perception was that the Foundation was Jung's mouthpiece, and this award to a known and blatant anti-Semite inevitably stirred up all the old resentments about Jung's own anti-Semitism. Hostile articles appeared in the American press and the entire episode of Jung and the Jews, which he had hoped dead and buried, was resurrected and raked over once more, to his considerable discredit.[43]

In the late 1940s Jung decided to publish his conclusions after twenty years of studying alchemy. The resulting volumes, *Mysterium Coniunctionis* and *Aion*, are widely regarded as the most esoteric and impenetrable of all his writings, but some of his disciples claim them as the supreme masterpieces in his *oeuvre*. He had begun with the insights of Herbert Silberer and Richard Wilhelm in the 1920s, and had then become massively learned in his own right, with a library of alchemical treatises superior to that held by the University of Basel.[44] When he first acquired these books on alchemy he had found them impenetrable, but then, realizing that they were written in a kind of code, he set himself the task of cracking it. His method was the same as that used to decipher an unknown foreign language: first he identified the key recurrent phrases, then he started a lexicon with cross-references. Again and again the same phrases came up: *solve et coagula, unum vas, lapis, prima materia, Mercurius*, etc. Eventually he felt satisfied that he had mastered the arcane lore, and it was then that the insight occurred to him that alchemy was really the pursuit of the unconscious by other means.[45]

The thing that convinced Jung that alchemy was a kind of allegory for the analytic process was the uncanny parallel between the individuation process and the passage from *unio mentalis* to *unus mundus* in alchemy. The threefold alchemical process involved, first, the liberation of the soul from matter, then the reunion of the liberated spirit with matter in a new and higher synthesis (typically symbolized by a dragon embracing a woman in her grave or a king dissolving in water), and finally the transforming union of the individual soul with the timeless flux of creation. This seemed an obvious metaphor for the integration of conscious and unconscious in the individuation process, with the fusion with the Self acting as *unus mundus*. Yet Jung eventually came to see that all 'holistic' processes could be described analogically by alchemy – the fusion of male and female, life and death, even good and evil.

A brief account of the alchemical parable needs to be offered, if only because Jung himself loved to dabble in the esoterica of alchemy and dwelt lovingly and in detail on its symbols. The central motif in the parable is the incestuous union of a king and queen, who introduce themselves, fully clothed, with a left-handed handshake, symbolizing incest and thus the union of like with like. Soon the king and queen divest themselves of clothes ready for sexual intercourse and enter the fountain of Mercury, here functioning as the water and by extension the unconscious, where they consummate their passion. Once immersed in the bath, the royal pair go on a night-sea journey and are engulfed by the sea. In the arcane language of alchemy they have returned to the *massa confusa* or primeval chaos in order to conceive the *lapis*. The king and queen die and meld into a being with two heads, the hermaphrodite. As 'punishment' for the incest, a state of putrefying blackness, the *nigredo* sets in. The soul departs from the body of king and queen and mounts heavenwards, later to descend as a healing force. Dew or *aqua sapientiae* then descends, prefiguring a divine birth, and the *nigredo* is replaced by whitening or *albedo*. The soul then returns from heaven to breathe life into the hermaphrodite, which is reborn as a *Rebis* or winged hermaphrodite.

That this is a convoluted paradigm of many mythologies and mystery religions is clear, and it requires no great feat of the imagination to see that it could also be read as a symbolic representation of the analytic process in therapy, complete with transference, individuation and integration. *Mysterium Coniunctionis* was thus Jung's *magnum opus* and bore the same relationship to his work in general as Whitehead's *Process and Reality*, Alexander's *Space, Time and Deity* or Sartre's *Critique de la Raison Dialectique* to theirs.[46] Alchemy seemed to him the knowledge-matrix in terms of which all his interests – Eastern philosophy, mandala symbolism, myth, fairy tales, dreams, religion and depth psychology – could be harmonized and shown to be aspects of a single whole. He was satisfied that he had succeeded where Goethe and Nietzsche had both failed.[47]

The core of Jung's belief as a doctor was the essential similarity of psychotic contents, whether they came from the present, the Middle Ages, from Europe or any of the other four continents.[48] This was of course based on the controversial notion of a collective unconscious, but Jung thought his studies in alchemy put the notion on a secure footing and provided the psychology of the unconscious with an historical basis. So, for instance, it could be shown that there was a congruence between alchemy and the Gnostic doctrine of Anthropos, even though it was certain that the alchemists knew directly nothing of Gnosticism.[49] So, too, the 'marriage *quaternio* of alchemy had its counterpart in the endogamy and cross-cousin marriages of the anthropologists and of fairy tales.[50] The mandala was the empirical equivalent of the metaphysician's *unus mundus*, and this in turn had its alchemical analogy in the *Lapis* or philosopher's stone.[51]

The central alchemical symbols of Rex (king) and Regina (queen) were merely another index of the Self, just as were the Christ of Christianity and the Anthropos of Gnosticism, and the Wise Old Man and Wise Old Woman of Jung's very first descent into the underworld of the unconscious. Alchemy also threw new light on mythology and fairytales. It was possible now to see that the American Indian myth of 'the man with the bearskin' was none other than Christ in the guise of a divine pilgrim, his clothes having been changed into a bearskin glistening with gold.[52] The wisdom of the alchemists, deriving from the collective unconscious, came from the same source as the trances of sorcerers and shamans, showing clearly that the search for the philosopher's stone was merely a lefthanded form of endeavour expressed more clearly in primitive societies by medicine men.[53]

Jung's mastery of alchemy also enabled him to reinterpret his life. The fascination with stones, going back to his childhood, now looked like an adumbration of the theme of the philosopher's stone. And the early visions of Philemon and the Wise Old Man now seemed to be imperfect versions of the central personage in alchemical lore – the spirit Mercury, alias Hermes Trismegistos, Thrice Greatest Hermes, identifiable with a number of other deities, including Thoth the Egyptian god of learning.[54] In alchemy Mercury is the all-embracing personality, uniting above and below, good and evil, base and sublime. He is elusive, ambivalent and with multiple meanings, which is why he is called *Mercurius duplex* and represented as a hermaphrodite. He symbolizes both the lowest *prima materia* and the highest *lapis philosophorum*, as well as the chthonic god of revelation and transformation.[55]

Jung claimed to have encountered Mercury in a number of guises: concealed in the 'world tree' painted by so many of his patients since Mercury is also the god of travel – and as his guide and interpreter through the underworld of the unconscious. But it was above all at Bollingen, with its simple regime of chopping wood, lighting fires and eating meals, that Jung sensed Mercury's presence, since he was also the god of household duties. Even more striking was the connection between stones, Bollingen and Merlin – for Jung simply another of Mercury's aliases. In 1950 Jung ordered some stones for an extension at Bollingen and a consignment of the wrong kind of stones was delivered. Taking advantage of this serendipitous occasion, he used the stones to build a monument which would express what Bollingen meant for him. On the stone monument he chiselled Latin verses, a Latin inscription and, inevitably, a homunculus. This carved stone, standing outside the tower as a kind of explanation of it, at once reminded him forcibly of Merlin and his cries of desperation after being trapped underground by the nymph Nimue. Metaphorically Merlin was crying out because he could not be understood in the Middle Ages, but his secret was carried on in alchemy in the figure of Mercury, waiting to be taken up again by Jung's psychology of the unconscious.[56]

Yet alchemy was something more than a guide to the esoteric meaning of Bollingen. Jung claimed that it pervaded his present dreams and made clear the meaning of distant, almost forgotten ones. While at work on *Mysterium Coniunctionis* he had a most complex dream. As in so many of his dreams, his house was involved. Once again he dreamed that another wing had been added, in one room of which was a zoological laboratory devoted to ichthyology. Also in the new wing was his mother's room, which contained a number of beds and turned out to be haunted.[57]

Opposite his mother's room was an area like the lobby of an hotel, where an invisible brass band played loudly. There was a clear contrast between this worldly place, representing Jung's everyday jollity, and the 'other world', of which the most important elements were the fish laboratory and the reception room for the spirits. Jung concluded that the spirit room represented the *coniunctio* while the fish laboratory stood for his preoccupation with Christ and the symbolism of the fish (Ichthus) which was to mark his next work, *Aion*. He further concluded that the dream was casting his parents in roles really destined for him: his father was a 'fisher of souls' as well as a Fisher King, struck with a mortal wound, while his mother was a guardian of departed spirits. He concluded that this meant that he had not yet got to the end of the mystery of the *coniunctio*, possibly because his wife Emma had not finished her proposed book on the Grail legend.

Later in the same dream Jung was troubled by the recurrent image of a fishskin cover on a bible. But the oneiric conundrum continued as he entered a house haunted by poltergeists, in the middle of which was a huge circular room like a mandala. From the centre a steep flight of steps led to a small door, which in turn gave on to a solitary chamber where Uriah – the husband of Bathsheba famously betrayed by King David – lived. The similarity of this dream of mysterious houses and secret chambers to Jung's other 'big dreams' is clear enough, but he chose to interpret it in particular rather than general terms. So he held that the fishskin bible referred to the unconscious, since fish were mute and unconscious; the theme of muteness also indicated that he, like Parsifal, had been dumb when in childhood he observed the psychic wound of his father, the 'Fisher King'; this was further symbolized by the poltergeists, which are usually associated with young people just before puberty – the age when he mutely beheld his father's suffering; the mandala ambience represented the 'other side'; while the abandoned Uriah prefigured the Christ abandoned by God who cried out on the cross: 'My God, My God, why hast thou forsaken me?' Here is a classic instance of the way in which Jungian dream interpretation could be said to make matters obscurer than ever, and Jung scarcely helps matters by remarking that not even this catalogue exhausted the meaning of the dream.

Jung's study of alchemy convinced him that his parents had been floundering in the darkness of ignorance and of a 'partial' view of the world: his mother was obsessed with the uncanny, which was only part of the truth – what Jung called *mysterium iniquitatis* – while his father was borne down by the burden of orthodox Christianity, again a partial truth. It was now possible for Jung to re-examine all the earlier dreams he had had about his parents. He remembered that he had been in the Tessin the night before his mother's death in January 1923 and dreamed that he was in a dark forest when suddenly a gigantic wolfhound burst out of the undergrowth. He realized that the 'Wild Huntsman' or Wotan had commanded the hound to carry away a human soul, and was bearing his mother away to join her ancestors. He went home immediately but did not feel mournful.[58]

With his deep knowledge of alchemy he was now able to reinterpret the experience. Wotan was simply another manifestation of Merlin or the spirit Mercury and death now appeared ambiguous, not just a dreadful tragedy but also a festive occasion, an example of *mysterium coniunctionis* or a kind of wedding whereby the soul attains its missing half and achieves wholeness. Having thus spirited away the terrors of death, Jung was able to feel more sympathy for his 'alienated' parents, and particularly for his father, of whom, he confesses, during the years 1896–1923 he had scarcely thought at all.

Jung had always shown a penchant for mysticism, but the experience of working on *Mysterium Coniunctionis* sparked an obsessive interest in the experience of ascetic saints and mystics, especially his favourite Nicholas of Klue or 'Brother Klaus'. Jung was fascinated by the 'miracle' of the years 1467–87 when Klaus reportedly lived without food or material sustenance for twenty years. He refused to accept that this was impossible and speculated that nourishment could take place by the passages of living molecules of albumen from one body to another. He based this hypothesis on the results obtained by an electrical engineer who measured the degree of ionization in the vicinity of a spiritualistic medium and found it sixty times the normal level.[59]

An even more evident result of the new alchemical mysticism was Jung's passion for quaternities. A wag once remarked that Jung's only true god was the number four, and certainly his obsession with that number has raised eyebrows then and since. A self-confessed Pythagorean, with the belief that numbers expressed ultimate reality, Jung had shown the shape of things to come in *Psychological Types* with the four functions of thinking, feeling, sensation and intuition. To that original quaternity he progressively added more and more, alleging that the human mind worked naturally in fours, because two pairs of opposites made up a balanced whole. He instanced Empedocles's four elements – earth, air, fire and water; Hippocrates's four humours – blood, phlegm, dark bile, light bile; the four winds, the four points of the compass, the four temperaments, the four groups of zodiacal signs and the plethora of tetradic cosmologies during the Middle Ages. There were four ascending models of woman (Eve, Helen of Troy, Mary and the Gnostic Sophia) and four of men (Lao-Tzu, Mani, Buddha and Christ). Literature, too, was full of quaternities, most notably the four Karamazov brothers (Ivan, Alyosha, Mitya and Smerdyakov). The Bible was a particularly fertile hunting ground, for there were four gospels, four living creatures before the throne of God, four rivers of Paradise and four generations of people – Adam to Noah, Noah to Abraham, Abraham to Moses, Moses to Christ.[60]

The hunt for quaternities became something of an obsession for Jung. He was delighted when his friend Wolfgang Pauli had a vision of the 'World Clock' divided into thirty-two portions, or four sectors with eight subsectors each.[61] In one series of dreams he analysed he found quaternity symbols in seventy-one dreams out of four hundred. He pointed out that mandalas manifested a tetradic pattern and that the writings of mystics were full of references to the number four. St Teresa of Avila's 'inner castle' or *imago dei*, for instance, manifested itself as a four-square city or garden and the golden flower of Chinese alchemy had four petals.[62]

Jung liked to trawl the byways of history and literature for tetralogies (like Wagner's *Ring* cycle) and tetrads, sometimes surpassing himself by finding examples of ogdoads or double quaternities, representing a totality that was at once heavenly and earthly, spiritual and corporeal.[63] It was not surprising that Jung's disciples sometimes felt the master was rigging the deck to force all phenomena into the mould of a quaternity. Jung would admit or exclude certain variables from his exposition according to whether inclusion or exclusion produced the desired fourfold answer.

Another favourite Jung variant on the quaternity theme was to argue that its usual structure was of the 3+1 type. So, for instance, three of the Evangelists had animal symbols but the fourth, Luke, was represented by an angel. Confusingly, he also liked to argue that the 3+1 structure that applied to the Evangelists was that of three Synoptic Gospels and one Gnostic (John). Mandalas, too, exhibited the 3+1 structure. Jung argued that this evinced the 'one world' relationship between mathematics and psychology, since the mathematical equation 3+1=4 referred to the three differentiated and one undifferentiated (unconscious) functions in the psychology of the individual. The integration of the unconscious 'fourth' into consciousness was one of the major tasks of the analytic process, since four represented the totality of personality – the end point of individuation.[64]

Jung's critics could overlook his excursions into numerology, which became more frequent as his interest in alchemy intensified. What seemed unforgivable to some was the way he used alchemy so as to appear to downgrade Christianity, whether by depersonalizing the figure of Christ, by alleging that Christianity's view of evil was erroneous, or more generally by regarding Christianity as a 'partial' and incomplete explanation of reality. This trend was a feature of *Mysterium Coniunctionis*, of *Aion* and of *Answer to Job*, his three great productions of the late 1940s.

The conventionally devout especially objected to Jung's portrayal of Christianity as merely a particularized instance of a general truth contained in alchemy. In Jung's view, the Christian story was a simpleminded claim to absolute truth by a partial version of the truth which had ossified misunderstanding and oversimplification into dogma. So, for example, the New Testament story of crucifixion, resurrection and ascension was simply a fairly crude instance of the alchemical process of death and rebirth. The crucifixion between two thieves, one good, one bad, symbolized the warring elements in the ego which had to be reconciled through integration with the Self. Christianity went wrong in imagining a transcendental Christ 'out there', whereas, truly understood, Christ was a symbol for the Self – *Christus intra nos*, to use the Pauline formula.

Again, properly understood, redemption means redeeming God or the numinous from the darkness of matter, not a transcendental God redeeming Man from his sins. 'The unavoidable internal contradictions in the image of a creator god can be reconciled in the unity and wholeness of the Self as the *coniunctio oppositorum* of the alchemists or as a *unio mystica*. In the experience of the Self it is no longer the opposites "God" and "Man" that are reconciled, as it was before, but rather the opposites within the God-image itself.'[65] For two millennia human beings had projected the ego into Christ, whereas Christ needed to be projected into the Self.[66]

Devout Christians were also scandalized to find Jung using the figurative talk in the marriage ceremony about how matrimony symbolized the marriage between Christ and his church as evidence that the core of the Christ story was the *hierosgamos* or sacred marriage of the sun and moon.[67]

Yet the heart of Jung's critique of Christianity was that, unlike alchemy, it provided no convincing account of the problem of evil. The Christian version of a transcendental god who was at once all good and all powerful made the existence of evil inexplicable, but Jung maintained it was only inexplicable because of the boneheadedness of theologians who had tried to drain all evil out of the notion of deity, decanting it in the form of a mysterious force of darkness called Satan.

Since the *mysterium coniunctionis* of alchemy involved the dialectical interpenetration of opposites which were then qualitatively raised to a higher synthesis, it followed that the portrait of Christ in conventional Christianity was seriously one-dimensional. Christianity, according to Jung, shared with Freudianism the fault of excessive concentration on the paternal principle, but thereafter the two ideologies diverged wildly: Christianity was allegedly a matter of all good and no evil while Freudianism concentrated on the dark side of man and could see no light. Both were necessary starting points but incomplete.[68]

The one Christian theologian who saw the truth was Origen, with his theory of *apocatastasis* – the idea that at the end of time Satan and all the demons would be saved and reconciled with God – but this view had been condemned as an extreme heresy.[69] Alchemy, a more complete explanation of reality than Christianity, would have balanced Christ with an Antichrist – which, of course, was the true meaning of the appearance of that personage in so much eschatological literature. Christ, lacking the dimension of evil, was inferior as a symbol of the Self to the *lapis* or philosopher's stone.[70] This was what enabled us to see the superiority of Mercury as symbol, for he was *Mercurius utriusque capax* (Mercury capable of both), a symbol of ambivalence superior to his divided and alienated Christian counterparts, the Holy Ghost as *summum bonum* (greatest good) and Satan as *summum malum* (the greatest evil). By its superior intellectual sophistication alchemy was able to solve problems that baffled Christian theologians.[71]

If in *Mysterium Coniunctionis* Jung seemed happy to spirit away the Christian god in the alchemical process, or dissolve him in Mercury's fountain, in *Aion* he seemed to have set himself the task of making Christianity a sub-class of astrology. Ostensibly an attempt to describe human history as the unfolding of a necessary process (again the echoes of Hegel!) which originated in the collective unconscious, *Aion* contained a core message that Christ had manifested himself at a predetermined moment (7 BC) when the point of spring entered the zodiacal sign of the Fishes. In Jung's words: 'A synchronicity exists between the life of Christ and the objective astronomical event, the entrance of the Spring equinox into the sign of Pisces. Christ is therefore the 'Fish' (just as Hammurabi before him was the 'Ram') and comes forth as the ruler of a new aeon.'[72]

It is a complex argument, depending on astrological terms like 'movement along the ecliptic' and the 'precession of the equinoxes'. Basically, though, Jung argues that Christ's birth occurred when the spring point of the Equinox was situated at the star called Al Rischa, known to astrologers as 'the knot' as it links the 'vertical fish' in the constellation of Pisces with the 'horizontal fish'. As the centuries wore on, the spring point moved along the ecliptic until in 1789–1818 it reached the tail of the horizontal fish. According to Jung this ushered in a period of enantiodromia or anti-Christianity. The birth of the Antichrist can be dated at the French Revolution, when a statue to the Goddess Reason was set up in Notre Dame Cathedral; Darwin was born in 1809, Marx in 1818, and much else. The spring point is not due to reach the last star in the 'horizontal fish' until AD 2813.[73]

According to Jung, it is an example of pure synchronicity that Christ was born under the sign of the fish – a notion not in currency in the first century of the Christian era – yet early Christianity was suffused with fish symbolism. Jesus took fishermen as his disciples, claimed he would make them fishers of men, fed the five thousand with loaves and fishes, and much more. Most intriguingly of all, *the* early Christian symbol was the fish (Ichthus), supposedly an acronym based on the Greek *Iesos Christos Theou Huios Soter* (Jesus Christ the Son of God Our Saviour). Much of *Aion* was accordingly taken up with an examination of fish symbolism in major religions and sects, in archetypal dreams, in mythology and in alchemy.[74]

Jung's gloss on the problem of the historical Jesus and his transmogrification in St Paul's Christology is typically idiosyncratic. He postulates first of all an illegitimate child who had a lifelong battle with the demon of power – hence the temptation in the desert. Jesus never quite overcame the power-complex, for if his kingdom was not of this world, it was still a kingdom.[75] Secondly, Jung interpreted Jesus's life in accordance with the Nietzschean canons of the morality of strenuousness. It was true that on the cross he gave himself up to despair when he realized that his life had been based on an illusion (hence 'My God, my God, why hast thou forsaken me?'), but he set the example of living heroically even if on mistaken premises.

Yet it took the popular and best-selling *Answer to Job* to bring to boiling point Christian dissatisfaction with Jung as a theologian. The personality of Job, who queried God's justice and won the moral argument with Yahweh, had always fascinated theologians and mystics: from Luther, Goethe and Blake to Kierkegaard, Jaspers, Ernst Bloch and Karl Barth. Jung's quarrel with God had lasted since the day he saw his father tortured by the demons of disbelief, and the two heart attacks of the mid-1940s convinced him that the time had come to attempt a definitive solution to the problem. In *Answer to Job* he produced a typical formulation. The question Christianity had never been able to answer was how an all-good, omnipotent God could permit evil. The usual solution was to deny God's omnipotence, but Jung postulated instead that the God of the Old Testament was not all-good, as indeed was only too evident from the story of Job. Yet, in an original twist, he suggested that God swapped omnipotence for goodness: Yahweh was all-powerful but not good, whereas after the Incarnation Christ was the god of love but as a consequence had to trade in his universal powers. The devil, who in Job's time was still one of the sons of God and on familiar terms with Yahweh, attained his true status as the adversary of Christ only after the Incarnation.[76]

Jung began with the proposition put forward by the Church Father Clement of Alexandria (Origen's teacher) – but later condemned as heresy – that God ruled the world with a right and left hand, the right being Christ and the left Satan. This, as Jung saw it, was a correct picture of the world as it was, but it resulted from the Incarnation, when God entered space and time, assumed flesh and became Man. The obvious question then was, why the Incarnation? Jung argued that this was an immediate and necessary consequence of Job's revealing the inadequacy of Yahweh: 'The immediate cause of the Incarnation lies in Job's revelation, and its purpose is the differentiation of Yahweh's consciousness.'[77]

In Jungian thought, God and the unconscious were one, but this had the result that from the beginning of time Man had suffered from God's unconsciousness. God had tempted Adam, told Abraham to sacrifice Isaac and tortured Job; it was surely this God of the Old Testament, too, who had sent the vision of the turd crashing on Basel Cathedral and who had caused the Holocaust. Because God was unaware of his unconsciousness, he made mankind suffer even more. What else but ignorance of what he was doing could explain or excuse God's listening to the transparent libels of Satan against Job, to say nothing of delivering the latter into the hands of the former for torment, with the single proviso that he be not killed?[78] Jung was fond of illustrating the ambivalence of God by reference to the writings of St John. He argues (in the teeth of the best scholarship) that the John of the Epistles, all love and Christian virtue, is also the John of the Book of Revelation, which is a cauldron of hatred teeming with visions of apocalyptic destruction. Because God's loving and compassionate nature is balanced in enantiodromia by hatred, cruelty and destruction, the catastrophe adumbrated in the Apocalypse can be avoided only if God becomes more conscious or becomes Man.[79]

The explanation for the Incarnation was that God was unconscious of his own omniscience, but his moral worsting by Job as it were played a searchlight on his plight.[80]

This was the insight Jung had had on the plains of Kenya – for the grazing of herds of zebra and antelope on the Athi plains would have had no more significance than the mere hurrying to and fro of atoms, endlessly, meaninglessly, if Man the perceiver had not been able to give the process meaning by relating it to the rest of Nature.[81] God concluded that to become more conscious he would have to become Man. This is the paradox of creation: God is incomplete without his creatures, for 'If God were conscious of Himself, he would not need conscious creatures.'[82] God can only reconcile the opposites in Himself and become whole through participation in the wholeness of a human being. God becomes the Self, and that in turn will ensure the salvation of the human race and its security from annihilation.

In ways unexplained, Yahweh was impelled to the wisdom of the Incarnation by the interpenetration of the masculine principle of perfection and the feminine principle of completeness. The feminine principle, which Jung, following the Gnostics, calls Sophia – supposedly a co-eternal and more or less hypostasized *pneuma* of feminine nature that existed before the Creation – gave Yahweh the insight to proceed with the Incarnation.[83]

At all events, one result of the Incarnation was that Satan, who had been given free rein in the story of Job, became marginalized. Yahweh now identifies with his light aspect and becomes the God of love or, rather, Yahweh is replaced by Christ.[84] At first, of course, Satan appears to be important, as he is now God's 'shadow'. And in a sense he is important, as the representative of the dark side, which human beings refuse to acknowledge in themselves or theologians in God. Jung liked to argue that Freud, in *The Future of an Illusion*, preached atheism and denied the existence of God and the devil, yet psychoanalysis itself was concerned with the dark side – the very demonic elements whose existence Freud denied.[85]

Yet there is something very unsatisfactory about Jung's treatment of the devil. When he wishes to score off Freud or Marxism or orthodox Christianity he underlines Satan's very real existence; when he is arguing from the individuation process, from alchemy, from Origen and apocatastasis, he regards him as a transitory phenomenon. The devil appears to exist as a powerful force before 'integration' but not thereafter. Tacking between the *ex ante* and *ex post* meanings of the devil enables Jung to validate just about any proposition whatever.[86]

This emphasis on Manichean dualism, with the Devil as the left hand of God, is attenuated as soon as Jung likens apocatastasis to the individuation process and thus 'psychologises' Satan by making him a personification of Christ's split-off side, a 'complex' in the language of the early Jung. The Incarnation thus becomes the first stage in a cosmic individuation process, as Jung frequently explained to Victor White.[87]

However, this divine individuation, like Origen's apocatastasis, seems reserved for the end of time. In the meantime, as the apocalyptic events in Revelations suggest, Satan is far from finished. It seems there will have to be a final reckoning based on the continuing clash between good and evil. The most important aspect of the Incarnation, for Jung, was the 'Christification' of Man that followed – 'ye are gods', was one of his favourite New Testament quotations – symbolized by the events at Pentecost, when the divine essence enters into Man.[88] But fighting this spirit is the devil, whose speciality is tempting Christified man into believing in his own completeness and omnipotence.[89]

The Devil was important to Jung's cosmology in another sense, for Satan reinforced his belief in quaternities. The number four, adding the feminine element of completeness to the alleged masculine perfection of the triad, signified the fusion of feminine and masculine, and was the formal reason why alchemy was intellectually superior to patriarchal Christianity. Jung often argued that Greek thought (especially Plato) and Christian dogma were deficient because of a fondness for incomplete triads: the Christian Trinity and Plato's three types of men in the *Republic*, for example (and it is hard not to see in his scorn for triads an arch reference to Freud's trio of ego, superego and id).[90] Ironically, whereas before the Incarnation the divine beings of most importance were God the Father and God the Son, after the Incarnation the Holy Ghost (Christified Man) and Satan take over as protagonists.

Instead of a Trinity, Jung proposed a divine quaternity. Using the parlance of contract bridge, God the Father would be North, God the Son West, the Holy Spirit South and the Devil East.[91] The fourth person adds the dark element to the Trinity and thus achieves totality, analogous to the integration of the personality in the individuation process. This was of course another old idea condemned as heresy in the early Christian church but revived as part of an essential secret wisdom by Jung.[92] Jung was adamant that his reformulation of a divine quaternity solved the problem of evil.[93]

Answer to Job, a surprising best-seller in the USA, evoked an avalanche of criticism from the most diverse quarters. It was not well received by the reviewers, against whom Jung railed angrily, and the snags of popularity soon became evident when one boneheaded correspondent wrote to him to suggest that his entire thesis in the book could be summed up as 'God is love'.[94] Jung's critics alleged that he was presenting as original insights a rehash of very old arguments: Walter Kaufman wrote scathingly that he 'managed to see himself as a pioneer who had the almost unheard-of courage to see that in some parts of the Bible God behaves in a way that is not all-good.'[95] Others alleged that completing the quaternity with Satan was just another of Jung's *a priori* 'makeshift soldering jobs' – another instance of entirely factitious and inorganic wholes and syntheses being created from disparate elements.[96] *Job*, on this view, was another in the long line of spurious 'integrations': religion and empiricism in analytical psychology; the ego and the unconscious in the archetype of the Self; spirit and matter in the symbols of alchemy; the singular and the universal in the collective unconscious.

Christians strongly objected to what they saw as Jung's blasphemy and arrogance. Along with other heresies, Jung embraced the idea that Christ was always divine and never a true human being, the crucifixion notwithstanding, and he added insult to injury by stating that the most beautiful expression of God's having to endure the reality of the world through being incarnated came in the movie about an all-black heaven, *Green Pastures*.[97] Jung himself pointed out that Protestantism concentrated solely on God the Son, the Saviour, ignoring the Father, but his Christian critics were concerned that the excessive concentration in Jungian thought on the third person in the Trinity, the Holy Ghost or Christ within us, logically meant that the authority of the Church, whether Catholic or Protestant, had no meaning.[98] But most of all, critics were concerned about the way Jung had appropriated a hotline to God. One wag remarked that 'Jung had now appointed himself psychiatrist to God, diagnosed a divine sickness and successfully cured the patient by applying his own theories.'[99]

The sharpest criticism of *Job* was that it was written for emotional relief and represented a working out of an unresolved Oedipus-complex; this would account for the careless argumentation and logic and the many lapses in scholarship. Walter Kaufman calls the book 'a long delayed adolescent rebellion against the Bible stories on which he had been raised, and particularly against God the Father . . . it would be difficult to find a clearer example of a man who never managed to resolve his Oedipus-complex.'[100] The thesis is that hatred of Yahweh subsumes hatred of his father and of Freud, and it receives support from two different quarters. First, the circumstantial fact of the anger so evident in *Job*: as Marilyn Nagy has well said, 'In *Answer to Job* Jung is angry at God in a way no unbeliever ever could be.'[101] Secondly, there is Jung's own testimony that the decision to grapple with the Job story was triggered by a dream about his father. In the dream he visited his father, who appeared as a genuinely learned biblical scholar, at a country house where two psychiatrists were also staying. His father began to expound some brilliant scholarship, but it was over the heads of the psychiatrists, who laughed and said his words were senile prattle. Jung claimed that he recognised the two psychiatrists as his shadow – professional medical men limited by their narrow training.[102]

If Jung had dismayed most of his Christian admirers with *Job*, he won back many of his Catholic sympathizers with his pronouncements on the dogma of the Assumption of the Blessed Virgin Mary, officially promulgated by Pope Pius XII in 1950 in the bull *Magnificentissimus Deus*. Jung immediately hailed the enunciation of this dogma as the most significant religious event since the Reformation.[103]

Jung's enthusiasm for the dogma of the Assumption puzzled many observers, some of whom regarded it as a harmless eccentricity. But it was very important to him in a psychological sense, as he went on to explain in a variety of essays and publications. Although the reasons for his enthusiasm make sense only as part of an interlocking system, it will be useful to disentangle the different threads in the argument. We may summarize these as follows: the 'nisus' of the unconscious; the enthronement of the feminine principle; the integration of matter; compensation or enantiodromia; the reinforcement of alchemical doctrine, and the underscoring of the quaternity.

Jung had made a careful study of Marian visions, especially those at Lourdes and Fatima, and he was convinced that their increasing frequency in the previous hundred years portended a yearning in the unconscious, a desire to express something hitherto inexpressible. The Assumption therefore satisfied a deep unconscious need.[104]

Jung had often castigated Christianity for being, like Freudianism, an exclusively patriarchal world-view, for the Church fathers were suspicious of mariolatry even as they accepted its need if Christianity was to become a world religion. Now, with this dogma, Christianity had left Freud far behind, even though the fact that Mary was now a goddess seemed to Jung to pose theological problems overlooked by the papal advisers. He praised Pius XII for cutting loose from apostolic authority and for embracing the feminine principle, thus making the Catholic Church the first integrated form of Christianity, marginalizing Protestantism as a narrow form of patriarchy. Doubtless, too, Jung was actuated by his own psychological agenda, for the idea that the Mother was assumed into heaven was in a sense a hit at the father and a score for the son – and hence another transposition of the Oedipus-complex.

Jung also thought that the fact that Mary had been assumed *bodily* into heaven meant that Christianity was at last jettisoning its age-old disdain for matter. The fault with alchemy had always been an over-emphasis on material forces, while Christianity had suffered from hypertrophy of the spiritual.[105]

Most central to Jung's cosmological concerns was the way the dogma of the Assumption reinforced all the conclusions he had drawn from his study of alchemy. Jung argued that it was the alchemical *zeitgeist* that had moved Pius XII to make a dogma out of Mary's *body*, thus raising a symbol of matter to the level of godhead. The Assumption was really the Christian version of the *hierosgamos* or sacred marriage, since the key link was not that between mariolatry and the old pagan cults of the goddess or Great Mother but between the Virgin and the Sophia of the Old Testament.[106] Just after the dogma of the Assumption was promulgated, Jung had a significant dream, which convinced him that the myth of Attis and Cybele was an analogy of the sacred marriage between Christ and Mary. In his dream a tree was brought into the hold of a ship. Jung interpreted this as the night sea-journey of the hero in the belly of the great fish-mother.[107]

Jung also thought that the dogma of the Assumption clinched the case for four as *the* mystical number, since it meant that the Catholic Church had tacitly abandoned the Trinity in favour of a quaternity. Although it was not strictly true that there was no feminine element in the Trinity – since Jung often argued that the Holy Ghost was one manifestation of Sophia[108] – nevertheless the perfection of God had now been fully achieved by God's union with Sophia in the guise of the Blessed Virgin Mary.[109] Mary was thus in effect a fourth member of the godhead, so that the Trinity was now a quaternity.

The problem about this explanation was that Jung had already explicitly identified Satan as the fourth member of the quaternity; if the Virgin Mary was now to be added to the godhead, surely that meant that the deity had to be conceived as a quinary. In that case, what price Jung's beloved mystical quaternity? His attempts to solve this problem were unsatisfactory to say the least. Without addressing the conundrum head-on, he mumbled inconsequentially about the quincunx and how it featured as a symbol of wholeness in China. When pressed hard on who exactly the members of his quaternity were, Jung disingenuously tried to seek refuge in the very Catholic apologetics he habitually assailed as inadequate. He argued that it must be Mary and not Satan who was the fourth person in the quaternity because the Devil represented Not-Being or *privatio boni*.[110] The sleight of hand here is notable: Jung does not give a direct answer to the question of who composes the quaternity but slides over into a hypothetical Catholic standpoint, full of premisses that he himself violently rejects.

Jung's thought on the role of Satan and the Virgin Mary in the quaternity is hopelessly confused and evasive. Impaled on a dilemma of his own making, he faced the further objection that all this obscurantism about the quaternity was in any case otiose. If, in accordance with strict Jungian canons, when we talk of God we are talking of the God-image, where is the urgency or even meaning about adding Satan or Mary to a mere image? Jung was so hard pressed on this point that he broke his own rules. Having repeatedly declared that the existence of a God-image tells us nothing about whether a transcendental deity exists 'out there', he tried to close the chaotic argument about quaternities by asserting that one *could* legitimately infer the reality of an original from the image.[111]

The controversy over the Assumption strengthened the friendship between Jung and the Catholic priest Father Victor White, who had first swum into his ken at the end of the war. White made several visits to Bollingen in the late 1940s, and the tenor of the close relationship between him and Jung is conveyed in the invitation to Bollingen Jung sent him in 1946, speaking of the rough comforts and the joys of the spartan life.[112]

Jung's taste for theology and White's for psychology made them a perfectly complementary pair. Yet this was another male friendship destined to go the way of all the others. The issue that eventually drove the two men apart was the problem of evil, and more specifically the Catholic theological notion that evil was mere *privatio boni* or absence of good. After White had spent ten days between 17 and 27 July 1952 at Bollingen the two men became estranged. Three years later Jung was angered by what he called an 'abysmally stupid' review of his theological work by Philip Toynbee in the London *Observer* in which he detected the hand or the influence of White. Apparently Jung was keener to end the relationship than White, for the priest, in acknowledging that friendly relations were no longer possible, signed off with a notable Freudian slip: 'Well, I will weary you *now* more.'[113]

Jung's 'theological decade', in which he returned to the problems bequeathed him by his father and addressed salient points of Christian doctrine, lasted from 1945–55. It may be, as a recent scholar has suggested, that Jung was by now actively trying to found a secular religion and was thus keen to refute the doctrines of the official religions.[114]

Amazingly, though, the joust with Catholic apologetics was not Jung's final theoretical period. In the last years of his life he increasingly devoted his time to concerns which would firmly establish him as a 'New Age' guru.

Chapter Twenty-Five

THE NEW AGE GURU

Throughout a long career Jung never lost his interest in parapsychology and the occult, but in the 1950s there was evidence that he considered this the one 'life task' he had not really solved. Having, to his own satisfaction at least, exposed the limitations of Christianity, its inferiority to alchemy and its inadequacy when providing an explanation for the problem of evil, he was ready to move on into the dark areas which the official religions of the West had repressed. As a result of his investigations, Jung became a prophet to all those who believed in astrology, numerology, palmistry, cheiromancy, eastern cults, white magic and even visitations from creatures from other planets.

By 1950 Jung was ready to abandon his earlier confidence that ghosts were aspects of a split-off complex in favour of a multicausal explanation. It is interesting to contrast the pronouncements of the younger Jung with those of the old man. In the 1930s Jung still believed that the explanation for wraiths, phantasms, ghouls and other spirits was psychological.[1] Fear of ghosts meant, psychologically speaking, the overpowering of consciousness by the autonomous contents of the unconscious, in a process similar to the onset of psychosis.[2] The ghostly figures which appeared in certain mediumistic seances bespoke the power of the mediums to constellate archetypal figures. From this Jung inferred that the images of our dream world could in certain circumstances be given physical form, and hypothesized that thoughts and emotions could be multifaceted: we perceived only their psychological aspects but they might also have physical ones.[3]

Eventually Jung came to feel that the psychological explanation for ghosts was unsatisfactory, since it covered some but not all of the known manifestations. At one time he was sympathetic to the view that ghosts represent some kind of residue from the past which a 'psychic' personality could make contact with, and was disposed to interpret apparitions as the heaped up sexuality of bygone eras producing an archaic fear.[4] Then he changed his mind and concluded that since the objective psyche had qualities transcending space and time, and since many instances of precognition and telepathy were utterly authentic, it was certain that psychic phenomena were not simply illusory effects of our mental processes; he even confessed to an open mind about so-called personal messages from the dead.[5] There is evidence during the 1950s that Jung underwent a titanic mental struggle on the subject, tacking between 'psychological' and 'objective' explanations of spirit phenomena. He still clung to the philosophically correct posture that even if we saw the ghost of a dead man, we could not prove the identity of the wraith and the man now dead. But since dreams from the unconscious unquestionably pointed to a continuation of life after death – and since telepathy, clairvoyance and 'second sight' were authentic phenomena inexplicable by mainstream twentieth-century science – then the sober conclusion seemed to be that parts of the psyche were not subject to the laws of space and time.[6]

During his last decade Jung wrestled incessantly with the epistemological dilemmas presented by the occult. A sceptic when it came to particular cases but a believer in the general truth of the existence of ghosts, he was fond of quoting the old saying: 'There is nothing quite true, and even this is not quite true.'[7] The problem with the late Jung was that he provided so many different explanations that in the end one was justified in concluding that he had not really advanced beyond the tautology that ghosts were ghosts. A statement such as the following shed darkness rather than light. He frequently asserted that they were phenomena that existed in their own right and were genuine manifestations of the unconscious.[8] One might ask straightaway how something that existed in its own right was also a manifestation of the unconscious. This seems to be a typical example of Jung placing an each-way bet.

Bit by bit Jung was forced reluctantly down the road towards a wholehearted embrace of occultism, with the corollary that ghosts are in some sense genuinely 'out there'. In his last years he declared himself an agnostic on the reality of spirit voices, uncertain whether they derived from the unconscious fantasies of the medium, from other members of the seance or genuinely from 'the other side'.[9] To his disciple Esther Harding he admitted that he was now convinced that ghosts could not be explained away psychologically, and that because the Self operates outside space and time, the obvious conclusion is that something of the human soul remains after death.[10] Finally, less than a year before his death, Jung explicitly rejected naturalistic explanations of ghostly phenomena.[11]

Jung's fascination with the occult looks at first sight omnivorous, but he drew the line at certain far reaches. He was not impressed by Gurdjieff, Ouspensky or Madame Blavatsky and described a biography of the self-styled 'Great Beast' Aleister Crowley as 'beastly beyond words'. It is true that he sometimes expressed a belief in demons, but this is rather like his oft-repeated assertion that he *knew* God existed – which he would then subvert by adding that when he said 'God' he meant of course the 'god-image'. For the most part Jung's interest lay in the interplay between conscious and unconscious or the twilight area between the mental and the physical, where the phenomena in question were not distinctly one or the other but occupied the area of William James's radical empiricism or 'neutral monism'.[12]

The sort of thing that caught Jung's attention was the Margery case. 'Margery' was the pseudonym of Mrs L.R.G. Crandon, a highly controversial US medium who died in 1941. The consensus of opinion was that psychic investigators had discredited the physical phenomena she produced as circus trickery, but Jung was adamant that no satisfactory explanation of her direct-voice mediumship had been given.[13]

The phenomenon of mediums speaking foreign languages unknown to them in their waking state suggested to Jung either cryptomnesia or messages from the unconscious, which was why glossolalia was associated with people in a state of ecstasy, why demons were held to speak in strange tongues and why people still employed archaic forms of language on ritual occasions.[14]

Jung felt that progress in parapsychology would come about only by identifying first of all those strange phenomena which were genuinely explicable in terms of the unconscious, and then proceeding to analyse the minority of cases which defied such an explanation. The story of the Pied Piper of Hamelin, for instance, was one which had long exercised the imagination. Jung started his analysis with the unexceptionable proposition that in world mythology heroes in whose death the people cannot or will not believe, or whose return is expected with fear or hope in the distant future, are invariably banished into a mountain. The vanished children who accompanied the Piper into the mountainside are in similar case, as they represent what has vanished from consciousness but is still alive in the unconscious, perfectly symbolized by the dark, unknown interior of the mountain. In short, the Pied Piper story shows a pagan spirit, not yet domesticated by Christianity, working in the unconscious.[15]

Much that was regarded as 'paranormal' could also be explained by archetypes and their constellation. Jung liked to play patience and kept a statistical record in a notebook of how the cards fell out. For many years he noticed that when he turned over a picture card it was always the jack or the king, with the queens always lurking among the cards he could not reach. This troubled him, until around 1950, when the queens suddenly seemed to turn up every time he played. He attributed this to the constellation of the feminine archetype following the promulgation of the dogma of the Assumption.[16] However, explanations via archetypes were not, in Jung's view, a facile 'open sesame' kind of universal answer.[17]

It was a central tenet of Jung's cosmology that the statistical probability on which mainstream science operated was valid only for phenomena which already exhibited the features of regularity and harmony that permitted the statistical method to be used.[18] Western science, in his view, went wrong in thinking that the statistical paradigm, which applied to most manifestations of matter, held good for *all* of them. The work of J.B. Rhine, with whom Jung continued a long and affectionate correspondence, convinced him that he was right, but his critics nettled him by demanding proof of his assertions.[19] Rhine suggested that Jung record all the parapsychological phenomena that had come his way in a lifetime as a psychotherapist; when this was added to the experiments of Aldous Huxley and others with mescalin, all the American studies on extra-sensory perception, and the material collated from societies for psychical research, the result would be a body of knowledge impervious to the assaults of scientific positivism. Yet Jung thought the idea futile.[20]

Jung was convinced that the *I Ching* gave meaningful answers but, as with his similar enthusiasm for the prophecies of Nostradamus, it is sometimes difficult to share his fervour. Jung's favourite symbol in the 1950s was water, chosen for its very ambivalence: something essential to life, for lack of which we would die of thirst, but also life-threatening because it is an alien element in which we could drown. Water also unites the above with the below, whether in the form of a waterfall or the ocean itself, and thus provides a key to arcane mythologies like those of ancient Egypt, India or China, to say nothing of Christianity or the beliefs of the Pueblo Indians.[21] However, water and the sea are symbols covering so much ground that they are open to myriad meanings. The sea could mean a literal sea, in which case it would make a difference whether it was the Pacific or the Dead Sea that was being referred to; it could be an inland 'sea' like Lake Superior; it could mean a sea of troubles, a sea of heartbreak, etc; or it could function as a general symbol of the unconscious (in Jungian terms) or sexuality (Freudianism).

It is well known that oracles rely for their reputation on giving advice so vague as to be meaningless, and it is hard to understand why Jung thought the *I Ching* was any different from the Pythoness at Delphi or the Sybil at Cumae. He argued that the *I Ching* was unique in that it consisted of readable archetypes and presented a picture of present and future exactly like dreams; the symbolism was the same and perhaps the most judicious conclusion would be that the *I Ching* was a kind of experimental dream.[22] Jung failed to see that in arguing along these lines he could never break out of the straitjacket of his own premises: the argument was circular in that one hypothesis (the reliability of the *I Ching*) was validated in terms of another (the existence of archetypes). By this time Jung simply took the reality of archetypes for granted and assumed that they were as much a part of the furniture of the real world as, say, the Alps.

It is sometimes suggested that Jung embraced astrology uncritically, but this is far from the case, and his attitude requires careful elucidation. It is true that he sometimes talked in an offhand way about the dawning of the age of Aquarius in a way calculated to appeal to the mass audience for astrology that undoubtedly exists, and also remarked, half-jokingly, that the true golden age for astrology was not the Middle Ages but the twentieth century.[23] Yet he was most insistent that in astrology above all one had to separate the wheat from the chaff. The Jungian theory of astrology involves at least five major propositions: the idea of the precession of the equinox; the idea that it was the seasons, not the stars, that had an influence on humans; the notion that astrology applies mainly to the macrocosm and not to individuals; the theory that astrology is primitive or projected psychology; and its link with the wider tenets of 'synchronicity'.

The idea of the precession of the equinox is based on the 'ecliptic' – the yearly great circle which the sun, from the standpoint of earth, appears to trace in a sky of fixed stars. The place on the ecliptic occupied by the Sun on 21 March is known as the Spring Equinox Point. In theory the Sun should return to the same point on 21 March each year but, because of the conical motion of the earth's axis, the Spring Equinox Point slips back along the ecliptic by a small amount each year (one degree of longitude every 72 years). The precession of the equinox is the slow western motion of the equinoctial points along the ecliptic – so slow that a complete revolution takes about 26,000 years and is known as a 'Platonic Year'. As a consequence, the vernal equinox moves clockwise through twelve zodiacal signs, the precession through each taking about 2,000 years (a 'Platonic Month'). Thus at the beginning of our era the vernal equinox entered the sign of Pisces and is now moving into Aquarius; Jung, though, remained uncertain when the transition would occur, sometimes nominating the decade between 1940–50, at others speaking more vaguely of the years between 2000 and 2200.[24]

The fallacy of popular astrology was that its horoscopic calculations did not take account of the precession but based them on the vernal equinox fixed by Hipparchus at 0 degrees Aries in about 125 BC; the actual vernal equinox, meanwhile, had long since moved out of Aries into Pisces. The astrological determination of time, therefore, did not correspond to any actual constellation in the heavens but was purely symbolic. Consequently, alleged correlations between individuals and planetary houses were purely fictitious, ruling out the possibility of causal connections with the actual positions of the stars. The only valid astronomical statements had to do with Platonic years.[25]

However, this still left intact the idea that there could be correlations between the characteristics of humans (or animals, come to that) and the different seasons in which they were born. For Jung it made a lot of difference whether one was born in spring or autumn, especially since he believed there were fluctuations in proton radiation at different times of the year. The importance of the zodiac was that it was a *seasonal* cycle; the stars were unimportant since Man had simply called the stars that were synchronous with a given season by names that reflected the qualities of that season. 'The fact that astrology nevertheless yields valid results proves that it is not the apparent positions of the stars which work, but rather the times which are measured or determined by arbitrarily named stellar positions.'[26]

The valid results of astrology Jung attributed to a kind of pre-established harmony between the outer and inner worlds, whose provenance was mysterious but most likely explicable on the thesis that the collective unconscious was 'star-driven'. What Jung meant by this was that the psyche as a whole, not the individual human, was affected by times or seasons (not by individual stars) and he liked to make an analogy with menstruation.[27]

This explained why astrological aeons had general features. In AD 900, for instance, the Spring Point was at the point of greatest extension of the Fishes in Pisces and Christianity was then at the height of its power. In AD 1500 the Spring Point was in the commisure, the ribbon between the two Fishes, and so the Reformation came about. Similarly, in the last hundred years the temporal power of both the Pope and the Dalai Lama reached their highest point within fifty years of each other and then lost it, again within fifty years of each other. The coming of the age of Aquarius will likewise coincide with a new period of human development – almost certainly, Jung thought, an era of collectivism.[28] The truths of astrology were general statements hinting at cosmic possibilities, often involving several layers of meaning, and usually symbolic rather than literal.[29]

The importance of astrology for Jung was that it was both a primitive form of psychology and an example of 'projected psychology'. Just as alchemy was an inchoate version of the psychology of transference, so astrology was a 5,000 year-old psychology which bespoke the human thirst for such knowledge before the necessary methodologies and the required level of intellectual sophistication for dealing with the unconscious were in place. Astrology was not mere superstition and it contained much that was valuable, but its hack practitioners had led it into a sidetrack, where authentic experiences were ignored in favour of credulous hypotheses.[30] This something that was worth knowing Jung called 'projected psychology'. His basic idea was that the stars and planets were used as mirrors to reflect our inner psychological patterns, but that foolish people, seeing the mirror-image, had mistaken it for the reality. In essence, hack astrologers thought that the stars affected and influenced human beings, but in fact humans had projected their psychological states onto the stars.[31]

To those who still think that Jung was credulous or 'soft on astrology', it is worth pointing out that he had many harsh things to say about the hack astrologers found in the columns of newspapers. Any notion that astrology could be used to predict an individual's future was false. What was an apt tool when used with intellectual rigour and fertile with suggestions for an ingenious and versatile mind was unreliable in the hands of the unimaginative and dangerous in the hands of a fool.[32]

However, Jung conceded that not all the mysteries of astrology were exhausted by his category of 'projected psychology' and that he had sometimes got fresh insights into a patient's character by casting his horoscope. Then there were the truly remarkable coincidences, such as the position of Mars in the zenith in the famous horoscope of Kaiser Wilhelm II. Jung concluded that astrology, like the *I Ching*, pointed decisively towards the general category of synchronicity – a conclusion reinforced by the failure of statistical probability adequately to explain astrology.

Synchronicity was another idea which confirmed Jung as a New Age guru. He had always been fascinated by coincidences of a significant kind and doubted that they could all be explained as chance events. Walking back to Küsnacht one day, he found that images of someone drowning kept flashing into his mind. When he arrived home he learned that his grandson's boat had capsized in the lake and he had nearly drowned. Then there was the time, at a wedding reception, when he fell into conversation with a stranger and made up an imaginary story to illustrate the point he was making about criminal psychology; a deathly hush fell on the company, and it later transpired that Jung had unwittingly told the stranger's life story.[33]

Even more striking were the synchronous events Jung observed while in session with his patients. One of his 'animus hound' female analysands recounted a dream in which someone had given her a golden scarab beetle. Just then Jung heard a tapping at the closed window behind him and saw a flying insect beating vainly against the glass. He opened the window and caught the insect as it flew in. It turned out to be a scarab beetle. Since the golden scarab was an Egyptian symbol of rebirth, Jung first surmized that synchronistic events might be activated by an archetype.[34]

On one occasion he held the therapeutic hour in his garden, with a woman patient whose dreams contained a plethora of sexual material. For once Jung was disposed to put a Freudian interpretation on the dream but the patient, *plus royaliste que le roi*, insisted on interpreting it symbolically in the orthodox Jungian way. She was resisting Jung's explanation when suddenly two sparrows fluttered to the ground and proceeded to mate.[35] Other events also seemed to Jung to transcend probability. On 1 April 1949 he had fish for lunch and was surprised to hear a reference to the custom of making an 'April fish' of someone. In the afternoon a former patient showed him some paintings of a fish, and next day another patient related a dream of a large fish.[36] All of this would, however, have been more convincing if Jung had not then been in the middle of his inquiry into fish symbolism in *Aion*.

Jung was impressed by how many 'synchronistic' phenomena there were and began to collect tales of significant coincidences and what might be termed 'archetypal serendipity'. Always interested in Abraham Lincoln, he liked to tell his followers the story of the young Abe's buying a barrel of rubbish for a dollar and finding within a copy of Blackstone's *Commentaries*, thus initiating his career as a lawyer.[37] But perhaps Jung's favourite story of synchronicity concerned a certain M. Descampes who, when a boy in Orleans, was given a slice of plum pudding by a M. de Fortgibu. Ten years later in a Paris restaurant Descampes ordered a piece of plum pudding and was told that the entire pudding had already been reserved by a M. de Fortgibu. Many years later Descampes was at a dinner party and was invited to try some plum pudding; he reflected wryly that the only thing missing was a M. de Fortgibu. At that moment the door opened and an old man, who had come to the wrong address, burst in on the party. His name was M. de Fortgibu.[38]

In some cases Jung thought that synchronicity could shade into numerology, especially if the beloved quaternity was involved. His uncanny experience after the near-fatal heart attack in 1944, when his doctor seemed to take his place and died in his stead, was presaged by a dream which occurred on the 4 April 1944 (4.4.44).[39] That synchronicity and the number four might have an organic relationship was also suggested by the idea that a version of physics revised along Jungian lines would include the four elements of space, time, causality and synchronicity.[40] But for those unhappy with the mysticism involved in the quaternity, Jung suggested that they look for evidence in the notion of *Zeitgeist*: why was it that at almost the same time Darwin and Wallace had near-identical views on evolution, or Newton and Leibnitz on calculus.[41]

In its simplest manifestation, synchronicity involved the coincidence of a psychic state with a corresponding and more or less simultaneous external event taking place outside the observer's field of perception, at a distance, and only verifiable afterwards. A famous example, often cited by Jung, was that of Emanuel Swedenborg. In 1759 he was staying with friends in Gothenburg. At 6 p.m. on a Saturday evening in July he had a vision of the great fire that broke out that night in Stockholm. He described the course of the fire in detail to his friends, and when couriers arrived from Stockholm on Monday and Tuesday with the news, his account was confirmed in every detail. When asked how he had known, he replied that the angels had told him.[42] Jung was intrigued, too, by the case of the RAF officer known to Sir Victor Goddard who had a precognitive dream about a plane crash – an incident well known from the movie *The Night My Number Came Up*.

Synchronicity also seemed to Jung an exciting idea in that it might prove to be a 'master-concept' explaining such things as extra-sensory perception and action at a distance. He cited the case of two English sisters, deprived of an expected inheritance, who made a waxen image of the heir they hated and threw it into the fire; that same night the inheritance – a mansion – burned down. In normal discourse we have to pose this as a mind-body problem: either the waxen image set fire to the mansion (but how?) or the imminence of the fire kindled the fantasy of the sisters (once again, how?). However, if we postulate that the contents of the collective unconscious are neutral as to mind and body and can take either form, it would seem to follow that they could also take both forms simultaneously.

Jung was often challenged for his evidence for synchronicity. Sometimes he disclaimed originality and referred his questioners to the Stoic and medieval idea of the 'sympathy of things': sometimes he cited Leibniz's idea of pre-established harmony; occasionally he referred to Schopenhauer's geographical analogy, whereby causal lines are lines of longitude and are intersected by lines of latitude or synchronicity.[43] Strangely, he did not refer to his most significant forerunner, Paul Kammerer (1881–1926) who, like Jung, believed in significant coincidences and kept a log-book of such events. Like Jung, too, he believed in a 'law of seriality' independent of the causality of physics and operating in an acausal way.[44]

When pressed for harder evidence, Jung cited four main sources: first, Chinese science and the *I Ching*; secondly, the new Western physics of relativity and quantum theory; thirdly, the experiments of J.B. Rhine and J.W. Dunne; fourthly, his own astrological experiments. Naturally, his critics pointed out that to cite the *I Ching* involved Jung in a circularity since he had previously validated the book of Chinese hexagrams by reference to synchronicity. At this point Jung was wont to drag in a farrago of Ancient Greek philosophers, neo-Platonists and Church fathers to buttress his argument.[45]

The defence via Western physics was more interesting, for here Jung had the support of a top-flight physicist, the Nobel Prize-winning Wolfgang Pauli, famous for the 'exclusion principle' of electrons in quantum theory. Pauli pointed out that quantum theory would eventually lead to even more far-reaching revisions of our notion of time than relativity theory itself, and influenced Werner Heisenberg, author of the 'indeterminacy principle' of subatomic particles, to take synchronicity seriously.[46] Heisenberg was an important catch, for he and Pauli, collaborators on the 'unified field theory' designed to harmonize the macrocosm of relativity with the microcosm of quantum physics, were widely recognized, on the death of Einstein, as the world's greatest physicists.

Yet the practical results of the Jung-Pauli collaboration were disappointing. Jung loved elaborate diagrams of the grid or latitude-longitude kind, preferably in quaternary form, linking quaternities such as the unitemporal and the eternal, the unique and the universal; or good and evil, spiritual and material; or space, time, causality and synchronicity. He and Pauli spent much time on these theoretical models and in their wilder flights sometimes 'modelled' a seven-dimensional space-time. Their favourite tetradic schema involved a north-south axis with indestructible energy as north and the space-time continuum as south; this was then intersected west-east by a line representing constant connection through effect or causality (west) and synchronicity (east), defined as inconstant connection through contingency, equivalence or meaning.[47]

Jung's own attempts to provide an empirical basis for synchronicity centred on astrology, which he had previously argued was validated by synchronicity. Shrugging off the circularity, Jung set to work on what he called his 'astrological experiment'. His aim was to see if the chance groupings of zodiac figures on a person's horoscope correlated meaningfully but acausally with psychic states and events. Jung zeroed in on marriage by examining the birth charts of a sample number of married couples, 180 in all. He failed to demonstrate any statistical relationship between planetary contacts and marriage, on the basis of a subjective association of ideas, yet noticed that in each batch of horoscopes he analysed he found the features he was looking for. Wishing to test further this curious finding that his subjective expectations were mirrored in the material, he decided to change the variables by selecting different experimenters. He chose three people whose psychological characteristics were well known to him and asked them to pick out by lot the horoscopes of the married couples. He found that the experimenters mysteriously chose couples whose horoscope mirrored their own emotional state. In his own case, he claimed to have found significant correlations – beyond what could be obtained by chance – in the first 150 cases, but then the results fell away and were insignificant, doubtless due to his declining interest in the project.[48]

Jung thought that when the experimenter had a strong emotional participation with his experiment, synchronicity took place, and that the emotion was usually due to an archetype being activated in the unconscious of the experimenter.[49] But perhaps all his experiment actually proved was that all researchers are bound to have some sort of attitude to the material they work with and that results can be affected by the hope, faith and expectations of the experimenters. In the case of the astrological experiment neither the testers nor those involved in the sample had neutral attitudes; they were all disposed to believe in astrology. Moreover, astrology itself was not acausal in its claims, so there was a fundamental contradiction in Jung's aims, in that the acausal principle of synchronicity was supposed to be validating the causal principle of astrology. It was in vain that Jung tried to wriggle out of the dilemma.

By all but true Jungian believers, the notion of synchronicity has generally been considered fatally flawed. The flaws arise from systematic ambiguity in Jung's use of the term, his typically turbid and confused exposition of a general idea, and insoluble paradoxes in the very conception itself. In the first place, Jung provided at least two major, but different, definitions of synchronicity. The first definition posits that there is a meaningful coincidence of certain psychic states and physical states or events: people have dreams and premonitions which come true, as in the case of J.W. Dunne's premonitory dream of the 1902 earthquake in Martinique, Swedenborg's vision of the Stockholm fire in 1759, or Sir Victor Goddard's RAF officer and the plane crash. The second definition covers cases of similar or identical thoughts and dreams occurring in different places at the same time, that is to say, meaningfully but not causally connected. Jung's many writings on the subject seem to imply a threefold conception of synchronicity: there is an interdependence of objective events; an interdependence of similar or identical thoughts; and a 'pre-established harmony' of physical and mental events. Whereas, in principle, the interdependence of physical events or mental processes might be susceptible to scientific laws, it was hard to see how the mind-matter divide could be so bridged, *and by the same general principle*. Philosophers have also objected that the very word 'meaningful' implies a mind to assign meaning, yet by talking about meaningful coincidence between physical events Jung was in effect smuggling in metaphysical assumptions about order and harmony in the universe, implying a transcendental meaning independent of human consciousness. Here the never very deeply buried vein of Platonism in Jung rose to the surface, yet there was a further problem in that Jung, as in his treatment of God, always denied transcendental entities in favour of psychological images.

Further confusion was added when Jung mixed even more ingredients in his turgid bouillabaisse: first, the idea of action at a distance derived from Pauli's theory of the sympathetic harmony of electrons in quantum theory and, secondly, the notion of two events that coincide in space and time but are then seen to have other, more meaningful, coincidences. To try to clear up the confusion Jung drew a distinction between 'synchronous' and 'synchronistic', but this simply made matters worse.[50] So, on Jung's view, precognitive experiences are 'evidently not synchronous but are synchronistic since they are experienced as psychic events *in the present*, as though the objective event already existed.'[51] On this Arthur Koestler remarked: 'One wonders why Jung created these unnecessary complications by coining a term which implies simultaneity, and then explaining that it does not mean what it means. But this kind of obscurity combined with verbosity runs through much of Jung's writing.'[52]

It was an oft reiterated theme of Jung's that the very notions of statistical probability and causality must admit of exceptions, otherwise they would be mathematical or *a priori* truths.[53] However, there are two cogent objections to Jung's position. In the first place, many mathematically minded philosophers, such as Bertrand Russell, have argued that the naïve 'cause and effect' notion of causality is otiose and could be replaced by a description of the physical universe relying solely on differential equations. In short, Jung's objection scarcely holds water. Secondly, there is the fundamental fallacy involved in arguing for acausality along causal lines; this is similar to the core paradox of the late Wittgenstein arguing for the inadequacy of language, by using the language of logical positivists arguing for a verification principle which could not itself be verified.

To try to save his beloved idea from intellectual extinction, Jung toyed with the idea of using synchronicity to explain schizophrenia, a subject in which he had taken little interest for nearly fifty years. He started from the proposition that synchronicity was triggered by the presence of an active archetype, usually occurring in individuals in highly emotional states – elated, ecstatic, shocked, depressed – or in individuals of creative genius or with a peculiar or pathological personality.[54] In such cases the threshold to the collective unconscious was habitually lowered, pointing clearly in the direction of schizophrenia and the *abaissement du niveau mental*. The lowering of the level of mental energy meant that synchronistic events were likely to be associated with persons near death or those suffering psychosis or near-psychosis. This would explain the detonations in book-cases of his early career as well as the appearance of the scarab when he had a female patient with a severe 'animus' problem. Jung's general theory of *unus mundus* – neither matter nor mind – fitted with this, as it allowed him to speculate that the archetypes were psychophysical entities or 'psychoids', whose trans-psychic reality meant they could take a physical as well as mental form: hence detonations in book-cases, ghosts and so on. This would also explain why when a person died clocks would stop, pictures fall off the wall, glass would crack.[55]

The idea that emotional states could alter space and time by 'contraction', leading to strong affects and the appearance of a 'gradient' allowing the unconscious to flow towards the conscious, seemed to open up exciting vistas in the area of schizophrenia. What a fittingly circular triumph it would be – a perfect *coniunctio oppositorum* – if the abiding interest of Jung's early years turned out to validate the obsession of his last years. However, he was soon forced to admit that this avenue of inquiry was a blind alley. Preposterously, it turned out that schizophrenics, who interpreted quite ordinary events as having especial significance for themselves, were indifferent to events that Jung classified as synchronistic. Prey to all kinds of chimerae themselves, they dismissed what he took as genuine synchronicity as mere delusions![56]

The very last occult or paranormal phenomenon to engage Jung's attention was unidentified flying objects, sometimes known as 'flying saucers'. Jung's interest, first quickened in 1951, became intense by the end of the 1950s. In some ways it can be seen as the culmination of an interest in science fiction and, particularly, in myths and reports of things seen in the skies. In 1948 he read a book about the Marian apparitions at Fatima and admitted that the book posed problems which he could not solve.[57] But his appetite for science fiction and speculative metaphysics of the more outlandish kind was becoming increasingly noticeable: he was very much struck by Philip Wylie's *When Worlds Collide*, John Wyndham's *The Midwich Cuckoos* and Teilhard de Chardin's *The Phenomenon of Man*, which he described as 'a great book'.[58]

In his last decade Jung was drawn more and more to the psychology of flying and space travel. Although he had begun by viewing aeroplanes as a symbol for the Trinity, he came to see them as a sign of neurotic evasion particularly favoured by men with a mother-complex, of whom he instanced Antoine de Saint-Exupéry. After a long talk with St-Exupéry's wife, he bracketed St-Exupéry with D.H. Lawrence as a man who overemphasized women and had therefore never grown up: 'Flight, you see, is really an act of evasion, an attempt to escape from the earth'.[59] He himself particularly disliked air travel, particularly by jet aircraft, as he took seriously the idea that the body went too fast for the soul, which had to catch it up; this was the true meaning of 'jet-lag'.[60]

The dream of space travel, according to Jung, contained all these elements plus some further, unique ingredients. Flights to outer space denoted both hyperanxiety caused by the world's intractable population problem and a desire to escape from ourselves, because it is easier to go to Mars or the Moon than to penetrate one's own being.[61] In Jung's view the depth psychologist was a greater hero than the explorer: a Victorian adventurer like H.M. Stanley could penetrate the Dark Continent of Africa, but this was a simple task when compared with penetrating the internal 'dark continent' of the unconscious. Jung also thought that human beings began to dream of interstellar communication at the precise moment when man's inhumanity to man was most evident, but that the fantasy of space travel was a kind of neurotic evasion of the life-task in the here and now.[62]

If Jung's explanation for space travel was more complex than his explanation for mere flight, the hermeneutic complexity increased tenfold when he came to deal with unidentified flying objects or UFOs. We can pin down fairly precisely the date when these first began to engage Jung's attention: February 1951. That month, having read some of the classic early works in this field – Donald Keyhoe's *Flying Saucers Are Real* and Gerald Heard's *Is Another World Watching?*, both published the year before – he wrote to Fowler McCormick about the recent spate of 'flying saucer' sightings: his opinion was that idle rumour was largely responsible, but this left the question of why rumour should take that particular form.[63]

But Jung was forced to find out more for himself, for in 1958 he had one of his celebrated 'big dreams' involving UFOs. Two metallically gleaming discs flew towards him, and it seemed to him that the dream was telling him that he was a projection of the UFO, whereas the conventional opinion was that UFOs were projections of the human unconscious. The UFO seemed to be the lens of a magic lantern with Jung's projected image on it, suggesting to him that his reality was guaranteed by a meditating yogi.[64]

The experience enabled Jung to interpret a dream reported to him by a medical colleague three months later. The man saw a large bird, which turned out to be a swan, that he wanted to photograph. Suddenly the swan crashed to the ground, leaving a plume of smoke like an aeroplane. Next a real aeroplane appeared to be flying through clouds of smoke or fog, and then a contraption like a helicopter descended towards the dreamer to fetch him; he saw shadowy figures, which he knew to be higher types of being, far more intelligent than Man, imbued with an absolute sense of justice, clearly visitors from another world. Jung's interpretation was typical multicausal amplification. The swan was a messenger of the gods, a symbol whose physical and spiritual meanings were conveyed by the alchemical spirit of Mercurius; the dreamer was aspiring to something higher, beyond, transcendental; the crash indicated that the something coming from beyond was disastrous, a fall of angels with apocalyptic consequences; and the motif of being carried off linked it with other UFO stories in which people were taken off to other planets.[65]

Around 1958, then, Jung decided to try to resolve the matter of UFOs once and for all. In his long essay, 'Flying Saucers. A Modern Myth of Things Seen in the Skies', he posed the question sharply. If they were real, what were they? If they were fantasy, why did fantasy take that form? Why was there a will to believe in UFOs? Why did the press promote news of their existence and pay no attention to sceptics? In short, why was it more desirable for flying saucers to exist than not?[66]

As with discussion about God, Jung regarded questions of transcendental existence as unimportant: just as it was the 'God-image' which was the crucial consideration, so what was significant about UFOs was their psychological implication. At various times Jung held different opinions about UFOs, not all of them compatible. He thought they reinforced the truths of psychology; they reinforced ideas in astrology and numerology; they acted as compensation for the decline of organized religion; they illustrated the *Zeitgeist*; and they were linked with archetypes and synchronicity.

Jung thought that UFO sightings, made by so many people at so many different times and places, were a more complex form of the phenomenon of the 'dancing sun' at Fatima in 1917 or the 'Angel of Mons' in 1914. Mons and Fatima were examples of collective visions – he was careful not to use the loaded phrase 'collective hysteria' – and in such cases one of two things happened: either a primary perception was followed by a phantasm – in other words, an objectively real physical process formed the basis of an accompanying myth; or a fantasy, originating in the unconscious, invaded the conscious mind with illusions and visions.[67]

Although Jung suspended judgement on the reality of UFOs, he made it clear that he had no very great opinion of the ability of the human mind to distinguish truth from illusion. He mentioned the panic caused by Orson Welles's 1938 radio broadcast of H.G. Wells's *War of the Worlds* and referred to the 'will to believe' he had observed at seances: on one occasion four out of five people present saw an object like a moon floating above the abdomen of the medium but the fifth (Jung himself) saw nothing. The argument that UFO witnesses were credible because they were in the main cool, rational and sceptical beings impressed Jung not at all; on his theory of compensation, the projections came from the unconscious, where the exact opposite would be the case.[68]

Doubtless mellowing in extreme old age, Jung accepted that UFOs could be read as endorsing either his theories or those of Freud. The circular shape of 'spaceships' linked them with mandalas, the symbol of totality, uniting inner opposites, the ultimate goal of the individuation process; it was no accident that Plato described the soul as having the shape of a sphere or that some early sects believed God was a circle. Because our consciousness cannot apprehend psychic totality, the mandalas were projected and their rounded wholeness was transmogrified into a spaceship controlled by intelligent beings. Jung gave many examples of UFOs seen in dreams and drew an analogy between the 'tear drop' volatile liquid of the alchemists and the behaviour of UFOs. Moreover, they have appeared in all eras and cultures: although 'flying saucers' were first publicized in 1947, the phenomenon was known long before, famous examples having been reported in Basel in 1566 and in Nuremburg in 1561. This suggested an obvious conclusion to Jung: 'From the dream examples and pictures it is evident that the unconscious, in order to portray its contents, makes use of certain fantasy elements which can be compared with the UFO phenomenon.'[69]

The surprise was to find Jung accepting that the rarer cigar-shaped UFOs were genuine phallic symbols and thus supportive of the Freudian picture of the unconscious, though he could not altogether resist the chance for another crack at psychoanalysis by suggesting ironically that perhaps the 'saucers' represented a repressed uterus coming down from the sky.

Jung also linked the appearance of 'flying saucers' with the great changes to be expected as the Age of Aquarius dawned and thought they provided further evidence that the ruling principle of the universe is number, as Pythagoras thought. His argument here is difficult to follow but it seems to hinge on two dreams, one of which seemed to presage the end of the world sometime in 1960–66, while the other warned him that he would die on 8 November.

More persuasive was Jung's idea that UFOs served to allay fears and enhance hopes and thus that their appearance filled the void left by the decline of organized religion in the West. UFOs answered a need for miracles, for a saviour, now that mankind feels alone after the 'death of God'. This also illustrates the action of the unconscious in compensating conscious fears.[70] Jung believed that Christians should be concentrating on convincing waverers in their own flock rather than taking their message to primitives; there would then be fewer UFO sightings.

Most of all, it was the spirit of the age that provoked the multiplicity of UFO sightings. Because of the weight of post-Second World War anxiety, unconscious contents of the psyche had projected themselves as unknown heavenly phenomena. Fear of catastrophe, whether from nuclear weapons or overpopulation, produced a 'sign from the heavens' – an obvious projection of a salvation fantasy, with the world expecting a redeeming supernatural event. Common interpretations of 'flying saucers' by ufologists, admittedly highly unconvincing, postulated that intruders from other planets or beneath the earth were acting as guardian angels, and were even prepared to intervene in earthly evolution at critical moments, to save *Homo sapiens* from self-destruction. But Jung pointed to the increasingly pessimistic *Zeitgeist* of the 1950s, when the early idea that visitors from outer space in UFOs were benevolent gradually gave way over the decade to the fear that they might be malevolent. He thought it significant that UFO sightings were principally an American phenomenon. Jung accounted for this by a mixture of American paranoia and high technology: science and futuristic technology had been developed to the highest point in the USA but no corresponding consciousness had developed; rather, and in compensation, there was a retreat into irrationality, into McCarthyism and anti-communist hysteria.[71] Certainly if we take the movies as a good index of the national unconscious, Jung's thesis is borne out, for the films of the 1950s dealing with beings from outer space and associated subjects – *The War of the Worlds, The Day the Earth Stood Still, Them, The Thing, When Worlds Collide, The Day the World Ended, Invasion of the Body Snatchers* – evince singular signs of post-nuclear guilt and paranoia.

Yet most of all Jung stressed the appearance of UFOs as caused by the triggering of an archetype. Although the phenomena might be precipitated by an adventitious physical cause, they were essentially a product of unconscious archetypes and therefore stood in need of psychological explanations. The obvious archetypes at play were those of the Self, of God – Elijah's ascent into heaven in the Bible clearly linked with the myth of things seen in the skies – and of the ship of death. In some UFO dreams the anima also played a major role, in the form of a young girl optimistic about the future – which

Jung interpreted as the compensating antidote to fears of universal catastrophe. Other UFO experiences were along the same lines, as when a UFO female 'spaceperson' speaks to the dreamer.[72]

Yet perhaps the aspect of the question that most exercised Jung was that of synchronicity. The debate about whether the primary stimulus in UFO sightings was a physical object or an unconscious fantasy could be sidestepped with the notion of synchronicity, which Jung thought was far the most likely explanation.[73] The UFOs could also be explained as a way of 'integrating' the antagonisms of the Cold War, since Jung thought it a meaningful coincidence that military aircraft from the USSR had a red star painted on the side, while American planes boasted a white five-pointed star. Red was regarded by the alchemists as a masculine colour and white as feminine; similarly, Russia was the land of 'Father Czars' and 'Father Stalin' while the USA was a matriarchy. UFOs would therefore represent the convergence which both sides unconsciously wished for.[74]

All these explanations tied up the conundrum of UFOs into very neat explanatory packages. Perhaps too neat for, as in the case of ghosts, Jung increasingly came to doubt that a purely psychological approach could explain all the sightings he read about in a rapidly swelling library on UFOs. The fact that UFOs possessed a surface visible to the naked eye and threw back a radar echo seemed to tell against the psychological thesis, but Jung pointed out that there were many cases when the human eye had picked up something which was not on a radar screen and, conversely, when radar had picked up things not available to the human eye. He thought that Heisenberg's uncertainty principle could account for this, and quantum mechanics in general could explain the 'saucers' apparent weightlessness, without bringing in the supererogatory idea that the UFOs came from outer space.

But if the objects could be picked up by radar and human vision, how could they be purely psychological in origin? Synchronicity was the obvious and general answer, but Jung advanced several ancillary arguments. One was the curious argument that their gravity-defying character would suggest that the UFOs were a kind of projection of the psyche itself, since the psyche was the one thing in Nature that was weightless. Another argument, deriving from reports of people who had seen UFOs in their dreams as 'flying spiders', was that the spider/UFO represented the ego trying to drag down the psyche so that the Self could not realize itself. Those impatient with Jung's far-fetched psychological explanations moved in for the kill at this point, protesting that a UFO could not represent either the Self or the ego, for this meant there were no identifying criteria and the 'saucers' could mean whatever anyone wanted them to mean. Jung's most convincing overall argument was that the idea of UFOs as hailing from another planet was itself an idea implanted by dreams, which he 'proved' from the dreams of patients who envisaged UFOs as interplanetary insects possessing a shell or carapace that shone like metal.[75]

Jung's general position on UFOs by the end of the 1950s was that what was seen was probably either a subjective hallucination or (where more than one person saw the apparition) a collective one. However, the more he read, the more he became sceptical about his own explanation. Reluctant to admit that there could ever be 'Close Encounters of the Third Kind', he speculated that UFOs, if physically real, might be some hitherto unknown phenomenon coming from the sea or beneath the earth; in other words, they were perfectly explicable occurrences as yet beyond the purview of science. In common with many scientists who have examined the riddle of UFOs, his most favoured physical explanation was ball lightning. He censured the United States Air Force for keeping secret its investigations into UFOs; this was a sure way to bring about another *War of the Worlds* panic.[76]

No sooner had Jung finished his essay on UFOs in 1958 than, by chance, he came upon the science-fiction novel *The Black Cloud* written by the distinguished British astronomer Fred Hoyle. Jung loved the book and felt that Hoyle had explained the essence of the UFO problem. The black cloud of the title was a cosmic cloud containing superhuman intelligence, with a diameter equal to the distance between the earth and the sun; the black cloud threatens mankind as it draws energy from the sun and away from the earth. In psychological terms the black cloud was the unconscious and the parable, in Jungian terms, was that Man (consciousness) was being overwhelmed by the unconscious.[77]

By this time Jung was heartily sick of the gullible and credulous attitude taken by most people towards UFOs and strongly denounced sensationalist literature on the subject, such as Desmond Leslie and George Adamski's *Flying Saucers Have Landed*. Yet he could be equally impatient with out-and-out sceptics. In January 1959 Charles

Lindbergh, the famous American aviator who in 1927 made the first solo nonstop transatlantic flight from New York to Paris, visited Jung at Küsnacht. In an evil hour Lindbergh took it into his head to ridicule Jung's interest in UFOs, pointing out that Donald Keyhoe's books, which had particularly influenced him, were wildly inaccurate factually. Jung listened politely but made no comment. Unable to take a hint, Lindbergh persevered and related a conversation with USAF General Spaatz. 'Slim,' Spaatz had said, 'don't you suppose that if there was anything true about this flying-saucer business, you and I would have learned about it by this time?' Finally nettled, Jung made a devastating reply: 'There are a great many things going on around this earth that you and General Spaatz don't know about.'[78]

Jung's long 'night-sea journey' in the realms of the paranormal after 1945 produced three very different conclusions: first, a conviction that the links between mind and body were much stranger even than hitherto dreamed of; secondly, a certainty that the insights he gained reinforced the truths of alchemy; and thirdly a feeling of angry scorn towards those who scoffed at experiments in occult or 'supernatural' areas.

Parapsychology convinced Jung that psychic phenomena could manifest themselves in physical form, and vice versa: this was why the study of psychosomatic medicine, so often derided by 'scientific' scoffers, was a key aspect of any depth psychology. Since the cross-over between the mental and the physical could not satisfactorily be explained in terms of conventional causality, Jung felt that the undoubted fact of psychosomatic causation was further evidence for synchronicity.[79] Certainly in his last years he seemed to return, by a roundabout route, to some of the modalities of his Freudian period. He became certain that tuberculosis was a psychosomatic illness, which explained why consumptive patients notoriously resisted psychoanalysis: 'It is in such cases often as if the patient had a pride and obstinacy in defending the achievement of a somatic answer to an insoluble psychological problem.'[80]

The more Jung investigated the paranormal in his final decade, the more he reinterpreted the puzzling events of his childhood, when he claimed he had had 'alchemical' experiences much more astonishing than anything he had revealed in his writings. This led him to interpret childhood as part Wordsworthian declining bliss and part a Platonic process of knowledge as recollection.

To question the wisdom of Jung's dalliance with the paranormal was to strike a deep well of rage and elicit a gushing torrent of invective; it is an invariable sign of Jung in full rage-ridden flight that his analogies are over the top.[81]

Jung sometimes went too far when investigating the occult and the preternatural, but he was merely living out Freud's sometimes expressed wish that he himself could have taken that route. Phenomena classed as 'supernatural' do need investigation by first-class minds, otherwise they will forever remain the preserve of cranks and charlatans. For this reason, Jung's courage and intellectual independence are to be applauded. As J.B.S. Haldane memorably remarked: 'The universe is not only queerer than we imagine – it is queerer than we *can* imagine.'

Chapter Twenty-Six

LAST YEARS

The amazing surge of creative energy in Jung's last decade, evinced in his wide-ranging excursions into the occult, took place, paradoxically, at a time of declining physical powers. After the near-fatal heart attack in 1944 he was never in robust health again. In 1949 he was laid up with a severe attack of gastric 'flu, and at one stage that year the house at Küsnacht resembled a hospital, with his secretary Marie-Jeanne Schmid prostrate with the same malady and his wife Emma with her arm in a sling, having broken it after slipping on a carpet.[1] In 1952, at the age of seventy-seven, he suffered from hepatitis, sustained a prolonged attack of 'flu and endured a long convalescence in Locarno. Barely recovered from that, he began having trouble with his heart – specifically arrhythmia and tachycardia brought on by overwork.[2] He was forced to cut his work rate to three hours of writing a day, four days of the week, which was the maximum he could do without disturbed sleep and symptoms of arrhythmia. Frustrated mentally, he next found that he could walk no more than a quarter of a mile a day without becoming exhausted; his large frame cried out for exercise, but his heart denied it.

In 1952 Jung made his farewell appearance at the Eranos conferences. Apart from motor tours to northern Italy, he was increasingly confined to the narrow Zürich-Bollingen grid. Even worse, he came under doctor's orders to give up tobacco. In the late 1940s his physician, Dr Jakob Stahel, ordered him to give up smoking, especially the American Granger tobacco and the Brazilian 'Gruner Heinrich' cigar he habitually smoked after lunch.[3] Jung pleaded for permission to smoke three pipes of tobacco a day and one or two cheroots; Stahel refused, but Jung smoked them anyway. He solved the problem of his general practitioner by getting rid of Stahel and signing up with a Swiss physician, Ignaz Tauber. Unlike Stahel and most other people, Tauber had the skin of a rhinoceros and could simply bounce off him Jung's many querulous sarcasms and scalding criticisms. He and his wife Elsbeth became two of Jung's closest friends in the 1950s.[4]

Tauber's battle to cut out Jung's smoking was no more successful than his predecessor's. He prescribed quidinal for his patient's tachycardia, but at first could make little headway against nicotine, for Jung made the 'concession' of smoking a pipe in the morning, a miniature cigar after lunch, another pipe at 4 p.m., another cigar after supper and a final pipe at 9.30 p.m. Under severe pressure from Tauber he gave up smoking completely for a few days until the craving led him to start smoking pipes again. In the end it was a premonitory dream, not the nagging of his physician, that made him kick the habit.[5] But the sacrifice caused him much anguish and to the end of his life he could be seen nostalgically twiddling an empty pipe in his hands.

Despite Jung's perverse talent for alienating male friends, he also had the happy knack of winning new supporters to fill the place of those who had fallen by the wayside. The friendship with Tauber held, as did those with Herbert Read and J.B. Priestley, who continued to popularize Jung's ideas in England.[6] A new, and quite unexpected, enthusiast was the American novelist Upton Sinclair, whose strong socialist commitment was evident in his novels *The Jungle*, *Metropolis*, *King Coal*, and *Oil*. Since Jung loathed socialism and regarded socialists as suffering, not so much from 'false consciousness' as from a 'false unconscious', it seemed unlikely that he would have anything to say to a man who had attempted to become a revolutionary governor of California and tried to found a communist colony at Englewood, New Jersey.[7] Yet a wary entente developed following a long critique of Sinclair's novel *A Personal Jesus* by Jung in the influential US journal *The New Republic*.[8] In reply Sinclair wrote Jung a personal letter, teasingly accusing him of feeling guilty that he had not written a life of Jesus himself and urging him to do so.

Jung replied guardedly that he was solely interested in psychology – in what people believe – not in what might or might not be historically true.[9] But he was sufficiently interested in Sinclair's work to agree to review another Sinclair novel for *The New Republic*, also on a theme of maximum interest to Jung, *Our Lady*. Again he was highly critical, accusing Sinclair of removing the quintessence of the Christian tradition while trying to extract it. It would not do to dismiss all of Christianity as a mere fantasy, for the psychological needs it fulfilled could not be met by any of the twentieth-century nostrums like science or existentialism.

Jung was always hypersensitive to criticism, which fed into his gloom about the postwar world and increased his pessimism. He tried to deal with his low opinion of the contemporary world by seeking solace in thoughts about the destiny of the Self. But he was a human being and could not operate for ever at such a lofty level. Inevitably, then, the stress of the postwar years found expression in many attacks, sometimes peevish, sometimes dithyrambic, on modern life, the Cold War and the materialism and technology, the ideology and even the culture of the 1950s. A frequent target in these years was existentialism, either in the person of its founder, Kierkegaard, or its Left Bank high priest Jean-Paul Sartre.[10] Another favourite butt for Jungian derision was modern art, poetry and novels. He sometimes went so far as to suggest that there was an organic connection between modernism in the arts and political totalitarianism. One discussion of Hitler and Stalin led on, as if by inevitable association of ideas, to the 'infernal' work of his old *bête noire* James Joyce.[11]

There was just a handful of modern favourites Jung was prepared to except from his blanket condemnation: Henry Moore (for his 'alchemical' sculptures), Hölderlin, Rilke and, especially, Gérard de Nerval, on whose *Aurélia* Jung had given one of his rare public lectures in Zürich in 1945.[12] He was fond of contrasting a 'hate figure' like the German surrealist painter Edgar Ende (whom he criticized for artistic cowardice, the avoidance of thought and meaning, and failure to find the universal behind the particular) with his beloved Rilke.[13]

However, Jung was prepared to stomach 'decadent' Westerners if that was the price for keeping communism at bay; for the theories of Marx, Engels and Lenin he always had the utmost loathing. In the light of subsequent history we know that he overrated the power of the communist states, but in the 1950s it seemed to him that Soviet Russia and Red China were insuperable monoliths, destined to endure well into the twenty-first century. As a result, much of his writing is peppered with a kind of visceral and, at times, unbalanced, hatred of all forms of socialism and egalitarianism, which he tended to see as simply less perfected versions of Stalinist communism.

Jung added no new ideas to his repertory of anti-communist philippic. His 1950s utterances are full of the old, familiar themes: communism as the destroyer of liberty, individualism and personal relations, even those between parents and children, in pursuit of a new 'atomized' Man in whom the human psyche is completely stifled; the impossibility of personal expression in communalized enterprises like collective farms; the loss of identity in standardized apartments and a homogenized political culture; the inevitable tendency of socialism to encourage people to seek the kingdom of heaven in the external world rather than in their own souls.[14]

But the West's superiority over the Soviet system was, in Jung's view, only marginal. The threat of nuclear war and the spectre of overpopulation and world famine were problems to which the West had no more answer than the East. And both systems were in thrall to Goddess Reason, to technology, increased production, GNP and welfarism. The West denounced communism vociferously but was really entirely bankrupt of countervailing ideas.[15]

Apart from the ever-present threat of global warfare, Jung thought that the West was faced by four main problems in its deep structure: technology, materialism, lack of individuality and lack of integration. The technological problem was twofold. In the first place modern technology estranged mankind from natural versatility of action, forcing its instincts to remain fallow and producing a 'slum mentality'. A start could be made by moving industry out of the cities and switching to a four-day week in factories on condition that workers spent the one or two days saved at agricultural work on their own plots.[16] The other problem about technology was that, like the sorcerer's apprentice, it was beyond human control; humans remained naked apes even as their inventions bordered on the miraculous.[17]

According to Jung, materialism, first enthroned by the Enlightenment and the French Revolution, consolidated by the scientific materialism of the nineteenth century and reaching its apogee in the cult of 'realism' in the twentieth century, had turned the clock back a full 2,000 years. The result was the recrudescence of despotism, trampling on human rights, of cruelty, indignity and a return of the slavery of the pre-Christian world, which solved its labour problems via the concentration camp.[18] Many agreed that materialism was rampant in the twentieth century but thought that Jung's analysis was hopelessly unhistorical. If freedom, human rights and dignity had been so highly valued in the *ancien régime* before the Enlightenment, it was difficult to see whence the pressure for revolution would have originated in the first place. Others alleged that Jung, with his Gnostic–alchemical worship of spirit, simply hated materialism of all kinds with a rare hatred and was not over-fastidious about the evidence he adduced to discredit it.

Yet the most serious malaise of the West was its 'split-off' aspect. Jung was fond of illustrating the world situation in the 1950s by the myth of Hercules in the underworld. Hercules's most celebrated feat while in the land of the dead was to rescue Theseus, whose flesh had stuck fast to a stone chair after Hades (aka Pluto and Dis) had ordered this punishment for the presumption of Theseus and Pirithous in bidding for the hand of his daughter. Because Theseus was held fast to his rocky seat, when Hercules tried to wrench him free he precipitated a mighty earthquake. This myth seemed to Jung to describe the contemporary world situation today.[19]

Sometimes the paradoxes Jung spun from his general psychological theories produced bizarre results. A proposal that the system of secret numbered accounts in Swiss banks be abolished, so as to enable nation-states to deal more effectively with international white-collar crime, was likely to be regarded by Jung and his followers as the action of 'criminals and personalities with latent pathology who, behind an appearance of normality, are undermined by unconscious illness and perverse tendencies . . . They are ruled by infantile wish-fantasies and personal affects and resentments.'[20] And while Jung appeared to denounce the excesses of capitalism, the denunciation took some highly idiosyncratic and enigmatic forms, showing clearly that his beloved theory of compensation could often end in absurdity.

However, it would be wrong to suggest that Jung viewed the

Europe of the 1950s entirely at the level of abstraction and offered merely cloudy generalities as prescriptions. He always took a keen interest in day-to-day world events and the complex practical moral issues thrown up by an increasingly fragmented and uncertain world. In 1951, as tensions rose, and the idea of a Russian invasion of Western Europe was taken very seriously in London and Washington, he declared himself passionately in favour of German rearmament: only dreamers, he said, favoured disarmament, especially since the result would be to hand Germany over to the Russians who, like the Nazis, posed as universal saviours and 'want to cure the whole world with their own disease.' Roundly denouncing disarmers and pacifists as 'dangerous dreamers' he again stretched the idea of compensation to snapping point: only profoundly warlike nations considered themselves peace-loving and whereas armed neutrality was plausible, the unarmed sort was not.[21]

Such statements smacked of an unregenerate pessimism, and Jung soon found himself unable to take comfort from any good actions performed by human beings: either such actions were compensation or they masked fear, of a terrible apocalypse to come. He was taken aback by the extraordinary worldwide response to the catastrophic floods in the Netherlands in February 1953, but argued that this positive sign for humanity masked fear of an even greater catastrophe. For the present fear was driving people towards collaboration, but the Dutch catastrophe also reminded them of the potential threat to world peace.[22]

The terrible year 1956 seemed to bear out all Jung's worst forebodings. In November, while Britain, France and Israel, to the fury of the United States, colluded in a backward-looking fit of gunboat diplomacy when faced with Egyptian president Nasser's nationalization of the Suez Canal, the Soviet Union sent its tanks into Budapest to crush the short-lived Hungarian experiment with 'socialism with a human face'. Jung condemned both the Anglo-French invasion of the Canal Zone and the Soviet invasion of Hungary, but especially the latter. The suppression of the Hungarian uprising he condemned forthrightly as a 'vile and abominable crime', while his initial pronouncement on Suez spoke only of 'unlawful measures' by Nasser which had provoked Britain and France to a warlike act.[23] In the long term Jung was delighted that the Hungarian uprising proved conclusively that all attempts to extirpate religion and substitute a secular ideology of salvation (the classless society as *parousia* or Second Coming, etc) were doomed to failure.[24]

The Chinese invasion of Tibet in 1959 also upset Jung, especially when he remembered his conversations in 1938 with a Tibetan abbot. Because of his many pronouncements on Tibetan Buddhism he was also associated in some people's minds with the cult of High Lamas on the Roof of the World, to the point where he was moved to rebuke a correspondent, who believed that the world was run from a Tibetan monastery by a cabal of 'elders' of whom Jung was one.[25] But when asked to add his name to a list of protesters about the Chinese invasion, he declined. A dignified refusal to go public about Tibet would have been acceptable but, as so often, Jung spoiled a reasonable case by impugning the motives of celebrities who did protest.[26]

Jung was forthright on the political issues of his final decade, and he was also increasingly asked his opinion on a range of social issues. Since he was by now, somewhat oddly, considered a champion of women, he was especially sounded on his attitude to a variety of 'women's issues'. He was in favour of licensed brothels and thought that if people did not wear moral blinkers, syphilis would have been extirpated long ago.[27] It was true that there was no clear dividing line between prostitution and crime, but this was mitigated by three considerations. First, prostitution was a social necessity, so the legal code was punishing something that was functional to sound well-being. Secondly, a crime-free society was mythical and any crimeless society would soon go to rack and ruin. Thirdly, punishment was itself an evil and in itself just as much a transgression as the crime it punished: it was justified only by the greatest good of the greatest number, so that crime versus punishment was simply one unavoidable and necessary evil pitted against another, with the important difference that society's evil had a justification lacking to the criminal, who practised individual evil.[28]

As for artificial insemination, Jung considered it a sign of the mental and moral deterioration of the world that such ideas were discussed at all. From the standpoint of psychology, the consequence of artificial insemination, even within wedlock and in legal circumstances, would be a form of illegitimacy, since the father would not be known. Besides, the whole process was redolent of the stud farm and reduced women to the status of cows or brood mares; he thought that the effect of such a conception on a woman's psychology would be akin to the effects of rape. Above all, the very idea of 'reifying' birth in this way devalued human beings and had a disastrous impact on human dignity.[29]

In 1959 Switzerland was in a ferment over a referendum on granting women the vote. The editor of the woman's page of the Zürich daily *Die Tat* wrote to ask Jung what effect the unconscious would have on the men taking part in such a referendum. Jung replied that he would expect unconscious resistance to the idea to be considerable, but in many men the unconscious desire for the maintenance of male privilege would be counterbalanced by a favourable attitude towards women and a proneness to feminine influence.[30] He decisively rejected the idea that to enfranchise women would 'masculinise' them; from his long clinical experience he felt able to state categorically that when women became 'masculinised', it was for reasons that had nothing to do with political activity. He spoke of the tenacity and toughness of female nature which had remained unaffected for thousands of years and would not be affected by the mere possession of a vote. Moreover, 'animus hounds' and domineering wives abounded in Switzerland even though they were unenfranchised; by contrast, there were countless women who had succeeded in public life without losing their femininity. Finally, in all ages there had been wise and shrewd women to whom even very clever men went for advice. In sum, there was no valid argument against giving women the vote.[31]

Yet another 'women's issue' was children, but Jung, a notably cold father, who never wrote anything significant on child psychology, always found the subject a bore. Jung once elicited a rare display of public exasperation from his wife, when he was explaining that children did not interest him as they had no symbolic material. 'Oh, Carl,' Emma cut in tartly, 'no one interests you who doesn't have symbolic material!'[32]

Swiss schoolteachers in the 1950s became increasingly worried about their charges' inability to concentrate and consulted Jung. He replied that the basic problem was the excessive noise of the modern world, so that the brain had to divert energies to filtering this out. Cinema, radio, television, the din of cars and aeroplanes all played their part; even in the 1930s, Jung claimed, the cacophony of 'muzak' in a New York hotel had been so great that he had had to give up on a conversation he was trying to hold.[33] Jung's hatred of noise found expression in an eloquent denunciation of its devotees – one with which many sorely harassed late twentieth-century citizens would surely agree. He repeated his charge that children's lack of concentration came about because all their important stimuli were external: radio, television, the gramophone.[34]

For Jung, noise was the degenerative symptom of urban civilization, compounded by the nerve-shattering din of technical gadgetry. What made the problem of noise even worse was its use as apotropaic magic. The more frightened people became by the nuclear arms race, the alarming pollution of water supplies, the steady increase of radioactivity and the sombre threat of overpopulation which further tempted world leaders to use the Bomb, the more their unconscious fear was reproduced at conscious level as a love of noise, which stops the fear from being heard. Noise was welcome because it drowned inner instinctive warnings of global catastrophe; like crowds, it gives the individual a feeling of security and wards off painful reflections; it scatters our anxious dreams, assures us we are all in the same boat, and enhances the idea that if we make such a racket nobody will dare to attack us.

Jung thought that people genuinely feared silence – the very expression 'deathly silence' was a giveaway – which was why there was so much whistling, humming, whispering and coughing and why the centre of social life was the dreaded cocktail party, an institution Jung loathed.[35] The real fear people entertained was what might come up from the depths if there was silence – all those things previously held at bay by noise.

With Jung's nose for what might be coming in the future, he also took a great interest in the new drug LSD, which he already knew as mescalin from the writings of Aldous Huxley. He thought that Huxley had blundered into a very dangerous field because, having got to know a bit of the collective unconscious, he had not learned how to balance this at the conscious level; Huxley was thus in the role of the sorcerer's apprentice in the fable, who had learned from his master how to summon the spirits without knowing how to get rid of them.[36]

Jung began investigating LSD by reading the accounts of those who had taken a 'trip'; there is no evidence that he ever took the drug himself, and to do so would have run counter to all we know of his personality. His initial interest was powered by the idea that the drug could produce an *abaissement du niveau mental* in which archetypes would come into the field of consciousness.[37] But he soon discovered that LSD trips could produce nothing of any use to psychology that could not be conjured by 'active imagination'. Mescalin/LSD provided a temporary short cut to a realm that could be reached more securely by the hard work and difficult training involved in his method. He rejected the idea that LSD could provide a *transcendental* experience; its only point was to convince sceptics that there was a realm of the unconscious. The obvious danger in taking LSD was that the drug could release a latent psychosis – much more common than manifest psychoses and thus more likely to be encountered during a 'trip'.

Jung was constantly seeking to fuse all knowledge, no matter how disparate, into a whole. Certainly Jung's writings in the 1950s are notable for the attempts to provide the psychological equivalent of Pauli's 'unified field theory'. Further refinements of the idea of God as internal, the 'God-image', were fused with ever more general theories about religion; and, paradoxically, the more Jung denounced the idea of a transcendental God, the more sympathetic he became to Catholicism for its emphasis on myth as a social phenomenon.[38] A new, and favourite, theory was that the word 'religion' itself came from the Latin *religere* – 'to ponder, take account of, observe' – rather than, as the Church Fathers thought, *religare* – 'to bind or connect'; he did not consider a third possibility, plausibly suggested by Robert Graves, that it derived from *rem legere* – literally 'to choose the thing'.[39]

The Hegelian drift of Jung's late thought is clear. Since the collective unconscious validated archetypes, and archetypes were the key to synchronicity, it seemed highly probable that the mind-body riddle could be solved only acausally, and that psychosomatic illnesses and miracle cures were themselves aspects of synchronicity. He had long been convinced that tuberculosis was psychogenic in origin and that many 'miracle cures' simply involved removing the psychic associations from the physical illness and prising free the patient from his 'complexes'. Consumption was a puzzling illness because of its obvious organic symptoms, but Jung himself had made annual visits to the famous sanatorium at Davos and had treated patients whose lesions had healed. Although reluctant to claim that all tumours had a purely psychological cause, he was persuaded that 'constellation' of the kind of archetype that produced synchronicity could explain the 'miracle cure' even in the case of organic disease.[40]

Convinced that a friend's tinnitus was psychosomatic in origin, Jung was honest enough to apply the same diagnosis to his own osteosclerosis.[41] And the experiments on epileptics by Wilder Penfield and Herbert Jasper seemed to him to offer further proof of *unus mundus* – that mind and matter were aspects of a more primal 'stuff'. Penfield and Jasper had succeeded in evoking an hallucinatory vision of coloured squares and circles (mandalas) by stimulating the occipital cortex of an epileptic, who previously had such visions only as a prelude to an attack. This suggested to Jung that there was no means of squaring the circle of mind-matter by causality: circularity would always occur if you postulated healing of an organic disease by archetypes but also postulated that the archetypes were located in the brain-stem. The acausal principle of synchronicity, it seemed to him, so far from being mystical mumbo-jumbo, was the answer to a whole range of phenomena to which conventional science could provide no answer.[42]

Intimations of Jung's own mortality seemed portended by a vivid dream in October 1952, when he dreamed of a huge black elephant uprooting a tree. He read this as a warning of death – he assumed his own – but later reinterpreted it when Toni Wolff died on 21 March 1953.[43] Although Toni had continued to work as a Jungian therapist and finally produced the work – *The Structures of the Feminine Psyche* – which Jung had long urged her to write, the distance between her and the Master had widened over the years. At least three major factors were at play in the rift. First, Toni Wolff had, so to speak, outlived her usefulness. She was largely responsible for Jung's successful encounter with the 'undiscovered self' in 1913–16; but for her he might have been trapped for ever in psychosis. But precisely because she had played the role of intermediary between Jung and his shadow, when he burst into the full sunlight of individuation after the years on the 'night-sea journey', Toni no longer had a vital role in his life.[44]

Secondly, the two had grown apart in their interests. Toni thought the study of alchemy was a blind alley and deplored the excessive attention Jung paid to the subject; Jung, in turn, was disappointed with her 'apostasy'.[45] Thirdly, and most obviously, as she approached sixty Toni lost her physical charms and began to suffer acutely from arthritis. Jung, who liked to have young and pretty women around him, grew bored with her and tried to avoid seeing her. He once remarked to Aniela Jaffé: 'Toni is coming today – I hope she doesn't stay long.' Towards the end Toni would often come over to Küsnacht for tea, but Jung would ignore her pointedly and read a paperback right through tea without exchanging a single word with her.[46]

Toni suffered terribly from his diminished attentions. A forty-a-day chainsmoker, she began to suffer rapid pulse movements and paroxysmal tachycardia in addition to her arthritis. The unhappier she became the more she imposed a Loyola-like regime on herself in the hope of achieving spiritual transcendence. When she called in Dr Gerhard Adler on 19 March 1953, she already knew she was dying. She struck Adler as bitter and disillusioned but she was still able to charm, telling him that it was pleasant to see someone arriving in Zürich who was not a neurotic.[47]

Toni's death shook Jung and brought on a recrudescence of arrhythmia and tachycardia, with a high pulse rate, still between 80 and 120 a month later.[48] But his public reaction was odd to say the least. He did not attend her funeral, an omission which elicited a variety of explanations from his entourage: he was too ill, he could not face it, it reminded him of his own imminent death, he disliked funerals and never went to them, and so on. He left it to Emma to represent him at the funeral, which, in her typically self-sacrificing way, she did. Privately, there was more reaction. On Easter Saturday 1953 he had a dream in which Toni appeared in a dress of kingfisher blue, the exact colour and image in which Philemon had originally appeared to him. This was a kind of symbolic acceptance that it was Toni who had enabled him successfully to wrestle with those figures from the unconscious. There were other possible Jungian 'amplifications' – Philemon and Toni as King and Queen, the kingfisher as the symbol of fidelity and happy sexual partnership, and so on.[49] At Bollingen Jung carved a stone for her, bearing the legend: 'She was the fragrance of the house.'[50]

Jung celebrated his eightieth birthday in July 1955, and for at least eighteen months before, elaborate preparations were under way to honour Switzerland's most famous citizen. A foretaste of the main celebrations came in Zürich on November 1953 when Jung was presented with the so-called *Codex Jung*. In 1945 he had learned that a collection of Gnostic manuscripts had been discovered in the village of Khenoboskion in Upper Egypt. Knowing of Jung's mania for Gnosticism, a wealthy admirer purchased them and arranged the formal presentation.[51] In 1955 itself Jung was fêted and lionized throughout Switzerland. Commemorative articles appeared in the newspapers, and the International Congress of Psychiatry was held in Zürich in his honour. Two lavish parties were held in July, one for psychologists and academic specialists, and the other for his friends and admirers. The second party, especially, was a great success: Jung so enjoyed having his students, neighbours, gardeners and all those close to him present in one room that he stayed far later than expected.[52]

However, all the celebrations were overshadowed by the rapidly declining health of his wife. Emma was diagnosed as having cancer early in 1955 and underwent a major operation, after which she was bedridden and needed careful nursing.[53] For a while she seemed to be in remission but then, in November, there was a sudden worsening of her condition and, after five days spent mostly in a coma, she died, leaving Jung devastated.[54] This time there could be no avoiding his duty and he was obliged to attend the funeral in Küsnacht church. Later he broke down in tears and kept repeating: 'She was a queen!' Acknowledging that she and Toni had been 'mystical sisters', he carved another stone for her at Bollingen on which were the words: 'She was the foundation of my house.'[55]

Given Jung's views on the aetiology of cancer, the depth of his guilt about Emma can only be guessed at; in his secret heart he surely knew that he had destroyed both her life and that of Toni Wolff as thoroughly as it was possible for a human to do by his habitual infidelities, his coldness, his ruthlessness and his rating of anima archetypes over flesh-and-blood women. He consoled himself with the thought of her inestimable importance to him, both spiritually and materially. After her death he had frequent dreams about her, which he read as evidence of the survival of the soul: in one he dreamed of her portrait, which he took to mean that he was seeing her completely objectively; in another he spent an entire day in Provence with her; in a third, he found her continuing her studies on the Holy Grail.

In financial terms Emma had been the salvation of Jung's life. Under Swiss law when he married her, a husband had complete access to his wife's money and could spend it as he wished without her consent. Jung's retreat into isolation after 1909 and the severance of ties with the Burghölzli and the world of academe was possible only because of the vast (but as yet unquantifiable) fortune Emma Rauschenbach brought into her marriage. Jung summed it up well in a moment of frank honesty to Father Victor White, when he admitted the importance of his wife's money.[56]

In 1952 Marie-Jeanne Schmid, the perfect secretary who had been with him for twenty years, left his employment to get married. Between then and her illness his wife Emma had acted as stopgap, but with her demise there was a gaping hole in Jung's domestic arrangements. Suddenly he remembered his female companion on the East African journey thirty years earlier. Ruth Bailey, now a woman of fifty-five, was living quietly in Cheshire when she got a phone call from Jung, asking her to come out to Küsnacht as companion-housekeeper on a 'temporary' basis. After a battle with Swiss immigration authorities, who could not see why Jung did not employ a Swiss woman, Ruth duly took up her position. She was under no illusions, for she had seen Jung the domestic tyrant in action before, berating Emma, to whom he owed everything material, for allowing a cauliflower to go off.[57] Aniela Jaffé, meanwhile, agreed to take over secretarial duties.

A close and friendly, though often stormy, relationship developed. Ruth Bailey could make him laugh, though he was subject to violent mood swings and could suddenly become intensely irritated with her jokes and stories. He was a martinet and a precisian and was liable to lose his temper if a single spoon was out of place. On the other hand he was clumsy and careless about the house and once nearly shot himself with his own service revolver. Most of all, as trencherman and 'heavy grubber', he was fanatical about food, and meals were a constant source of tension. He prided himself on his own talents as a cook and would often insist on being driven into Zürich to get the right base for a sauce; some of his elaborate sauces contained no fewer than thirteen ingredients.[58]

Both gourmet and gourmand, a man who infuriated waiters in restaurants by poring over menus for half an hour, often changing his mind several times before coming to a final decision, Jung was already notorious in his circle for the secret meals he had in his rooms at the Eranos conferences, over and above the regular three meals provided for all participants.[59] Ruth Bailey initially found mealtimes a trial, and matters came to a head when she used two tomatoes while preparing a dish of spaghetti. When Jung threw a scene over this, Bailey calmly announced that she would be leaving next day. The following morning Jung ate humble pie, apologized and pleaded with her to stay.[60] He would call Jaffé and Bailey into his study in the morning and dictate the day's lunch and dinner menus, but Bailey, quickly noting his absent-mindedness, learned to ignore him and tended to serve what was most convenient for her.

Cross-grained, dyspeptic, and with a shorter fuse than any man Bailey had ever known, Jung asked her to ignore his frequent rages, adding, however, that there would never be any trouble if she always did exactly what he wanted. She also noticed a tendency towards miserliness, for he complained about petty expenditures, went in for penny-pinching economies and prowled around the house switching off electric lights. He was maniacal about punctuality and neatness, traits which, allied with the 'nearness' over money, seemed almost to make him a textbook case of Freud's 'anal-erotic' category. When he sensed that Jaffé and Bailey were becoming indispensable to him, he accused them of having a secret lust for power.[61] Both Jaffé and Bailey noticed that he cheated when playing patience and chided him with this.[62] He got his revenge by mutterings about women as 'power devils'.

Both Bailey and Jaffé learned to put up with Jung's temper tantrums, his impossibly demanding punctiliousness, his prima donna antics, with his dogmatic opposition to sleeping pills and his maddening insistence, whenever he had lost something, that it had been spirited away by supernatural forces. They indulged his fantasy, based on conversations with a necessarily deferential gardener, Herman Muller, that ordinary people understood him better than intellectuals did. Jaffé turned a blind eye to the way he was doctoring the record for posterity by, for example, burning great piles of incriminating letters from former mistresses.[63] Bailey tended to be tougher on him, rebuking him publicly for the cold and formal manners that existed between him and his daughters, all of whom were frightened of him, and none of whom had dared to kiss him until Bailey insisted that they do so and derided Jung for his stiffness.[64]

Peaceful co-existence between Jung and the two women he depended on was soon established at Küsnacht. At Bollingen, where Jung increasingly wished to be, it was less easy, as the quarters were more cramped and the women, naturally, did not share Jung's taste for 'roughing it'. He insisted on spending one week in every month at Bollingen, so the luckless Bailey was under severe pressure for that week; Aniela Jaffé used to walk the half hour from Bollingen station to the tower every Wednesday and try to get a week's worth of secretarial chores completed in a single gruelling day.[65]

At Bollingen Jung amused himself by supervising yet another set of extensions to the tower, which he explained as being necessary because they symbolized the extensions of consciousness achieved in old age.[66] In the tower there was still no running water or electricity and no telephone – an invention he had come to detest. He liked to boast that if a sixteenth-century time traveller should suddenly appear, the only things he would find strange would be the kerosene and matches. From his point of view the primitive conditions enabled him to get in touch with ancestral voices.[67]

Things were less pleasant for Ruth Bailey, who found adjusting to the oil-lamps, wood-fires and water from the pump far from easy. It was small consolation when Jung paid her the – for him – mighty compliment of saying that she had the most marvellous gift: the gift of silence. However, her cooking chores were lighter, for Jung liked to supervise a roast on the grill, and at lunch times would content himself with a simple meal: perhaps an enriched Knorr or Maggi packet-soup, a cheese board, bread, butter, fruit and coffee. He loved wine, especially burgundy, and would sip the occasional liqueur, but maintained his lifelong distaste for cocktails. He liked to gaze out on the lake and observe the animal life. Feeding the birds was a major pleasure, and once Jaffé noticed that he had put out a bowl of milk for a ring-snake. The birds seemed to reciprocate the warm feeling: Bailey noted that on one occasion a tomtit landed on Jung's head and actually tried to make a nest in his white hair. As for snakes, the real serpent in paradise at Bollingen was the Swiss airforce, whose fighter squadrons based at Dubendorf had taken to screaming low over the lake before vanishing behind the mountains, thus increasing Jung's mania about noise.[68]

Back at Küsnacht the stream of celebrities and 'names' making pilgrimages to see the greatest living psychologist showed no signs of abating. Moravia paid a second visit, Konrad Lorenz lunched with Jung in Zürich, Ian Fleming, creator of James Bond, fell under his spell and was influenced by his thoughts on numerology and astrology. Among the many American visitors were Charles Lindbergh and Claire Myers Owens, one of the principal popularizers of 'psychological religion' in the USA.[69]

Some of the visitors recorded valuable impressions of Jung, man and prophet. The novelist Hugo Charteris sketched an unflattering portrait of Jung in old age: 'Mr Jung's hands (were) getting bulbous, jointed with rheumatism, he (could not) stand for long periods . . . When he laughed, he laughed completely like a hippo waiting for a bun. No dentures. Only four eye teeth, ground to needle sharpness and gums like hard wet wool.'[70]

The Latin American diplomat and writer Miguel Serrano, who had extensive conversations with Jung at Locarno on 28 February 1959 and later the same year at Küsnacht, reported him sunk in deep pessimism about the future of the world. Jolande Jacobi filled in the details on the sage's gloomy forebodings: she told Serrano that Jung was convinced that global warfare or some similar catastrophe would take place in 1964, as he now thought this was when the entry into the Age of Aquarius would occur; he was also increasingly inclined to believe that UFO sightings might actually be the prelude to the landing of beings from outer space, which for humanity as a whole would be like the coming of the white man to Africa.[71]

By 1959 he had concluded that he could offer no more therapeutic help to anyone and that his writing days were over; he did, however, agree to collaborate with Aniela Jaffé on the autobiographical memoir that eventually became *Memories, Dreams and Reflections*.

In 1959 Jung was a surprise choice as one of the interviewees for the BBC *Face to Face* programme, an oddly heterogeneous collection of encounters with celebrities, including on the one hand Bertrand Russell and Lord Birkett and on the other media people such as Gilbert Harding, Tony Hancock and Adam Faith. The interview, conducted at Küsnacht by the journalist John Freeman, was a great success and introduced Jung to a new audience.[72] When asked if he believed in God, he replied forthrightly: 'I don't believe, I know.' This went down well with the orthodox Christians among the BBC viewers, but Jung had to spend a lot of time explaining to his followers that when he said 'God', he meant, of course, the 'God-image'.[73]

Freeman got on well with Jung and remained on friendly terms, while the BBC was so delighted with the programme that it planned a follow-up venture, this time with Jung interviewed by a psychiatrist. Jung did not like the idea at all, fearing that his would-be interlocutor would not be open-minded or competent, that the interview would degenerate into confrontation or mere 'gladiator games'.[74] He stalled successfully, and the programme was never made.

In January 1960 Jung suffered another severe heart attack, which he played down as 'a slight embolism and heart cramps'. He was confined to bed for a month and forbidden all mental activity; presumably he did not count Buddhism under this heading, as he spent the time rereading his favourite Buddhist texts.[75] He had only just recovered when he heard the shattering news that Father Victor White was dying of cancer. The two men had come to the parting of the ways in 1955 when Jung pointedly invited White to Küsnacht, where acquaintances came, rather than to Bollingen, the domain of friends. White, who knew the Jungian code better than any man, riposted by not even bothering to call at Küsnacht when he came to Zürich to lecture at the Jung Institute in 1955. He still expected to go on corresponding with Jung, but when three of his letters went unanswered, all contact ceased.

On receipt of the news of White's illness, Jung wrote him a letter, but it was an odd production to send to a seriously ill man, as it was an impersonal missive, full of talk about shadows and archetypes.[76] The letter Jung should have written to White was the one he sent to the Mother Prioress of the hospice where White lay dying, stressing that he knew of apparently hopeless cases involving tumours where 'miracle cures' had taken place.[77] To the same woman he laid bare some of his deepest unease, especially about the early and unexpected death of so many of the talented and original people he had known: Honegger, Gross, Sigg, Baynes, Zimmer, Neumann, Wilhelm, Pauli.[78]

The Mother Prioress wrote back to say that Jung's cold letter had served only to upset Father White. Jung then wrote her a graceful apology, and finally reached down into himself and found the words with which to reach White. 'I want to assure you of my loyal friendship. I shall not forget all the useful things I have learned through our many talks and through your forbearance with me. I was often sorry to be a *petra scandali*.'[79] White replied on 8 May 1960, thanking Jung for his 'wonderful and comforting letter'. He died on 22 May.

July 1960 was the occasion of Jung's eighty-fifth birthday. Once again there were lavish celebrations, including a celebratory dinner on 25 June 1960 at the Grand Dolder, Zürich, organized by Cornelia Brunner.[80] Küsnacht gave him the freedom of the town – a rare honour in Switzerland, where such marks of favour are extraordinary. Some observers thought he was already fading fast, though there is little sign of declining powers in his correspondence. His somewhat notorious utterance to an artless correspondent who wrote asking what one could do to help in the present parlous condition of the world – 'Help yourself and you help the world'[81] – could be read as senility, but more likely it was merely an extreme example of Jung's aversion to all organized political activity.

In his last years Jung made many motoring trips into the Alps, Austria and Italy, always with Ruth Bailey and accompanied either by his old American friend Fowler McCormick or by his daughters and sons-in-law: by this time he was a great-grandfather, with nineteen grandchildren and eight great-grandchildren. It was a favourite conceit of Jung's that he and his companions belonged to what he called 'The International Touring and Culinary Association', as he loved to stop at favourite restaurants on these tours.[82]

His last venture into Italy came after a second long illness in 1960; by now even Jung's ox-like strength was being taxed by infections, from which he took a long time to recover. Sensing that the end could not be far away, he had expressed a particular wish to see his beloved Alps up close. His daughter Marianne and her husband drove him on a roundabout route through the Alpine peaks to Lugano and then as far as Milan and the Lombardy plain. As the Alps faded into the distance, Jung said, with tears in his eyes, 'I think that's the last time I shall meet the mountains'. He saw many new places, including the Cathedral at Monza, but tired easily. Marianne and Ruth Bailey remembered how he would sit for long stretches in the car without saying anything. One afternoon, when they had become concerned about his taciturnity, he suddenly broke the silence by saying, jokingly, 'It is always a pleasure to carry out the duties of this Association'.[83]

Jung had always thought that one should recognize in death a goal worth striving for, since shrinking from death robs the second half of life of meaning.[84] He faced the end with equanimity and was rewarded with a premonitory dream of death. He saw what he described as the 'other Bollingen' bathed in a glow of light, and a voice told him that it was now complete and ready for habitation. Then, far below on the ground, he saw a mother wolverine teaching its cub to dive and swim in a pool. Since he had often dreamed of this 'other Bollingen', the meaning seemed clear: he must soon pass into another element and learn a different way of adaptation, like the young wolverine.[85]

As trees in the Jungian symbolic system always signified death, his last recorded dream was also of the 'fey' variety. He saw a big, round block of stone in a high, barren place, on which was inscribed: 'This shall be a sign unto you of wholeness and oneness.' There was also a lot of pottery on the right-hand side of a square, and another square, of trees, all fibrous roots, with gold threads gleaming through, sprouting up from the ground and surrounding him. To the end Jung's taste for dream interpretation did not desert him. The symbol of the round stone indicated wholeness; the pottery connoted the canopic jars in which the dismembered corpse of the God Osiris was stored, ready for resurrection; and the tree roots stood for the invisible aspects of life.[86]

Against all the odds, Jung survived an embolism on 17 May 1961, but grew weaker and weaker. The fatal heart attack came on 6 June. Jung's last recorded words, to Ruth Bailey, were, 'Let's have a really good red wine tonight.'[87] It was not to be, for Jung died at three forty-five that afternoon. The funeral, attended by a vast assembly, took place in the parish church at Küsnacht. The Reverend Werner Meyer, pastor of Küsnacht, spoke of Jung as a prophet who had stemmed the tide of rationalism. Two of his disciples, the theologian Hans Schar and the economist Eugen Bohler, delivered eloquent panegyrics. Jung's body was then cremated and the ashes deposited in the family grave in Küsnacht cemetery. There lay the remains of his father, mother, sister and wife in a tomb Jung had designed himself, complete with family coat of arms and Latin inscriptions. Tributes poured in from around the world: an especially valued one came from the Indian prime minister Jawaharlal Nehru, a distant and unobtrusive admirer.[88] As with all great prophets, the disciples set to work to fashion a thaumatology, alleging that a violent thunderstorm had broken out in Küsnacht two hours after his death. The legend of Jung, the man-God, was already in the making.

BIBLIOGRAPHY

Abraham, H.C. & Freud, E.L., eds, *The Freud-Abraham Letters, 1907–26* (1965)

Abraham, Karl, *Clinical Papers and Essays on Psychoanalysis* (1953)

Acheson, Dean, *Present at the Creation. My Years in the State Department* (NY 1966)

Adler, Alfred, *Superiority and Social Interest* (ed. H.L. & R.R. Ansbacher, 1965)

Adler, Gerhard, *The Living Symbol. A Case Study in the Process of Individuation* (NY 1961)

Alexander F. & Selesnik, S., *A History of Psychiatry* (NY 1961)

Alexander, Franz, Eisensten Samuel & Grotjahan, eds, *Psychoanalytic Pioneers* (1966)

Allen, Gay Wilson, *William James. A Biography* (1967)

Appignanesi, Lisa & Forrester, John, *Freud's Women* (1992)

Aronson, Alex, *Psyche and Symbol in Shakespeare* (Bloomington, Indiana 1972)

Arraj, James, *St John of the Cross and Dr C.G. Jung: Christian Mysticism in the Light of Jungian Psychology* (Oregon 1986)

Axelrod, Stephen Gould, *Robert Lowell: Life and Art* (Princeton 1978)

Aziz, Robert, *C.G. Jung's Psychology of Religion and Synchronicity* (NY 1990)

Baedeker, Karl, *Switzerland and the Adjacent Portions of Italy, Savoy and Tyrol. Handbook for Travellers* (Leipzig 1899)

Bancroft, Mary, *Autobiography of a Spy* (NY 1983)

Barbey, Bernard, *P.C. Du Géneral: Journal du Chef de l'Etat Major Particulier du General Guisan* (Neuchatel 1988)

Barnaby H. & D'Acierno, P., eds., *C.G. Jung and the Humanities: Towards a Hermeneutics of Culture* (1990)

Bauer, Jan, *Alcoholism and Women: The Background and the Psychology* (Toronto 1982)

Baynes, H.G., *Analytical Psychology and the English Mind* (1950)

Becker, Raymond de, *The Understanding of Dreams* (1968)

Bennet, E.A., *Meetings with Jung* (1982)

Bennet, E.A., *Jung* (1961)

Bertin, Celié, *Marie Bonaparte* (1983)

Bickman, Martin, *The Unsounded Centre: Jungian Studies in American Romanticism* (Chapel Hill, NC 1980)

Binion, Ralph, *Frau Lou* (Princeton 1968)

Binswanger, Ludwig, *Sigmund Freud. Reminiscences of a Friendship* (NY 1957)

Bleuler, Eugen, *Dementia Praecox or the Group of Schizophrenias* (NY 1950)

Bleuler, Manfred, *The Schizophrenic Disorders* (Yale 1978)

Bloch, Ernst, *Prinzip Hoffnung* (Frankfurt 1959)

Bolen, J.S. *The Tao of Psychology: Synchronicity and the Self* (NY 1979)

Bolen, J.S., *The Goddesses in Everywoman* (SF 1984)

Boss, Medar, *The Meaning and Content of Sexual Perversions* (NY 1949)

Bottome, Phyllis, *Alfred Adler* (1939)

Bouttes, Jean Louis, *Jung. La Puissance d'une Illusion* (Paris 1990)

Bouvier, Nicholas, Craig, Gordon & Gossman, Lionel, *Geneva, Zürich, Basel: History, Culture and National Identity* (Princeton 1994)

Bowers, Kenneth & Meichenbaum, Donald, ed., *The Unconscious Reconsidered* (1984)

Boyle, Andrew, *Montagu Norman* (1967)

Branson, Clark, *Howard Hawks: a Jungian Study* (Santa Barbara 1987)

Brennan, Anne & Brewi, Janice, *Celebrate the Mid-Life: Jungian Archetypes and Mid-Life Spirituality* (NY 1989)

Brennan, Anne & Brewi, Janice, *Mid-life: Psychological and Spiritual Perspectives* (NY 1982)

Brill, A.A., *Freud's Contribution to Psychiatry* (NY 1944)

Brill, A.A., *Lectures on Psychoanalysis and Psychiatry* (1938)

Brivic, Sheldon, *Joyce Between Freud and Jung* (1980)

Brome, Vincent, *Jung. Man and Myth* (1978)

Brome, Vincent, *Ernest Jones. Freud's Alter Ego* (1982)

Brome, Vincent, *J.B. Priestley* (1988)

Brunner, Cornelia, *Anima as Fate* (Dallas 1986)

Buber, Martin, *The Eclipse of God* (NY 1952)

Buber, Martin, *I and Thou* (NY 1958)

Burkhardt, Frederick & Bowers, F., *The Works of William James: Essays in Psychical Research* (Harvard 1986)

Burnham, John, *Psychoanalysis in American Medicine* 1894–1918 (NY 1976)

Burnham, John & William McGuire, *Jelliffe: American Psychologist and Physician. His Correspondence with Sigmund Freud and C.G. Jung* (1983)

Burrow, Trigant, *A Search For Man's Sanity: The Selected Letters of Trigant Burrow* (1958)

Campbell, Joseph, *The Mythic Image* (Princeton 1974)

Campbell, Joseph, ed. *The Mysteries: Papers from the Eranos Yearbooks* (Princeton 1955)

Campbell Joseph & Moyers, Bill, *The Power of Myth* (NY 1988)

Caprio, Betty, *The Woman Sealed in the Tower* (NY 1982)

Carotenuto, Aldo, *The Vertical Labyrinth: Individuation in Jungian Psychology* (Toronto 1985)

Carotenuto, Aldo, *A Secret Symmetry: Sabina Spielrein between Jung and Freud* (1984)

Carotenuto, Aldo, ed., *Sabina Spielrein, Tagebuch Einer Heimlichen Symmetrie. Sabina Spielrein Zwischen Jung und Freud* (Freiburg 1986)

Carroll, L. Patrick & Dyckmann, Katherine Marie, *Chaos or Creation: Spirituality in Mid-Life* (NY 1986)

Catillejo, I. Claremont de, *Knowing Women: a Feminine Psychology* (NY 1973)

Champernowne, Irene, *A Memoir of Toni Wolff* (SF 1980)

Charet, F.X., *Spiritualism and the Foundations of C.G. Jung's Psychology* (NY 1993)

Churchill, Winston, *The Second World War* (1954)

Cirlot, J.E., *A Dictionary of Symbols* (1972)

Clark, Ronald, *Freud. The Man and the Cause* (1980)

Cobb, Noel, *Prospero's Island: The Secret Alchemy at the Heart of the Tempest* (1984)

Cocks, Geoffrey, *Psychotherapy and Psychoanalysis in the Third Reich* (1985)

Cocks, Geoffrey, *Psyche and Swastika: Neue Deutsche Seelenheillunde 1933–1945* (LA 1975)

Coleman, Arthur & Libby, *The Father: Mythology and Changing Roles* (Chicago 1988)

Collier, Peter & Horowitz, Favid, *The Rockefellers. An American Dynasty* (1976)

Conger, John, P., *Jung and Reich: The Body as Shadow* (Berkeley 1988)

Connolly, Cyril, *The Golden Horizon* (1953)

Cornillier, P., *La Survivance de L'Áme et son Evolution Après la Mort* (Paris 1920)

Coursen, H.R., *The Compensating Psyche: A Jungian Approach to Shakespeare* (Lanham, Md. 1986)

Coward, Harold G., *Jung and Eastern Thought* (NY 1985)

Cox, David, *Jung and St Paul: A Study of the Doctrine of Justification by Faith and its Relation to the Concept of Individuation* (1959)

Craig, Gordon A., *The Triumph of Liberalism* (NY 1988)

Curtius, Ernst Robert, *Critical Essays on European Literature* (Princeton 1973)

Daly, Mary, *Gyn/Ecology: the Metaethics of Radical Feminism* (Boston 1978)

Decker, Hannah, *Freud in Germany: Revolution and Reaction in Science, 1893–1907* (NY 1977)

Desoille, Robert, *Exploration de l'Affectivité Subconsciente par la Méthode du Rêve Eveillé* (Paris 1938)

Devereux, George, ed., *Psychoanalysis and the Occult* (NY 1953)

Donahue, A.K. & Hillman, J., eds, *Freud. The Cocaine Papers* (Vienna 1963)

Donington, Robert, *Wagner's Ring and its Symbols: The Music and the Myth* (1963)

Donn, Linda, *Freud and Jung: Years of Friendship, Years of Loss* (NY 1988)

Douglas, Claire, *Translate the Darkness: The Life of Christiana Morgan, the Veiled Woman in Jung's Circle* (NY 1993)

Dourley, John P., *The Psyche as Sacrament: C.G. Jung and Paul Tillich* (Toronto 1981)

Dry, A., *The Psychology of Jung. A Critical Interpretation* (1961)

Dubois, Paul, *Les Psychonéuroses et leur Traitement Moral* (Paris 1904)

Dupont, Judith, ed., *The Clinical Diary of Sandor Ferenczi* (Cambridge, Mass. 1988)

Duverger, Maurice, *The Study of Politics* (1972)

Dyer, Donald R., *Cross–Currents of Jungian Thought* (1991)

Eder, David, *Memoirs of a Modern Pioneer* (1945)

Edinger, Edward F., *The Creation of Consciousness: Jung's Myth for Modern Men* (Toronto 1984)

Edinger, Edward F., *Encounter with the Self: A Jungian Commentary on William Blake's Illustration of the Book of Job* (Toronto 1986)

Edinger, Edward F., *The Bible and the Psyche: Individuation Symbolism in the Old Testament* (Toronto 1986)

Edinger, Edward F., *The Christian Archetype: A Jungian Commentary on the Life of Christ* (Toronto 1987)

Edinger, Edward F., *Goethe's Faust: Notes for a Jungian Commentary* (Toronto 1990)

Edinger, Edward F., *Ego and Archetype: Individuation and the Religious Function of the Psyche* (Baltimore 1972)

Edinger, Edward F., *Melville's Moby Dick: A Jungian Commentary: An American Nekyia* (NY 1978)

Edinger, Edward F., *Anatomy of the Psyche: Alchemical Symbolism in Psychotherapy* (Lasalle, Illinois, 1985)

Eissler, K.R., *Talent and Genius* (NY 1971)

Eissler, K.R., *Victor Tausk's Suicide* (NY 1983)

Eissler, K.R., *Psychologische Aspekte Des Briefwechsels Zwischen Freud und Jung* (Stuttgart 1982)

Eliade, Mircea, *The Forge and the Crucible: The Origins and Structure of Alchemy* (1962)

Ellenberger, Henri, *The Discovery of the Unconscious* (1970)

Ellmann, Richard, *James Joyce* (1959)

Erikson, Erik, *Identity, Youth and Crisis* (NY 1968)

Erikson, Erik, *Life History and the Historical Moment* (NY 1975)

Erikson, Erik, *Identity and the Life Cycle* (NY 1959)

Erikson, Erik, *Childhood and Society* (1950)

Evans, R.I., *Jung on Elementary Psychology* (1979)

Evans, R.I., *Conversations with Carl Jung and Reactions from Ernest Jones* (Princeton 1974)

Ferenczi, Sandor, *Final Contributions to the Problems and Methods of Psychoanalysis* (NY 1955)

Ferenczi, Sandor, *First Contributions to Psychoanalysis* (1980)

Ferenczi, Sandor, & Rank, Otto, *The Development of Psychoanalysis* (NY 1925)

Ferenczi, Sandor, *Further Contributions to the Theory and Technique of Psychoanalysis* (1969)

Fierz-David, Linda, *Women's Dionysian Initiation: The Villa of Mysteries in Pompeii* (1988)

Fierz-David, Linda, *The Dream of Poliphilo* (1988)

Filoramo, Giovanni, *A History of Gnosticism* (Oxford 1990)

Fink, Augusta, *I-Mary* (Tucson 1983)

Flournoy Théodore, *From India to the Planet Mars* (NY 1900)

Flournoy Théodore, *The Philosophy of William James* (1911)

Flournoy, Olivier, *De Théodore Flornoy à la Psychanalyse, Suivi d'une Correspondance entre Théodore Flournoy et Helène Smith* (Neuchatel 1986)

Fodor, Nandor, *Freud, Jung and Occultism* (NY 1971)

Fordham, Michael, *Explorations into the Self* (1985)

Fordham, Michael, *Contact with Jung* (1963)

Fordham, Michael, *Jungian Psychotherapy* (1978)

Forel, Auguste, *Out of my Life and Work* (1937)

Forel, Auguste, *Rückbuck Auf Mein Leben* (Zurich 1935)

Frank, Ludwig, *Afte Utstorungen* (Munich 1913)

Franz, Marie-Louise, von, *An Introduction to the Interpretation of Fairy Tales* (NY 1970)

Franz, Marie-Louise, von, *C.G. Jung. His Myth in our Time* (1975)

Franz, Marie-Louise, von, *The Psychological Meaning of the Redemption Motif in Fairy Tales* (Toronto 1980)

Franz, Marie-Louise, von, *The Golden Ass of Apulcius* (Dallas 1980)

Franz, Marie-Louise, von, *The Passion of Perpetua* (Dallas 1980)

Franz, Marie-Louise, von, *Alchemy: An Introduction to the Symbolism and the Psychology* (Toronto 1980)

Franz, Marie-Louise, von, *Puer Aeternus: A Psychological Study of the Adult Struggle with the Paradise of Childhood* (Santa Monica 1981)

Franz, Marie-Louise, von, *The Way of the Dream* (Toronto 1987)

Franz, Marie-Louise, von, *On Dreams and Death: A Jungian Interpretation* (Boston 1986)

Franz, Marie-Louise, von, *On Divination and Synchronicity: The Psychology of Meaningful Chance* (Toronto 1980)

Freeman, Erika, *Insights: Conversations with Theodor Reik* (New Jersey 1971)

Freedman, Ralph, *Herman Hesse: Pilgrim of Crisis* (1979) pp. 224–25

Freud, Martin, *Glory Reflected* (1957)

Frey-Rohn, Liliane, *From Freud to Jung* (1974)

Galbraith, J.K., *Economics, Peace and Laughter* (1971)

Gallant, Christine, *Blake and the Assimilation of Chaos* (Princeton 1978)

Gallup, Donald, ed., *The Journals of Thornton Wilder* (Yale 1985)

Gardner, Robert L., *The Rainbow Serpent: Bridge to Consciousness* (Toronto 1990)

Garrison, Jim, *The Darkness of God: Theology after Hiroshima* (1982)

Garzonio, Marco, *Gesù E Le Donne* (1990)

Gay, Peter, *Freud. A Life for our Time* (1988)

Gay, Peter, *Reading Freud: Explorations and Entertainments* (1990)

Gay, Peter, *A Godless Jew: Freud, Atheism and the Making of Psychoanalysis* (1987)

Gedo, John E., *Portraits of the Artist* (NY 1983)

Glaser, Hermann, ed. *The German Mind of the Nineteenth Century* (NY 1981)

Glatzer, Nahum, *The Dimensions of Job: A Study and Selected Readings* (1969)

Glover, Ernest, *Freud or Jung?* (1950)

Godard, Jerry C., *Mental Forms Creating: William Blake Anticipates Freud, Jung and Rank* (1985)

Golberg, A., ed. *Progress in Self Psychology* (1989)

Goldenberg, Naomi R., *Returning Words to Flesh: Feminism, Psychoanalysis and the Resurrection of the Body* (Boston 1990)

Goldbrunner, Josef, *Individuation: Die Tiefen Psychologie von Carl G. Jung* (Munich 1947)

Gordon, Rosemary, *Dying and Creating: A Search for Meaning* (1978)

Graves, Robert, *The White Goddess* (1948)

Green, Martin, *The Von Richtofen Sisters* (NY 1974)

Greene, Liz, *The Astrology of Fate* (1984)

Gregory, Anita, *The Strange Case of Rudi Schneider* (NY 1985)

Griffin, David Ray, *Archetypal Process: Self and Divine in Whitehead, Jung and Hillman* (Evanston, Illinois, 1989)

Grose, Peter, *The Gentleman Spy. The Life of Allen Dulles* (1995)

Grosskurth, Phyllis, *Melanie Klein* (1986)

Grosskurth, Phyllis, *The Secret Ring: Freud's Inner Circle and the Politics of Psychoanalysis* (1991)

Gruber, F., *Zane Grey* (NY 1970)

Guisan, Henri, *Bericht an die Bundesversammlung Über den Aktivdienst 1939–1945* (Berne 1946)

Gutreil, Emil A., ed., *The Autobiography of Wilhelm Stekel: The Life Story of a Pioneer Psychoanalyst* (NY 1950)

Häberlin, Paul, *Stutt Einer Autobiographie* (Frauenfeld 1956)

Häberlin, Paul, *Aus Meinem Huttenbuch, Erlebuisse und Bedanken Einen Bemsjagen* (Frauenfeld 1956)

Hale, Nathan G., *James Jackson Putnam* (1971)

Hale, Nathan G., *Freud and the Americans* (1971)

Hall, J.A., *Jungian Dream Interpretation* (Toronto 1983)

Hannah, Barbara, *Encounters with the Soul* (Santa Monica 1981)

Hannah, Barbara, *C.G. Jung: His Life and Work, A Biographical Memoir* (1976)

Harding, Esther, *Women's Mysteries, Ancient and Modern* (1935)

Harding, Esther, *The Parental Image* (NY 1964)

Hawthorn, Jeremy, *Multiple Personality and the Disintegration of Literary Character* (1983)

Heisig, James W., *Imago Dei. A Study of C.G. Jung's Psychology of Religion* (1979)

Henke, James, *The Ego King: An Archetypal Approach to Elizabethan Political Theory and Shakespeare's Henry VI Plays* (Salzburg 1977)

Herzog, E., *Psyche and Death* (1966)

Hillman, James, *The Dream and the Underworld* (NY 1979)

Hillman, James, *Facing the Gods* (Dallas 1980)

Hillman, James, ed., *Puer Papers* (Dallas 1979)

Hillman, James, *Anima: An Anatomy of a Personified Notion* (Dallas 1985)

Hillman, James, *Loose Ends* (Dallas 1975)

Hillman, James, *Revisioning Psychology* (NY 1975)

Hochheimer, W., *The Psychotherapy of C.G. Jung* (1969)

Hodin, J.P., *Modern Art and the Modern Mind* (Cleveland 1972)

Hoeller, Stephan A., *Jung and the Lost Gospels* (Wheaton, Illinois, 1989)

Hoeller, Stephan, A., *The Gnostic Jung and the Seven Sermons to the Dead* (Illinois 1983)

Hogenson, George B., *Jung's Struggle with Freud* (Notre Dame, Ind. 1983)

Holl, Adolf, *Der Fisch am der Tiefe, oder die Freuden der Keuscheit* (Hamburg 1990)

Holland, Norman, *Psychoanalysis and Shakespeare* (NY 1966)

Homans, P., *Jung in Context* (1979)

Hostie, Raymond, *Religion and the Pscyhology of Jung* (1957)

Hughes, Stuart, *Consciousness and Society* (NY 1977)

Humbert, Eli, *C.G. Jung* (Wilmette, Illinois, 1988)

Hurswitz, Emanuel, *Otto Gross: Paradiessucher Zwischer Freud und Jung* (Frankfurt 1979)

Hutchins, Patricia, *James Joyce's World* (1957)

Hyslop, James, *Science and a Future Life* (1907)

Izod, John, *The Films of Nicholas Roeg: Myth and Mind* (1992)

Jacobi, Jolande, *Complex/Archetype/Symbol in the Psychology of C.G. Jung* (Princeton 1959)

Jacobi, Jolande, *The Way of Individuation* (1967)

Jacoby, Mario, *The Analytic Encounter: Transference and Human Relationship* (Toronto 1984)

Jacoby, Mario, *Individuation and Narcissism: the Psychology of the Self in Jung and Kohut* (1990)

Jacoby, Mario, *Longing for Paradise: Psychological Perspective on an Archetype* (Boston 1980)

Jaffé, Aniela, *C.G. Jung. Word and Image* (Princeton 1979)

Jaffé, Aniela, *The Myth of Meaning* (NY 1971)

Jaffé, Aniela, *Apparitions: an Archetypal Approach to Death, Dreams and Ghosts* (Dallas 1979)

Jaffé, Aniela, *Jung's Last Years and other Essays* (Dallas 1984)

Jaffé, Aniela, *From the Life and Work of C.G. Jung* (1972)

Jaffé, Aniela, *Was C.G. Jung a Mystic?* (1989)

James, Henry, ed., *The Letters of William James*, 2 vols (Boston 1920)

James, William, *The Principles of Psychology* (NY 1890)

James, William, *The Varieties of Religious Experience* (1935)

James, William, *Pragmatism* (1907)

James, William, *Memories and Studies* (1911)

James, William, *Essays on Radical Empiricism* (1912)

Jekels, L., *Selected Papers* (NY 1952)

Jensen, Ferne, ed., *C.G. Jung, Emma Jung and Toni Wolff: A Collection of Remembrances* (San Francisco 1982)

Johnson, Robert A., *He: Understanding Masculine Psychology* (NY 1986)

Johnson, Robert A., *We: Understanding the Psychology of Romantic Love* (1984)

Jones, Ernest, *The Life and Work of Sigmund Freud*, 3 vols (1957)

Jones, Ernest, *Free Associations* (1959)

Jung, Emma, *Animus and Anima* (NY 1957)

Kammerer, Paul, *Das Gesetz Der Serie* (Stuttgart 1919)

Kanai, Hayao, *The Japanese Psyche: The Major Motifs in the Fairy Tales of Japan* (Dallas 1988)

Kaufman, Louis, *Moe Berg. Athlete, Scholar, Spy* (1974)

Kaufmann, Walter, *Discovering the Mind* (1980)

Kerenyi, Karl, *Hermes, Guide of Souls* (Dallas 1986)

Kerenyi, Karl, *Zeus and Hera: The Archetypal Image of Father, Husband and Wife* (1975)

Kerenyi, Karl, *Dionysos: Archetypal Image of Indestructible Life* (1976)

Kerr, John, *A Most Dangerous Method. The Story of Jung, Freud and Sabina Spielrein* (1994)

Kesten, Hermann, ed., *The Thomas Mann Diaries, 1918–21, 1933–39* (NY 1982)

Keyserling, Hermann, *The Travel Diary of a Philosopher*, 2 vols (NY 1925)

Keyserling, Hermann, *The World in the Making* (NY 1927)

Keyserling, Hermann, *America Set Free* (NY 1929)

Kirsch, James, *The Reluctant Prophet* (LA 1973)

Kirsch, James, *Shakespeare's Royal Self* (1966)

Kline, Paul, *Fact and Fantasy in Freudian Theory* (1972)

Kluger, Rivkah Scharf, *Satan in the Old Testament*, (Evanston, Illinois, 1967)

Kluger, Rivkah Scharf, *Psyche and the Bible* (NY 1974)

Knapp, Bettina, *Dream and Image* (NY 1957)

Knapp, Bettina, *Theatre and Alchemy* (Detroit 1980)

Knapp, Bettina, *Archetype, Dance and the Writer* (NY 1983)

Knapp, Bettina, *Archetype, Architecture and the Writer* (Bloomington, Indiana, 1986)

Knapp, Bettina, *Word, Image, Psyche* (Alabama 1985)

Knapp, Bettina, *Music, Archetype and the Writer: A Jungian View* (1988)

Knipe, Rita, *The Water of Life: A Jungian Journey through Hawaiian Myth* (Honolulu 1989)

Koestler, Arthur, *The Lotus and the Robot* (1960)

Koestler, Arthur, *The Case of the Midwife Toad* (1971)

Koestler, Arthur, *The Roots of Coincidence* (1974)

Kretschmer, Ernst, *Körperbau und Charakter* (Berlin 1921)

Kretschmer, Ernst, *Gestalten und Bedanken* (Stuttgart 1963)

Kris, Ernst, *The Origins of Psychoanalysis* (1954)

Kugler, *The Alchemy of Discourse* (1982)

La Dage, Alta J., *Occult Psychology: A Comparison of Jungian Psychology and the Moden Qabalah* (St Paul, Minnesota, 1978)

Lauscher, Hermann, ed., *Gesammelte Werke* (Frankfurt 1970)

Lauter, Estella & Rapprecht, Carol, *Feminist Archetypal Theory: Interdisciplinary Revisions of Jungian Thought* (Knoxville 1985)

Le Rider, J., *Otto Gross: Révolution sur le Divan* (Paris 1988)

Leach, Maria & Fried Jeropme, eds., *Dictionary of Folklore, Mythology and Legend* (NY 1972)

Lee, M. Owen, *Death and Rebirth in Virgil's Arcadia* (NY 1989)

Lenormand, Henri René, *Théâtre Complet* (Paris 1930)

Leonard, Linda, *The Wounded Woman* (1982)

Leppmann, Wolfgang, *Rilke: A Life* (NY 1984)

Lieberman, *Act of Will. Otto Rank* (1985)

Livingstone, Angela, *Lou Andreas-Salomé* (1984)

Lockhart., R.A., *Words as Eggs* (Dallas 1983)

Lovell, Stanley, *Of Spies and Stratagems* (NY 1963)

Luke, Helen, M., *Old Age* (NY 1987)

Luke, Helen, M., *Dark Wood to White Rose: A Study of Meanings in Dante's Divine Comedy* (New Mexico 1975)

McDougall, William, *An Outline of Psychology* (1923)

McDougall, William, *Psychoanalysis and Social Psychology* (1936)

McCormick, Donald, *The Life of Ian Fleming* (1993)

McGann, Diarmid, *Journeying within Transcendence: A Jungian Perspective on the Gospel of John* (NY 1988)

McGann, Diarmid, *The Journeying Self: The Gospel of Mark through a Jungian Perspective* (NY 1985)

McGuire, William, *Bollingen: An Adventure in Collecting the Past* (1982)

McGuire, William, ed., *Analytical Psychology. Notes on a Seminar given in 1925 by C.G. Jung* (1990)

Maddox, Brenda, *A Married Man. A Life of D.H. Lawrence* (1994)

Maidenbaum, Ariel & Martin, Stephen, *Lingering Shadows: Jungians, Freudians and Antisemitism* (Boston 1991)

Maier, C.A., *Soul and Body: Essays on the Theories of C.G. Jung* (Santa Monica 1986)

Malcolm, Janet, *Psychoanalysis: The Impossible Profession* (1982)

Marti, Hans, *Urbild und Versfassung* (Berne 1958)

Martin, Luther M., & Goss, James, ed., *Essays on Jung and the Study of Religion* (NY 1985)

Masson, Jeffrey, *Against Therapy: Emotional Tyranny and the Myth of Psychological Healing* (NY 1989)

Mattoon, Mary Ann, *Understanding Dreams* (Dallas 1984)

Meier, C.A., *The Unconscious in its Empirical Manifestations* (Boston 1984)

Meier, C.A., *The Meaning and Significance of Dreams* (Boston 1987)

Mellon, Paul, *Reflections in a Silver Spoon* (1992)

Meyer, Adolf, *Collected Papers*, 2 vols (Baltimore 1950)

Micale, Mark, ed., *Beyond the Unconscious. Essays of Henri F. Ellenberger in the History of Psychiatry* (Princeton 1993)

Micale, Mark & Porter, Roy, *Discovering the History of Psychiatry* (1994)

Middelkoop, Pieter, *The Wise Old Man: Healing Through Inner Images* (Boston 1985)

Mileck, Joseph, *Herman Hesse, Life and Art* (1978)

Milford, Nancy, *Zelda. A Biography* (1970)

Miller, David, *Hells and Holy Ghosts* (Nashville, Tenn., 1989)

Miller, David, *Christs: Meditations on Archetypal Images in Christian Theology* (NY 1981)

Miller, Karl, *Doubles* (1985)

Mitchell, Juliet, *Psychoanalysis and Feminism* (1974)

Mitchell, Juliet & Rose, Jacqueline, eds., *Feminine Sexuality: Jacques Lacan and the Ecole Freudienne* (1982)

Mitzman, Arthur, *The Iron Cage: An Historical Interpretation of Max Weber* (NY 1970)

Moacanin, Radmila, *Jung's Psychology and Tibetan Buddhism* (1986)

Mommsen, Wolfgang & Osterhammel, ed., *Max Weber and his Contemporaries* (1987)

Moore, Robert L., ed., *Carl Jung and Christian Spirituality* (NY 1988)

Moreau, Christain, *Freud et L'Occultisme* (Toulouse 1976)

Moser, Fanny, *Spuk: Irrglaube oder Wahrglaube* (Zürich 1950)

Murr, Priscilla, *Shakespeare's Antony and Cleopatra* (NY 1988)

Nagy, Marilyn, *Philosophical Issues in the Psychology of C.G. Jung* (NY 1991)

Naifeh, Steven & Smith, Gregory White, *Jackson Pollock* (1990)

Neumann, Erich, *The Archetypal World of Henry Moore* (1959)

Neumann, Erich, *Creative Man* (Princeton 1979)

Neumann, Erich, *Amor and Psyche: The Psychic Development of the Feminine* (1956)

Neumann, Erich, *The Great Mother: An Analysis of the Archetype* (1955)

Neumann, Erich, *The Origins and History of Consciousness* (Princeton 1954)

Newman, Kenneth D., *The Tarot: A Myth of Male Initiation* (NY 1983)

Nichols, Sallie, *Jung and Tarot: An Archetypal Journey* (Maine 1980)

Noll, Richard, *The Jung Cult. Origins of a Charismatic Movement* (Princeton 1994)

Nunberg, Herman, *Memoirs* (1946)

Oberndor, C.P., *A History of Psychoanalysis in America* (1953)

O'Connor, Peter, *Understanding Jung* (1985)

Olney, James, *Metaphors of the Self* (1972)

Olney, James, *The Rhizome and the Flower* (1980)

O'Neill, Timothy R, *The Individuated Hobbit* (1980)

Ott, Hugo, *Heidegger* (1993)

Owen, A.R.G., *Can we Explain the Poltergeist?* (NY 1964)

Owens, Claire Myers, *Awakening to Good* (Boston 1958)

Pauson, Marian, *Jung the Philosopher* (1988)

Papadopoulos, Renos, ed., *Carl Gustav Jung: Critical Assessments*, 4 vols (1992)

Papadopoulos, R.K. & Saayman, G.S. eds., *Jung in Modern Perspective* (1985)

Peat, David, *Synchronicity: The Bridge Between Matter and Mind* (Toronto 1987)

Peierls, Rudolph, *Birds of Passage* (Princeton 1985)

Perera, Sylvia Brinto, *The Scapegoat Complex: Towards a Mythology of Shadow and Guilt* (Toronto 1986)

Perera, Sylvia Brinto, *Descent of the Goddess* (1981)

Perry, Ralph Barton, *The Thought and Character of William James* (1935)

Peters, H.F., *My Sister, My Spouse* (NY 1962)

Pfeiffer, Ernst, *Sigmund Freud and Lou Andreas-Salomé* (NY 1972)

Pfister, Oscar, trans. C.R. Payne, *The Psychoanalytic Method* (1917)

Pfister, Oscar, trans. C. R. Payne, *Psychoanalysis and Faith*

Philp, H.L., *Jung and the Problem of Evil* (1958)

Piaget, Jean, *Play, Dreams and Imitation in Childhood* (NY 1962)

Pocock, J.G.A., *The Machiavellian Moment* (1975)

Powers, Thomas, *Heisenberg's War* (1993)

Prince, Morton, *The Unconscious* (NY 1914)

Progoff, I., *Jung's Psychology and its Social Meaning* (1953)

Progoff, I., *Synchronicity and Human Destiny* (1972)

Quinn, Susan, *A Mind of Her Own* (1988)

Radolph, K., *Gnosis* (SF 1985)

Raine, Kathleen, *The Human Face of God: William Blake and The Book of Job* (1982)

Rank, Otto, *The Double* (Chapel Hill, NC, 1971)

Read, Herbert, ed. *A Search for Man's Soul. The Letters of Trigant Burrow* (1958)

Read, Herbert, *Icon and Idea* (1955)

Read, Herbert, *The Form of Things Unknown* (1960)

Rhine, J.B., *Extra-sensory Perception* (1940)

Rhine, J.B., *New Frontiers of the Mind* (1937)

Rhine, J.B., *The Reach of the Mind* (1948)

Richards, David, *The Hero's Quest for the Self: an Archetypal Approach to Hesse's Demian and Other Novels* (Lanham, Md, 1987)

Ricoeur, Paul, *Freud and Philosophy* (1970)

Rieff, Philip, *The Triumph of the Therapeutic: Uses of Faith after Freud* (NY 1966)

Rieff, Philip, *Freud: The Mind of the Moralist* (NY 1959)

Riese, Hertha, ed., *Historical Explorations in Medicine and Psychiatry* (NY 1978)

Rivière, Joan, *The Inner World. Collected Papers, 1920–1958* (1991)

Roazen, P., *Freud and his Followers* (1975)

Roazen, P., *Erik Erikson. The Power and Limits of a Vision* (1976)

Robertson. R., *C.G. Jung and the Archetypes of the Collective Unconscious* (NY 1987)

Robinson, Forrest G., *Love's Story Told: A Life of Henry A. Murray* (Harvard 1992)

Rolfe, Eugene, *Encounter with Jung* (Boston 1989)

Rosenberg, Samuel, *Why Freud Fainted* (NY 1978)

Rosenzweig, Saul, *Freud, Jung and Hall the King-Maker: The Expedition to America*, 1909 (Seattle 1992)

Ross, Dorothy G., *G. Stanley Hall: The Psychologist as Prophet* (1972)

Roustang, Francois, *Dire Mastery: Discipleship from Freud to Lacan* (Baltimore 1976)

Rubins, Jack L., *Karen Horney* (NY 1978)

Ruitenbeek, Hendrik M., *Heirs to Freud* (NY 1966)

Rush, Anne Kent, *Moon, Moon* (NY 1976)

Rycroft, Charles, *A Critical Dictionary of Psychoanalysis* (1972)

Saliba, David, *A Psychology of Fear: The Nightmare Formula of E.A. Poe* (Lanham, Md., 1980)

Samuels, Andrew, *A Critical Dictionary of Jungian Analysis* (1986)

Samuels, Andrew, *Jung and the Post-Jungians* (1985)

Samuels, Andrew, ed., *The Father: Contemporary Jungian Perspectives* (1985)

Sandner, Donald, *Navajo Symbols of Healing* (1979)

Sanford, John A., *The Strange Trial of Mr Hyde: A New Look at the Nature of Human Evil* (SF 1987)

Sanford, John A., *The Kingdom Within: A Study of the Inner Meaning of Jesus' Sayings* (NY 1970)

Sanford, John A., *King Saul, the Tragic Hero: A Study in Individuation* (NY 1985)

Sanford, John A., *Evil. The Shadow Side of Reality* (NY 1987)

Segaller, Stephen, *Yung: the Wisdom of the Dream* (1989)

Scholem. G., ed. *The Correspondence of Walter Benjamin and Gershom Scholem 1932–1940* (NY 1989)

Schultz, Duane, *Intimate Friends, Dangerous Rivals: The Turbulent Relationship between Freud and Jung* (LA 1990)

Schur, Max, *Freud: Living and Dying* (1972)

Schwarz, Urs, *The Eye of the Hurricane. Switzerland in World War Two* (Boulder, Colorado, 1980)

Schwartz-Salant, Nathan & Stein, Murray, *Transference and Counter-Transference* (Wilmette, Illinois, 1984)

Segen, Emilio, *From X-Rays to Quarks* (NY 1980)

Serrano, Miguel, *Jung and Hesse* (1966)

Sharp, B., *The Survival Papers: Anatomy of a Mid-Life Crisis* (Toronto 1988)

Shepherd, Michael, *Sherlock Holmes and the Case of Dr Freud* (1985)

Shorter, Bani, *An Image Darkly Forming* (1987)

Sinclair, Upton, *The Autobiography of Upton Sinclair* (1963)

Singer, June, *A Psychological Interpretation of William Blake* (NY 1970)

Singer, June, *Androgyny. The Opposites Within. Towards a New Theory of Sexuality* (1976)

Smart, Frances, *Neurosis and Crime* (1970)

Smelser, Neil & Erikson, Erik, eds, *Themes of Work and Love in Adulthood* (Harvard 1980)

Smith, R. Harris, *OSS, The Secret History of America's First Central Intelligence Agency* (1972)

Spiegelman, Marvin J., *The Knight* (Arizona 1982)

Spiegelman, Marvin & Vasavada, Arvind, *Hinduism and Jungian Psychology* (Phoenix, Az., 1987)

Spiegelman, Marvin & Miyuki, Mokusen, *Buddhism and Jungian Psychology* (Phoenix, Az., 1984)

Staude, John Raphael, *The Adult Development of C.G. Jung* (1981)

Steele, Robert, *Freud and Jung. Conflicts of Interpretation* (1982)

Stein, Murray, ed., *Jungian Analysis* (1984)

Stein, Murray, *In Midlife: A Jungian Analysis* (Dallas 1983)

Steiner, Gustav, *Erinnerungen an Carl Gustav Jung* (Basel 1965)

Stekel, Wilhelm, *The Autobiography of a Psychoanalyst* (1950)

Stepansky, Paul, *In Freud's Shadow: Adler in Context* (1983)

Stepansky, Paul, *Freud: Appraisals and Re-Appraisals* (New Jersey 1988)

Stern, Paul J., *C. G. Jung. The Haunted Prophet* (1976)

Stevens, Anthony, *Archetypes: A Natural History of the Self* (1982)

Stevens, Anthony, *On Jung* (1990)

Stevens, Anthony, *Jung* (1994)

Stevens, Anthony, *Private Myths. Dreams and Dreaming* (1995)

Stevens, Anthony, *The Roots of War* (1989)

Stineman, Esther L., *Mary Austin, Mary Austin: Song of a Maverick* (New Haven 1989)

Stolorow, Robert D., & Atwood, George E., *Faces in a Cloud: Subjectivity in Personality Theory* (NY 1979)

Storr, Anthony, *The Dynamics of Creation* (1972)

Storr, Anthony, *Jung* (1973)

Storr, Anthony, *The Art of Psychotherapy* (1979)

Storr, Anthony, *Solitude: A Return to the Self* (1988)

Storr, Anthony, *The School of Genius* (1988)

Sulloway, Frank J., *Freud, Biologist of the Mind* (NY 1979)

Tabori, Cornelius, *My Occult Diary* (1951)

Tedlock, E.W., Jr., *Frieda Lawrence: Memoirs and Correspondence* (1964)

Teichmann, Howard, *Smart Aleck* (1976)

Thipgen, Corbett H. & Cleckley, Harvey, *The Three Faces of Eve* (NY 1957)

Tillich, Paul, *Carl G. Jung 1875–1961. A Memorial Meeting* (NY 1967)

Trub, Hans, *Heilung Aus Der Begegnung Eine Auseinandersetzung Mit Der Psychologie C.G. Jungs* (Stuttgart 1962)

Turner, Dixie, *A Jungian Psychoanalytic Interpretation of William Faulkner's As I Lay Dying* (Washington 1981)

Ulanov, A.B., *Receiving Women: Studies in the Psychology and Theology of the Feminine* (Philadelphia 1981)

Uhsadel, Walter, *Evangelische Seezsorge* (Zürich 1966)

Van der Post, Laurens, *Jung and the Story of our Time* (1977)

NOTES

KEY TO ABBREVIATIONS USED IN NOTES

CGJS: *C.G. Jung Speaking*: *Interviews and Encounters*, ed. William McGuire & R.F.C. Hull (1977)

CW: *The Collected Works of C.G. Jung*, 21 vols (eds. Herbert Read, Michael Fordham, Gerhard Adler, 1953–83)

ETG: *Jung*, *Erinnerunnger, Traume*, *Gedanken* (Aniela Jaffé, ed., Zürich 1961)

F-Abraham: *A Psychoanalytic Dialogue*: *The Letters of Sigmund Freud and Karl Abraham 1907–1926* (eds. Hilde C. Abraham & Ernst L. Freud, 1965)

F-Ferenczi: *The Correspondence of Sigmund Freud and Sandor Ferenczi, Vol.1.1908–1914* (eds. Eva Brabant, Ernst Falzeder, Patrizia Giampieri-Deutsch, 1993)

F-Jones: *The Correspondence of Sigmund Freud and Ernest Jones* (ed. Andrew Paskauskas, 1993)

F-Jung: *The Freud-Jung Letters* (ed. William McGuire, trans. Ralph Manheim & R.F.C. Hull, 1974)

F-Pfister: *Psychoanalysis and Faith: The Letters of Sigmund Freud and Oscar Pfister*, ed. Ernst L. Freud & Heinrich Meng, (1963)

Letters: Gerhard Adler Ed., with Aniela Jaffé, *C. G. Jung* Letters, 2 vols (1975)

MDR: *C.G. Jung, Memories, Dreams, Reflections*, recorded and edited by Aniela Jaffe (1963)

SE: *The Standard Edition of the Complete Psychological Works of Sigmund Freud*, 24 vols (ed. James Strachey, 1953–74)

Seminars 1. *Dream Analysis. Notes of a Seminar Given in 1928–30 by C.G. Jung* (ed. William McGuire, 1984)

Seminars 2. *Nietzsche's Zarathustra. Notes of a Seminar given in 1934–1939 by C.G. Jung* (ed. James L. Jarott, 1989)

1: A SWISS CHILDHOOD

1. Hans Marti, *Urbild und Versfassung* (Bern 1958).
2. CW 10 p.540. *Seminars*, i. pp.20–21, 36.
3. CW 10 pp.485, 483.
4. CW 10 p.224; CW 10 p.485.
5. CW 10 p.482.
6. Maurice Duverger, *The Study of Politics* (1972) p.31.
7. CW 10 p.485.
8. CW 10 p.486.
9. J.K. Galbraith, *Economics, Peace and Laughter* (1971) p.329.
10. CW 10 pp.200, 228–29; CGJS p.153; CGSJ p.407.
11. CW 9 ii. pp.224–32.
12. Jung to Schmid, 25 February 1958, *Letters*, ii. pp.418–20.
13. SE 14 p.61.
14. MDR p.220.
15. Aniela Jaffé, 'Details about C.G.Jung's family,' *Spring* (1983) pp.35–43.
16. Jung to Ewald Jung, 30 December 1959, *Letters*, ii. pp.527–29.
17. For the Family Romance see SE 14 pp.236–41.
18. *Letters*, ii. pp.527–29; MDR pp.221–22; Jung to Henry Corbin, 4 May 1953, *Letters*, ii. pp.115–116; Gustav Steiner, *Erinnerungen an Carl Gustav Jung* (Basel 1965) pp.122–23.
19. ETG p.399.
20. *Letters*, ii. pp.115–116.
21. *Seminars*, i. p.518.
22. Henri Ellenberger, *The Discovery of the Unconscious* p.661.
23. SE 17 p.149.
24. Brian Feldman, 'Jung's Infancy and Childhood and its influence upon the development of Analytical Psychology', *Journal of Analytical Psychology* 37 (1992) pp.255–74.

25. MDR p.22.
26. MDR p.23; Jaffe, 'Details about C.G. Jung's family', loc. cit.
27. MDR p.23; Vincent Brome, *Jung* p.31.
28. D.W. Winnicott's review of MDR in *The Journal of Psychoanalysis* 45 (1964) pp.450–55; cf. also Winnicott, *Psychoanalytic Explorations* (Harvard 1989) pp.482–92.
29. J.Satinover, 'At the mercy of a mother: abandonment and restitution in psychosis and psychotic character', *Chiron. A Review of Jungian Analysis* (1985) pp.47–86.
30. MDR p.24; cf. also Guenter Loose, 'Jung's Childhood Prayer', *Spring* (1966) pp.76–80; Gordon A. Craig, *The Triumph of Liberalism* (N.Y.1988) pp.69–70; Karl Baedeker, *Switzerland and the Adjacent Portion of Italy, Savoy and Tyrol. Handbook for Travellers* (Leipzig 1899) p.4.
31. MDR pp.25–26.
32. Jacques Lacan, 'The Meaning of the Phallus', in Juliet Mitchell & Jacqueline Rose, eds., *Feminine Sexuality: Jacques Lacan and the Ecole Freudienne* (1982) pp.75–85.
33. Feldman, 'Jung's Infancy', loc. cit. p.266.
34. MDR pp.33–34.
35. Anthony Stevens, *On Jung* (1990) p.104; Stevens, op.cit. pp.98–102.
36. A. Tilander, 'Why did C.G. Jung write his autobiography?' *Journal of Analytical Psychology* 36 (1991) pp.111–24.
37. MDR p.30.
38. MDR p.29–32.
39. MDR pp.32–33.
40. *Seminars*, 2 i. p.197.
41. CGJS p.166; *Seminars*, i. p.210; CW 18 pp.171–72.
42. Albert Oeri, 'Some Youthful Memories of C.G. Jung', *Spring* (1970) pp.182–89.
43. MDR p.34.
44. ibid.
45. Stevens, op. cit.p.258.
46. Aniela Jaffé, 'The Creative Phases in Jung's Life', *Spring* (1972) pp.162–90.
47. Daniel Noel, 'Veiled Kabir: C.G. Jung's Phallic Self-Image', *Spring* (1974) pp.224–42.
48. Feldman, 'Jung's Infancy', loc. cit.p.269.
49. *Seminars*, 2 ii. p.1191; CW 10 p.371.
50. *Seminars*, i. p.71.
51. CW 9 i. p.269; CW 10 p.370.
52. *Seminars*, i. p.63.
53. Colin Wilson, *Jung, Lord of the Underworld* (1975) p.18.
54. MDR p.58; CGJS p.413; Stern, *Haunted Prophet*, op.cit. p.26.
55. MDR pp.60–61; *Seminars*, i. p.87.
56. Feldman, 'Jung's Infancy', loc.cit. p.272.

2: A TROUBLED ADOLESCENCE

1. Hannah p.60.
2. Albert Oeri, 'Ein Paar Jungenderinnerungen', in *Die Kulturelle Bedeutung der Komplexen Psychologie* (Berlin 1925) pp.524–26; cf also Oeri, 'Some Youthful Memories of C.G. Jung', *Spring* (1970) pp.182–89; CGJS pp.4–5, 81.
3. Paul Mellon, *Reflections in a Golden Spoon* (1992) pp.179–80.
4. Jean Delay, *La jeunesse d'André Gide* (Paris 1956), i. pp.193–99.
5. J. Coolidge, 'School Phobia' in *Basic Handbook of Child Psychiatry* (NY 1979).
6. MDR pp.45–46.
7. ibid. p.50.
8. ibid. p.64.
9. ibid p.52.
10. Jung to Walter Benet, 13 June 1955, *Letters*, ii. p.257.
11. MDR pp.53, 62, 96.
12. ibid. pp.64–65.
13. Van der Post p.86; Stevens, *On Jung* p.105.
14. Jung to Pastor L. Memper, 29 September 1953, *Letters*, ii pp.128–29.
15. MDR pp.83–84.
16. CGJS p.4; Oeri in *Spring* (1970) loc.cit.
17. CW 17 p.136.
18. James L. Jarrett, 'Schopenhauer and Jung', *Spring* (1981) pp.193–204.
19. MDR pp.74–77.
20. Jung to Aniela Jaffé, 22 December 1942, *Letters*, i. p.325–26.
21. MDR pp.85–86.
22. Jung to Freud, *F-Jung* p.95.
23. Aniela Jaffé p.19.
24. MDR pp.93–95.
25. CW 17 pp.137–43.
26. ibid. p.100.
27. ibid. p.221.
28. Marilyn Nagy, *Philosophical Issues in the Psychology of C.G. Jung* (NY 1991) p.12.
29. Jung to Rudolph Jung, 11 May 1956, *Letters*, ii. p.297; Russell Lockhart, 'Cancer in Myth and Dream', *Spring* (1977) pp.1–26; cf. C.B. & M.B. Bahnson, 'Cancer as an Alternative to Psychosis: A Theoretical Model of Somatic and Psychological Regression', in D.M. Histen & L.L. Leshan, eds, *Psychosomatic Aspects of Neoplastic Disease* (Philadelphia 1964) pp.184–202.
30. MDR p.101.

3: STUDENT DAYS

1. Stefanie Zumstein-Preiswerk, *C.G. Jung's Medium; Die Geschichte der Nelly Preiswerk* (Munich 1975) pp.53, 74.
2. Martin Ebon, 'Jung's First Medium', *Psyche* 7 (1976) pp.3–12; Henri F. Ellenberger, 'Jung's Medium', *Journal of the History of Behavioural Sciences* 12 (1976) pp.34–42.
3. CW i. pp.44–61.
4. William McGuire, ed. *Analytical Psychology. Notes of a seminar given in 1925 by C.G. Jung* (1990) pp.3–4.
5. CW i. p.17–43.
6. MDR pp.108–09.
7. Vincent Brome, *Jung. Man and*

Myth (1978) p.65.
8. Aldo Carotenuto, *A Secret Symmetry: Sabina Spielrein between Jung and Freud* (1984) p.105.
9. CW 7 p.123.
10. Carotenuto, *A Secret Symmetry* p.105.
11. Henri F. Ellenberger, 'The Story of Helene Preiswerk: A Critical Study with New Documents', *History of Psychiatry* 2 (1991) pp.41–52; cf. also Mark Micale ed., *Beyond the Unconscious: Essays of Henri F. Ellenberger on the History of Psychiatry* (Princeton 1993) pp.291–305.
12. Zumstein-Preiswerk, op.cit. p.67.
13. James Hillman, 'Some Early Background to Jung's Ideas', *Spring* (1976) pp.123–36.
14. Oeri in *Spring* (1970) loc.cit. pp.185–88; CGJS pp.7–9.
15. *Seminars*, 2 i. p.592.
16. Adolf Portmann, 'Jung's Biology Professor: Some Reflections', *Spring* (1976) pp.148–54.
17. *Seminars*, i. p.387.
18. MDR p.106.
19. Gustav Steiner, *Erinnerungen an Carl Gustav Jung*, op.cit. pp.146–50.
20. *Zofingia Lectures* (1983) pp.3–47.
21. ibid. p.54.
22. ibid. pp.59–111; cf. also Marilyn Nagy, 'Self and Freedom in Jung's lecture on Ritschl', *Journal of Analytical Psychology* 35 (1990) pp.443–457.
23. Steiner, *Erinnerungen*, op.cit. pp.151–63.
24. Jung to Joseph Rychlak, 27 April 1959, *Letters*, ii. pp.500–02; Jung to Friedrich Seifert, 31 July 1935, *Letters*, i. p.194.
25. Van der Post p.104.
26. MDR p.111.
27. *Seminars*, 2.i. pp.509–11.
28. MDR p.114.
29. Kerr, *Most Dangerous Method*, op.cit. p.53.
30. Ellenberger, *The Discovery of the Unconscious* (1970) pp.126–33.
31. William James, *The Principles of Psychology* (NY 1890) pp.201–209.
32. Theodore Flournoy, *From India to the Planet Mars* (NY 1900) p.119.
33. Morton Prince, *The Unconscious* (NY 1914) pp.147–310; cf. also T.W. Mitchell, 'The Division of the Self and Co-Consciousness', in *Problems of Personality. Studies Presented to Dr Morton Prince* (NY 1925) pp.191–203.
34. Corbett H. Thipgen & Harvey Cleckley, *The Three Faces of Eve* (NY 1957).
35. CW i. p.125.
36. Henri Ellenberger, 'Jung's Medium', *Journal of the History of Behavioural Sciences* 12 (1976) p.42; Kerr, *Most Dangerous Method*, op.cit. pp.54–55; M. Ebon, 'Jung's First Medium', *Psyche* 7 (1976) p.147; William B. Goodheart, 'C.G. Jung's First "Patient"', *Journal of Analytical Psychology* 29 (1984) pp.1–34 (at p.34).
37. For Flournoy see Edouard Claparède, 'Theodore Flournoy: his life and his works', *Archives de Psychologie* 18 (1923) pp.1–25; James S. Witzig, 'Theodore Flournoy', *Journal of Analytical Psychology* 27 (1982) pp.131–48. For Jung's admiration see Hannah op.cit. p.48.
38. MDR p.113.
39. ibid.
40. Jung to Karl Schmid, 25

February 1958, *Letters*, ii. pp.418–20; CGJS p.217; ibid. p.207; Philip Wolff-Windegg, 'C.G. Jung, Bachofen, Burkhardt and Basel', *Spring* (1976) pp.137–47.

4: BURGHÖLZLI APPRENTICESHIP

1. Manfred Bleuler, 'Eugen Bleuler', *Archives of Neurology and Psychiatry* 26 (1934) pp.610–28.
2. Manfred Bleuler, 'Eugen Bleuler's Conception of Schizophrenia – An Historical Sketch', *Bulletin of the Isaac Ray Medical Library* 1 (1953) pp.47–60.
3. Auguste Forel, *Out of My Life and Work* (1937).
4. CW 18 p.202.
5. Anne Marie Wetley, *Auguste Forel* (Salisbury 1953).
6. *Seminars*, 2 ii. p.1270.
7. Stern, *Haunted Prophet*, op.cit. p.76–77.
8. *Seminars*, i. p.660.
9. Ellenberger, *Discovery*. op.cit. p.667.
10. CW 1 p.71.
11. CW 18 p.201.
12. CW 1 pp.81–84, 102–05.
13. CW 1 pp.1–12.
14. CW 1 pp.109–31.
15. CW 1 pp.159–214.
16. CW 1 p.218.
17. CW 1 p.56, 69, 78, 92, 98, 99, 170, 185.
18. Manfred Bleuler, 'My Father's Conception of Schizophrenia', *Bulletin of the New York State Asylum* 7 (1931) pp.1–16. Cf. also Manfred Bleuler, *The Schizophrenic Disorders* (Yale 1978); C.A. Meier, *The Unconscious in its Empirical Manifestations* (Boston 1984) pp.124–25, 128–35.
19. CW 3 pp.75–95.
20. ibid.
21. MDR pp.126–27; CW 3 p.266.
22. MDR p.130; CW 3 pp.264–65.
23. CW 3 pp.234–37; cf. also R. Noll, 'Multiple Personality, Dissociation and C.G. Jung's Complex Theory', *Journal of Analytical Psychology* 34 (1989) pp.353–70.
24. CW 3 p.227.
25. CW 3 p.36, 69, 97.
26. Manfred Bleuler to Gerhard Adler, 27 April 1971, *Letters*, ii. p.356.
27. CW 3 p.67.
28. CW 3 p.73.
29. CW 3 p.172.
30. CW 3 pp.163–65.
31. CW 3 pp.219–25.
32. SE 7 p.178.
33. CW 2 pp.353–407.
34. CW 3 pp.18, 254.
35. MDR pp.118–20.
36. MDR p.120.
37. C.A. Meier, 'The Association Experiment as Developed by C.G. Jung', in Meier, *The Unconscious in its Empirical Manifestations* (Boston 1984) pp.65–149.
38. CW 2 pp.410–11.
39. CW 2 pp.554–80.
40. CW 3 p.39.
41. CW 3 pp.99–146.
42. MDR p.117–118.
43. SE 5 p.515.
44. CW 3 pp.25–34.
45. SE 7 pp.7–122.
46. CW 2 pp.288–317.

47. Anthony Storr, *Jung* (1973) p.30.
48. CW 3 p.95.
49. CW 7 p.144.
50. Oeri, 'Reminiscences', *Spring* (1970) p.188.
51. MDR p.140.
52. ibid pp.121–23.
53. Eugen Bleuler, *Dementia Praecox or the Group of Schizophrenias* (NY 1950) pp.1–2.

5: SEX AND MARRIAGE

1. Van der Post, *Jung and the Story of Our Time* (1977) p.112.
2. CW2 pp.584–85.
3. *Seminars*, i. p.97.
4. Aniela Jaffe, 'Details about Jung's Family', *Spring* (1983) pp.35–43.
5. Ferne Jensen, ed., *C.G. Jung, Emma Jung and Toni Wolff. A Collection of Remembrances* (SF 1982) p.34.
6. Stern, *Haunted Prophet* pp.70–71.
7. Carotenuto, *A Secret Symmetry* p.12.
8. CW 3 p.162; cf. also Olivier Flournoy, *Théodore et Léopold. De Théodore Flournoy à la psychanalyse. Suivi d'une correspondance entre Théodore Flournoy et Helène Smith* (Neuchâtel 1986).
9. Jung to J.B. Rhine, 27 November 1934, *Letters*, i. pp.180–81.
10. Zumstein-Preiswerk, *C.G. Jung's Medium*, op. cit. pp.100–104.
11. ibid. p.104.
12. Kerr, *Dangerous Method*, op. cit. p.56.
13. Brome, *Jung* p.83.
14. Gerhard Wehr, *Jung: A Biography* (Boston 1987); CW 2 p.174.
15. John C. Burnham & William McGuire, eds, *Jelliffe: American Psychologist and Physician. His Correspondence with Sigmund Freud and C.G. Jung* (1983); *Seminars*, i. p.xvi.
16. CW 8 p.366.
17. CGJS p.326; CW 18 pp.67–68; Jung to Carl Seelig, 25 February 1953, *Letters*, ii. p.109.
18. Gustav R. Heyer, 'C.G. Jung: Ein Lebensbild', in *Aus Meiner Werkstatt* (Munich 1966) p.167.
19. Wilson, *Lord of the Underworld* p.89.
20. CW 9 ii. p.11.
21. Stevens op. cit p.162.
22. CW 17 p.191. CW 7 p.198.
23. CW 10 p.132. Jung to Freud, 30 January 1910, *F-Jung* p.289.
24. MDR p.136.
25. CW 17 p.195.
26. ibid. pp.194–6.
27. Stern, *Haunted Prophet* pp.78–79.
28. Storr, *Jung* p.10.
29. Walter Kaufmann, *Discovering the Mind* (Vol.3. 1980) p.372.
30. Stern op.cit. p.72.
31. William McGuire, 'Jung's Complex Reactions (1907): Word Association Experiments Performed by Binswanger'. *Spring* (1984) pp.1–34.
32. Hannah, *Jung* p.74.
33. Sonu Shamdasani, 'A Woman Called Frank', *Spring* (1990) pp.26–56 (at p.54).
34. Jung to Freud, 18 May 1911, *F-Jung* pp.424–25.

35. CW 2 pp.235–46.
36. Emma Jung, *Animus and Anima* (NY 1957) p.40.
37. CW 3 pp.57–58.
38. ibid. pp.58–62.
39. Jung to Freud, 29 December 1906, *F-Jung* pp.14–15.
40. ibid p.15.
41. Freud to Jung, 1 January 1907, *F-Jung*. pp.17–18; Jung to Freud, 8 January 1907, ibid. p.20.
42. *New Yorker*, 23 May 1964.
43. Stern, *Haunted Prophet* p.139.
44. Maggy Anthony, *The Valkyries* (1990) p.31; Brome, *Jung* p.170.
45. Ellenberger, *Discovery* pp.78, 159.
46. CW 1 pp.186–87.
47. Sabina Spielrein, 'Beitrage zur kenntnis der kindlichen seele', *Zentralblatt für Psychanalyse und Psychotherapie* 3 (1912) pp.57–72.
48. Kerr, *Dangerous Method* p.34.
49. SE 3 pp.58–60.
50. Abraham to Freud, 15 January 1914, *F-Abraham* p.163.
51. Jung to Freud, 4 June 1909, *F-Jung* p.228.
52. CW 4 p.316.
53. Freud to Jung, 23 October 1906, *F-Jung* p.7.
54. CW 4 pp.20–21.
55. Bruno Bettelheim, introduction to Carotenuto, *A Secret Symmetry*, op.cit. p.xvii; Carotenuto, *A Secret Symmetry* pp.146–47; *New York Times Book Review*, 16 May 1982; Kerr, *Dangerous Method* pp.32–33, 68–69.
56. Adolf Holl, *Der Fisch am der Tiefe, oder Die Freuden der Keuschheit* (Hamburg 1990) pp.71–81.
57. Peter Swales, 'What Jung *Didn't* Say', *Harvest* 38 (1992) pp.30–37.
58. Bettelheim in Carotenuto, *A Secret Symmetry* p.xxviii.
59. Kerr op. cit. pp.223–27.
60. Bettelheim in Carotenuto op. cit. pp.xx-xxi, xxvii; Aldo Carotenuto, 'More about Sabina Spielrein', *Spring* (1985) p.129–36.
61. Freud to Jung, 9 March 1909, *F-Jung* p.210.
62. Paul Homans in *Journal of the History of Behavioural Sciences* 19 (July 1983) pp.240–44.
63. CW 3 p.46; CW 1 p.98.
64. Bettelheim in Carotenuto, op. cit. p.xxvi.
65. Jung to Freud, 4 June 1909, *F-Jung* pp.72–73.
66. CW 2 p.86.
67. Carotenuto, *A Secret Symmetry* pp.104, 106; Jung to Freud, 6 July 1907, *F-Jung* pp.72–73.
68. Sabina Spielrein, *Tagebuch einer heimlich Symmetrie. Sabine Spielrein zwischen Jung und Freud* (ed. Carotenuto, Freiburg 1986) p.189.
69. Spielrein to Freud, 11 June 1909, *A Secret Symmetry*, op. cit. p.93.
70. Carotenuto, *A Secret Symmetry* pp.101–02.

6: FIRST CONTACTS WITH FREUD

1. Freud to Jung, 11 April 1906, *F-Jung* p.3.
2. CW 4 pp.3–9.
3. Jones, *Freud*, op. cit, ii. p.124.
4. CW 3 pp.3–4; SE 7 p.261.
5. For Franz Riklin see *Spring*

(1970) pp.1–14; C.A. Meier, *The Unconscious in its Empirical Manifestations* (Boston 1984) pp.107–09.
6. Stern, *Haunted Prophet* p.144.
7. *New York Times Book Review*, 24 January 1988; Peter Gay, *Freud. A Life for Our Time* (1988) p.757–59.
8. Kerr, *Dangerous Method* pp.127–28.
9. Gay, *Freud*, op. cit. pp.179–80.
10. CW 2. p.406.
11. Freud to Jung, 6 December 1906, *F-Jung* pp.12–13.
12. SE 12 pp.159–71.
13. Lisa Appignanesi & John Forrester, *Freud's Women* (1992) pp.189, 204.
14. Carotenuto, *A Secret Symmetry* p.101.
15. Jung to Freud, 27 October 1906, *F-Jung* pp.8–9.
16. Kerr, op.cit. p.122.
17. Jung to Freud, 5, 23 October 1906, 4 December 1906, *F-Jung* pp.4–5, 6–7, 9–10, 10–11.
18. Freud to Jung, 7, 27 October, 6 December 1906, ibid. pp.5–6, 8–9, 11–13.
19. Freud to Jung, 30 December 1906, ibid pp.16–17.
20. Jung to Freud, 8 January 1907, ibid. pp.20–22.
21. Ernest Jones, *Free Associations* (1959) p.165.
22. Freud to Jung, 1 January 1907, *F-Jung* pp.17–19.
23. Gay, *Freud* p.200.
24. McGuire, 'Jung's Complex Reactions', *Spring* (1984) pp.1–34.
25. Martin Freud, *Glory Reflected* (1957) pp.108–09.
26. Jones, *Freud*, ii. p.32.
27. CW 16 p.72.
28. Vincent Brome, *Ernest Jones. Freud's Alter Ego* (1982) p.93.
29. MDR pp.146–47.
30. Ludwig Binswanger, *Sigmund Freud.Reminiscences of a Friendship* (NY 1957) pp.2–3.
31. Martin Freud op.cit. pp.108–09.
32. Max Graf, 'Reminiscences of Professor Sigmund Freud', *The Psychoanalytic Quarterly* 2 (1942) p.472.
33. Jones, *Free Associations*, op.cit p.167.
34. Jung to Freud, 31 March 1907, *F-Jung* pp.25–26.
35. Freud to Jung, 7 April 1907, ibid. pp.27–29.
36. John Billinsky, 'Jung and Freud', *Andover Newton Quarterly* 10 (1969) p.39–43.
37. Brome, *Jung* p.264.
38. Billinsky, loc. cit p.42.
39. Peter Swales, 'Freud, Minna Bernays and the Conquest of Rome', *New American Review* 1 (1982) pp.1–23.
40. Appignanesi & Forrester, *Freud's Women*, op.cit. p.50.
41. Jones, *Freud*, i. pp.139, 271, ii. pp.386–87; Ronald Clark, *Freud: The Man and the Cause* (1980) p.52; Gay, *Freud* pp.752–53.
42. Erika Freeman, *Insights: Conversation with Theodor Reik* (New Jersey 1971) p.116.
43. Carotenuto, *A Secret Symmetry* p.104.
44. Peter Gay, 'The Dog that did not Bark in the Night', in Gay, *Reading Freud: Explorations and Entertainments* (1990) p.164–79; cf. also Gay, 'Sigmund and Minna? The Biographer as Voyeur', in *New York Times Book Review*, 27 January 1989; Alan C. Elms, 'Freud and Minna', *Psychology Today* 16 (1982) p.40–46.

45. Kerr, *Dangerous Method* p.137.
46. Jung to Freud, 4 June 1909, *F-Jung* p.229.
47. Jung to Freud, 31 March 1907, ibid, pp.25–26. Jung to Freud, 11 April 1907, ibid. pp.30–32.
48. Freud to Jung, 14 April 1907; Jung to Freud, 17 April 1907, ibid. pp.32–37; Freud to Jung, 21 April 1907, ibid. pp.38–42; Jung to Freud, 13 May 1907; Freud to Jung, 23 May 1907, ibid. pp.43–48.
49. Jung to Freud, 4 June 1907; Freud to Jung, 6 June 1907, ibid. pp.56–60.
50. Jung to Freud, 12 June 1907; Freud to Jung, 14 June 1907, ibid. pp.62–65.
51. ibid.
52. Jung to Freud, 31 March 1907, ibid. pp.25–26.
53. Jung to Freud, 11 April 1907, ibid. pp.30–32; Freud to Jung, 24, 30 May 1907, ibid. p.49–51, 55–56.
54. SE 11 pp.214–15.
55. Jung to Freud, 28 June, 6 July 1907, *F-Jung* pp.65–68, 71–74.
56. CW 7 p.248.
57. Ellenberger, *Discovery*, op. cit pp.797–98.
58. Jones, *Freud*, ii. p.126.
59. John C. Burnham & William McGuire, *Jelliffe: American Psychoanalyst and Physician. His Correspondence with Sigmund Freud and C. G. Jung* (1983) pp.187–88.
60. Freud to Jung, 2 September 1907, *F-Jung* p.82; Jung to Freud, 28 October 1907, ibid. p.95; Jung to Freud, 31 March 1907; Freud to Jung, 7 April 1907, ibid. pp.25–26, 27–29; Freud to Jung, 19 September 1907; Jung to Freud, 25 September 1907, ibid. pp.87–90.
61. Karl Abraham, *Clinical Papers* (1953) p.37.
62. Jung to Freud, 19 August 1907, *F-Jung* pp.78–79.
63. Freud to Jung, 27 August 1907, ibid. pp.79–80.
64. *F-Abraham* pp.xv, 13.
65. A.A. Brill, *Lectures on Psychoanalytic Psychiatry* (NY 1946) pp.26–27.
66. A.A. Brill, *Freud's Contribution to Psychiatry* (NY 1944) pp.30, 42–43, 97–98.
67. Brome, *Jung* p.100.
68. Jung to Freud, 19 August 1907; Freud to Jung, 27 August 1907, *F-Jung* pp.79–80.
69. Paul E. Stepansky, 'The Empiricist as Rebel. Jung, Freud and the Burdens of Discipleship', *Journal of the History of the Behavioural Sciences* 12 (1976) p.216–39
70. Kerr, *Dangerous Method* p.154.

7: SABINA SPIELREIN

1. Jung to Freud, 10 October 1907, 15 February 1908, *F-Jung* pp.101, 117–118.
2. Carotenuto, *Secret Symmetry* pp.107–08; Carotenuto, *Tagebuch*, op.cit. pp.189–92.
3. Sabina Spielrein, 'Die Destruktion als Ürsache des Werdens'. *Jahrbuch für psychoanalystische und psychopathologische Forchungen* 4 (1912) pp.465–503.
4. Sabina Spielrein, 'Extraits inédits d'un journal', (trans. Jeanne

Moll) in *Le Bloc-Notes de la Psychoanalyse* 3 (1983) p.147–70 (at pp. 166–67).
5. Spielrein to Jung, 19, 26, 27 January 1908, *Secret Symmetry* pp. 80–82.
6. *Secret Symmetry* p.11; ibid. pp.8, 17.
7. Spielrein, 'Extraits inédits', loc. cit. p.156.
8. Carotenuto, *Tagebuch* pp.194–95.
9. Jung to Freud, 20 February 1908, *F-Jung* p.122.
10. CW 10 p.540; *Secret Symmetry* p.106.
11. Freud to Jung, 27 January, 25 February 1908, *F-Jung* pp.115–116, 125–26; Freud to Jung, 3 March 1908; Jung to Freud, 18 April 1908; Freud to Jung, 19 April 1908, ibid. p.128–29, 138–39, 140–41.
12. Jung to Freud, 22 January 1908; Freud to Jung, 25 January 1908, ibid. pp.111–113.
13. Jones, *Free Associations* p.165.
14. Freud to Jung, 25 January, 17 February, 18 February 1908, *F-Jung* pp.112–113, 119–22.
15. Jung to Freud, 20 February 1908, ibid. pp.122–24.
16. Jung to Freud, 25 September 1907, ibid. pp.89–90.
17. Jung to Freud, 11 April 1908, ibid. p.136.
18. SE 10 pp.153–318.
19. Jones, *Freud*, ii. pp.47–52.
20. Kerr, *Dangerous Method* p.80.
21. Jones, *Free Associations* p.166.
22. Jung to Freud, 30 April 1908; Freud to Jung, 3 May 1908, *F-Jung* pp.143–46.
23. Jones, *Freud* ii. pp.46, 138; Brome, *Ernest Jones* p.55.
24. Abraham to Freud, 4 April 1908, *F-Abraham* p.32.
25. SE 14 p.27.
26. Jones, *Freud*, ii. pp.47–52.
27. Freud to Jung, 3 May 1908; Jung to Freud, 7 May 1908; Freud to Jung, 10 May 1908, *F-Jung* pp.145, 149, 150.
28. Jung to Abraham, 3, 30 January 1908, *Letters* i. pp.4–7.
29. Abraham to Freud, 11 May 1908, *F-Abraham* pp.35–37.
30. Freud to Abraham, 3 May 1908, *F-Abraham* p.34.
31. Freud to Putnam, 8 July 1915 in Nathan Hale, *James Jackson Putnam* (1971) p.189.
32. SE 14 p.43.
33. Freud to Abraham, 23 July 1908, *F-Abraham* pp.46–47.
34. Abraham to Freud, 11 May 1908, *F-Abraham* p.36.
35. Abraham to Freud, 16, 31 July 1908, *F-Abraham* p.44–45, 48.
36. Freud to Abraham, 11, 20, 23 July, 29 September 1908, ibid.pp.43, 46, 47, 51–52.
37. Ellenberger, *Discovery* pp.799–800.
38. Abraham to Freud, 18 December 1908; Freud to Abraham, 26 December 1908, *F-Abraham* pp.61–62.
39. CW 3 pp.327–28.
40. Arthur Mitzman, 'Anarchism, Expressionism and Psychoanalysis', *New German Critique* 10 (1977) pp.77–104.
41. Emanuel Hurwitz, *Otto Gross – Paradiessucher zwischen Freud und Jung* (Frankfurt 1979).
42. E.W. Tedlock, Jr, *Frieda Lawrence*: *Memoirs and Correspondence* (1964) pp.94–102; cf. also Martin Green, *The Von Richtofen Sisters* (NY 1974) pp.32–47.
43. Arthur Mitzman, *The Iron Cage*: *An Historical Interpretation of*

Max Weber (NY 1970) pp.280–82.
44. Freud to Jung, 18 April 1908; Jung to Freud, 24 April 1908, *F-Jung* pp.141–42; *F-Jones* p.1; Freud to Jung, 3, 6 May 1908, *F-Jung* pp.146–47; Jung to Freud, 14, 25 May 1908, *F-Jung* pp.151, 153; Freud to Jung, 19, 29 May 1908, *F-Jung* pp.152, 154; A.K. Donahue & J. Hillman, eds., *Freud. The Cocaine Papers* (Vienna 1963).
45. Jones, *Free Associations* pp.172–73.
46. Carotenuto, *Secret Symmetry* p.107.
47. Jung to Freud, 19 June 1908, *F-Jung* pp.155–56; Jung to Freud, 26 June 1908, ibid. p.160.
48. Freud to Jung, 21, 30 June 1908, ibid. pp.157, 162.
49. Jung to Freud, 19 June 1908, ibid. pp.155–56.
50. Jung to Freud, 9 September 1908, 3 June 1909; Freud to Jung, 30 June 1909, ibid. pp.171, 227, 238.
51. CW 6 pp.273–88; CW 4 pp.304–21.
52. Freud to Jung, 7 April 1911; Jung to Freud, 19 April 1911, *F-Jung* pp.414, 416.
53. Jung to Freud, 21 August, 9 September 1908, *F-Jung* pp.169–71.
54. Brome, *Jung* p.107.
55. Freud to Abraham, 29 September 1908, *F-Abraham.* pp.51–52. Freud to Abraham, 11 October 1908, *F-Abraham* p.54; Freud to Jung, 15 October 1908, *F-Jung* pp.172–73.
56. Binswanger, *Freud*, op.cit. p.31.
57. Fritz Wittels, *Sigmund Freud* (1924) p.138.
58. Freud to Jung, 21 December 1908, 7 January 1909; Freud to Jung, 26 December 1908, *F-Jung* pp.18–89, 193–95, 190–91.
59. SE 10 pp.3–149.
60. Jung to Freud, 3 December 1908, *F-Jung* p.184.
61. CW 17 pp.10–34.
62. Brome, *Jung* p.298.
63. Freud to Jung, 8 November 1908, *F-Jung* p.175.
64. Jung to Freud, 27 November 1908, ibid. p.180.
65. Jung to Freud, 19 January 1909, ibid. p.198.
66. Jones, *Freud*, ii. p.50; Freud to Jung, 25 January 1909, *F-Jung* p.202; Jung to Speilrein, 4 December 1908, Carotenuto, *Tagebuch* pp.195–96; Carotenuto, *Secret Symmetry* pp.168–69; Kerr, *Dangerous Method* p.207.
67. Jung to Mrs Spielrein quoted in Spielrein to Freud, 11 June 1909, Carotenuto, *Secret Symmetry* p.94.
68. *Secret Symmetry* pp.96–97; cf. John Kerr, 'The Devils' Elixirs: Jung's "Theology" and the Dissolution of "Freud's Poisoning Complex,"' *Psychoanalytic Review* 75 (1988) pp.1–33.
69. Freud to Jung, 22 January 1909, *Jung* p.201.
70. Jung to Freud, 21 March 1909, *F-Jung* p.214.
71. Paul Häberlin, *Stutt einer Autobiographie* (Frauenfeld 1956); cf. also Häberlin, *Aus meinem Huttenbuch, Erlebuisse und bedanken eines bemsjagen* (Frauenfeld 1956).
72. Jung to Freud, 7 March 1909, *F-Jung* pp.207–08; Freud to Jung, 9 March 1909, ibid. p.211; Jung to Freud, 11 March 1909, ibid.

pp.212–13;. MDR p. 152; Jones, Freud, iii. pp.383–411.
73. Jung to Freud, 2 April 1909, *F-Jung* pp.215–16.
74. Freud to Jung, 16 April 1909, ibid. pp.218–19.
75. Jung to Freud, 12 May 1909, ibid. p.20.
76. MDR pp.147–48.
77. SE 15 p.59.
78. SE 18 pp.177–93, 197–200; SE 22 pp.31–56.
79. SE 22 pp.43, 47, 54.
80. Edoardo Weiss, *Sigmund Freud as a Consultant:Reflections of a Pioneer's Psychoanalysis* (NY 1970) p.71; Emilio Serradio, 'Freud's Occult Fascination', *Tomorrow* 6 (1958) pp.9–16; George Devereux ed., *Psychoanalysis and the Occult* (NY 1953); Henrik M. Ruitenbeek, *Heirs to Freud* (NY 1966).
81. Jones, *Freud*, ii. pp.13–14.
82. Jones, *Freud*, ii. p.138; Jones, *Free Associations* p.165.
83. Cornelius Tabori, *My Occult Diary* (1951) pp.213–19; Freud to Romain Rolland, 19 January 1930, in Ernest Freud, ed. *Letters* p.393; Jones, *Freud*, ii. p.392.
84. MDR pp.159–60; Robert Grinnell, 'Reflections on the Archetypes of Consciousness', *Spring* (1970) pp.15–39. William McGuire, ed., *Analytical Psychology* (1990) pp.38–39.
85. Kaufmann, *Discovering the Mind*, op. cit. p.358.
86. *Seminars*, i. pp.193–94.
87. Jung to Père Bruno de Jésus-Marie, 20 November 1956, *Letters*, ii. pp.336–38.
88. Jung to Freud, 2 April 1909, *F-Jung* p.216.
89. Freud to Jung, 3 June 1909, ibid. p.226.
90. Jung to Freud, 4 June 1909, ibid. pp.228–29.
91. Freud to Jung, 7 June 1909, ibid. p.231.
92. Jung to Freud, 12 June 1909, ibid. p.232.
93. Freud to Spielrein, 8 June 1909, *Secret Symmetry* p.114.
94. Spielrein to Freud, 10 June 1909, ibid. p.93.
95. Freud to Jung, 18 June 1909, *F-Jung* pp.234–35.
96. Jung to Freud, 21 June 1909, ibid. p.236.
97. Freud to Spielrein, 24 June 1909, *Secret Symmetry* p.115.
98. Freud to Jung, 30 June 1909, *F-Jung* p.238.
99. SE 12 p.170.
100. Kerr, *Dangerous Method* p.122.

8: VOYAGE TO AMERICA

1. A. Koelsch, 'Freud Discovers America', *Virginia Quarterly Review* 46 (1970) pp.115–32
2. Dorothy Ross, *Stanley Hall. The Psychologist as Prophet* (1972) passim, esp. pp.383–94.
3. SE 20 p.51.
4. Freud to Ferenczi, 10 January 1909, *F-Ferenczi* p.33.
5. Freud to Jung, 17 January 1909, *F-Jung* p.196.
6. Freud to Ferenczi, 17 January, 2, 28 February, 9 March 1909, *F-Ferenczi* pp.36, 41, 47–48, 49.
7. Freud to Jung, 18 June 1909, *F-Jung* pp.234–35.
8. Jung to Freud, 12 June 1909, *F-Jung* pp.232–33.

9. MDR p.153; Jung to Jones, 19 December 1953, *Letters*, ii. p.144.
10. Clark, *Freud* p.265.
11. Max Schur, *Freud, Living and Dying* (1972) pp.80–82; Jones, *Freud*, i.p.317; Jones, *Free Associations* p.222.
12. SE 21 pp.182–83.
13. Bettelheim, introduction to Carotenuto, *Secret Symmetry* p.xxxii.
14. Paul Roazen, *Freud and his Followers* (1975) p.258; Binswanger, *Sigmund Freud. Reminiscences of a Friendship* (1957) p.49.
15. Jones, *Freud*, ii p.90.
16. MDR p.154.
17. Billinsky, 'Jung and Freud', loc.cit.p.42.
18. CW 18 p.452.
19. MDR pp.155–56.
20. Winnicott loc.cit.p.452.
21. Bennet, *Jung*, op.cit.p.41.
22. *New York Times*, 30 August 1909.
23. Hale, *Freud and the Americans*, op.cit.pp.390–91; Jones, *Free Associations* pp.230–31.
24. Jung to Emma Jung, 31 August 1909, in Aniela Jaffé, *C.G. Jung. Word and Image* (Princeton 1979) p.47.
25. Freud to Jones, 26 February 1911, *F-Jones* p.92.
26. Jung to Emma Jung, 6 September 1909, MDR pp.336–37.
27. *Lectures and Addresses Delivered before the Departments of Psychology and Pedagogy in Celebration of the Twentieth Anniversary of the Opening of Clark University, September 1909*, 2 vols (Worcester, Mass, 1910).
28. *Boston Evening Transcript*, 8 September 1909; *Worcester Telegram*, 8 September 1909.
29. SE 11 pp.20–52.
30. *Boston Evening Transcript*, 11 September 1909.
31. CW 17 pp.129–41.
32. Jones, *Freud*, ii. p.53–59.
33. Jung to Emma Jung, 8 September 1909, MDR p.337.
34. William Koelsch, *Incredible Day Dreams. Freud and Jung at Clark* (1984) unpaged.
35. SE 14 pp.30–31, SE 20 p.52
36. Jung to Emma Jung, 14 September 1909, MDR p.338.
37. SE 20 p.252.
38. Jung to Virginia Payne, 22 July 1949, *Letters*, i. pp.530–32.
39. Jones, *Freud*, ii p.59.
40. James to Calkins in Ralph Barton Perry, *The Thought and Character of William James; As revealed in unpublished correspondence and notes, together with his published writings*, 2 vols (Boston 1935), ii. p.123; James to Flournoy, 28 September 1909 in Henry James, ed., *The Letters of William James*, 2 vols (Boston 1920), ii. p.327–28.
41. George E. Gifford, 'Freud and the Porcupine', *Harvard Alumni Medical Bulletin* 46 (1972).
42. Jung to Emma Jung in Jaffe, *Jung. Word and Image*, op. cit. pp.49–51.
43. MDR p.338.
44. CW 17 p.135.
45. Jung to Emma Jung, 22 September 1909, MDR p.339; Jung to Emma Jung, 25 September 1909, MDR pp.339–40.
46. Jung to Freud, 1, 14 October 1909, *F-Jung* pp.247–50; Freud

to Jung, 27 April 1911, ibid. p.419.
47. CW 8 p.125.
48. Homans, *Jung in Context*, op. cit. p.148.
49. Koelsch, 'Freud Discovers America', loc. cit. p.126.
50. Erik Erikson, *Identity, Youth and Crisis* (NY 1964) p.20.
51. 'Does Consciousness Exist?' in William James, *Essays in Radical Empiricism* (1912) p.33; James, *The Varieties of Religious Experience* (1935); James, *Pragmatism* (1907) p.133.
52. Jones to Freud, 5 December 1912, *F-Jones* p.180.
53. Eugene Taylor, 'William James and C.G. Jung', *Spring* (1980) pp.157–68 (at pp.164–65).
54. James, *Memories and Studies* (1911) pp.209–26.
55 CW 18 pp.25–26.
56. James, *Pragmatism* p.12.
57. CW 6 p.353.
58. See e.g. CW 7 pp.32, 199; CW 9. i. p.264; 9 ii. p.179; CW 10 pp.90, 162, 164, 168, 170, 171; CW 13 p.50; CW 15 pp.34, 46, 48; CW 16 pp.46, 173; CW 18 pp.192, 479.
59. Théodore Flournoy, *The Philosophy of William James* (1911).
60. James Hyslop, *Science and A Future Life* (1906) pp.113 ff.
61. CW 13 p.41; Jung to Kunkel, 10 July 1946, *Letters*, i. p.430.
62. *Seminars*, i. p.644; CGJS pp.332, 536; CW 18 pp.194, 682.
63. James, *Varieties of Religious Experience* p.199.
64. *Seminars*, i. p.645.

9: STORMCLOUDS GATHER

1. Kerr, *Dangerous Method* p.269.
2. Jung to Freud, 22 November 1909, *F-Jung* p.268.
3. SE 10 passim, esp. 190–207.
4. Jung to Freud, 14 October, 8 November 1909, *F-Jung* pp.251–52, 258.
5. Jung to Freud, 8 November 1909; Freud to Jung, 11 November 1909, *F-Jung* pp.257, 260.
6. Jung to Freud, 2 December 1909; Freud to Jung, 19 December 1909, ibid., pp.270, 277; Jung to Freud, 25 December 1909, ibid. p.279.
7. Jung to Freud, 30 January 1910, ibid. p.289.
8. Jung to Freud, 11 February 1910, ibid. pp.293–94.
9. Jung to Freud, 20 February 1910, ibid. pp.297–98.
10. Jung to Freud, 20 February, 2 March 1910, ibid. pp.296–98.
11. Freud to Jung, 6 March 1910, ibid. p.300.
12. Freud to Ferenczi, 3 March 1910, *F-Ferenczi* p.147.
13. Emma Jung to Freud, 8 March 1910; Jung to Freud, 9 March 1910, *F-Jung* pp.301–02.
14. Willi Hoffer, obituary of Pfister in *International Journal of Psychoanalysis* 39 (1958) p.616; Peter Gay, *A Godless Jew: Freud, Atheism and the Making of Psychoanalysis* (1987) p.74. Freud to Pfister, 17 March 1910, *F-Pfister* p.35.
15. Jones, *Free Associations* p.215.
16. SE 11 pp.139–52.
17. Sandor Ferenczi, *Final*

Contributions to the Problems and Methods of Psychoanalysis (NY 1980) pp.300–305.
18. Fritz Wittels, *Sigmund Freud. His Personality. His Teaching and His School* (1924) pp.139–40.
19. Emil A. Gutreil, ed., *The Autobiography of Wilhelm Stekel: the Life Story of a Pioneer Psychoanalyst* (NY 1950) p.128.
20. Jones, *Freud*, ii. pp.70–77.
21. Clark, *Freud* p.298.
22. Ferenczi to Freud, 5 April 1910, *F-Ferenczi* p.158; Freud to Ferenczi, 5 April 1910, ibid. p.158.
23. Jung to X, 9 April 1959, *Letters*, i. p.19.
24. Edoaurd Claparède, ed., *VIeme Congrès International de Psychologie 1909. Rapport et Comptes Rendus* (Geneva 1910).
25. Jung to Freud, 30 April 1910, *F-Jung* p.307.
26. Jung to Freud, 17 April 1910; Freud to Jung, 2 May 1910; Jung to Freud, 5 May 1910, ibid. pp.307, 314, 316.
27. Jung to Freud, 2 June 1910, ibid. p.325; Freud to Abraham, 5 June, 3 July 1910, *F-Abraham* pp.89–91.
28. Freud to Ferenczi, 5 June 1910; Ferenczi to Freud, 12 June 1910, *F-Ferenczi* pp.177,182.
29. Jones to Freud, 30 March 1910; Freud to Jones, 22 May 1910, *F-Jones* pp.49,59.
30. Freud to Pfister, 2 May 1910, *F-Pfister* p.37.
31. Freud to Jung, 19 June 1910, *F-Jung* p.330.
32. Jung to Freud, 6 August 1910; Freud to Jung, 10 August 1910, *F-Jung* pp.341,345–46.
33. Jung to Freud, 29 October 1910, 13 November 1910, 29 November 1910, *F-Jung* pp.364,371,374–75.
34. Freud to Jung, 23 October 1910, ibid. pp.360–61.
35. SE 20 p.51.
36. Bleuler to Freud, 19 October 1910 in Franz Alexander and Sheldon Selesnik, 'Freud-Bleuler Correspondence', *Archives of General Psychology* 12 (1965) pp.1–9 (at p.5).
37. P. Cornillier, *La survivance de l'âme et son évolution après la mort. Comptes-rendus d'Expériences* (Paris 1920); H.R. Lenormand, *'L'Amour Magicien,' in Théâtre Complet* (Paris 1930), vi. pp.1–113.
38. CW 5 pp.447–462.
39. Freud to Jung, undated; Jung to Freud, 26 June 1910, *F-Jung* pp.332–338.
40. Homans, *Jung in Context* pp.37,49,50,56.
41. Binswanger, *Freud*, op.cit.p.26.
42. Jung to Freud, 10 August 1910, *F-Jung* pp.345–46.
43. Freud to Ferenczi, 14 August 1910, *F-Ferenczi* p.202.
44. Binswanger, op.cit.p.26.
45. *Collected Papers of Adolf Meyer* (Baltimore 1950),i.pp.223ff.
46. Hans Walser, 'An Early Psychoanalytical Tragedy.J.J. Honegger and the Beginnings of Training Analysis', *Spring* (1974) pp.243–55.
47. Freud to Pfister, 12 July 1909, *F-Pfister* p.26.
48. Francois Roustang, *Dire Mastery: Discipleship from Freud to Lacan* (Baltimore 1976) pp.87–88.
49. Jung to Freud, 15 November, 25 December 1909, 30 January

1910; Freud to Jung, 2 January, 2 February 1910, *F-Jung* pp.262,279,289,282,291.
50. Jung to Freud, 6 April 1910; Freud to Jung, 12 April 1910, ibid.pp.304–06.
51. Walser, loc.cit.p.253.
52. Jung to Freud, 24 May 1910, *F-Jung* pp.319–20.
53. Jung to Freud, 2,17 June 1910; Freud to Jung, 9,19 June 1910, ibid. pp.325–330.
54. Jung to Freud, 7 November 1910, ibid.pp.369–70.
55. Jung to Freud, 31 March 1911, *F-Jung* p.412.
56. Jung to Freud, 19 April 1911, ibid.p.413; Freud to Jung, 2 April 1911, ibid.p.413.
57. Jung to Freud, 12 June 1911; Freud to Jung, 15 June 1911, ibid. pp.427, 430.
58. Aldo Carotenuto, 'Lettera a Honegger', *Rivista di Psicologia Analitica* 8 (1977) pp.33–38.
59. Herman Nunberg, *Memoirs* (NY 1969) p.116.
60. Walser, loc. cit. p.251.
61. SE 11 pp.221–227.
62. Jung to Freud, 8 September 1910; Freud to Jung, 24 September 1910, *F-Jung* pp.351–54; Sonu Shamdasani, 'A Woman Called Frank', *Spring* (1990) pp.26–56 (at p.54).
63. Carotenuto, *Secret Symmetry* p.35.
64. Jung to Freud, 24 July, 6 August 1910, *F-Jung* pp.341–42.
65. Freud to Abraham, 30 August 1910, *F-Abraham* op.cit.
66. *Secret Symmetry* pp.4, 6.
67. Kerr, *Dangerous Method* p.297.
68. *Secret Symmetry*, p.14.
69. ibid. pp.14–15.
70. ibid. pp.18–20.
71. Freud to Jung, 29 September 1910, *F-Jung* pp.355–56.
72. *Secret Symmetry*, ibid.
73. SE 4 pp.194–96.
74. Gay, *Freud* p.132.
75. Jung to Freud, 11 August 1910, *F-Jung* p.346.
76. MDR pp.268–69.
77. Freud to Jung, undated, June 1910, *F-Jung* p.334.
78. MDR pp.284–85.
79. *Secret Symmetry* p.30.
80. MDR pp.138–40; *Secret Symmetry* pp.33–34.
81. ibid. p.38.
82. Freud to Ferenczi, 23 December 1912, *F-Ferenczi* p.446.
83. Stevens, *On Jung* p.160.
84. Van der Post pp.174–75; Maggy Anthony, *The Valkyries* p.27.
85. Jung to Freud, 13, 23 December 1910, *F-Jung* pp.378–79, 383; Bleuler to Freud, 13 October 1910 in Franz Alexander & Selesnik, 'Freud-Bleuler Correspondence', *Archives of General Psychology* 12 (1965) p.3.
86. Freud to Binswanger, 1 January 1911 in Binswanger, op.cit. p.28; Jones, *Freud*, ii. p.140.
87. Freud to Jung, 3 December 1910, *F-Jung* p.376.
88. Freud to Jung, 17 February 1911, ibid. p.393.
89. Freud to Ferenczi, 29 December 1910, *F-Ferenczi* p.246.

10: THE RIFT DEEPENS

1. Jones, *Free Associations* pp.219–20; Freud to Ferenczi, 10 April 1911, 17 October 1992, *F-Ferenczi* pp.268, 411.
2. Freud to Jung, 25 November 1910; Jung to Freud, 29 November 1910, *F-Jung* pp.372–75.
3. Freud to Jung, 3, 22 December 1910, ibid. pp.376–77, 382; Jung to Freud, 18 January 1911; Freud to Jung, 22 January 1 March 1911, ibid. pp.384–87, 398–400.
4. Jung to Freud, 18, 31 January, 28 February 1911; Freud to Jung, 17 February 1911, ibid. pp.384–85, 389, 396–98, 394; Jung to Freud, 7 March 1911, ibid. p.402.
5. Eugen Bleuler, *Dementia Praecox or the Group of Schizophrenias* (1911).
6. CW 3 p.197–202.
7. SE 14 p.36.
8. CW 5 pp.xi, 33, 455.
9. CW 5 pp.171–206, 447–50, 455–57.
10. CW 5 pp.180–81.
11. CW 5 pp.154–55; CW 5 pp.128–37.
12. CW 3 p.190.
13. CW 5 pp.419–20.
14. CW 5 pp.141, 256.
15. CW 5 p.258.
16. CW 5 pp.100–101, 157–58; Cf. CW 8 p.150.
17. Jones to Freud, 26 November 1911, *Freud-Jones* p.120.
18. Homans, *Jung in Context* p.66.
19. Kerr, *Dangerous Method* p.329.
20. CW 5 pp.259, 378.
21. CW 15 p.139; cf. CW 5 pp.210, 212, 316, 350, 358, 381.
22. William McGuire ed. *Analytical Psychology*, op.cit. p.27.
23. CW 5 pp.31–32.
24. Joseph Wheelwright in *Psychological Perspectives* 2 (1975) pp.171–76.
25. William McGuire, letter in *Journal of Analytical Psychology* 21 (1976) pp.94–95.
26. Jung to Freud, 11 May 1911, *F-Jung* p.421; SE 12 pp.225–26; Jung to Freud, 8 May, 12 June 1911; Freud to Jung, 15 June 1911, *F-Jung* pp.421–29.
27. Jung to Freud, 12 June 1911, *F-Jung* pp.426–27.
28. Jung to Freud, 8 May 1911, ibid. p.421.
29. Freud to Ferenczi, 11 May 1911, *F-Ferenczi* p.274.
30. Ferenczi to Freud, 13, 27 May 1911; Freud to Ferenczi, 14, 21, 28 May, ibid. pp.277–86.
31. Freud to Jung, 15 June 1911, *F-Jung* p.428.
32. Freud to Jung, 13 July 1911; Jung to Freud, 11, 19 July 1911; ibid. pp.432–35.
33. Freud to Jung, 21 July 1911; Jung to Freud, 26 July 1911, ibid. pp.436–37; Jung to Freud, 8 March 1911, ibid. p.401.
34. Jung to Freud, 29 August 1911, *F-Jung* pp.438–39.
35. Jones, *Freud*, ii. pp.89–102.
36. Hale, *Putnam* op.cit. pp.39–40.
37. SE 13 pp.1–162.
38. SE 14 p.45; Jones, *Freud*, ii. pp.85–86.
39. SE 12 p.81.
40. Brome, *Jung* p.134.
41. Freud to Ferenczi, 5 October 1911; Ferenczi to Freud, 18 October 1911; *F-Ferenczi* pp.302–04.
42. Roazen, *Freud and his Followers*, op. cit. p.176.

43. Wittels, *Freud* pp.150–51; Max Graf, 'Reminiscences of Professor Sigmund Freud', *Psychoanalytic Quarterly* 11 (1942) pp.471–73.
44. Carotenuto, *Secret Symmetry* p.48.
45. Carotenuto, *Tagebuch* pp.199–200.
46. Kerr, *Dangerous Method* p.333.
47. Jung to Spielrein, 21/22 September 1911, Carotenuto, *Tagebuch* p.202.
48. Freud to Jung, 12 October 1911, *F-Jung* p.447; Jung to Freud, 4, 6, 30 October 1911, ibid. pp.444–46, 452.
49. Freud to Jung, 13 October 1911, ibid. pp.448–49.
50. Jung to Freud, 17 October 1911; Freud to Jung, 20 October 1911, ibid. pp.450–51.
51. Freud to Jung, 2 November 1911, ibid. pp.453–54.
52. Freud to Abraham, 29 October 1911, *F-Abraham* p.108.
53. L. Donn, *Jung and Freud. Years of Friendship. Years of Loss* (NY 1983) pp.137–38.
54. Ferenczi to Freud, 19 October 1911; Freud to Ferenczi, 19, 21 October 1911, *F-Ferenczi* pp.304–07.
55. Ferenczi to Freud, 23 October 1911, ibid. p.307.
56. Emma Jung to Freud, 30 October 1911, *F-Jung* pp.452–53.
57. Emma Jung to Freud, 6 November 1911, ibid. p.455–57.
58. Emma Jung to Freud, 14 November 1911, ibid. pp.462–63.
59. Emma Jung to Freud, 24 November 1911, ibid. p.467.
60. Stern, *Haunted Prophet* pp.137–39.
61. Carotenuto, *Tagebuch* pp.202–04, Jung to Freud, 12 November 1911, *F-Jung* pp.458–59; Kerr, *Dangerous Method* pp.367–72.
62. Jung to Freud, 17 October 1911, *F-Jung* p.450.
63. Stern, *Haunted Prophet* p.106.
64. Jung to Freud, 14 November 1911, *F-Jung* pp.460–61.
65. Alexander & Selesnik, eds., 'Freud-Bleuler Correspondence', *Archives of General Psychiatry* 12 (1965) p.5.
66. Jung to Freud, 24 November 1911, *F-Jung* pp.466–67.
67. Freud to Jung, 30 November 1911, ibid. pp.468–69.
68. Jung to Freud, 11 December 1911, ibid. pp.470–71.
69. Freud to Jung, 17 December 1911, ibid, p.473.
70. Kerr, *Dangerous Method* p.381.
71. Spielrein to Jung, 15 December 1917, 16 January 1918, *Secret Symmetry* pp.60, 71.
72. *Secret Symmetry* pp.xxxiv–xxxv.
73. ibid. p.41; *Tagebuch* p.206.
74. Kerr, *Dangerous Method* p.379.
75. CW 5 p.531.
76. SE 12 pp.14–78.
77. Jung to Freud, 14 November, 11 December 1911, *F-Jung* pp.461, 471.
78. Phyllis Grosskurth, *The Secret Ring: Freud's Inner Circle and the Politics of Psychoanalysis* (1991) pp.43–44.
79. Freud to Jung, 31 December 1911, *F-Jung* pp.475–76.
80. Jung to Freud, 2, 9 January 1912; Freud to Jung, 10 January 1912; ibid. p.476–79.
81. SE 12 p.342–44.
82. Ellenberger, *Discovery* p.816.

11: THE KREUZLINGEN GESTURE

1. Jung to Freud, 9 January 1912, *F-Jung* pp.478–79; Freud to Jung, 10 January 1912, ibid. p.479.
2. *Neue Zürcher Zeitung*, 2, 3, 10, 13 January 1912.
3. *Neue Zürcher Zeitung*, 10 January 1912.
4. *Neue Zürcher Zeitung*, 15, 17 January 1912.
5. *Neue Zürcher Zeitung*, 27, 28, 31 January, 1 February 1912.
6. SE 12 p.99.
7. SE 12 p.111.
8. Freud to Jung, 18 February 1912, *F-Jung* pp.484–85.
9. Jung to Freud, 25 February 1912, ibid. pp.487–88.
10. Freud to Jung, 29 February 1912, ibid. pp.488–89.
11. Jung to Freud, 3 March 1912, ibid. pp.490–91.
12. Freud to Jung, 5 March 1912; Jung to Freud, 10 March 1912, ibid. pp.492–94.
13. Carotenuto, *Secret Symmetry* p.42.
14. Carotenuto, *Tagebuch* p.208; Diary entry, 22 February 1912 in *Secret Symmetry* p.43.
15. Jung to Spielrein, 18, 25 March 1912, *Tagebuch* pp.206–08.
16. Jung to Freud, 22 March 1912; Freud to Jung, 24 March 1912, *F-Jung* pp.496–97.
17. CW 18 p.761.
18. MDR p.286.
19. *Seminars*, 2 ii. p.948.
20. Jung to Freud, 27 April, 8 May 1912; Freud to Jung, 14 May 1912, *F-Jung* pp.502–04.
21. Jung to Freud, 8 May 1912, ibid. p.503.
22. Stern, *Haunted Prophet* pp.107–08.
23. Binswanger, *Freud* pp.37–40.
24. Jones, *Freud*, ii. pp.94–102, 143–62; Schur, *Freud. Living and Dying*, op. cit. pp.260–64.
25. Gay, *Freud* p.229.
26. Kerr, *Dangerous Method* pp.409–10.
27. Freud to Ferenczi, 26 November 1912, *F-Ferenczi* p.434.
28. Clark, *Freud* p.319.
29. Jung to Freud, 8 June 1912, *F-Jung* p.509.
30. Freud to Abraham, 3 June 1912, *F-Abraham* op. cit.
31. Jung to Freud, 18 July 1912, ibid. p.511.
32. Freud to Spielrein, 14 June 1912, *Secret Symmetry* p.116.
33. *F-Pfister* pp.56–57.
34. Grosskurth, *The Secret Ring* op.cit. Freud to Ferenczi, 28 July 1912, *F-Ferenczi* pp.398–99.
35. Ferenczi to Freud, 8 August 1912, ibid. p.401.
36. Freud to Putnam, 20 August 1912, Hale, *Putnam* op.cit. p.146.
37. Abraham to Freud, 9 August 1912; Freud to Abraham, 11 August 1912, *F-Abraham* pp.121 -22; Freud to Jones, 22 July, 1 August 1912; Jones to Freud, 18 September, 30 October 1912, *F-Jones* pp.143,147,160–61,165.
38. Freud to Jones, 22 September 1912, ibid.pp.162–63.
39. *Seminars*, i. p.vii.
40. Kirstie Miller, 'The Letters of C.G. Jung and Medill and Ruth McCormick', *Spring* (1990) pp.1–25.
41. 'Glimpses of a Freudian Odyssey', *Psychoanalytic Quarterly* 2 (1933) pp.318–29.
42. Jung to Jelliffe, 13 May 1912 in John C.Burnham & William

McGuire, *Jelliffe. American Psychoanalyst and Physician. His Correspondence with Sigmund Freud and C.G. Jung* (1983) p.190.
43. *Seminars*, i. p.213.
44. Jung to Burrow, 26 December 1912, *Letters*, i. p.24.
45. *New York Times*, 29 September 1912.
46. *Jung and the Wisdom of the Dream*, op.cit.
47. Laurie Lathrop, 'What Happened at St Elizabeth's?' *Spring* (1984) pp.45–50.
48. CW 18 p.552.
49. *Seminars* i. p.59.
50. CW 18 pp.38–391CW 7 p.201; CW 5 p.125.
51. CW 4 pp.118–22.
52. CW 4 p.123.
53. ibid. pp.164–65.
54. ibid. pp.106–07.
55. ibid. p.134.
56. ibid. p.166.
57. ibid. p.178.
58. ibid. p.182.
59. ibid. p.251.
60. ibid. pp.152–53.
61. Clark, *Freud* p.322.
62. CW 4 p.89.
63. ibid. p.86.
64. ibid. p.197.
65. Putnam to Jones, 24 October 1912, Hale, *Putnam* pp.276–77.
66. Jones to Freud, 14 November 1912, *F–Jones* p.175.
67. Jung to Jelliffe, 28 November 1912 in Burnham & McGuire, *Jelliffe*, op.cit. p.191.
68. Jones, *Freud*, ii. p.455; Mireille Cigali in *Le Bloc–Notes de la Psychoanalyse* 9 (1989) pp.221–23.
69. Jung to Freud, 11 November 1912, *F–Jung* pp.515–16.
70. Freud to Jung, 14 November 1912, *F–Jung* pp.517–19.
71. Freud to Jung, 27 January 1913, ibid. p.541.
72. W. Stekel, *The Autobiography of a Psychoanalyst* (1950) p.142.
73. *F–Abraham* p.125.
74. Jones, *Freud*, ii. p.145.
75. Freud to Ferenczi, 26 November 1912, *F–Ferenczi* pp.433–35.
76. Jung to E.A. Bennet, 1953, *Letters*, ii. p.133.
77. MDR p.153.
78. Freud to Binswanger, 1 January 1913, Binswanger, *Freud* p.49.
79. Jones, *Freud*, i. p.348.
80. Schur, *Freud*, op.cit. pp.264–72.
81. Kerr, *Dangerous Method* pp.429–30.
82. Freud to Jones, 8 December 1912, *F–Jones* p.182.
83. Freud to Abraham, 3 December 1912, *F–Abraham* p.128.
84. Jung to Freud, 26 November 1912, *F–Jung* p.523.
85. Lou–Andreas Salomé, *The Freud Journal* (Kay-Wilmers, ed., 1987) pp.43, 58.
86. Freud to Ferenczi, 29 November 1912, *F–Ferenczi* p.437.
87. Freud to Jung, 29 November 1912, *F–Jung* pp.523–24.
88. Stern, *Haunted Prophet* p.108; Kerr, *Dangerous Method* p.432.
89. Jung to Freud, 3 December 1912, *F–Jung* pp.525–27.
90. Kerr, *Dangerous Method* p.433; Kaufmann op.cit. p.340.
91. Freud to Jones, 8 December 1912, *F–Jones* p.182.
92. Freud to Ferenczi, 9 December 1912, *F–Ferenczi* p.440.
93. Freud to Jung, 9 December 1912, *F–Jung* pp.532–33.
94. Gay, *Freud* p.234.
95. Jung to Freud, 11–14 December 1912, *Freud–Jung* p.533.
96. Freud to Jung, 16 December 1912, ibid. p.534.

97. Jung to Freud, 18 December 1912, ibid. pp.534–35.
98. Gay, *Freud* p.235.
99. Freud to Jung, 22 December 1912, *F–Jung* pp.536–37; Freud to Ferenczi, 23 December 1912, *F–Ferenczi* p.446.
100. Freud to Jones, 26 December 1912, *F–Jones* p.186.
101. Jung to Freud, 3 January 1913; Freud to Jung, 3 January 1913, *F–Jung* p.539.
102. Jung to Freud, 6 January 1913, ibid. p.540.

12: GUERRE À OUTRANCE

1. CW 4 p.191.
2. CW 4 p.287.
3. CW 4 p.289.
4. Andrew Boyle, *Montagu Norman* (1967) pp.91–95.
5. Jung to Freud, 3 March 1913, *F-Jung* p.545.
6. MDR p.269.
7. *Seminars*, 2.ii. p.1252.
8. Jones to Freud, 25 April 1913, *F-Jones* p.191; Freud to Ferenczi, 7 March, 8 June 1913, *F-Ferenczi* pp.473, 491.
9. *Seminars*, i. p.216.
10. Jones to Freud, 18 March 1913, *F-Jones* p.195; Freud to Abraham, 27 March 1913, *F-Abraham* p.137.
11. Freud to Abraham, 1 June 1913, *F-Abraham* p.141.
12. Freud to Pfister, 1 January 1913, *F-Pfister* op.cit.
13. Freud to Ferenczi, 19 May 1913, *F-Ferenczi* p.487.
14. Freud to Putnam, 1 January 1913, Hale, *Putnam* p.153.
15. Clark, *Freud* p.333.
16. Ellenberger, *Discovery* pp.817–18.
17. CW 4 p.247.
18. CW 4 pp.338–39.
19. Freud to Ferenczi, 3 August 1913, *F-Ferenczi* p.502.
20. Lou-Andreas Salome, *The Freud Journal* (1987), op.cit pp.168–70.
21. SE 14 p.45.
22. SE 12 p.317–26.
23. SE 14 p.60; Ellenberger, op.cit. p.815.
24. Jones, *Free Associations* p.225.
25. Jones, *Freud*, ii.pp.101–03, 148.
26. Brome, *Jung* p.136.
27. Jung to Freud, 27 October 1913, *F-Jung* p.550.
28. Jung to Maeder, 29 October 1913, *Letters*, i. p.28.
29. Jones to Freud, 4 November 1913; Freud to Jones 1913, *F-Jones* pp.234, 238; Freud to Abraham, 2, 6, 19 November 1913; Abraham to Freud, 4 November 1913, *F-Abraham* pp.153–57.
30. Freud to Ferenczi, 30 October, 4 November 1913; Ferenczi to Freud, 3 November 1913, *F-Ferenczi* pp.516–17.
31. Freud to Abraham, 9 November 1913, *F-Abraham* p.157.
32. Freud to Jones, 17 November 1913, *F-Jones* p.239.
33. Freud to Jones, 15 November 1913; Jones to Freud, 24 November 1913, ibid. p.243.
34. Jones to Freud, 29 November 1913; Freud to Jones, 4, 31 December 1913, ibid. pp.244–47, 250.
35. SE 20 p.208.
36. SE 14 p.58.
37. SE 11 pp.214–15.
38. SE 17 pp.53–54.

39. SE 14 p.60.
40. Lou-Andreas Salomé, *Freud Journal*, op.cit.
41. SE 20 pp.52–53.
42. SE 14 p.62.
43. SE 14 p.63.
44. SE 17 pp.115–116; SE 7 pp.142–43.
45. SE 14 p.80.
46. SE 16 p.269.
47. SE 14 pp.80–81; SE 14 p.65.
48. SE 14 p.66.
49. Ferenczi, *Further Contributions to the Theory and Technique of Psychoanalysis* (1969) pp.211, 258, 421, 449; *Final Contributions to the Problems and Methods of Psychoanalysis* (1955) p.264.
50. SE 2 p.45
51. Jones, *Freud*, iii. p.273.
52. Lou-Andreas Salomé, *Freud Journal*, op.cit. pp.38–39; Jones, *Freud*, ii. p.113.
53. SE 13 p.xiii.
54. Freud to Spielrein, 20 January, 8 May 1913, *Secret Symmetry* pp.118–20.
55. Freud to Spielrein, 28 August, 29 September 1913, *Secret Symmetry* pp.120–21.
56. *F-Jones* passim.
57. Freud to Abraham, 24 April 1914, *F-Abraham* p.173.
58. Freud to Jones, 17 May, 2 June 1914, *F-Jones* pp.279, 286.
59. SE 13 pp.211–36, Jones to Freud, 18 May 1914, *F-Jones* pp.281–82.
60. *F-Abraham* pp.181–84; *F-Jones* pp.277–78.
61. Freud to Abraham, 26 July 1914, *F-Abraham* p.186, *F-Jones* pp.288–92 passim.
62. J.B. Hobman, *David Eder: Memoirs of a Modern Pioneer* (1945); Jones to Freud, 17 July 1914, *F-Jones* pp.293–94.
63. *F-Jung* p.551.
64. CGJS p.344.
65. Jones to Freud, 3 August, 15 November 1914, *Freud-Jones* pp.298, 302–03.
66. Hannah, *Jung* pp.111–112.
67. Kerr, *Dangerous Method*, passim, esp. pp.3–15.
68. A.A. Brill, 'A Psychoanalyst scans his Past', *The Journal of Nervous and Mental Diseases* 95 (1942) p.547.
69. Herman Nunberg, *Memoirs* (NY 1946) p.46.
70. Herbert Leman, 'Jung contra Freud/Nietzsche contra Wagner', *International Review of Psychoanalysis* 13 (1986) pp.201–09.
71. Homans, *Jung in Context* p.54.
72. SE 22 p.144.
73. Freud to Ferenczi, 5 August 1913, *F-Ferenczi* p.505.
74. Homans, op.cit. pp.37, 48–50.
75. Freud to Jung, 4 October 1909, *F-Jung* p.248.
76. SE 9 pp.9–10.
77. Jung to Freud, 28 October 1907, 8 November 1907, 11 November 1908, 14 December 1909, 11 February 1910, *F-Jung* pp.94–95, 97, 177, 275, 294.
78. Roazen, *Freud and his Followers* p.252.
79. Homans op.cit. pp.56–58.
80. Jones, *Free Associations* p.215.
81. Abraham to Freud, 26 February 1924; Freud to Abraham, 4 March 1924, 5 November 1925, *F-Abraham* p.399.
82. SE 5 p.483.
83. SE 12 pp.300–301.
84. SE 18 p.22.
85. SE 20 p.53.
86. Paul E. Stepansky, 'The Empiricist as Rebel: Jung, Freud

and Burdens of Discipleship', *Journal of the History of Behavioural Sciences* 12 (1976) pp.216–39; K.R. Eissler, 'Eine Angebliche Disloyalitat Freuds Einem Freunde Gegenüber', *Jahrbuch der Psychoanalyse* 19 (1986) pp.71–88; Hannah S. Decker, 'A Tangled Skein: the Freud-Jung Relationship', in Wallace and Pressley eds. *Essays in the History of Psychiatry* pp.103–111.

87. Binswanger, *Freud* pp.9, 53–55.

13: THE DESCENT INTO THE UNDERWORLD

1. Jung to Poul Bjerre, 17 July 1914, *Letters*, ii. pp.xxix-xxx; Jung to Hans Schmid, 6 November 1915, *Letters*, i. pp.31–32.
2. MDR pp.166–67.
3. MDR pp.168–69.
4. CGJS p.232.
5. CGJS pp.233–34.
6. Jung to Freud, 11 February 1910, Jung to Freud, 11 February 1910, *F-Jung* p.294.
7. MDR p.173.
8. MDR pp.173–74.
9. Kaufman, op.cit. p.360; Stevens, *On Jung* p.157.
10. MDR p.175.
11. Hannah, *Jung* p.117.
12. Kaufman op.cit. p.360.
13. Van der Post p.169.
14. MDR p.176.
15. MDR p.177.
16. MDR pp.177–78.
17. N. Fodor, 'Jung's Sermons to the Dead', *Psychoanalytic Review* 51 (1964).
18. Jung to Paul Schmidt, 5 January 1942, *Letters*, i. pp.309–10.
19. Stern, *Haunted Prophet* p.122.
20. Stevens, *On Jung* p.175.
21. Elliott Jacques, 'Death and the Midlife Crisis', in *Work, Creativity and Social Justice* (1970) pp.38–63.
22. MDR pp.172, 181.
23. MDR pp.182–83.
24. E.M. Brenner, 'Gnosticism and Psychology. Jung's Septem Sermones ad Mortuos', *Journal of Analytical Psychology* 35 (190) pp.397–419; J. Heisig, 'Septem Sermones. Play and Theory', *Spring* (1972) pp.206–18; Judith Hubback, 'Septem Sermones ad Mortuos', *Journal of Analytical Psychology* 11 (1966) pp.95–111; Stephen Hoeller, *The Gnostic Jung and Seven Sermons to the Dead* (Wheaton, Ill. 1982); K. Radolph, *Gnosis* (SF 1985).
25. Mary Williams, 'The Poltergeist Man', *Journal of Analytical Psychology* 8 (1963) pp.123–43
26. CW 8 pp.69–71; CW 7 pp.280–91; cf. R.F.C. Hull, 'Prefatory Note to Two Posthumous Papers of C.G. Jung', *Spring* (1970) pp.166–69.
27. Jung to Hans Schmid, 6 November 1915, *Letters*, i. pp.30–32.
28. Brome, *Jung* p.161.
29. Van der Post p.177.
30. Hannah, *Jung* pp.119–20.
31. MDR p.179.
32. MDR pp.179–80.
33. Kerr, *Dangerous Method* pp.503–06.
34. Freud to Spielrein, 15 May 1914,

20 April 1915, *Secret Symmetry* pp.122–23.
35. Jung to Spielrein, 10 October 1917, Carotenuto, *Tagebuch* p.214.
36. Jung to Spielrein, 21, 25 January 1918, ibid. pp.218–20.
37. Spielrein to Jung, 26–27 January 1918, *Secret Symmetry* p.87.
38. Spielrein to Jung, 27–28 January 1918, *Secret Symmetry* p.85; Jung to Spielrein, 3 April 1919, *Tagebuch* p.224
39. Jung to Spielrein, 1 September 1919, *Secret Symmetry* p.190.
40. Appignanesi & Forrester, *Freud's Women*, op.cit.p.223.
41. Spielrein to Jung, 28 January 1918, *Secret Symmetry* p.88.
42. Jung to Spielrein, 3 April 1919, *Tagebuch* p.222.
43. MDR p.178.
44. *Spring* (1970) pp.1–14.
45. Stern, *Haunted Prophet* p.144.
46. C.A. Meier, *The Meaning and Significance of Dreams* (Boston 1987) esp. pp.7–15, 83–117.
47. Jung to Maeder, 26 February 1918, *Letters*, i. p.34.
48. Peter Collier & David Horowitz, *The Rockefellers. An American Dynasty* (1976) p.73.
49. P. Hamann, ed. *Ermanno Wolf-Ferrari* (1986).
50. Collier and Horowitz, op.cit.
51. Stern, *Haunted Prophet* pp.148–52.
52. Joseph Mileck, *Herman Hesse, Life and Art* (1978) pp.100–102.
53. SE 14 pp.275–300.
54. Jung to Jelliffe, 5 March, July 1915 in Burnham & McGuire, *Jelliffe Correspondence*, op.cit.pp.197–98; CW 10 p.233.
55. Hannah, *Jung* p.132
56. Jung to Oeri, 2 January 1929, *Letters*, i.p.57.
57. Jung to Miss Bonditch, 22 October 1916, *Letters*, i.p.57.
58. Foreign Office Reports 566/1868.
59. MDR p.187.
60. CW 9. i. pp.355–84; 9. ii. pp.232–65; CW 11 pp.79–105; CW 13 p.22–26.
61. *Seminars*, i. p.645.
62. ibid.
63. *Seminars*, i. p.52.
64. CW 6 p.80.

14: THE PSYCHOLOGY OF TYPES

1. Van der Post p.230.
2. CW 8 p.318.
3. Jung to Marianne Jung, 1 July 1919, *Letters*, i. pp.36–37.
4. Jaffé, *Word and Image*, op. cit. pp.140–42.
5. Brome, *Jung* p.176.
6. Richard Ellmann, *James Joyce* (1959) pp.480–83.
7. MDR p.225.
8. *Seminars*, i. p.233.
9. Jung to Emma Jung, 15 March 1920, MDR pp.340–41; *Seminars*, 2 ii. p.422.
10. Jaffé, *Word and Image* pp.150–51.
11. *Seminars*, 2 i. pp.46–47.
12. MDR p.230.
13. MDR p.232.
14. CW 18 p.789.
15. Michael Fordham, *Contact with Jung* (1963) p.182.
16. ibid. pp.180–81.
17. CW 18 pp.320–26.
18. Fanny Moser, *Spuk: Irrglaube oder Wahrglaube* (Zurich 1950) pp.250–61.

19. Wilson, *Lord of the Underworld* p.13.
20. CW 18 p.318.
21. CGJS p.383.
22. CW 10 p.69.
23. CW 12 p.333; cf. also Mary Williams, 'The Poltergeist Man', *Journal of Analytical Psychology* 8 (1963) pp.103–21; A.R.G. Owen, *Can We Explain the Poltergeist*? (NY 1964)
24. CW 8 p.318; Aniela Jaffé, 'C.G. Jung and Parapsychology', in J.R. Smythies, ed., *Science and ESP* (1967) p.267.
25. CW 6 pp.260–62.
26. CW 6 p.16; CW 6 pp.64–218.
27. CW 6 p.353.
28. CW 6 pp.356–59.
29. CW 6 pp.363–66.
30. CW 18 p.15; CGJS p.312.
31. CW 6 pp.383–87.
32. CW 6 pp.388–91.
33. CGJS pp.310–11.
34. CW 18 p.28.
35. CW 6 pp.395–98.
36. CW 6 pp.530–32.
37. CW 18 p.20.
38. Jung to Ernst Hauhart, 18 February 1957, *Letters*, ii. pp.346–48; Jung to Frau Vetter, 12 March 1932, *Letters*, i. pp.89–90.
39. CW 7 p.42.
40. Jung to Robert Kroon, 9 June 1960, *Letters*, ii. pp.564–65; CW 6 p.510.
41. Kaufman, *Discovering the Mind*, op.cit. p.309.
42. Stern, *Haunted Prophet* p.164.
43. CW 6 pp.71–72.
44. *Seminars*, i. p.12.
45. CW 6 p.487.
46. Ernest Glover, *Freud or Jung*? (1950) pp.102–04.
47. CW 6 pp.516–17.
48. CW 7 p.44; *Seminars*, 2 ii. p.xvi.
49. CW 6 p.288.
50. Storr, *Jung* pp.77–79.
51. Freud to Jones, 19 May 1921, *F-Jones* p.424.
52. Lou-Andreas Salomé to Freud, 20 June 1918, 30 January 1919, in Ernst Pfeiffer, ed., *Sigmund Freud and Lou-Andreas Salomé Letters* (1972) pp.82, 89; cf. also Karl Abenheimer, 'Lou-Andreas Salomé's Main Contribution to Psychoanalysis', *Spring* (1971) pp.22–37.

15: THE GLOBETROTTER

1. Hellmutt Wilhelm and Rudolf Ritsema 'I Ching', *Spring* (1970) pp.91–125.
2. MDR pp.342–45.
3. Ralph Freedman, *Herman Hesse*: *Pilgrim of Crisis* (1979) pp.224–25; Joseph Mileck, *Herman Hesse*. *Life And Art* (1978) p.103; Benjamin Nelson, 'Hesse and Jung. Two Newly Discovered Letters', *Psychological Review* 50 (1963) pp.15–16.
4. Wilson, *Lord of the Underworld* p.112.
5. Fordham, *Contact with Jung* pp.182–83; *Seminars*, i. p.65.
6. MDR p.212.
7. MDR p.291.
8. MDR p.219.
9. MDR p.214.
10. Ellen Y. Siegelman, 'The Tower as Artifact and Symbol in Jung and Yeats', *Psychological Perspectives* 18 (1987) pp.52–69.
11. Hannah, *Jung* p.153–56.

12. MDR p.292; MDR pp.217–19.
13. CW 18 p.554.
14. Augusta Fink, *I-Mary* (Tucson 1983); Esther L. Stineman, *Mary Austin, Mary Austin: Song of a Maverick* (New Haven 1989).
15. *New York Herald Tribune*, 23 December 1924.
16. William McGuire, 'Jung in America 1924–1925', *Spring* (1978) pp.37–53.
17. Brenda Maddox, *A Married Man. A Life of D.H. Lawrence* (1994) pp.327–57.
18. Miguel Serrano, *Jung and Hesse* (1966) p.59.
19. Esther Harding, 'Frances Wickes', *Journal of Analytical Psychology* 13 (1968) p.68.
20. Segaller, Stephen: *Jung: the Wisdom of the Dream* (1989) p.134.
21. MDR p.233; CW 10 p.89.
22. CW 18 p.274.
23. CW 10 p.68; Jung to Miguel Serrano, 14 September 1960, *Letters*, ii. pp.592–97.
24. CW 11 p.317.
25. MDR p.238.
26. CW 18 p.10; MDR pp.235–37.
27. CGJS p.77; CW 10 p.65; CW 13 pp.98–100.
28. MDR p.234.
29. CW 5 p.480; McGuire, 'Jung in America', loc. cit. p.44; MDR p.255.
30. *Seminars*, i. p.4; Jung to Jelliffe, 17 January 1925, *Jelliffe*, op. cit. pp.212–13.
31. CGJS pp.30–31.
32. *Seminars*, i. p.xvi.
33. Jung to Jolande Jacobi, 20 November 1928, *Letters*, i. p.55; Fordham, *Contact with Jung* p.181.
34. Van der Post p.52.
35. Jung to Hans Kuhn, 1 January 1926, *Letters*, i. pp.42–44.
36. MDR p.239.
37. Hannah, *Jung* pp.168–69.
38. CW 18 p.275; CW 9. i. p.95; MDR p.241; CW 10 p.62.
39. CGJS pp.32–36.
40. Jung to Allen Gilbert, 20 April 1946, *Letters*, i. pp.422–23.
41. *Seminars*, i. p.307
42. CW 9 i. p.143; CW 10 p.62.
43. CW 9. i. pp.169–70; *Seminars*, i. p.220.
44. CW 18 p.240; CW 10 pp.71–72; Jung to Frances Wilkes, 9 August 1926, *Letters*, i. p.44.
45. CW 18 p.10.
46. CW 10 p.71; CW 8 p.407.
47. *Seminars*, 2. i. p.248.
48. CW 15 p.18; CW 18 p.318.
49. CW 15 p.8; *Seminars*, i. pp.320–21; CW 10 pp.63–64; CW 18 pp.285–86.
50. *Seminars*, i. p.20; CGJS p.215; MDR pp.245–47.
51. *Seminars*, 2. i. p.187.
52. CW 18 p.555.
53. *Seminars*, 2. i. p.175–76.
54. CW 8 pp.304–05.
55. CW 9.i. pp.268–69.
56. Jung to Karl Schmid, 25 February 1958, *Letters*, ii. pp.418–20.
57. Jung to Hans Kuhn, 1 January 1926, *Letters*, i. pp.42–44.
58. CW 10 pp.61–62.
59. *Seminars*, 2. i. p.754.
60. *Seminars*, i. p.70.
61. *Seminars*, i. p.649.
62. *Seminars*, 2. i. p.674.
63. CW 15 p.17.
64. MDR p.254; CGJS p.294.
65. Brome, *Jung* p.211.
66. *Seminars*, i. p.678.
67. *Seminars*, i. pp.133–34.
68. Hannah, *Jung* p.180.
69. CGJS p.142; MDR p.256.

70. *Seminars*, 2. i. p.673.
71. *Seminars*, 2. ii. p.1530.
72. *Seminars*, i. p.338.
73. *Seminars*, i. p.337.
74. CGJS p.142.
75. Van der Post op.cit. p.50.

16: THE DOCTRINE

1. Jung to Frances Wilkes, 9 August 1926, *Letters*, i. p.44; Jung to Louis London, 24 September 1926, *Letters*, i. p.45.
2. Brome, *Jung* p.200.
3. Ibid. pp.19–20, 225, 250–51.
4. Stern, *Haunted Prophet* p.130.
5. Michael Fordham, 'Memories and Thoughts about C.G. Jung', *Journal of Analytical Psychology* 20 (1975) pp.103–13.
6. *Jung and the Wisdom of the Dream*, op.cit. p.95.
7. Kaufman, op.cit. pp.375, 442.
8. Stern op.cit. p.131.
9. CGJS p.250.
10. SE 16 p.376.
11. CW 16 p.41.
12. CW 11 pp.334–35.
13. CW 16 p.100.
14. J. Henderson, 'C.G. Jung: a reminiscent picture of his method', *Journal of Analytical Psychology* 20 (1975) p.114–21.
15. Janet Malcolm, *Psychoanalysis: the Impossible Profession* (1982) p.40.
16. SE 17 pp.159–68.
17. CW 16 p.66.
18. CW 4 p.335.
19. CW 7 p.84.
20. CW 8 p.399.
21. CW 8 p.399.
22. CW 7 p.74.
23. CW 16 pp.20, 26–27.
24. CW 17 pp.65–132.
25. MDR pp.115–117.
26. CW 11 p.554.
27. CW 16 pp.19, 87.
28. SE 12 p.207.
29. Erich Neumann, *The Origins and History of Consciousness* (Princeton 1954).
30. CW 9.i. p.3.
31. CGJS p.398; CW 9 i. pp.3–53; CW 7 pp.64–138; CW 10 pp.3–28; CW 18 pp.36–39.
32. David Holt, 'Jung and Marx', *Spring* (1973) pp.52–66.
33. Edward Edinger, *Ego and archetype: Individuation and the Religious Function of the Psyche* (Baltimore 1972).
34. CW 13 p.46; Jolande Jacobi, *The Way of Individuation* (1967).
35. CW 9. i. pp.3–41; CW 10 pp.194–243.
36. CW i. p.284; Sylvia Brinton Perera, *The Scapegoat Complex: Towards a Mythology of Shadow and Guilt* (Toronto 1986); John Sanford, *Evil. The Shadow Side of Reality* (NY 1987).
37. CW 7 pp.123–241, 269–304.
38. CW 7 p.193.
39. CW 7 p.297.
40. CW 7 p.164.
41. CW 13 p.265.
42. CW 8 pp.133, 185; CW 9 i. p.42; Jolande Jacobi, *Complex/Archetype/Symbol in the Psychology of C.G.Jung* (Princeton 1959).
43. CW 7 pp.156–62.
44. CW 9. i. p.29.
45. CW 9. i. pp.27–28, 285; CW 7 pp.187–91.
46. CW 17 p.198.
47. CW 9 i. p.287.
48. CW 7 p.192.

49. CW 7 p.195.
50. *Seminars*, 2 i. pp.300–12.
51. Pieter Middelkoop, *The Wise Old Man* (Boston 1985).
52. Erich Neumann, *The Great Mother* (Princeton 1955); Jean Shinoda Bolen, *The Goddesses in Everywoman* (SF 1984).
53. CW 9 i. p.79; Jung to Elizabeth Metzer, 7 February 1942, *Letters*, i. p.313; Jung to Swami Devatunanda, 9 February 1937, *Letters*, i. pp.226–27.
54. Jung to Mircea Eliade, 19 January 1955, *Letters*, ii. pp.210–12.
55. CW 10 p.10; CW 11 pp.148–50.
56. Anthony Stevens, *Archetypes. A Natural History of the Self* (NY 1983).
57. Jung to Henri Flournoy, 29 March 1949, *Letters*, i. pp.524–26.
58. Jung to Flournoy, 29 March 1949, op. cit; Jung to van dem Bergh von Eysinga, 13 February 1954, *Letters*, i. pp.151–54.; CGJS p.293.
59. Jung to A.D. Cornell, 9 February 1960, *Letters*, i. pp.537–43.
60. CW 9. i. pp.255–72; Jung to Victor White, 10 April 1954, *Letters*, ii. pp.163–74.
61. CW 13 pp.193–250; Karl Kerenyi, *Hermes. Guide of Souls* (Dallas 1987); Ralph Metman, 'The Trickster Figure in Schizophrenia', *Journal of Analytical Psychology* 3 (1958) pp.5–28; A Plant, 'A Case of Tricksterism Illustrating Ego Defences', *Journal of Analytical Psychology* 4 (1959) pp.119–36.
62. CW 9. i. p.267.
63. *Jung and the Wisdom of the Dream* op.cit. p.94.
64. Stevens, *On Jung* p.114.
65. CW 9. i. pp.23–71, 290–384; CW 7 pp.173–241; CW 10 pp.247–305; CW 11 pp.148–200, 273–96; Edward Edinger, *Ego and Archetype*: *Individuation and the Religious Function of the Archetype* (Baltimore 1972); Mario Jacoby, *Longing for Paradise*: *Psychological Perspective on an Archetype* (Boston 1980).
66. CW 10 p.463.
67. CW 14 pp.535, 546; CW 9 p.275; CW 7 p.171.
68. CW 8 p.226; Jung to Dorothea Hoch, 30 April 1953, *Letters*, ii. p.113–114; Jung to Arnival Vasavada, 22 November 1954, ibid. pp.194–96.
69. Gerhard Adler, *The Living Symbol. A Case Study in the Process of Individuation* (NY 1961); Aldo Carotenuto, *The Vertical Labyrinth*: *Individuation in Jungian Analysis* (Toronto 1981).
70. CW 11 pp.190, 468.
71. CW 9 ii. p.68.
72. CW 12 p.19; CW 12 pp.94–98; CW 9 ii. p.164; CW 10 p.138.
73. CW 7 pp.123–304; CW 9 ii. pp.3–7; CW 8 pp.159–234; CW 17 pp.49–62.
74. CW 7 p.144; CW 9. i. p.282.
75. CW 9. i. pp.278–80.
76. Jung to Dr N (unknown), 2 December 1937, *Letters*, i. pp.239–40.
77. CW 16 pp.152, 191–92.
78. Jung to Morton Kelsey, 3 May 1958, *Letters*, ii. pp.434–36.
79. CW 7 p.175.
80. CW 11 p.151; Stevens, *On Jung* p.28.
81. Andrew Samuels, ed., *The Father. Contemporary Jungian*

Perspectives (NY 1988); Arthur & Libby Coleman, *The Father; Mythology and Changing Roles* (Chicago 1988).

82. CW 9. i. p.281.
83. CW 3 p.271.
84. CW 7 pp.140–41.
85. CW 18 p.181.
86. CW 8 p.402.
87. CW 14 p.531.
88. Jung to E.A. Bennet, 22 May 1960, *Letters*, ii. p.558; cf. Bennet, *Jung* pp.95–103.
89. A. Dry, *The Psychology of Jung. A Critical Interpretation* (1961) p.119.
90. Erich Fromm, *The Art of Being* (1993) p.84.
91. R. Hobson, 'The Archetypes of the Collective Unconscious', in Michael Fordham, ed., *Analytical Psychology. A Modern Science* (1973) p.70.
92. Jung to E.A. Bennet, 22 May 1960, *Letters*, ii. p.558.
93. Marilyn Nagy, *Philosophical Issues in the Psychology of C.G. Jung* (NY 1991) p.266; CW 9 ii. p.177; Demaris Wehr, *Jung and Feminism* (1990) p.72; Glover, op.cit. p.51; J.R. Staude, *The Adult Development of C.G. Jung* (1981) p.102.
94. Hans Trub, *Heilung aus der begegnung eine auseinanderersetzung mit der psychologie C.G. Jungs* (Stuttgart 1962).
95. Homans, *Jung in Context* op.cit. p.208.
96. Glover, op.cit. p.174.
97. CGJS p.262; MDR p.320; CW 9 i.p.267; Paul Kline, *Fact and Fantasy in Freudian Theory* (1972) p.324; Stevens, *On Jung* p.264.
98. CW 7 pp.148–51
99. CW 7 pp.170–71.

17: VALKYRIES AND OTHER WOMEN

1. *New York Herald Tribune*, 30 December 1928.
2. Aniela Jaffé, *Word and Image* p.140.
3. Jung to Oscar Schmitz, 20 October 1928, *Letters*, i. pp.53–54.
4. Chauncey Goodrich, 'Transatlantic Dispatches from and about Zürich', *Spring* (1983) pp.183–90.
5. Jung to Christiana Morgan, 13 September 1929; Jung to G.A. Farner, 29 June 1934, *Letters*, i. pp.70–71, 168.
6. Jung to Jelliffe, 21 July 1927, *Jelliffe*, op.cit. p.225.
7. CGJS p.38; *Neue Freie Presse*, 23 February 1928.
8. CGJS p.50; 'Transatlantic', *Spring* (1983) op.cit. p.199.
9. Hannah, *Jung* pp. 205–206.
10. MDR pp.265–68; CGJS p.184.
11. MDR p.268.
12. A. Tilander, 'Why did C.G. Jung write his Autobiography?' *Journal of Analytical Psychology* 36 (1991) pp.111–124 (at p.121).
13. Jung to Mary Foote, 28 March 1933, *Letters*, ii. p.xxxiii; Jung to Erich Neumann, 19 December 1938, *Letters*, i. pp. 250–52.
14. Aniela Jaffé, 'The Creative Phases in Jung's Life', *Spring* (1972) pp.162–90.
15. CW 15 p.54.
16. Jung to Richard Wilhelm, 6, 22 April 1929, *Letters*, i.pp.62–64.

17. Jung to Richard Wilhelm, 10 September 1929, ibid. i. pp.67–68.
18. CW 15 p.62.
19. MDR pp.342–45.
20. Stern, *Haunted Prophet* p.131.
21. Jung to van der Hoop, 2 March 1934, *Letters*, i. pp.146–47.
22. Stern, *Haunted Prophet* p.146.
23. Gerhard Wehr, *Rudolf Steiner* (Freiburg 1982).
24. Katharine Grant Watson, 'A Visit to C.G. Jung', *Christian Community* 1 (1976) p.19.
25. Jung to Frau M. Patzelt, 29 November 1935, *Letters*, i. p.203.
26. Hannah, *Jung* p.204.
27. Jung to Keyserling, 19 June 1927, 12 May 1928, *Letters*, i. pp.47–50; Miguel Serrano, *Jung and Hesse*, op.cit. pp.28, 66; Jung to Keyserling, 25 August 1928, *Letters*, i. p. 52–53; Jung to Keyserling, 20 October 1928, *Letters*, i. pp.54–55; Jung to Keyserling, 20 December 1929, 9 September 1930, *Letters*, i.pp.72–73,76; Jung to Keyserling, 23 April 1931, ibid.pp.82–83; Jung to Keyserling, 24 December 1931, ibid. pp.85–86; Jung to Keyserling, 13, 20 August 1921, ibid.pp.84–85.
28. Stern op.cit. p.208.
29. Rupert Hart-Davis, *Hugh Walpole. A Biography* (1952) p.314.
30. Jung to Hugh Walpole, 15 August, 14 November 1930, *Letters*, i.pp.75,78–79.
31. CW 15 pp.87–88.
32. Jung to Robert Walter Corti, 12 September 1929, *Letters*, i.pp.69–70.
33. Vincent Brome, 'H.G. Wells and C.G. Jung', *Spring* (1975) pp.56–59.
34. *Neue Zürcher Zeitung*, 18 November 1928.
35. *Seminars*, i. pp.188,617.
36. Vera Krasovskaya, *Nijinsky* (1979); Romola Nijinsky, *Nijinsky* (1980); Tamara Nijinsky, *Nijinsky and Romola* (1991) pp.391–2.
37. Howard Teichmann, *Smart Aleck* (1976).
38. CW 15 pp.109–34.
39. Richard Ellmann, *James Joyce* (1959) pp.641–42.
40. Jung to Joyce, 27 September 1932, *Letters*, i.pp.98–99.
41. William O.Walcott, 'Carl Jung and James Joyce. A Narrative of Encounters', *Psychological Perspectives* 1 (1970) pp.21–31.
42. Roazen, *Freud and His Followers* p.354.
43. Ellmann, *Joyce*, op.cit. p.693.
44. CGJS pp.239–40.
45. Ellmann, op.cit. p.692; Jung to Gus Claritas, 23 February 1957, *Letters*, ii. pp.348–49.
46. S.R. Brivic, *Joyce between Freud and Jung* (1980).
47. Ellmann, op.cit. pp.525, 691; CGJS p.241; Robert D. Neumann, 'The Transformative Quality of the Feminine in the "Penelope" episode of Ulysses', *Journal of Analytical Psychology* 31 (1986) pp.63–74; Thomas Cowan, 'On Finnegan's Wake', *Spring* (1972) pp.43–59; William O. Walcott, 'The Paternity of James Joyce's Stephen Daedalus', *Journal of Analytical Psychology* 10 (1965) pp.79–95; Patricia Hutchins, *James Joyce's World* (1957) pp.184–85.
48. Nancy Milford, *Zelda. A Biography* (1970) p.179.

49. Maggy Anthony, *The Valkyries. The Women around Jung* (1990) pp.33–34; Tina Keller, 'Beginnings of Active Imagination. Analysis with C.G. Jung and Toni Wolff, 1915–1928', *Spring* (1982) pp.279–82.
50. *Letters*, ii.
51. Anthony, *Valkyries*, op.cit. pp.38–39; cf. L. Fierz-David, *Woman's Dionysian Initiation* (1988); The Dream of Poliphilo (1988).
52. Donald Gallup, ed., *The Journals of Thornton Wilder* (Yale 1985) p.144.
53. Van der Post p. 230.
54. Anthony op.cit. pp.45–48.
55. ibid. pp.56–61.
56. Jung to Olga Frobe-Kapteyn, 29 January 1934, *Letters* i. pp.139–40.
57. William McGuire, 'The Arcane Summer Schools', *Spring* (1980) pp.146–55.
58. Brome, *Jung* p.252.
59. Ernst Kretschmer, *Gestalten und Gedanken* (Stuttgart 1963) p.135.
60. Aniela Jaffé, 'C.G. Jung and the Eranos Conferences', *Spring* (1977) pp.201–12.
61. ibid. p.211.
62. Mary Bancroft, 'Jung and his Circle', *Psychological Perspectives* 6 (1975) ppp.115–25.
63. Anthony op.cit. pp.85–86.
64. Edward Foote, 'Who was Mary Foote?' *Spring* (1974) pp.256–58.
65. Hannah, *Jung* p.191.
66. Brome, *Jung* p.225.
67. Bancroft, loc.cit.
68. Anthony, op.cit. pp.85–86.
69. Brome, *Jung* p.225.
70. CW 10 p.39; CW 9 i. p.271.
71. CW 17 p.198; CW 10 p.39.
72. CW 9. i.p.30.
73. CW 10 p.40.
74. CW 9. i.p.70.
75. CW 9. i. p.70.
76. CW 10 p.41.
77. Jung to Georgette Bower, 8 December 1928, *Letters*, i. p.248; CW 13 pp.39–43.
78. Jung to Carol Jeffrey, 18 June 1958, *Letters*, ii. pp.454–56.
79. Demaris Wehr, *Jung and Feminism* (1990) p.116.
80. CW 16 p.174.
81. CW 7 p.205.
82. CW 7 p.210.
83. CW 10 p.44.
84. CW 7 p. 209.
85. James Hyslop, *Science and a Future Life* (1907) p.113.
86. CW 7 p.208.
87. CW 9. ii. p.15; CW 9 i. pp.290–91; CW 18 p.147.
88. D.W. Fritz, 'The Animus-Possessed Wife of Bath', *Journal of Analytical Psychology* 23 (1978) pp.63–89.
89. Jung to Carol Jeffrey, 18 June 1958, *Letters*, ii. pp.454–56.
90. CW 10 p.123; CW 10 pp.117–118; CW 7 p.206; Jung to Cary Baynes, 12 April 1959, *Letters*, ii. p. 496.
91. *Seminars*, ii. pp.14–15.
92. CW 10 p.127.
93. *Daily Mail*, 25–29 April 1955.
94. CGJS p.245.
95. Jung to Mary Bancroft, August 1955, *Letters*, ii p.270; *Seminars* i. p.14.
96. Robert Hopcke, 'Jung's Attitudes towards Homosexuality', *Spring* (1987) p.154–61; Mitch Walker, 'Jung and Homophobia', *Spring* (1991) pp.55–70; Robert Hopcke, 'Jung and Homosexuality. A Clear Vision', *Journal of Analytical Psychology* 33 (1988) pp.65–80.

97. CW 9. i. p.94.
98. CW 9. i. p.87.
99. CW 9 i. p.89.
100. CW 9 i. p.91; Edward Whitmont, *The Symbolic Quest* (NY 1969) p.100; CW 10 p.132; CW 9. i. pp.71–72.
101. CW 8 pp.397–98.
102. Marco Garzonio, *Gesù e le donne* (1990).
103. CW 9 ii. p.22; CW 9 ii. p. 268.
104. Jung to Walter Lenino, 21 April 1949, *Letters*, i. pp.498–99.
105. Jung to Gustav Senn, 13 October 1941, *Letters*, i. p.305; Fordham, *Contact with Jung* p.213.
106. Juliet Mitchell, *Psychoanalysis and Feminism* (1974).
107. Naomi Goldenberg, 'A Feminist Critique of Jung', *Signs. Journal of Women in Culture and Society* 2 (1976) pp.443–449; Mary Daly, *Gyn/Ecology: the Metaethics of Radical Feminism* (Boston 1978) p. 280.
108. CW 7 p. 186; CW 9 i. pp.99–100; CW 7 p. 187; CW 9. i. p.98; CW 7 pp.208–09; Demaris Wehr, *Jung and Feminism*, op.cit. p.65; H. Binswanger, 'Positive Aspects of the Animus', *Spring* (1963) pp.82–101; Edward Whitmont, *The Return of the Goddess* (1983) p.189; Andrew Samuels, *Jung and the Post-Jungians* (1985) p.210; Katherine Bradway, 'Gender Identity and Gender Roles: their place in Analytic Practice', in Murray Stein, *Jungian Analysis* (1982) p.279; cf. J. Hillman, *Anima: An Anatomy of a Personified Notion* (Dallas 1985).
109. J. Singer, *Androgyny: Towards a New Theory of Sexuality* (1977); M. Mattoon, *Jungian Psychology in Perspective* (NY 1981).
110. CW 9 ii. pp.20–21.
111. Stevens, *On Jung* p.218.
112. Anne Kent Rush, *Moon, Moon* (NY 1976).
113. Jean Bolen, *Goddesses in Every Woman* (1984); Linda Leonard, *The Wounded Woman* (1982); Sylvia Perera, *Descent of Goddesses* (1981); Bani Shorter, *An Image Darkly Forming* (1987); Ann Ulanov, *Receiving Women* (1981); Estella Lauter & Carol Rapprecht, *Feminist Archetypal Theory: Interdisciplinary Revisions of Jungian Thought* (Knoxville 1985).
114. Demaris Wehr, *Jung and Feminism*, op.cit. p.106.
115. CW 8 p.396; Jung to Zwi Werblowsky, 28 March 1951, *Letters*, ii. pp.15–17.
116. CW 9. i. p.87; CW 10 p.122.
117. Serrano, *Jung and Hesse* p.58.
118. Jung to Carol Jeffrey, 18 June 1958, *Letters*, ii. pp.454–56; CW 9 i. p.95; CW 10 p.129.

18: THE SHADOW OF THE NAZIS

1. CW 11 p.347; *Daily Sketch*, 15 October 1936; *Observer*, 18 October 1936.
2. Adolf Guggenbuhl-Craig, 'America's Political Fantasies', *Spring* (1992) pp.61–67 (at p.63); *Seminars*, 2 i. p.581.
3. CW 9 ii. p.181.
4. Jung to Samuel Schmalhausen, 19 October 1934, *Letters*, i. p.174.
5. CW 11 p.320.

6. CW 10 p.262.
7. Jung to Baroness Vera von der Heyett, 13 February 1958, *Letters*, ii. p.417.
8. CW 15 p.15; CW 18 p.541; CW 7 p.204; *Seminars*, i. p.175.
9. *Seminars*, 2 i. p.374.
10. *Seminars* i. p.165.
11. *Seminars*, 2 i. pp.485–87.
12. *Seminars*, 2 i. pp.467–69.
13. *Seminars*, 2 i. p.690; CW 18 p.569.
14. *Seminars*, 2 i. p.583.
15. *Seminars*, 2 i. p.592.
16. Jung to Evelyn Bohler, 8 January 1956, *Letters*, ii. pp.284–86.
17. CW 18 p.593.
18. CW 9.i. 267; CW 10 pp.254–55.
19. CW 18 p.572.
20. CW 18 p.343.
21. CW 18 p.343.
22. CW 10 p.231–33; CW 11 p.47; *Seminars*, 2 i. p.589.
23. MDR p.223.
24. CW 10 p.280; CW 9 ii. p.181.
25. CW 9 i. p.127.
26. CGJS pp.134–35; *Seminars*, 2 i. p.584.
27. CW 10 p.226.
28. CW 18 p.596.
29. CGJS p.203.
30. CW 10 p.278.
31. *Seminars*, 2 i. pp.554, 585.
32. *Seminars*, i. p.25.
33. CW 11 p.235.
34. *Observer*, 11 October 1936.
35. Cyril Connolly, *The Golden Horizon* (1953) pp.397–409.
36. *Seminars*, 2 ii. p.1542.
37. CGJS p.117.
38. CGJS pp.115, 129–31.
39. CW 18 pp.127, 165.
40. CGJS p.126–28.
41. *Seminars*, i. p.188; CW 18 pp.281, 575; CGJS pp.117–119.
42. CGJS pp.120–21, 128–29, 140.
43. *Seminars*, 2 ii. p.1523.
44. *Seminars*, 2 i. p.376.
45. CW 18 p.575.
46. *Seminars*, 2 i. pp.376, 496–97.
47. CW 18 pp.544–45; CW 18 p.570.
48. CW 10 pp.537, 296.
49. CW 10 p.210.
50. CW 18 p.578; *Seminars*, 2 i. p.377.
51. CW 18 p.597; CW 10 p.213.
52. Jung to Miguel Serrano, 14 September 1960, *Letters*, ii. pp.592–97.
53. CW 10 p.13.
54. CW 9 ii. p.175.
55. *Seminars*, 2 i. p.475.
56. CW 10 p.185.
57. CW 10 p.184.
58. CW 18 p.164; CGJS pp.300–301.
59. CGJS p.151.
60. CW 10 p.206–07.
61. CW 10 pp.166, 353.
62. CGJS p.196.
63. CW 10 p.237.
64. Andrew Samuels, 'National Psychology, National Socialism and Analytical Psychology. Reflections on Jung and Antisemitism', *Journal of Analytical Psychology* 37 (1992) pp.3–28, 127–48 (at p.133).
65. CW 10 p.236.
66. Geoffrey Cocks, 'C.G. Jung and German Psychotherapy', *Spring* (1979) pp.221–227 (at pp.224–25).
67. Van der Post p.198.
68. Jung to M.H. Goering, 16 November 1937, *Letters*, i. p.238.
69. Fordham, *Contact with Jung* op.cit. p.82.
70. Seminars 2 i p.581.
71. Jaffè, *From the Life and Work* p.91.
72. Hugo Ott, *Martin Heidegger, a political life* (1993).

73. Jung to Gustav Richard Keyer, 20 April 1934, *Letters*, i. pp.157–58.
74. *New Yorker*, 23 May 1964.
75. Jung to Paul Bjerre, 22 January 1934; Jung to Alphonse Maeder, 22 January 1934, *Letters*, ii. pp.135–37.
76. Jung to Rudolph Alless, 23 November 1933, *Letters*, i. pp.131–32; Jung to M.H. Goring, 7 June 1934, ibid. p.163; Jones, *Freud*, iii. p.187.
77. Ernst Kretschmer, *Gestalten und Gedanken* (Stuttgart 1963) pp.133–36.
78. *Neue Zürcher Zeitung*, 27 February 1934.
79. *Neue Zürcher Zeitung*, 13, 14, 15 March 1934.
80. F. Alexander & S. Selesnik, *A History of Psychiatry* (NY 1961) pp.407–09; Grossman, 'C.G. Jung and National Socialism', *Journal of European Studies* 9 (1979) pp.231–59.
81. Hermann Kesten, ed., *Thomas Mann Diaries, 1918–1921, 1933–1939* (NY 1982) pp.201, 235.
82. Geoffrey Cocks, 'C.G. Jung and German Psychotherapy', *Spring* (1979) pp.221–227; Cocks, 'Psychotherapy and the Third Reich: A Research Note', *Journal of the History of Behavioural Sciences* 14 (1978) pp.33–36.
83. Kaethe Draper, 'Psychoanalysis in Hitler's Germany: 1933–1945', *American Imago* 29 (1972) pp.199–214.
84. Geoffrey Cocks, *Psychotherapy in the Third Reich* (1985); *Psyche and Swastika. Neue Deutsche Seelenheillunde 1933–1945* (LA 1975).
85. Wolfgang Giegerich, 'Postscript to Cocks', *Spring* (1979) pp.228–31.
86. Jeffrey Masson, *Against Therapy: Emotional Tyranny and the Myth of Psychological Healing* (1989) pp.135–52.
87. J. Kirsch, 'Carl Gustav Jung and the Jews; the real story', *Journal of Psychology and Judaism* 6 (1982) p.117.
88. Jung to van der Hoop, 3 January 1936, *Letters*, i. pp.207–08.
89. Aniela Jaffé, *From the Life and Work*, op.cit. p.83.
90. Jung to Max Guggenheim, 28 March 1934, *Letters*, i. pp.155–56; Ellenberger, *Discovery* p.677.
91. CW 10 p.237.
92. Hermann Kesten, ed., *Thomas Mann Diaries*, op.cit. p.235 (under 16 March 1935).
93. CW 10 p.353.
94. CW 18 p.600.
95. CGJS p.122.
96. CW 10 pp.165–66; Jung to A. Pupato, 2 March 1934, *Letters*, i. pp.147–48.
97. Jung to B. Cohen, 28 April 1934, *Letters*, i. pp.159–60; CW 10 pp.533–34.
98. Jung to James Kirsch, 26 May 1934, *Letters*, i. pp.160–63.
99. Jung to B. Cohen, 26 March 1934, ibid. i. pp.154–55; Jung to Gerhard Adler, 9 June 1934, ibid. i. pp.164–65.
100. Jung to Abraham Aaron Robuck, 19 December 1936, ibid. i. pp.223–224.
101. Jung to C.E. Benda, 19 June 1934, ibid. i. pp.167–68; CW 6 p.80.
102. CW 7 p.149.
103. Jones, *Freud*, ii. p.55.
104. Ernest Harms, 'Carl Gustav Jung – Defender of Freud and

the Jews', *Psychiatric Quarterly* 20 (1946) pp.198–230.
105. R. Raymond, 'On Carl Gustav Jung's psychosocial basis of morality during the Nazi era', *Journal of Psychology and Judaism* 6 (1982); J. Kirsch, 'Carl Gustav Jung and the Jews: the real story', ibid.; F. Dalal, 'Jung: a racist', *British Journal of Psychotherapy* 4 (1988); cf. A. Samuels, 'Jung and Antisemitism', *Continuum* 1 (1990) pp.45–52; A. Maidenbaum, *Lingering Shadows: Freud, Jung and Antisemitism* (Boston 1991).
106. Clark, *Freud* p.493.
107. G. Scholem, ed., *The Correspondence of Walter Benjamin and Gershom Scholem 1932–1940* (NY 1989) pp.197, 203.
108. Andrew Samuels, 'National Psychology, etc', loc.cit, *Journal of Analytical Psychology* 37 (1992) p.15.
109. Margrit Burri, 'Repression, Falsification and Bedevilling of German Mythology', *Spring* (1978) pp.88–104.
110. Jaffé, *From the Life and Work*, op.cit. pp.97–98.
111. CW 10 p.539.
112. Jung to Henry A. Murray, 6 October, 19 December 1938, 6 March 1939, *Letters*, ii. pp.xxiv-xxv; Jung to J.H. van der Hoop, 14 January 1946, *Letters*, i. pp.404–06; Jung to Allen Gilbert, 8 January 1934, *Letters*, i. p.134.

19: THE WORLD OF DREAMS

1. *Neue Zürcher Zeitung*, 26, 27 November 1932.
2. Jung to Elizabeth von Sury, 14 November 1933, *Letters*, i. pp.130–31.
3. Stern, *Haunted Prophet* pp.223–226.
4. Jung to Medard Boss, 27 June 1947, *Letters*, ii. p.xl-xlii.
5. Medard Boss, *The Meaning and Content of Sexual Perversions* (NY 1949) p. xi.
6. CW 16 p.149; Jung to Mr 0, 30 April, 2 May 1947, *Letters*, i. pp.458–60.
7. Jung to Jolande Jacobi, 13 March 1956, *Letters*, ii. pp.293–94.
8. *Seminars*, i. p.208; CW 4 p.240.
9. CW 8 pp.294–96.
10. Mary Ann Mattoon, *Understanding Dreams* (Dallas 1984), C.A. Meier, *The Meaning and Significance of Dreams* (Boston 1987) pp.83–117.
11. Meier ibid. pp.7–15.
12. CW 12 pp.47–48.
13. CW 10 p.23.
14. James A. Hall, *Jungian Dream Interpretation: A Handbook of Theory and Practice* (Toronto 1983).
15. CW 13 p.347.
16. CW 18 p.173.
17. CW 18 pp.229–34.
18. CW 9. i. pp.355–84.
19. CW 3 p.242; CW 8 pp.290–91; CW 7 p.178; CW 10 pp.152–53.
20. CW 8 pp.290–93; Jung to H.J. Barett, 27 December 1956, *Letters*, ii. p.341.
21. CW 18 p.144.
22. CGJS p.41; CW 18 pp.216–26;

CW 8 pp.250, 263; CW 16 p.153.
23. CW 7 pp.179–81.
24. Jung to P. Schmid, 21 December 1934, *Letters*, i. p.182; CW 12 p.154; Jung to Keyserling, 10 May 1932, *Letters*, i. pp.92–93; CW 18 p.210.
25. Glover, *Freud or Jung* op.cit. p.111.
26. MDR p.281.
27. Jung to Emma Asbeck, 7 May 1947, *Letters*, i. pp.460–61; MDR pp.137–38.
28. CW 16 p.253.
29. CW 18 p.207.
30. CW 18 p.208.
31. CW 16 pp.150–51; CW 17 pp.60–62.
32. CW 9. i. pp.279–80.
33. MDR p.222.
34. CGJS pp.376–77.
35. CW 9 i. p.364; MDR p.189; MDR p.190.
36. Jung to Richard Wilhelm, 26 April 1929; Jung to Alice Crowley, 20 July 1942, *Letters*, i. pp.62–63, 319.
37. Jung to Victor White, 30 January 1948, ibid. i. pp.490–93.
38. MDR p.135; CGJS p.69; Jung to Frau N, 26 April 1930, *Letters*, i. p.74.
39. Jung to Miss N, 14 October 1954, *Letters*, ii. pp.187–88.
40. Jung to C.R. Birnie, 14 May 1948, *Letters*, i. pp.500–501.
41. Jung to Eugen Bohler, 23 February 1956, *Letters*, ii. p.291.
42. Jung to O. Schrenk, 8 December 1952, ibid. pp.99–100.
43. Jung to Aniela Jaffé, 22 December 1942, *Letters*, i. pp.325–26.
44. Jung to Herr N, 22 March 1939, *Letters*, i. pp.264–66; Jung to Wilhelm Laiblin, 19 March 1934, ibid. pp.153–54.
45. Jung to Grant Wilson, 25 January 1954, *Letters*, ii. p.146.
46. Jung to Herr N, 2 November 1960, ibid. p.608; CW 17 p.102.
47. SE 19 pp.108–38.
48. CW 18 p.190.
49. CW 16 p.134.
50. CW 8 pp.250, 263; CW 16 p.153; CW 7 pp.187, 199; CW 11 pp.26–27.
51. *Seminars*, i. p.30; CW 13 pp.300–301; CW 17 p.103; CW 16 p.32.
52. *Seminars*, i. p.30.
53. CW 16 p.160.
54. CW 4 p.237.
55. *Seminars*, 2 ii. p.414; CW 18 pp.183–290; CW 9 pp.290–390; CW 12 pp.39–223.
56. CW 15 p.70; *Seminars*, i. p.540.
57. CW 18 p.247; CW 16 p.157.
58. CW 13 p.348; Jung to Kurt Plachte, 10 January 1929, *Letters*, i. pp.59–62.
59. Paul Ricoeur, *Freud and Philosophy* (1970) p.464.
60. *Seminars*, 2 ii. pp.414, 440.
61. CW 5 p.378; *Seminars*, i. p.645.
62. Jung to Mr N, 5 July 1932, *Letters*, i. pp.95–97.
63. *Seminars*, i. pp.574–82.
64. Storr, *Jung* p.112.

20: AMERICA, AMERICA

1. Van der Post pp.45–46.
2. Hannah, *Jung* p.234.
3. Jung to Dieter Meyer, 26 January 1959, *Letters*, ii.p.479.
4. CW 18 pp.1–415.
5. Paul Roazen, *Erik Erikson* (1976) pp.8–9.
6. Jung to Henry Murray, 10

September 1935, *Letters*, i.pp.198–200.
7. Hannah, *Jung* p. 236.
8. *New York Times*, 4 October 1936.
9. Kaufman pp.427–28.
10. Roazen, *Freud and his Followers* p.302.
11. Robert Grinnell, 'Jung at Yale', *Spring* (1976) pp.155–56.
12. Jung to Heinrich Zimmer, 14 December 1936, *Letters*, i.pp.222–223; Fordham, *Contact with Jung* p.187; Jung to Abraham Aaron Roback, 29 September 1936, *Letters*, i.p.219.
13. *Time*, 9 November 1936.
14. *Observer*, 18 October 1936.
15. *Daily Sketch*, 15 October 1936; Jung to Jolande Jacobi, 27 October 1936, *Letters*, i.pp.220–221; CW 9.i.p.48.
16. Robert Grinnell, 'Jung at Yale', loc.cit.
17. CW 10 p.231; Jung to J.B. Rhine, 18 September 1945, *Letters*, i.pp.378–79.
18. Steven Naifeh & Gregory White Smith, *Jackson Pollock* (1990) pp.327–336.
19. Jelliffe to Jung, 5 July 1932, *Jelliffe*, op.cit. p.237; Jung to Jelliffe, 7 June 1932, ibid.p.236.
20. William McGuire, 'How Jung counselled a Distressed Parent', *Spring* (1981) pp.185–91; Stephen Gould Axelrod, *Robert Lowell: Life and Art* (Princeton 1978) pp.22, 241.
21. Jung to Henry Murray, 19 December 1938, 6 March 1939, *Letters*, ii.p.xxv.
22. Jelliffe to Merrill Moore, 18 May 1936, *Jelliffe*, op.cit. pp.263, 270.
23. Jelliffe to Jones, 15 December 1937, ibid.p.270.
24. Stern, *Haunted Prophet* p.226.
25. CGJS p.344.
26. Stern, op.cit. p.181.
27. Jung to John Barrett, 11 February 1954, *Letters*, ii.pp.150–51.
28. Jung to John Weir Perry, 8 February 1954, ibid.p.150; *Seminars*, i.p.666; ibid.p.684.
29. CW 10 p.506.
30. *New York Times*, 22 September 1912.
31. CGJS pp.222–223.
32. CGJS p.14.
33. Jung to Freud, 6 April 1910, *F-Jung* pp.304–05.
34. CGJS p.123
35. *Seminars*, i. p.243; Jung to Erich Neumann, 28 February 1952, *Letters*, ii. pp.41–43.
36. Fordham, *Contact with Jung* p.152.
37. *New York Sun*, 27 February 1931.
38. Jung to F. von Tischendorf, 19 April 1958, *Letters*, ii. pp.430–33.
39. CW 18 p.48.
40. CW 18 p.47; CW 10 p.49.
41. CW 10 pp.511–13.
42. Jung to William Matthew, 26 September 1945, *Letters*, i. pp.380–81.
43. CW 10 p.514.
44. CW 10 p.48; CW 10 pp.46, 13.
45. CW 18 p.551.
46. CW 10 p.46.
47. CW 10 pp.46–47.
48. CW 10 pp.508–10.
49. *Seminars*, 2 ii. p.1093; CW 11 p.179.
50. Jung to Robert Edmond Jones, 6 January 1931, *Letters*, i. p.81.
51. CW 10 pp.503–04.
52. CW 18 p.35; *Seminars*, i. p.706.
53. Roazen, *Freud and His Followers* p.386.

54. *Seminars*, i. p.542.
55. J.J. Clarke, *In Search of Jung* (1992).
56. *Seminars*, i. pp.542–43.
57. Fordham, *Contact with Jung* pp.166–67.
58. *Seminars*, i. p.695.
59. CW 10 p.93; *Seminars*, i. p.12.
60. Jung to Werner Kaegi, 7 November 1932, *Letters*, i. p.102; Jung to Frances Wilkes, 14 December 1956, *Letters*, ii. pp.338–39; CW 15 p.117.
61. CGJS p.221; Ellenberger, *Discovery* p.880; Jung to Heinrich Berunn, 27 August 1960, *Letters*, ii. p.586; cf. J.P. Hodin, *Modern Art and the Modern Mind* (Cleveland 1972).
62. CW 18 p.274; Jung to Walter Mertens, 24 November 1932, *Letters*, i. pp.107–08.
63. CW 15 pp.138–39
64. Michael Fordham, 'Memories and Thoughts about C.G. Jung', *Journal of Analytical Psychology* 20 (1975) p.109; Jung to Herbert Read, 2 September 1960, *Letters*, ii. pp.589–91.
65. M.L. Franz, *C.G Jung: his Myth in Our Time* (1975) p.84; Aniela Jaffé, *From the Life and Work*, op.cit. p.116.
66. CW 17 pp.115–116; *Seminars*, i. p.74.
67. CGJS p.249.
68. Jung to Serge Moreux, 20 January 1950, *Letters*, i. p.542; CGJS p.274; Alan Watts, *In My Own Way* (NY 1972) p.394; CW 15 p.88; cf. James Kirsch, 'The Enigma of Moby Dick', *Journal of Analytical Psychology* 3 (1958) pp.131–48.
69. Jung to Zwi Werblowsky, 21 May 1953, *Letters*, ii. pp.116–117; Jung to Ellen Gregori, 3 August 1957, ibid. ii. p.382; CW 15 pp.87–88.
70. Robert S. Steele & Susan V. Swinney, 'Zane Grey, Carl Jung and the Journey of the Hero', *Journal of Analytical Psychology* 23 (1978) pp.63–89; cf. F. Gruber, *Zane Grey* (NY 1970).
71. CGJS pp.82–83; Michael Shepherd, *Sherlock Holmes and the Case of Dr Freud* (1985).
72. Jaffé, *From the Life and Work*, op.cit. p.131; M–L. Von Franz, 'The Library of C.G. Jung', *Spring* (1970) pp.190–95.
73. CW 15 p.104.
74. CW 15 p.102.
75. CW 15 p.103.

21: THE LURE OF THE ORIENT

1. Jung to Erich Neumann, 4 April 1938, *Letters*, i. p.243.
2. Miguel Serrano, *Jung and Hesse* p.52.
3. Wehr, *Jung* p.309.
4. Alfred Adler, *Superiority and Social Interest* (1965) pp.72–73.
5. CW 11 p.488; Jung to A. Vetter, 25 January 1932, *Letters*, i. p.87.
6. CW 10 pp.521.
7. *Seminars*, 2, i. p.676.
8. CW 10 pp.521–22.
9. CW 10 pp.516–17.
10. Jung to Maag, 30 June 1933, *Letters*, i. pp.126–27.
11. MDR p.260.
12. Jung to Boshi Sen, 24 February 1938, *Letters*, i. pp.241–42.
13. CW 12 p.96.
14. CGJS p.406.

15. Jung to Boshi Sen, 24 February 1938, *Letters*, i. pp.241–42.
16. MDR p.257.
17. Serrano, *Jung and Hesse* pp.48–50.
18. MDR p.264.
19. CW 10 p.464.
20. Van der Post p.57.
21. CW 10 pp.525–26; MDR p.261.
22. CW 10 p.22.
23. Jung to Georg Krauskopf, 31 December 1949, *Letters*, i. p.538; MDR p.261; CW 13 p.53; CW 11 pp.576–78.
24. MDR p.196.
25. *Seminars*, 2 ii. p.1212.
26. CW 18 p.531; CW 10 p.49.
27. Jung to V. Vijayatunga, August 1957, *Letters*, ii. pp.385–86.
28. Jung to Bernard Aschner, 28 March 1951, *Letters*, ii. pp.14–15.
29. *Seminars*, 2 ii. p.1276.
30. MDR p.257; MDR p.293; CW 11 p.493; Jung to Rev.W.P. Witcutt, 24 August 1960, *Letters*, ii. p.582.
31. Jung to Mr N (anon), 25 October 1935; Jung to Kendig Cully, 25 September 1937, *Letters*, i. pp.200–201, 237.
32. CW 10 p.527; Serrano, *Jung and Hesse* p.50.
33. MDR pp.258–59.
34. CW 10 p.528.
35. CW 9 i. p.506; CW 11 p.484.
36. Alan Watts, *Psychotherapy East and West* (1973) p.94; cf. Kaufman pp.399–402.
37. CW 10 p.528.
38. Jung to Adolf Keller, August 1956, *Letters*, ii. p.322.
39. Jung to Karl Kotscham, 16 May 1958, ibid. ii. p.438.
40. CW 15 p.58.
41. Jung to Subrahamanya Iyer, 9 January 1939, *Letters*, i. pp.254–55.
42. Jung to Dr S, 1 April 1948, ibid. i. p.496.
43. CW 13 p.7.
44. CW 13 p.15.
45. Jung to Frau N, 26 April 1955, *Letters*, ii. p.247.
46. Jung to Ronald Waddell, 6 December 1960, ibid. ii. p.613.
47. Jung to Pastor Jahn, 7 September 1935, *Letters*. i. p.196; CW 11 pp.537, 570–72; CW 8 p.198.
48. *Encounter*, August, October 1960, February 1961; cf. Arthur Koestler, *The Lotus and the Robot* (1960).
49. Jung to Melvin Lasky, 19 October 1960, *Letters*, ii. pp.600–603; Jung to Daisetz Suzuki, 22 September 1933, *Letters*, i. pp.127–28.
50. Jung to Oskar Schmitz, 26 May 1923, *Letters*, i. pp.39–41; Jung to Subramanya Iyer, 16 September 1937, *Letters*, i. pp.235–36; Jung to Georgette Boner, 17 March 1947, *Letters*, i. p.451.
51. Jung to Gualthernus Mees, 15 September 1947, *Letters*, i. pp.477–78.
52. CW 9 i. p.113.
53. CW 9 i. pp.114–115; Jung to William Hamilton Smith, 26 January 1953, *Letters*, ii. p. 103.
54. Jung to Frau N, 30 May 1960, ibid. ii. p. 561.
55. MDR p.284.
56. CW 18 pp.287–88; CW 11 p.480; CW 14 p.109; Jung to Walter Robert Corti, 30 April 1929, *Letters*, i. pp.64–66.
57. CW 18 p.733.
58. MDR p.320.
59. CW 14 p.548.
60. CW 12 p.8.
61. Jung to Kurt Plachte, 10

January 1929, *Letters*, i. pp.59–62.
62. Jung to Mr N, 20 October 1954, *Letters*, ii. pp.183–84.
63. Jung to Pastor Walter Bernet, 13 June 1955; Jung to Pastor Amstutz, 23 May 1955, ibid. ii. pp.257–64, 254–55.
64. CW 11 pp.468, 190; Jung to Pastor Niederer, 1 October 1953, *Letters*, ii. pp.129–30.
65. CW 18 p.736.
66. CW 10 pp.214–15.
67. Jung to Gerhard Frei, 13 January 1948, *Letters*, i. p.487; Jung to Pastor Walter Bernet, 13 June 1955, *Letters*, ii. pp.257–64.
68. Martin Buber, *Eclipse of God: Studies in the Relationship between Religion and Philosophy* (NY 1952) pp.83–84; Buber, *I and Thou* (NY 1958) p.79.
69. CW 18 p.667; Ferne Jensen, ed., *C.G. Jung, Emma Jung and Toni Wolff*, op.cit. p.120.
70. Marilyn Nagy, *Philosophical Issues in the Psychology of C.G. Jung* (NY 1991) p.92.
71. CW 14 p.541; CW 14 p.551.
72. *Seminars,* i. 521; *Seminars*, i. p.531.
73. Jung to W.E. Hocking, 5 May 1939, *Letters*, i. pp.269–70.
74. *Seminars*, 2 ii. p.1351.
75. Jung to Walter Uhsadel, 18 August 1936, *Letters*, i. pp.216–17.
76. *Seminars*, 2 i. p.98.
77. Jung to Dorothée Hoch, 3 July 1952, *Letters*, ii. pp.74–76.
78. CW 11 p.22; Jung to Adolf Keller, 20 March 1951, *Letters*, ii. pp.9–10.
79. Jung to Maag, 12 June 1933, *Letters*, i. pp.124–25.
80. CW 11 p.465; Jung to Paul Métraux, 23 May 1945, *Letters* i. p.368.
81. Jung to Pastor Jakob Amstutz, 28 March 1953, *Letters*, ii. p.112.
82. *Seminars*, i. p.516; Van der Post p.54.
83. Jung to Pastor H. Wregmann, 19 December 1943, *Letters*, i. pp. 339–40.
84. Jung to Dr H,17 March 1951, *Letters*, ii. pp.6–9.
85. *Seminars*, 2 ii. p.1024.
86. CW 18 p.267–71.
87. Jung to Jolande Jacobi, 24 June 1935, *Letters*, i. p.191.
88. CW 11 p.22.
89. *Seminars*, i. p.22; CW 18 p.371.
90. Jung to Josef Rudin, 14 March 1953, *Letters*, ii. p.110.
91. CW 18 pp.645–47.
92. Jung to H. Oberhaunsli, 16 December 1933, *Letters*, i. pp.133–34.

22: FREUD: FINAL ACCOUNTS

1. Hannah, *Jung* pp.255–56.
2. Jung to Edwin Schmid, 18 April 1938, *Letters*, i.p.244.
3. Robert McCully, 'Remarks on the last contact between Freud and Jung', *Quadrant* 20 (1987) pp.73–74.
4. Martin Freud, *Glory Reflected.* op.cit. p.217.
5. Jung to George Charles Montagu, 10 August 1960, *Letters*, ii.pp.579–80.
6. Michael Fordham, 'Memories and Thoughts and C.G.Jung', *Journal of Analytical Psychology* 20 (1975) p.103.

7. Van der Post p.148.
8. Michael Molnar, ed. *Freud Diary 1929–39* (1992) p.245.
9. Roy Grinker, 'Reminiscences of a Personal Contact with Freud', *American Journal of Orthopsychiatry* 10 (1940) p.852.
10. SE 23 esp. pp.85–90.
11. SE 22 pp.43, 47, 54; SE 6 pp.260–61; SE 18 p.181.
12. Jones, *Freud*, ii.pp.21,184; SE 6 pp.260–61.
13. SE 23 p.300.
14. SE 18 p.165.
15. SE 6 p.257.
16. SE 6. pp.260–61; SE 17 p.243.
17. Hannah, *Jung* p.258.
18. Fordham, *Contact with Jung* p.71.
19. Hannah, *Jung* pp.259–60.
20. CW 15 p.48.
21. Roazen, *Freud and his Followers* p.19; Freud to Jones, 22 October 1927, *F-Jones* p.635.
22. Homans, *Jung in Context* p.168.
23. CW 15 pp.41–47.
24. CW 9 i.p.277; CW 15 p.41.
25. Jung to Christian Jenssen, 29 May 1933, *Letters*, i.pp.121–22.
26. CW 18 p.126; MDR p.162.
27. Jung to Ernst Hanhart, 18 February 1957, *Letters*, ii.pp.346–48.
28. MDR p.149; Ellenberger, *Discovery* p.462.
29. CW 15 p.34.
30. Jung to Robert Loeb, 26 August 1941, *Letters*, i.pp.301–02.
31. *F-Ferenczi* p.314.
32. Jung to Ernst Hauhart, 18 February 1957, *Letters*, ii.pp.346–48.
33. Jung to Allen Gilbert, 4 March 1930, *Letters*, i.p.73.
34. CW 10 p.165. Jung to Zuri Werblowsky, 28 March 1951, *Letters*, ii.pp.15–17.
35. CW 11 p.481. CW 7 p.28; CW 10 p.170; CW 16 p.35; CW 11 p.516. CW 10 p.172.
36. CW 13 p.302; MDR p.149.
37. CW 11 pp.515–16.
38. CW 10 p.163.
39. CW 13 p.345; CW 10 p.170; CW 10 p.161.
40. CW 10 p.171; CW 10 p.162.
41. Jung to John Weir Perry, 8 February 1954, *Letters*, ii. pp.148–50.
42. CW 10 p.167.
43. CW 3 p.187; CW 7 pp.45, 118, 290; CW 11 pp.330, 333; CW 4 p.335; CW 10 p.161; CW 6 pp.60–62; Jung to Dr S, 16 October 1930, *Letters*, i. pp.77–78; CW 16 pp.178–9.
44. CW 16 p.20; Fordham, *Contact with Jung* p.174.
45. CGJS p.280; CW 7 p.54.
46. CW 16 p.66; MDR pp.150–51; CW 16 p.152.
47. Hermann Lauscher, ed. *Gesammelte Werke* (Frankfurt 1970) p.432.
48. Jung to Hesse, 18 September 1934, *Letters*, i. pp.171–74; Jung to Emanuel Meier, 24 March 1950, *Letters*, i. p.552.
49. Theodore Ziolkowski, ed., *My Belief. Essays on Life and Art by Herman Hesse* (1974) pp.359–60.
50. Jung to Benjamin Nelson, 19 June 1960, *Letters*, ii. pp.307–09.
51. Franz Alexander, Samuel Eisenstein & Martin Grotjahan, eds, *Psychoanalytic Pioneers* (1966) p.226.
52. Jung to Dr N, 5 February 1934, *Letters*, i. pp.142–43.
53. Jung to Wilhelm Bitter, 12 July 1958, *Letters*, ii. pp.457–58.
54. Jung to Max Frischknecht, 8 February 1946, *Letters*, i. pp.408–12.

55. SE 12 p.207.
56. MDR p.162; Jung to Smith Ely Jelliffe, 24 February 1936, *Letters*, i. pp. 210–11.
57. SE 13 p.146; CW 11 p.338; CW 9 i. p.61.
58. SE 12 p.91–96, 99–108, 111–120, 147–56.
59. CW 16 p.164.
60. CW 7 p.131.
61. CW 7 pp.129–34; CW 18 p.155.
62. CW 18 pp.138–39.
63. Erik Erikson, *Life History and the Historical Moment* (NY 1975) p.105.
64. CW 18 p.151.
65. SE 11 pp.141–52.
66. CW 18 pp.140–43, 149–53.
67. CW 18 p.143.
68. CW 18 p.141; CW 16 p.175.
69. CW 16 pp.230–34.
70. CW 16 p.234.
71. CW 16 p.185–86.
72. CW 18 p.161.
73. Michael Fordham, *Jungian Psychotherapy* (NY 1978); Mario Jacoby, *The Analytic Encounter: Transference and Human Relationship* (Toronto 1984).
74. Stevens, *On Jung* p.235.
75. CW 12 p.232.
76. CW 18 pp.284–85.
77. CW 14 pp.518–19, 526.
78. CW 16 p.207; CW 12 p.244.
79. CW 16 pp.171–72.
80. CW 16 p.18.
81. CW 16 p.222.
82. CW 16 pp.262–63, 218–19.
83. CW 14 p.528.
84. CW 18 p.159.
85. CW 12 pp.228–30.
86. CW 12 pp.360–70.
87. CW 12 pp.35–36.
88. Wilson, *Lord of the Underworld* pp.105–06.
89. Demaris Wehr, *Jung and Feminism* pp.70–71.
90. SE 11 pp.221–27.
91. SE 12 p.116; CW 4 pp.198–99.
92. SE 19 pp.274–75; SE 21 pp.247–48.
93. CW 11 p.351.
94. Jung to Hans Conrad Banzinger, 26 November 1934, *Letters*, i. pp.178–80.
95. Jung to Hans Illing, 26 January 1955, *Letters*, ii. pp.218–221; Erich Fromn, *Gesamtausgabe* 8 pp.130,411.
96. Charles Rycroft, *A Critical Dictionary of Psychoanalysis* (1972) p. ix; P. Rieff, *The Triumph of the Therapeutic. Uses of Faith after Freud* (1973) p.98.
97. P. Ricoeur, *Freud and Philosophy*, op.cit. p.176.
98. Samuels, *Jung and the Post-Jungians* pp.123–28; Corbett L. Kugler, 'The Self in Jung and Kohut', in A. Golberg, ed. *Progress in Self Psychology* (1989).
99. Erik Erikson, *Identity: Youth and Crisis* (NY 1968) pp.58, 223; Erikson, *Identity and the Life Cycle* (NY 1959) p.372; cf. Paul Roazen, *Erik Erikson. The Power and Limits of a Vision* (1976) p.154.
100. Erikson, *Identity and the Life Cycle* pp.59, 129; Roazen, *Erik Erikson* p.190.
101. CGJS p.269; Jung to Edith Schroder, April 1957, *Letters*, ii. pp.358–59.

23: WARTIME

1. CGJS p.134.
2. CW 11 p.482–83; CW 12 p. 481; *Seminars*, 2 ii. pp.1275–76.
3. *Seminars*, 2 i. p.554; Jung to X, 16 February 1939, *Journal of Analytical Psychology* 39 (1992) pp. 149–51; CW 18 pp.604–05.
4. CW 18 p. 578; CW 18 p.605.
5. Carl Zuckmayer, *A Part of Myself* (NY 1970); CGJS p.132.
6. MDR p.201.
7. Jung to Erich Neumann, 20 January 1939, *Letters*, i. pp.258–59.
8. Paul Mellon, *Reflections in a Silver Spoon*. op.cit. pp.161–63.
9. ibid. pp.158, 164.
10. Hannah, *Jung* p.262.
11. ibid. p.265.
12. CGJS pp.180–82.
13. Jay Sherry, 'Jung, the Jews and Hitler', *Spring* (1986) pp.163–75 (esp. pp.171–73).
14. *Seminars*, 2 i. p.586. cf. Philippe Marguerat, *La Suisse face au IIIeme Reich. Réduit national et dissuasion économique 1940–1945* (Lausanne 1991); Willi Gautschi, *General Henri Guisan. Die Schweizerische Armeeführung im zweiten weltkrieg* (Zurich 1989).
15. Jung to Ed Lauchenauer, 16 January 1940, *Letters*, i. p.282.
16. Jung to Esther Harding, 28 September 1939, ibid. i. p.276.
17. Aniela Jaffé, 'Details about C.G. Jung's Family', *Spring* (1983) pp.35–43.
18. Jung to Esther Harding, 28 September 1939, *Letters*, i. p.276; CW 18 pp.596–97.
19. Urs Schwarz, *The Eye of the Hurricane. Switzerland in World War Two* (Boulder, Colorado, 1980) p.10; cf. Edgar Bonjour, *Geshichte der Schweizerischen neutralität vier jahrunderte eidgenössicher aussenpolitik*, 6 vols (Basel 1970); Georg Kreis, *Auf den sruren von la charite. Die Schweizerische armeeführung um spannungsfeld des Deutsch–Französischen gegensatzes 1936–1941* (Basel 1976).
20. Jung to J.H. van der Hoop, 14 January 1946, *Letters*, i. pp.404–06.
21. Jung to Mrs N, 5 October 1939, ibid. i. pp.277–78.
22. ibid.
23. Maggy Anthony, *The Valkyries*, op.cit. p.88.
24. Mary Bancroft, *Autobiography of a Spy* (NY 1983).
25. Joseph Garlinski, *The Swiss Corridor* (1989); Mary Bancroft, 'Jung and his Circle', *Psychological Perspectives* 6 (1975) p.123.
26. Peter Grose, *Gentleman Spy. The Life of Allen Dulles* (1995) pp.164–65.
27. Jung to Gottlieb Duttweiler, 4 December 1939, *Letters*. i. pp.279–80.
28. *Neue Zürcher Zeitung*, 21 December 1939.
29. Schwarz, *The Eye of the Hurricane*, op.cit. pp.69–71; Markus Heininger, *Dreizehn gründe warum die Schweiz im zweiten weltkrieg nicht erobert wurde* (Zürich 1989).
30. Mellon, *Reflections*, op.cit. pp.166–70.
31. Rudolph Peierls, *Birds of Passage* (Princeton 1985) pp.48–49.

32. Emilio Segne, *From X-Rays to Quarks* (NY 1980) p.155; Victor Weisskopf, *The Joy of Insight* (NY 1991) p.85; Thomas Powers, *Heisenberg's War* (1993) pp.184–85.
33. Jung to Henriette Goodrich, 20 May 1940, *Letters*, i. p.282.
34. *Neue Zürcher Zeitung*, 29 June 1940; cf. Erwin Bucher, *Zwischen bundesbrat und general. Schweizer politik und armee in zweiten weltkrieg* (St Gallen 1991).
35. Henri Guisan, *Bericht an die Bundesversammlung über den Aktivdienst 1939–1945* (Berne 1946) p.33.
36. ibid. p.37.
37. C. Oser, *Histoire de la neutralité Suisse* (Neuchatel 1970).
38. Scharwz, *The Eye of the Hurricane*, op.cit. p.62; Klaus Urner, *'Die Schweiz muss noch geschluckt werden!' Hitlers aktionsplane gegen die Schweiz* (Zürich 1990).
39. Dean Acheson, *Present at the Creation. My Years in the State Department* (NY 1969) p.48.
40. Schwarz, op.cit. pp.32–34; Oswald Ingglin, *Die stille krieg. Der wirt schaftskrieg zwischen Grossbritannien und der Schweiz im zweiten weltkrieg* (Zürich 1991); Peter Kamber, *Schlesse auf die befreier. Die ilufguerilla der Schweiz gegen die Allierten 1943–1945* (Zürich 1993).
41. Jung to P.W. Martin, 20 August 1945, *Letters*, i. p.377; Jung to H.G. Baynes, 12 August 1940, ibid. i. pp.288–89; Jung to H.G. Baynes, 9 December 1940, ibid. i. pp.289–90.
42. CW 18 pp.582–86.
43. Jung to Mary Mellon, 18 April 1941, *Letters*, i. pp.297–98.
44. Jung to H.G. Baynes, 27 May 1941, ibid. i. pp.299–300.
45. Jung to Robert Loeb, 26 August 1941, ibid. i. pp.301–02.
46. Jung to Olga Koenig-Fachsenfeld, 5 May 1941, ibid. i. p.299; Jung to Elined Kotschnig, 18 February 1941, ibid. i. pp.294–95.
47. CW 16 p.103.
48. Kerr, *Dangerous Method* p.478.
49. Jung to Fritz Kunkel, 10 July 1946, ibid. i. pp.430–33.
50. Aniela Jaffé, *Word and Image*, op. cit. p.112.
51. Bernard Barbey, *P.C. du Général: Journal du chef de l'état major particulier du Général Guisan 1940–1945* (Neuchâtel 1948) p.128.
52. Jung to J.B. Rhine, 5 November 1942; Jung to Wellman Schmiel, 5 November 1942; June to Frausirka Baumgarten-Tramer, *Letters*, i. pp.321–23.
53. Jung to Mary Mellon, 24 September 1945, ibid. i. p.363.
54. Jung to Karl Kerenyi, 10 March 1941, ibid. i. pp.295–96.
55. Stern, *Haunted Prophet* pp.174, 234–36.
56. Jung to Alice Crowley, 20 July 1942, *Letters*, i. p.319.
57. CGJS p.183.
58. Philip Wolff-Windegg, 'C.G. Jung – Bachofen, Burkhardt and Basel', *Spring* (1976) pp.137–47 (at p.147).
59. Jung to Arnold Kunzli, 4 February 1943, *Letters*, i. pp.328–29.
60. Jung to Joseph Rychlak, 27 April 1959, *Letters*, ii. pp.500–502; Jung to Arnold Kunzli, 13 February 1943, *Letters*, i. p.330.
61. Stern, op. cit. p.235.

62. Jung to Arnold Kunzli, 28 February 1943, *Letters*, i. pp.331–332; Kaufmann p.290.
63. Ott, *Heidegger*, op. cit.
64. SE 19 p.57.
65. *Seminars*, 2 i. p.582.
66. Jung to Rudolph Pannwitz, 27 March 1937, *Letters*, i. pp.231–32; Jung to Arnold Kunzli, 16 March 1943, *Letters*, i. pp.333–34; Jung to Mitchel Bedord, 31 December 1952, *Letters*, ii. p.102; Jung to Willi Brerni, 26 December 1953, *Letters*, ii. p.145.
67. Marie-Louise Franz, *Jung and the Myth of Our Time* p.64; Jon Kimche, *Spying for Peace; General Guisan and Swiss Neutrality* (1960); Pierre Braunschweig, *Geheimer draht nach Berlin. Die nachrichenlinie Masson Schellenberg und ser Schweizerische nachrichtendienst im zweiten weltkrieg* (Zürich 1991); Hans Rudolf Kurz, *Nachrichenzentrum Schweiz. Die Schweiz im nachrichtendienst des zweiten weltrieges* (Frauenfeld 1972).
68. Jung to Kerenyi, 2 May 1943, *Letters*, i. p.334; Stern, op. cit p.233.
69. R. Harris Smith, *OSS. The Secret History of America's First Central Intelligence Agency* (1972) p.204; Stanley Lovell, *Of Spies and Stratagems* (NY 1963) p.127; Thomas Powers, *Heisenberg's War* (1993) pp.381–405.
70. Louis Kaufman, *Moe Berg. Athlete, Scholar, Spy* (1974) pp.193–95; Jung to Allen Dulles, 1 February 1945, *Letters*, i. pp.356–57.
71. Maggy Anthony, *The Valkyries* p.88; Christopher Andrew & Oleg Gordievsky, *KGB. The inside story of its foreign operations from Lenin to Gorbachev* (1990) p.224–25.
72. Mary Bancroft, 'Jung and his Circle', loc. cit. pp.122–25.
73. Schwarz, *The Eye of the Hurricane* pp.34–36; Winston Churchill, *The Second World War* (1954), vi. p.616.
74. Jung to Markus Fierz, 12 January 1949, *Letters* i. p.518.
75. MDR pp.270–71.
76. Jung to Kristine Mann, 11 February 1945, *Letters*, i. pp.356–57.
77. Brome, *Jung* p.243.
78. MDR p.272.
79. MDR p.273.
80. Hannah, *Jung* pp.278–83.
81. MDR p.275.
82. Hannah, *Jung* p.284.
83. Aniela Jaffé, 'The Creative Phases in Jung's Life,' *Spring* loc. cit.

24: THE THEOLOGIAN

1. Jung to Albert Oeri, 7 May 1945, *Letters*, i. pp.367–68. Jung to Anon, 7 October 1946, ibid. pp.443–45.
2. CW 10 p.239.
3. CW 10 pp.239–41.
4. CGJS pp.149, 236.
5. Jung to Hermann Ullmann, 25 May 1945, *Letters*, i. pp.369–70; CW 10 pp.195–97.
6. CW 10 p.238.
7. Jung to Emma von Pelet, 15

January 1944, *Letters*, i. pp.341–42.

8. Jung to Horst Scharschuch, 1 September 1952, *Letters*, ii. pp.81–83.
9. Jung to Allen Dulles, 1 February 1945, *Letters*, i. pp.356–57.
10. Jung to Eugene Henley, 20 April 1946, ibid. i. pp.424–25; Jung to P.W. Martin, 20 August 1945; Jung to Hermann Keyserling, 10 December 1945; Jung to J.H. van der Hoop, 14 January 1946; Jung to Fritz Blanke, 2 May 1945, ibid. i. pp.377, 401, 404–06, 363–65.
11. Jung to Eugene Henley, 20 April 1946, ibid. i. p.424–25.
12. Jung to J.H. van der Hoop, 14 January 1946, ibid. i. pp.404–06.
13. Jung to Victor White, 13 February 1946, ibid. i. pp.412–14.
14. Jung to N, 6 July 1946, ibid. i. p.428.
15. Jung to Anon, 10 July 1946, ibid. i. p.434; Jung to Mrs N, 19 November 1955, *Letters*, ii. pp.278–79; Jung to Eleanor Bertine, 25 July 1946, *Letters*, i. pp.436–37; Paul Mellon, *Reflections in a Silver Spoon* (1992) pp.170–73, 221–22, 342–45.
16. Stern, *Haunted Prophet* pp.248–49.
17. Hannah, *Jung* p.296.
18. Vincent Brome, *J.B. Priestley* (1988) pp.182–84, 288, 308, 340, 415, 430; Jung to J.B. Priestley, 9 August 1946, *Letters*, i. p.440. Jung to J.B.Priestley, 17 July 1946, ibid. i. p.435.
19. Martin Gilbert, *Never Despair* (1988) pp.260–67.
20. Jung to Ernest Anderes, 22 September 1946; Jung to Victor White, 6 November 1946; Jung to Jolande Jacobi, *Letters*, i. pp.442–43, 448–49.
21. Jung to Victor White, 18 December 1945, *Letters*, i. p.450.
22. Jung to Frau N, 11 July 1944, ibid. i. p.343.
23. Jung to Jakob Stahel, 17 March 1947; Jung to Victor White, 27 March 1947, ibid. i. pp.451–53.
24. Jung to Eleanor Bertine, 17 April 1947, ibid. i. pp.454–55.
25. CGJS p.169; CGJS pp.185–86.
26. Aniela Jaffé, 'C.G. Jung and the Eranos Conferences', *Spring* (1977) pp.201–12 (at p.206); Jung to Alvine von Keller, 25 January 1949, *Letters*, ii. p.513.
27. Jung to Mrs N, 31 August 1945, *Letters*, i. pp.377–78.
28. Jung to Wilhelm Bitter, 23 August 1959, *Letters*, ii. p.513.
29. Jung to Fritz Versaz, 31 October 1946, *Letters*, i. pp.446–48.
30. Jung to Dorothy Thompson, 23 September 1949, *Letters*, i. pp.534–37.
31. CW 9. i. p.253; CW 10 pp.298–99; Jung to Victor White, 10 April 1954, *Letters*, ii. pp.163–74.
32. CW 8 p.222.
33. Marie-Louise von Franz, *Jung and his Myth*, op. cit. p.265.
34. Jung to Henry Murray, 2 July 1948, *Letters*, i. pp.503–05; Jung to Dorothy Thompson, 23 September 1949, ibid. i. pp.534–37.
35. Jung to Henry Murray, 2 July 1948, ibid. i. pp.503–05.
36. I. Progoff, *Synchronicity and Human Destiny* (1973) pp.151–52.
37. CW 10 p.537; cf. Jim Garrison, *The Darkness of God; Theology after Hiroshima* (1982).

38. Jung to Dorothy Hoch, 23 September 1952, *Letters*, ii. pp.83–86; Jung to Willi Bremi, 11 December 1953, ibid. ii. pp.140–43.
39. Kathleen Raine, *The Human Face of God: William Blake and the Book of Job* (1982).
40. CW 15 p.97; Jung to Piloo Nawavutty, 11 November 1948, *Letters*, i. pp.512–14; Jung to Esther Harding, 8 July 1947, ibid. i. pp.468–69.
41. Jung to Dr S, 5 December 1951, *Letters*, ii. p.30.
42. CGJS p.195; Jung to Dorothy Thompson, 23 September 1949, *Letters*, i. pp.534–37.
43. *Saturday Review of Literature*, 11, 18 June 1949.
44. CGJS p.146.
45. MDR p.196.
46. MDR p.210.
47. Jung to Herbert Bowman. 18 June 1958, *Letters*, ii. pp.453–54.
48. CW 14 p.xviii.
49. CW 16 pp.216–17.
50. CW 16 pp.222–227.
51. CW 14 pp.463–64.
52. Jung to Fritz Blanke, 2 May 1945, *Letters*, i. pp.363–65.
53. Jung to Willi Bremi, 11 December 1953, *Letters*, ii. pp.140–43; CW 13 p.301.
54. Jung to Rudolf Bernoulli, 5 October 1944, *Letters*, i. p.351.
55. CW 13 pp.207–50.
56. MDR pp.215–16.
57. MDR p.204.
58. MDR p.209; MDR p.291.
59. CW 18 p.660–61; Jung to Fritz Blanke, 2 May 1945, 10 November 1948, *Letters* i, pp.363–65,511.
60. CW 9 ii.pp.232–65; CW 11 pp.37–38,52–53,64–67; Jung to Stephen Abrams, 2 October 1957, *Letters*, ii. pp.398–400.
61. CW 12 pp.203–04.
62. CW 11 pp.52,54,58.
63. CW 14 p.11.
64. CW 14 p.212; *Seminars*, i.p. 121. CW 14 p.505; Jung to Herbert Read, 17 October 1948, *Letters*,i.pp.509–10; Jung to Philip Wylie, 22 December 1957, *Letters*, ii. pp.404–05; MDR p.354.
65. MDR pp.311–12.
66. CW 9 ii.p.43; Jung to Herbert Bowman, 18 June 1958, *Letters*, ii. pp.453–54.
67. Jung to Willi Bremi, 11 December 1953, *Letters*, ii. pp.140–43.
68. Jung to R.F.C.Hull, 27 December 1958, ibid.ii. p.470.
69. Jung to John Trinick, 26 October 1957, ibid.ii. pp.400–401.
70. CW 12 pp.345–431.
71. CW 16 p.192.
72. MDR p.210.
73. CW 9.ii.pp.72–94.
74. CW 9 ii.p.114.
75. Jung to A.Zazine, 3 May 1939, *Letters*,i. pp.267–69.
76. MDR p.202; CW 9 ii.p.42; Jung to Bernhard Martin, 7 December 1954, *Letters*, ii. pp.197–99.
77. CW 11 p.406.
78. Jung to Pastor Wegmann, 6 December 1945, *Letters*, i. pp.395–98.
79. CW 11 p.458.
80. CW 11 p.405.
81. Jung to Erich Neumann, 5 January 1952, *Letters*, ii. pp.32–35; MDR pp.240–41.
82. MDR p.312.
83. CW 11 pp.455–56.
84. Jung to Morton T. Kelsey, 27 December 1958, *Letters*, ii. p.471–73.

85. CW 10 p.172.
86. Jung to Erich Neumann, 5 January 1952, *Letters*, ii.pp.32–35.
87. Jung to Victor White, 24 November 1953, ibid.ii. pp.134–38.
88. CW 11. p.432.
89. CW 11 p.429; Jung to H.G. Baynes, 22 January 1942, *Letters* p.311–12.
90. CW 11 pp.59–61; CW 12 p.26.
91. CW 11 p.175.
92. CW 11 p.170.
93. CW 18 p.715.
94. Jung to James Kirsch, 29 January 1953; Jung to Anon, 7 May 1960, *Letters*, ii. pp.104, 556–57.
95. Kaufman p.414.
96. Stern, *Haunted Prophet* p.256.
97. CW 11 pp.179, 399; CW 18 pp.717–18.
98. Jung to Morton Kelsey, 27 December 1958, *Letters*, ii. pp.471–73; CW 11 pp.432–33.
99. Brome, *Jung* p.254.
100. Kaufman pp.414, 421.
101. Nagy, *Philosophical Issues* p.146.
102. MDR p.207.
103. CW 9 ii. p.109; Jung to Hans Schar, 16 November 1951, *Letters*, ii. pp.28–29; Van der Post p.58; Neumann to Jung, 5 December 1951, ibid. ii. pp35–36; CW 11 pp.458–59.
104. CW 11 p.461.
105. CW 14 p.169; CW 18 p.731; Jung to Victor White, 24 November 1953, *Letters*, ii. pp.137–38; CW 9 i. pp.108–09.
106. CW 9 i. p.108; CW 11 p.267.
107. Jung to Victor White, 25 November 1950, *Letters*, i. pp.566–68.
108. Jung to A. Vetter, 8 April 1932, ibid. i. pp.90–91.
109. CW 13 p.96.
110. CW 18 p.712.
111. CW 18 p.713.
112. Jung to Victor White, 13 April 1946, *Letters*, i. p.419; Jung to Victor White, 25 November 1950, ibid. i. pp.566–68; F.X. Charet, 'A Dialogue between Psychology and Theology. The Correspondence of C.G. Jung and Victor White', *Journal of Analytical Psychology* 35 (1990) pp.412–441; Jung to Victor White, 30 April 1952; Jung to Simon Doniger, November 1955, *Letters*, ii. pp.58–60, 281–82; Jung to Victor White, 31 December 1949, *Letters*, i. pp.539–41; CW 11 pp.299–310; Victor White, *God and the Unconscious* (1952); cf. also White, *Soul and Psyche* (1960).
113. Jung to Victor White, 30 June 1952, 19 January 1955, *Letters*, ii. pp.71–74, 212–14; *Observer*, 9 January 1955; Charet, 'A Dialogue', loc.cit.
114. Richard Noll, *The Jung Cult. Origins of a Charismatic Movement* (Princeton 1994).

25: THE NEW AGE GURU

1. CW 8 pp.315–17.
2. CW 12 p.333.
3. Jung to L.M. Boyers, 30 September 1932, *Letters*, i. pp.99–100.
4. *Seminars* i. p.154.
5. Jung to J.H. Barrett, 12 October 1956, *Letters*, ii. pp.333–334.
6. CGJS pp.376–77; Jung to Mrs Otto Milbrand, 6 June

1958, ibid. ii. p.445.
7. Jung to J.H. Barret, 12 October 1956, *Letters*, ii. pp.333–34.
8. CW 18 p.313.
9. Jung to Edward Steiner, 5 June 1958, *Letters*, ii. p.444.
10. Jung to Esther Harding, 5 December 1951, ibid. ii. p.29.
11. Jung to Olga von Hoenig Faschsenfeld, 30 November 1960, ibid. ii. pp.611–12.
12. Jung to Fernando Cassari, 13 July 1954, ibid. ii. p.180; Jung to John Symonds, 13 October 1953, ibid. ii. p.130; CGJS p.155.
13. Jung to Mark Wyman Richardson, 14 June 1934, *Letters*, i. pp.432–33.
14. Jung to Fritz Kunkel, 10 July 1946, ibid. i. pp.432–33; Jung to E.V. Tenney, 23 February 1955, *Letters*, ii. pp.227–229.
15. CW18 pp.344–45; Jung to Melvin Lasky, September 1956, *Letters*, ii. pp.330–332.
16. Hugo Debrunner, 'Changes in the Handline of C.G. Jung', *Spring* (1974) p.193–99.
17. Jung to Baroness Tinti, 10 January 1936, *Letters*, i. pp.208–09.
18. CW 18 p.510.
19. Jung to J.B. Rhine, 9 August 1954, 18 February 1953, *Letters*, ii. pp.106–07.
20. Jung to J.B. Rhine, 22 September 1953, ibid. ii. pp.126–27.
21. Ira Progoff, *Jung, Synchronicity and Human Destiny* (NY 1973) pp.21–45; Jung to Johanna Michaels, 20 January 1939, *Letters*, i. pp.259–61.
22. Jung to W.P. Witcutt, 24 August 1960; Jung to Michael Fordham, 3 January 1957; *Letters*, ii. pp.582–83, 343–44.
23. Jung to Lucas Menz, 22 February 1955, ibid. ii. pp.225–26; CW 10 p.370.
24. CW 9 ii. pp.93–94.
25. Jung to Hans Bender, 10 April 1958, *Letters*, ii. pp.428–29.
26. Jung to B. Baur, 29 January 1934, *Letters*, i. pp.138–39.
27. *Seminars*, i. pp.424–25.
28. *Seminars*, i. p.422–23; Jung to Corti, 12 September 1929, *Letters*, i. pp.69–70; *Seminars*, 2 i. pp.375–76.
29. Jung to André Barbault, 26 May 1954, *Letters*, ii. pp.175–77.
30. Jung to L. Oswald, 8 December 1928, *Letters*, i. p.56.
31. Jung to B.V. Raman, 6 September 1947, ibid. i. pp.475–76; Van der Post p.242.
32. Jung to Robert Kroon, 15 November 1958, *Letters*, ii. pp.463–64.
33. Jung to Hans Bauden, 10 April 1958, ibid. ii. pp.428–29, C.T. Frey-Wehdin, 'Reflections on C.G. Jung's Concept of Synchronicity', *Journal of Analytical Psychology* 21 (1976) pp.37–49; M.L. Franz, *On Divination and Synchronicity: the psychology of meaningful chance* (Toronto 1980).
34. CW 8 pp.525–26.
35. CGJS pp.182–83.
36. MDR p.136.
37. Progoff, *Synchronicity and Human Destiny*, op. cit. pp.170–72.
38. CW 8 p.431.
39. MDR p.273.
40. CW 8 pp.465–67, 512; Jung to Stephen Abrams, 21 October 1957, *Letters*, ii. p.398–400.
41. Jung to Evelyn Thorne, 23 March 1955, ibid. ii. pp.233–34.
42. CW 8 p.526.
43. Jung to A.D. Cornell, 9 February 1960, *Letters*, ii.

pp.537–43; Jung to Hans Bender, 10 April 1958, ibid. ii. pp.428–29.

44. Paul Kammerer, *Das Gesetz der Serie* (Stuttgart 1919); Arthur Koestler, *The Case of the Midwife Toad* (1971).
45. CW 11 pp.589–608; CW 8 pp.485–504; Jung to Pascual Jordan, 10 November 1934, *Letters*, i. pp.176–78.
46. Jung to Pauli, 29 October 1934, *Letters*, i. pp.174–76; Jung to Vann Gillmor, 3 February 1960, *Letters*, ii. p.535.
47. CW 9 ii. pp.61–63; CW 8 p.514; Jung to J.R. Smythies, 29 February 1952, *Letters*, ii. pp.44–47.
48. Arthur Koestler, *The Roots of Coincidence* (1974) p.101; CW 8 pp.432–34; Progoff, *Synchronicity and Human Destiny*, op. cit. pp.98–106; Jung to Stephen Abrams, 20 June 1957, *Letters*, ii. pp.373–74; CW 8 pp.459–84.
49. CW 18 p.497; Jung to Hans Bender, 6 March 1958, *Letters*, ii. pp.420–21.
50. CW 8 pp.528–30; Jung to André Barbault, 26 May 1954; Jung to Hans Bender, 12 February 1958, *Letters*, ii. pp.175–77, 415–16; CW 8 pp.441, 511; MDR p.356; CW 8 p.518; CW 8 p.441.
51. CW 8 p.445.
52. Koestler, *Roots of Coincidence* op.cit. p.95.
53. Jung to Hans Bender, 12 February 1958, *Letters*, ii. pp.415–16; CW 18 p.499; Jung to Edward Whitmont, 4 March 1950, *Letters*, i. pp.546–48.
54. Jung to A.D. Cornell, 9 February 1960, *Letters*, ii. pp.537–43.
55. CW 8 p.446; Jung to Hans Bender, 12 February 1958, *Letters*, ii. pp.415–16.
56. Jung to L. Kling, 14 January 1958, ibid. ii. pp.409–10.
57. Jung to P. Bachler, 8 March 1948, *Letters*, i. pp.493–94.
58. Jung to Philip Wylie, 27 June 1947, *Letters*, ii. pp. xxxviii–xxxiv; Jung to Gerhard Adler, 3 June 1958, *Letters*, i. pp.443–444; Miguel Serrano, *Jung and Hesse* pp.100–101.
59. *Seminars*, i. pp.574–82; Serrano, *Jung and Hesse* p.59.
60. Jung to Roger Lais, 11 February 1961, *Letters*, ii. p.626.
61. Serrano, *Jung and Hesse* p.102.
62. Jung to Miguel Serrano, 14 September 1960, *Letters*, ii. pp.592–97.
63. Jung to Fowler McCormick, 22 February 1951, ibid. ii. p.6.
64. Jung to Beatrice Hinkle, 6 February 1951, ibid. ii. pp.3–4; MDR p.298; Harold G. Coward, 'Jung's Encounter with Yoga', *Journal of Analytical Psychology* 23 (1978) pp.339–357.
65. Jung to Dr H.A.F. 16 January 1959, *Letters*, ii. pp.476–77.
66. CW 10 pp.309–10.
67. CW 10 p.314.
68. Jung to J.E. Schulte, 24 May 1958, *Letters*, ii. p.443; CW 10 p.320.
69. CW 10 p.406.
70. CW 10 pp.344–45; CW 10 p.350; CW 10 pp.409, 366; CW 18 pp.626–27; Jung to James Kirsch, 29 April 1958, *Letters*, ii. p.433.
71. CW 10 p.414; CW 18 pp.630–31; CW 10 p.383.
72. CW 10 pp.390–99; CW 10 pp.367–68, 376–80
73. CW 10 pp.413, 417.

74. CW 10 p.417.
75. CW 10 pp.352–60, 415–17.
76. CW 18 p.627.
77. Jung to Anon, 2 January 1958, *Letters*, ii. p.407; CW 10 pp.426–31; Jung to Aniela Jaffé, 4 January 1958, *Letters*, ii. p.408; Jung to K.W. Bash, 12 December 1958, ibid. ii. p.468. Jung to Charles Harnett, 12 December 1957, ibid. ii. p.403. Jung to Walter Schaffner, 16 February 1961, ibid. ii. pp.627–28.
78. CGJS p.395.
79. C.A. Meier 'Psychosomatic Medicine from the Jungian point of view', *Journal of Analytical Psychology* 8 (1963) pp.103–21.
80. Jung to Gerhard Frei, 17 January 1949, *Letters*, i. p.522; Jung to Paul Campbell, 19 December 1952, *Letters*, ii. pp.100–101.
81. Jung to Dr N, 27 October 1941, *Letters*, i. pp.306–07; Jung to M.R. Brabard-Isaac, 22 July 1939, ibid. i. pp.274–75; Jung to Calvin Hall, 6 October 1954, *Letters*, ii. pp.184–87.

26: LAST YEARS

1. Jung to Victor White, 31 December 1949, *Letters*, i. pp.539–41.
2. Jung to Victor White, Spring 1952, *Letters*, ii. pp.50–51; Jung to James Kirsch, 18 November 1952, ibid. ii. pp.91–92; Jung to Aniela Jaffé, 16 September 1953, ibid. ii. pp.125–26.
3. Jaffé, *From the Life and Work* p.129.
4. Stern, *Haunted Prophet* pp.239, 242–44.
5. Jung to Ignaz Tauber, 23 January, 4 February, 13 March 1953, *Letters*, ii. p.103, 105, 109–10.
6. Jung to Herbert Read, 17 October 1948, *Letters*, i. pp.509–10; Jung to J.B. Priestley, 8 November 1954, *Letters*, ii. pp.192–93; *New Statesman*, 30 October 1954; *Times Literary Supplement*, 6 August 1954.
7. Upton Sinclair, *The Autobiography of Upton Sinclair* (1963).
8. *The New Republic*, 27 April 1953.
9. Jung to Upton Sinclair, 24 November 1952, *Letters*, ii. p.94–97; *The New Republic*, 21 February 1955; *Time*, 7 March 1955; Jung to Upton Sinclair. *Letters*, ii. pp.230–32.
10. Jung to Mitchel Bedford, 31 December 1952; Jung to Fritz Meerwein, July 1955; Jung to Hugo Charteris, 9 January 1960, *Letters*, ii pp.102, 269–70, 531–32.
11. Jung to Horst Scharschurch, 1 September 1952; Jung to Noel Pierre, 3 December 1952, ibid. ii. pp.81–83, 98; cf.Ernst Robert Curtius, *Critical essays on European Literature* (Princeton 1973).
12. Jung to Fraud Oswald, 1 November 1954; Jung to René Kipfer, 21 October 1960, *Letters*, ii pp.193–94, 604–05; CW 18 p.779.
13. Jung to Martin Elsasser, 28

January 1937, *Letters*, i. pp.225–226; Jung to Ellen Gregori, 3 August 1957, *Letters*, ii. p.382.
14. *Neue Zürcher Zeitung*, 2 June 1963; CGJS pp.201–04; Jung to Heinz Westmann, 12 July 1947, *Letters*, i. p.472.
15. CW 10 pp.263–68, 298–99; Jung to Evelyn Böhler, 8 January 1956, *Letters*, ii. pp.284–86.
16. CW 18 p.614.
17. Jung to Leo Holliday, 6 November 1960, *Letters*, ii. pp.608–09.
18. CW 9 ii. p.233.
19. Jung to Max Imboden, 30 January 1958, *Letters*, ii. pp.411–13.
20. Von Franz, *Jung and his Myth in Our Time*, op. cit. p.268.
21. CW 18 p.612; Jung to Fritz Pfaflin, 22 March 1951, *Letters*, ii. pp.11–12.
22. Jung to Frau van Schrarendijk-Berlage, 11 February 1953, ibid. ii. p.105.
23. CW 18 p.636; CW 10 p.290; Jung to Jolande Jacobi, 6 November 1956, *Letters*, ii. p.336.
24. CW 10 p.262.
25. Jung to Anon, 10 October 1956, *Letters*, ii p.353.
26. Jung to Jean Vontobel-Ruosch, 28 April 1959, *Letters*, ii. pp.502–03.
27. CW 7 p.261.
28. Jung to Wilhelm Bitten, 7 December 1960, Letters, ii. p.614–15.
29. Jung to E.Roenne-Peterson, 16 March 1953, ibid. ii. p.111.
30. Jung to Claire Schenter, 10 January 1959, *Letters*, ii. pp.475–76.
31. Jung to Verena Ballmer-Suter, 24 January 1959, ibid. ii. pp.477–78.
32. CW 18 p.132–33, Maggy Anthony, *The Valkyries* p.17; Jean Piaget, *Play, Dreams and Imitation in Childhood* (NY 1962) p.212; Jung to P.F.Jenny, 1 July 1954, *Letters*, ii. p.178.
33. CGJS p.249.
34. Jung to Karl Oftinger, September 1957, *Letters*, ii. pp.388–91.
35. CGJS p.249; Jung to Karl Oftinger, September 1957, *Letters*, ii. pp.388–91.
36. Jung to Victor White, 10 April 1954, ibid. ii. pp.163–74.
37. Michael Fordham, 'Memories and Thoughts about C.G. Jung', *Journal of Analytical Psychology* 20 (1975) p.113.
38. Jung to Benhard Martin, 7 December 1954; Jung to B.A. Snowdon, 7 May 1955; Jung to Pastor Amstutz, 23 May 1955; Jung to William Lachat, 29 June 1955; Jung to Robert Smith, 29 July 1960, ibid. ii. pp.197–99, 252–55, 267–68, 271–72, 570–73.
39. Jung to Pastor Tanner, 12 February 1959; Jung to Gunter Wittwer, 10 October 1959, ibid. ii. pp.482–83, 517; Robert Graves, *The White Goddess* (1948) passim.
40. Jung to Paul Campbell, 19 December 1952; Jung to Wilhelm Bitten, 17 April 1959; Jung to J.A.F. Swobododa, 23 January 1960, *Letters*, ii. pp.100–101, 498–50, 533–34.
41. Jung to Dr S, 30 August 1951, ibid. ii. p.50.
42. Jung to John Gruesen, 4 June 1955, ibid. ii. p.256.

43. Jung to James Kirsch, 28 May 1953, ibid. ii. pp.117–118.
44. Van der Post p.177.
45. Glin Bennet, 'Domestic Life with C.G. Jung', *Spring* (1986) pp.177–89 (at p.181); J.J. Clarke, *In Search of Jung* (1992) p.77.
46. Bennet loc.cit. p.182; Brome, *Jung* p.257.
47. ibid. p.258.
48. Hannah, *Jung* p.313.
49. Maggy Anthony, *The Valkyries* p.35.
50. Van der Post p.178.
51. Wehr, *Jung* pp.365–70.
52. Von Franz, *Jung and the Myth of Our Time* p.6.
53. Jung to Victor White, May 1955, *Letters*, ii. p.251.
54. Jung to Gerald Sykes, 21 November 1955, ibid. ii. p.280.
55. Van der Post p.178.
56. Jung to Erich Neumann, 15 December 1955, *Letters*, ii. p.284; Jung to Victor White, 2 April 1955, ibid. ii. pp.238–42.
57. Bennet, 'Domestic Life', loc. cit. p.184.
58. *Jung and the Wisdom of the Dream* p.90.
59. Wehr, *Jung* p.273.
60. Bennet, loc. cit. p.185.
61. Jaffé, *From the Life and Work* p.115.
62. Bennet, loc. cit. p.183; Brome, *Jung* p.249; Jung to Mary Bancroft, August 1955, *Letters*, ii. p.270.
63. Jaffé, op. cit. pp.105, 114, 117, 125.
64. Bennet, loc. cit. p.181.
65. Jaffé, op.cit. pp.132–36.
66. MDR p.213; Jung to Aniela Jaffé, 18 March 1957, *Letters*, ii. p.351.
67. MDR p.224.
68. Jaffé, op. cit. pp.135–36; Bennet, loc. cit. p.186; Jung to Aniela Jaffé, 6 April 1954, *Letters*, ii. pp.162–63.
69. CGJS pp.xv, 236; Wehr, *Jung* p.418; Donald McCormick, *The Life of Ian Fleming* (1993) pp.43–44; Claire Myers Owen, *Awakening to Good* (Boston 1958) pp.207–220.
70. Brome, *Jung* p.264; *Daily Telegraph*, 21 January 1960.
71. Serrano, *Jung and Hesse* pp.48, 65; CW 18 p.38.
72. Jung to Emma von Plet, 6 January 1960, *Letters*, ii. p.531; Jung to Ralf Winkler, 5 June 1957, ibid. ii. pp.366–67; Jung to James Kirsh, 12 November 1959, *Letters*, ii. p.520–23; *Observer*, 25 October 1959; *The Listener*, 21 January 1960.
73. Jung to M. Leonard, 5 December 1959, *Letters*, ii. pp.525–26.
74. Jung to Hugh Burnett, 30 June 1960, ibid. ii. pp.573–74.
75. Jung to Eugen Böhler, 25 February 1960, ibid. ii. p.544.
76. Jung to Victor White, 25 March 1960, ibid. ii. pp.544–46.
77. Jung to Mother Prioress, 26 March 1960, ibid. ii. p.547.
78. Same to same, 6 February 1960, ibid. ii. p.536.
79. Same to same, 29 April 1960; Jung to Victor White, 30 April 1960, ibid. ii. pp.553–55.
80. Jung to Cornelia Brunner, 28 June 1960, ibid. ii. p.568.
81. Jung to Anon, 14 February 1961, ibid. ii. p.627.
82. CGJS p.411; J. Hillman, *Loose Ends* (Dallas 1975) p.146; *Revisioning Psychology* (NY 1975) p.260.
83. Jung to Fowler McCormick,

December 1960, *Letters*, ii. p.621; Brome, *Jung* p.268.
84. CW 8 p.402.
85. Hannah, *Jung* p.346.
86. ibid. p.347.
87. Bennet, 'Domestic Life', loc. cit. p.188.
88. Serrano, *Jung and Hesse* p.103.

INDEX

The abbreviations **CGJ** and **SF** have been used for Carl Gustav Jung and Sigmund Freud in the index. The main entries for both have been arranged alphabetically in sections and subheadings are arranged chronologically in each section, except for **writings** which are in alphabetical order. Likewise, other subheadings have been arranged chronologically.

The abbreviation IPA has been used for International Psychoanalytic Association.